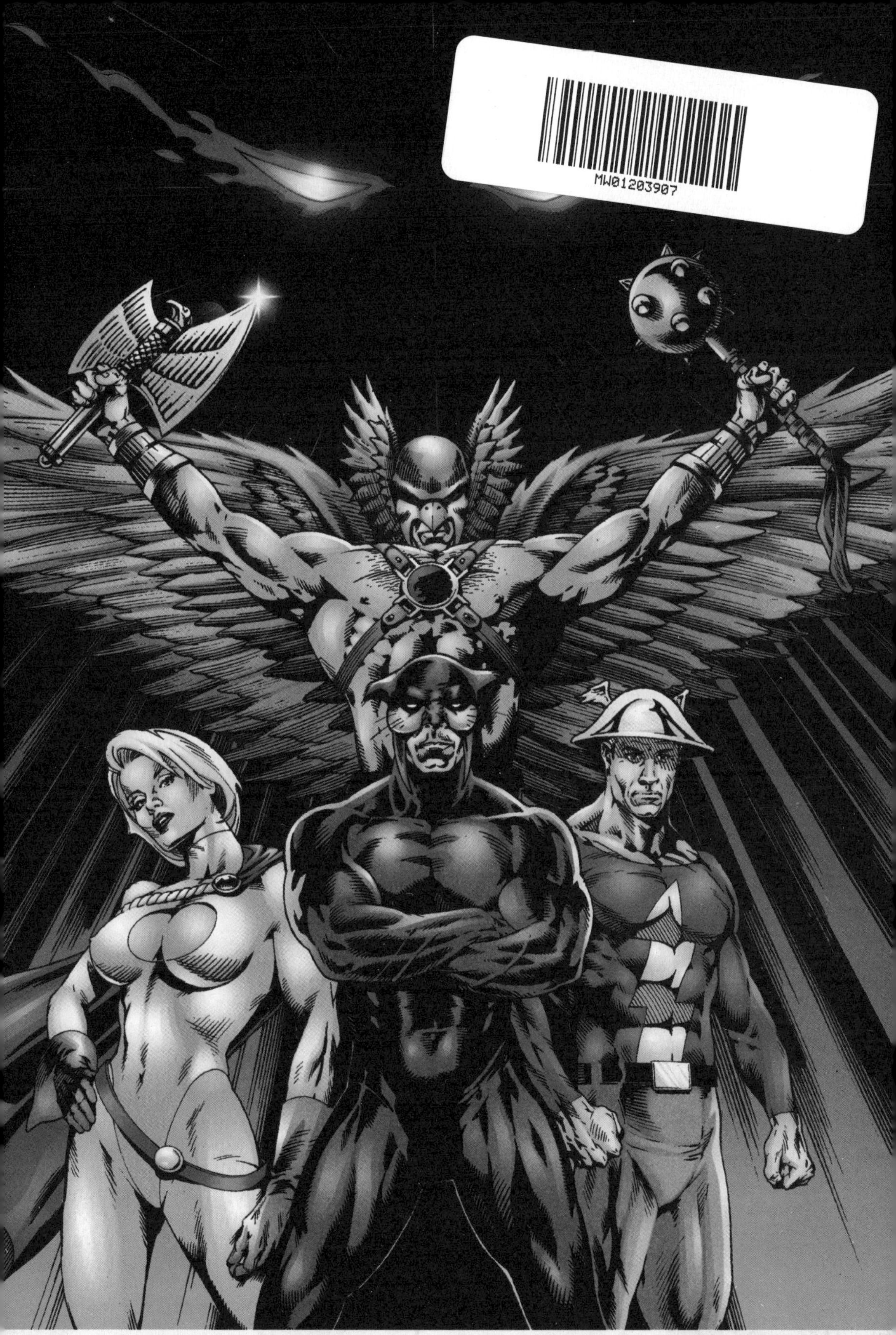

JSA PRINCES OF DARKNESS

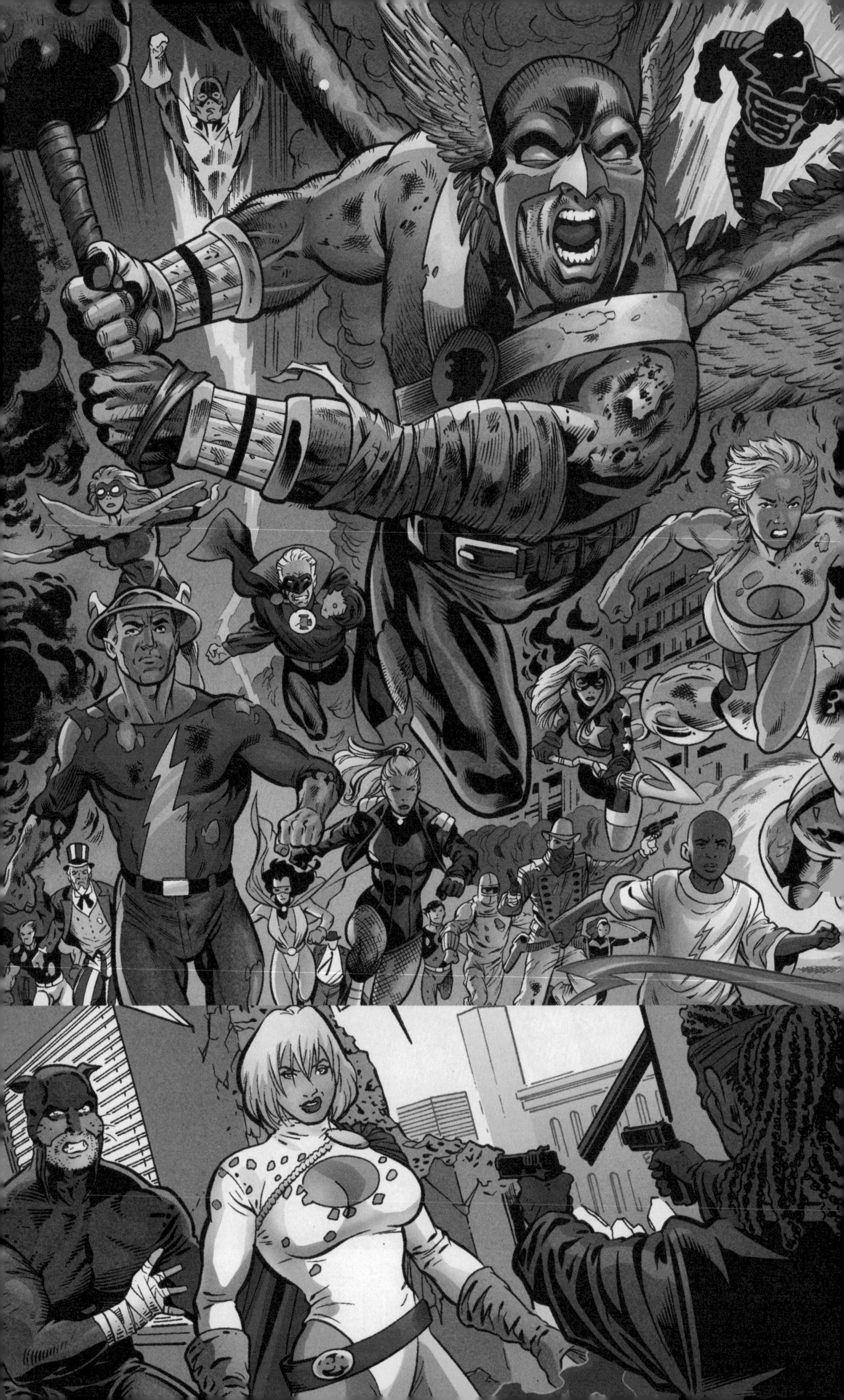

JSA PRINCES OF DARKNESS

GEOFF JOHNS DAVID GOYER WRITERS LEONARD KIRK DON KRAMER SAL VELLUTO PENCILLERS

KEITH CHAMPAGNE BOB ALMOND WADE von GRAWBADGER INKERS JOHN KALISZ COLORIST

KEN LOPEZ LETTERER MICHAEL BAIR CARLOS PACHECO & JESUS MERINO ORIGINAL COVERS

Dan DiDio Senior VP-Executive Editor   Peter Tomasi Editor-original series   Stephen Wacker Associate Editor-original series   Robert Greenberger Senior Editor-collected edition
Robbin Brosterman Senior Art Director   Paul Levitz President & Publisher   Georg Brewer VP-Design & DC Direct Creative   Richard Bruning Senior VP-Creative Director
Patrick Caldon Executive VP-Finance & Operations   Chris Caramalis VP-Finance   John Cunningham VP-Marketing   Terri Cunningham VP-Managing Editor   Stephanie Fierman
Senior VP-Sales & Marketing   Alison Gill VP-Manufacturing   Rich Johnson VP-Book Trade Sales   Hank Kanalz VP-General Manager, WildStorm   Lillian Laserson Senior VP & General Counsel
Jim Lee Editorial Director-WildStorm   Paula Lowitt Senior VP-Business & Legal Affairs   David McKillips VP-Advertising & Custom Publishing   John Nee VP-Business Development
Gregory Noveck Senior VP-Creative Affairs   Cheryl Rubin Senior VP-Brand Management   Jeff Trojan VP-Business Development, DC Direct   Bob Wayne VP-Sales

There has always been a need for heroes. In the dawning days of World War II, America produced a generation of heroes the likes of which had never before been seen. The mightiest of them banded together to protect the innocent as the Justice Society of America. For a decade they fought the good fight, retiring from the public spotlight when their day had passed.

But now the need for heroes has never been greater. So the JSA lives once more, led by the survivors of the original team who are training a new generation of crime-fighters. Under their elders' guidance, these younger heroes not only learn how to harness their power but also come to understand who paved their way and the tremendous legacy that they have inherited.

Since its re-formation, the JSA has rediscovered old friends, fought familiar enemies, and buried some of their comrades. The team has also reestablished its roots in New York City, with their headquarters doubling as meeting place and museum open to the public.

As we begin, the JSA is..

CAPTAIN MARVEL

Entrusted by the wizard Shazam with the combined magical might of Solomon, Hercules, Atlas, Zeus, Achilles, and Mercury, teenager Billy Batson needs only speak his mentor's name to be transformed into Captain Marvel, the World's Mightiest Mortal. Batson currently shares the power of Shazam with several other champions, joining a long line of warriors who have acted as Shazam's avatars over the millennia.

DR. FATE

Nabu, a Lord of Order, was exiled to Earth in 3,500 B.C. Once here, he took the guise of an Egyptian sorcerer and served as an advisor to Prince Khufu. Later, his essence and powers were entombed in a golden helmet and amulet. In 1940, Kent Nelson assumed the golden armaments and became the first Dr. Fate. Several others have worn the mantle since then, and its current possessor is Hector Hall, the son of Hawkman.

DR. MID-NITE

A medical prodigy, Pieter Anton Cross refused to work within the system. Treating patients on his own, he came into contact with a dangerous drug that altered his body chemistry, letting him see light in the infrared spectrum. Although he was blinded in an explosion intended to kill him, he continues to protect the weak in the assumed identity of Dr. Mid-Nite.

THE FLASH

The first in a long line of super-speedsters, Jay Garrick is capable of running at velocities near the speed of light. A scientist, Garrick has also served as mentor to other speedsters and heroes over several generations.

GREEN LANTERN

Engineer Alan Scott found a lantern carved from a meteorite known as the Starheart. Fulfilling a prophecy to grant power, Scott tapped into the emerald energy and fought injustice as the Green Lantern. He has gone through many changes but is currently a living embodiment of the Starheart.

HAWKMAN and HAWKGIRL

Thousands of years ago, in ancient Egypt, Prince Khufu and his Princess Chay-Ara discovered an alien spacecraft from the planet Thanagar. The ship was powered by a mysterious anti-gravity element, which they called Nth metal. The unearthly energies of the Nth metal, enhanced by the strength of their love, transformed the souls of the Prince and Princess. For centuries, they were reincarnated, life after life, destined to meet one another and rekindle their love... until today. Today, he is Carter Hall, archaeologist and adventurer. She is Kendra Saunders, trained to inherit the mantle of Hawkgirl. But Kendra has no recollection of her past lives or her past love with Carter, nor any interest whatsoever in renewing that love.

HOURMAN

Rick Tyler struggled for a while before accepting his role as the son of the original Hourman. It hasn't been an easy road — he endured addiction to the Miraclo drug that increases his strength and endurance, and nearly died of leukemia. Now, after mastering the drug, he uses a special hourglass to see one hour into the future.

JAKEEM THUNDER

Keystone City's Jakeem Williams was raised by his aunt after his mother died and his father disappeared. He developed a serious attitude and did poorly in school, but secretly he wasn't happy about it. Asking the Flash for his autograph, Jakeem came into possession of a pen that was actually the vessel for a 5th-Dimensional being known as the Thunderbolt. Jakeem became his new partner and is now learning how best to use his position of power.

MR. TERRIFIC

Haunted by the death of his wife, Olympic gold medal-winning decathlete Michael Holt was ready to take his own life. Instead, inspired by the Spectre's story of the original Mr. Terrific, he rededicated himself to ensuring fair play among the street youth using his wealth and technical skills.

POWER GIRL

She thought herself a princess of ancient Atlantis or a survivor of the doomed planet Krypton, but Karen Starr is now less certain of her origins than of her commitment to justice. Her enhanced strength and powers of flight and invulnerability are matched only by her self-confidence, which borders on arrogance.

SAND

The ward of original Sandman Wesley Dodds and the nephew of Dodds's lifelong partner Dian Belmont, Sandy Hawkins was transformed through a bizarre experiment into a crazed silicon monster. Revived from a state of suspended animation and cured of his condition some years ago, Sandy has become a geomorph, able to transform his body into sand and to control silicon to a limited degree.

THE STAR-SPANGLED KID

When Courtney Whitmore first discovered the cosmic converter belt once worn by the JSA's original Star-Spangled Kid, she saw it as an opportunity to cut class and kick some butt. Now, she is slowly — *very* slowly — beginning to learn about the awesome legacy she has become a part of.

WILDCAT

A former heavyweight boxing champ, Ted Grant, a.k.a. Wildcat, prowls the mean streets defending the helpless. One of the world's foremost hand-to-hand combatants, he has trained many of today's best fighters — including Black Canary, Catwoman, and the Batman.

FRIENDS OF THE JSA

AIR WAVE

Harold Jordan is a cousin of Hal Jordan, Earth's best-known Green Lantern. Harold's father was the first Air Wave so it's no surprise that Harold follows in the family tradition. He has the ability to become living energy and travel along the electromagnetic spectrum. Briefly calling himself Maser, he served with the Captains of Industry and was subsequently captured and used by Kobra. After the JSA defeated Kobra, they freed Air Wave, who has happily returned to action.

ATOM SMASHER

Al Rothstein never wanted anything more than to become a member of the Justice Society of America. Although his grandfather was the super-villain known as Cyclotron, Al is trying to live up to the legacy of a hero — his godfather, the original Atom. Al inherited his superhuman strength and the ability to increase his mass from his grandfather's atomic-powered physiology.

DOVE

Dawn Granger possesses power gifted by a Lord of Order, replacing the first Dove, Don Hall. She teamed for a time with Don's brother Hank, the super-powered Hawk, until Hank went insane. Becoming a being known as Monarch, Dove seemingly died, only to recently return to life. She now tries to find a sense of balance between being Dawn and Dove.

OBSIDIAN

Son of the first Green Lantern, and brother of the Outsiders' Jade, Todd developed power over shadow. Taking the costumed identity of Obsidian, he has served with incarnations of Infinity, Inc. and the Justice League. His psyche, though, was fractured as a result of the abuse handed out by his adoptive father, Jim Rice, and gradually, the shadow realm he traversed drove him mad. He has battled the JSA and remains embittered, even after Jim sacrificed his life to stop Obsidian from committing further damage.

THE SHADE

His origins clouded through deliberate obfuscation, this English-born man has at times played the roles of both hero and villain. Over a century ago, he had an odd experience that left him with power over shadow and seeming immortality. As a result, he has made a bizarre assortment of alliances through the years, but of late has come to the aid of Earth's champions.

AND, AT THE TIME OF THIS STORY, THEIR OPPONENTS

BLACK ADAM

Teth-Adam was the first to wield the mystical powers bestowed by the wizard Shazam. As Mighty Adam, he battled evil during Egypt's 15th Dynasty until the power ultimately corrupted him. Shazam imprisoned Adam in a scarab that was lost for centuries. A few years ago, two archaeologists, C.C. and Mary Batson, unearthed the scarab. Teth-Adam's powers and soul took root in the body of his descendant, Theo Adam, a thief and murderer. Now Theo struggles for redemption.

ECLIPSO

The first Spirit of God's wrath, Eclipso found himself an outcast. A god of revenge, he was then trapped in a black diamond for millennia until accidentally freed by scientist Bruce Gordon. Repeatedly, Eclipso sought dominion over humanity but met defeat time and again. After Gordon and Eclipso were no longer mystically tethered, Eclipso grew more savage, hungering for a chance to crush lives until the Spectre once more imprisoned him in the black diamond.

FLAW & CHILD

The Lords of Order and Chaos have agents in many realities including the mystic realm of the Gemworld. There, the powerful youth known only as Child served Chaos, and he in turn was served by the brutish crystal behemoth Flaw. They worked with a dark noble, Wrynn, who grew in power and became the villainous mage Mordru. As a result, they now serve their creation.

KOBRA

Spiritual leader of a worldwide cult whose members are legion, the terrorist Kobra seeks to rule the world, convinced it is his destiny. He has been opposed by Earth's heroes, meeting defeat at the hands of Batman, the Outsiders and the JSA. In one of his more recent acts, he blew up an airplane that carried Atom Smasher's mother, making him a target for vengeance. He had been tried and freed, sowing seeds for several gambits in an attempt to emerge victorious.

MORDRU

Child, a servant of Chaos, recruited dark nobleman Wrynn to join his cause. Wrynn studied and developed vast magical powers, renaming himself Mordru. The mage tried to take over the Gemworld but was defeated by Princess Amethyst. Mordru then sought additional power, crossing into Earth's realm and killing the Lords' agents in an attempt to obtain Dr. Fate's mystic helm. The JSA rose to Fate's defense and a major battle played out in America, one that claimed the lives of Scarab and Kid Eternity. The mage was trapped within Fate's helmet, a gateway into another reality, until just days earlier...

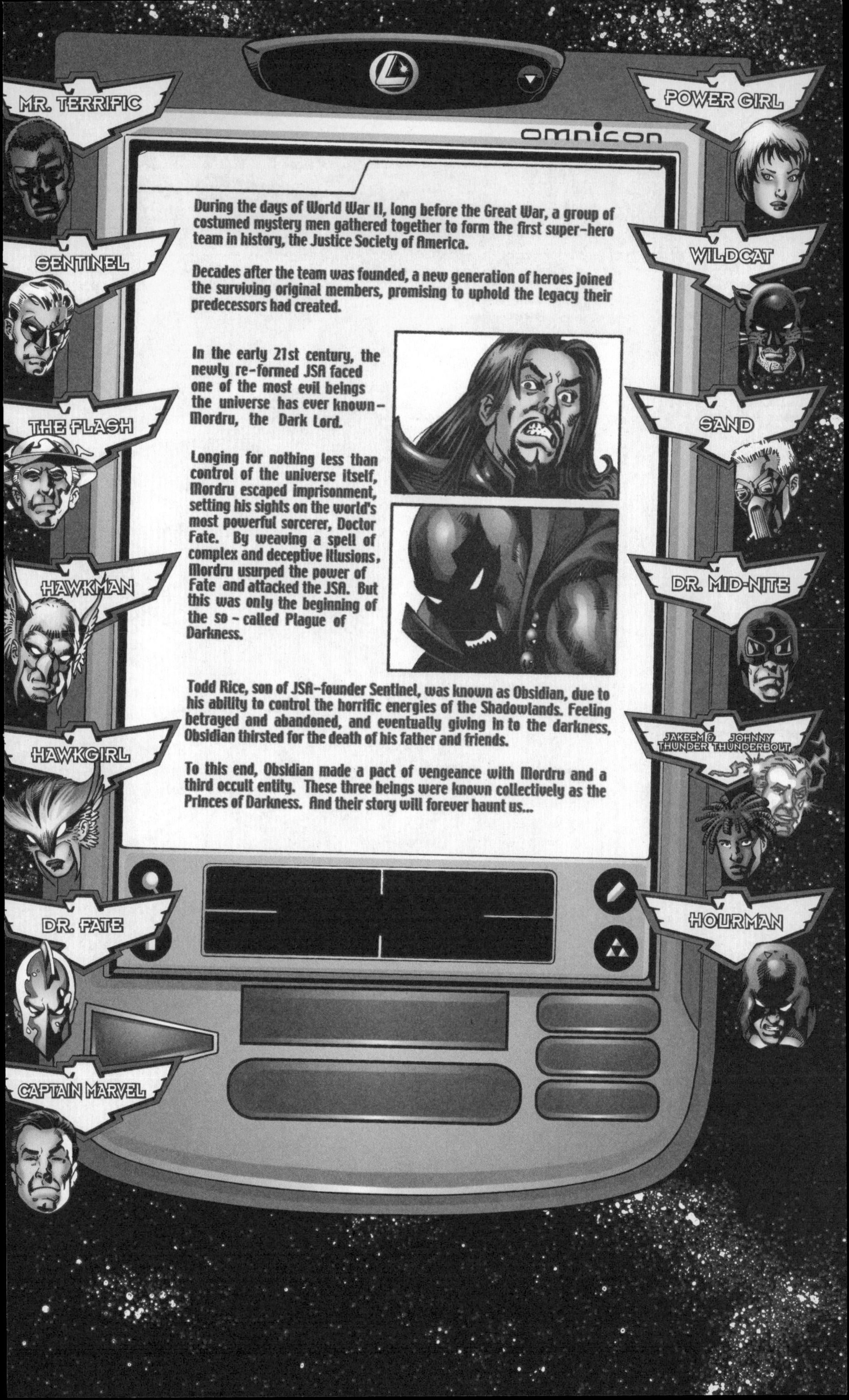
omnicon
During the days of World War II, long before the Great War, a group of costumed mystery men gathered together to form the first super-hero team in history, the Justice Society of America.
Decades after the team was founded, a new generation of heroes joined the surviving original members, promising to uphold the legacy their predecessors had created.
In the early 21st century, the newly re-formed JSA faced one of the most evil beings the universe has ever known— Mordru, the Dark Lord.
Longing for nothing less than control of the universe itself, Mordru escaped imprisonment, setting his sights on the world's most powerful sorcerer, Doctor Fate. By weaving a spell of complex and deceptive illusions, Mordru usurped the power of Fate and attacked the JSA. But this was only the beginning of the so-called Plague of Darkness.
Todd Rice, son of JSA-founder Sentinel, was known as Obsidian, due to his ability to control the horrific energies of the Shadowlands. Feeling betrayed and abandoned, and eventually giving in to the darkness, Obsidian thirsted for the death of his father and friends.
To this end, Obsidian made a pact of vengeance with Mordru and a third occult entity. These three beings were known collectively as the Princes of Darkness. And their story will forever haunt us...
MR. TERRIFIC
POWER GIRL
SENTINEL
WILDCAT
THE FLASH
SAND
HAWKMAN
DR. MID-NITE
HAWKGIRL
JAKEEM & THUNDER
JOHNNY THUNDERBOLT
DR. FATE
HOURMAN
CAPTAIN MARVEL

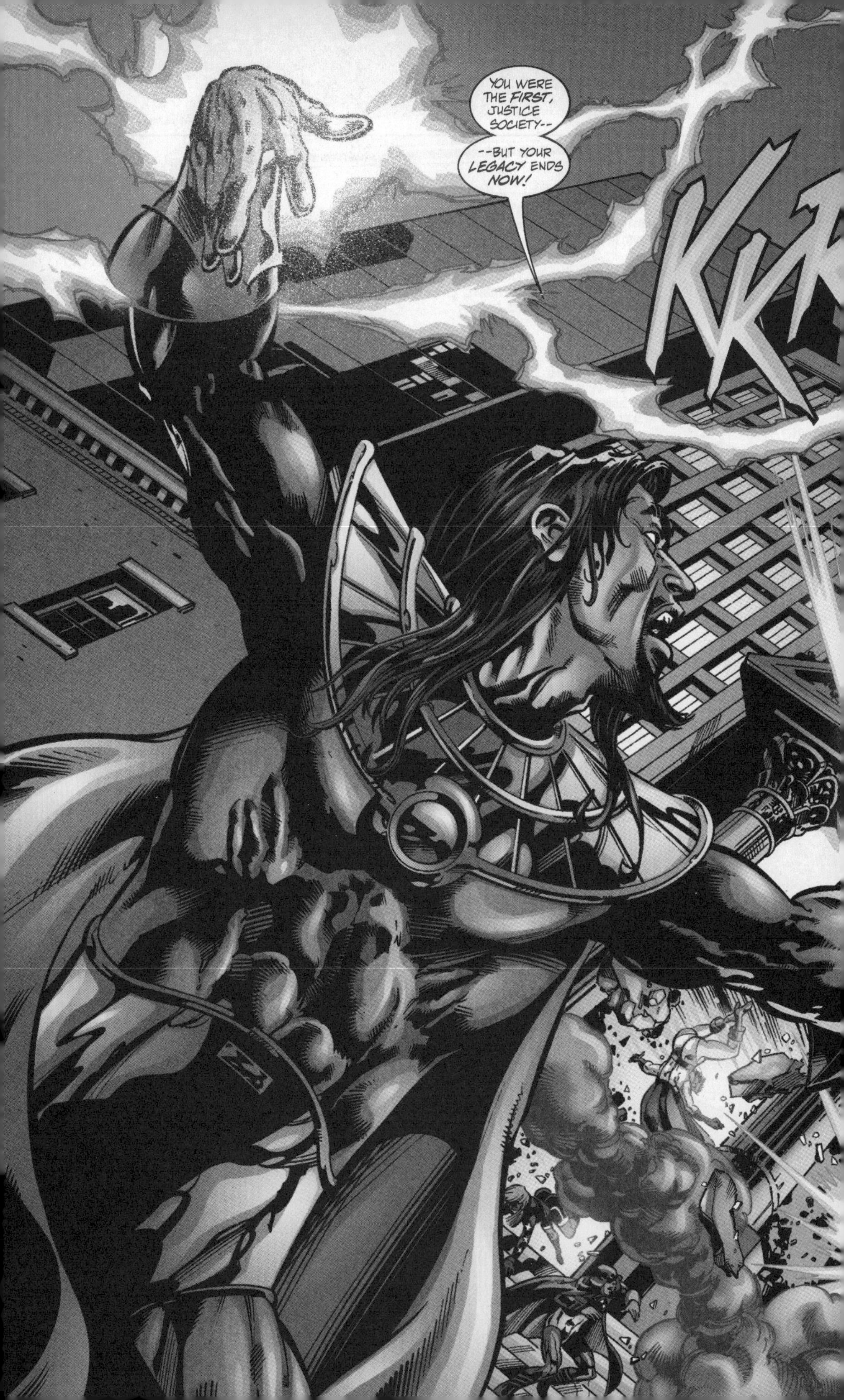
YOU WERE THE FIRST, JUSTICE SOCIETY--
--BUT YOUR LEGACY ENDS NOW!
KKR

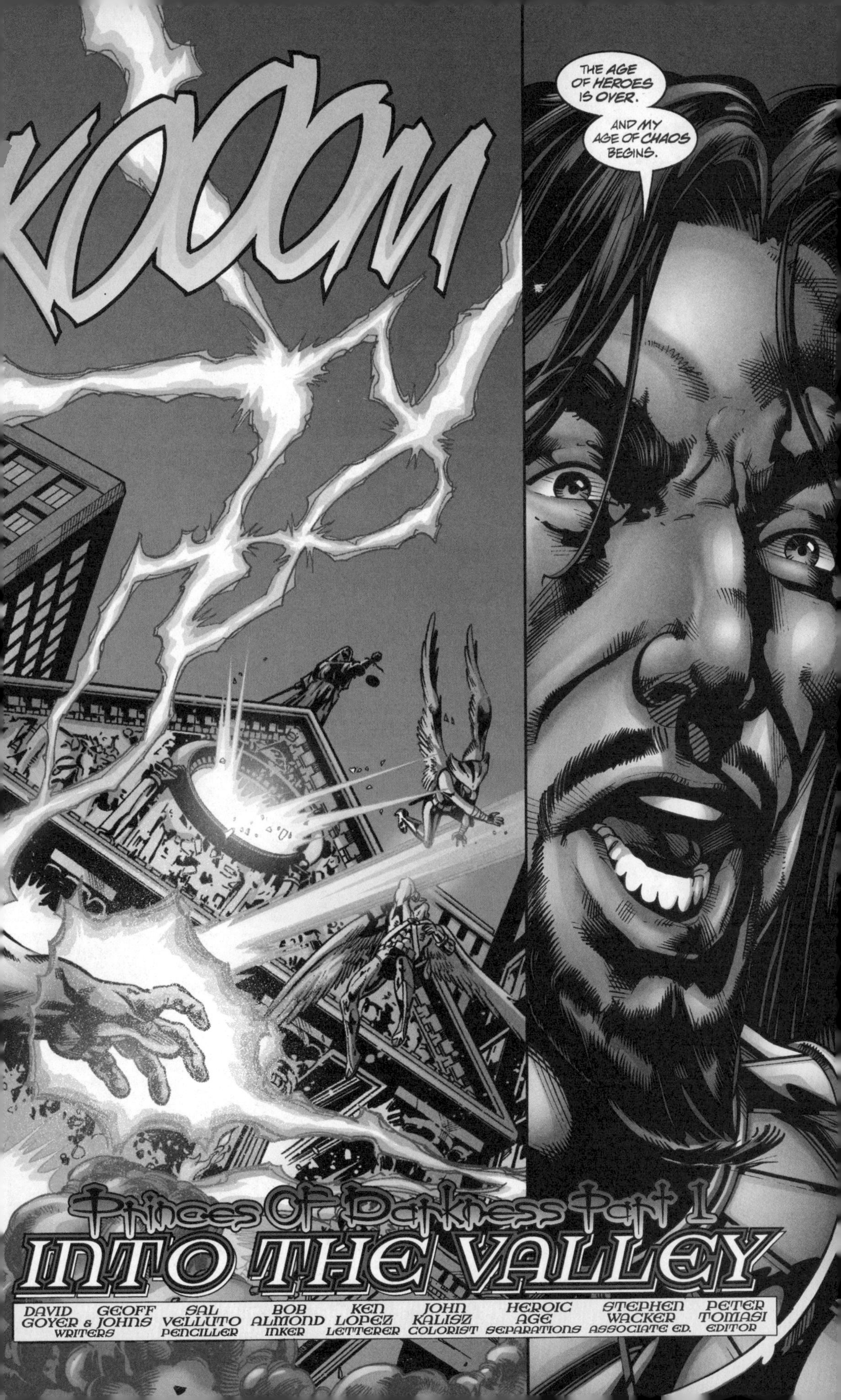
KOOOM
THE AGE OF HEROES IS OVER.
AND MY AGE OF CHAOS BEGINS.
Princes Of Darkness Part 1
INTO THE VALLEY
DAVID GOYER & GEOFF JOHNS WRITERS
SAL VELLUTO PENCILLER
BOB ALMOND INKER
KEN LOPEZ LETTERER
JOHN KALISZ COLORIST
HEROIC AGE SEPARATIONS
STEPHEN WACKER ASSOCIATE ED.
PETER TOMASI EDITOR

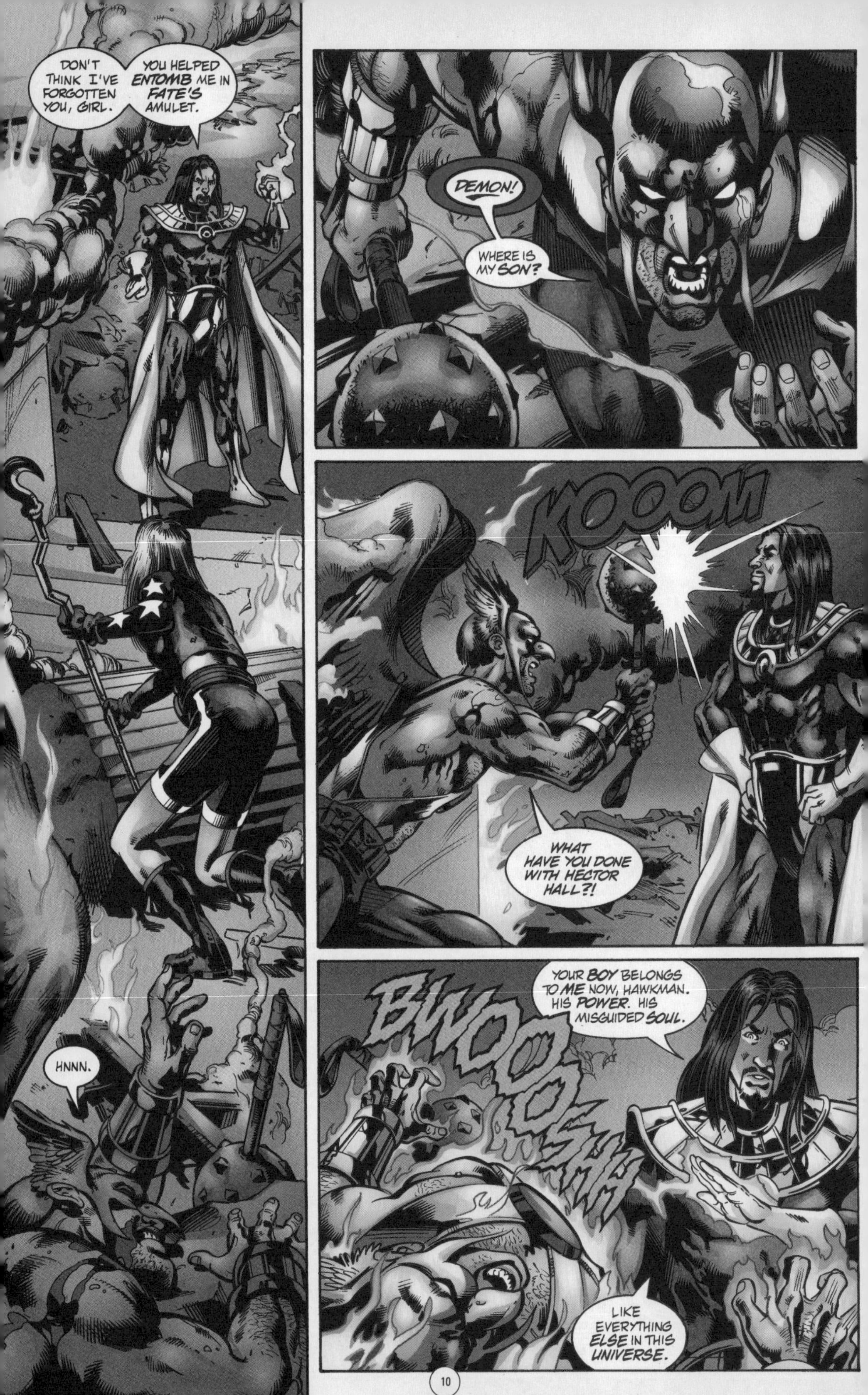
DON'T THINK I'VE FORGOTTEN YOU, GIRL.
YOU HELPED ENTOMB ME IN FATE'S AMULET.
HNNN.
DEMON!
WHERE IS MY SON?
KOOOM
WHAT HAVE YOU DONE WITH HECTOR HALL?!
BWOOOSHH
YOUR BOY BELONGS TO ME NOW, HAWKMAN. HIS POWER. HIS MISGUIDED SOUL.
LIKE EVERYTHING ELSE IN THIS UNIVERSE.

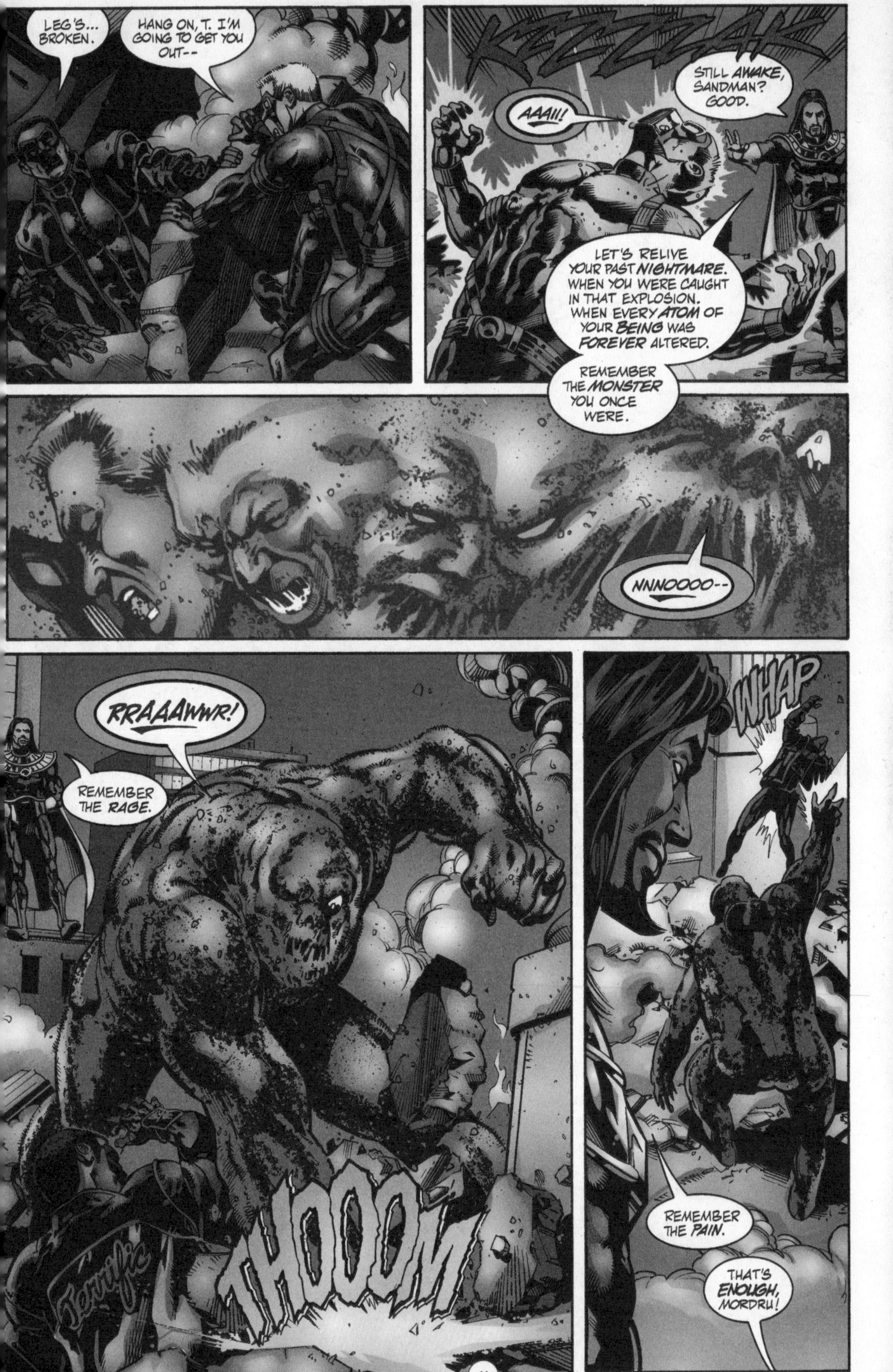
LEG'S... BROKEN.
HANG ON, T. I'M GOING TO GET YOU OUT--
KRZZZZAK
AAAI!!
STILL AWAKE, SANDMAN? GOOD.
LET'S RELIVE YOUR PAST NIGHTMARE. WHEN YOU WERE CAUGHT IN THAT EXPLOSION. WHEN EVERY ATOM OF YOUR BEING WAS FOREVER ALTERED.
REMEMBER THE MONSTER YOU ONCE WERE.
NNNOOOO--
RRAAAWWR!
REMEMBER THE RAGE.
THOOOM
Terrific
WHAP
REMEMBER THE PAIN.
THAT'S ENOUGH, MORDRU!

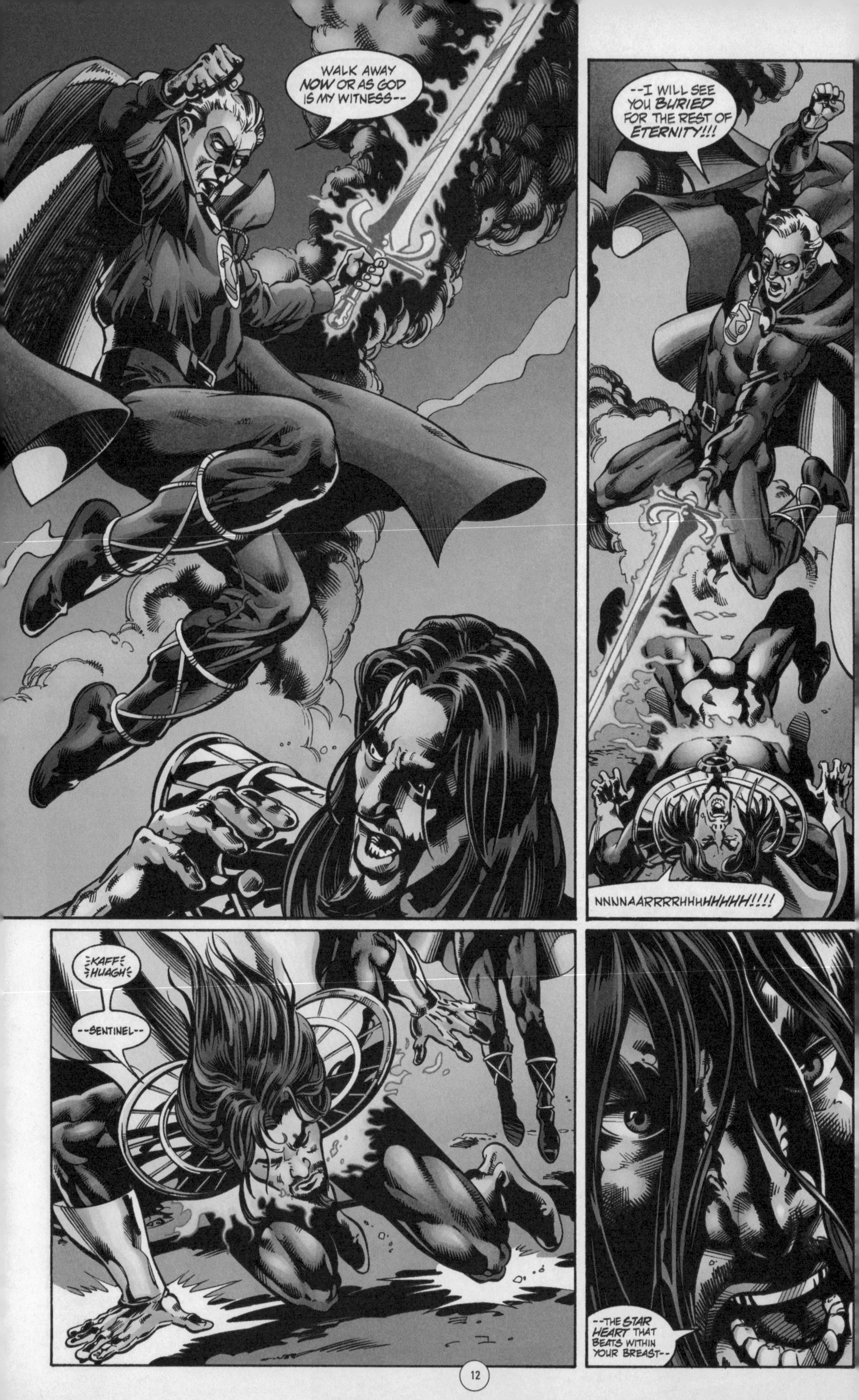

WALK AWAY NOW OR AS GOD IS MY WITNESS--
--I WILL SEE YOU BURIED FOR THE REST OF ETERNITY!!!
NNNNAARRRRHHHHHHHH!!!!
KAFF HUAGH
--SENTINEL--
--THE STAR HEART THAT BEATS WITHIN YOUR BREAST--

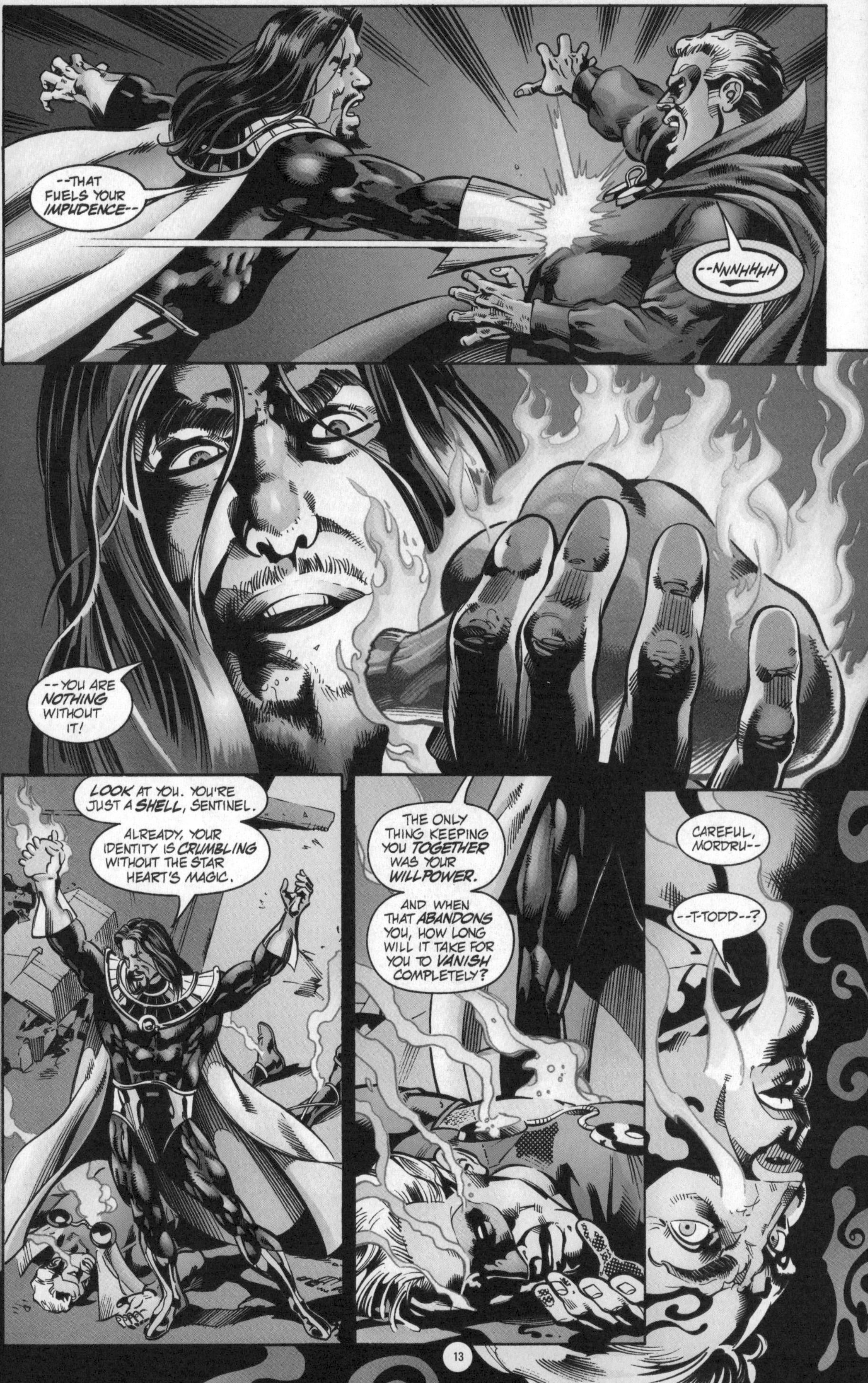
--THAT FUELS YOUR IMPUDENCE--
--NNNHHHH
--YOU ARE NOTHING WITHOUT IT!
LOOK AT YOU. YOU'RE JUST A SHELL, SENTINEL.
ALREADY, YOUR IDENTITY IS CRUMBLING WITHOUT THE STAR HEART'S MAGIC.
THE ONLY THING KEEPING YOU TOGETHER WAS YOUR WILLPOWER.
AND WHEN THAT ABANDONS YOU, HOW LONG WILL IT TAKE FOR YOU TO VANISH COMPLETELY?
CAREFUL, MORDRU--
--T-TODD--?

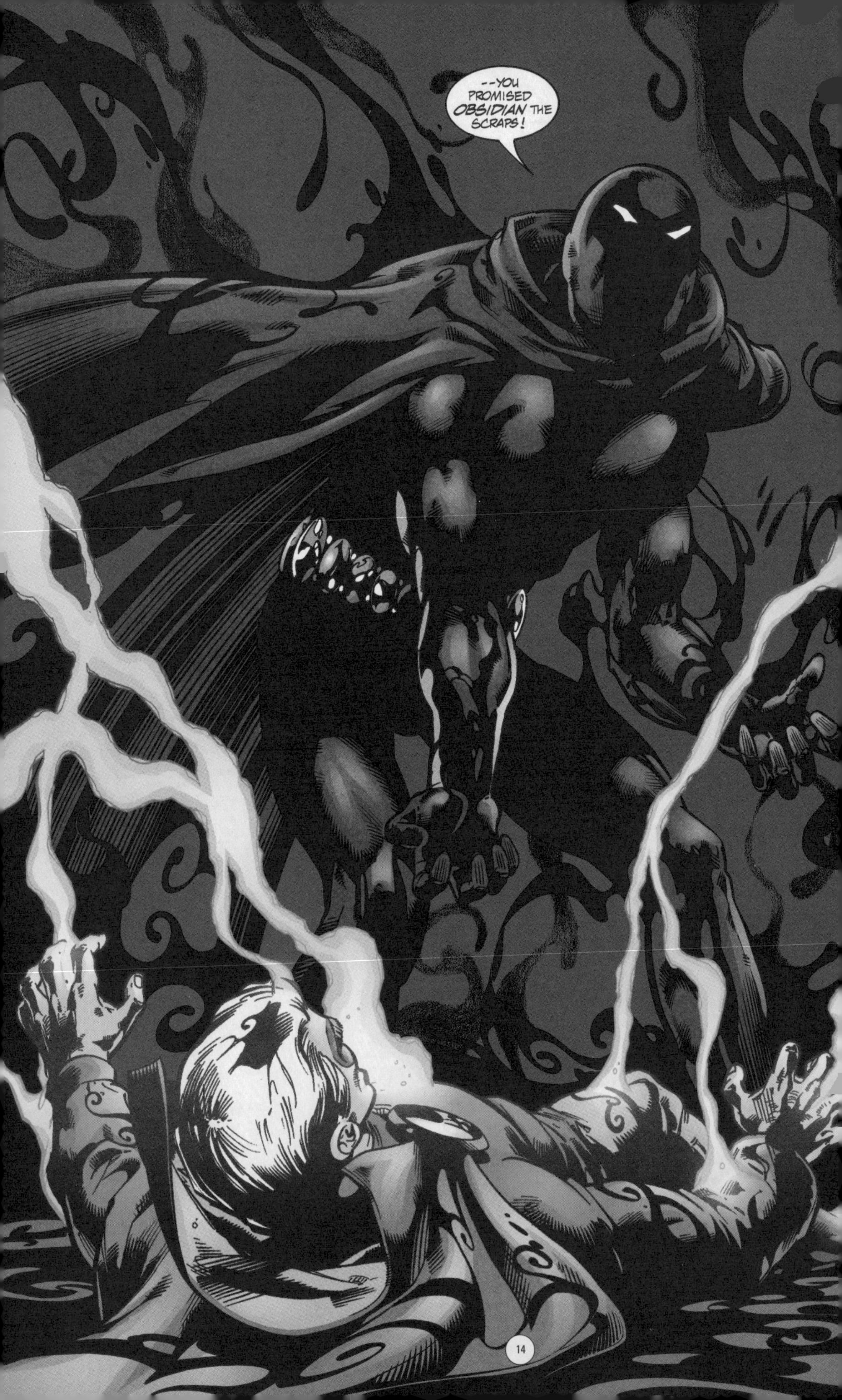
--YOU PROMISED OBSIDIAN THE SCRAPS!

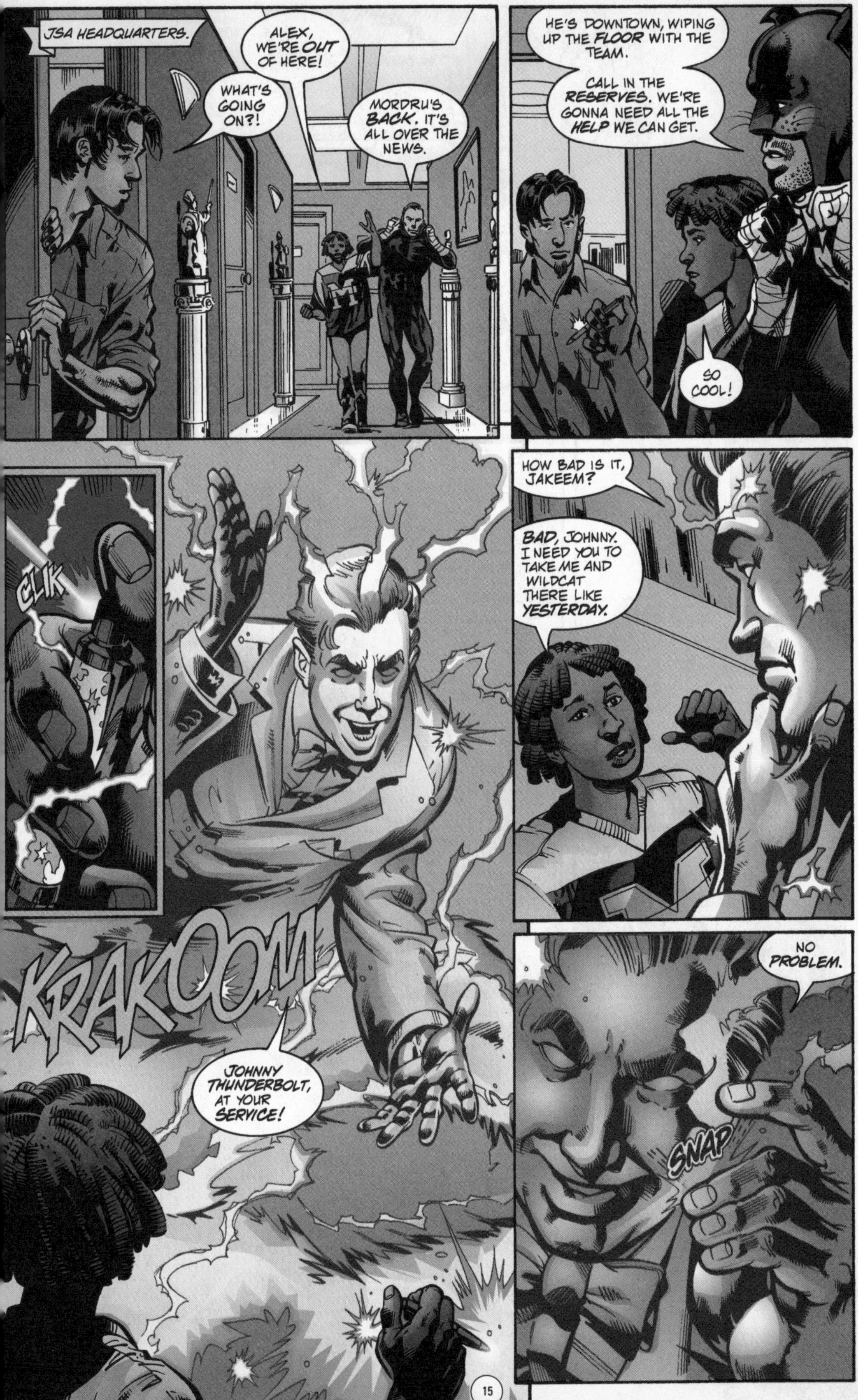

JSA HEADQUARTERS.
ALEX, WE'RE OUT OF HERE!
WHAT'S GOING ON?!
MORDRU'S BACK. IT'S ALL OVER THE NEWS.
HE'S DOWNTOWN, WIPING UP THE FLOOR WITH THE TEAM.
CALL IN THE RESERVES. WE'RE GONNA NEED ALL THE HELP WE CAN GET.
SO COOL!
CLIK
KRAKOOM
JOHNNY THUNDERBOLT, AT YOUR SERVICE!
HOW BAD IS IT, JAKEEM?
BAD, JOHNNY. I NEED YOU TO TAKE ME AND WILDCAT THERE LIKE YESTERDAY.
NO PROBLEM.
SNAP

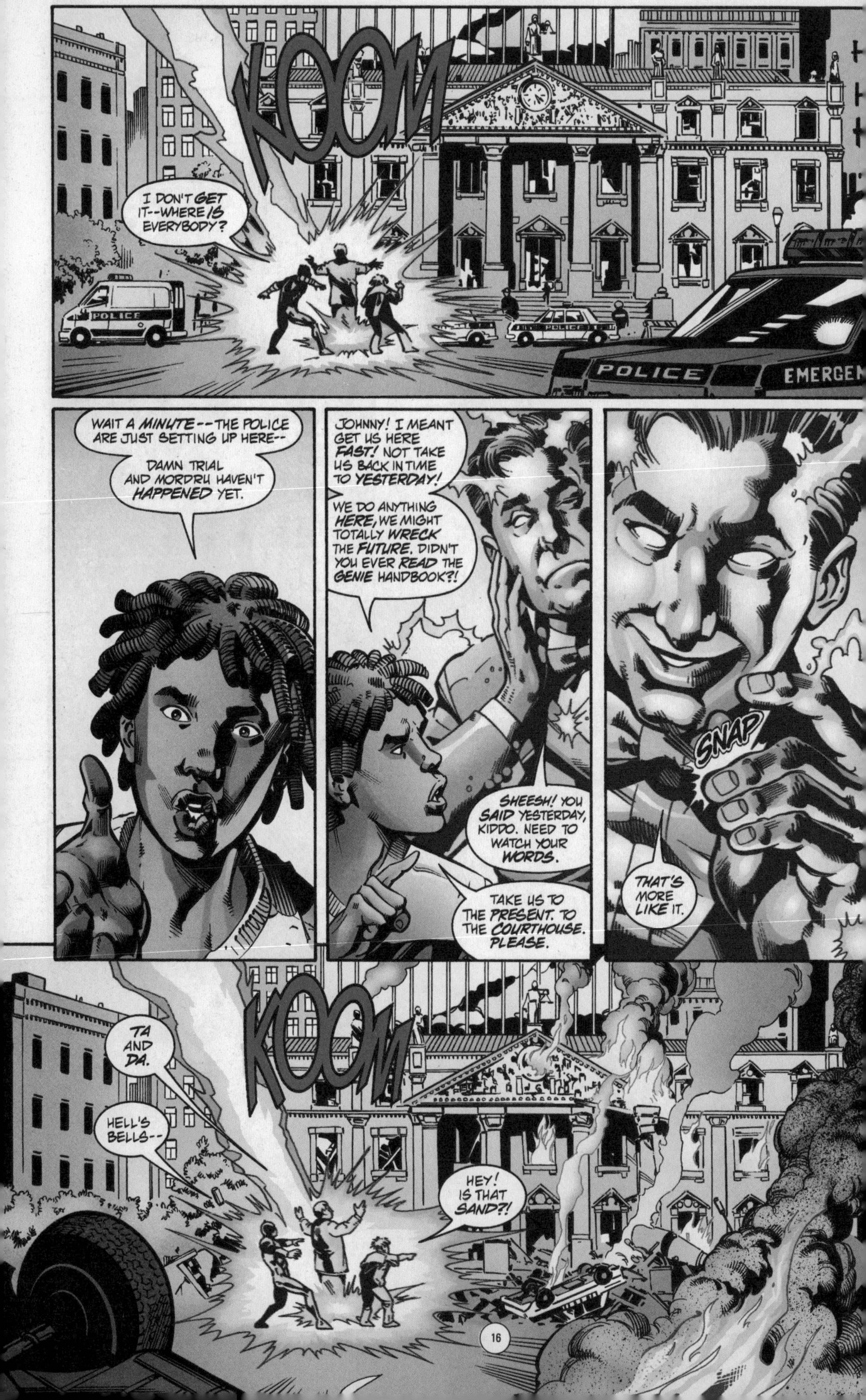
KOOM
I DON'T GET IT--WHERE IS EVERYBODY?
POLICE
POLICE
EMERGEN
WAIT A MINUTE--THE POLICE ARE JUST SETTING UP HERE--
DAMN TRIAL AND MORDRU HAVEN'T HAPPENED YET.
JOHNNY! I MEANT GET US HERE FAST! NOT TAKE US BACK IN TIME TO YESTERDAY!
WE DO ANYTHING HERE, WE MIGHT TOTALLY WRECK THE FUTURE. DIDN'T YOU EVER READ THE GENIE HANDBOOK?!
SHEESH! YOU SAID YESTERDAY, KIDDO. NEED TO WATCH YOUR WORDS.
TAKE US TO THE PRESENT. TO THE COURTHOUSE. PLEASE.
SNAP
THAT'S MORE LIKE IT.
KOOM
TA AND DA.
HELL'S BELLS--
HEY! IS THAT SAND?!

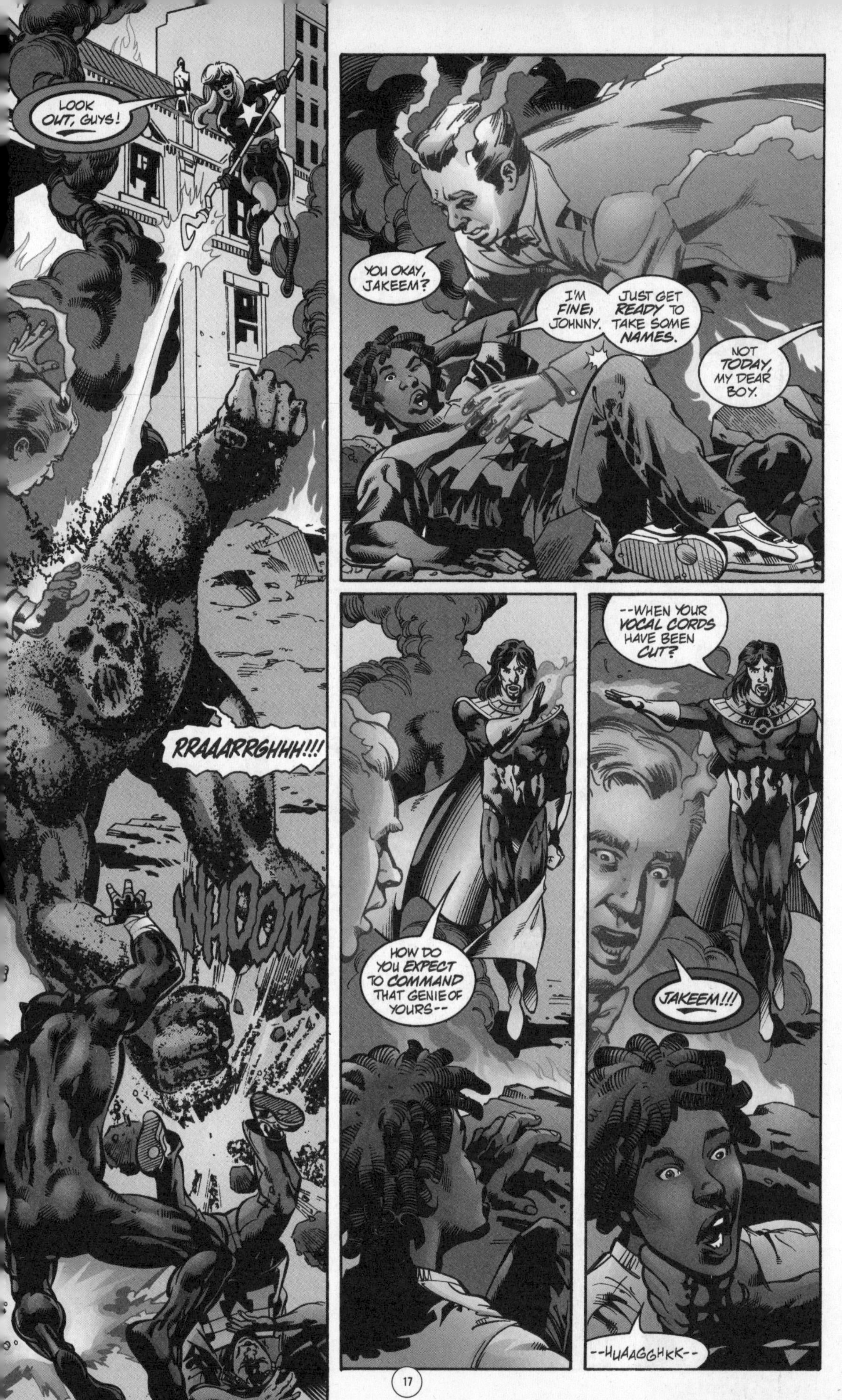

LOOK OUT, GUYS!
RRAAARRGHHH!!!
WHOOM
YOU OKAY, JAKEEM?
I'M FINE, JOHNNY.
JUST GET READY TO TAKE SOME NAMES.
NOT TODAY, MY DEAR BOY.
HOW DO YOU EXPECT TO COMMAND THAT GENIE OF YOURS--
--WHEN YOUR VOCAL CORDS HAVE BEEN CUT?
JAKEEM!!!
--HUAAGGHKK--

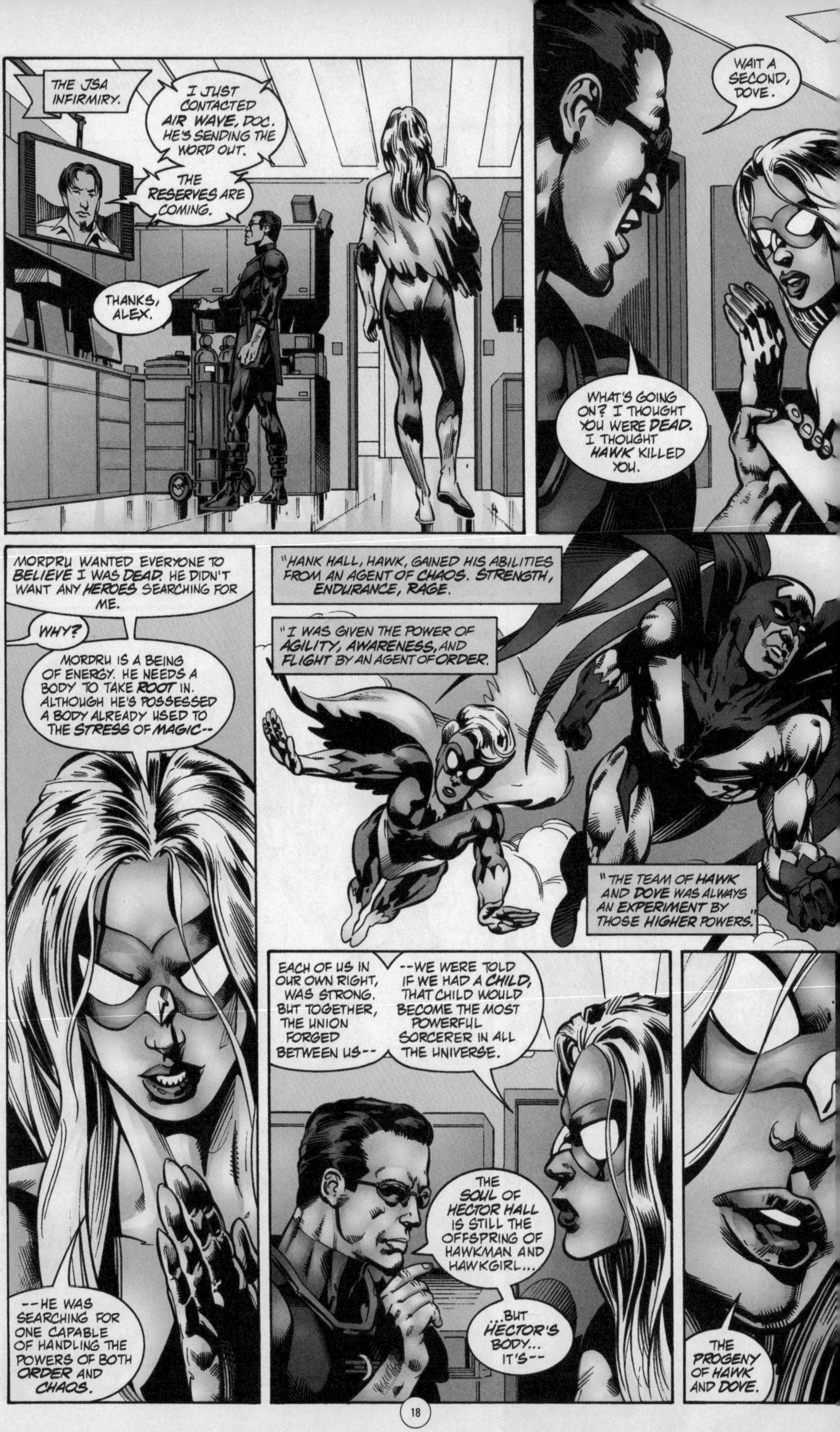
THE JSA INFIRMIRY.
I JUST CONTACTED AIR WAVE, DOC. HE'S SENDING THE WORD OUT.
THE RESERVES ARE COMING.
THANKS, ALEX.
WAIT A SECOND, DOVE.
WHAT'S GOING ON? I THOUGHT YOU WERE DEAD. I THOUGHT HAWK KILLED YOU.
MORDRU WANTED EVERYONE TO BELIEVE I WAS DEAD. HE DIDN'T WANT ANY HEROES SEARCHING FOR ME.
WHY?
MORDRU IS A BEING OF ENERGY. HE NEEDS A BODY TO TAKE ROOT IN. ALTHOUGH HE'S POSSESSED A BODY ALREADY USED TO THE STRESS OF MAGIC--
--HE WAS SEARCHING FOR ONE CAPABLE OF HANDLING THE POWERS OF BOTH ORDER AND CHAOS.
"HANK HALL, HAWK, GAINED HIS ABILITIES FROM AN AGENT OF CHAOS. STRENGTH, ENDURANCE, RAGE.
"I WAS GIVEN THE POWER OF AGILITY, AWARENESS, AND FLIGHT BY AN AGENT OF ORDER.
"THE TEAM OF HAWK AND DOVE WAS ALWAYS AN EXPERIMENT BY THOSE HIGHER POWERS.
EACH OF US IN OUR OWN RIGHT, WAS STRONG. BUT TOGETHER, THE UNION FORGED BETWEEN US--
--WE WERE TOLD IF WE HAD A CHILD, THAT CHILD WOULD BECOME THE MOST POWERFUL SORCERER IN ALL THE UNIVERSE.
THE SOUL OF HECTOR HALL IS STILL THE OFFSPRING OF HAWKMAN AND HAWKGIRL...
...BUT HECTOR'S BODY... IT'S--
THE PROGENY OF HAWK AND DOVE.

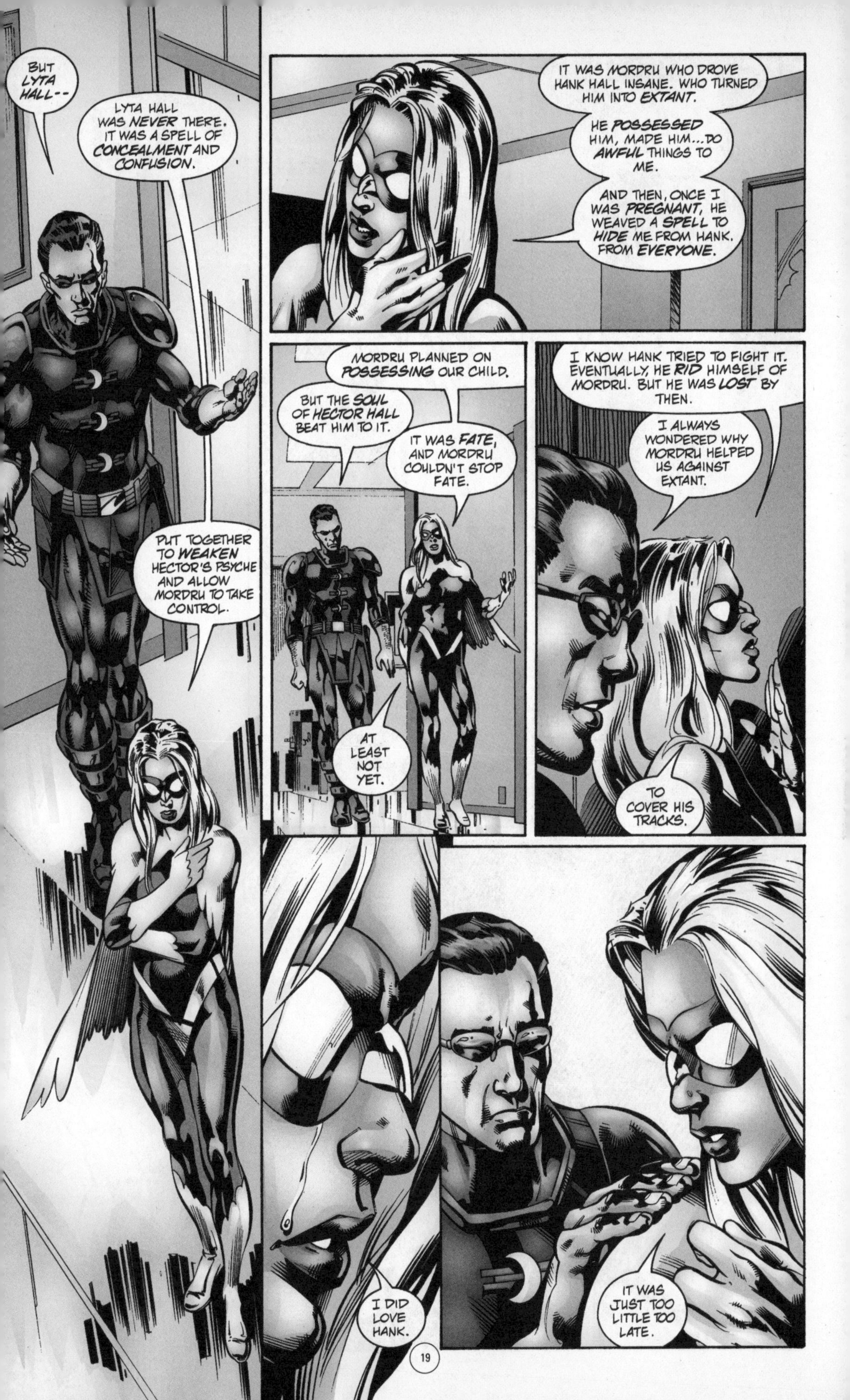

BUT LYTA HALL--
LYTA HALL WAS NEVER THERE. IT WAS A SPELL OF CONCEALMENT AND CONFUSION.
PUT TOGETHER TO WEAKEN HECTOR'S PSYCHE AND ALLOW MORDRU TO TAKE CONTROL.
IT WAS MORDRU WHO DROVE HANK HALL INSANE. WHO TURNED HIM INTO EXTANT.
HE POSSESSED HIM, MADE HIM...DO AWFUL THINGS TO ME.
AND THEN, ONCE I WAS PREGNANT, HE WEAVED A SPELL TO HIDE ME FROM HANK. FROM EVERYONE.
MORDRU PLANNED ON POSSESSING OUR CHILD.
BUT THE SOUL OF HECTOR HALL BEAT HIM TO IT.
IT WAS FATE, AND MORDRU COULDN'T STOP FATE.
AT LEAST NOT YET.
I KNOW HANK TRIED TO FIGHT IT. EVENTUALLY, HE RID HIMSELF OF MORDRU. BUT HE WAS LOST BY THEN.
I ALWAYS WONDERED WHY MORDRU HELPED US AGAINST EXTANT.
TO COVER HIS TRACKS.
I DID LOVE HANK.
IT WAS JUST TOO LITTLE TOO LATE.

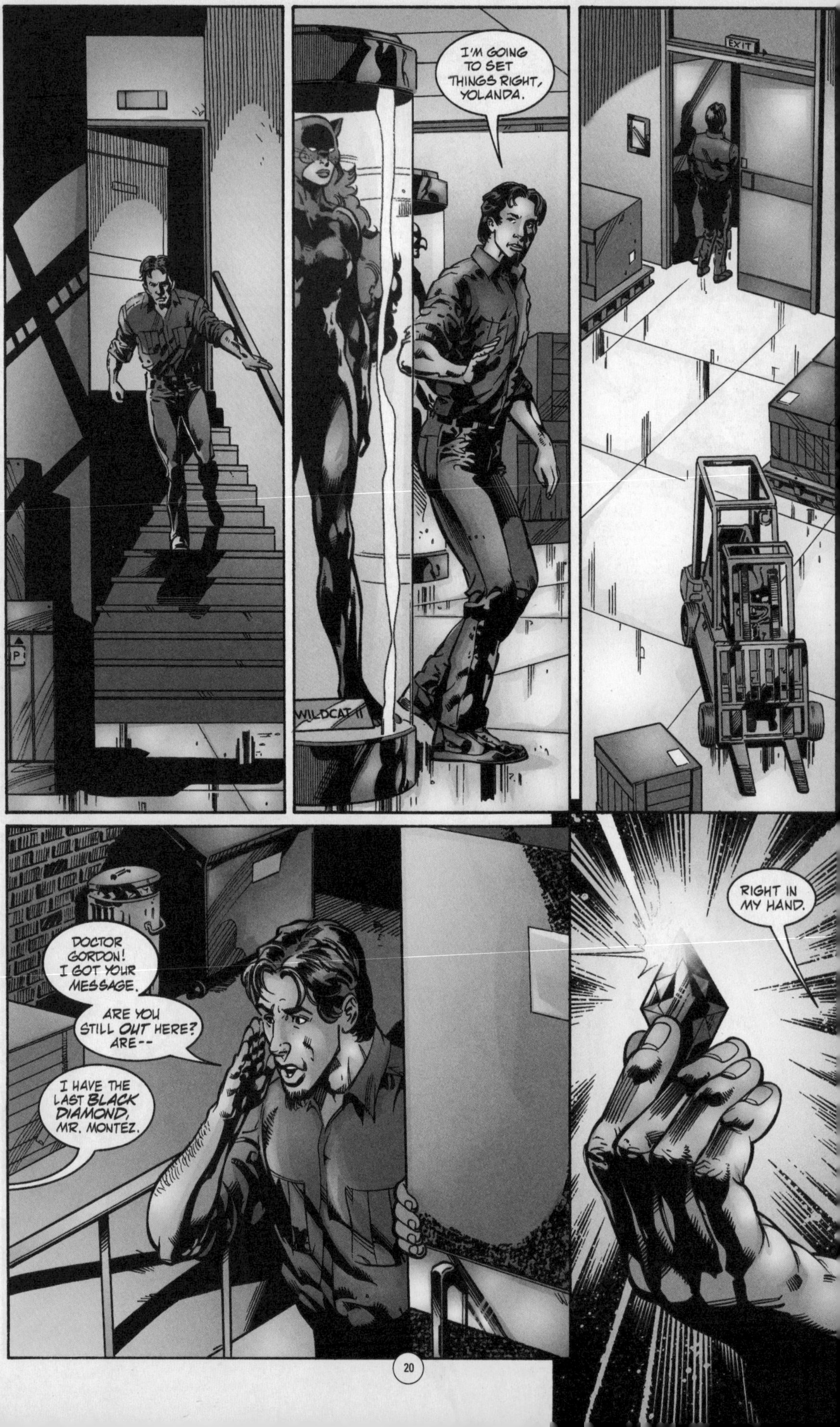
I'M GOING TO SET THINGS RIGHT, YOLANDA.
WILDCAT II
EXIT
DOCTOR GORDON! I GOT YOUR MESSAGE.
ARE YOU STILL OUT HERE? ARE--
I HAVE THE LAST BLACK DIAMOND, MR. MONTEZ.
RIGHT IN MY HAND.

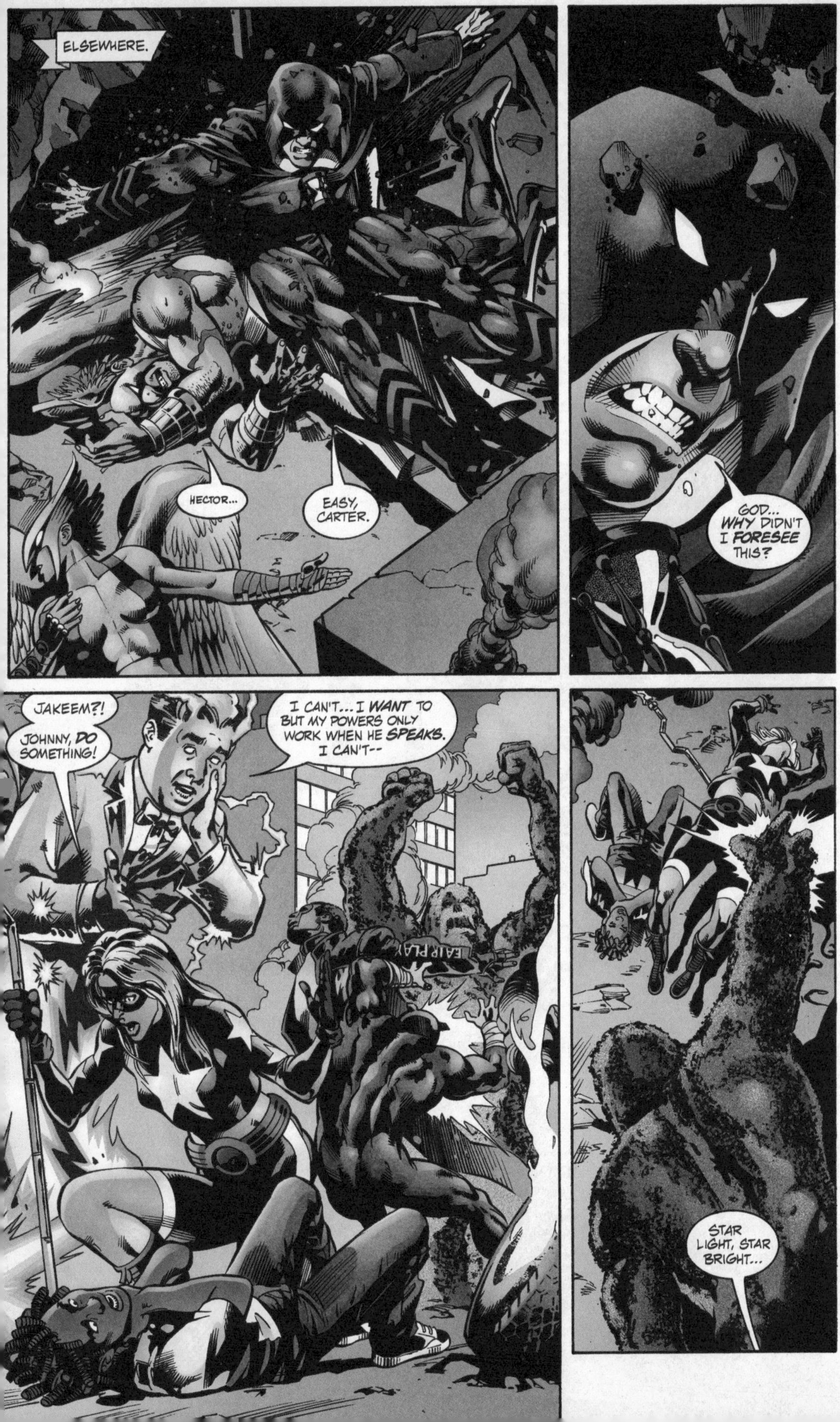
ELSEWHERE.
HECTOR...
EASY, CARTER.
GOD... WHY DIDN'T I FORESEE THIS?
JAKEEM?!
JOHNNY, DO SOMETHING!
I CAN'T... I WANT TO BUT MY POWERS ONLY WORK WHEN HE SPEAKS. I CAN'T--
FAIR PLAY
STAR LIGHT, STAR BRIGHT...

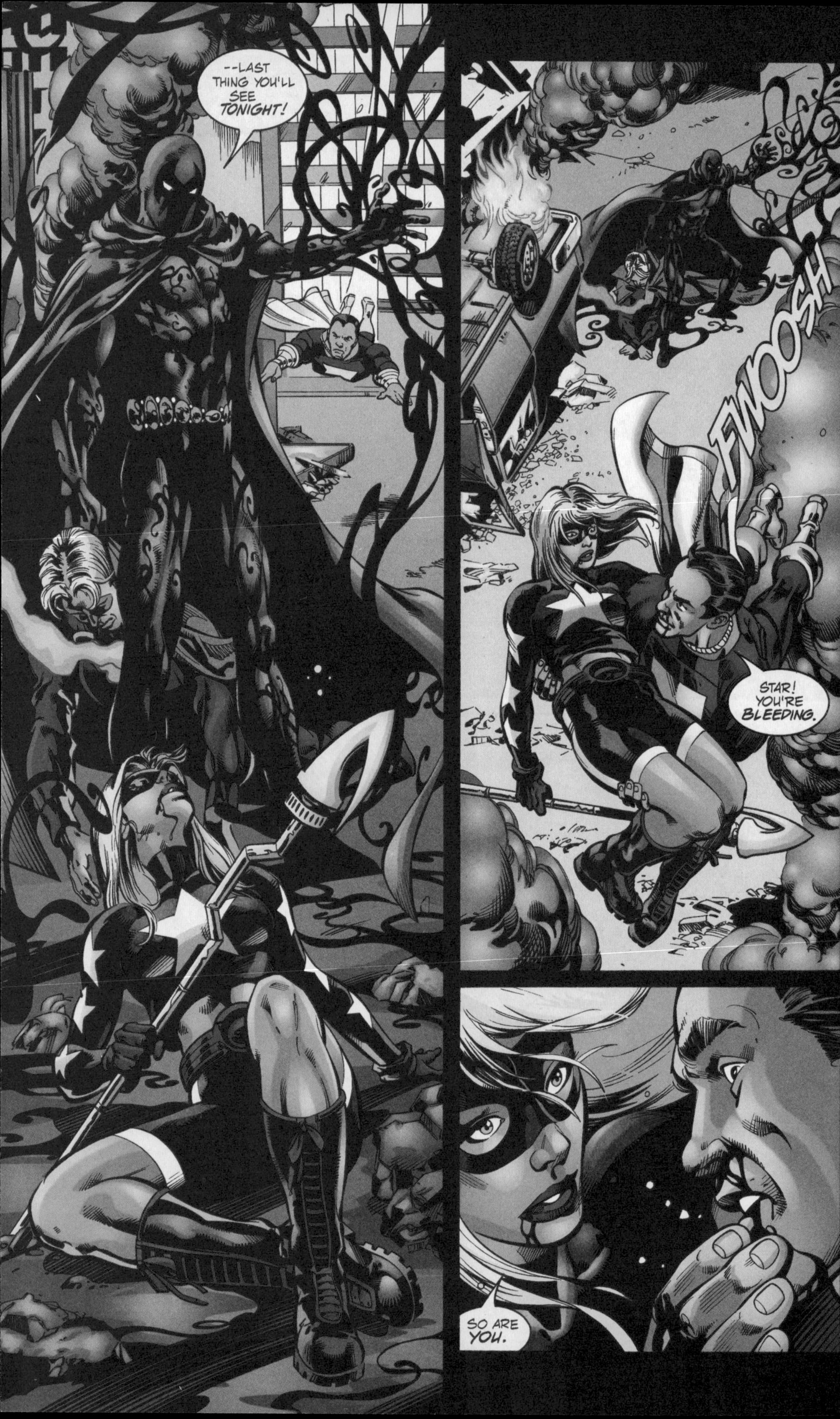
--LAST THING YOU'LL SEE TONIGHT!
FWOOSH
STAR! YOU'RE BLEEDING.
SO ARE YOU.

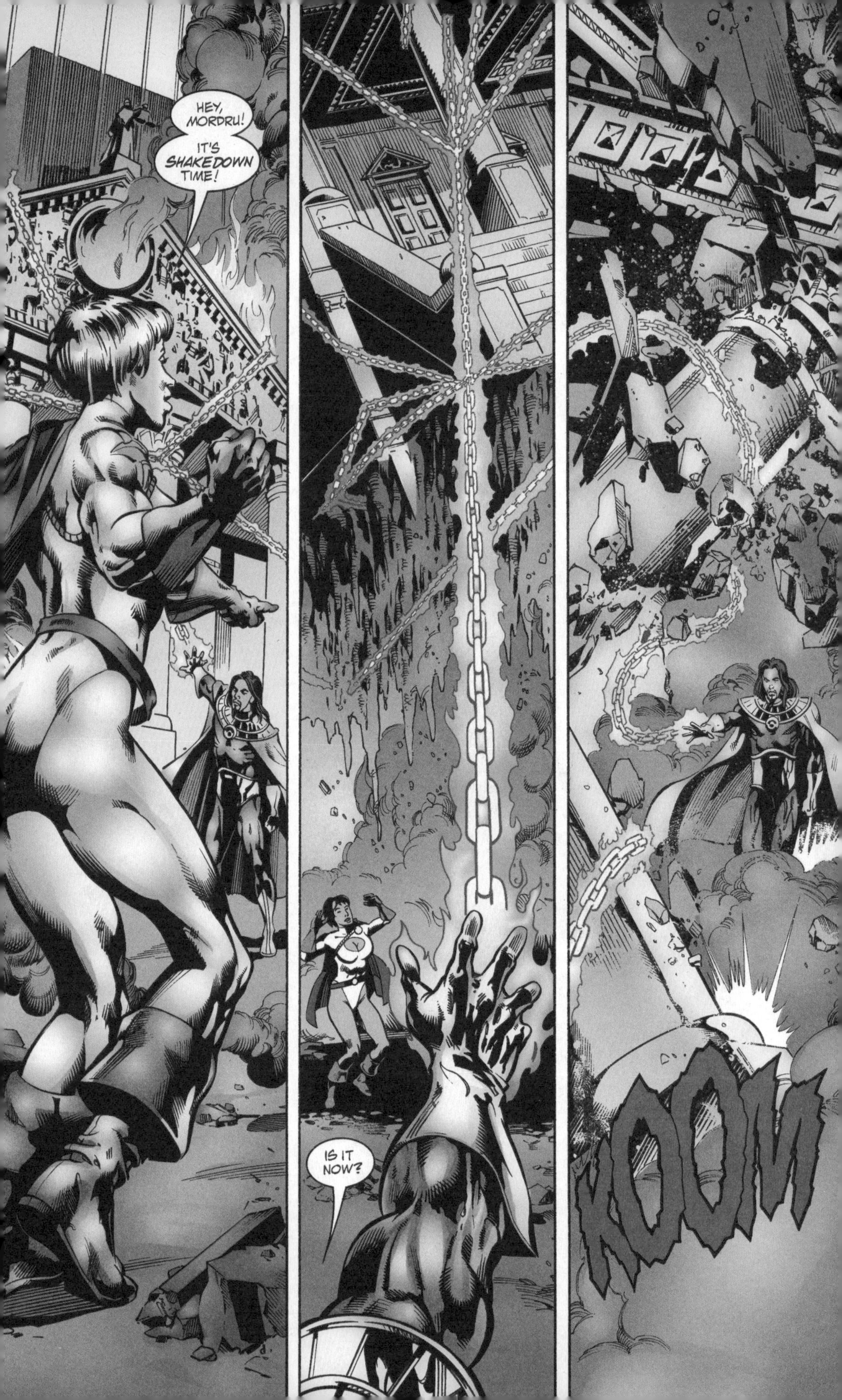

HEY, MORDRU!
IT'S SHAKEDOWN TIME!
IS IT NOW?
KROOM

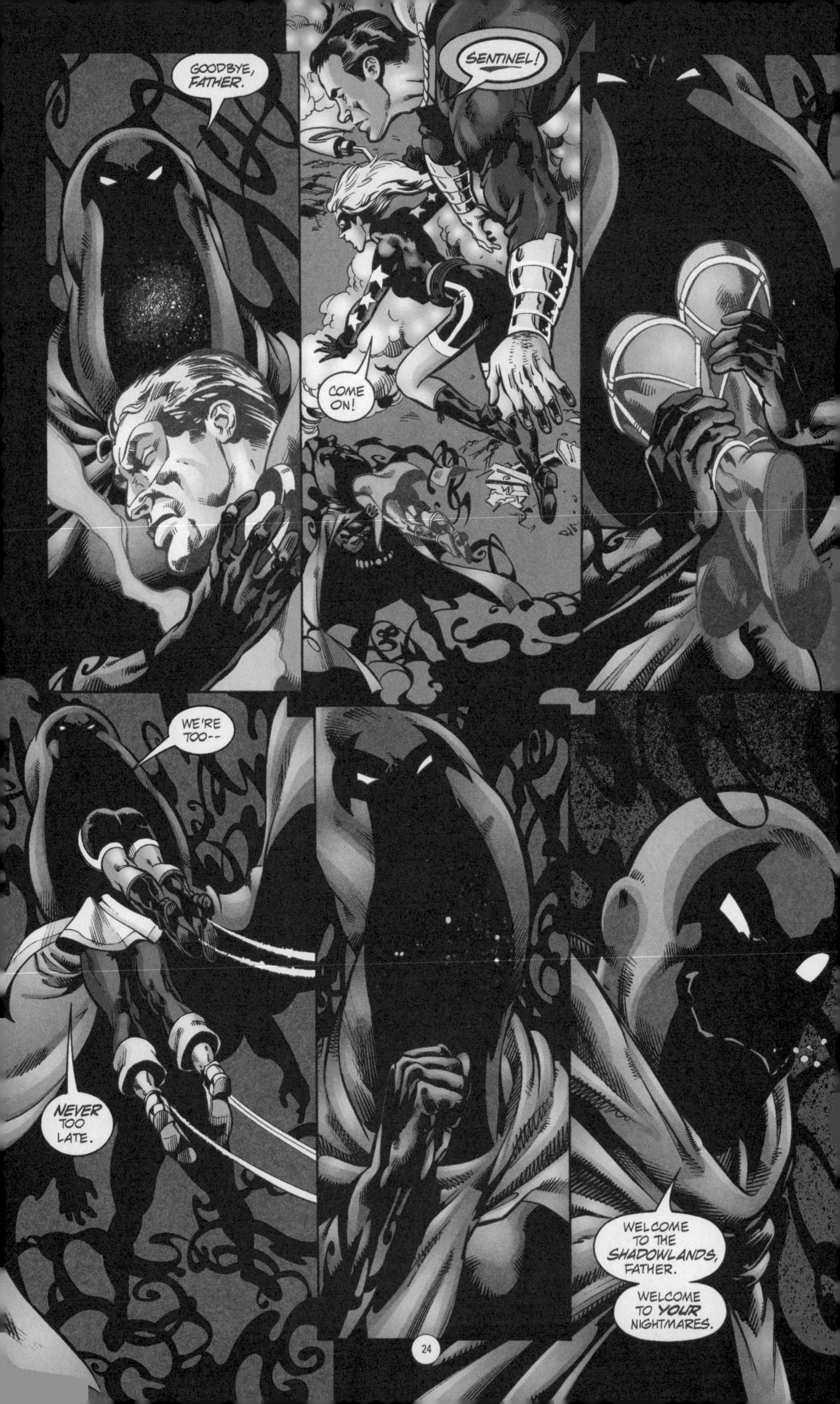
GOODBYE, FATHER.
SENTINEL!
COME ON!
WE'RE TOO--
NEVER TOO LATE.
WELCOME TO THE SHADOWLANDS, FATHER.
WELCOME TO YOUR NIGHTMARES.

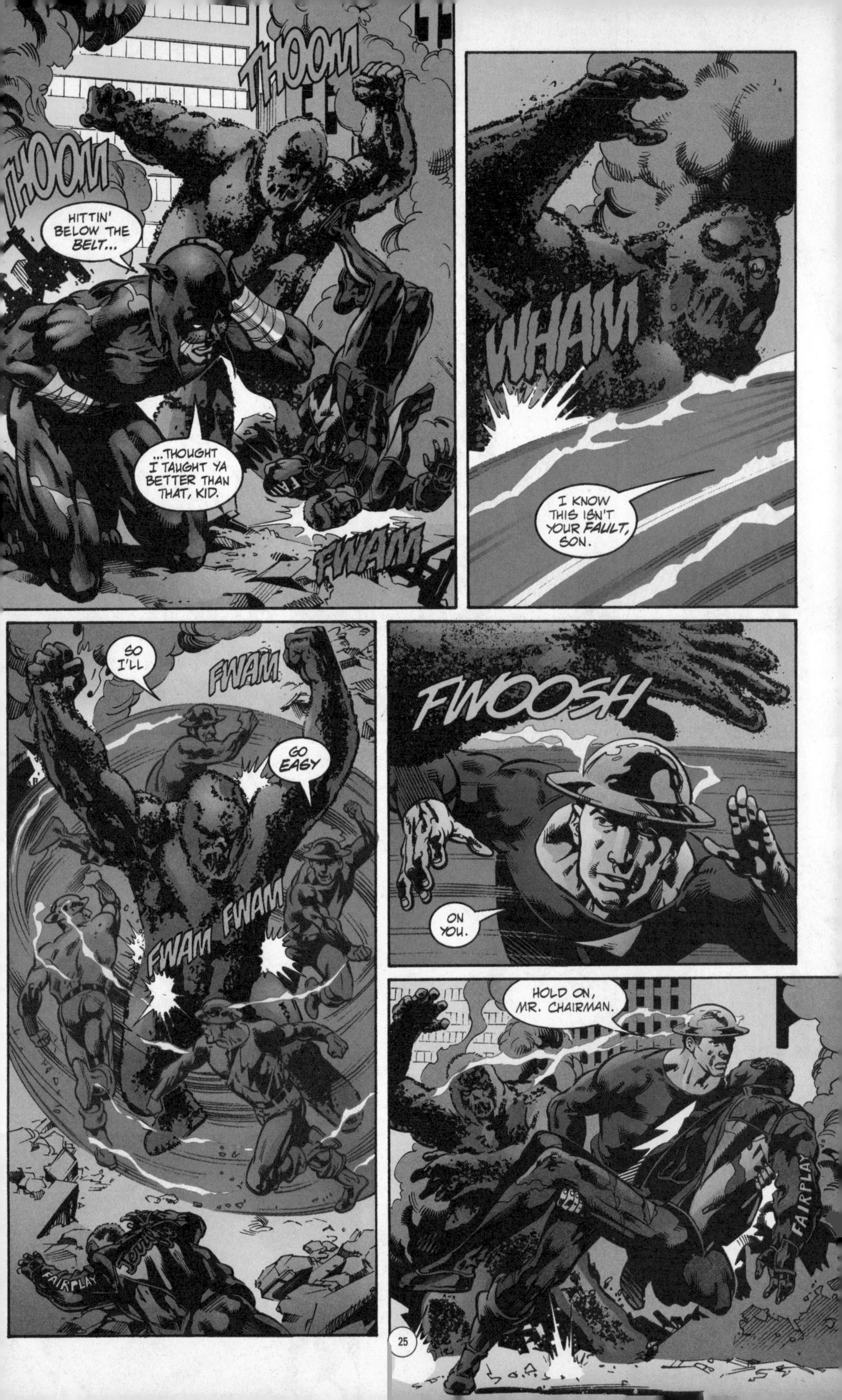
THOOM
THOOM
HITTIN' BELOW THE BELT...
...THOUGHT I TAUGHT YA BETTER THAN THAT, KID.
FWAM
WHAM
I KNOW THIS ISN'T YOUR FAULT, SON.
SO I'LL
FWAM
GO EASY
FWAM
FWAM
FWAM
FAIRPLAY
FWOOSH
ON YOU.
HOLD ON, MR. CHAIRMAN.
FAIRPLAY

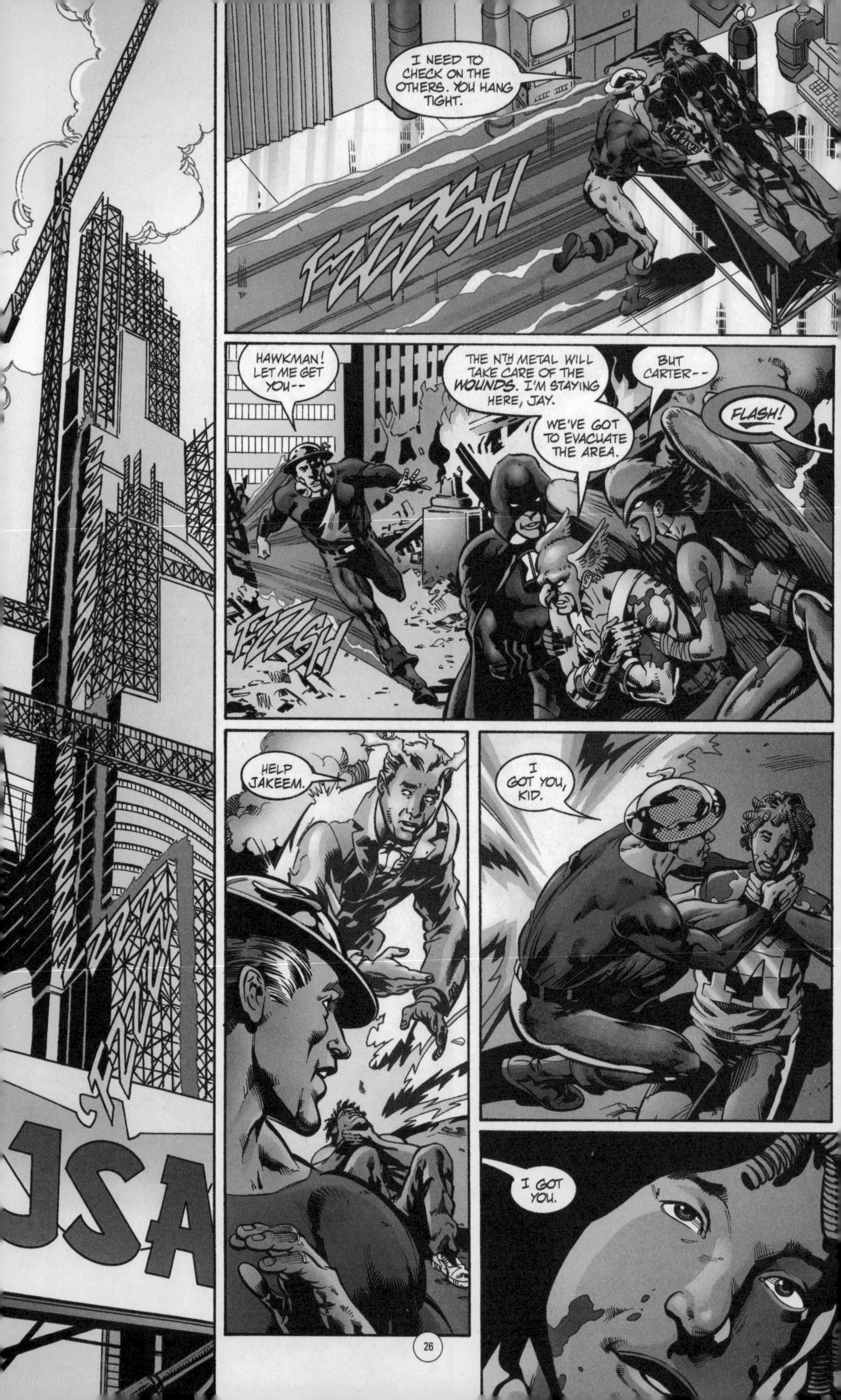

I NEED TO CHECK ON THE OTHERS. YOU HANG TIGHT.
FZZZSH
HAWKMAN! LET ME GET YOU--
THE NTH METAL WILL TAKE CARE OF THE WOUNDS. I'M STAYING HERE, JAY.
WE'VE GOT TO EVACUATE THE AREA.
BUT CARTER--
FLASH!
FZZSH
HELP JAKEEM.
I GOT YOU, KID.
I GOT YOU.
JSA

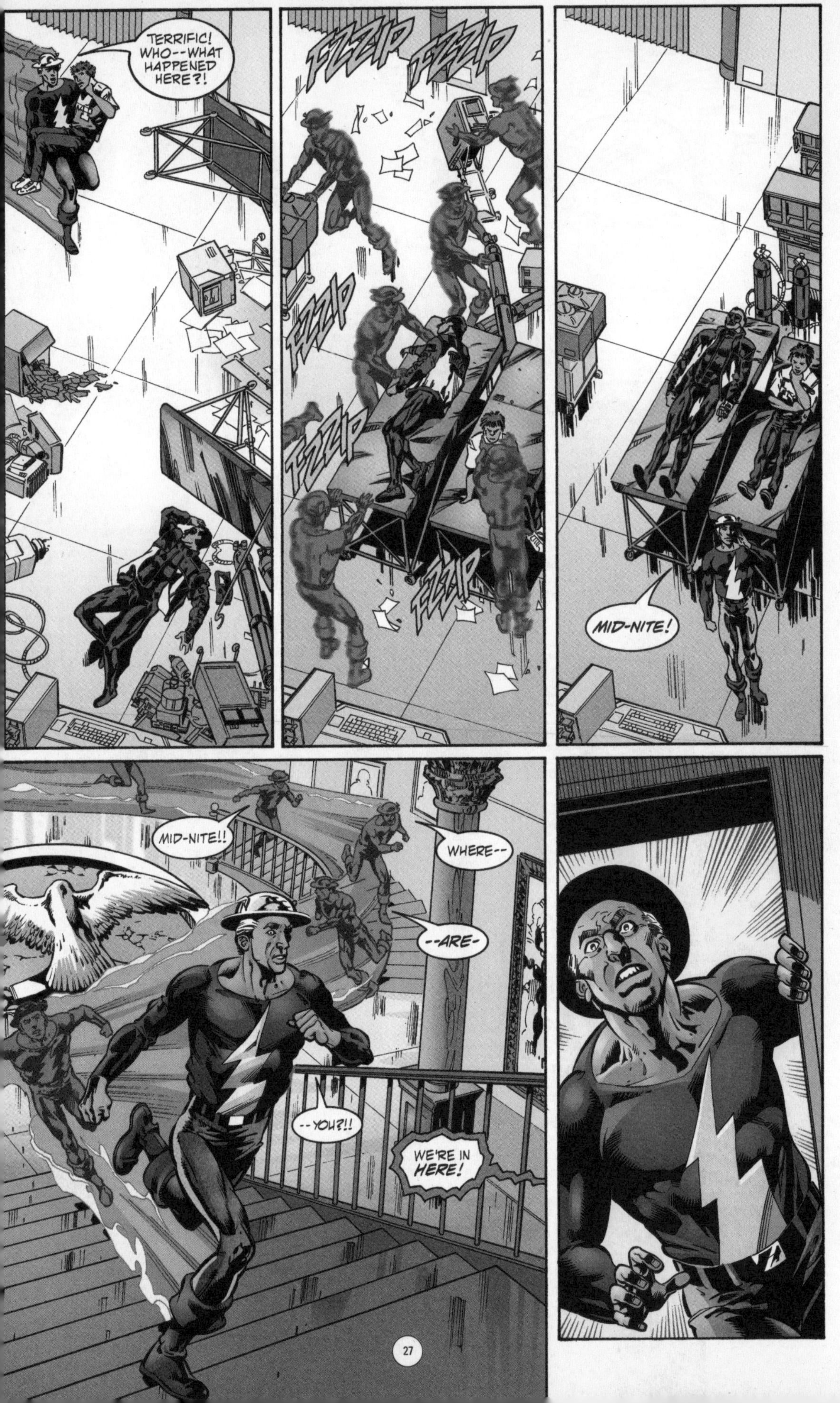
TERRIFIC! WHO--WHAT HAPPENED HERE?!
FZZIP FZZIP
FZZIP
FZZIP
FZZIP
MID-NITE!
MID-NITE!!
WHERE--
--ARE-
--YOU?!!
WE'RE IN HERE!

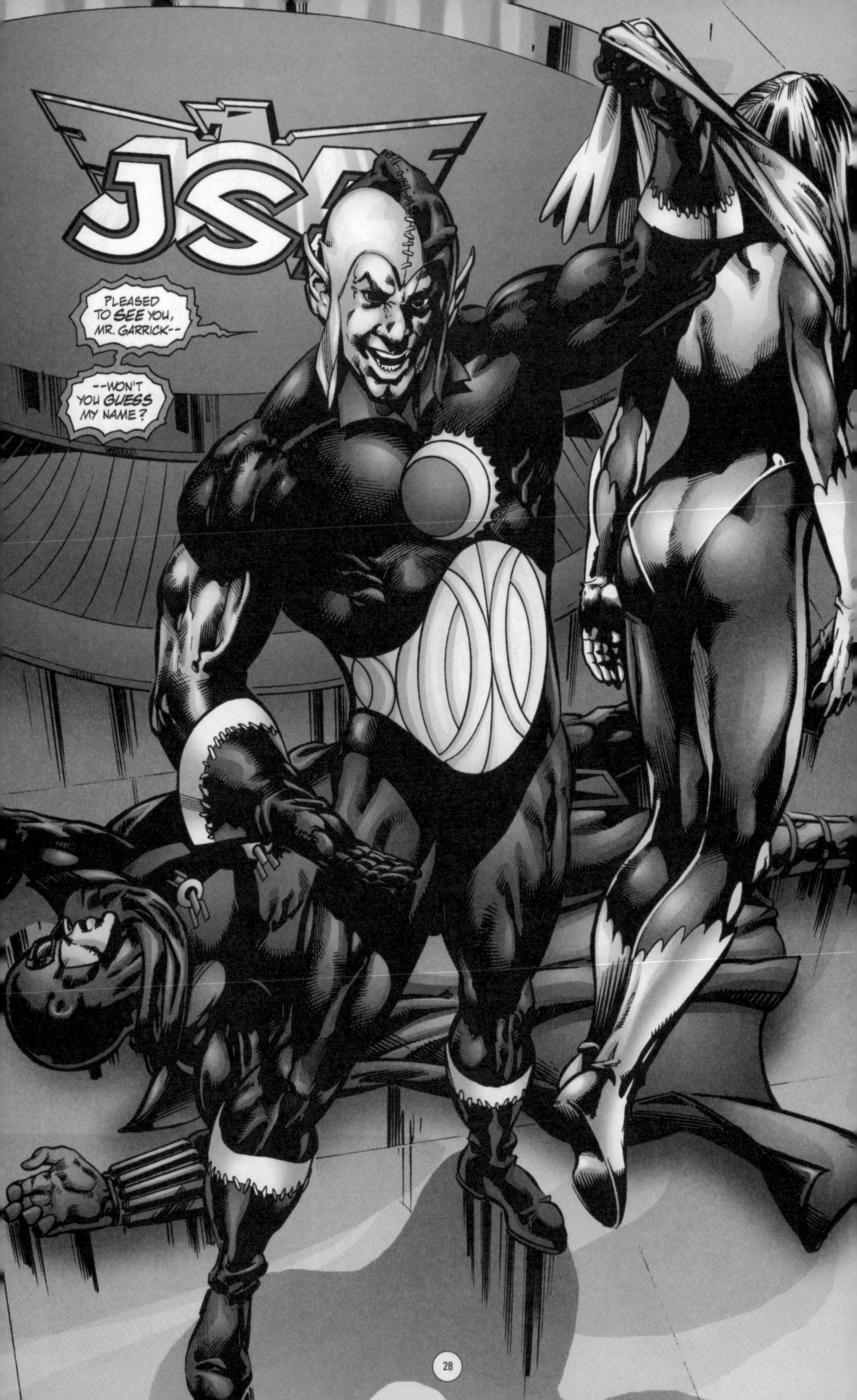
JSA
PLEASED TO SEE YOU, MR. GARRICK--
--WON'T YOU GUESS MY NAME?

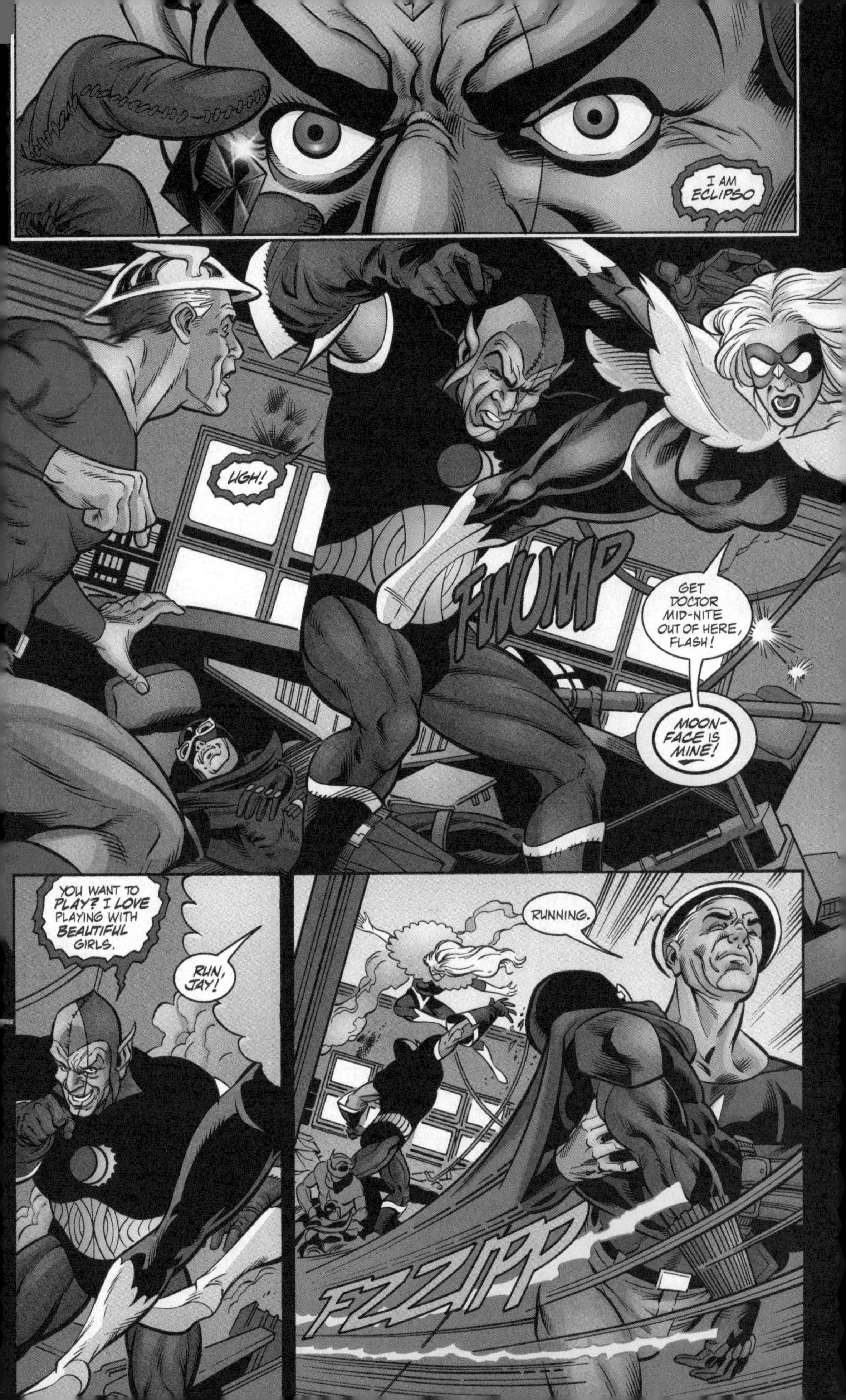
I AM ECLIPSO
UGH!
FWUMP
GET DOCTOR MID-NITE OUT OF HERE, FLASH!
MOON-FACE IS MINE!
YOU WANT TO PLAY? I LOVE PLAYING WITH BEAUTIFUL GIRLS.
RUN, JAY!
RUNNING.
FZZIPP

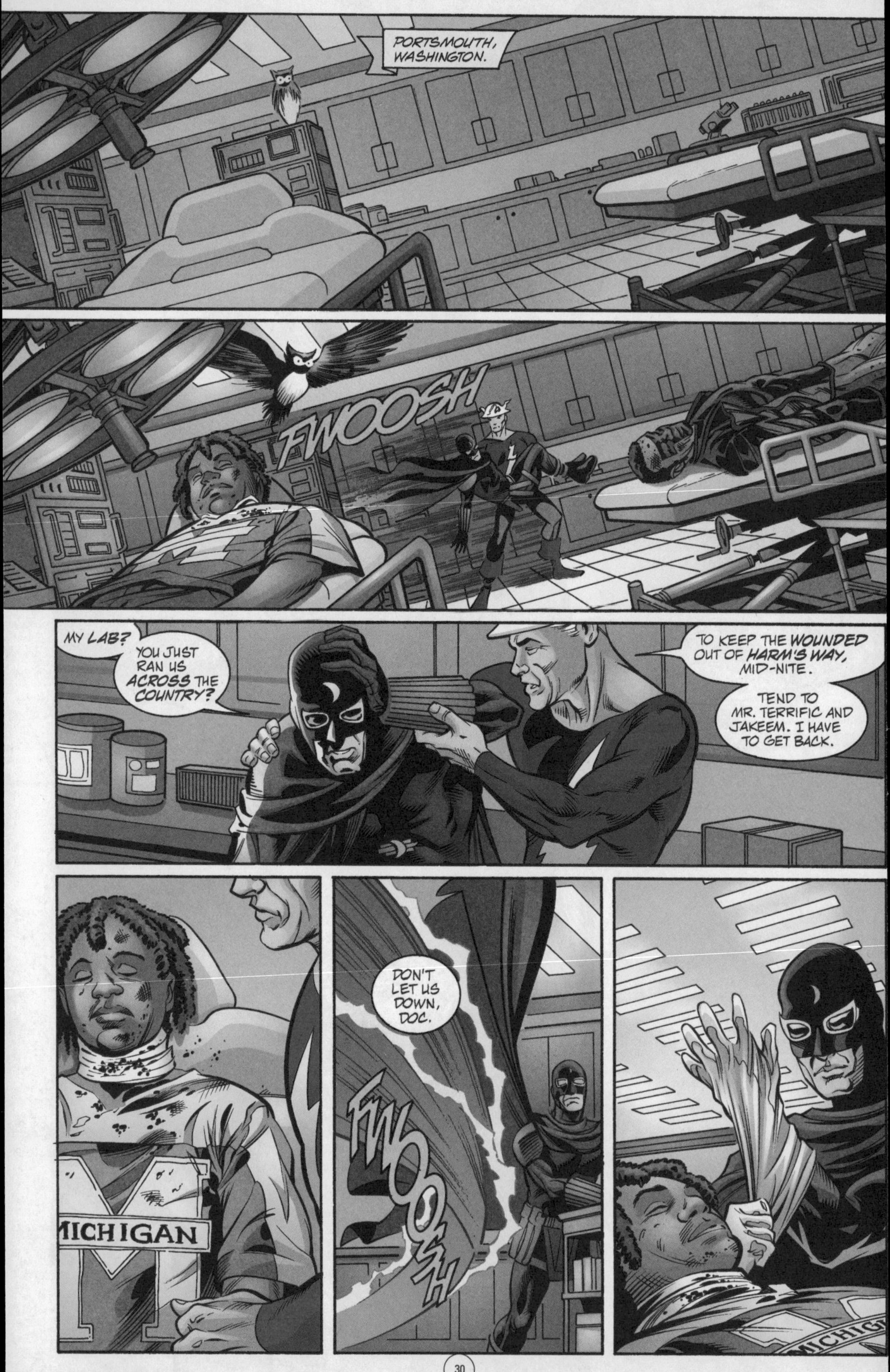
PORTSMOUTH, WASHINGTON.
FWOOSH
MY LAB? YOU JUST RAN US ACROSS THE COUNTRY?
TO KEEP THE WOUNDED OUT OF HARM'S WAY, MID-NITE.
TEND TO MR. TERRIFIC AND JAKEEM. I HAVE TO GET BACK.
MICHIGAN
DON'T LET US DOWN, DOC.
FWOOOSH

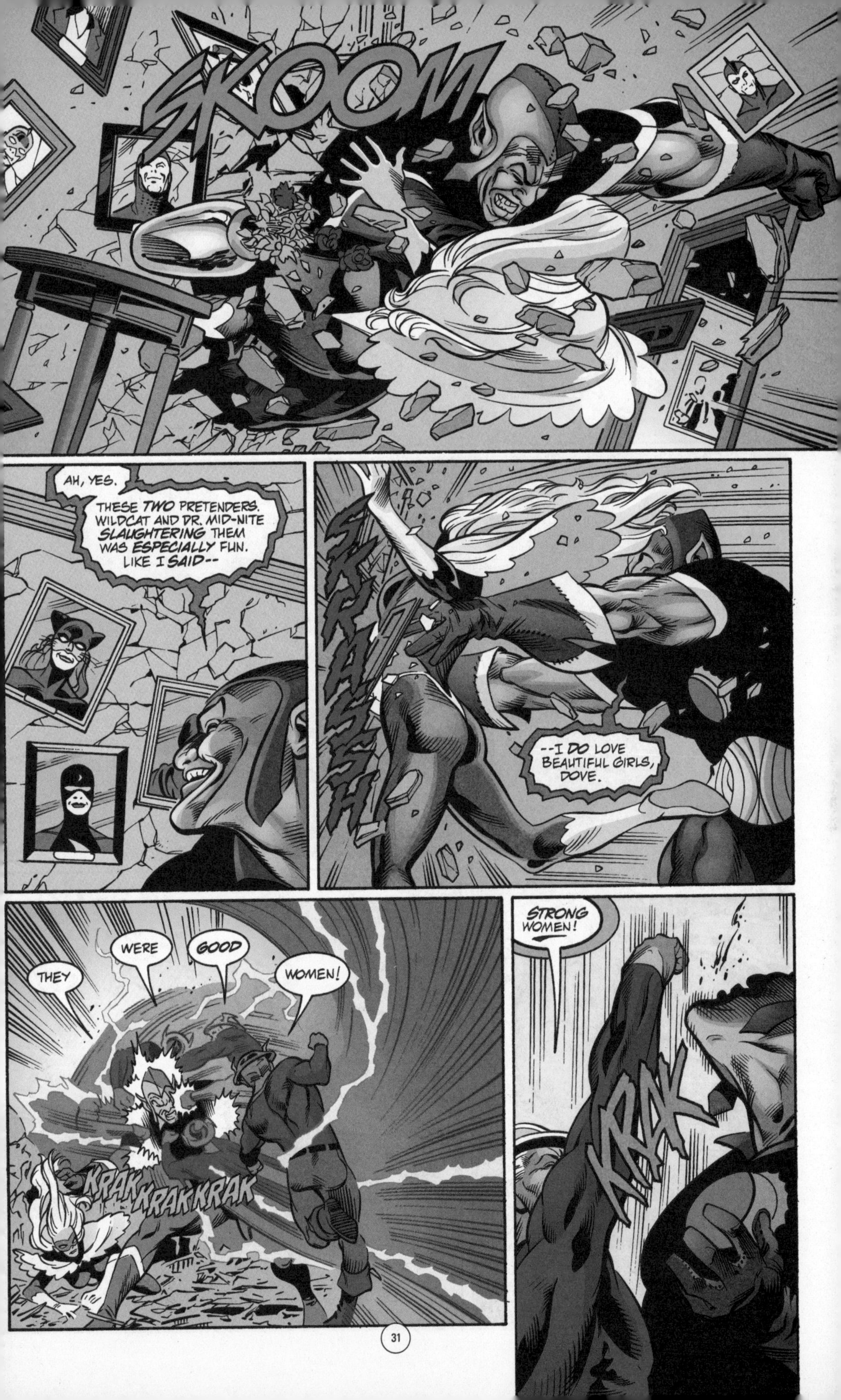
SKOOM
AH, YES.
THESE TWO PRETENDERS. WILDCAT AND DR. MID-NITE SLAUGHTERING THEM WAS ESPECIALLY FUN. LIKE I SAID--
SKRASHSH
--I DO LOVE BEAUTIFUL GIRLS, DOVE.
THEY
WERE
GOOD
WOMEN!
KRAK KRAK KRAK
STRONG WOMEN!
KRAK

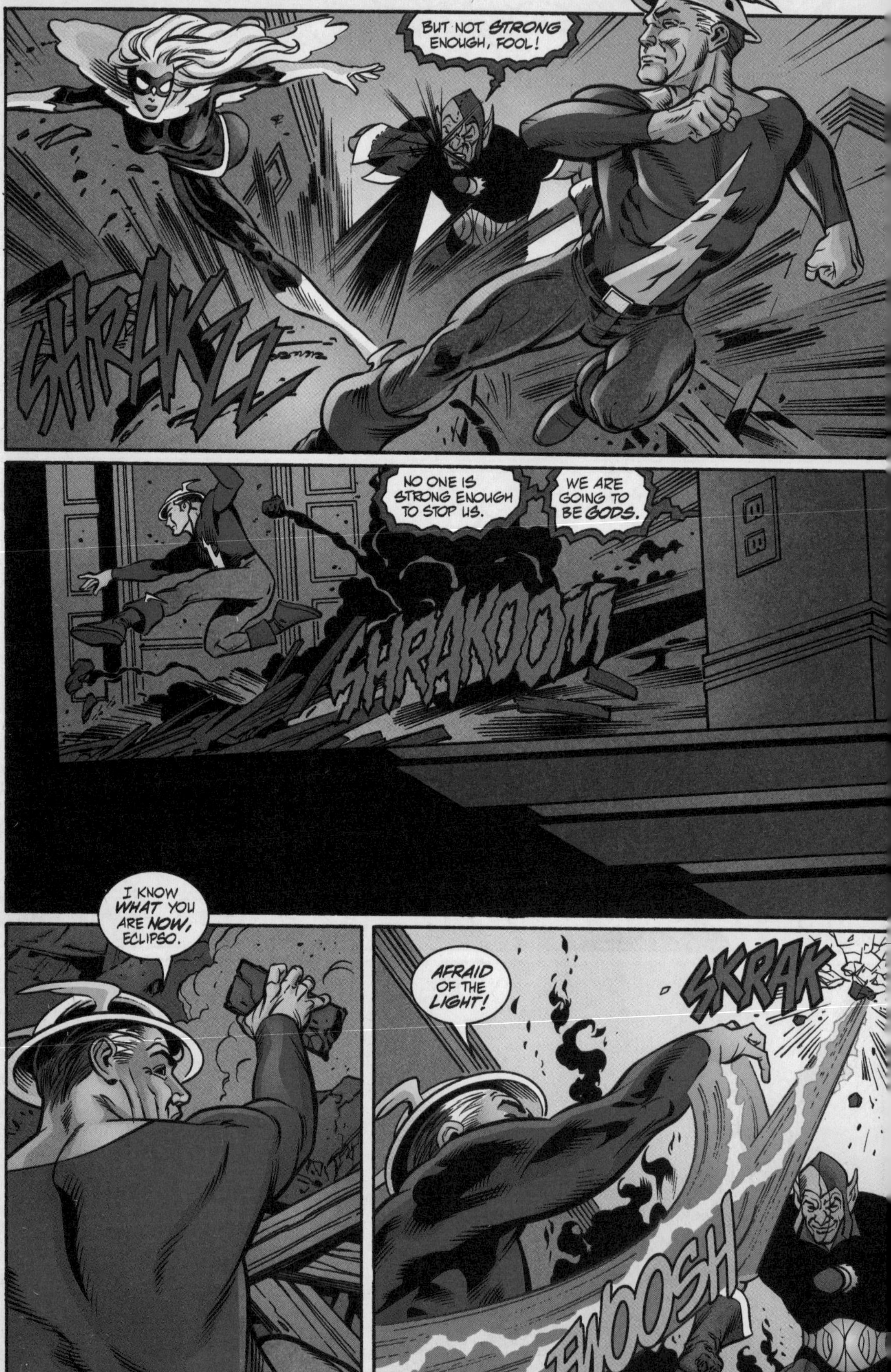

BUT NOT STRONG ENOUGH, FOOL!
SHRAKZZ
NO ONE IS STRONG ENOUGH TO STOP US.
WE ARE GOING TO BE GODS.
SHRAKOOM
I KNOW WHAT YOU ARE NOW, ECLIPSO.
AFRAID OF THE LIGHT!
SKRAK
FWOOSH

YAAHH!

SSSSS

HURTS?

GOOD.

FWIP FWIP FWIP

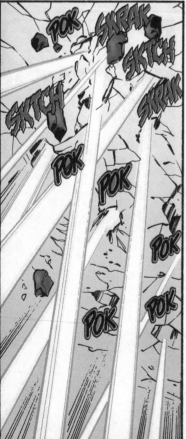

POK
SKRAK
SKTCH
SKTCH
SKRAK
POK
POK
POK
POK POK

ENJOY THE SUNLIGHT WHILE YOU CAN.

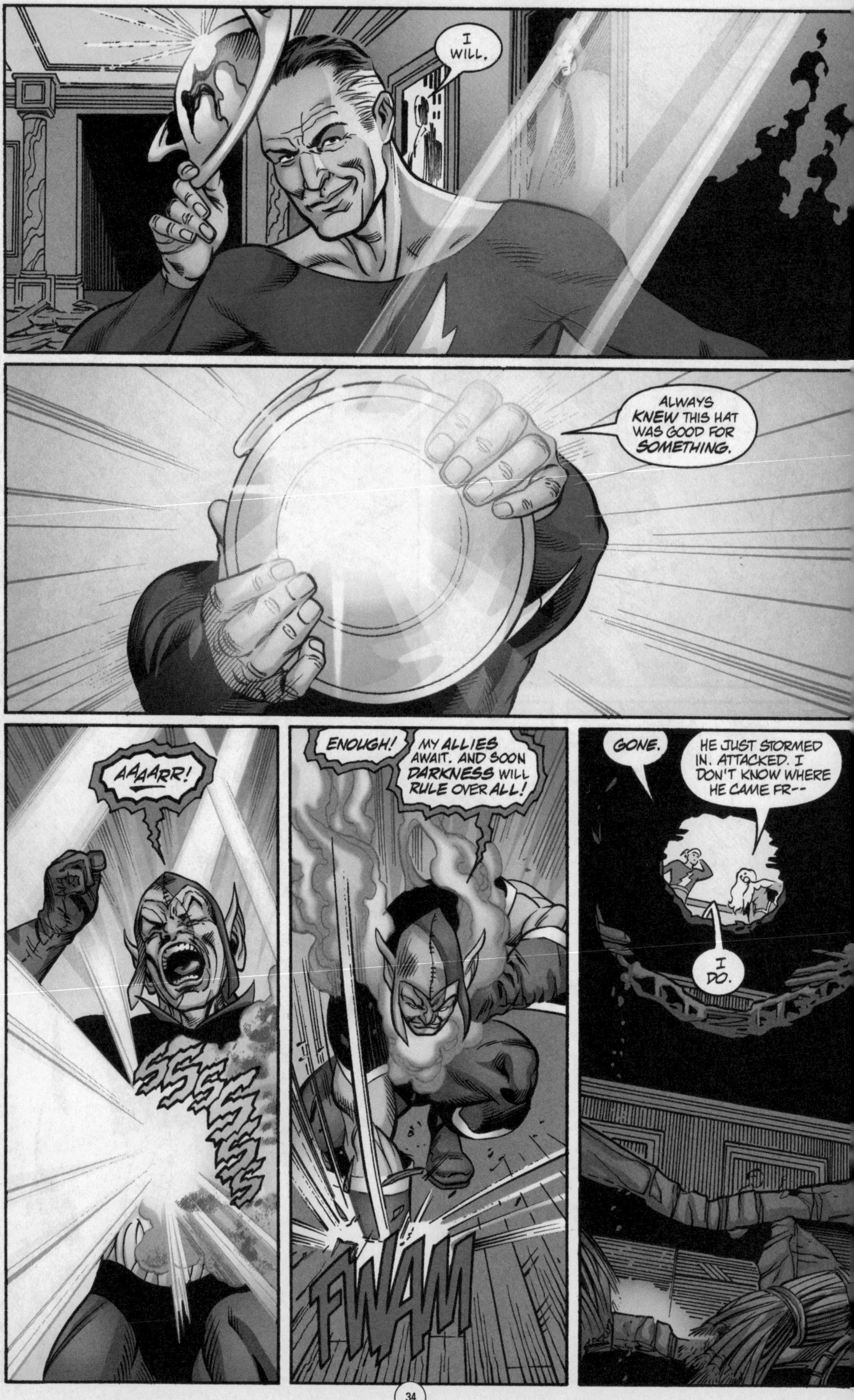
I WILL.
ALWAYS KNEW THIS HAT WAS GOOD FOR SOMETHING.
AAAARR!
SSSSSSS
ENOUGH!
MY ALLIES AWAIT. AND SOON DARKNESS WILL RULE OVER ALL!
FWAM
GONE.
HE JUST STORMED IN. ATTACKED. I DON'T KNOW WHERE HE CAME FR--
I DO.

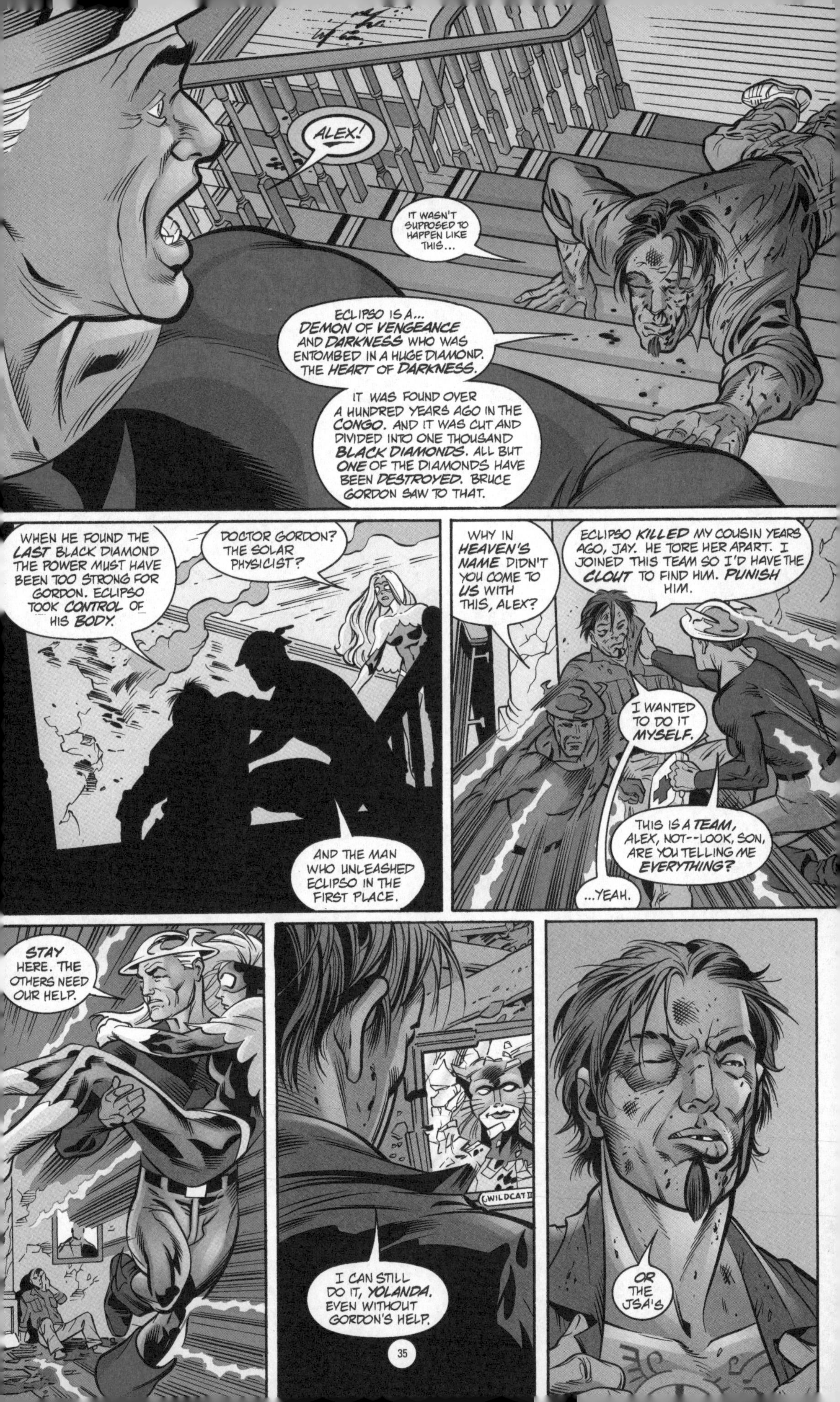
ALEX!
IT WASN'T SUPPOSED TO HAPPEN LIKE THIS...
ECLIPSO IS A... DEMON OF VENGEANCE AND DARKNESS WHO WAS ENTOMBED IN A HUGE DIAMOND. THE HEART OF DARKNESS.
IT WAS FOUND OVER A HUNDRED YEARS AGO IN THE CONGO. AND IT WAS CUT AND DIVIDED INTO ONE THOUSAND BLACK DIAMONDS. ALL BUT ONE OF THE DIAMONDS HAVE BEEN DESTROYED. BRUCE GORDON SAW TO THAT.
WHEN HE FOUND THE LAST BLACK DIAMOND THE POWER MUST HAVE BEEN TOO STRONG FOR GORDON. ECLIPSO TOOK CONTROL OF HIS BODY.
DOCTOR GORDON? THE SOLAR PHYSICIST?
AND THE MAN WHO UNLEASHED ECLIPSO IN THE FIRST PLACE.
WHY IN HEAVEN'S NAME DIDN'T YOU COME TO US WITH THIS, ALEX?
ECLIPSO KILLED MY COUSIN YEARS AGO, JAY. HE TORE HER APART. I JOINED THIS TEAM SO I'D HAVE THE CLOUT TO FIND HIM. PUNISH HIM.
I WANTED TO DO IT MYSELF.
THIS IS A TEAM, ALEX, NOT--LOOK, SON, ARE YOU TELLING ME EVERYTHING?
...YEAH.
STAY HERE. THE OTHERS NEED OUR HELP.
WILDCAT II
I CAN STILL DO IT, YOLANDA. EVEN WITHOUT GORDON'S HELP.
OR THE JSA'S

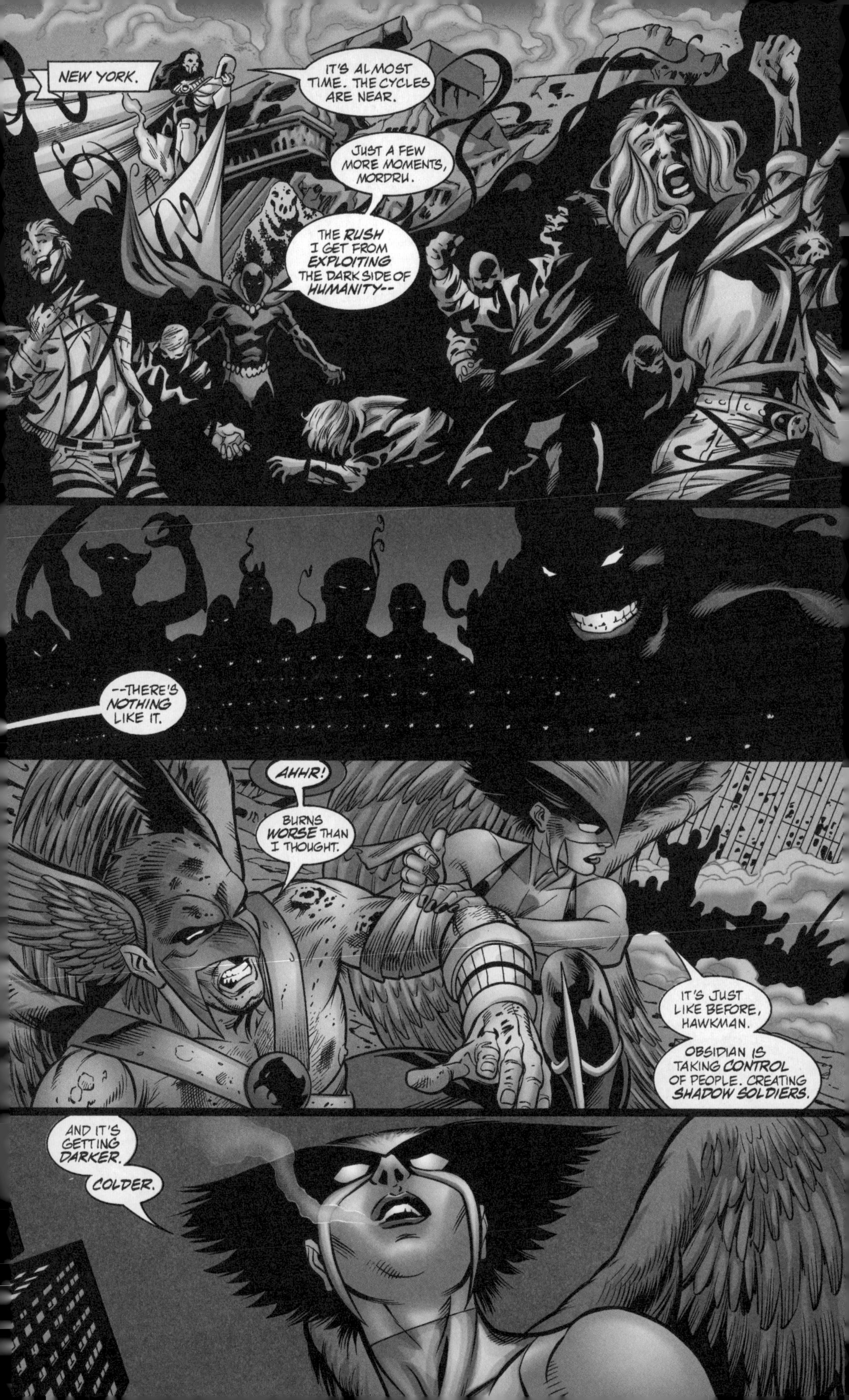

NEW YORK.
IT'S ALMOST TIME. THE CYCLES ARE NEAR.
JUST A FEW MORE MOMENTS, MORDRU.
THE RUSH I GET FROM EXPLOITING THE DARK SIDE OF HUMANITY--
--THERE'S NOTHING LIKE IT.
AHHR!
BURNS WORSE THAN I THOUGHT.
IT'S JUST LIKE BEFORE, HAWKMAN.
OBSIDIAN IS TAKING CONTROL OF PEOPLE. CREATING SHADOW SOLDIERS.
AND IT'S GETTING DARKER.
COLDER.

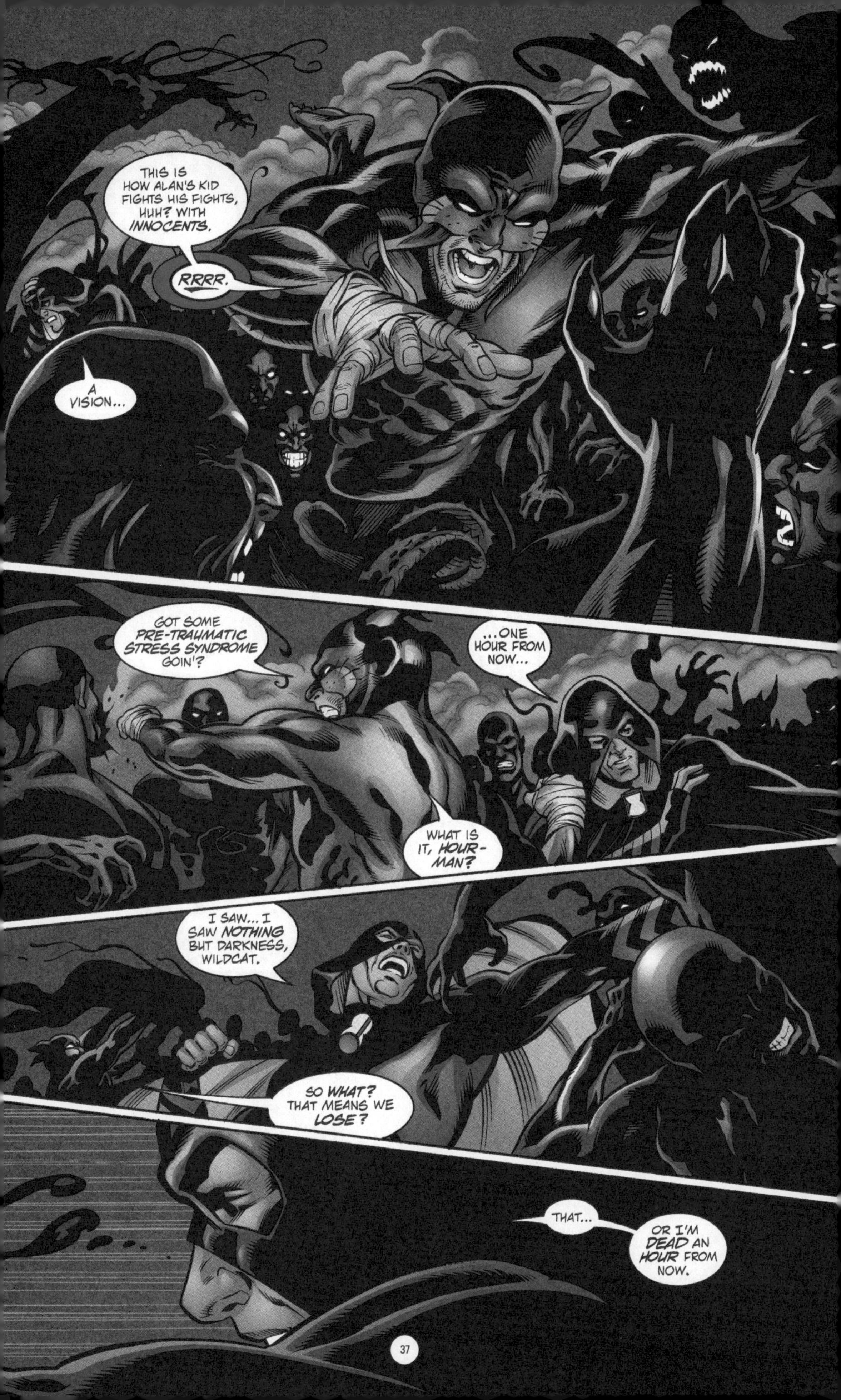
THIS IS HOW ALAN'S KID FIGHTS HIS FIGHTS, HUH? WITH INNOCENTS.
RRRR.
A VISION...
GOT SOME PRE-TRAUMATIC STRESS SYNDROME GOIN'?
...ONE HOUR FROM NOW...
WHAT IS IT, HOUR-MAN?
I SAW... I SAW NOTHING BUT DARKNESS, WILDCAT.
SO WHAT? THAT MEANS WE LOSE?
THAT...
OR I'M DEAD AN HOUR FROM NOW.

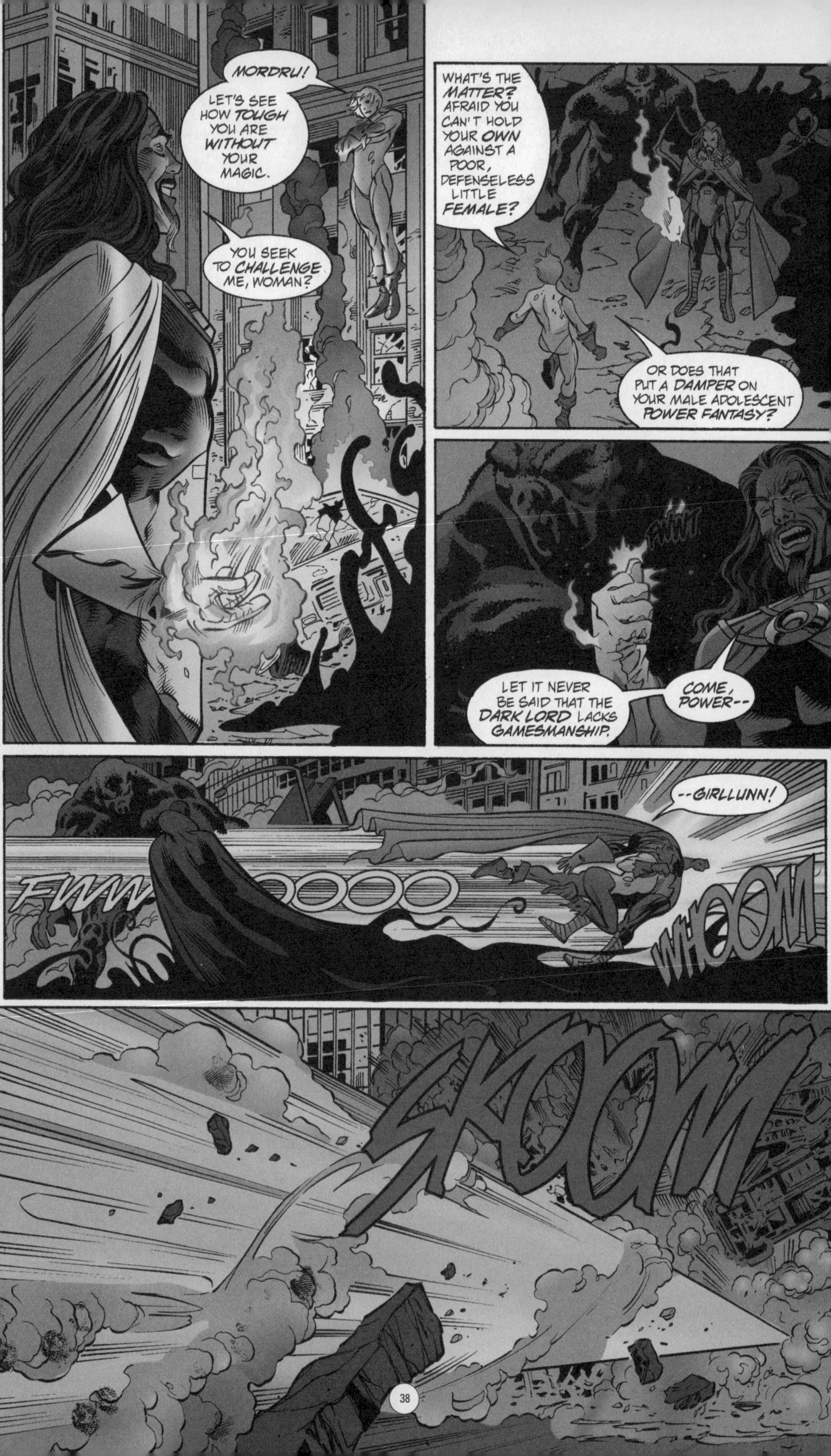
MORDRU!
LET'S SEE HOW TOUGH YOU ARE WITHOUT YOUR MAGIC.
YOU SEEK TO CHALLENGE ME, WOMAN?
WHAT'S THE MATTER? AFRAID YOU CAN'T HOLD YOUR OWN AGAINST A POOR, DEFENSELESS LITTLE FEMALE?
OR DOES THAT PUT A DAMPER ON YOUR MALE ADOLESCENT POWER FANTASY?
FWIT
LET IT NEVER BE SAID THAT THE DARK LORD LACKS GAMESMANSHIP.
COME, POWER--
--GIRLLUNN!
FWWOOOOO
WHOOM
SKOOM

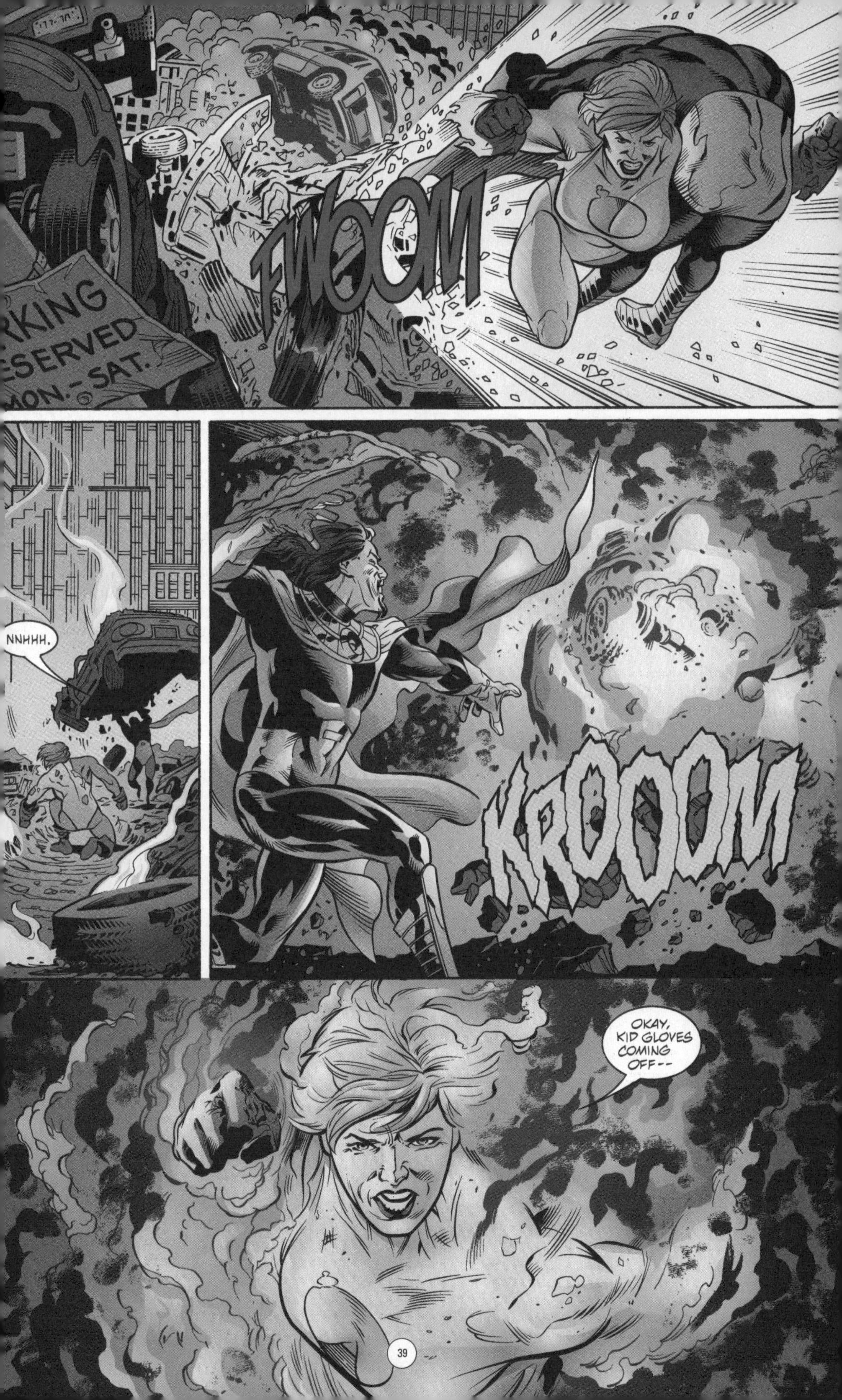
RKING
ESERVED
MON.-SAT.
FWOOM
NNHHH.
KROOOM
OKAY, KID GLOVES COMING OFF--

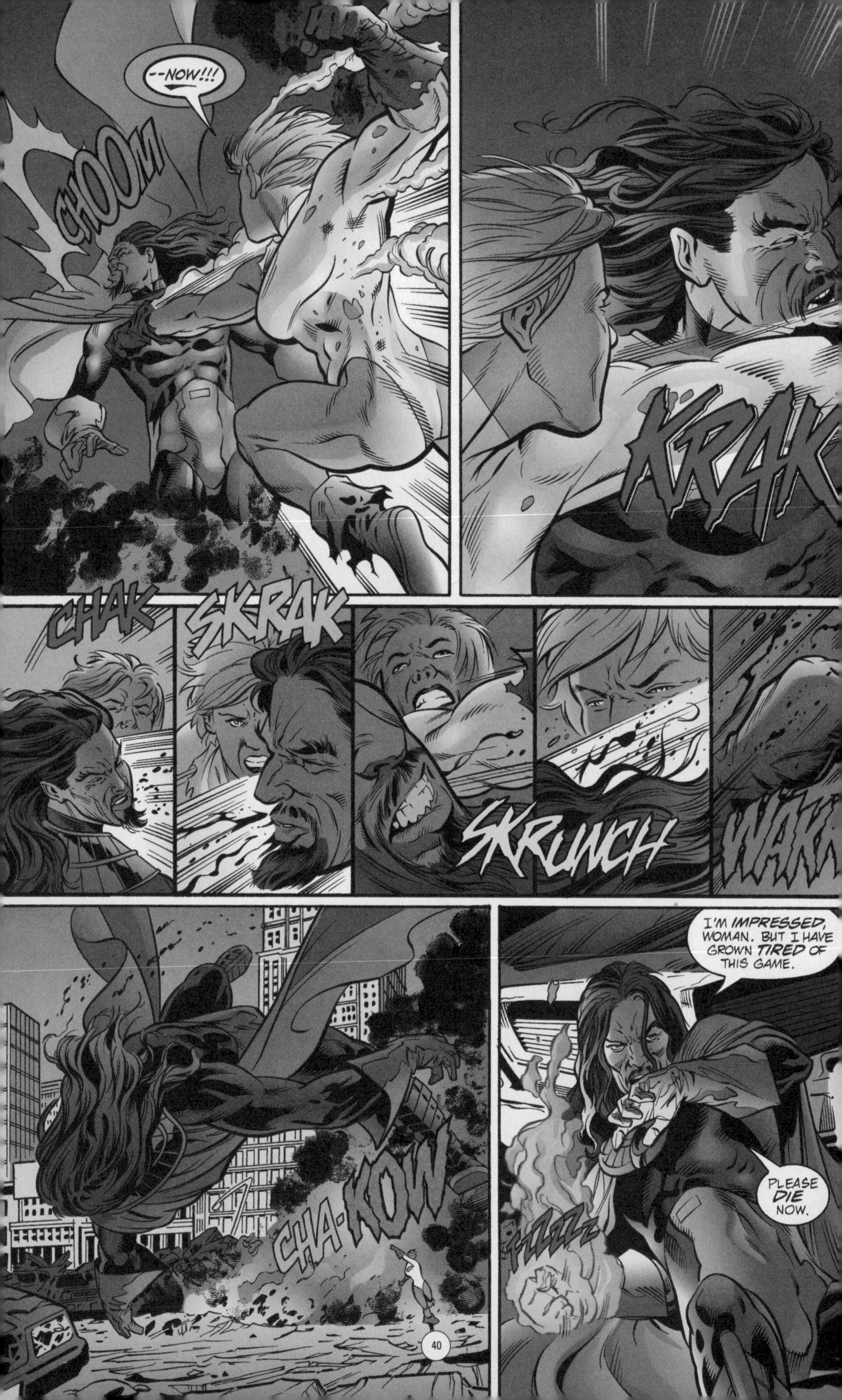

--NOW!!!
CHOOM
KRAK
CHAK
SKRAK
SKRUNCH
WAKK
CHA-KOW
I'M IMPRESSED, WOMAN. BUT I HAVE GROWN TIRED OF THIS GAME.
FZZZZZ
PLEASE DIE NOW.

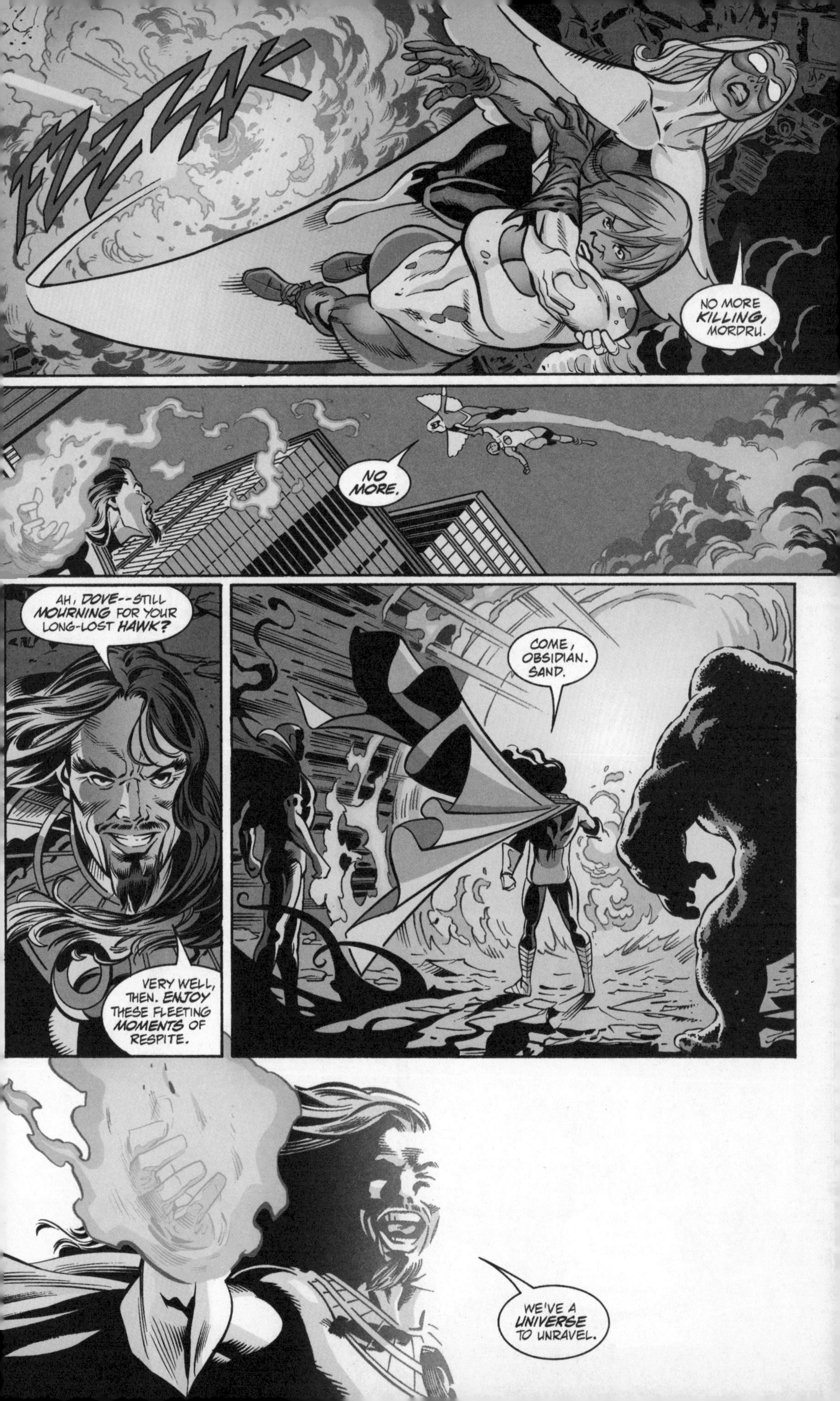
FZZZAK
NO MORE KILLING, MORDRU.
NO MORE.
AH, DOVE--STILL MOURNING FOR YOUR LONG-LOST HAWK?
VERY WELL, THEN. ENJOY THESE FLEETING MOMENTS OF RESPITE.
COME, OBSIDIAN. SAND.
WE'VE A UNIVERSE TO UNRAVEL.

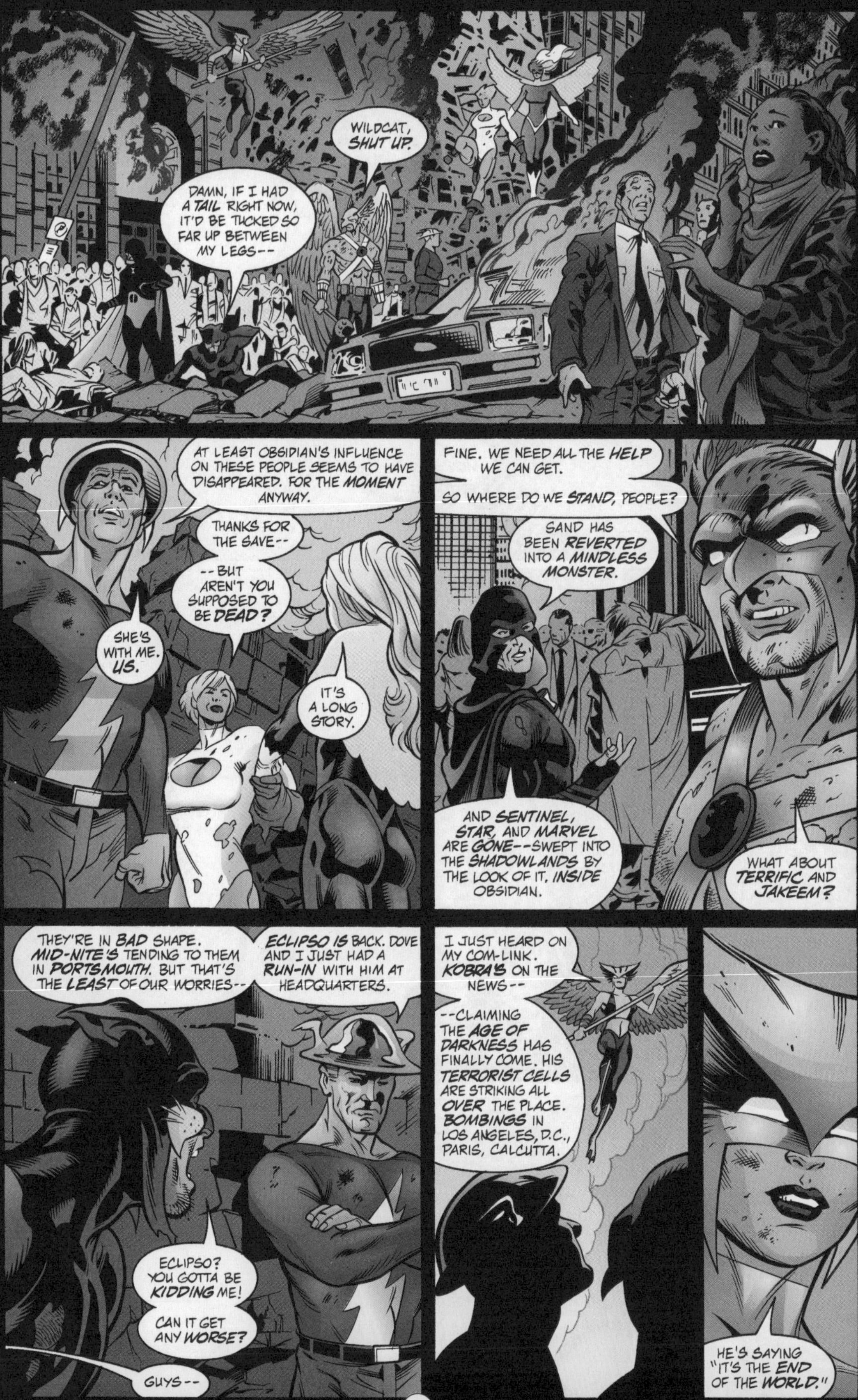
DAMN, IF I HAD A TAIL RIGHT NOW, IT'D BE TUCKED SO FAR UP BETWEEN MY LEGS--
WILDCAT, SHUT UP.
AT LEAST OBSIDIAN'S INFLUENCE ON THESE PEOPLE SEEMS TO HAVE DISAPPEARED. FOR THE MOMENT ANYWAY.
THANKS FOR THE SAVE--
--BUT AREN'T YOU SUPPOSED TO BE DEAD?
SHE'S WITH ME. US.
IT'S A LONG STORY.
FINE. WE NEED ALL THE HELP WE CAN GET.
SO WHERE DO WE STAND, PEOPLE?
SAND HAS BEEN REVERTED INTO A MINDLESS MONSTER.
AND SENTINEL, STAR, AND MARVEL ARE GONE--SWEPT INTO THE SHADOWLANDS BY THE LOOK OF IT. INSIDE OBSIDIAN.
WHAT ABOUT TERRIFIC AND JAKEEM?
THEY'RE IN BAD SHAPE. MID-NITE'S TENDING TO THEM IN PORTSMOUTH. BUT THAT'S THE LEAST OF OUR WORRIES--
ECLIPSO IS BACK. DOVE AND I JUST HAD A RUN-IN WITH HIM AT HEADQUARTERS.
ECLIPSO? YOU GOTTA BE KIDDING ME!
CAN IT GET ANY WORSE?
GUYS--
I JUST HEARD ON MY COM-LINK. KOBRA'S ON THE NEWS--
--CLAIMING THE AGE OF DARKNESS HAS FINALLY COME. HIS TERRORIST CELLS ARE STRIKING ALL OVER THE PLACE. BOMBINGS IN LOS ANGELES, D.C., PARIS, CALCUTTA.
HE'S SAYING "IT'S THE END OF THE WORLD."

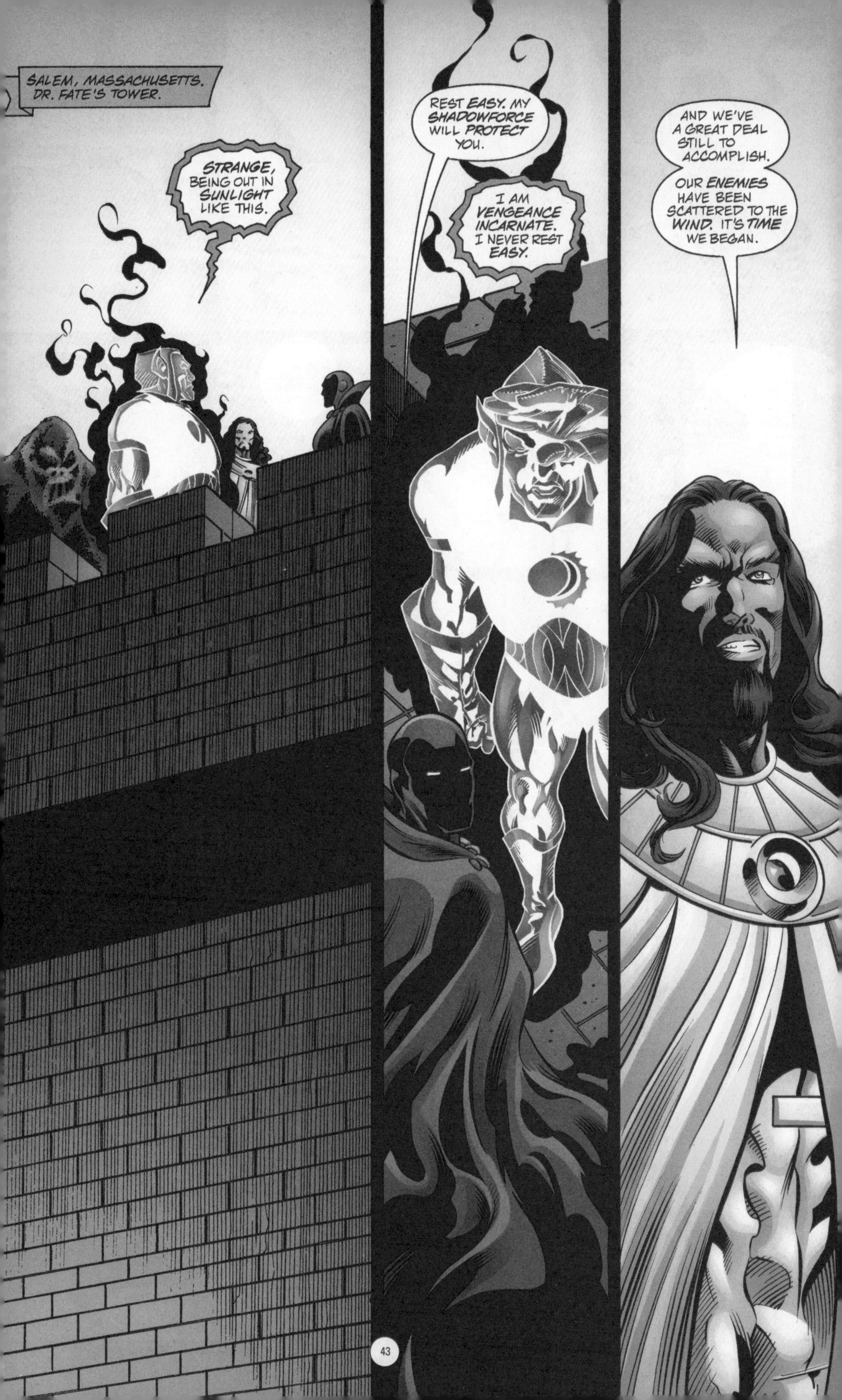
SALEM, MASSACHUSETTS. DR. FATE'S TOWER.
STRANGE, BEING OUT IN SUNLIGHT LIKE THIS.
REST EASY. MY SHADOWFORCE WILL PROTECT YOU.
I AM VENGEANCE INCARNATE. I NEVER REST EASY.
AND WE'VE A GREAT DEAL STILL TO ACCOMPLISH.
OUR ENEMIES HAVE BEEN SCATTERED TO THE WIND. IT'S TIME WE BEGAN.

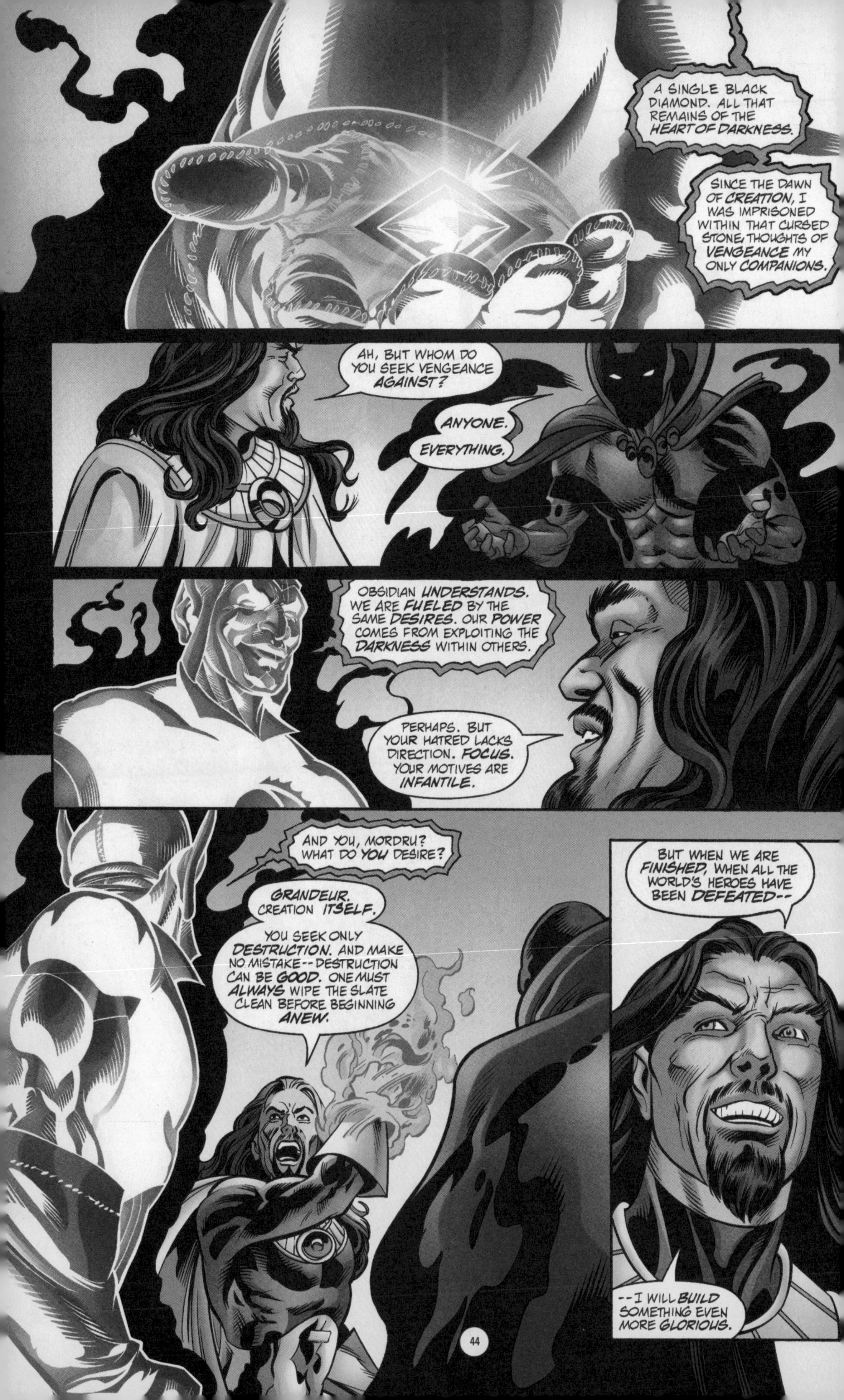
A SINGLE BLACK DIAMOND. ALL THAT REMAINS OF THE HEART OF DARKNESS.
SINCE THE DAWN OF CREATION, I WAS IMPRISONED WITHIN THAT CURSED STONE, THOUGHTS OF VENGEANCE MY ONLY COMPANIONS.
AH, BUT WHOM DO YOU SEEK VENGEANCE AGAINST?
ANYONE.
EVERYTHING.
OBSIDIAN UNDERSTANDS. WE ARE FUELED BY THE SAME DESIRES. OUR POWER COMES FROM EXPLOITING THE DARKNESS WITHIN OTHERS.
PERHAPS. BUT YOUR HATRED LACKS DIRECTION. FOCUS. YOUR MOTIVES ARE INFANTILE.
AND YOU, MORDRU? WHAT DO YOU DESIRE?
GRANDEUR. CREATION ITSELF.
YOU SEEK ONLY DESTRUCTION. AND MAKE NO MISTAKE--DESTRUCTION CAN BE GOOD. ONE MUST ALWAYS WIPE THE SLATE CLEAN BEFORE BEGINNING ANEW.
BUT WHEN WE ARE FINISHED, WHEN ALL THE WORLD'S HEROES HAVE BEEN DEFEATED--
--I WILL BUILD SOMETHING EVEN MORE GLORIOUS.

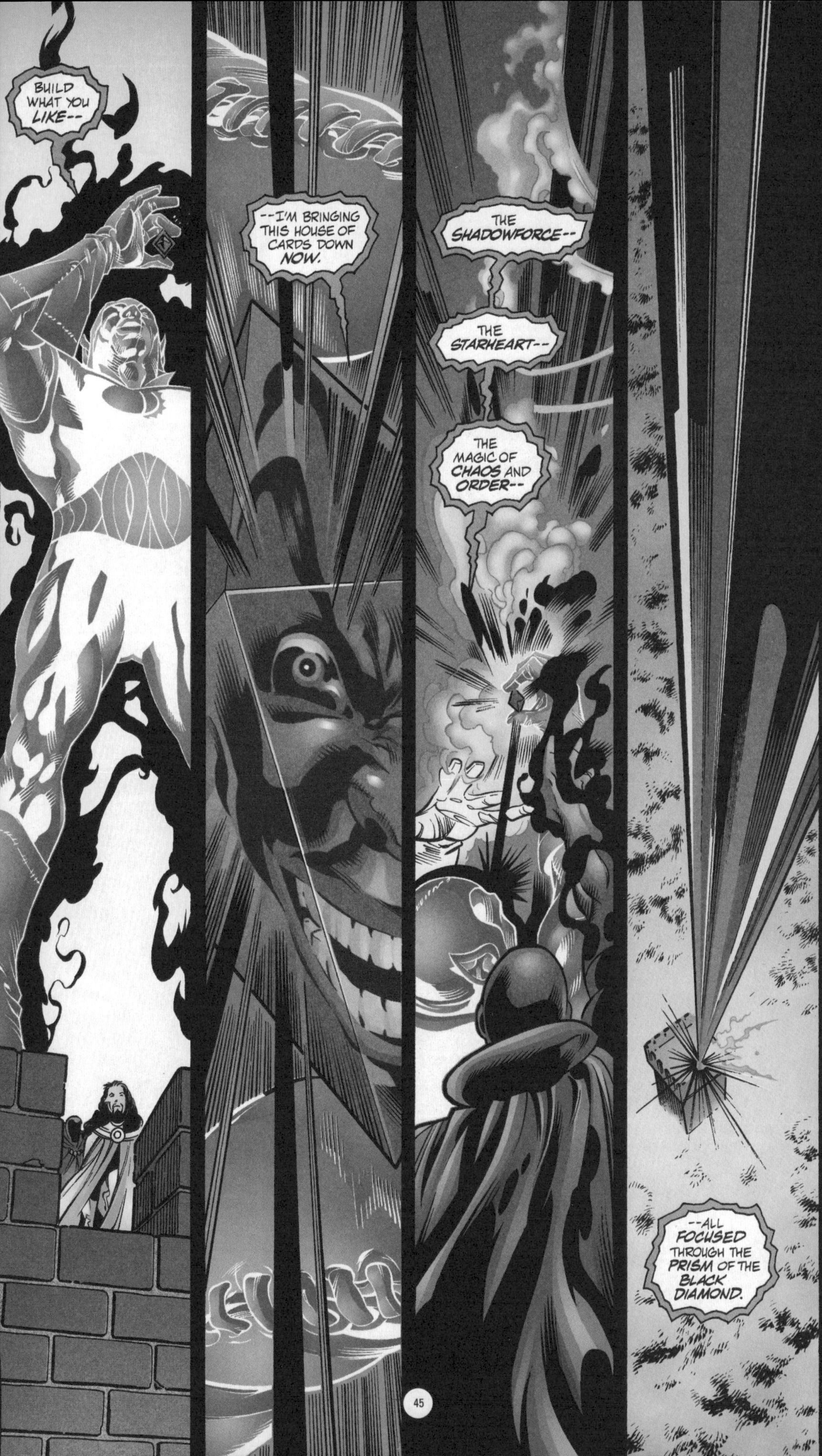
BUILD WHAT YOU LIKE--
--I'M BRINGING THIS HOUSE OF CARDS DOWN NOW.
THE SHADOWFORCE--
THE STARHEART--
THE MAGIC OF CHAOS AND ORDER--
--ALL FOCUSED THROUGH THE PRISM OF THE BLACK DIAMOND.

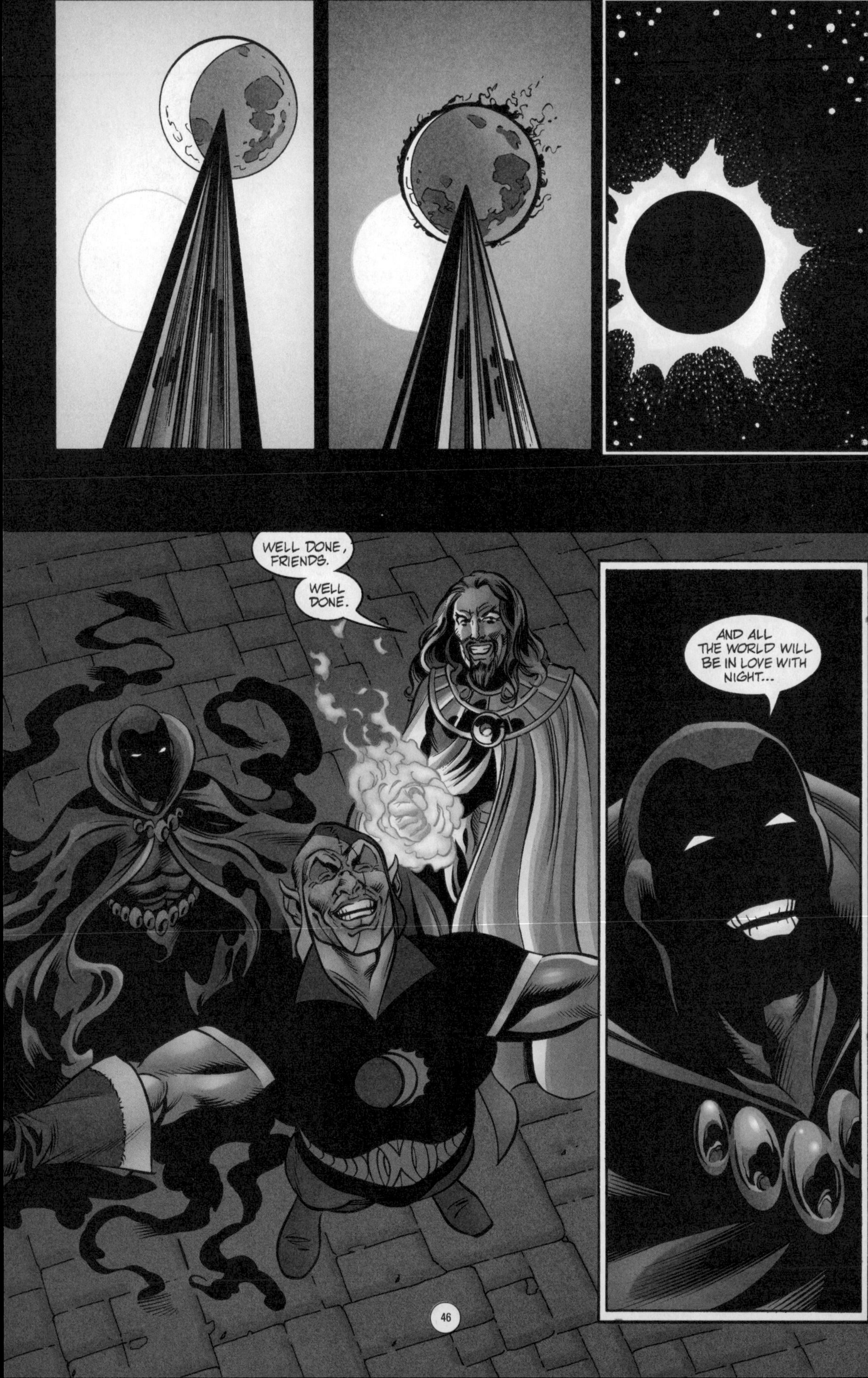
WELL DONE, FRIENDS.
WELL DONE.
AND ALL THE WORLD WILL BE IN LOVE WITH NIGHT...

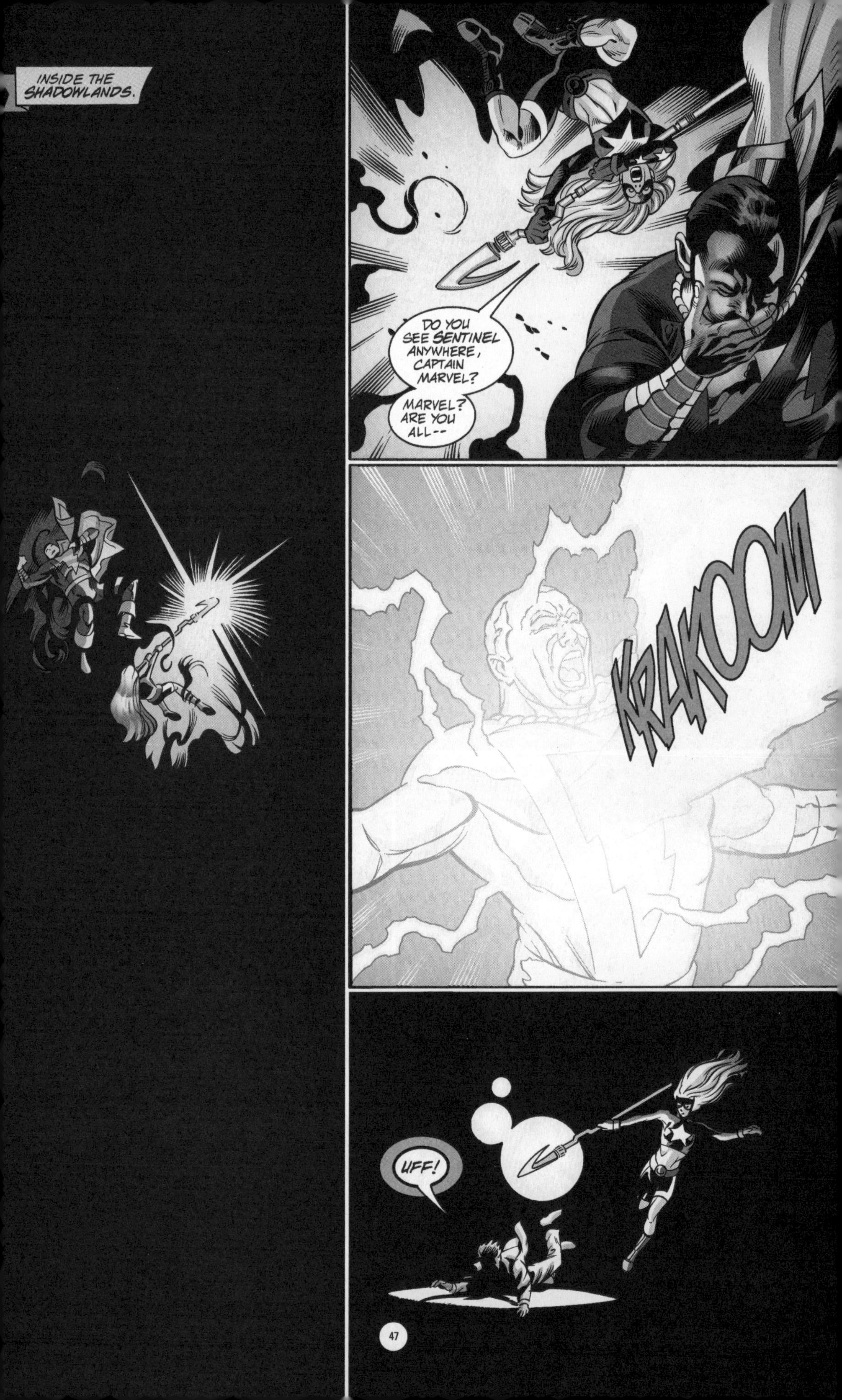
INSIDE THE SHADOWLANDS.
DO YOU SEE SENTINEL ANYWHERE, CAPTAIN MARVEL?
MARVEL? ARE YOU ALL--
KRAKOOM
UFF!

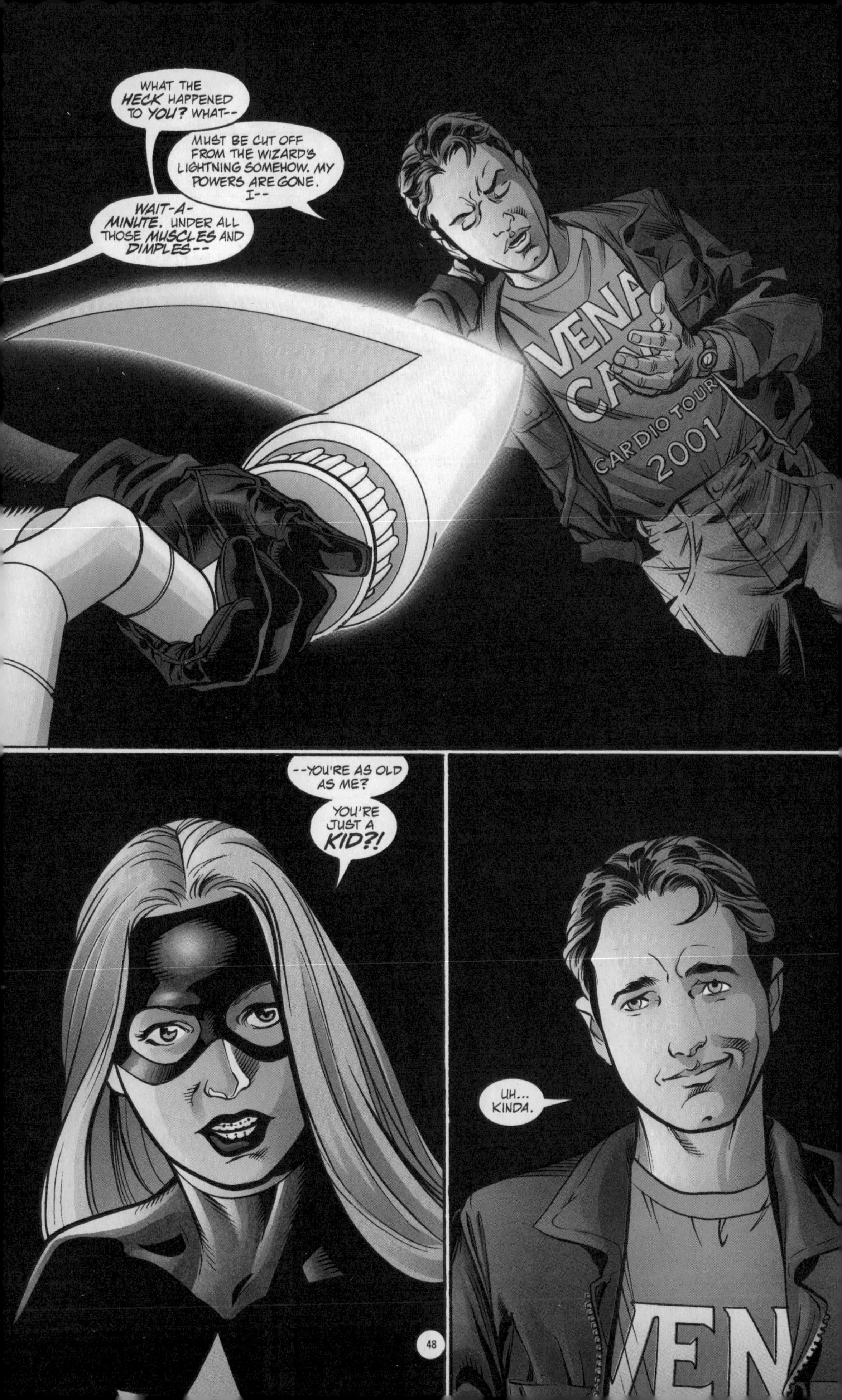
WHAT THE HECK HAPPENED TO YOU? WHAT--
MUST BE CUT OFF FROM THE WIZARD'S LIGHTNING SOMEHOW. MY POWERS ARE GONE. I--
WAIT-A-MINUTE. UNDER ALL THOSE MUSCLES AND DIMPLES--
VENA CA CARDIO TOUR 2001
--YOU'RE AS OLD AS ME?
YOU'RE JUST A KID?!
UH... KINDA.
VEN

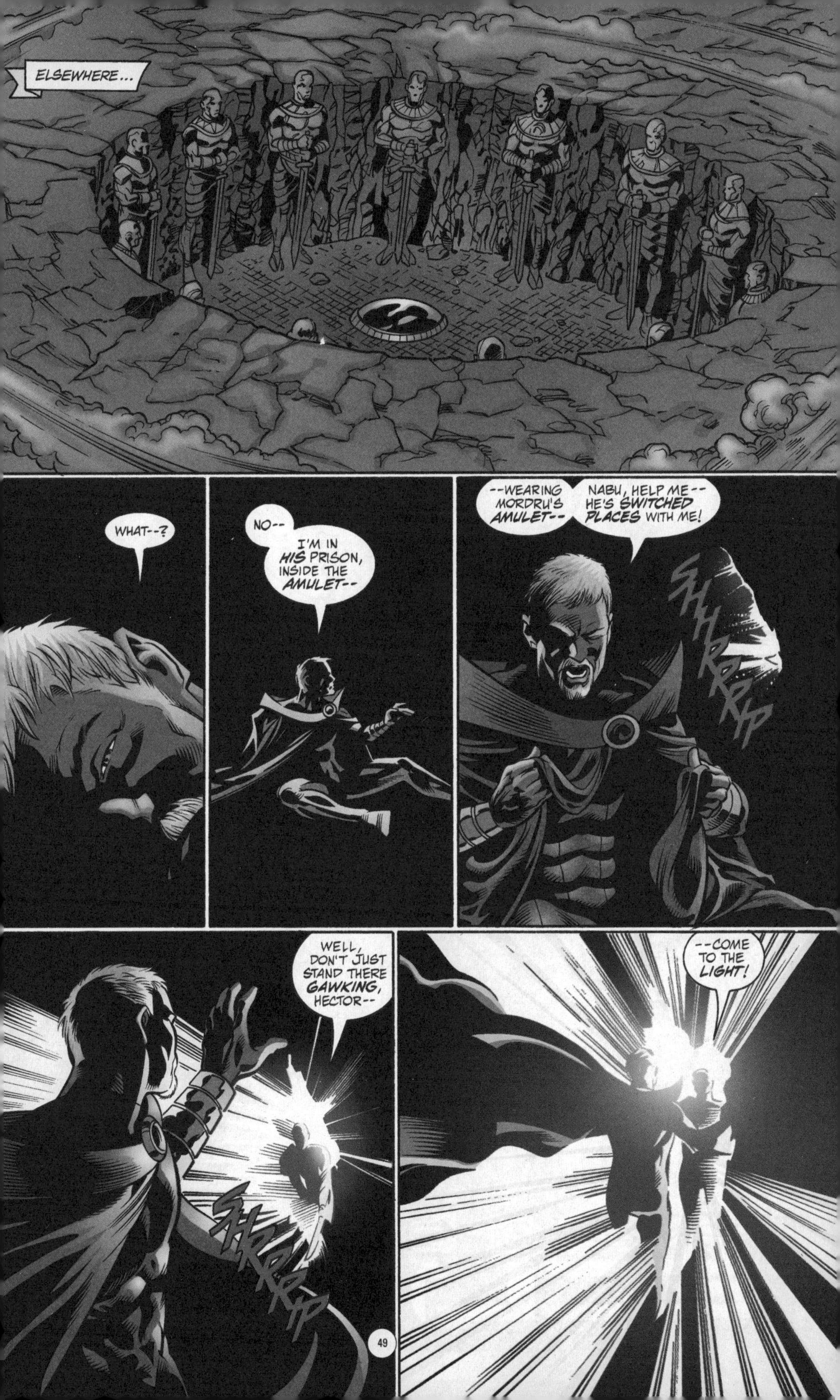
ELSEWHERE...
WHAT--?
NO--
I'M IN HIS PRISON, INSIDE THE AMULET--
--WEARING MORDRU'S AMULET--
NABU, HELP ME-- HE'S SWITCHED PLACES WITH ME!
SHHRRRIP
WELL, DON'T JUST STAND THERE GAWKING, HECTOR--
SHHRRRIP
--COME TO THE LIGHT!

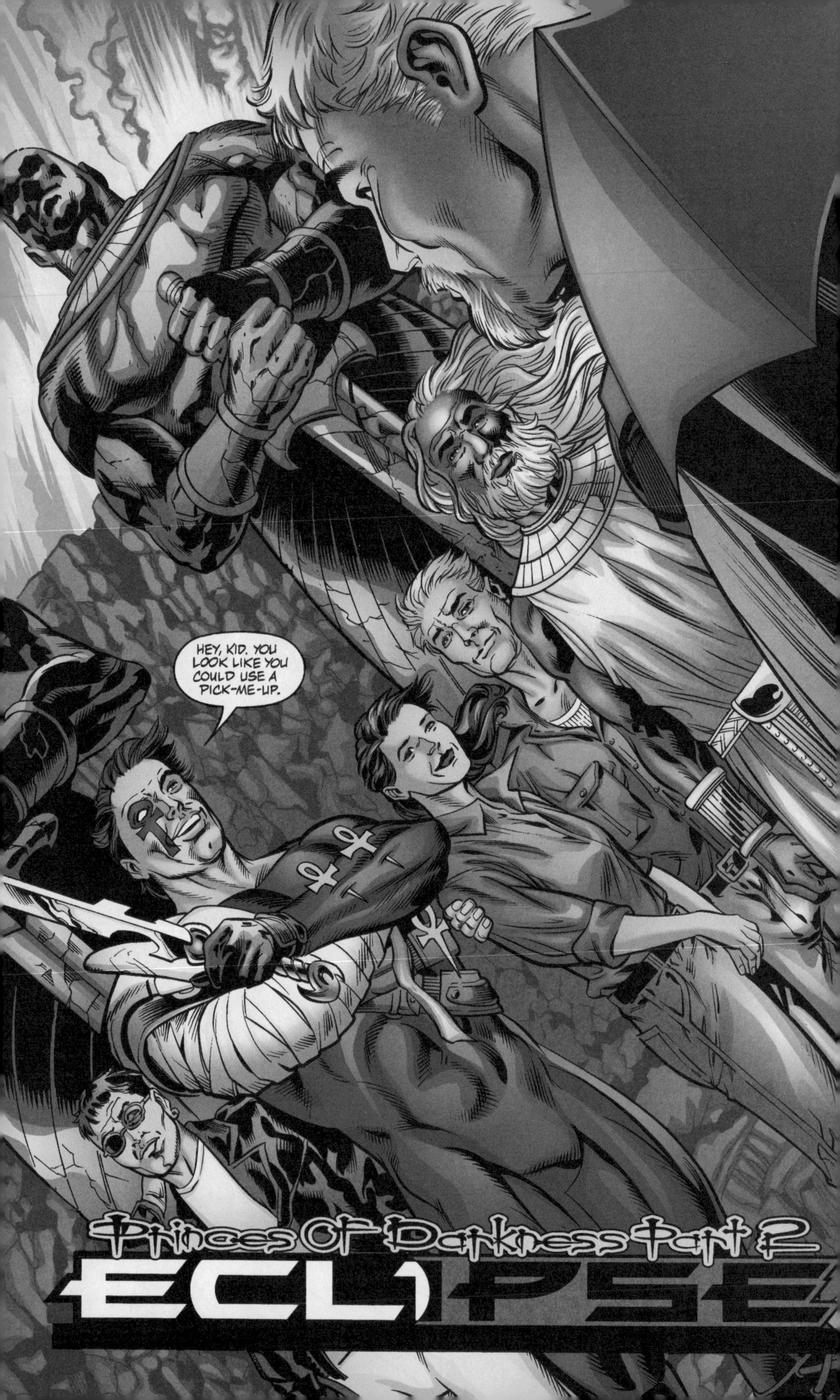
HEY, KID. YOU LOOK LIKE YOU COULD USE A PICK-ME-UP.
Princes Of Darkness Part 2
ECLIPSE

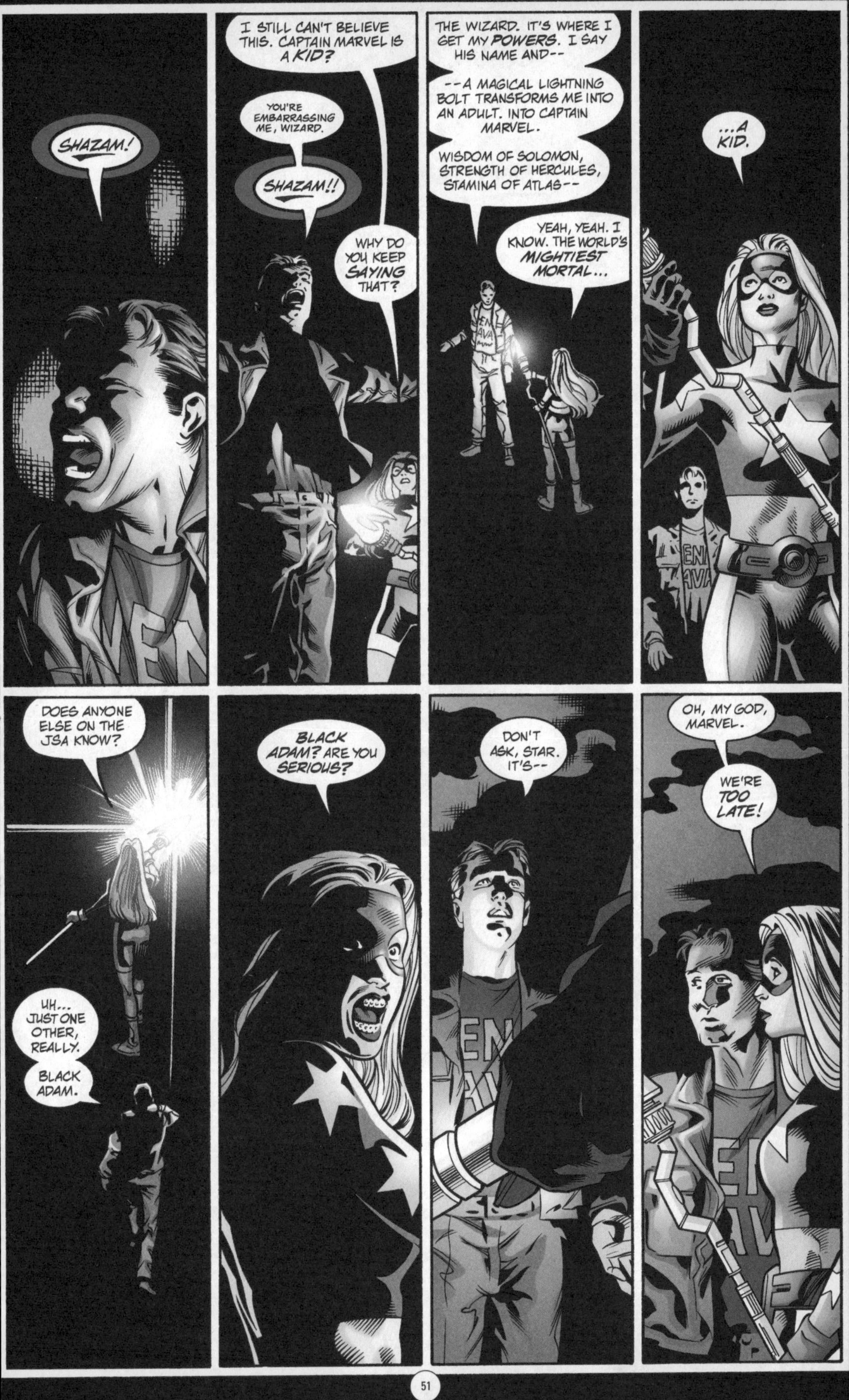
SHAZAM!
I STILL CAN'T BELIEVE THIS. CAPTAIN MARVEL IS A KID?
YOU'RE EMBARRASSING ME, WIZARD.
SHAZAM!!
WHY DO YOU KEEP SAYING THAT?
THE WIZARD. IT'S WHERE I GET MY POWERS. I SAY HIS NAME AND--
--A MAGICAL LIGHTNING BOLT TRANSFORMS ME INTO AN ADULT. INTO CAPTAIN MARVEL.
WISDOM OF SOLOMON, STRENGTH OF HERCULES, STAMINA OF ATLAS--
YEAH, YEAH. I KNOW. THE WORLD'S MIGHTIEST MORTAL...
...A KID.
DOES ANYONE ELSE ON THE JSA KNOW?
UH... JUST ONE OTHER, REALLY.
BLACK ADAM.
BLACK ADAM? ARE YOU SERIOUS?
DON'T ASK, STAR. IT'S--
OH, MY GOD, MARVEL.
WE'RE TOO LATE!

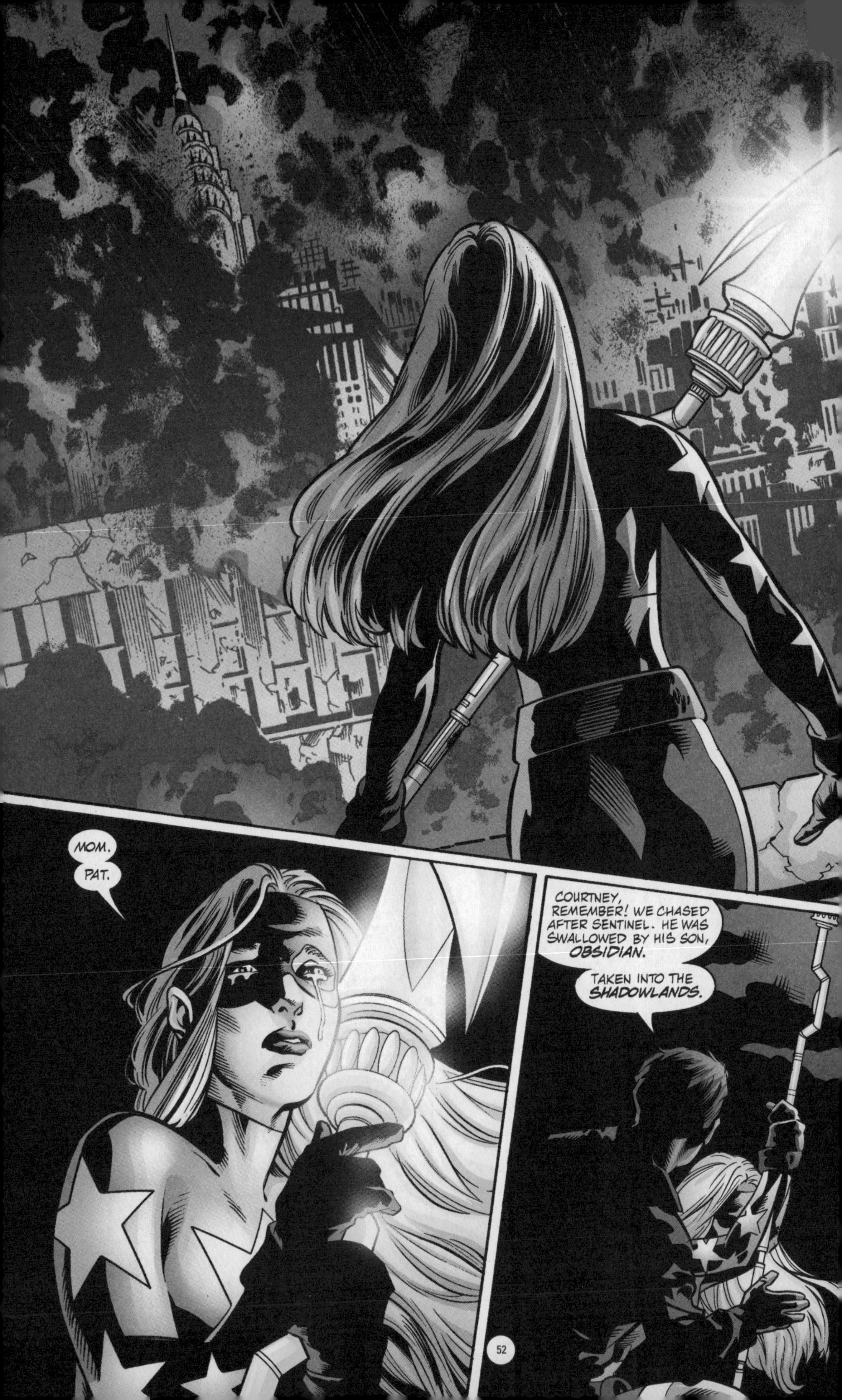
MOM.
PAT.
COURTNEY, REMEMBER! WE CHASED AFTER SENTINEL. HE WAS SWALLOWED BY HIS SON, OBSIDIAN.
TAKEN INTO THE SHADOWLANDS.

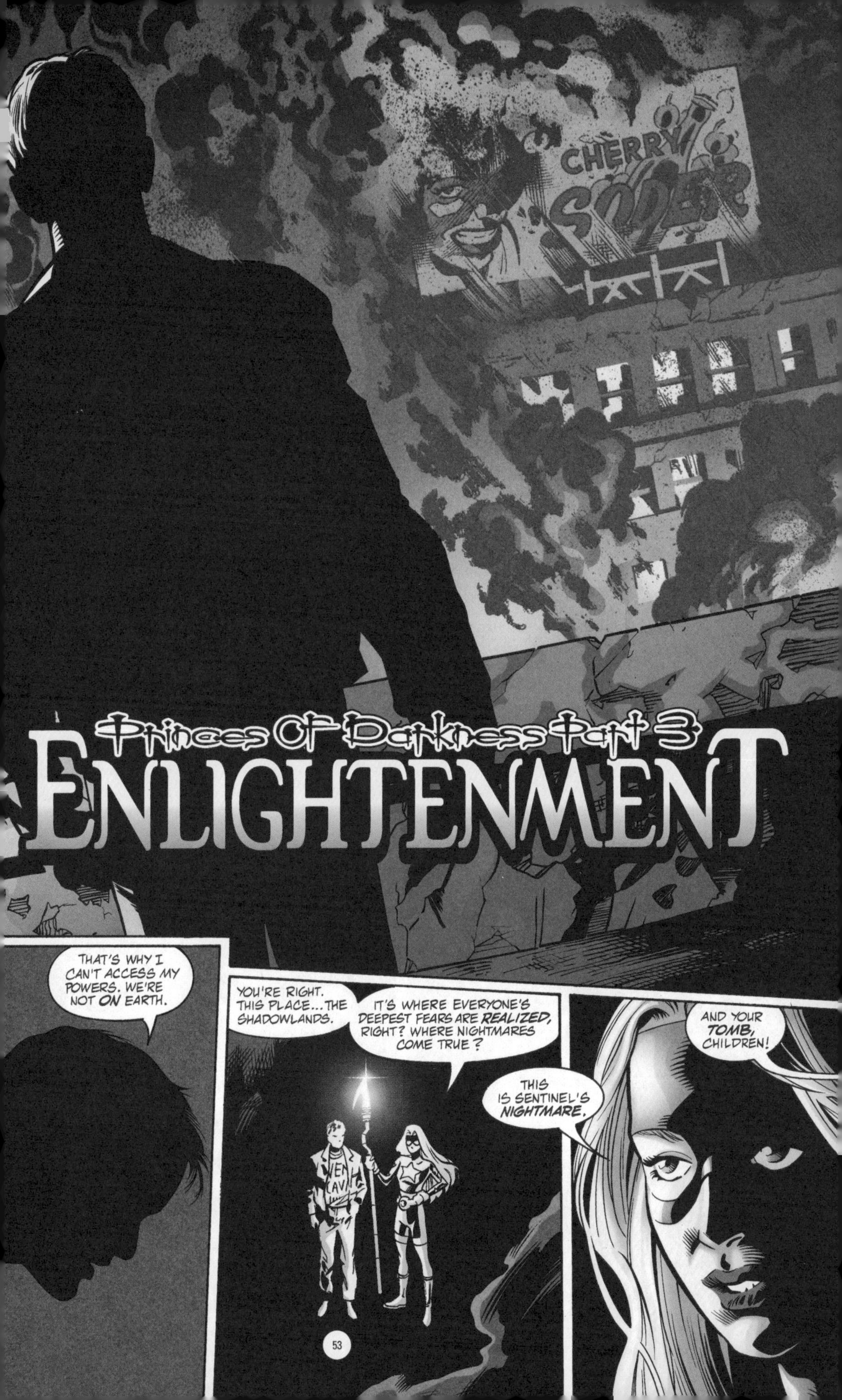

CHERRY
Princess Of Darkness Part 3
ENLIGHTENMENT
THAT'S WHY I CAN'T ACCESS MY POWERS. WE'RE NOT ON EARTH.
YOU'RE RIGHT. THIS PLACE... THE SHADOWLANDS.
IT'S WHERE EVERYONE'S DEEPEST FEARS ARE REALIZED, RIGHT? WHERE NIGHTMARES COME TRUE?
THIS IS SENTINEL'S NIGHTMARE.
AND YOUR TOMB, CHILDREN!

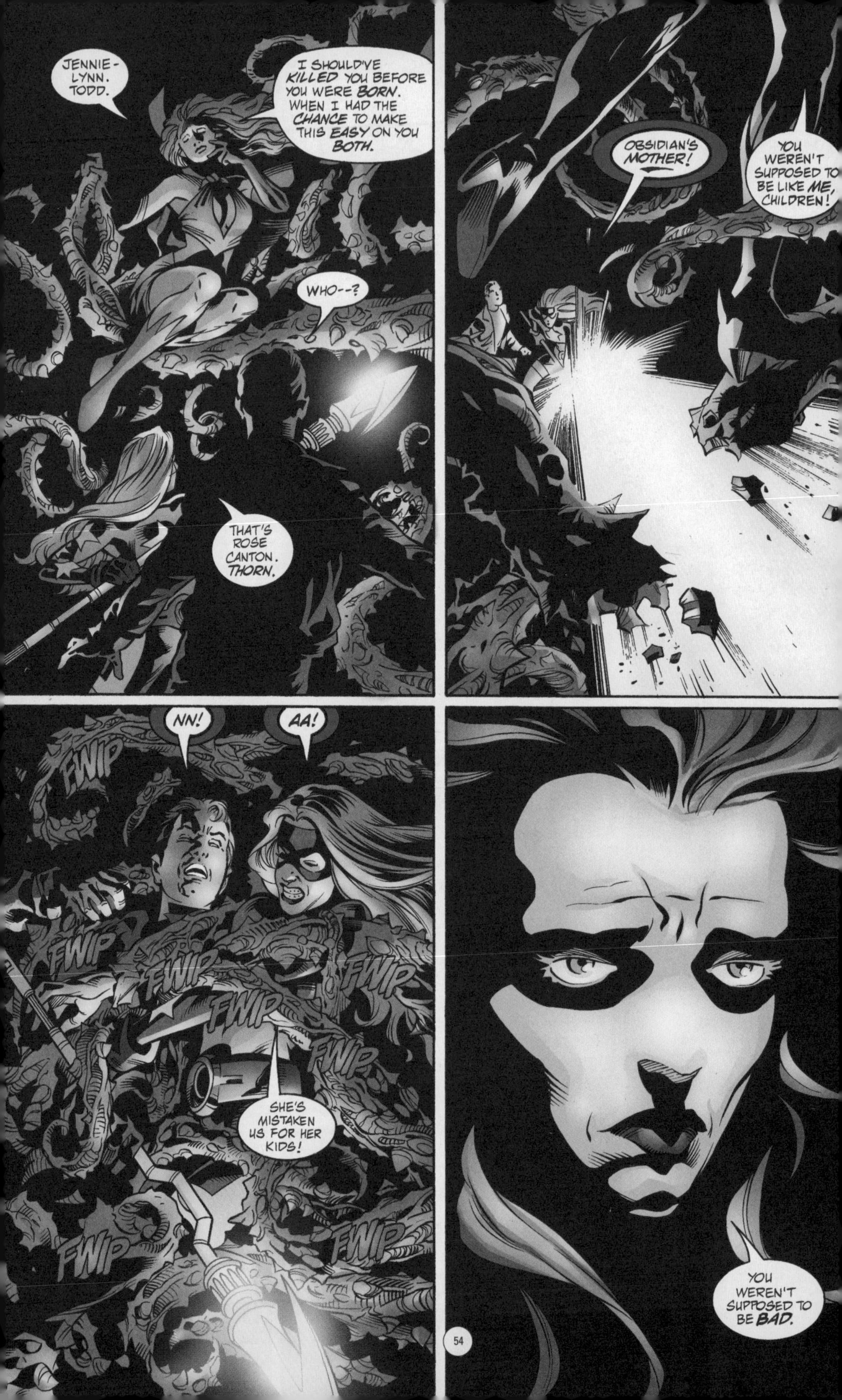

JENNIE-LYNN. TODD.
I SHOULD'VE KILLED YOU BEFORE YOU WERE BORN. WHEN I HAD THE CHANCE TO MAKE THIS EASY ON YOU BOTH.
WHO--?
THAT'S ROSE CANTON. THORN.
OBSIDIAN'S MOTHER!
YOU WEREN'T SUPPOSED TO BE LIKE ME, CHILDREN!
NN!
AA!
FWIP
FWIP
FWIP
FWIP
FWIP
FWIP
SHE'S MISTAKEN US FOR HER KIDS!
FWIP
FWIP
YOU WEREN'T SUPPOSED TO BE BAD.

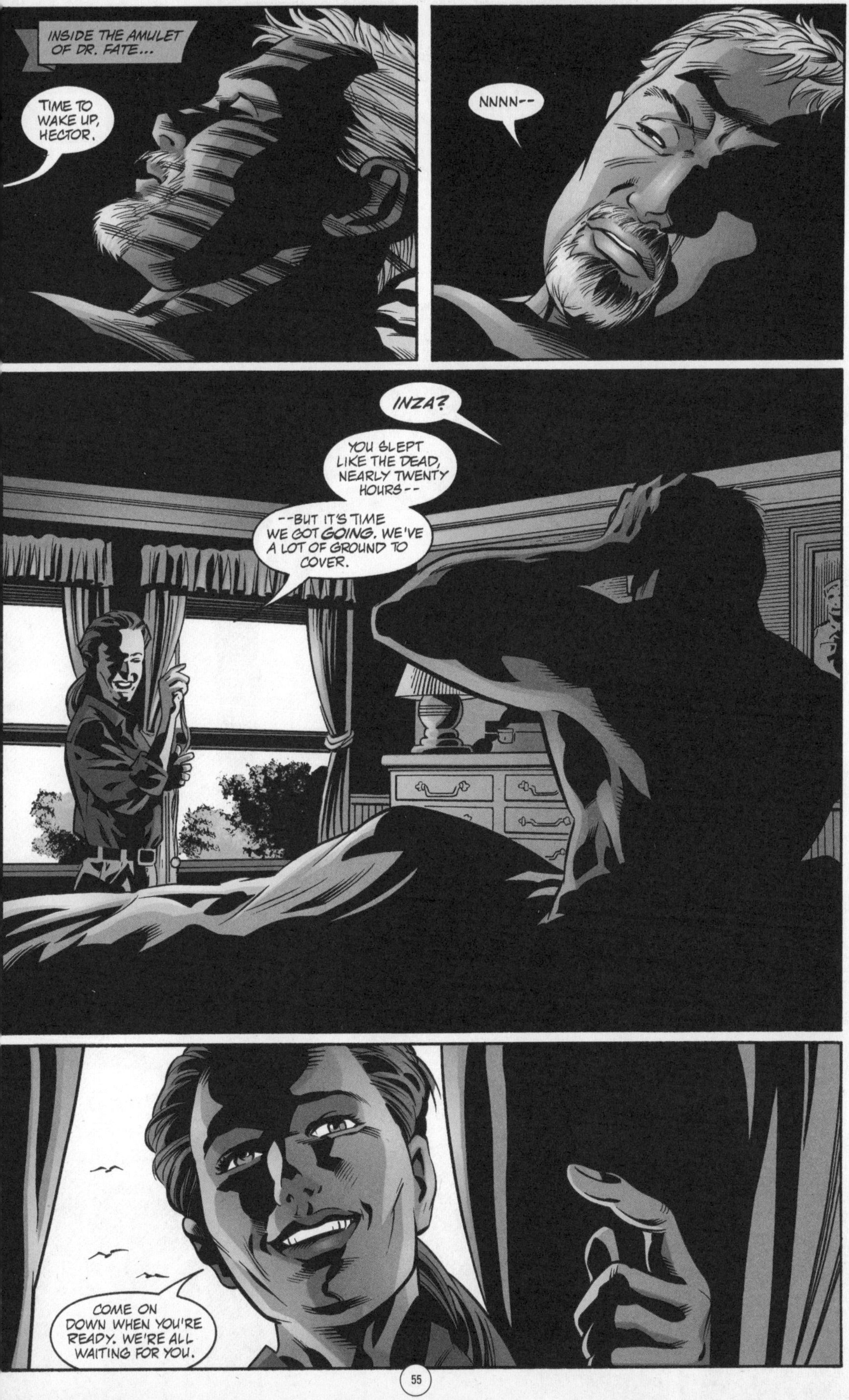

INSIDE THE AMULET OF DR. FATE...
TIME TO WAKE UP, HECTOR.
NNNN--
INZA?
YOU SLEPT LIKE THE DEAD, NEARLY TWENTY HOURS--
--BUT IT'S TIME WE GOT GOING. WE'VE A LOT OF GROUND TO COVER.
COME ON DOWN WHEN YOU'RE READY. WE'RE ALL WAITING FOR YOU.

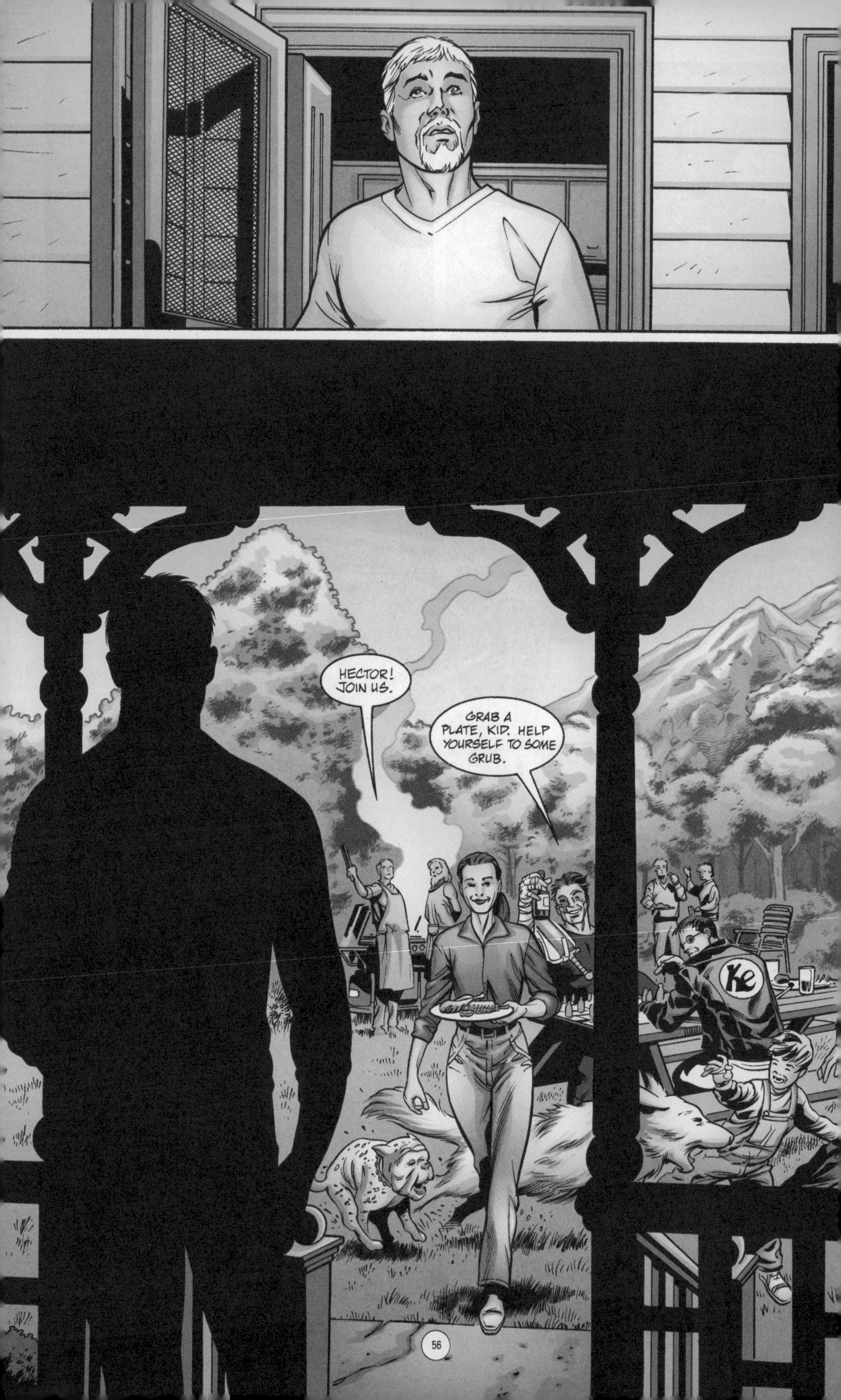
HECTOR! JOIN US.
GRAB A PLATE, KID. HELP YOURSELF TO SOME GRUB.

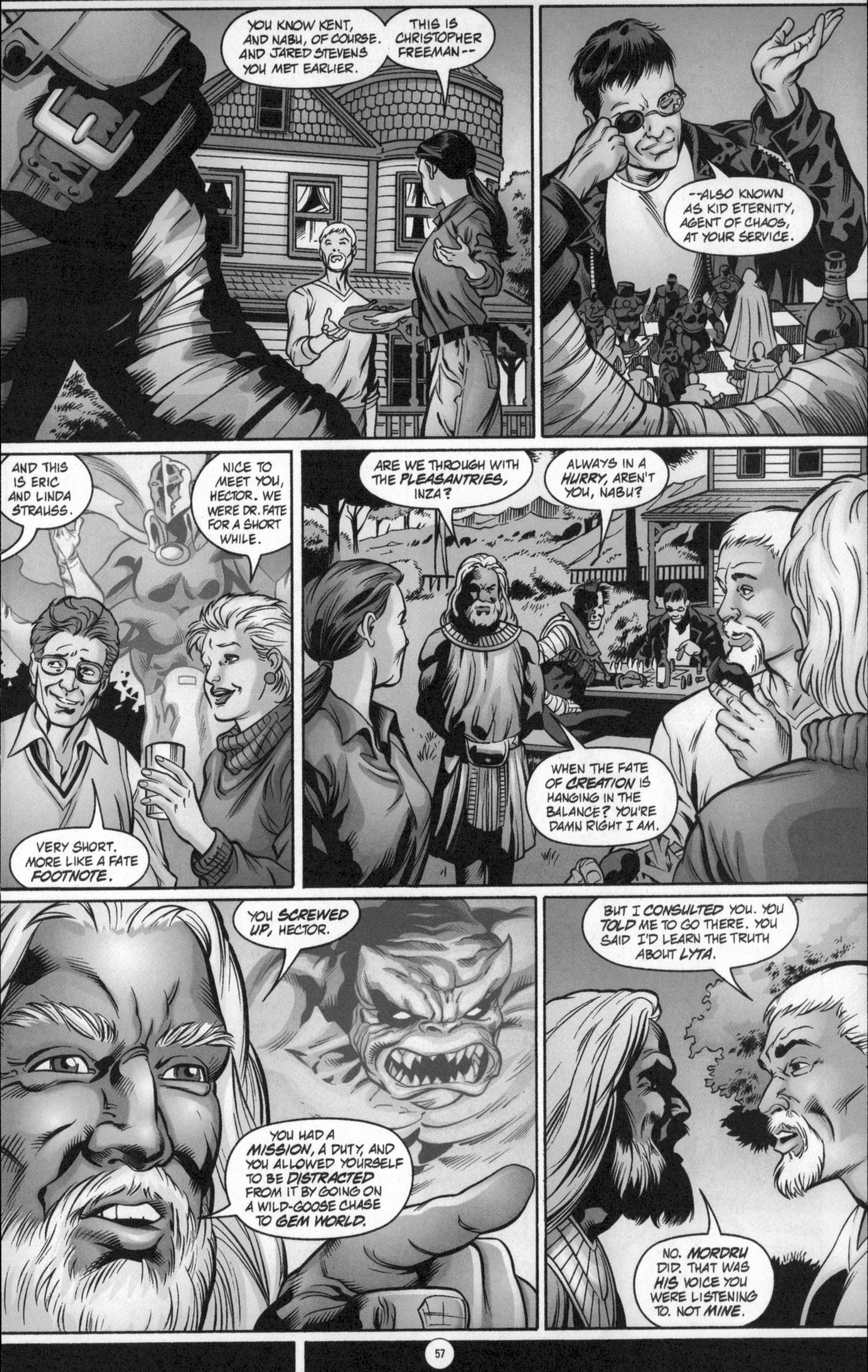
YOU KNOW KENT, AND NABU, OF COURSE. AND JARED STEVENS YOU MET EARLIER.
THIS IS CHRISTOPHER FREEMAN --
--ALSO KNOWN AS KID ETERNITY, AGENT OF CHAOS, AT YOUR SERVICE.
AND THIS IS ERIC AND LINDA STRAUSS.
NICE TO MEET YOU, HECTOR. WE WERE DR. FATE FOR A SHORT WHILE.
VERY SHORT. MORE LIKE A FATE FOOTNOTE.
ARE WE THROUGH WITH THE PLEASANTRIES, INZA?
ALWAYS IN A HURRY, AREN'T YOU, NABU?
WHEN THE FATE OF CREATION IS HANGING IN THE BALANCE? YOU'RE DAMN RIGHT I AM.
YOU SCREWED UP, HECTOR.
YOU HAD A MISSION, A DUTY, AND YOU ALLOWED YOURSELF TO BE DISTRACTED FROM IT BY GOING ON A WILD-GOOSE CHASE TO GEM WORLD.
BUT I CONSULTED YOU. YOU TOLD ME TO GO THERE. YOU SAID I'D LEARN THE TRUTH ABOUT LYTA.
NO. MORDRU DID. THAT WAS HIS VOICE YOU WERE LISTENING TO. NOT MINE.

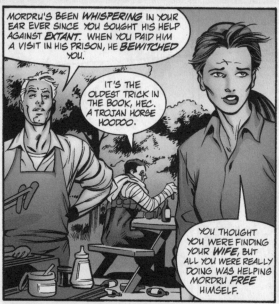

MORDRU'S BEEN *WHISPERING* IN YOUR EAR EVER SINCE YOU SOUGHT HIS HELP AGAINST *EXTANT.* WHEN YOU PAID HIM A VISIT IN HIS PRISON, HE *BEWITCHED* YOU.

IT'S THE OLDEST TRICK IN THE BOOK, HEC. A TROJAN HORSE HOODOO.

YOU THOUGHT YOU WERE FINDING YOUR *WIFE,* BUT ALL YOU WERE REALLY DOING WAS HELPING MORDRU *FREE* HIMSELF.

I WOULDN'T FEEL TOO BAD. YOU'RE NOT THE *ONLY* ONE HERE THAT GOT *SUCKER-PUNCHED.*

I GOT MY *SPIRIT-TUSH* FRIED BUT GOOD-- AND *JARED--* HELL, HE MANAGED TO GET *SKEWERED* WITH HIS OWN BLADE.

SMOOTH, JARED.

LISTEN, YOU LITTLE *LATTE-SLURPING FRUITCAKE!* THERE WERE EXTENUATING *CIRCUMSTANCES!*

WE *ALL* HAD CIRCUMSTANCES, SO GIVE IT A *REST,* BOYS.

SOME OF US WERE MORE ALIGNED WITH *ORDER,* SOME WITH *CHAOS.* BUT WHAT THE MANTLE OF FATE *REALLY* NEEDED WAS A *VESSEL* BORN OF *BOTH.*

A FATE-CHILD.

SOMEONE WHO COULD ACT AS A *FULCRUM* BETWEEN THE TWO *FORCES.*

MORDRU'S INTENTION WAS TO *SHED* HIS CURRENT HOST'S BODY AND LEAP INTO THE *CHILD'S.*

UNFORTUNATELY FOR HIM, YOUR WANDERING *SOUL* MANAGED TO TAKE ROOT *FIRST.*

HE'S HAD TO *IMPROVISE* SINCE THEN. TRICK YOU, EXPLOIT YOUR *WEAKNESSES.*

WAIT A MINUTE-- YOU SAID MORDRU WASN'T ABLE TO ABANDON HIS *CURRENT* HOST. SO WHOSE BODY IS HE IN *NOW?*

MORDRU USURPED THE *BODY* OF A LORD OF ORDER NAMED *ARION.*

ARION'S SOUL IS THE *KEY.* IF YOU CAN *LIBERATE* IT, YOU'LL KNOCK MORDRU OFF-BALANCE. HE'LL HAVE TO GRAPPLE FOR CONTROL OF HIS CURRENT BODY. HE'LL BE *VULNERABLE.*

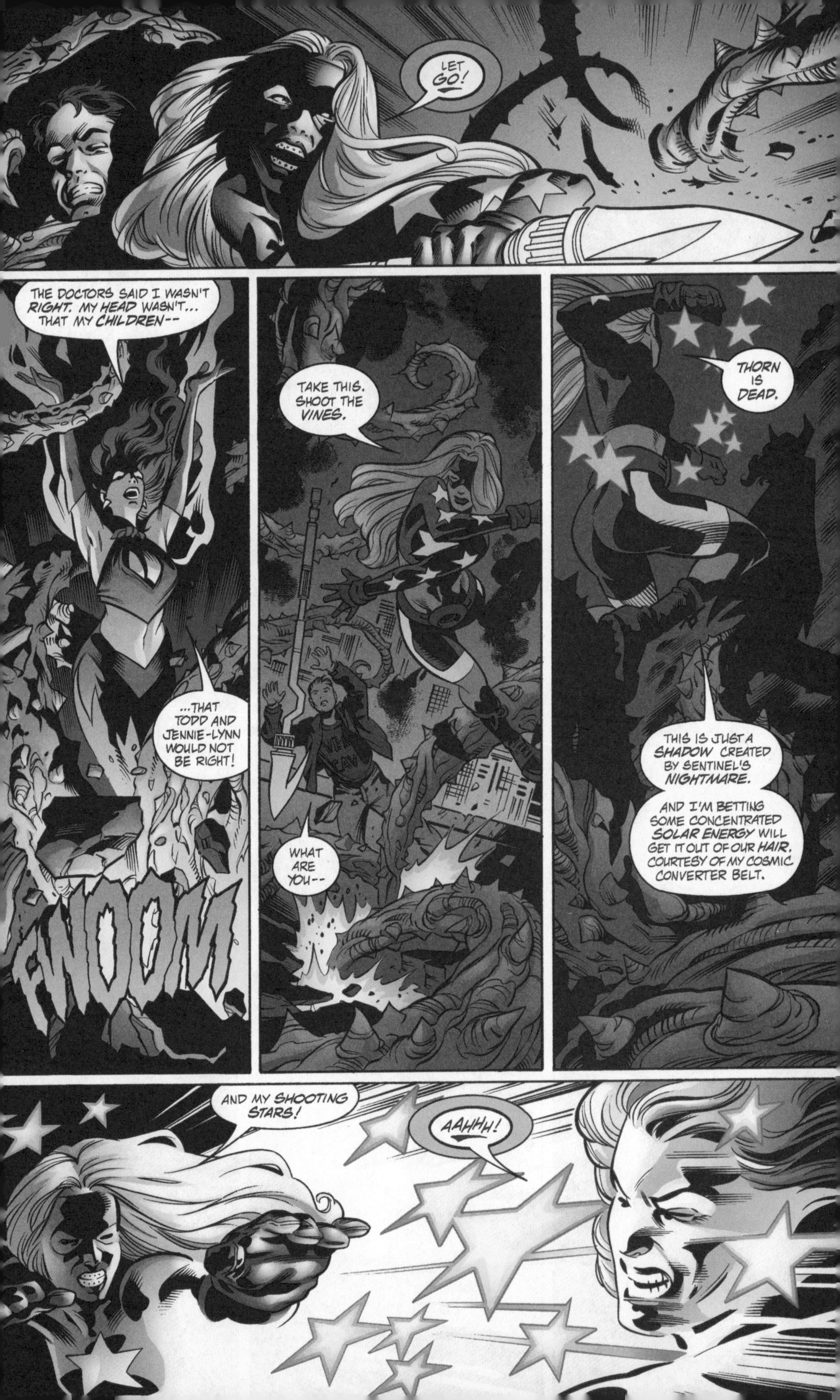
LET GO!
THE DOCTORS SAID I WASN'T RIGHT. MY HEAD WASN'T... THAT MY CHILDREN--
...THAT TODD AND JENNIE-LYNN WOULD NOT BE RIGHT!
FWOOM
TAKE THIS. SHOOT THE VINES.
WHAT ARE YOU--
THORN IS DEAD.
THIS IS JUST A SHADOW CREATED BY SENTINEL'S NIGHTMARE.
AND I'M BETTING SOME CONCENTRATED SOLAR ENERGY WILL GET IT OUT OF OUR HAIR. COURTESY OF MY COSMIC CONVERTER BELT.
AND MY SHOOTING STARS!
AAHHH!

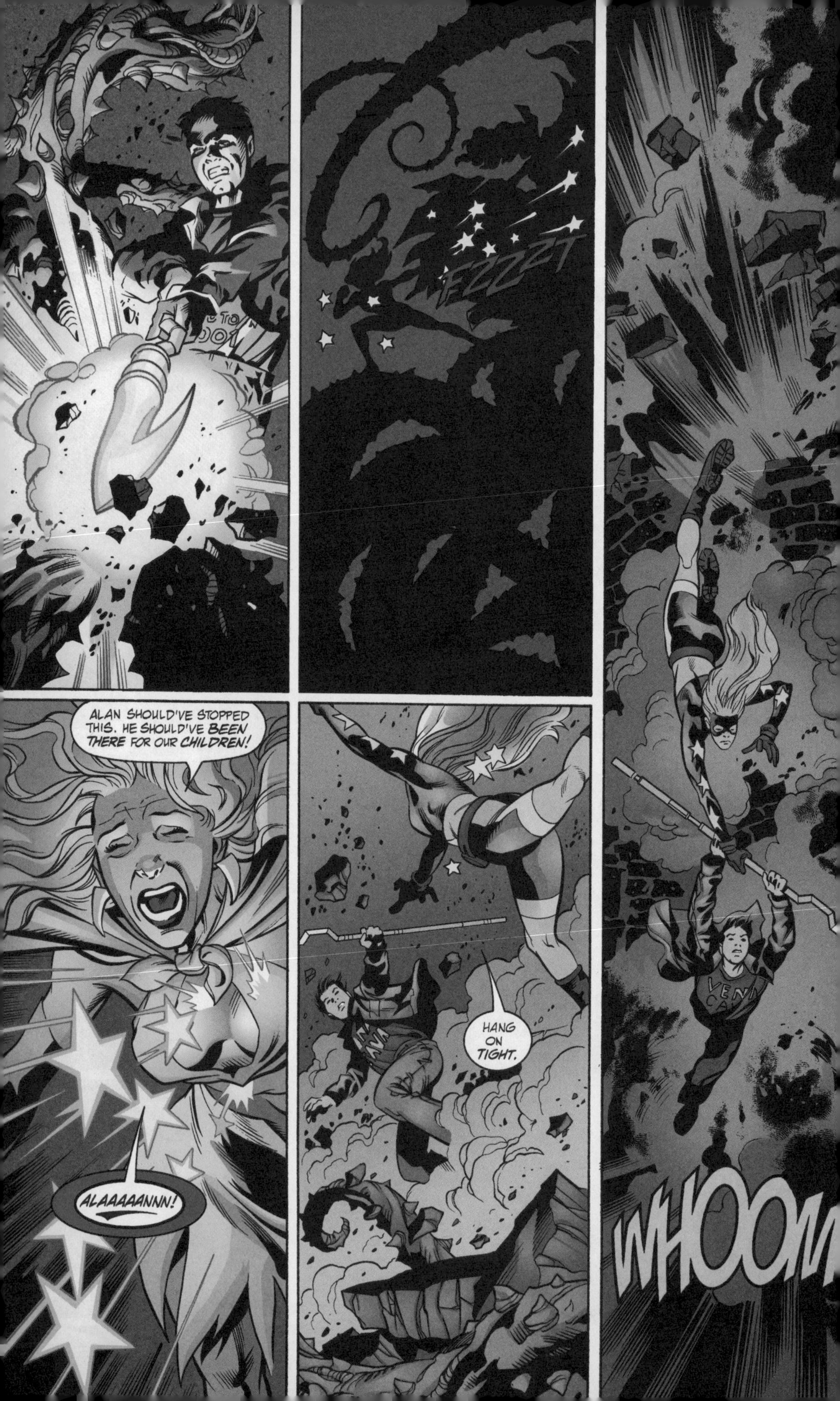
FZZZT
ALAN SHOULD'VE STOPPED THIS. HE SHOULD'VE BEEN THERE FOR OUR CHILDREN!
ALAAAAANNN!
HANG ON TIGHT.
WHOOM

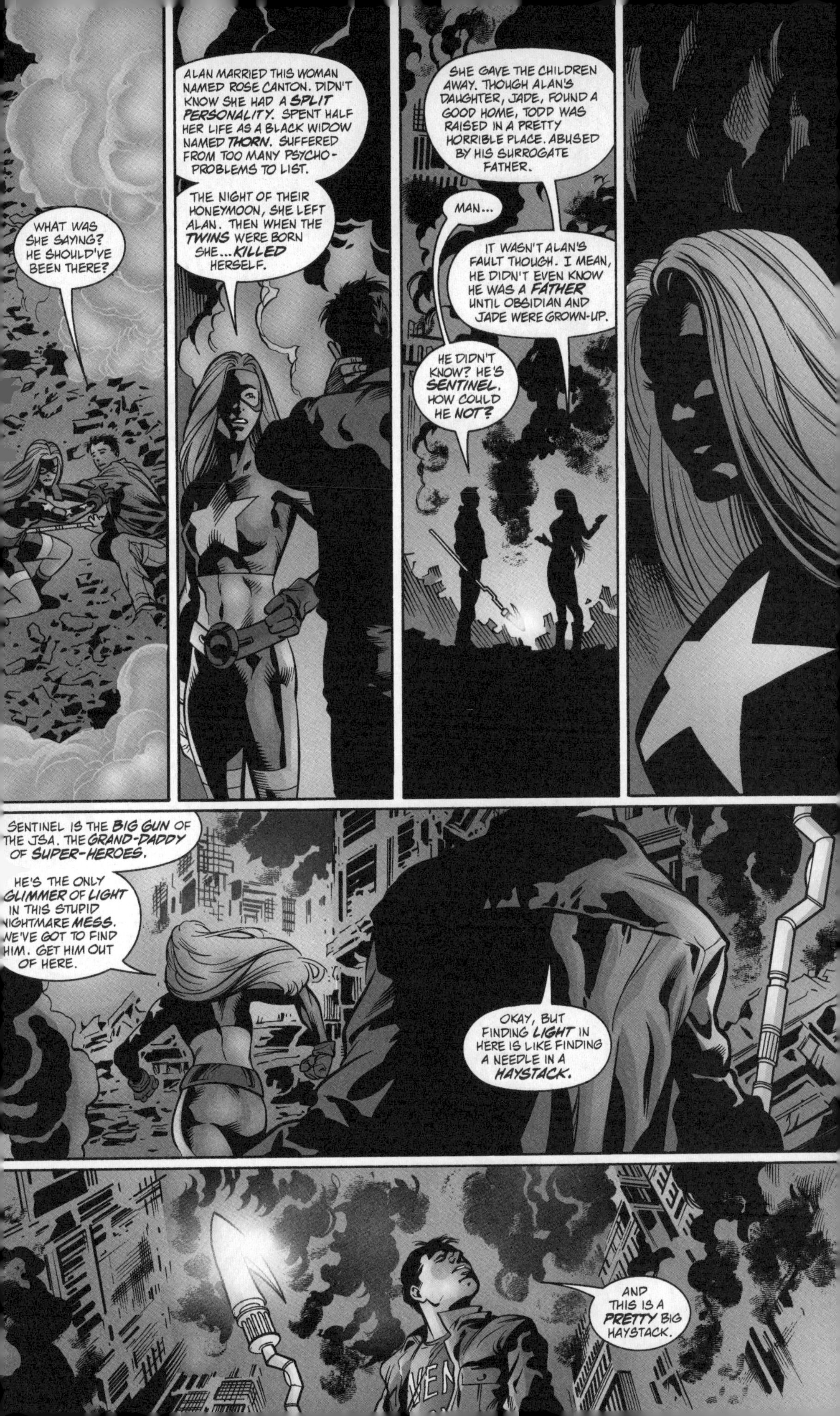
WHAT WAS SHE SAYING? HE SHOULD'VE BEEN THERE?
ALAN MARRIED THIS WOMAN NAMED ROSE CANTON. DIDN'T KNOW SHE HAD A SPLIT PERSONALITY. SPENT HALF HER LIFE AS A BLACK WIDOW NAMED THORN. SUFFERED FROM TOO MANY PSYCHO-PROBLEMS TO LIST.
THE NIGHT OF THEIR HONEYMOON, SHE LEFT ALAN. THEN WHEN THE TWINS WERE BORN SHE... KILLED HERSELF.
SHE GAVE THE CHILDREN AWAY. THOUGH ALAN'S DAUGHTER, JADE, FOUND A GOOD HOME, TODD WAS RAISED IN A PRETTY HORRIBLE PLACE. ABUSED BY HIS SURROGATE FATHER.
MAN...
IT WASN'T ALAN'S FAULT THOUGH. I MEAN, HE DIDN'T EVEN KNOW HE WAS A FATHER UNTIL OBSIDIAN AND JADE WERE GROWN-UP.
HE DIDN'T KNOW? HE'S SENTINEL. HOW COULD HE NOT?
SENTINEL IS THE BIG GUN OF THE JSA. THE GRAND-DADDY OF SUPER-HEROES.
HE'S THE ONLY GLIMMER OF LIGHT IN THIS STUPID NIGHTMARE MESS. WE'VE GOT TO FIND HIM. GET HIM OUT OF HERE.
OKAY, BUT FINDING LIGHT IN HERE IS LIKE FINDING A NEEDLE IN A HAYSTACK.
AND THIS IS A PRETTY BIG HAYSTACK.

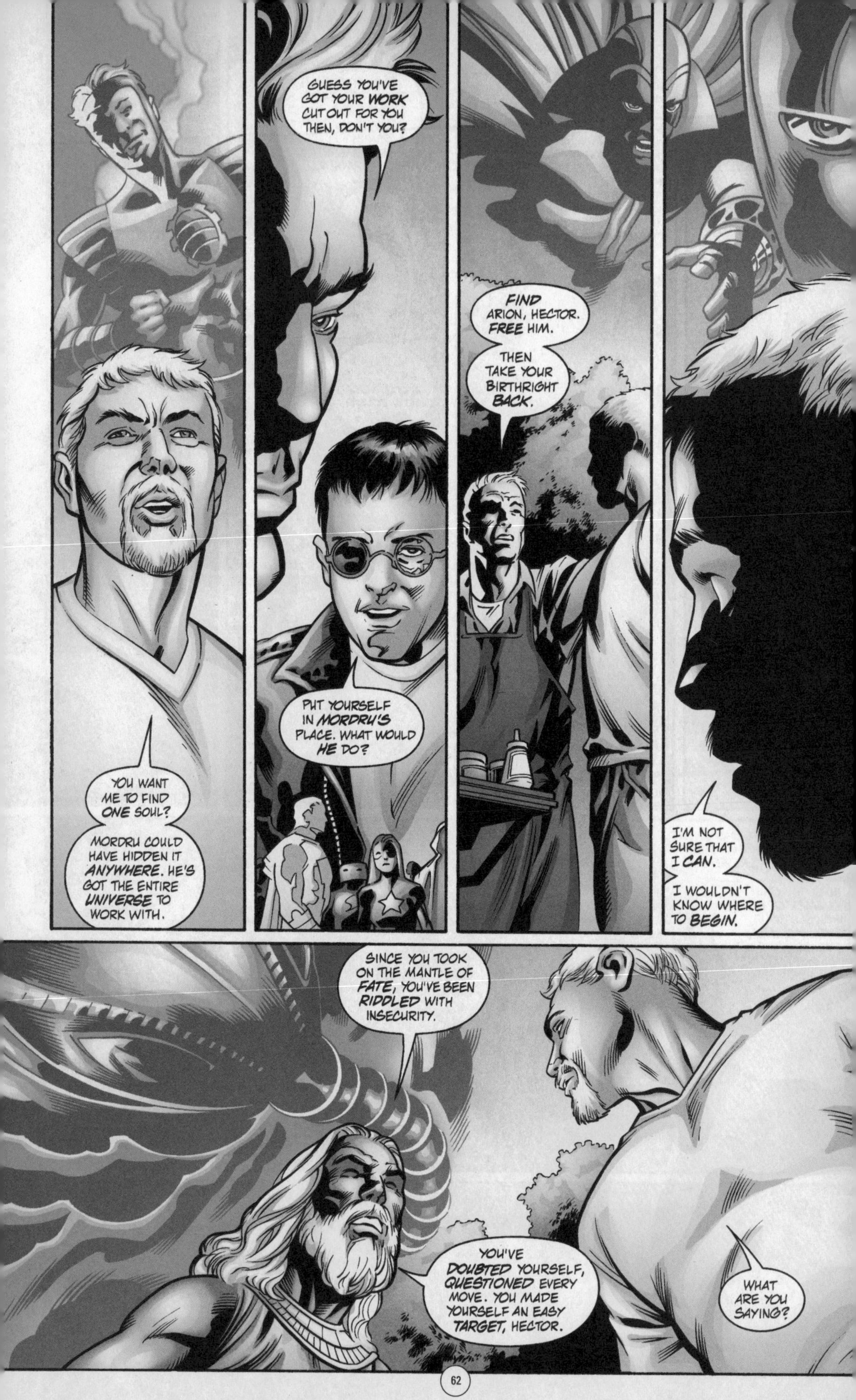

YOU WANT ME TO FIND ONE SOUL?
MORDRU COULD HAVE HIDDEN IT ANYWHERE. HE'S GOT THE ENTIRE UNIVERSE TO WORK WITH.
GUESS YOU'VE GOT YOUR WORK CUT OUT FOR YOU THEN, DON'T YOU?
PUT YOURSELF IN MORDRU'S PLACE. WHAT WOULD HE DO?
FIND ARION, HECTOR. FREE HIM.
THEN TAKE YOUR BIRTHRIGHT BACK.
I'M NOT SURE THAT I CAN.
I WOULDN'T KNOW WHERE TO BEGIN.
SINCE YOU TOOK ON THE MANTLE OF FATE, YOU'VE BEEN RIDDLED WITH INSECURITY.
YOU'VE DOUBTED YOURSELF, QUESTIONED EVERY MOVE. YOU MADE YOURSELF AN EASY TARGET, HECTOR.
WHAT ARE YOU SAYING?

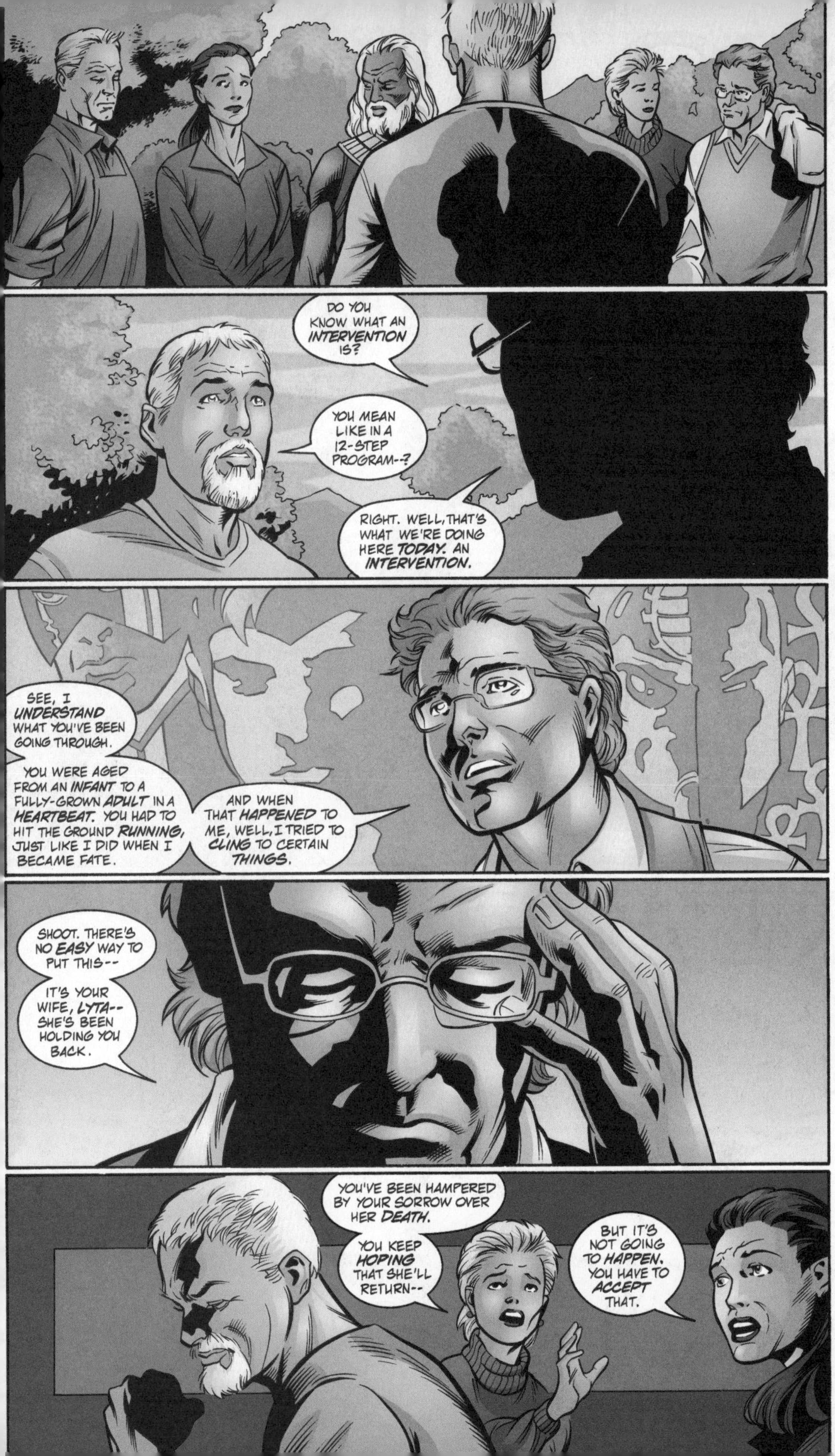
DO YOU KNOW WHAT AN INTERVENTION IS?
YOU MEAN LIKE IN A 12-STEP PROGRAM--?
RIGHT. WELL, THAT'S WHAT WE'RE DOING HERE TODAY. AN INTERVENTION.
SEE, I UNDERSTAND WHAT YOU'VE BEEN GOING THROUGH.
YOU WERE AGED FROM AN INFANT TO A FULLY-GROWN ADULT IN A HEARTBEAT. YOU HAD TO HIT THE GROUND RUNNING, JUST LIKE I DID WHEN I BECAME FATE.
AND WHEN THAT HAPPENED TO ME, WELL, I TRIED TO CLING TO CERTAIN THINGS.
SHOOT. THERE'S NO EASY WAY TO PUT THIS--
IT'S YOUR WIFE, LYTA-- SHE'S BEEN HOLDING YOU BACK.
YOU'VE BEEN HAMPERED BY YOUR SORROW OVER HER DEATH.
YOU KEEP HOPING THAT SHE'LL RETURN--
BUT IT'S NOT GOING TO HAPPEN. YOU HAVE TO ACCEPT THAT.

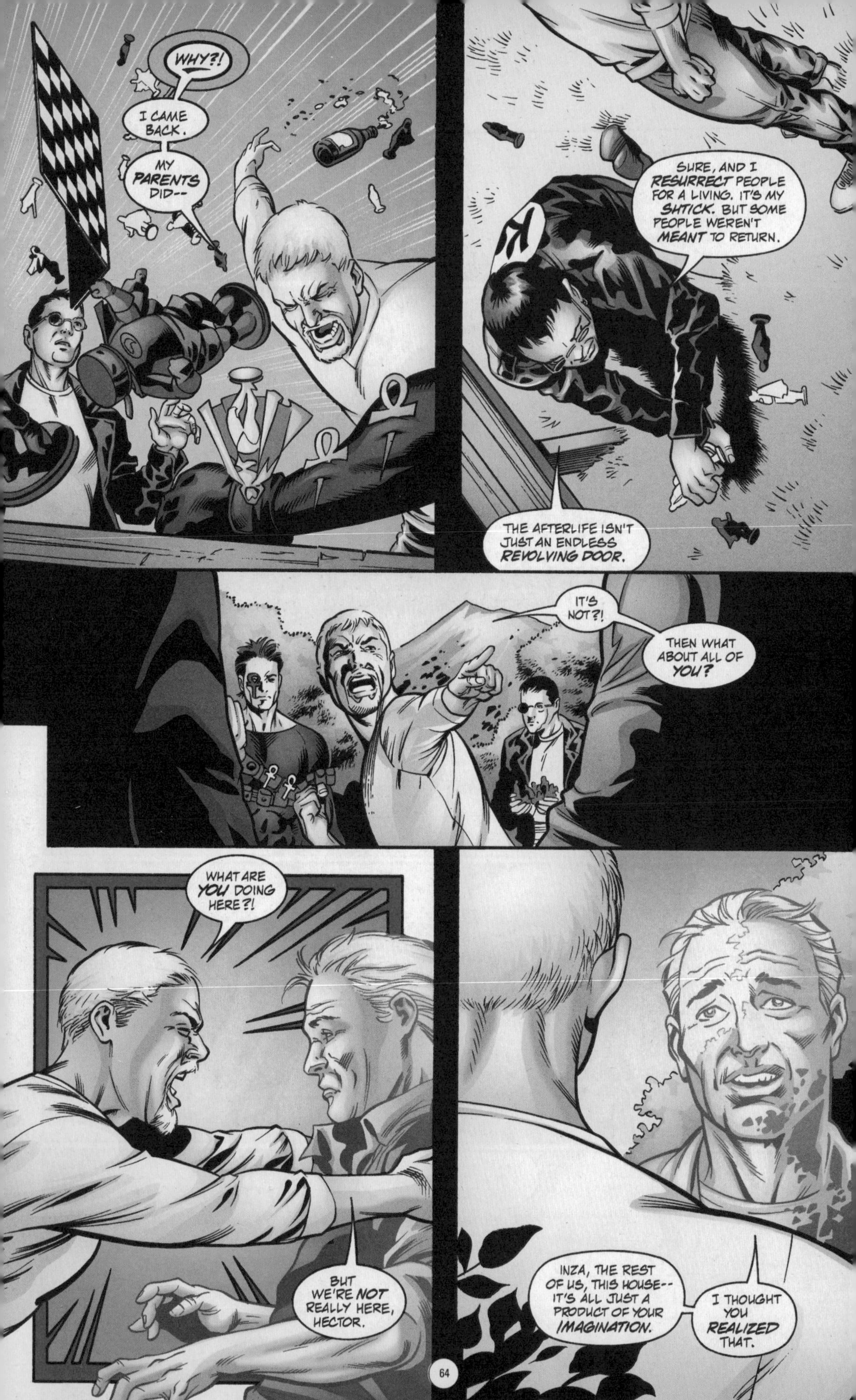
WHY?!
I CAME BACK.
MY PARENTS DID--
SURE, AND I RESURRECT PEOPLE FOR A LIVING. IT'S MY SHTICK. BUT SOME PEOPLE WEREN'T MEANT TO RETURN.
THE AFTERLIFE ISN'T JUST AN ENDLESS REVOLVING DOOR.
IT'S NOT?!
THEN WHAT ABOUT ALL OF YOU?
WHAT ARE YOU DOING HERE?!
BUT WE'RE NOT REALLY HERE, HECTOR.
INZA, THE REST OF US, THIS HOUSE-- IT'S ALL JUST A PRODUCT OF YOUR IMAGINATION.
I THOUGHT YOU REALIZED THAT.

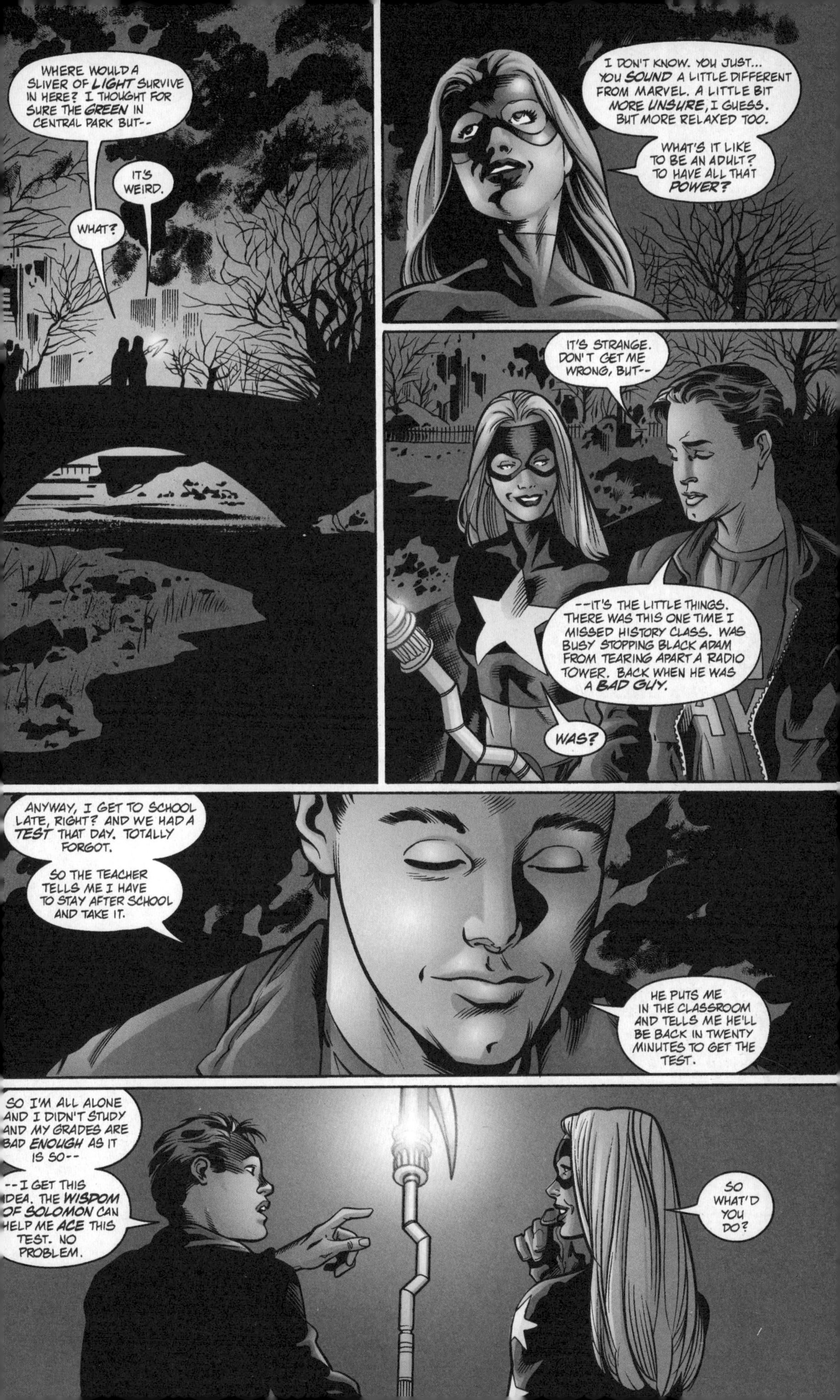
WHERE WOULD A SLIVER OF LIGHT SURVIVE IN HERE? I THOUGHT FOR SURE THE GREEN IN CENTRAL PARK BUT--
IT'S WEIRD.
WHAT?
I DON'T KNOW. YOU JUST... YOU SOUND A LITTLE DIFFERENT FROM MARVEL. A LITTLE BIT MORE UNSURE, I GUESS. BUT MORE RELAXED TOO.
WHAT'S IT LIKE TO BE AN ADULT? TO HAVE ALL THAT POWER?
IT'S STRANGE. DON'T GET ME WRONG, BUT--
--IT'S THE LITTLE THINGS. THERE WAS THIS ONE TIME I MISSED HISTORY CLASS. WAS BUSY STOPPING BLACK ADAM FROM TEARING APART A RADIO TOWER. BACK WHEN HE WAS A BAD GUY.
WAS?
ANYWAY, I GET TO SCHOOL LATE, RIGHT? AND WE HAD A TEST THAT DAY. TOTALLY FORGOT.
SO THE TEACHER TELLS ME I HAVE TO STAY AFTER SCHOOL AND TAKE IT.
HE PUTS ME IN THE CLASSROOM AND TELLS ME HE'LL BE BACK IN TWENTY MINUTES TO GET THE TEST.
SO I'M ALL ALONE AND I DIDN'T STUDY AND MY GRADES ARE BAD ENOUGH AS IT IS SO--
--I GET THIS IDEA. THE WISDOM OF SOLOMON CAN HELP ME ACE THIS TEST. NO PROBLEM.
SO WHAT'D YOU DO?

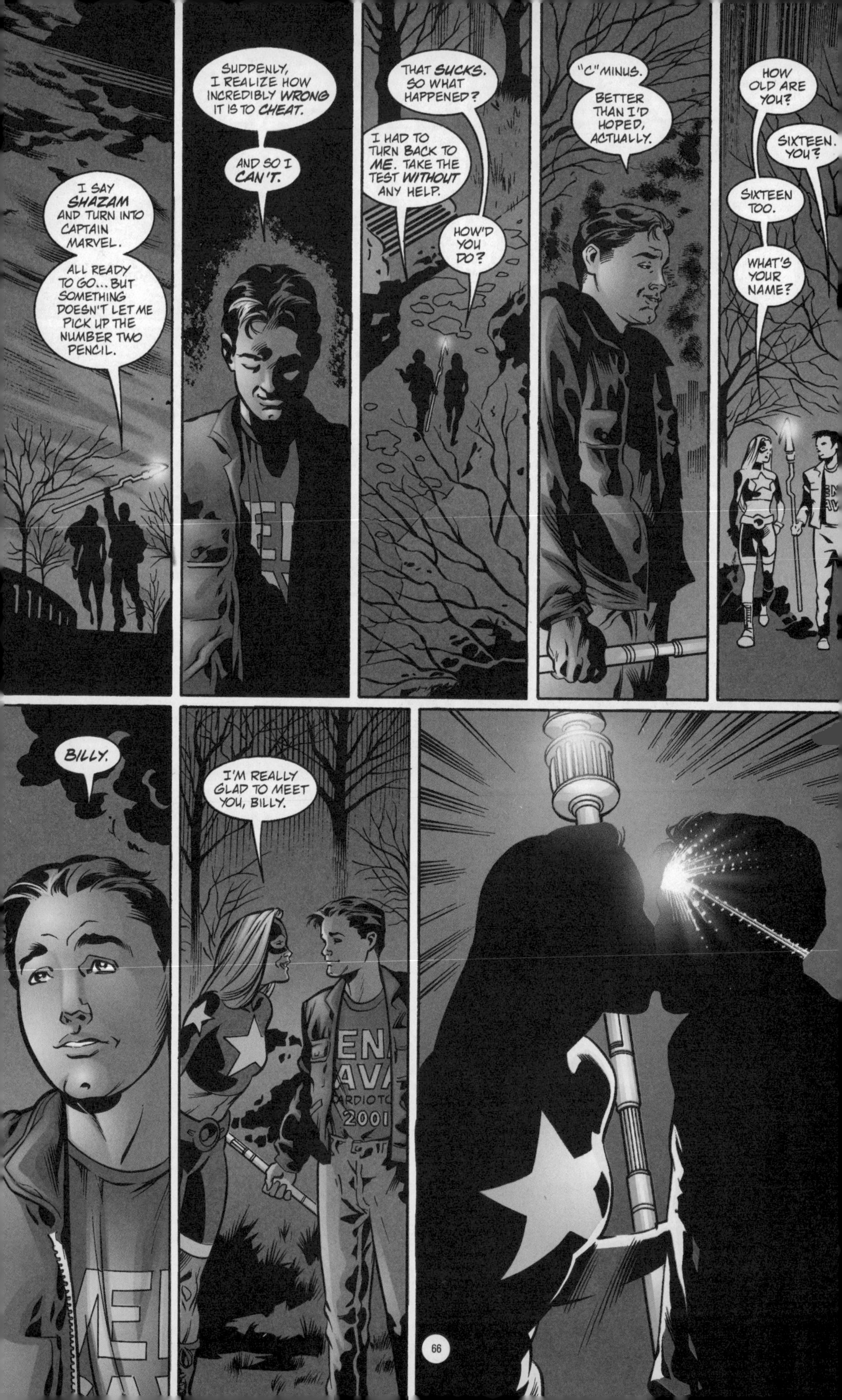

I SAY SHAZAM AND TURN INTO CAPTAIN MARVEL.
ALL READY TO GO... BUT SOMETHING DOESN'T LET ME PICK UP THE NUMBER TWO PENCIL.
SUDDENLY, I REALIZE HOW INCREDIBLY WRONG IT IS TO CHEAT.
AND SO I CAN'T.
THAT SUCKS. SO WHAT HAPPENED?
I HAD TO TURN BACK TO ME. TAKE THE TEST WITHOUT ANY HELP.
HOW'D YOU DO?
"C" MINUS.
BETTER THAN I'D HOPED, ACTUALLY.
HOW OLD ARE YOU?
SIXTEEN. YOU?
SIXTEEN TOO.
WHAT'S YOUR NAME?
BILLY.
I'M REALLY GLAD TO MEET YOU, BILLY.

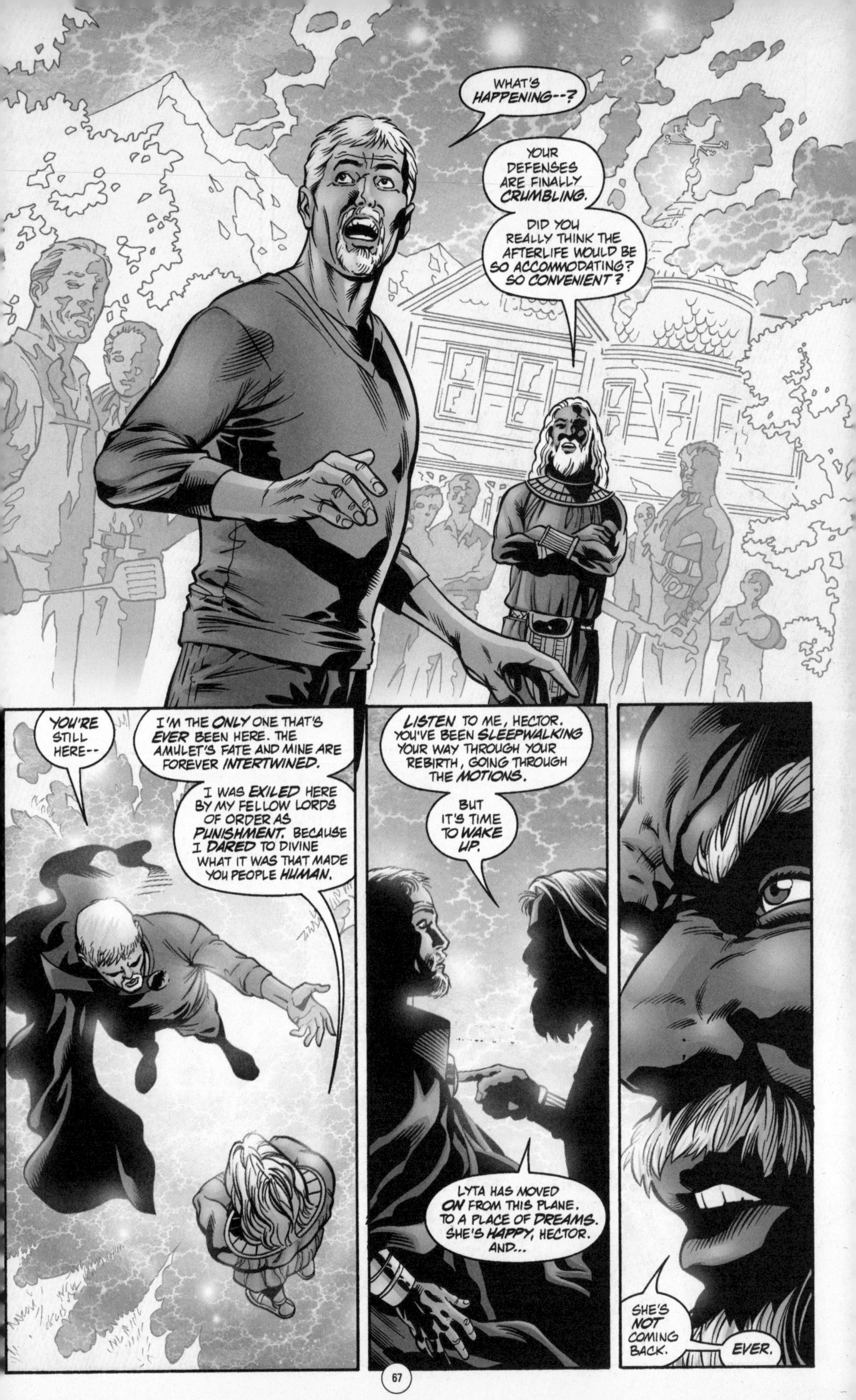
WHAT'S HAPPENING--?
YOUR DEFENSES ARE FINALLY CRUMBLING.
DID YOU REALLY THINK THE AFTERLIFE WOULD BE SO ACCOMMODATING? SO CONVENIENT?
YOU'RE STILL HERE--
I'M THE ONLY ONE THAT'S EVER BEEN HERE. THE AMULET'S FATE AND MINE ARE FOREVER INTERTWINED.
I WAS EXILED HERE BY MY FELLOW LORDS OF ORDER AS PUNISHMENT. BECAUSE I DARED TO DIVINE WHAT IT WAS THAT MADE YOU PEOPLE HUMAN.
LISTEN TO ME, HECTOR. YOU'VE BEEN SLEEPWALKING YOUR WAY THROUGH YOUR REBIRTH, GOING THROUGH THE MOTIONS.
BUT IT'S TIME TO WAKE UP.
LYTA HAS MOVED ON FROM THIS PLANE. TO A PLACE OF DREAMS. SHE'S HAPPY, HECTOR. AND...
SHE'S NOT COMING BACK.
EVER.

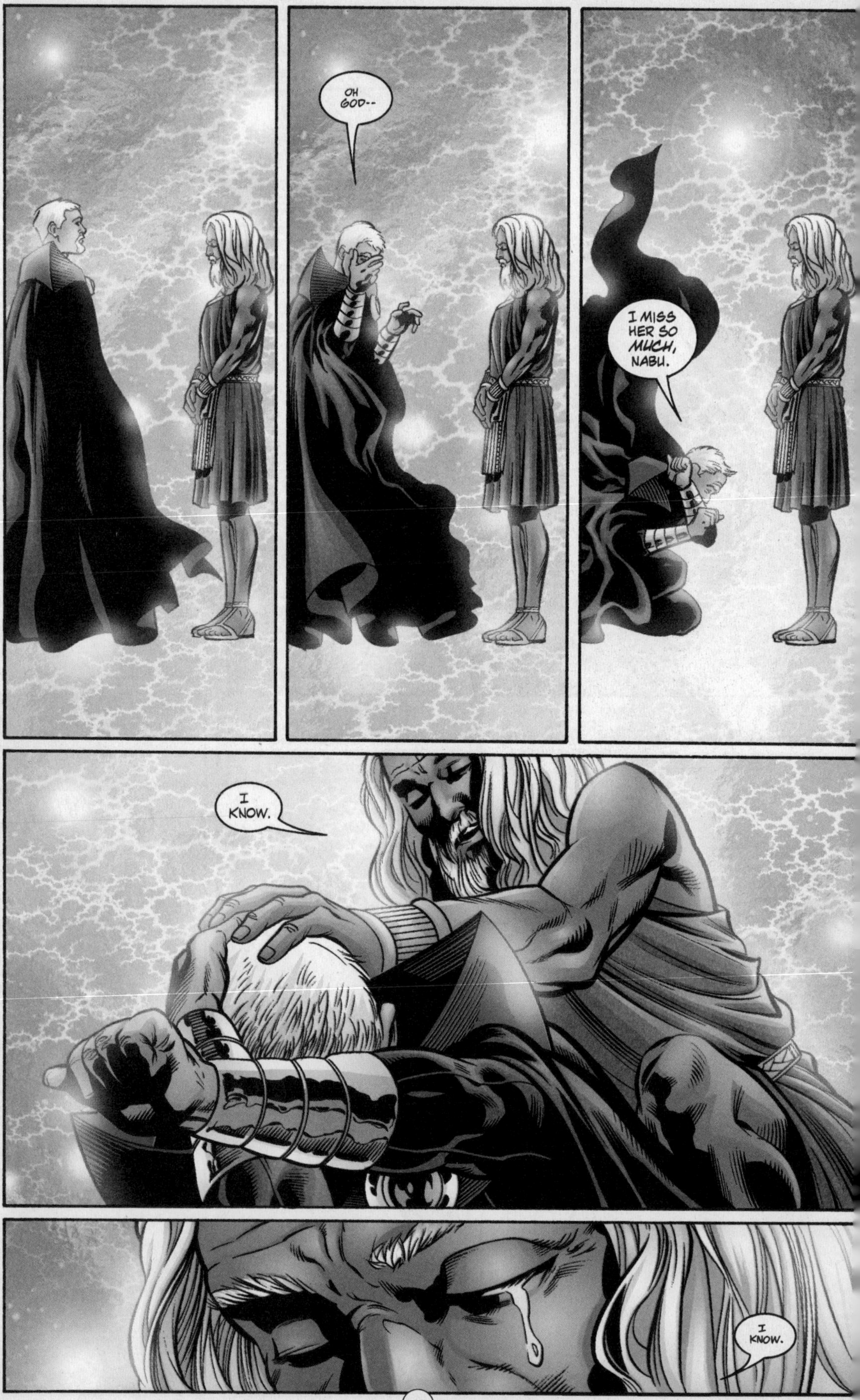
OH GOD--
I MISS HER SO MUCH, NABU.
I KNOW.
I KNOW.

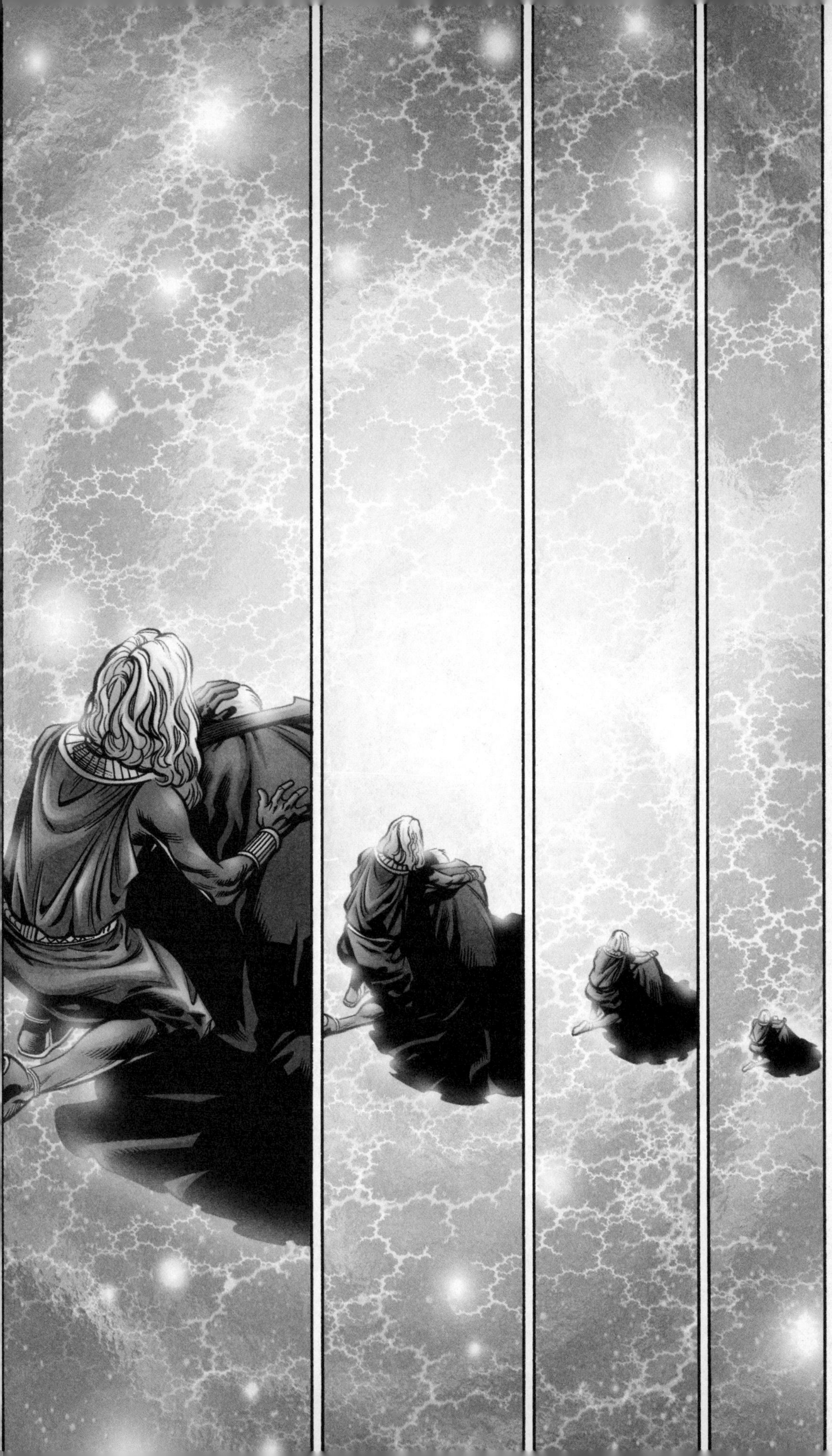

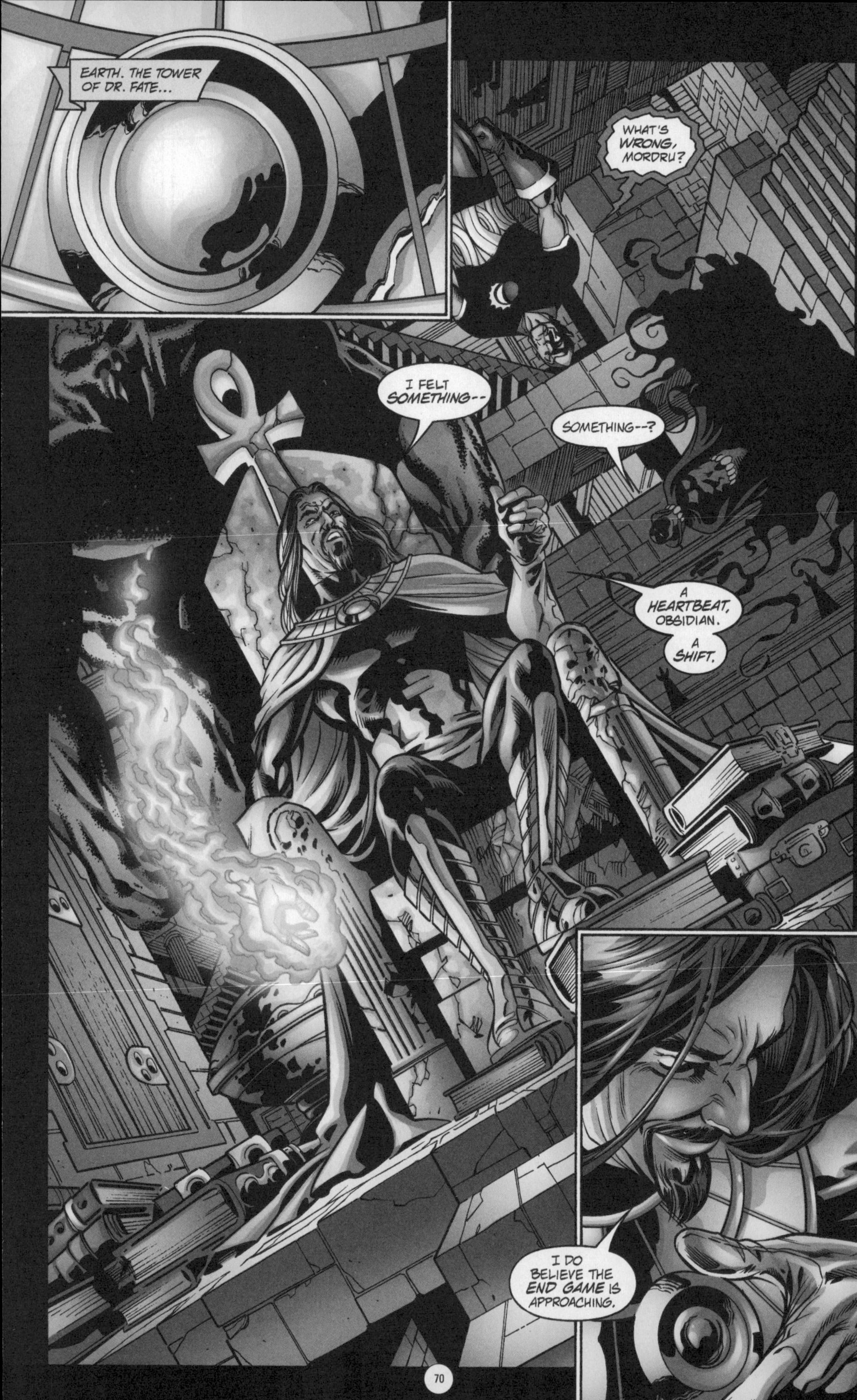
EARTH. THE TOWER OF DR. FATE...
WHAT'S WRONG, MORDRU?
I FELT SOMETHING--
SOMETHING--?
A HEARTBEAT, OBSIDIAN. A SHIFT.
I DO BELIEVE THE END GAME IS APPROACHING.

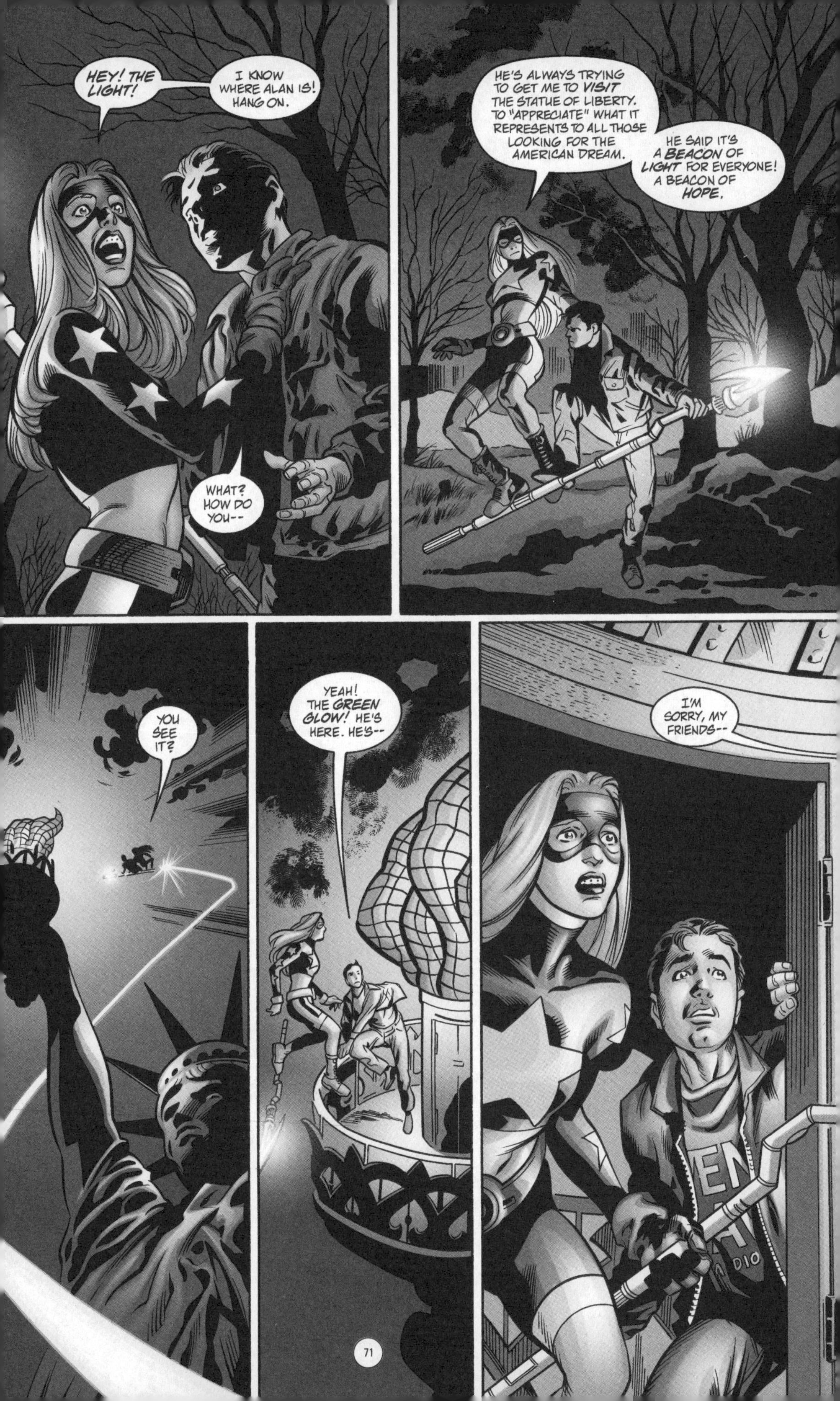
HEY! THE LIGHT!
I KNOW WHERE ALAN IS! HANG ON.
WHAT? HOW DO YOU--
HE'S ALWAYS TRYING TO GET ME TO VISIT THE STATUE OF LIBERTY. TO "APPRECIATE" WHAT IT REPRESENTS TO ALL THOSE LOOKING FOR THE AMERICAN DREAM.
HE SAID IT'S A BEACON OF LIGHT FOR EVERYONE! A BEACON OF HOPE.
YOU SEE IT?
YEAH! THE GREEN GLOW! HE'S HERE. HE'S--
I'M SORRY, MY FRIENDS--

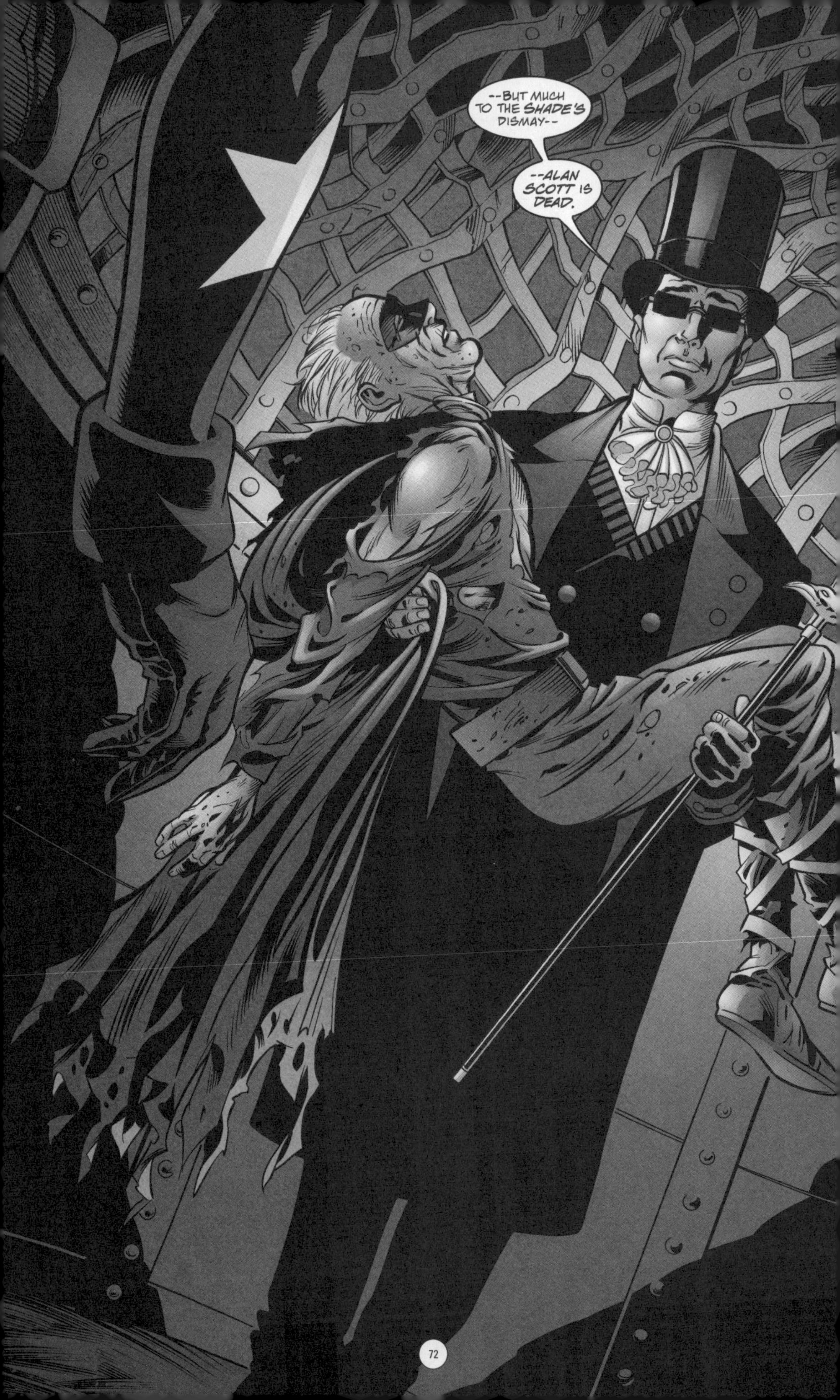
--BUT MUCH TO THE SHADE'S DISMAY--
--ALAN SCOTT IS DEAD.

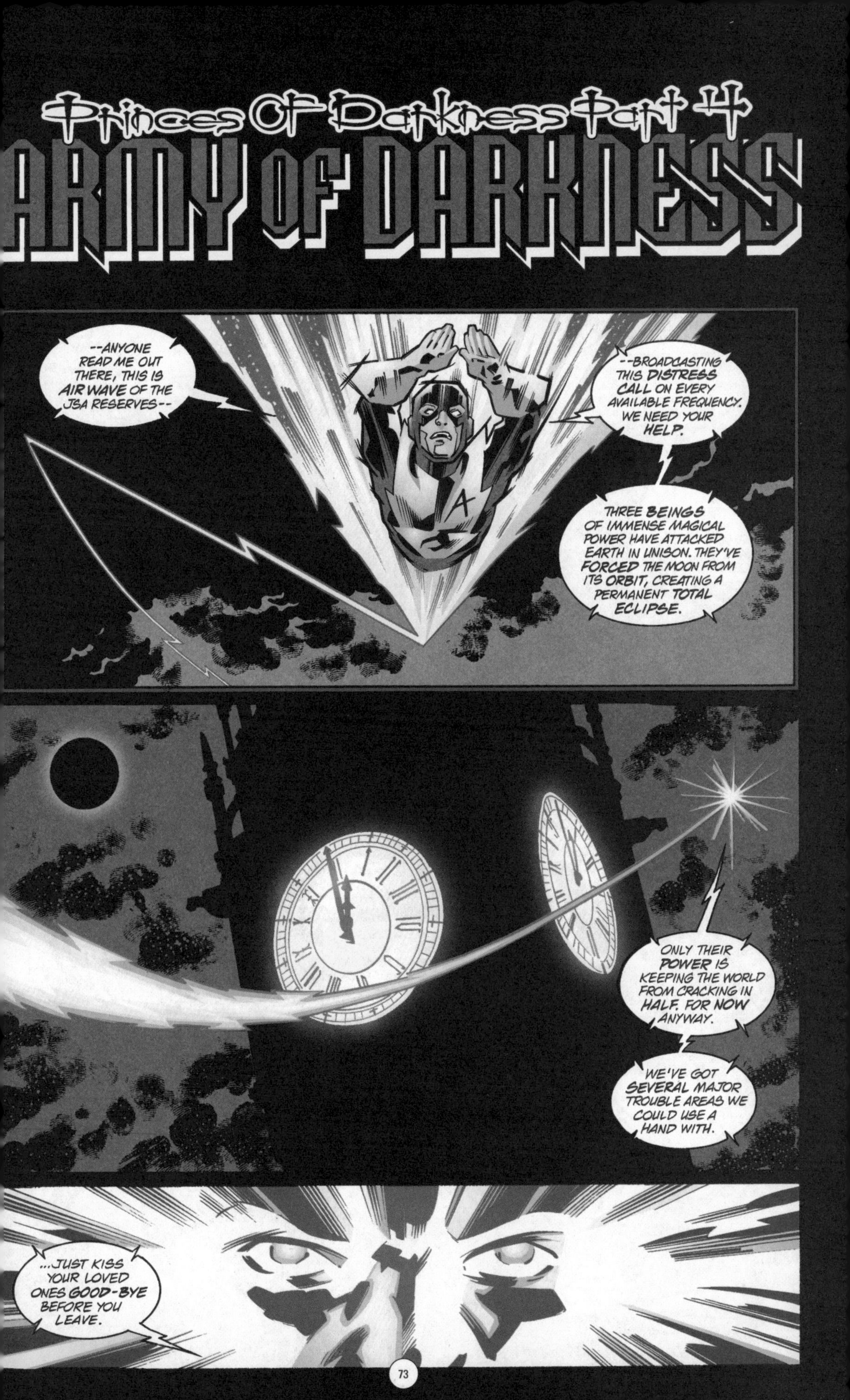
Princes Of Darkness Part 4
ARMY OF DARKNESS
--ANYONE READ ME OUT THERE, THIS IS AIR WAVE OF THE JSA RESERVES--
--BROADCASTING THIS DISTRESS CALL ON EVERY AVAILABLE FREQUENCY. WE NEED YOUR HELP.
THREE BEINGS OF IMMENSE MAGICAL POWER HAVE ATTACKED EARTH IN UNISON. THEY'VE FORCED THE MOON FROM ITS ORBIT, CREATING A PERMANENT TOTAL ECLIPSE.
ONLY THEIR POWER IS KEEPING THE WORLD FROM CRACKING IN HALF. FOR NOW ANYWAY.
WE'VE GOT SEVERAL MAJOR TROUBLE AREAS WE COULD USE A HAND WITH.
...JUST KISS YOUR LOVED ONES GOOD-BYE BEFORE YOU LEAVE.

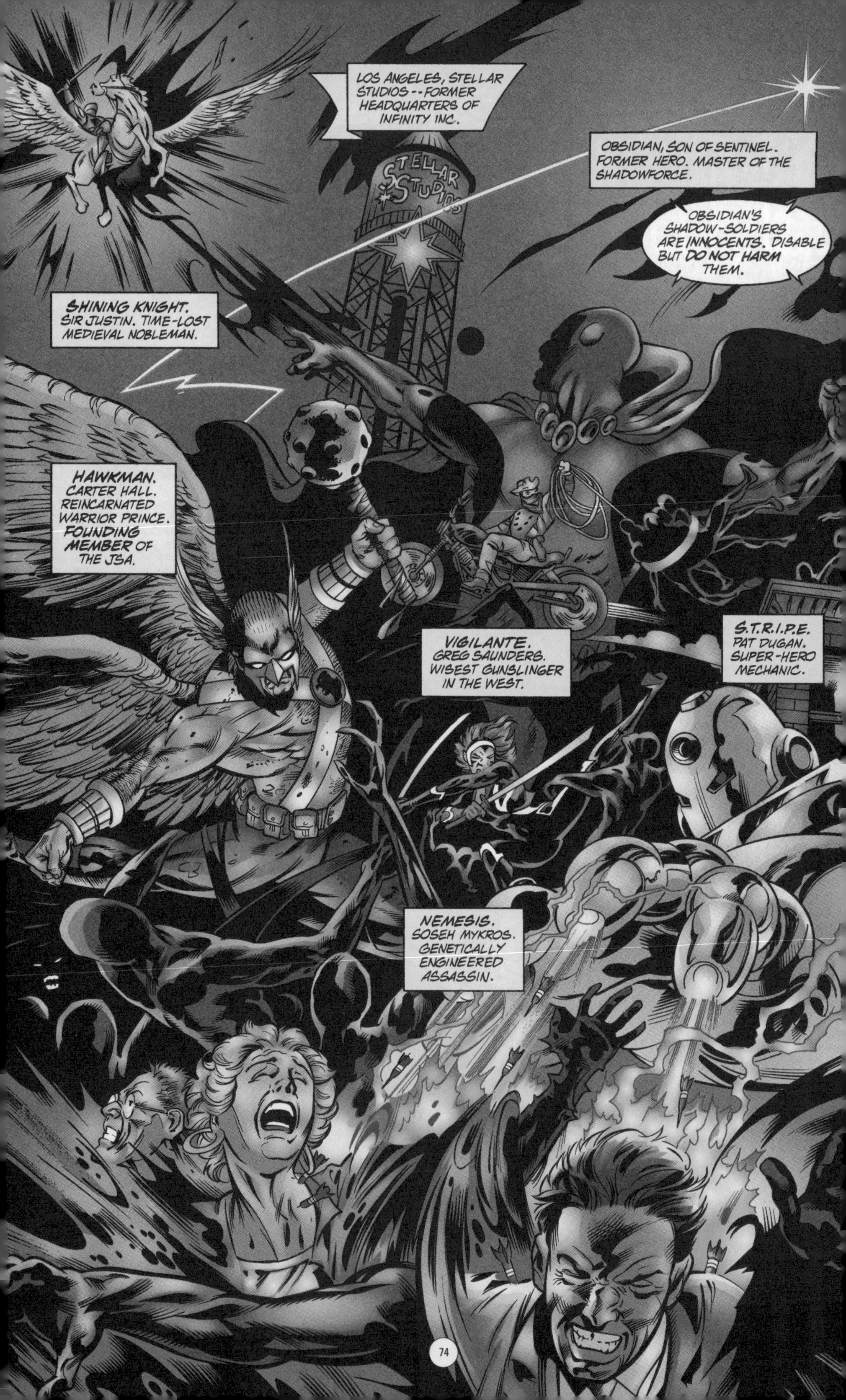

LOS ANGELES, STELLAR STUDIOS -- FORMER HEADQUARTERS OF INFINITY INC.
STELLAR STUDIOS
OBSIDIAN, SON OF SENTINEL. FORMER HERO. MASTER OF THE SHADOWFORCE.
OBSIDIAN'S SHADOW-SOLDIERS ARE INNOCENTS. DISABLE BUT DO NOT HARM THEM.
SHINING KNIGHT. SIR JUSTIN. TIME-LOST MEDIEVAL NOBLEMAN.
HAWKMAN. CARTER HALL. REINCARNATED WARRIOR PRINCE. FOUNDING MEMBER OF THE JSA.
VIGILANTE. GREG SAUNDERS. WISEST GUNSLINGER IN THE WEST.
S.T.R.I.P.E. PAT DUGAN. SUPER-HERO MECHANIC.
NEMESIS. SOSEH MYKROS. GENETICALLY ENGINEERED ASSASSIN.

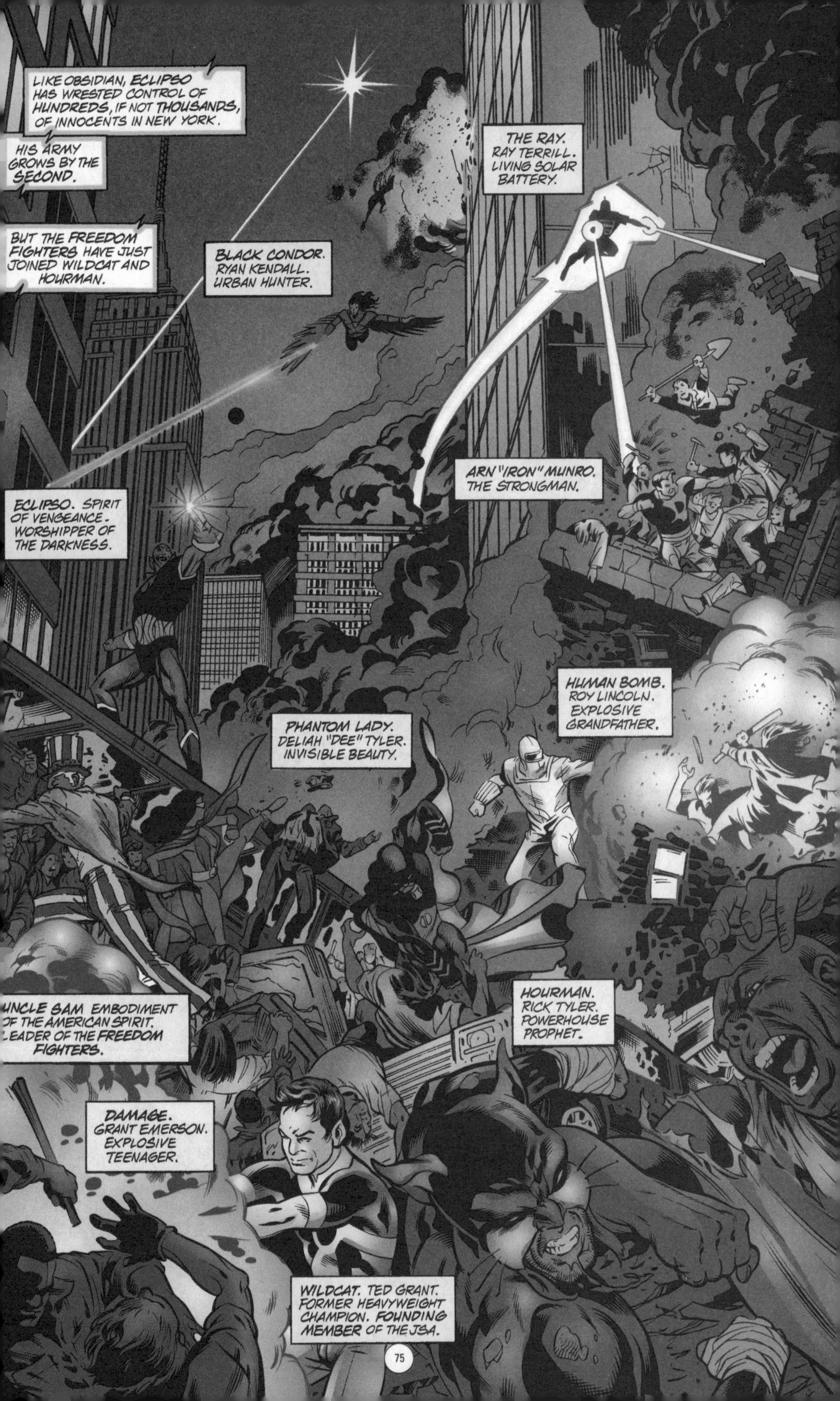
LIKE OBSIDIAN, ECLIPSO HAS WRESTED CONTROL OF HUNDREDS, IF NOT THOUSANDS, OF INNOCENTS IN NEW YORK.
HIS ARMY GROWS BY THE SECOND.
BUT THE FREEDOM FIGHTERS HAVE JUST JOINED WILDCAT AND HOURMAN.
BLACK CONDOR. RYAN KENDALL. URBAN HUNTER.
THE RAY. RAY TERRILL. LIVING SOLAR BATTERY.
ARN "IRON" MUNRO. THE STRONGMAN.
ECLIPSO. SPIRIT OF VENGEANCE. WORSHIPPER OF THE DARKNESS.
HUMAN BOMB. ROY LINCOLN. EXPLOSIVE GRANDFATHER.
PHANTOM LADY. DELIAH "DEE" TYLER. INVISIBLE BEAUTY.
UNCLE SAM EMBODIMENT OF THE AMERICAN SPIRIT. LEADER OF THE FREEDOM FIGHTERS.
HOURMAN. RICK TYLER. POWERHOUSE PROPHET.
DAMAGE. GRANT EMERSON. EXPLOSIVE TEENAGER.
WILDCAT. TED GRANT. FORMER HEAVYWEIGHT CHAMPION. FOUNDING MEMBER OF THE JSA.

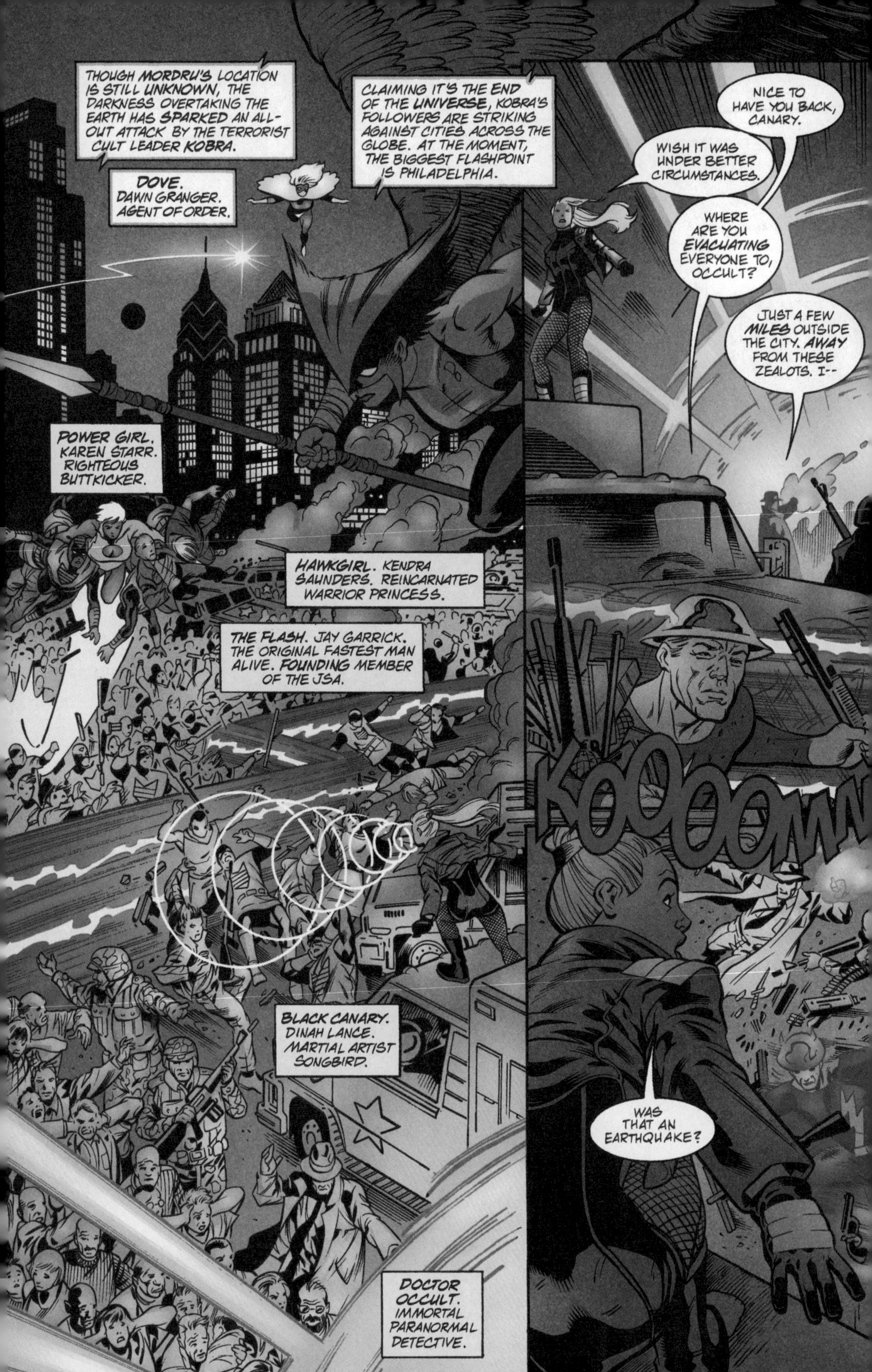
THOUGH MORDRU'S LOCATION IS STILL UNKNOWN, THE DARKNESS OVERTAKING THE EARTH HAS SPARKED AN ALL-OUT ATTACK BY THE TERRORIST CULT LEADER KOBRA.
CLAIMING IT'S THE END OF THE UNIVERSE, KOBRA'S FOLLOWERS ARE STRIKING AGAINST CITIES ACROSS THE GLOBE. AT THE MOMENT, THE BIGGEST FLASHPOINT IS PHILADELPHIA.
DOVE. DAWN GRANGER. AGENT OF ORDER.
POWER GIRL. KAREN STARR. RIGHTEOUS BUTTKICKER.
HAWKGIRL. KENDRA SAUNDERS. REINCARNATED WARRIOR PRINCESS.
THE FLASH. JAY GARRICK. THE ORIGINAL FASTEST MAN ALIVE. FOUNDING MEMBER OF THE JSA.
BLACK CANARY. DINAH LANCE. MARTIAL ARTIST SONGBIRD.
DOCTOR OCCULT. IMMORTAL PARANORMAL DETECTIVE.
NICE TO HAVE YOU BACK, CANARY.
WISH IT WAS UNDER BETTER CIRCUMSTANCES.
WHERE ARE YOU EVACUATING EVERYONE TO, OCCULT?
JUST A FEW MILES OUTSIDE THE CITY. AWAY FROM THESE ZEALOTS. I--
KOOOOMM
WAS THAT AN EARTHQUAKE?

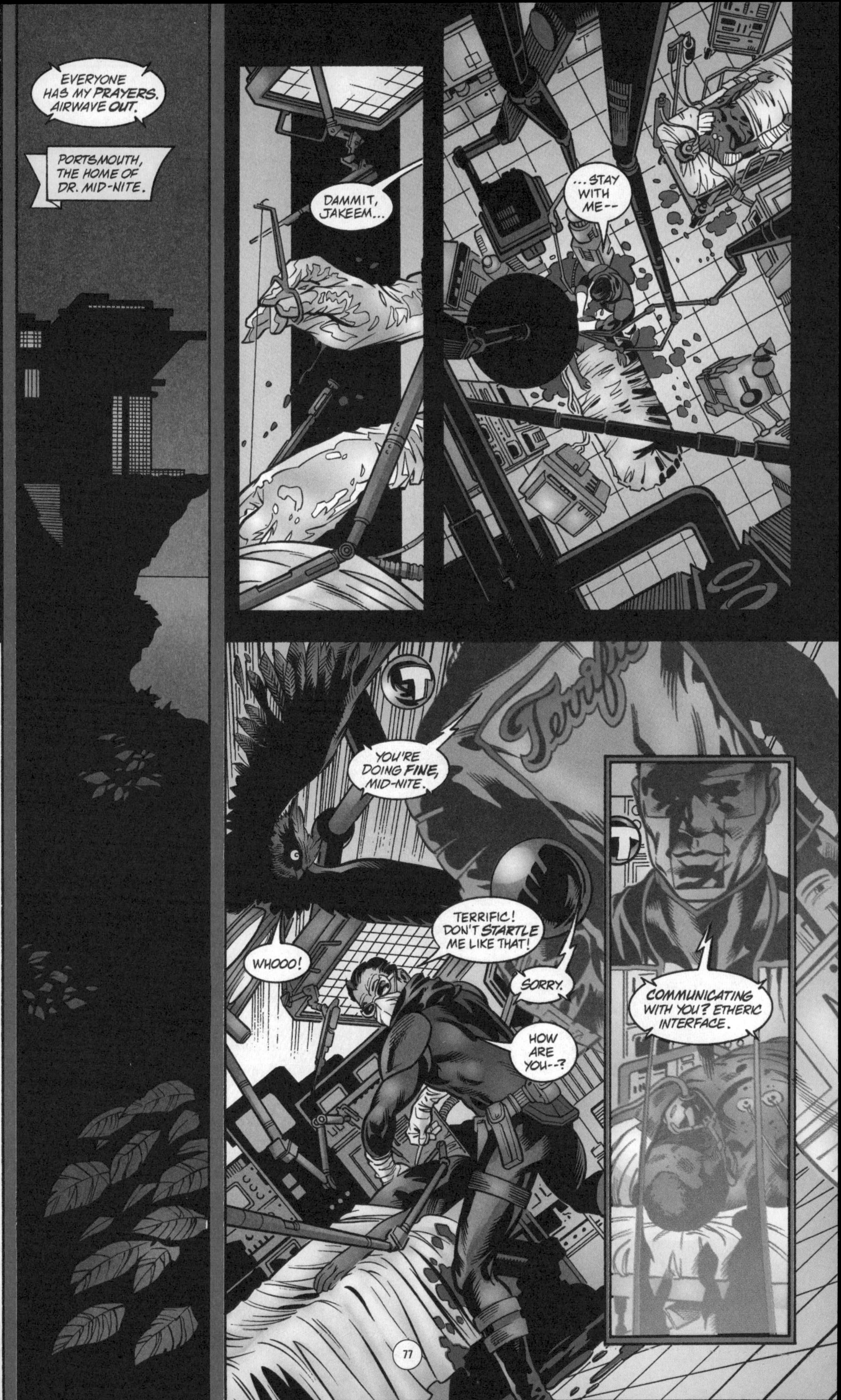

EVERYONE HAS MY PRAYERS. AIRWAVE OUT.
PORTSMOUTH, THE HOME OF DR. MID-NITE.
DAMMIT, JAKEEM...
...STAY WITH ME--
YOU'RE DOING FINE, MID-NITE.
WHOOO!
TERRIFIC! DON'T STARTLE ME LIKE THAT!
SORRY.
HOW ARE YOU--?
COMMUNICATING WITH YOU? ETHERIC INTERFACE.

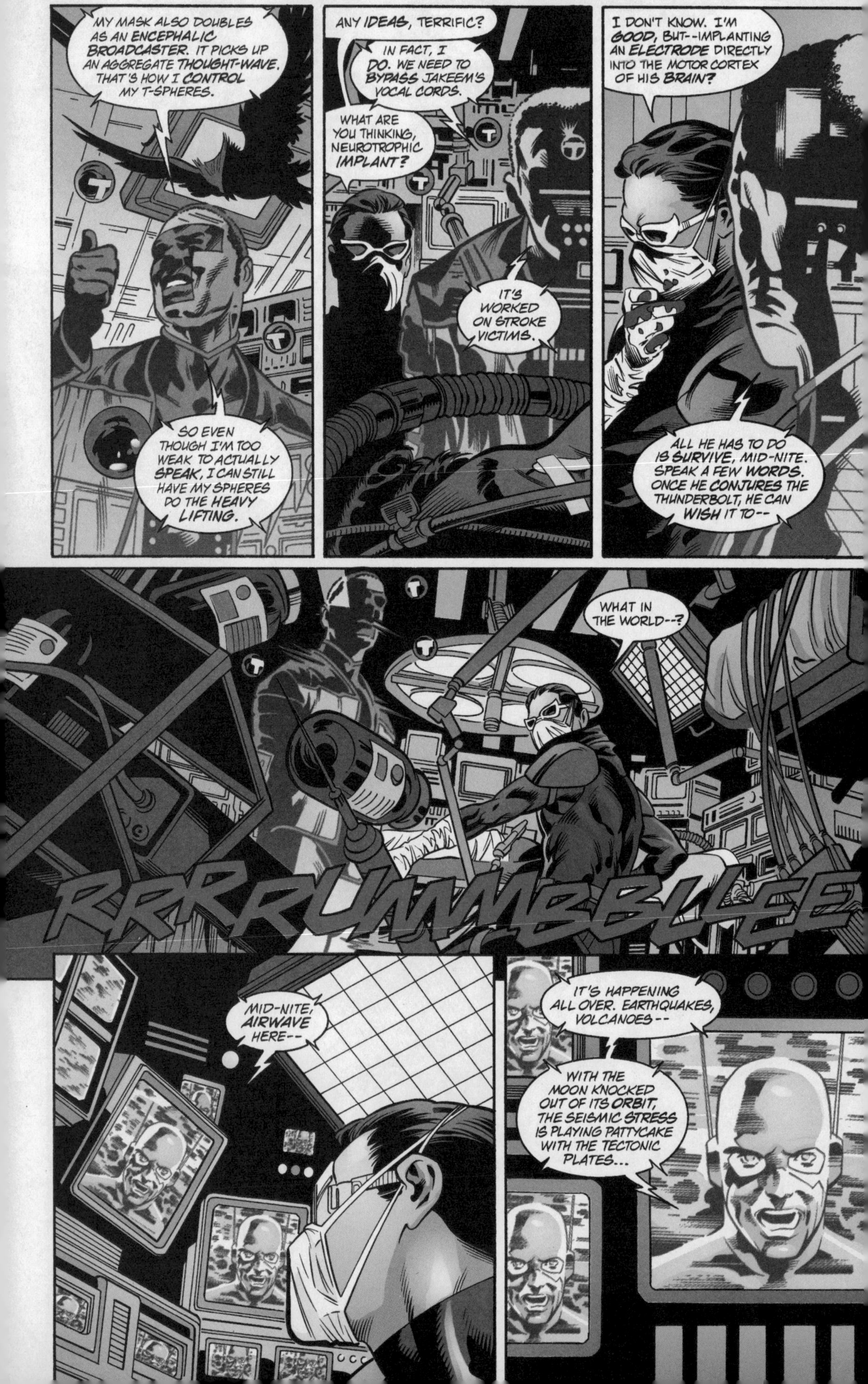
MY MASK ALSO DOUBLES AS AN ENCEPHALIC BROADCASTER. IT PICKS UP AN AGGREGATE THOUGHT-WAVE. THAT'S HOW I CONTROL MY T-SPHERES.
SO EVEN THOUGH I'M TOO WEAK TO ACTUALLY SPEAK, I CAN STILL HAVE MY SPHERES DO THE HEAVY LIFTING.
ANY IDEAS, TERRIFIC?
IN FACT, I DO. WE NEED TO BYPASS JAKEEM'S VOCAL CORDS.
WHAT ARE YOU THINKING, NEUROTROPHIC IMPLANT?
IT'S WORKED ON STROKE VICTIMS.
I DON'T KNOW. I'M GOOD, BUT--IMPLANTING AN ELECTRODE DIRECTLY INTO THE MOTOR CORTEX OF HIS BRAIN?
ALL HE HAS TO DO IS SURVIVE, MID-NITE. SPEAK A FEW WORDS. ONCE HE CONJURES THE THUNDERBOLT, HE CAN WISH IT TO--
WHAT IN THE WORLD--?
RRRRUMMBBLLEE
MID-NITE, AIRWAVE HERE--
IT'S HAPPENING ALL OVER. EARTHQUAKES, VOLCANOES--
WITH THE MOON KNOCKED OUT OF ITS ORBIT, THE SEISMIC STRESS IS PLAYING PATTYCAKE WITH THE TECTONIC PLATES...

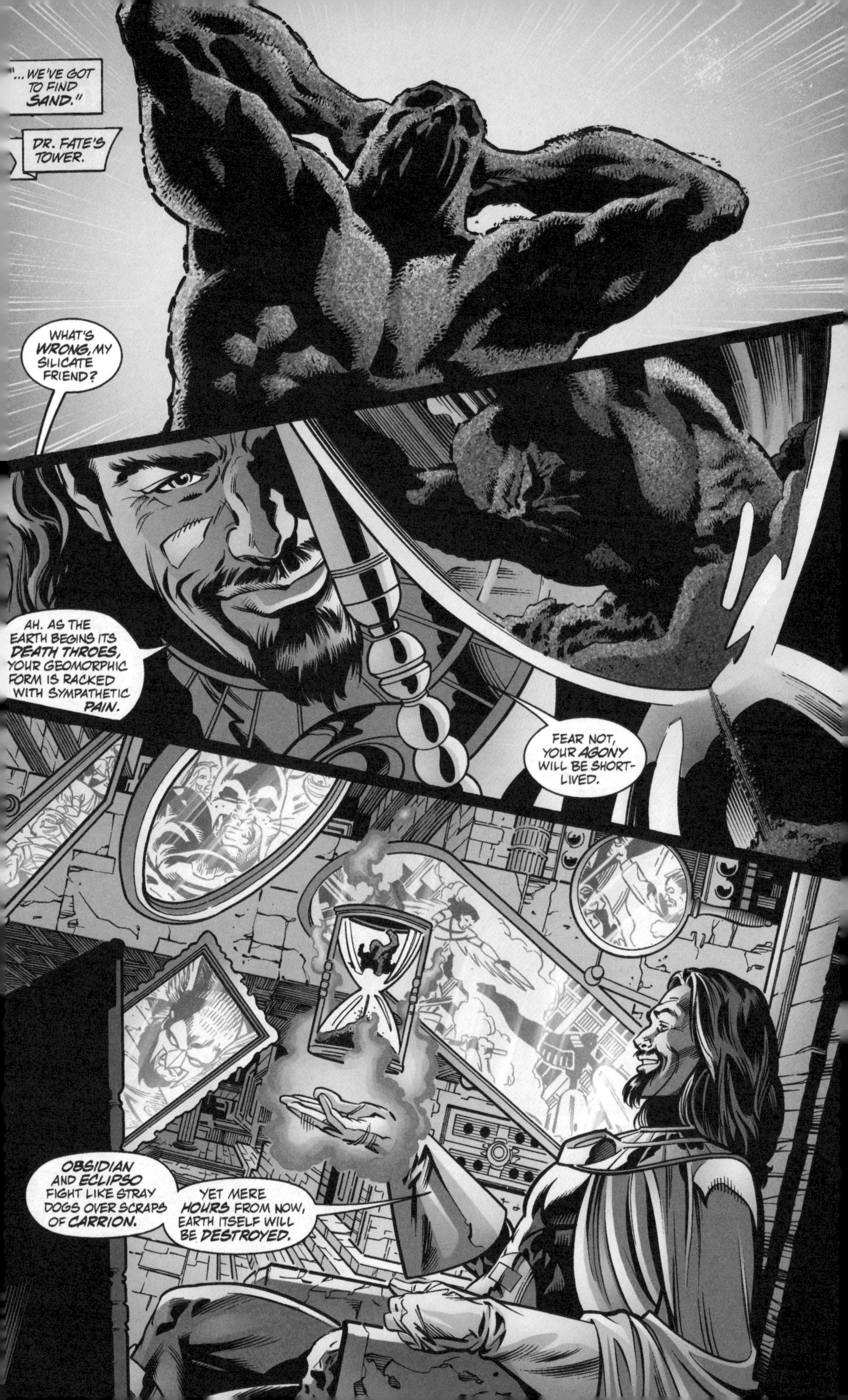
"...WE'VE GOT TO FIND SAND."
DR. FATE'S TOWER.
WHAT'S WRONG, MY SILICATE FRIEND?
AH. AS THE EARTH BEGINS ITS DEATH THROES, YOUR GEOMORPHIC FORM IS RACKED WITH SYMPATHETIC PAIN.
FEAR NOT, YOUR AGONY WILL BE SHORT-LIVED.
OBSIDIAN AND ECLIPSO FIGHT LIKE STRAY DOGS OVER SCRAPS OF CARRION.
YET MERE HOURS FROM NOW, EARTH ITSELF WILL BE DESTROYED.

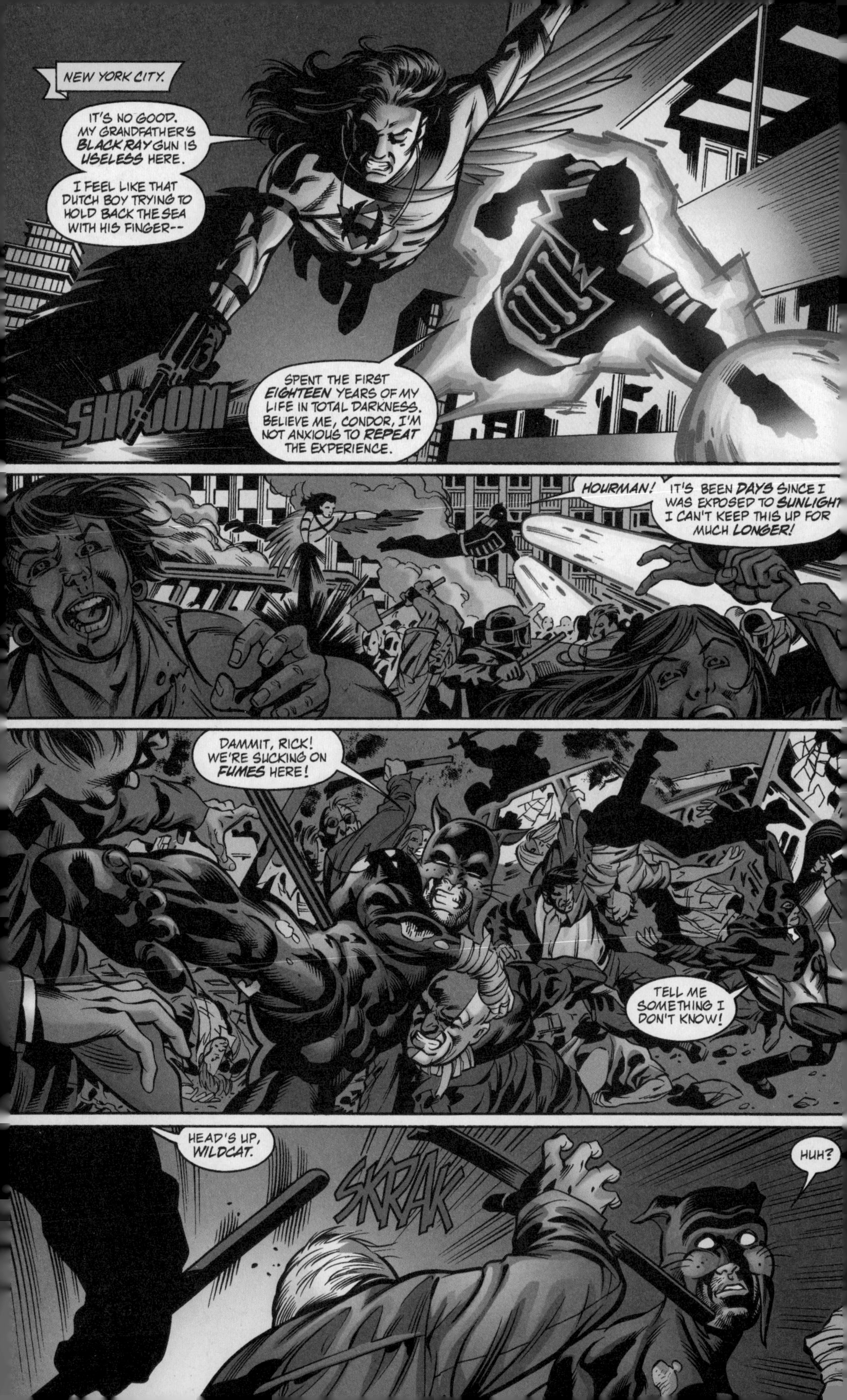
NEW YORK CITY.
IT'S NO GOOD. MY GRANDFATHER'S BLACK RAY GUN IS USELESS HERE.
I FEEL LIKE THAT DUTCH BOY TRYING TO HOLD BACK THE SEA WITH HIS FINGER--
SPENT THE FIRST EIGHTEEN YEARS OF MY LIFE IN TOTAL DARKNESS. BELIEVE ME, CONDOR, I'M NOT ANXIOUS TO REPEAT THE EXPERIENCE.
HOURMAN!
IT'S BEEN DAYS SINCE I WAS EXPOSED TO SUNLIGHT. I CAN'T KEEP THIS UP FOR MUCH LONGER!
DAMMIT, RICK! WE'RE SUCKING ON FUMES HERE!
TELL ME SOMETHING I DON'T KNOW!
HEAD'S UP, WILDCAT.
SKRAK
HUH?

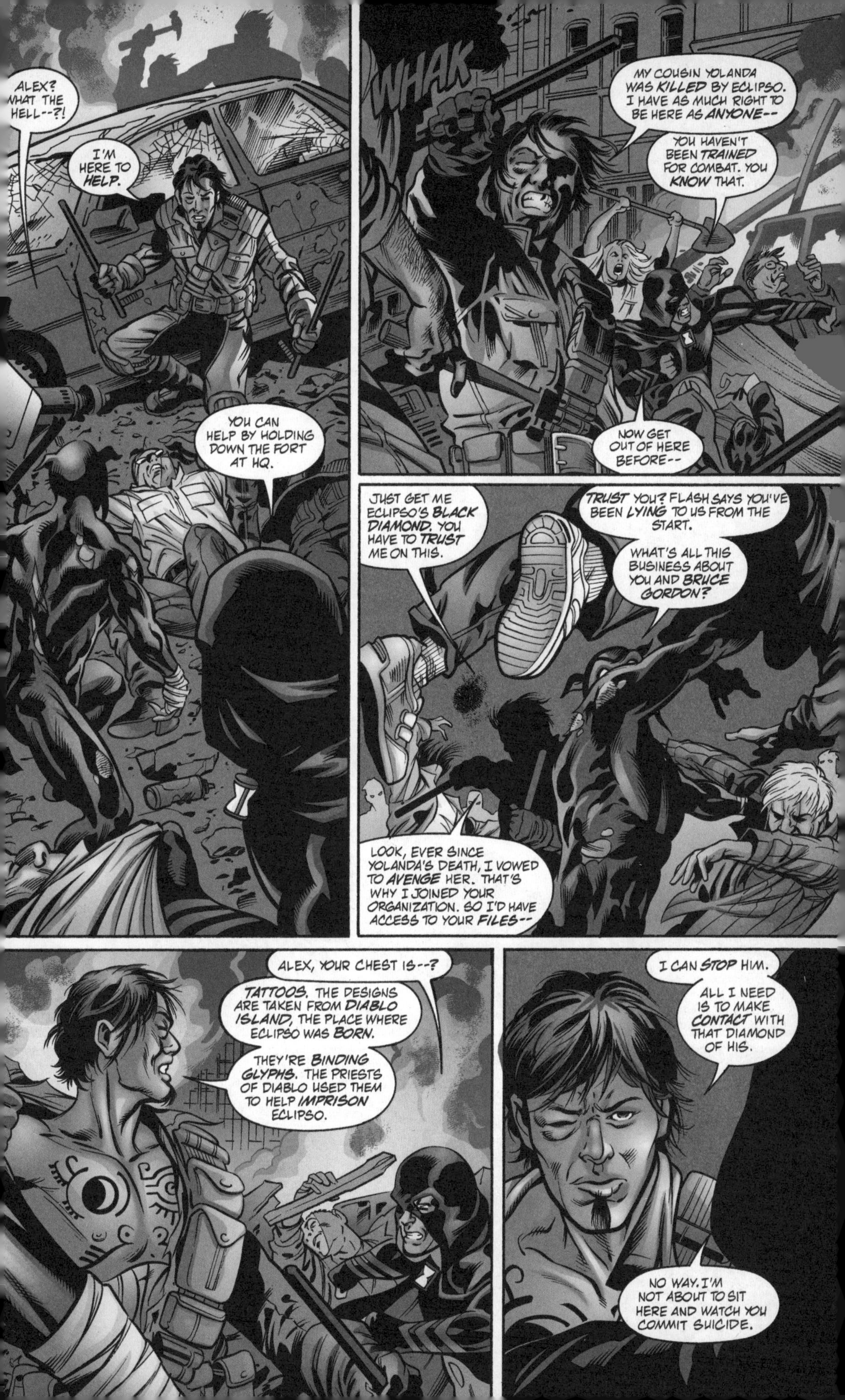
ALEX? WHAT THE HELL--?!
I'M HERE TO HELP.
YOU CAN HELP BY HOLDING DOWN THE FORT AT HQ.
WHAK
MY COUSIN YOLANDA WAS KILLED BY ECLIPSO. I HAVE AS MUCH RIGHT TO BE HERE AS ANYONE--
YOU HAVEN'T BEEN TRAINED FOR COMBAT. YOU KNOW THAT.
NOW GET OUT OF HERE BEFORE--
JUST GET ME ECLIPSO'S BLACK DIAMOND. YOU HAVE TO TRUST ME ON THIS.
TRUST YOU? FLASH SAYS YOU'VE BEEN LYING TO US FROM THE START.
WHAT'S ALL THIS BUSINESS ABOUT YOU AND BRUCE GORDON?
LOOK, EVER SINCE YOLANDA'S DEATH, I VOWED TO AVENGE HER. THAT'S WHY I JOINED YOUR ORGANIZATION. SO I'D HAVE ACCESS TO YOUR FILES--
ALEX, YOUR CHEST IS--?
TATTOOS. THE DESIGNS ARE TAKEN FROM DIABLO ISLAND, THE PLACE WHERE ECLIPSO WAS BORN.
THEY'RE BINDING GLYPHS. THE PRIESTS OF DIABLO USED THEM TO HELP IMPRISON ECLIPSO.
I CAN STOP HIM.
ALL I NEED IS TO MAKE CONTACT WITH THAT DIAMOND OF HIS.
NO WAY. I'M NOT ABOUT TO SIT HERE AND WATCH YOU COMMIT SUICIDE.

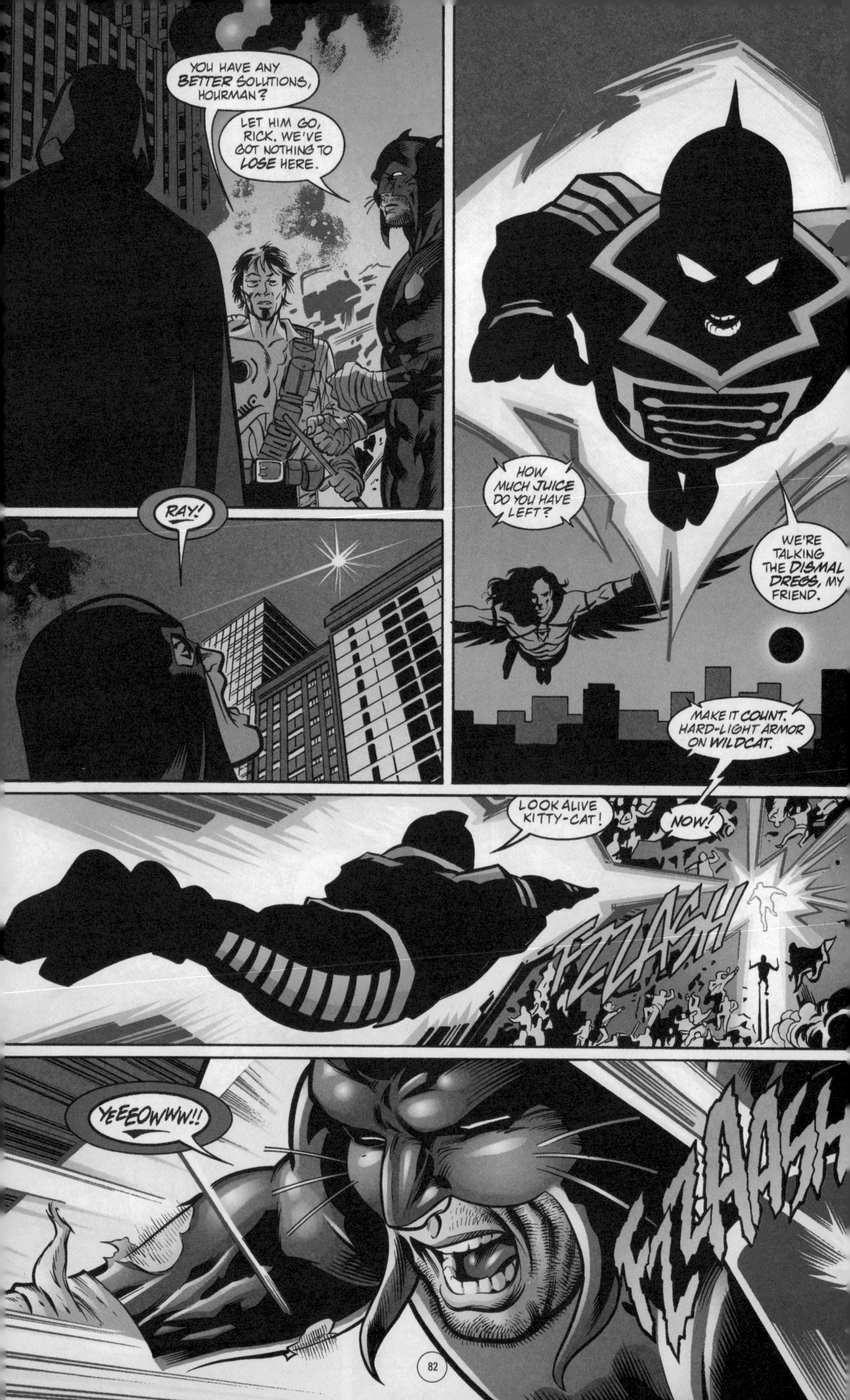

YOU HAVE ANY BETTER SOLUTIONS, HOURMAN?
LET HIM GO, RICK. WE'VE GOT NOTHING TO LOSE HERE.
RAY!
HOW MUCH JUICE DO YOU HAVE LEFT?
WE'RE TALKING THE DISMAL DREGS, MY FRIEND.
MAKE IT COUNT. HARD-LIGHT ARMOR ON WILDCAT.
NOW!
LOOK ALIVE KITTY-CAT!
FZZASH
YEEEOWWW!!
FZZASH

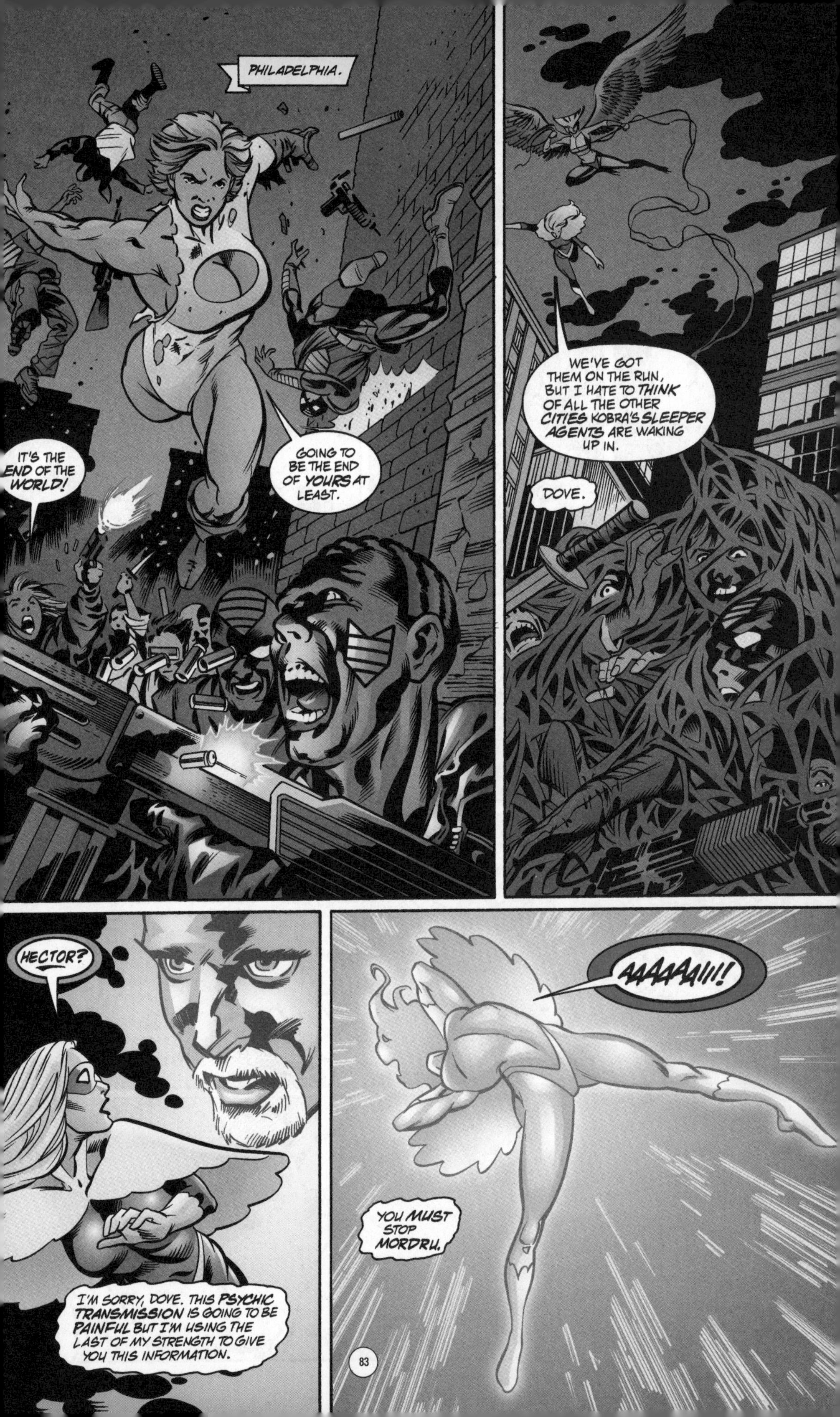
PHILADELPHIA.
IT'S THE END OF THE WORLD!
GOING TO BE THE END OF YOURS AT LEAST.
WE'VE GOT THEM ON THE RUN, BUT I HATE TO THINK OF ALL THE OTHER CITIES KOBRA'S SLEEPER AGENTS ARE WAKING UP IN.
DOVE.
HECTOR?
I'M SORRY, DOVE. THIS PSYCHIC TRANSMISSION IS GOING TO BE PAINFUL BUT I'M USING THE LAST OF MY STRENGTH TO GIVE YOU THIS INFORMATION.
AAAAAIII!
YOU MUST STOP MORDRU.

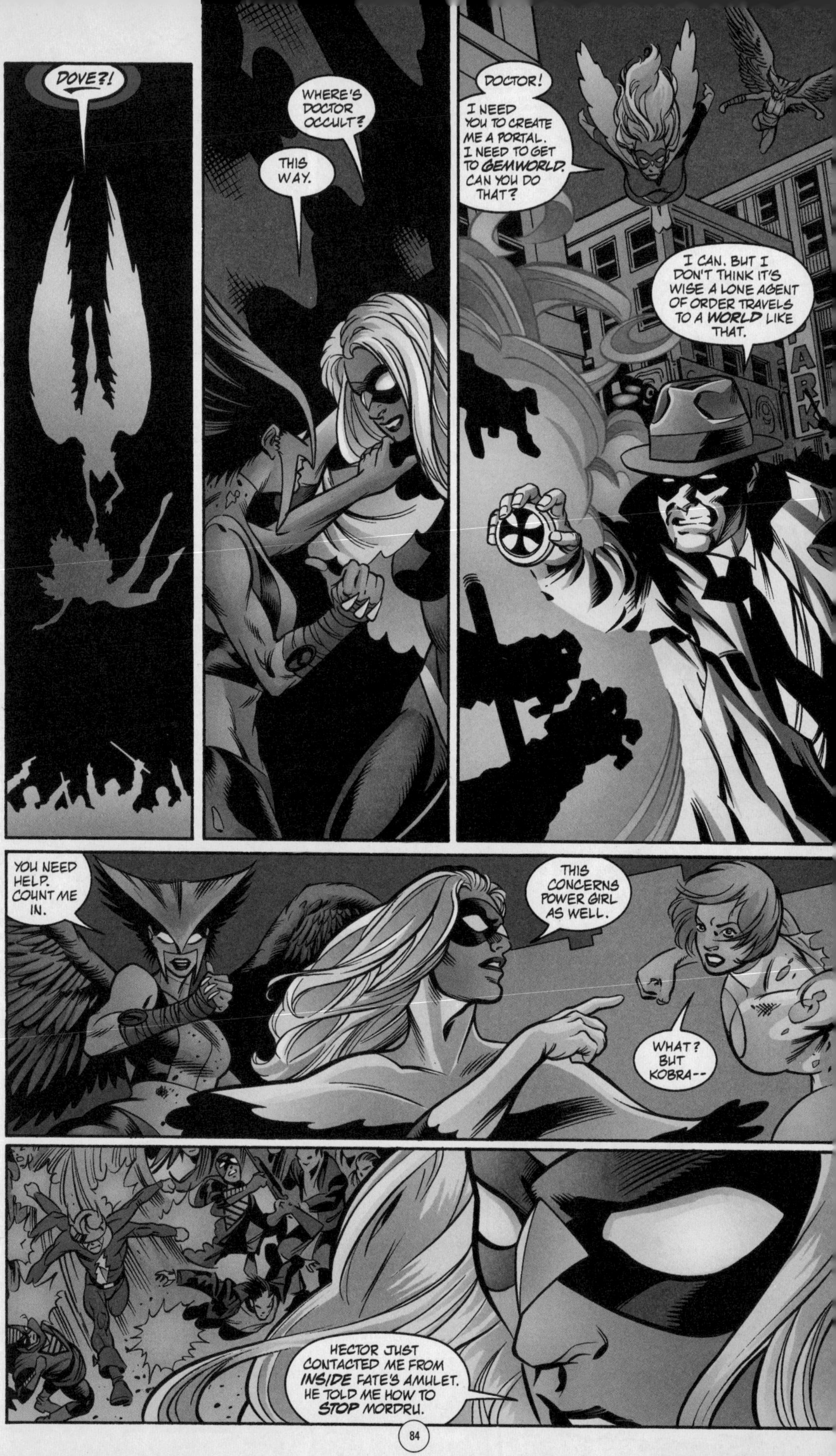
DOVE?!
WHERE'S DOCTOR OCCULT?
THIS WAY.
DOCTOR! I NEED YOU TO CREATE ME A PORTAL. I NEED TO GET TO GEMWORLD. CAN YOU DO THAT?
I CAN. BUT I DON'T THINK IT'S WISE A LONE AGENT OF ORDER TRAVELS TO A WORLD LIKE THAT.
YOU NEED HELP. COUNT ME IN.
THIS CONCERNS POWER GIRL AS WELL.
WHAT? BUT KOBRA--
HECTOR JUST CONTACTED ME FROM INSIDE FATE'S AMULET. HE TOLD ME HOW TO STOP MORDRU.

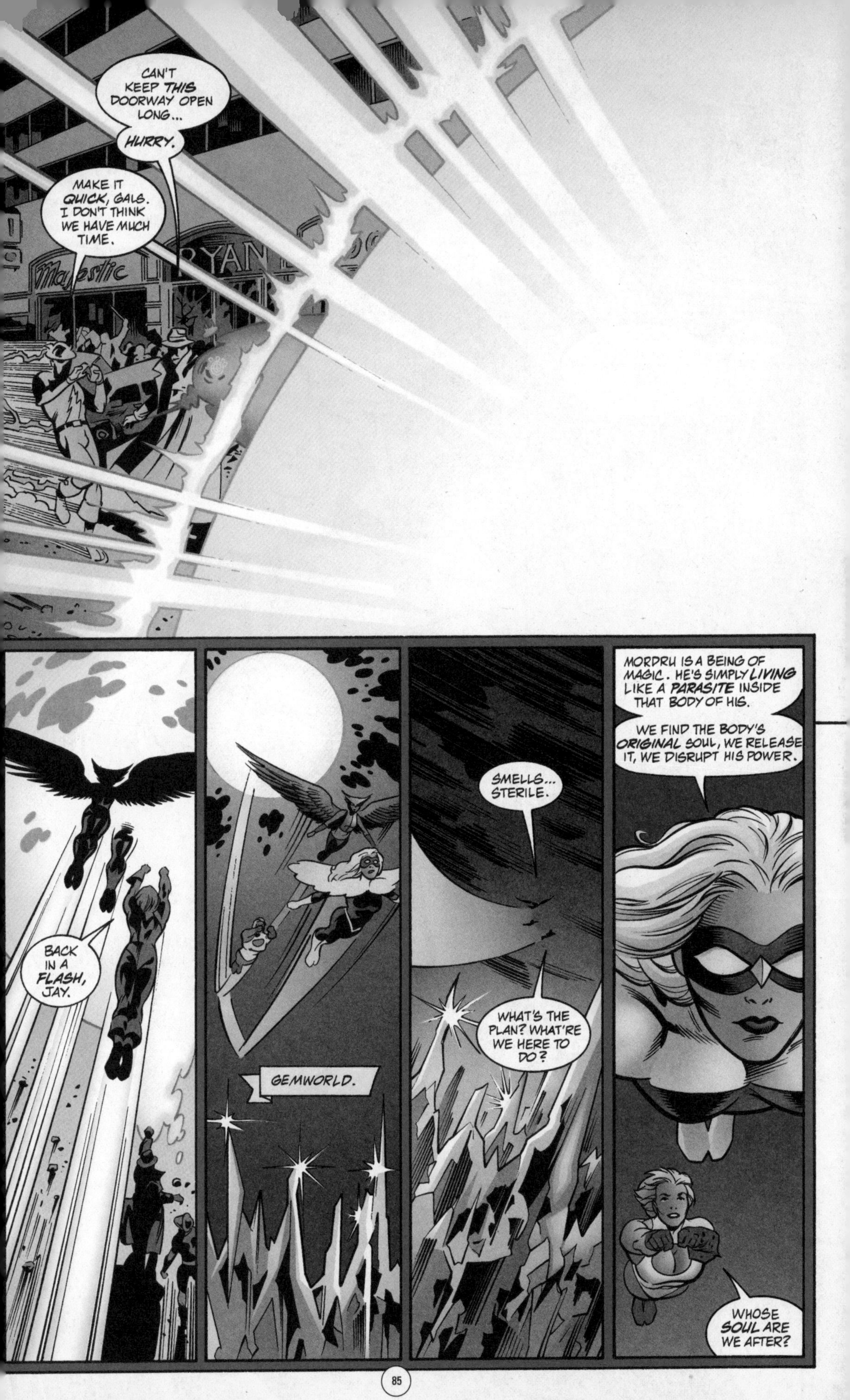

CAN'T KEEP THIS DOORWAY OPEN LONG...
HURRY.
MAKE IT QUICK, GALS. I DON'T THINK WE HAVE MUCH TIME.
Majestic
BACK IN A FLASH, JAY.
GEMWORLD.
SMELLS... STERILE.
WHAT'S THE PLAN? WHAT'RE WE HERE TO DO?
MORDRU IS A BEING OF MAGIC. HE'S SIMPLY LIVING LIKE A PARASITE INSIDE THAT BODY OF HIS.
WE FIND THE BODY'S ORIGINAL SOUL, WE RELEASE IT, WE DISRUPT HIS POWER.
WHOSE SOUL ARE WE AFTER?

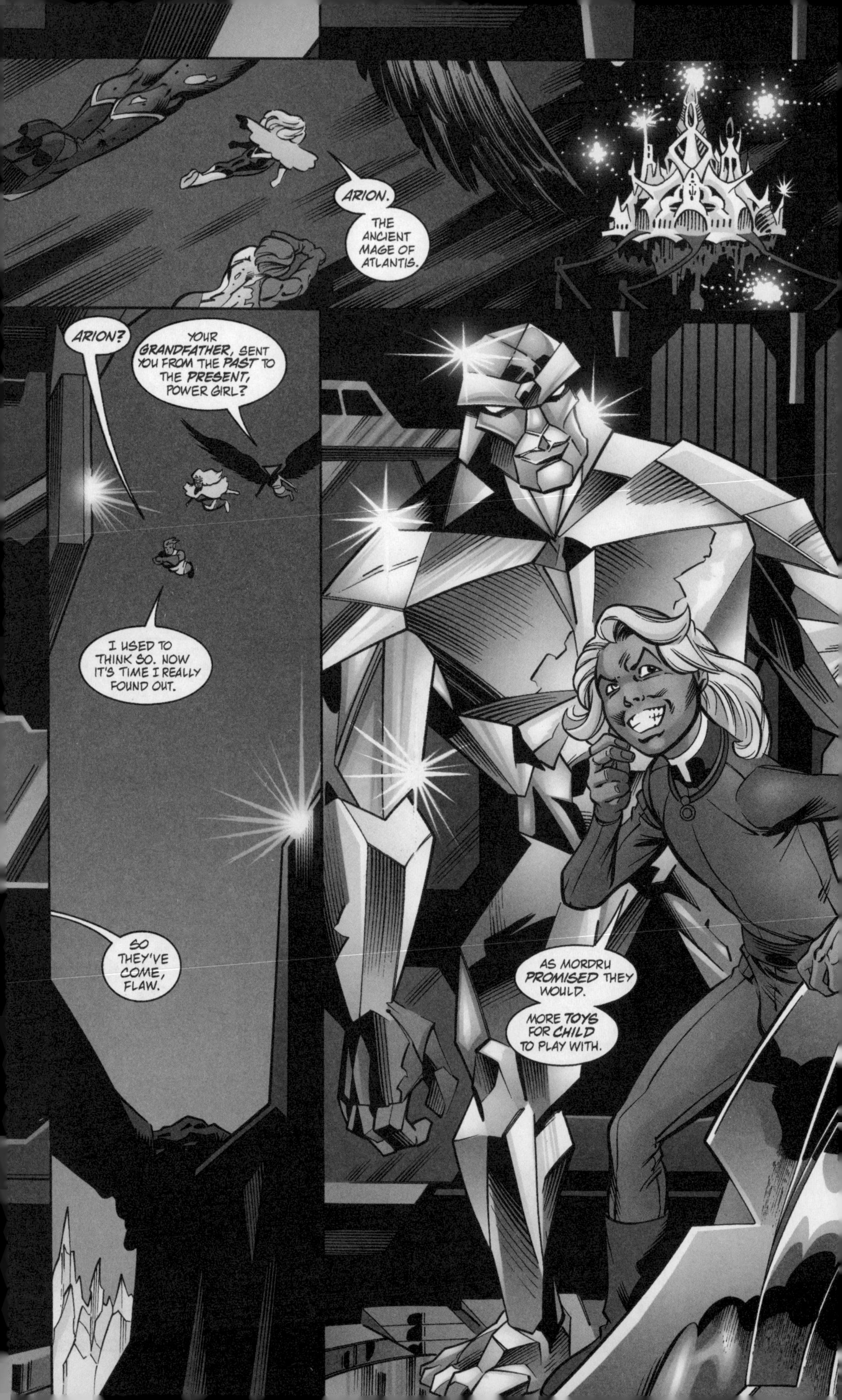
ARION.
THE ANCIENT MAGE OF ATLANTIS.
ARION?
YOUR GRANDFATHER, SENT YOU FROM THE PAST TO THE PRESENT, POWER GIRL?
I USED TO THINK SO. NOW IT'S TIME I REALLY FOUND OUT.
SO THEY'VE COME, FLAW.
AS MORDRU PROMISED THEY WOULD.
MORE TOYS FOR CHILD TO PLAY WITH.

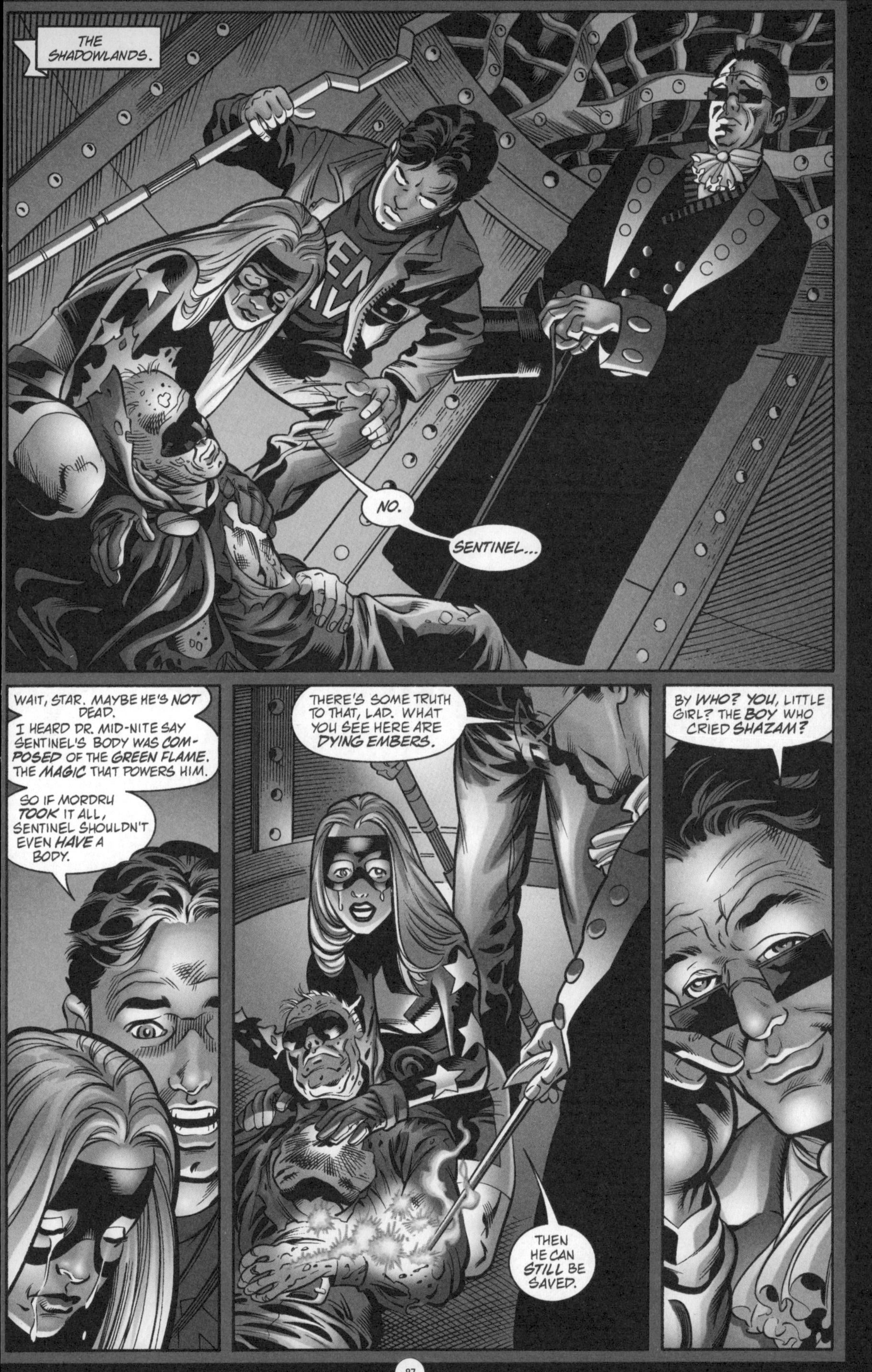

THE SHADOWLANDS.
NO.
SENTINEL...
WAIT, STAR. MAYBE HE'S NOT DEAD.
I HEARD DR. MID-NITE SAY SENTINEL'S BODY WAS COMPOSED OF THE GREEN FLAME. THE MAGIC THAT POWERS HIM.
SO IF MORDRU TOOK IT ALL, SENTINEL SHOULDN'T EVEN HAVE A BODY.
THERE'S SOME TRUTH TO THAT, LAD. WHAT YOU SEE HERE ARE DYING EMBERS.
THEN HE CAN STILL BE SAVED.
BY WHO? YOU, LITTLE GIRL? THE BOY WHO CRIED SHAZAM?

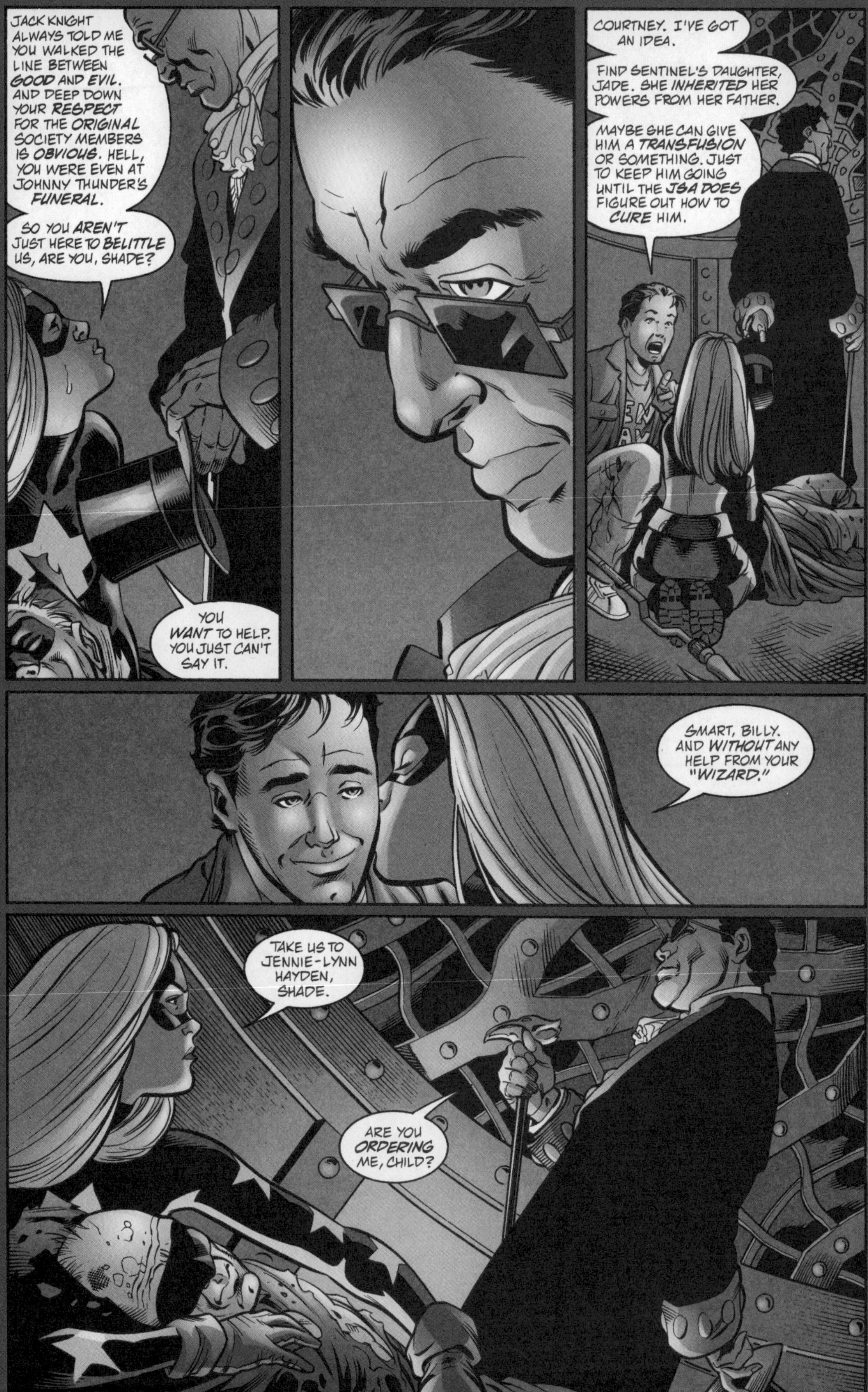
JACK KNIGHT ALWAYS TOLD ME YOU WALKED THE LINE BETWEEN GOOD AND EVIL. AND DEEP DOWN YOUR RESPECT FOR THE ORIGINAL SOCIETY MEMBERS IS OBVIOUS. HELL, YOU WERE EVEN AT JOHNNY THUNDER'S FUNERAL.
SO YOU AREN'T JUST HERE TO BELITTLE US, ARE YOU, SHADE?
YOU WANT TO HELP. YOU JUST CAN'T SAY IT.
COURTNEY. I'VE GOT AN IDEA.
FIND SENTINEL'S DAUGHTER, JADE. SHE INHERITED HER POWERS FROM HER FATHER.
MAYBE SHE CAN GIVE HIM A TRANSFUSION OR SOMETHING. JUST TO KEEP HIM GOING UNTIL THE JSA DOES FIGURE OUT HOW TO CURE HIM.
SMART, BILLY. AND WITHOUT ANY HELP FROM YOUR "WIZARD."
TAKE US TO JENNIE-LYNN HAYDEN, SHADE.
ARE YOU ORDERING ME, CHILD?

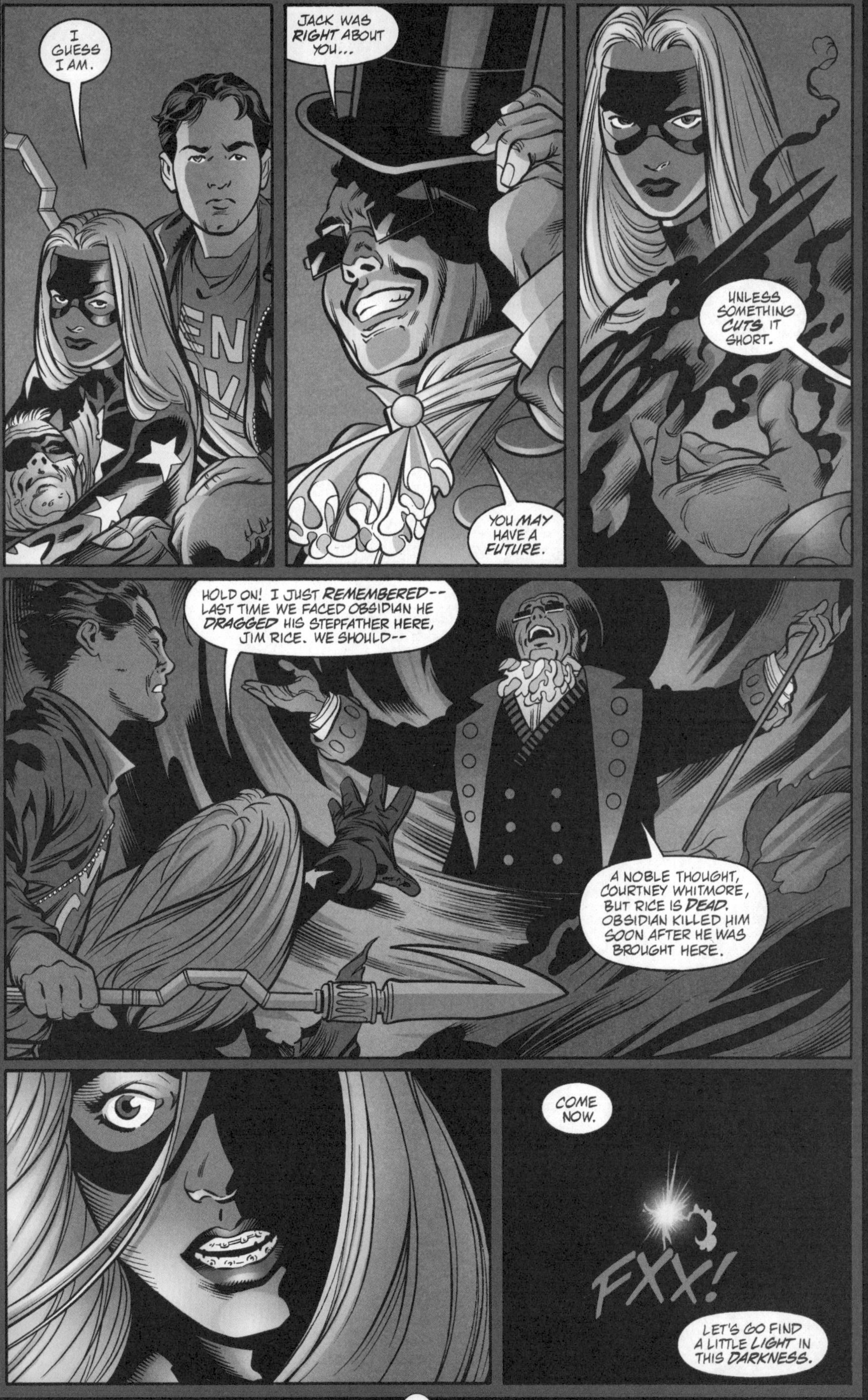

I GUESS I AM.
JACK WAS RIGHT ABOUT YOU...
YOU MAY HAVE A FUTURE.
UNLESS SOMETHING CUTS IT SHORT.
HOLD ON! I JUST REMEMBERED-- LAST TIME WE FACED OBSIDIAN HE DRAGGED HIS STEPFATHER HERE, JIM RICE. WE SHOULD--
A NOBLE THOUGHT, COURTNEY WHITMORE, BUT RICE IS DEAD. OBSIDIAN KILLED HIM SOON AFTER HE WAS BROUGHT HERE.
COME NOW.
FXX!
LET'S GO FIND A LITTLE LIGHT IN THIS DARKNESS.

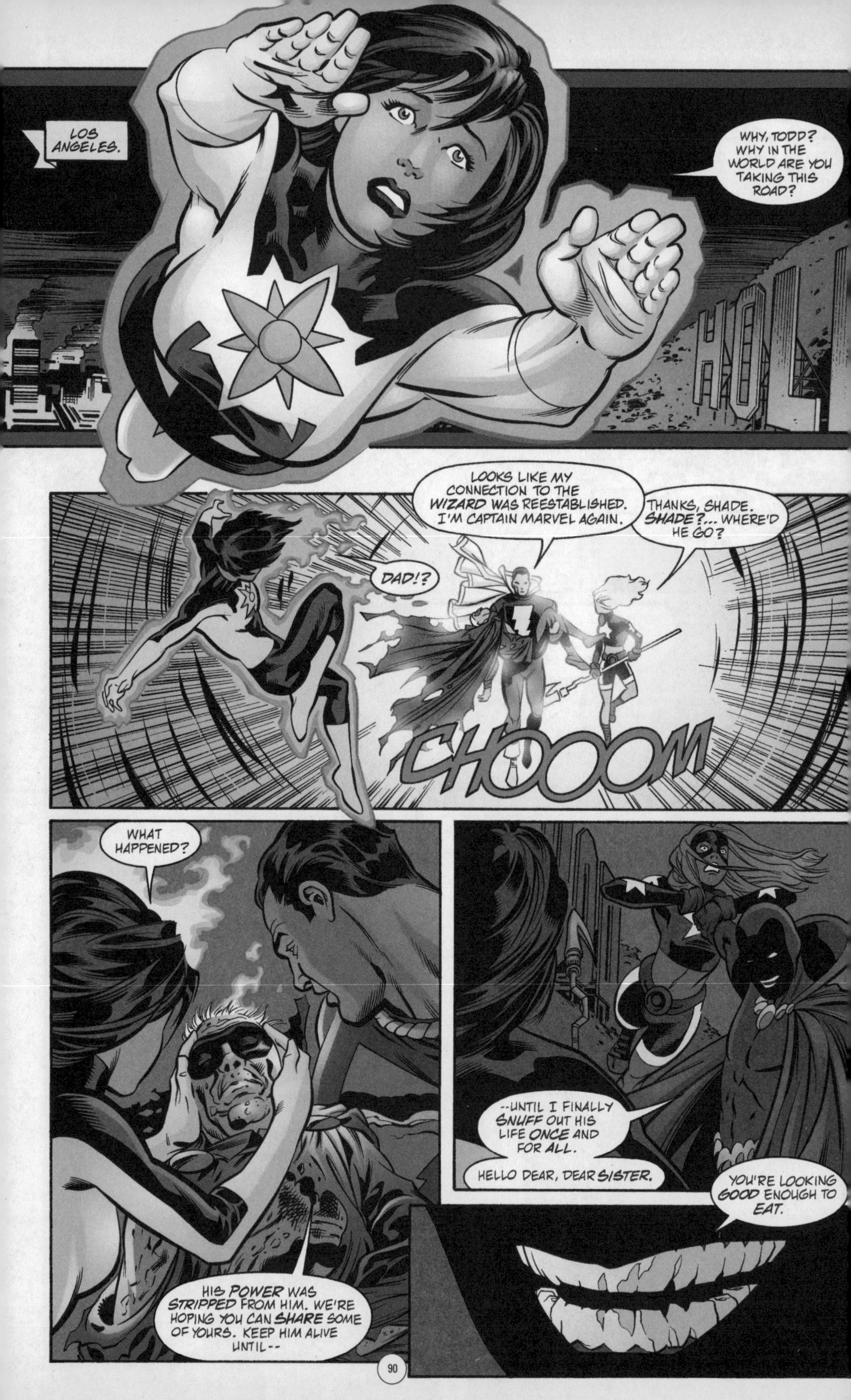

LOS ANGELES.
WHY, TODD? WHY IN THE WORLD ARE YOU TAKING THIS ROAD?
LOOKS LIKE MY CONNECTION TO THE WIZARD WAS REESTABLISHED. I'M CAPTAIN MARVEL AGAIN.
THANKS, SHADE. SHADE?... WHERE'D HE GO?
DAD!?
CHOOOM
WHAT HAPPENED?
HIS POWER WAS STRIPPED FROM HIM. WE'RE HOPING YOU CAN SHARE SOME OF YOURS. KEEP HIM ALIVE UNTIL--
--UNTIL I FINALLY SNUFF OUT HIS LIFE ONCE AND FOR ALL.
HELLO DEAR, DEAR SISTER.
YOU'RE LOOKING GOOD ENOUGH TO EAT.

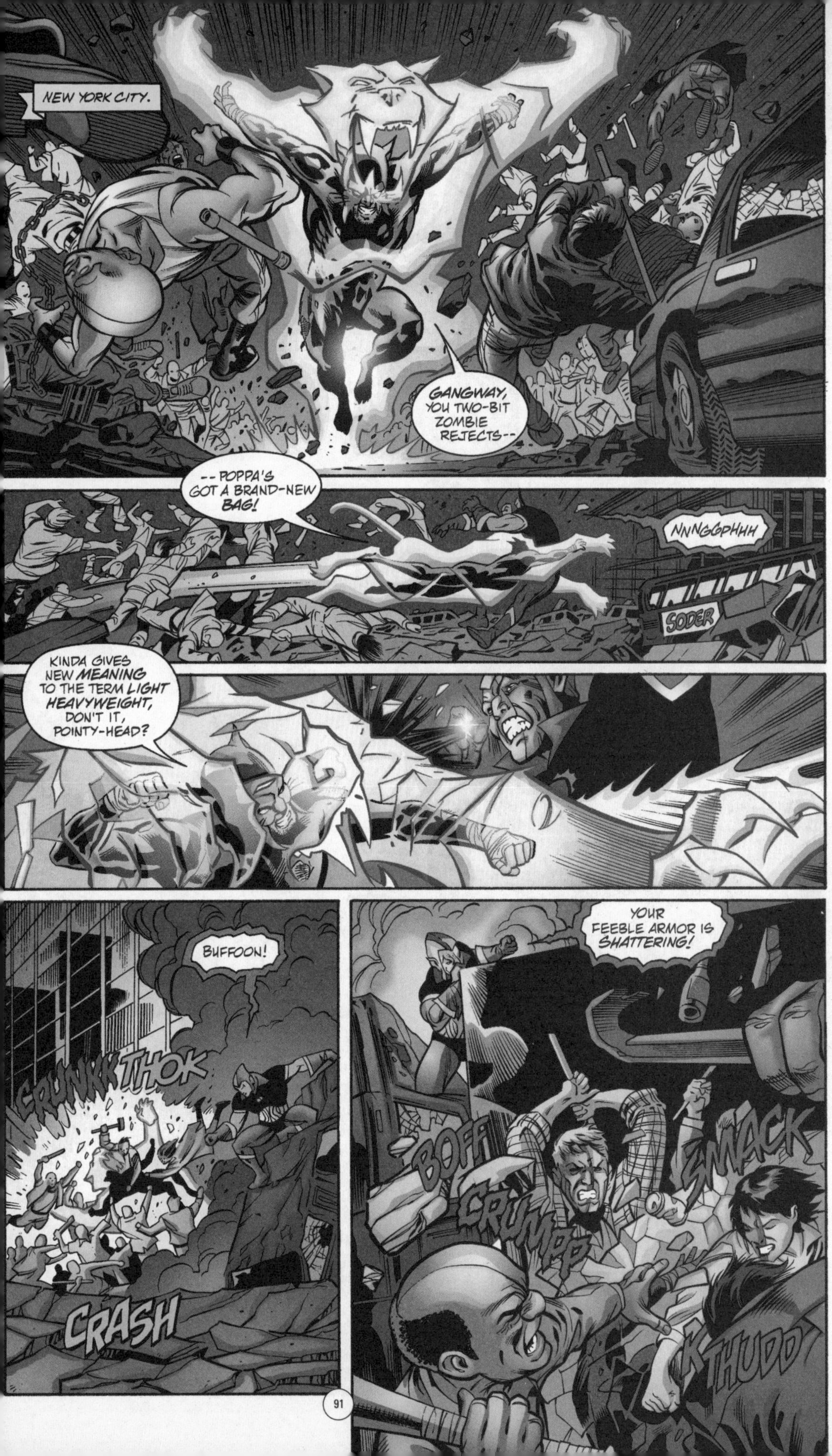
NEW YORK CITY.
GANGWAY, YOU TWO-BIT ZOMBIE REJECTS--
--POPPA'S GOT A BRAND-NEW BAG!
NNNGGPHHH
SODER
KINDA GIVES NEW MEANING TO THE TERM LIGHT HEAVYWEIGHT, DON'T IT, POINTY-HEAD?
BUFFOON!
CRUNKK THOK
CRASH
YOUR FEEBLE ARMOR IS SHATTERING!
BOFF
SMACK
CRUMPP
KTHUDD

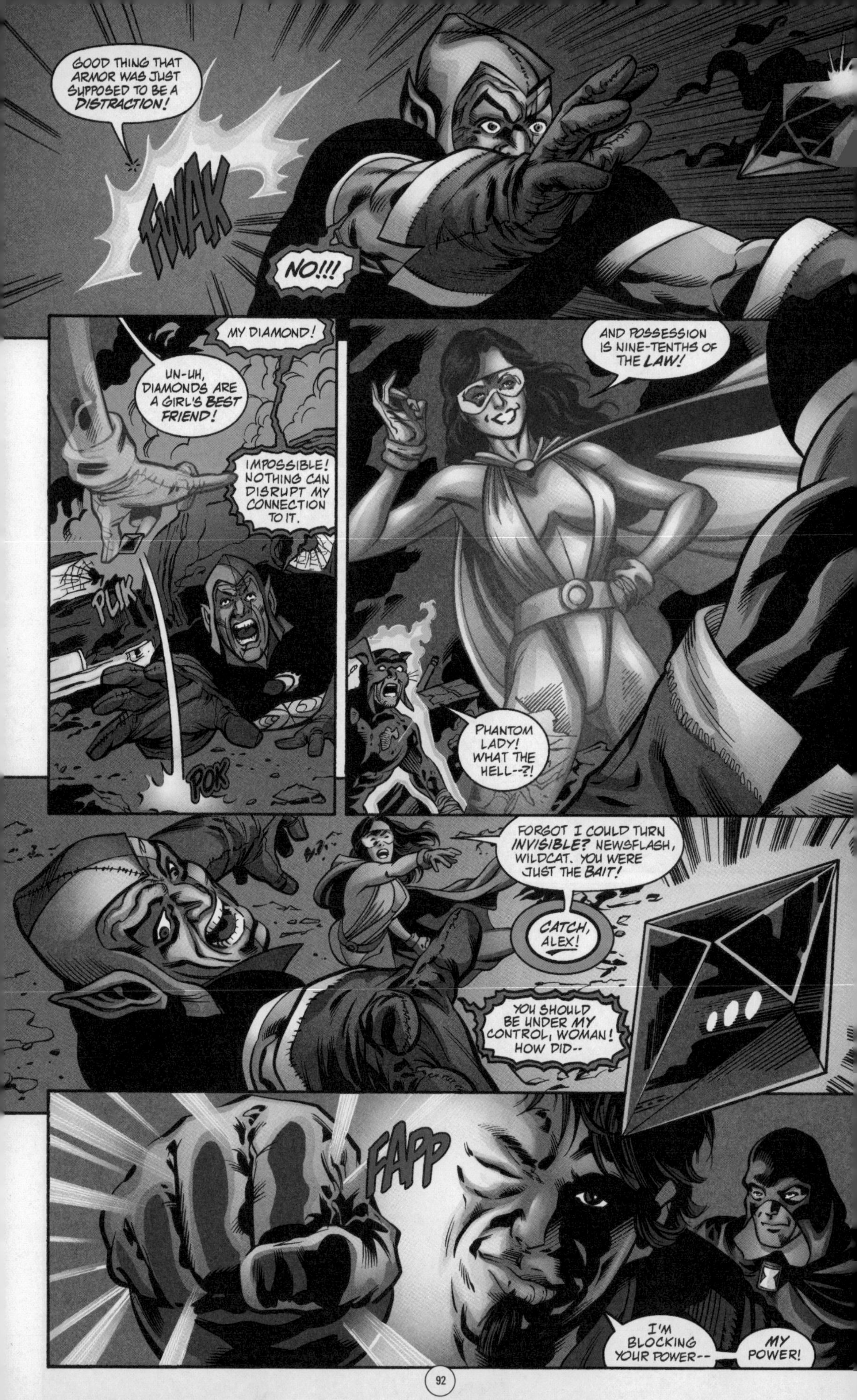

GOOD THING THAT ARMOR WAS JUST SUPPOSED TO BE A DISTRACTION!
FWAK
NO!!!
MY DIAMOND!
UN-UH, DIAMONDS ARE A GIRL'S BEST FRIEND!
IMPOSSIBLE! NOTHING CAN DISRUPT MY CONNECTION TO IT.
PLIK
POK
AND POSSESSION IS NINE-TENTHS OF THE LAW!
PHANTOM LADY! WHAT THE HELL--?!
FORGOT I COULD TURN INVISIBLE? NEWSFLASH, WILDCAT. YOU WERE JUST THE BAIT!
CATCH, ALEX!
YOU SHOULD BE UNDER MY CONTROL, WOMAN! HOW DID--
FAPP
I'M BLOCKING YOUR POWER--
MY POWER!

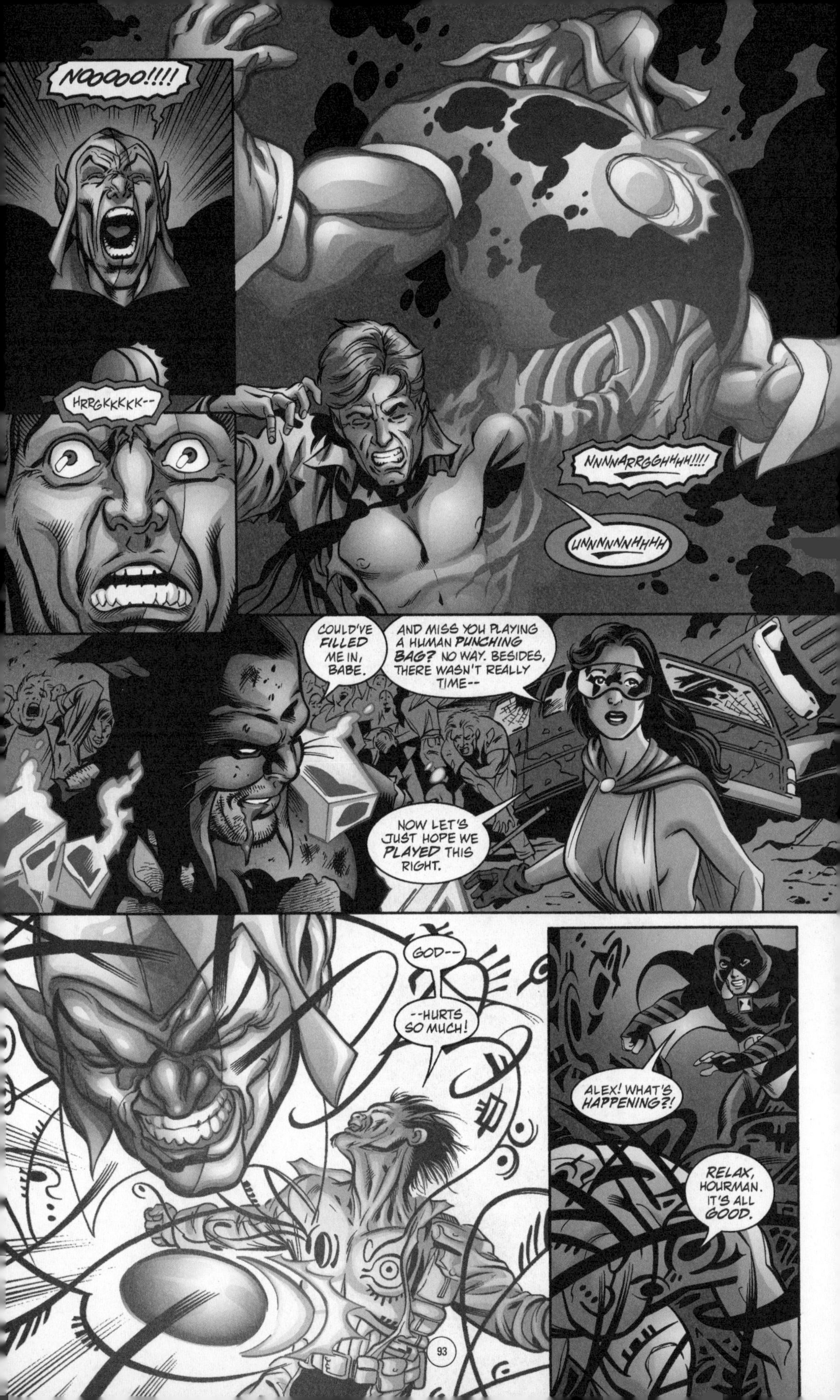
NOOOOO!!!!
HRRGKKKKK--
NNNNARRGGHHHH!!!!
UNNNNNNHHHH
COULD'VE FILLED ME IN, BABE.
AND MISS YOU PLAYING A HUMAN PUNCHING BAG? NO WAY. BESIDES, THERE WASN'T REALLY TIME--
NOW LET'S JUST HOPE WE PLAYED THIS RIGHT.
GOD--
--HURTS SO MUCH!
ALEX! WHAT'S HAPPENING?!
RELAX, HOURMAN. IT'S ALL GOOD.

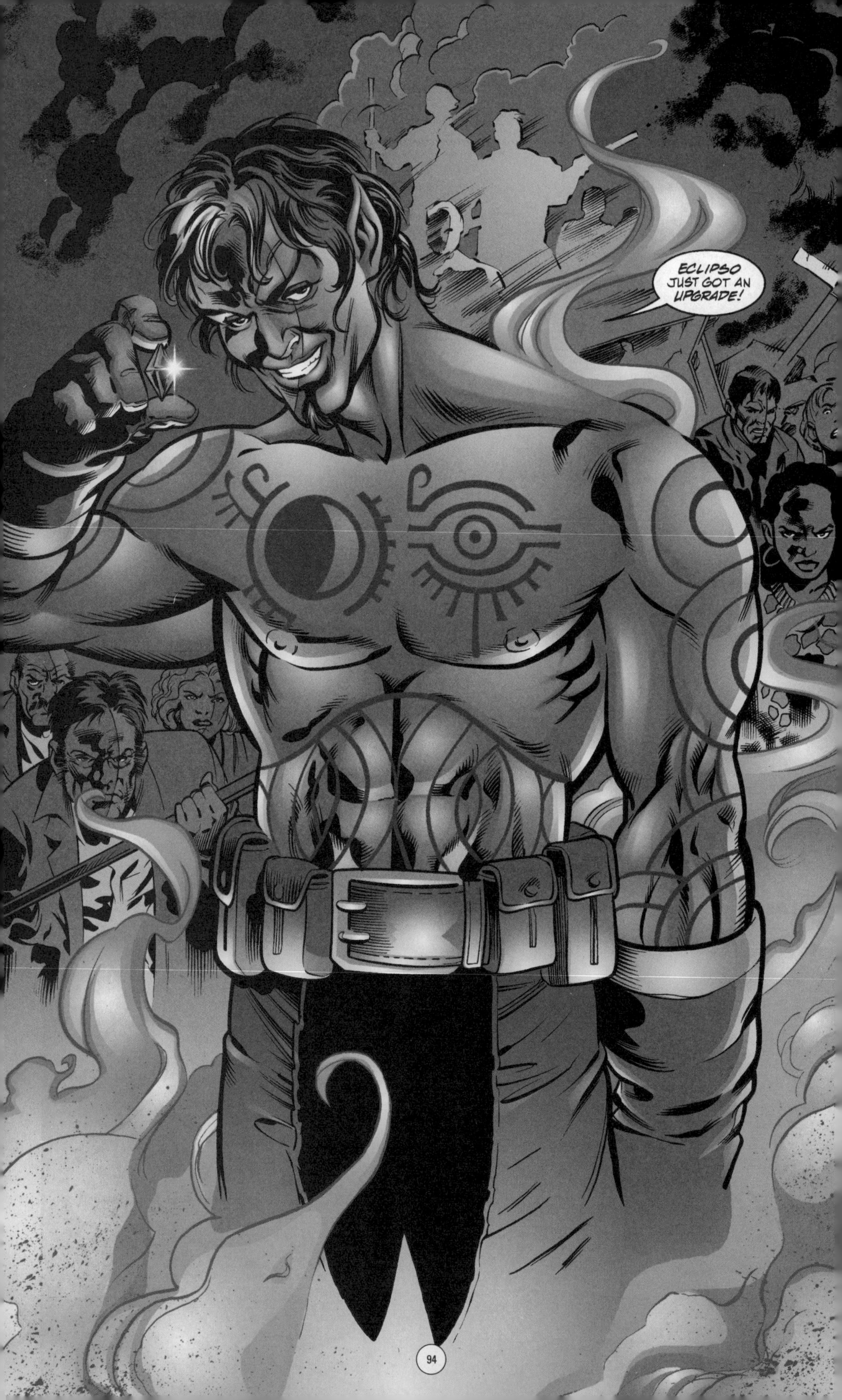
ECLIPSO JUST GOT AN UPGRADE!

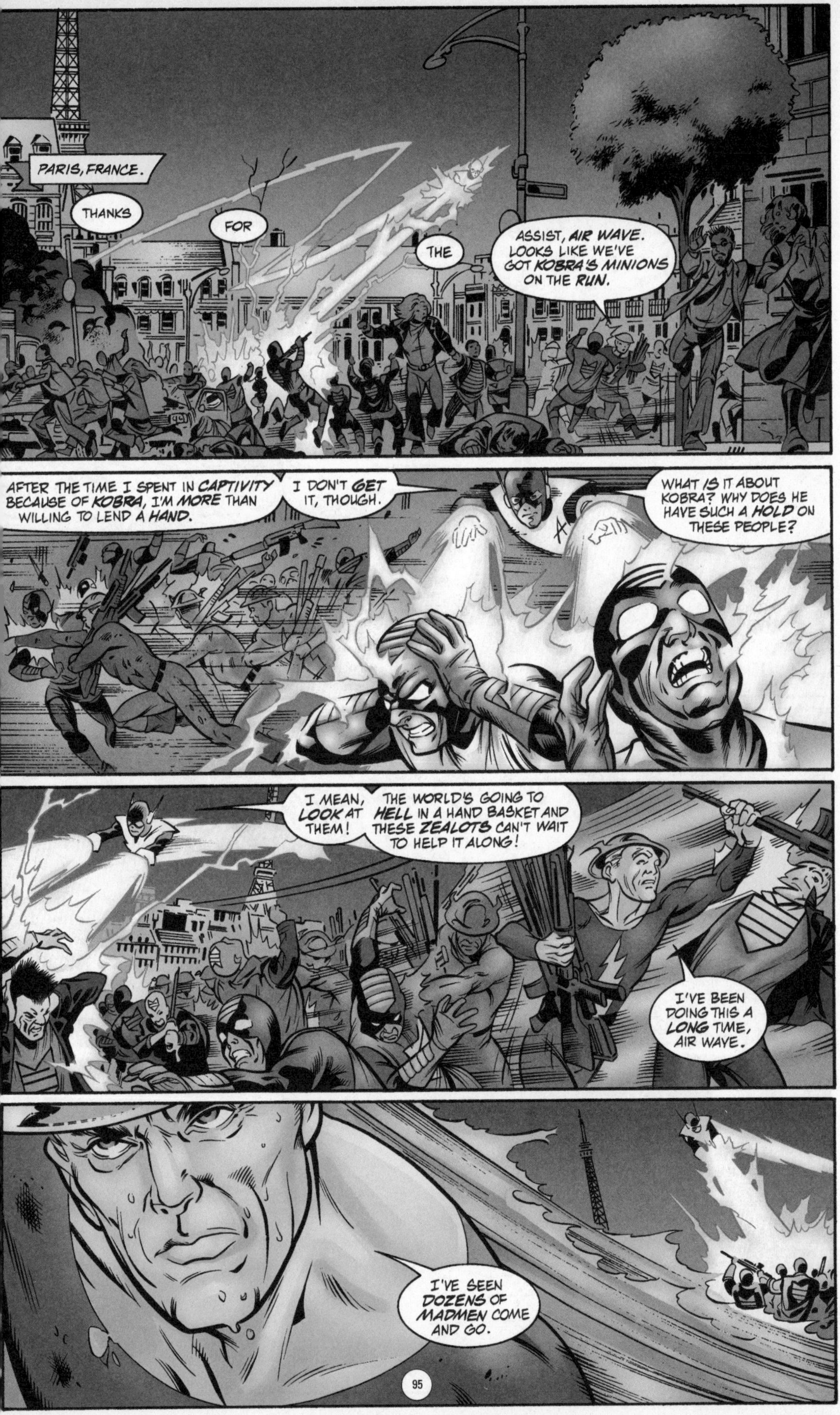
PARIS, FRANCE.
THANKS
FOR
THE
ASSIST, AIR WAVE. LOOKS LIKE WE'VE GOT KOBRA'S MINIONS ON THE RUN.
AFTER THE TIME I SPENT IN CAPTIVITY BECAUSE OF KOBRA, I'M MORE THAN WILLING TO LEND A HAND.
I DON'T GET IT, THOUGH.
WHAT IS IT ABOUT KOBRA? WHY DOES HE HAVE SUCH A HOLD ON THESE PEOPLE?
I MEAN, LOOK AT THEM!
THE WORLD'S GOING TO HELL IN A HAND BASKET AND THESE ZEALOTS CAN'T WAIT TO HELP IT ALONG!
I'VE BEEN DOING THIS A LONG TIME, AIR WAVE.
I'VE SEEN DOZENS OF MADMEN COME AND GO.

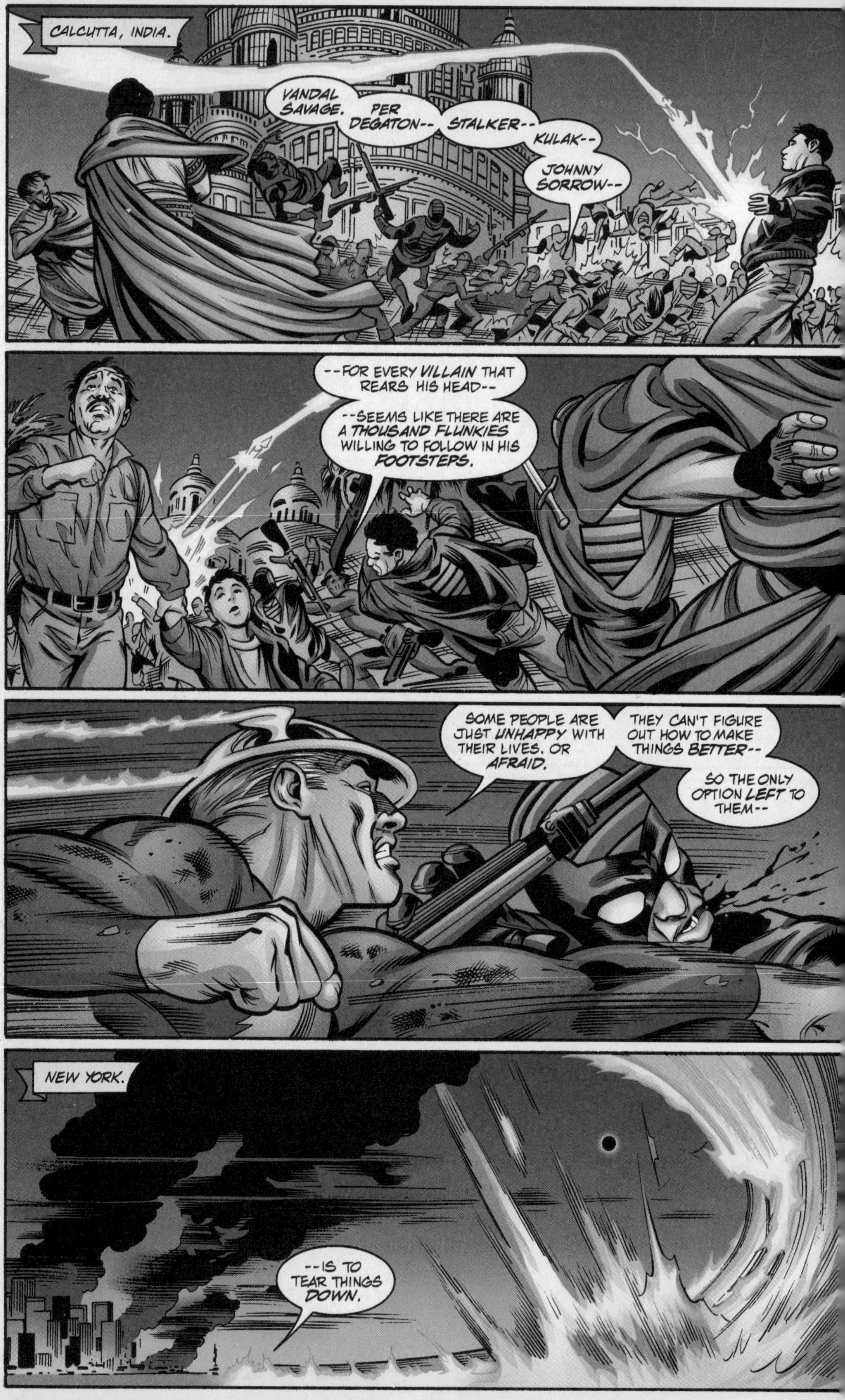
CALCUTTA, INDIA.
VANDAL SAVAGE.
PER DEGATON--
STALKER--
KULAK--
JOHNNY SORROW--
--FOR EVERY VILLAIN THAT REARS HIS HEAD--
--SEEMS LIKE THERE ARE A THOUSAND FLUNKIES WILLING TO FOLLOW IN HIS FOOTSTEPS.
SOME PEOPLE ARE JUST UNHAPPY WITH THEIR LIVES. OR AFRAID.
THEY CAN'T FIGURE OUT HOW TO MAKE THINGS BETTER--
SO THE ONLY OPTION LEFT TO THEM--
NEW YORK.
--IS TO TEAR THINGS DOWN.

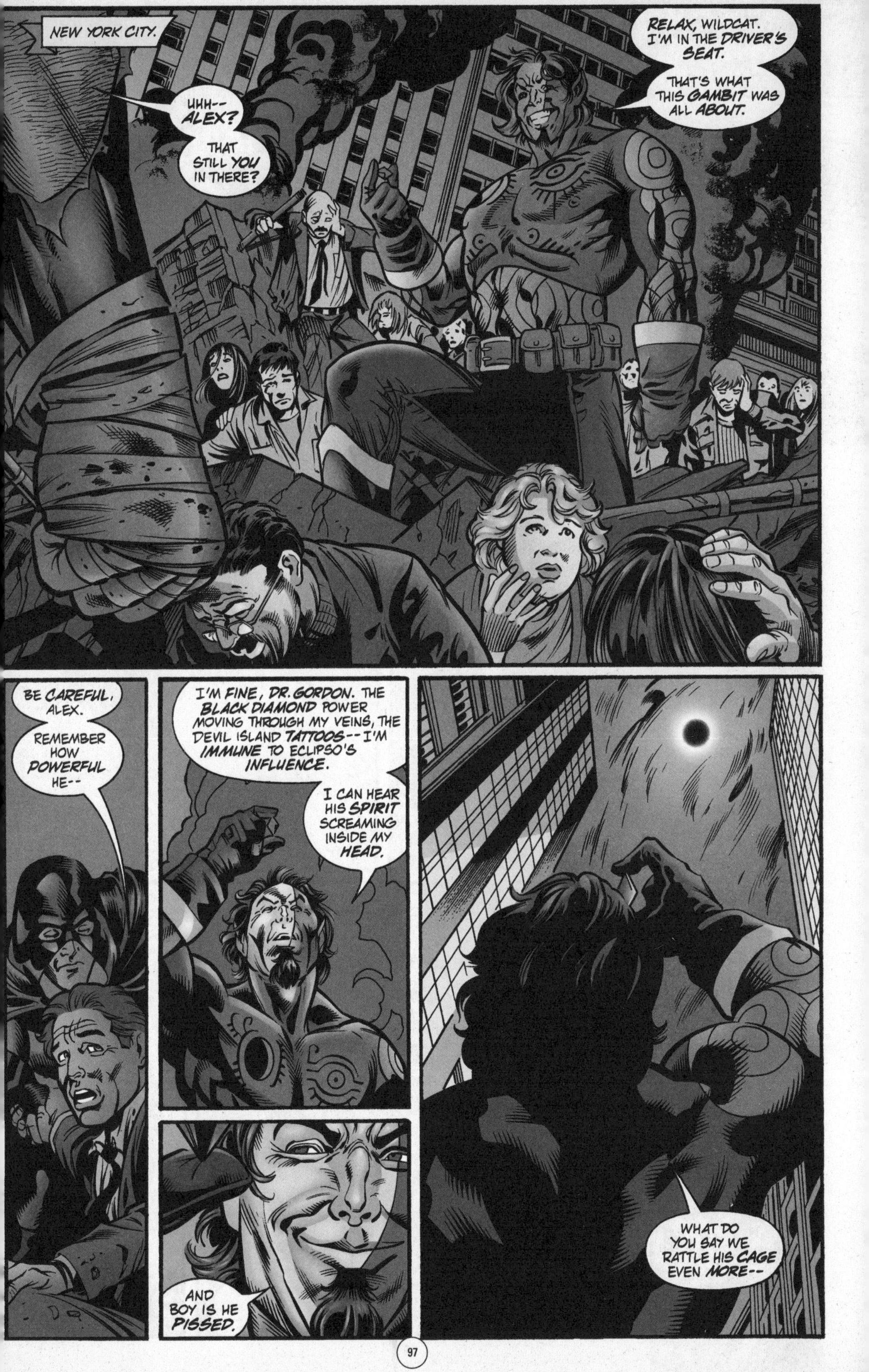
NEW YORK CITY.
UHH-- ALEX?
THAT STILL YOU IN THERE?
RELAX, WILDCAT. I'M IN THE DRIVER'S SEAT.
THAT'S WHAT THIS GAMBIT WAS ALL ABOUT.
BE CAREFUL, ALEX.
REMEMBER HOW POWERFUL HE--
I'M FINE, DR. GORDON. THE BLACK DIAMOND POWER MOVING THROUGH MY VEINS, THE DEVIL ISLAND TATTOOS-- I'M IMMUNE TO ECLIPSO'S INFLUENCE.
I CAN HEAR HIS SPIRIT SCREAMING INSIDE MY HEAD.
AND BOY IS HE PISSED.
WHAT DO YOU SAY WE RATTLE HIS CAGE EVEN MORE--

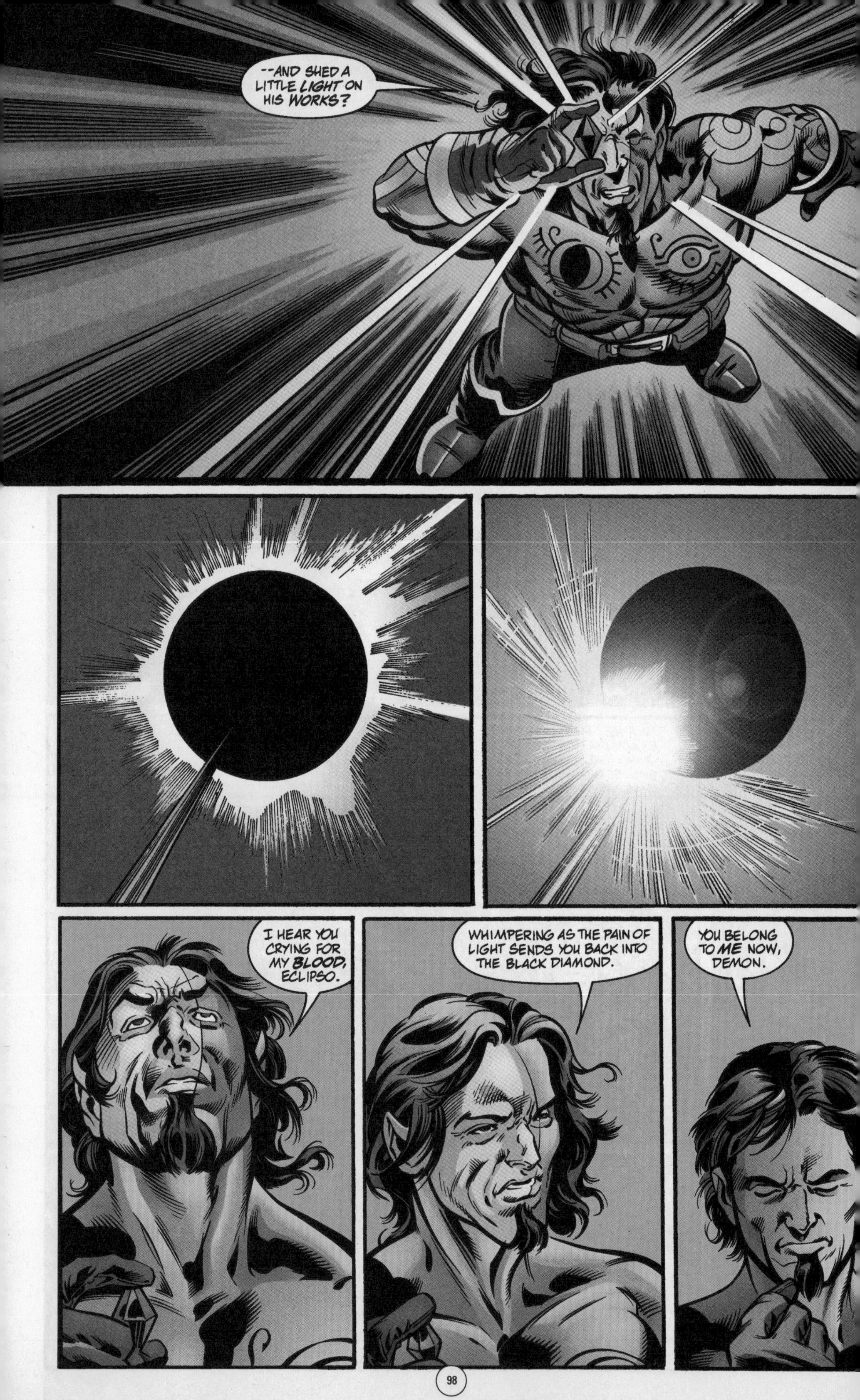
--AND SHED A LITTLE LIGHT ON HIS WORKS?
I HEAR YOU CRYING FOR MY BLOOD, ECLIPSO.
WHIMPERING AS THE PAIN OF LIGHT SENDS YOU BACK INTO THE BLACK DIAMOND.
YOU BELONG TO ME NOW, DEMON.

Princes Of Darkness Part 5
THE LAST LIGHT

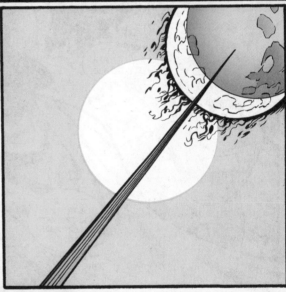

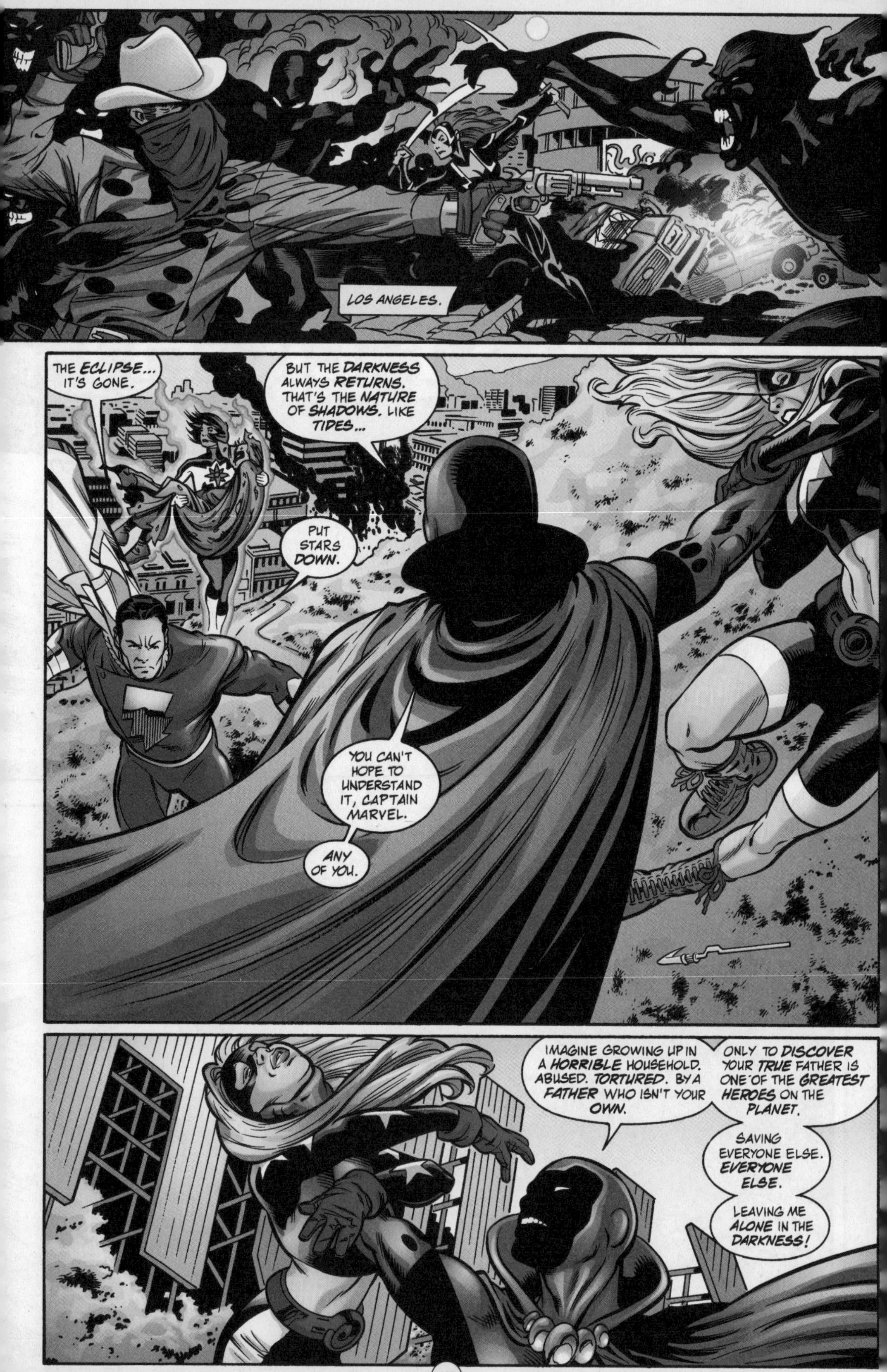

LOS ANGELES.
THE ECLIPSE... IT'S GONE.
BUT THE DARKNESS ALWAYS RETURNS. THAT'S THE NATURE OF SHADOWS. LIKE TIDES...
PUT STARS DOWN.
YOU CAN'T HOPE TO UNDERSTAND IT, CAPTAIN MARVEL.
ANY OF YOU.
IMAGINE GROWING UP IN A HORRIBLE HOUSEHOLD. ABUSED. TORTURED. BY A FATHER WHO ISN'T YOUR OWN.
ONLY TO DISCOVER YOUR TRUE FATHER IS ONE OF THE GREATEST HEROES ON THE PLANET.
SAVING EVERYONE ELSE. EVERYONE ELSE.
LEAVING ME ALONE IN THE DARKNESS!

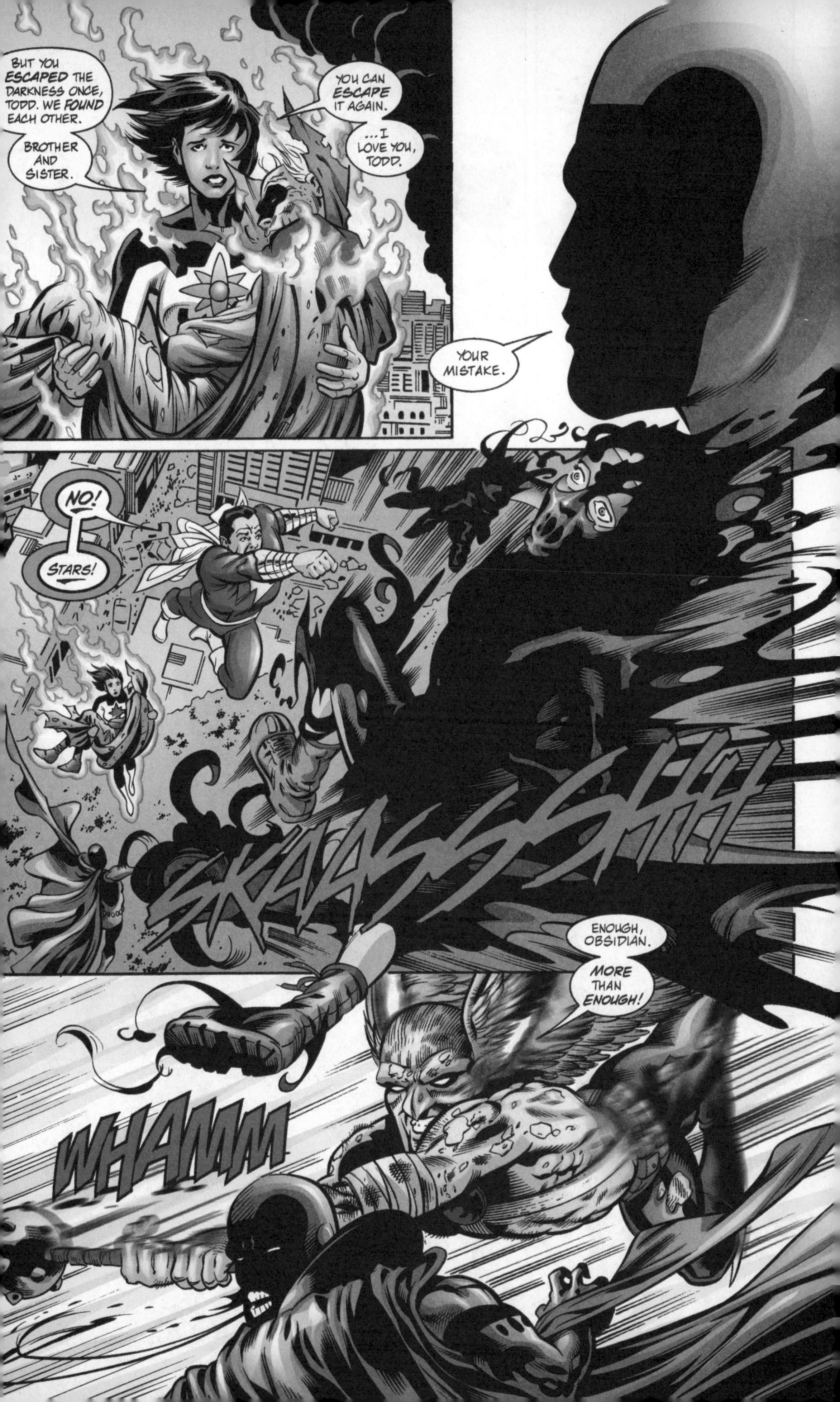

BUT YOU ESCAPED THE DARKNESS ONCE, TODD. WE FOUND EACH OTHER.
BROTHER AND SISTER.
YOU CAN ESCAPE IT AGAIN.
...I LOVE YOU, TODD.
YOUR MISTAKE.
NO!
STARS!
SKAASSSHH
ENOUGH, OBSIDIAN.
MORE THAN ENOUGH!
WHAMM

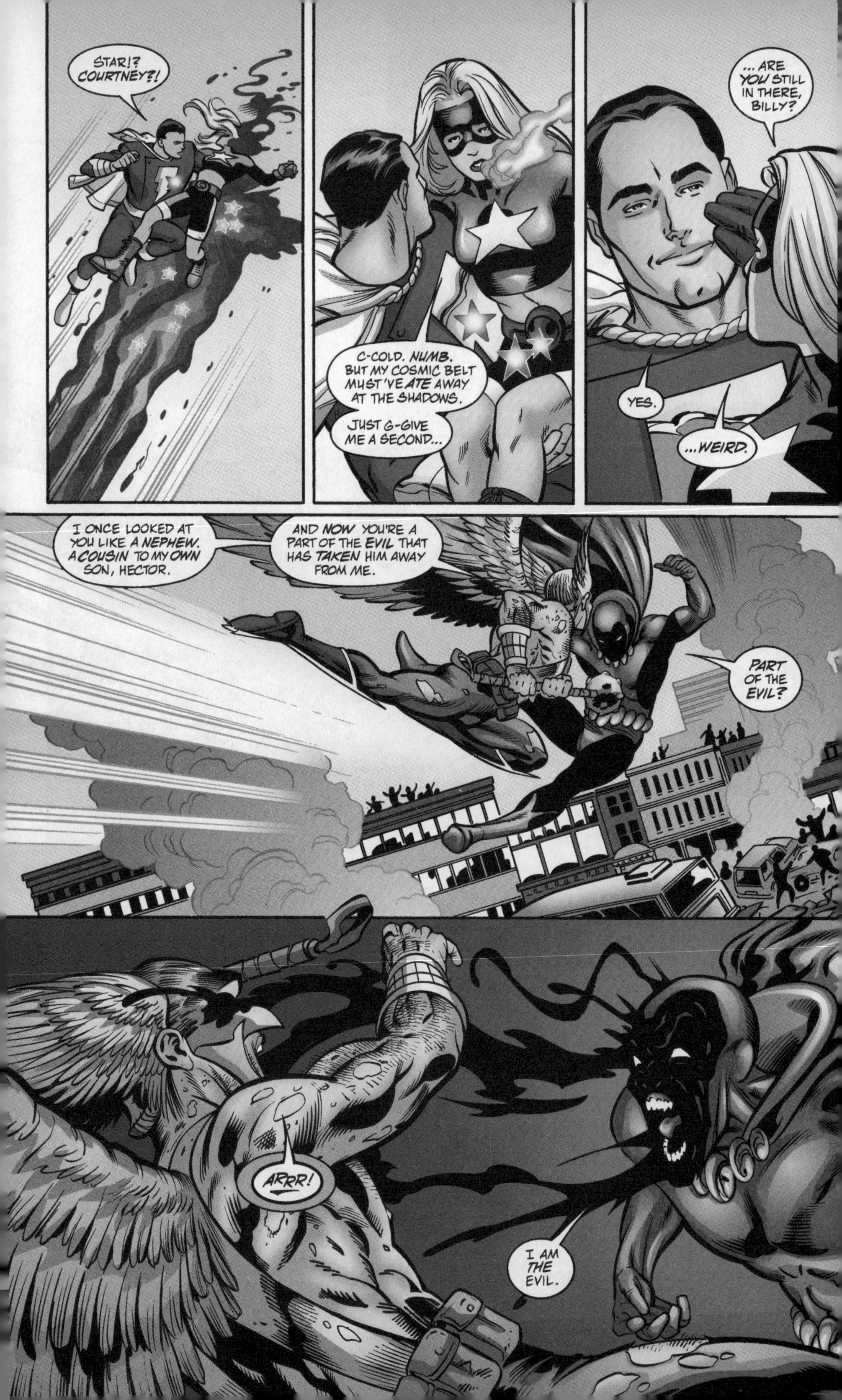
STAR!? COURTNEY?!
C-COLD. NUMB. BUT MY COSMIC BELT MUST'VE ATE AWAY AT THE SHADOWS.
JUST G-GIVE ME A SECOND...
...ARE YOU STILL IN THERE, BILLY?
YES.
...WEIRD.
I ONCE LOOKED AT YOU LIKE A NEPHEW. A COUSIN TO MY OWN SON, HECTOR.
AND NOW YOU'RE A PART OF THE EVIL THAT HAS TAKEN HIM AWAY FROM ME.
PART OF THE EVIL?
ARRR!
I AM THE EVIL.

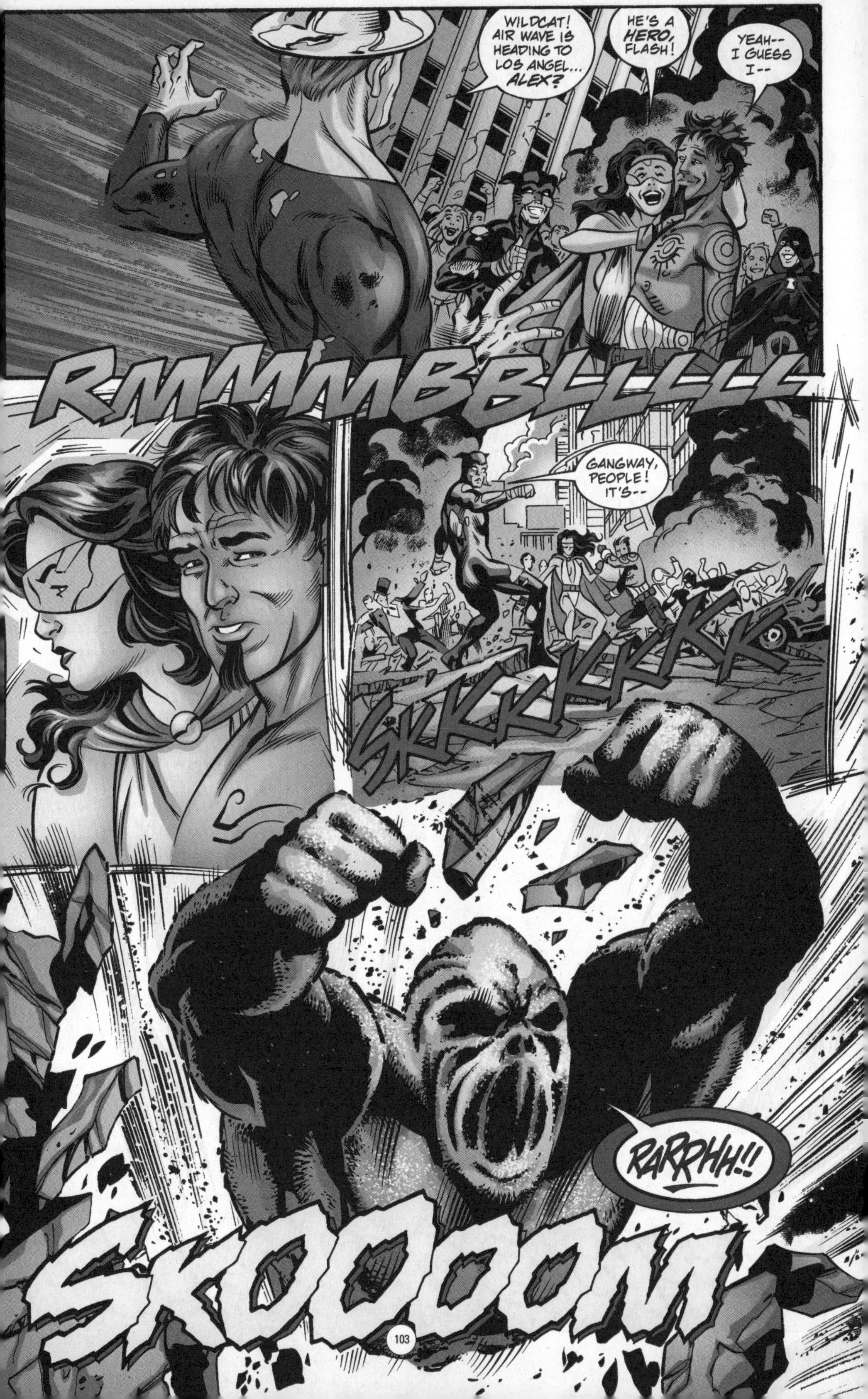
WILDCAT! AIR WAVE IS HEADING TO LOS ANGEL... ALEX?
HE'S A HERO, FLASH!
YEAH-- I GUESS I--
RMMMBBLLLL
GANGWAY, PEOPLE! IT'S--
SKKKKKKKKK
RARRHH!!
SKOOOOM

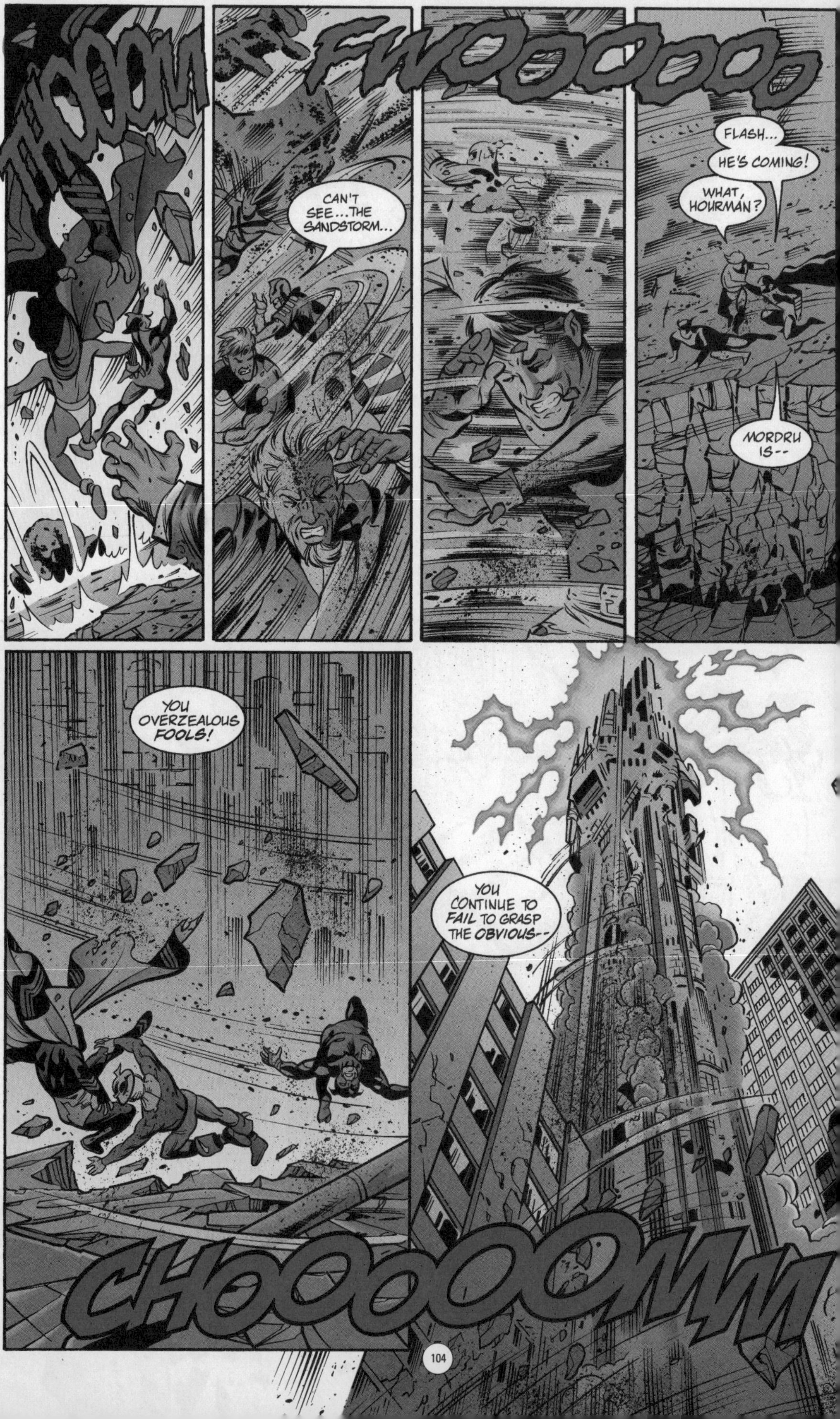
THOOOM
FWOOOOOOOO
CAN'T SEE...THE SANDSTORM...
FLASH...
HE'S COMING!
WHAT, HOURMAN?
MORDRU IS--
YOU OVERZEALOUS FOOLS!
YOU CONTINUE TO FAIL TO GRASP THE OBVIOUS--
CHOOOOOMM

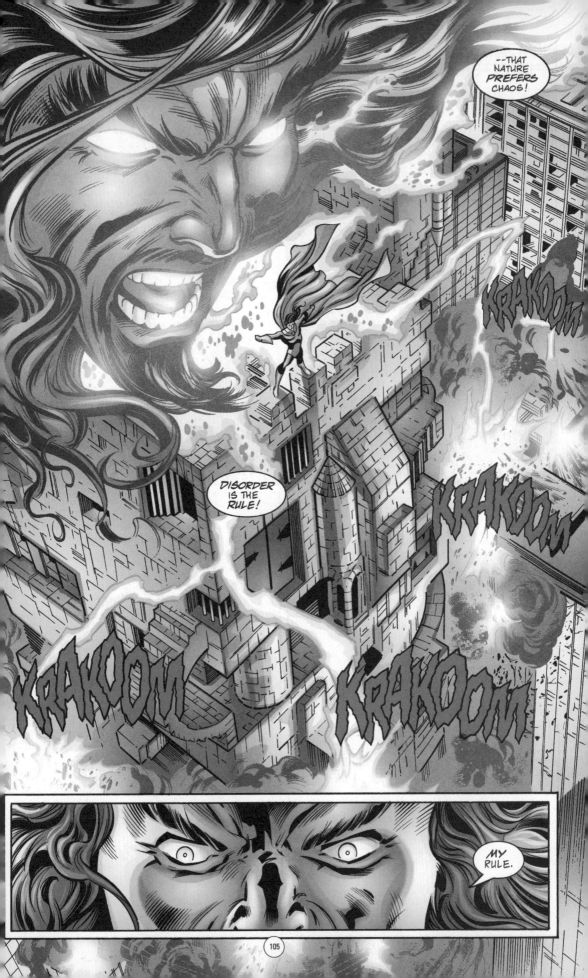

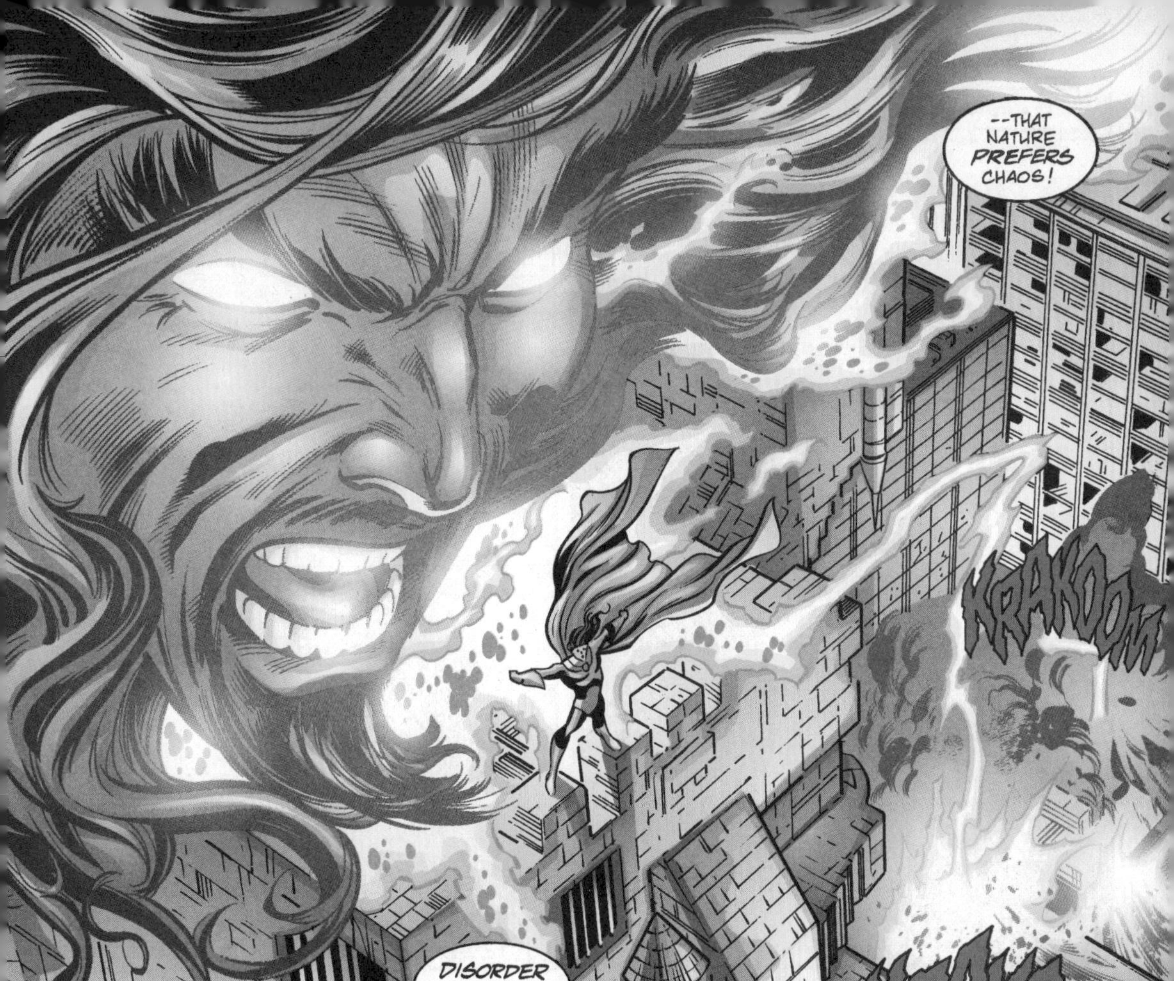
--THAT NATURE PREFERS CHAOS!
KRAKOOM
DISORDER IS THE RULE!
KRAKOOM
KRAKOOM
KRAKOOM
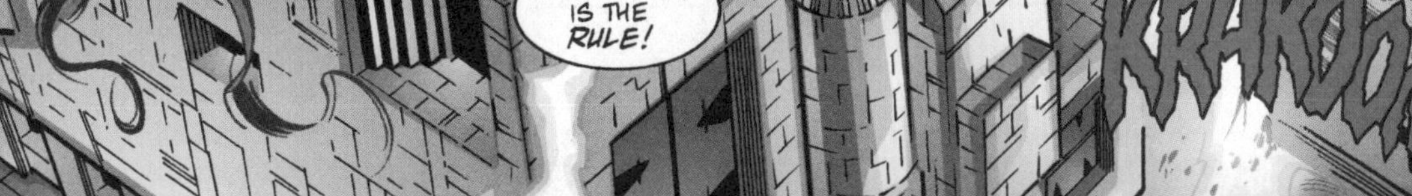
MY RULE.

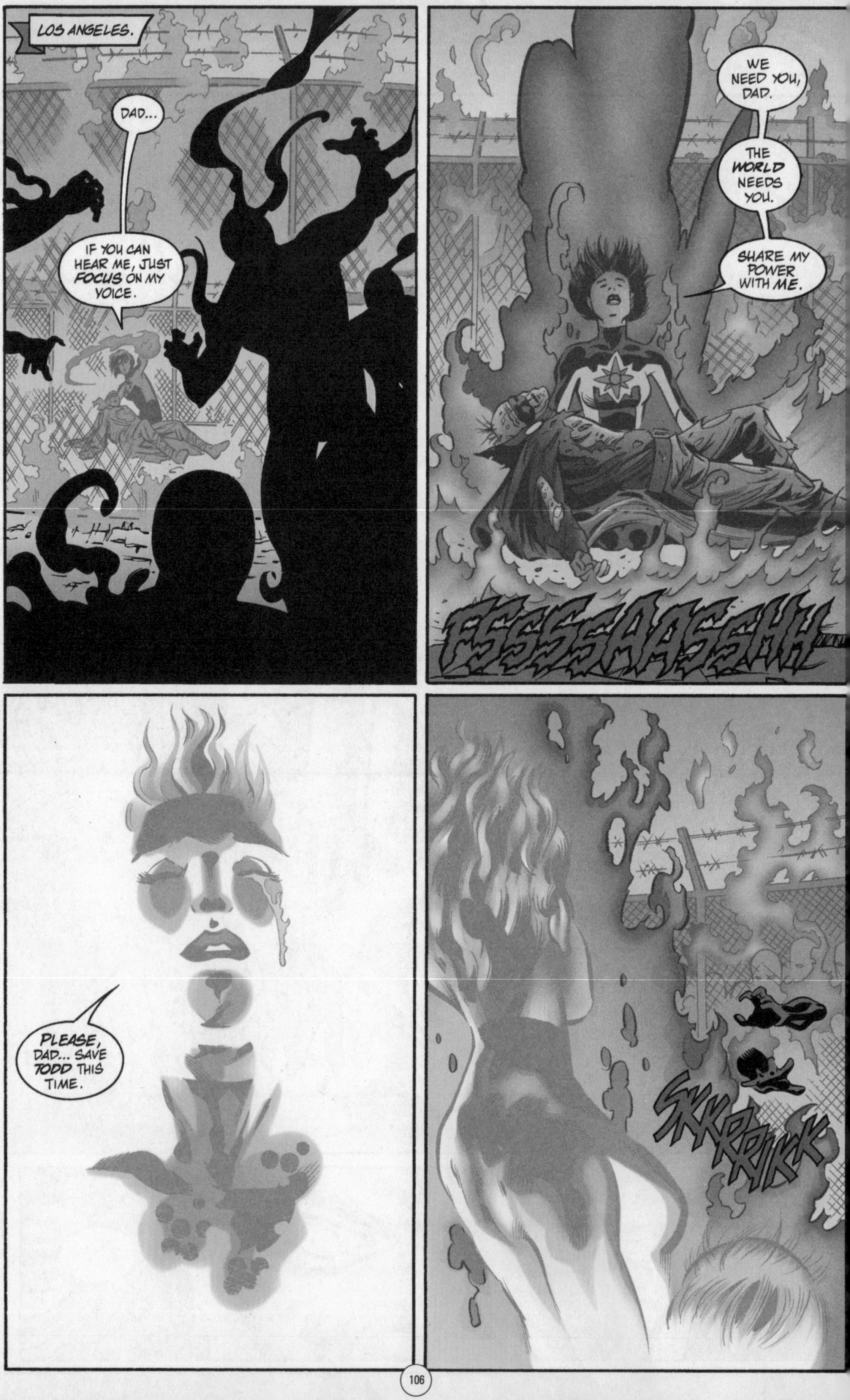
LOS ANGELES.
DAD...
IF YOU CAN HEAR ME, JUST FOCUS ON MY VOICE.
WE NEED YOU, DAD.
THE WORLD NEEDS YOU.
SHARE MY POWER WITH ME.
FSSSAASSHH
PLEASE, DAD... SAVE TODD THIS TIME.
SKKRRIKK

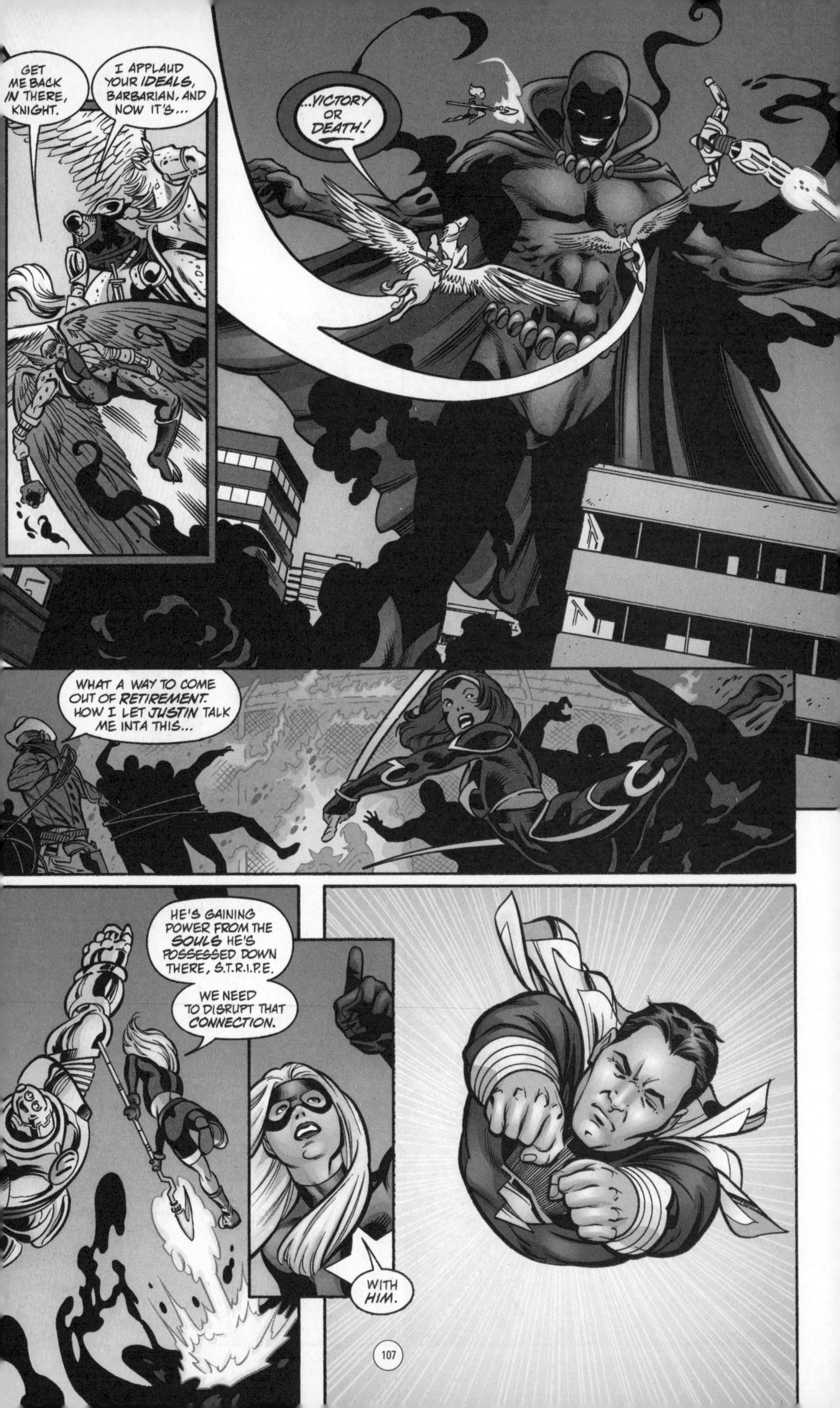
GET ME BACK IN THERE, KNIGHT.
I APPLAUD YOUR IDEALS, BARBARIAN, AND NOW IT'S...
...VICTORY OR DEATH!
WHAT A WAY TO COME OUT OF RETIREMENT. HOW I LET JUSTIN TALK ME INTA THIS...
HE'S GAINING POWER FROM THE SOULS HE'S POSSESSED DOWN THERE, S.T.R.I.P.E.
WE NEED TO DISRUPT THAT CONNECTION.
WITH HIM.

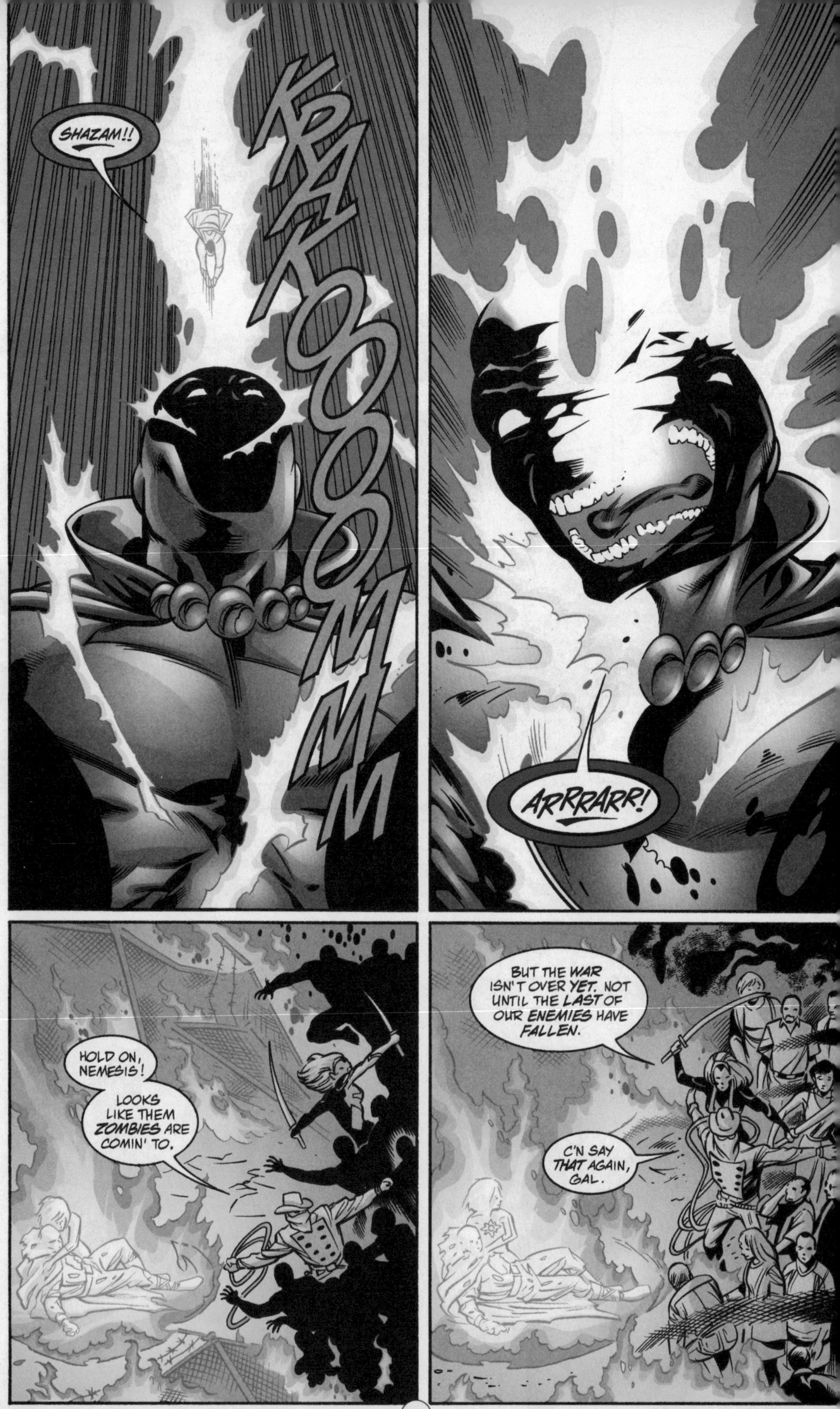

SHAZAM!!
KRAKOOOOOMMM
ARRRARR!
HOLD ON, NEMESIS!
LOOKS LIKE THEM ZOMBIES ARE COMIN' TO.
BUT THE WAR ISN'T OVER YET. NOT UNTIL THE LAST OF OUR ENEMIES HAVE FALLEN.
C'N SAY THAT AGAIN, GAL.

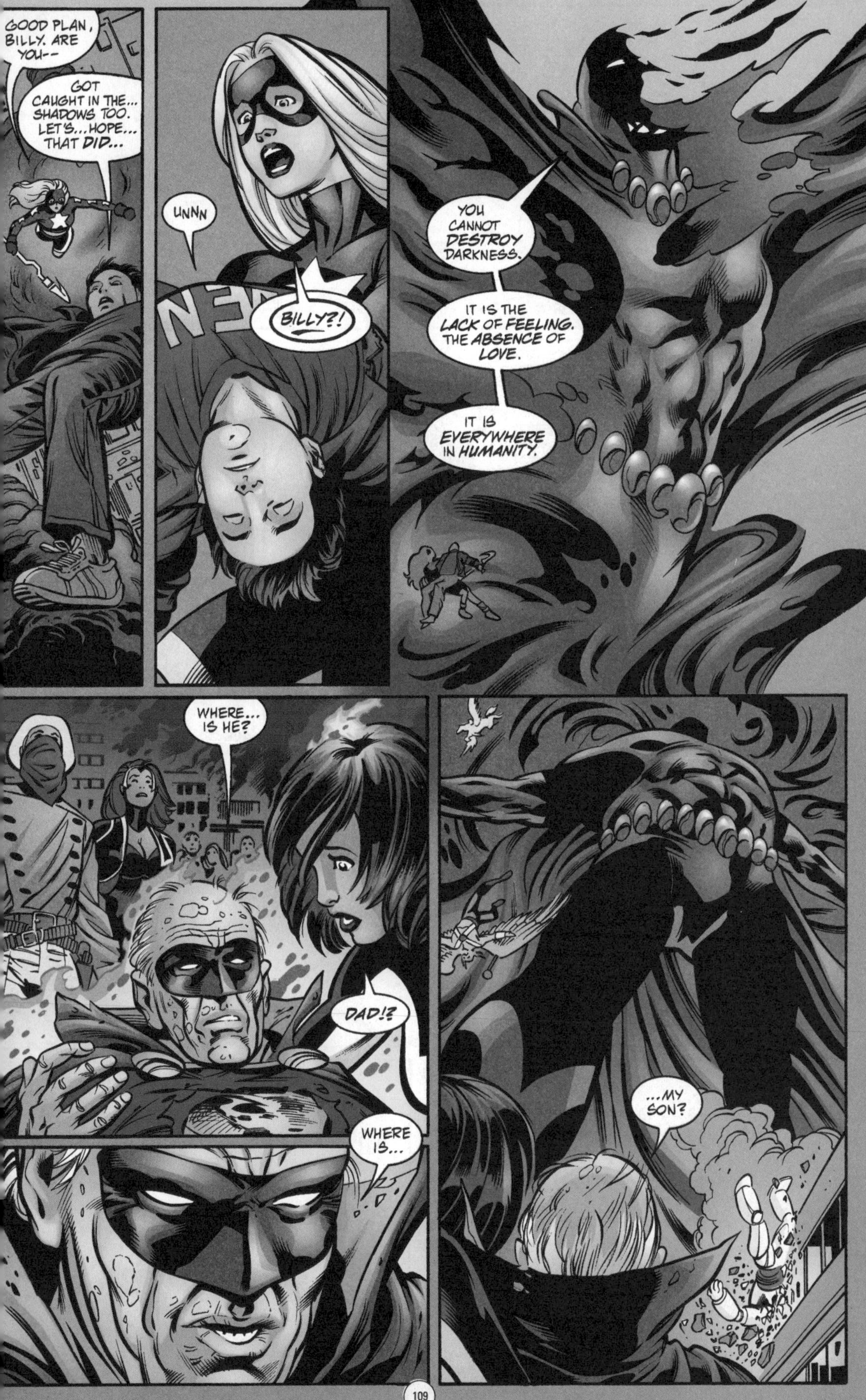

GOOD PLAN, BILLY. ARE YOU--
GOT CAUGHT IN THE... SHADOWS TOO. LET'S...HOPE... THAT DID...
UNNN
BILLY?!
YOU CANNOT DESTROY DARKNESS.
IT IS THE LACK OF FEELING. THE ABSENCE OF LOVE.
IT IS EVERYWHERE IN HUMANITY.
WHERE... IS HE?
DAD!?
WHERE IS...
...MY SON?

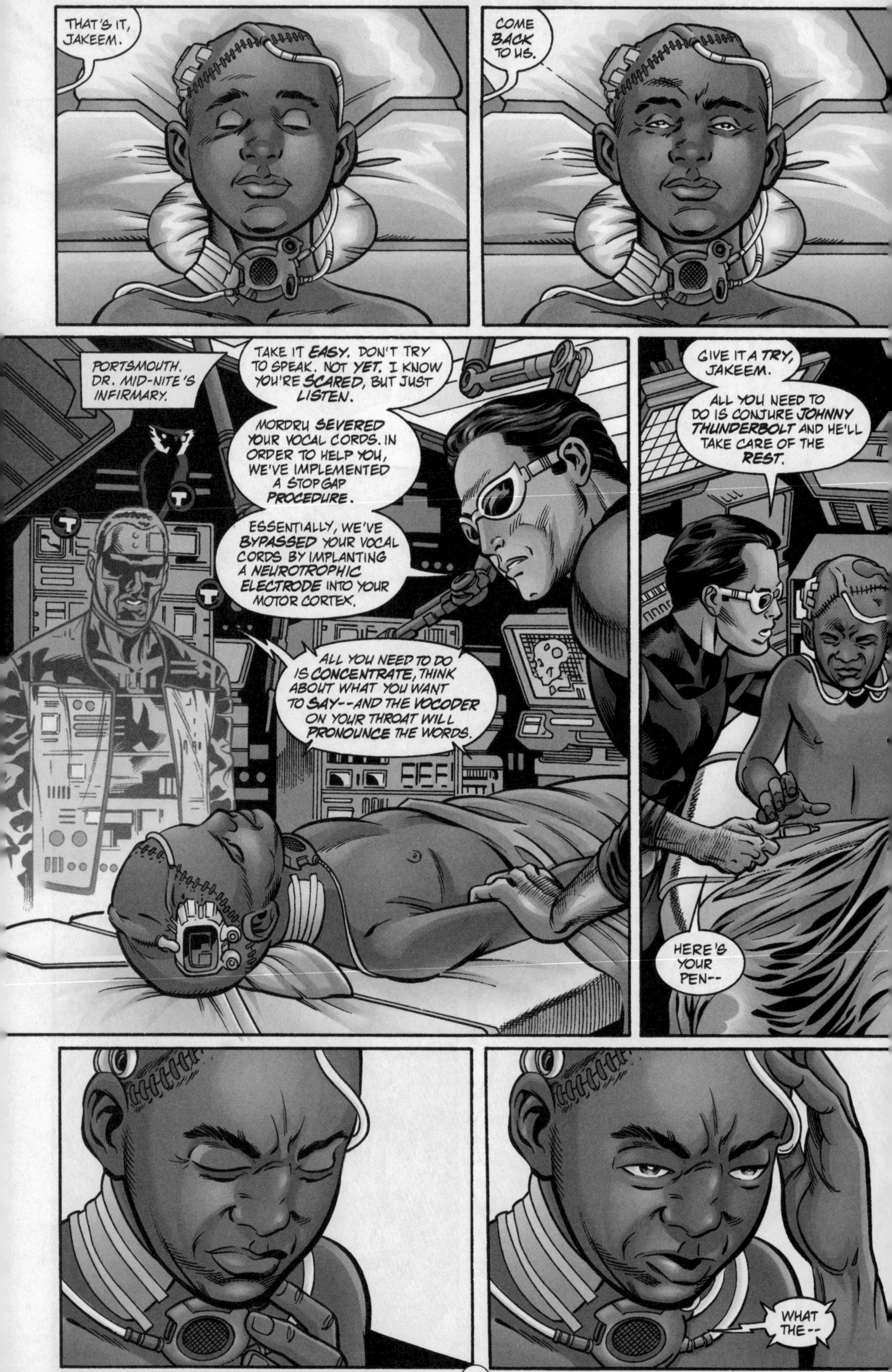
THAT'S IT, JAKEEM.
COME BACK TO US.
PORTSMOUTH. DR. MID-NITE'S INFIRMARY.
TAKE IT EASY. DON'T TRY TO SPEAK. NOT YET. I KNOW YOU'RE SCARED, BUT JUST LISTEN.
MORDRU SEVERED YOUR VOCAL CORDS. IN ORDER TO HELP YOU, WE'VE IMPLEMENTED A STOPGAP PROCEDURE.
ESSENTIALLY, WE'VE BYPASSED YOUR VOCAL CORDS BY IMPLANTING A NEUROTROPHIC ELECTRODE INTO YOUR MOTOR CORTEX.
ALL YOU NEED TO DO IS CONCENTRATE, THINK ABOUT WHAT YOU WANT TO SAY--AND THE VOCODER ON YOUR THROAT WILL PRONOUNCE THE WORDS.
GIVE IT A TRY, JAKEEM.
ALL YOU NEED TO DO IS CONJURE JOHNNY THUNDERBOLT AND HE'LL TAKE CARE OF THE REST.
HERE'S YOUR PEN--
WHAT THE--

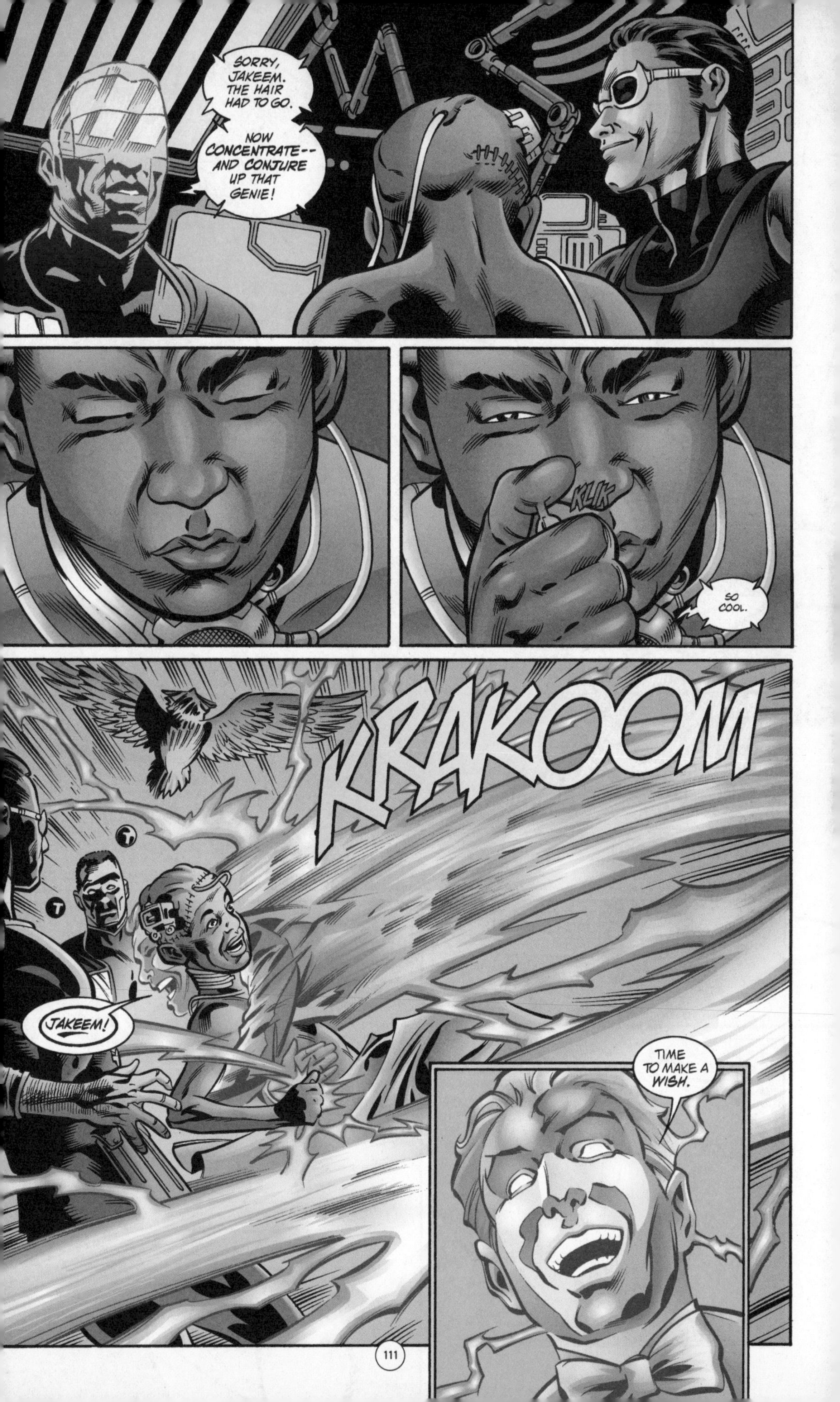

SORRY, JAKEEM. THE HAIR HAD TO GO.
NOW CONCENTRATE-- AND CONJURE UP THAT GENIE!
KLIK
SO COOL.
KRAKOOM
JAKEEM!
TIME TO MAKE A WISH.

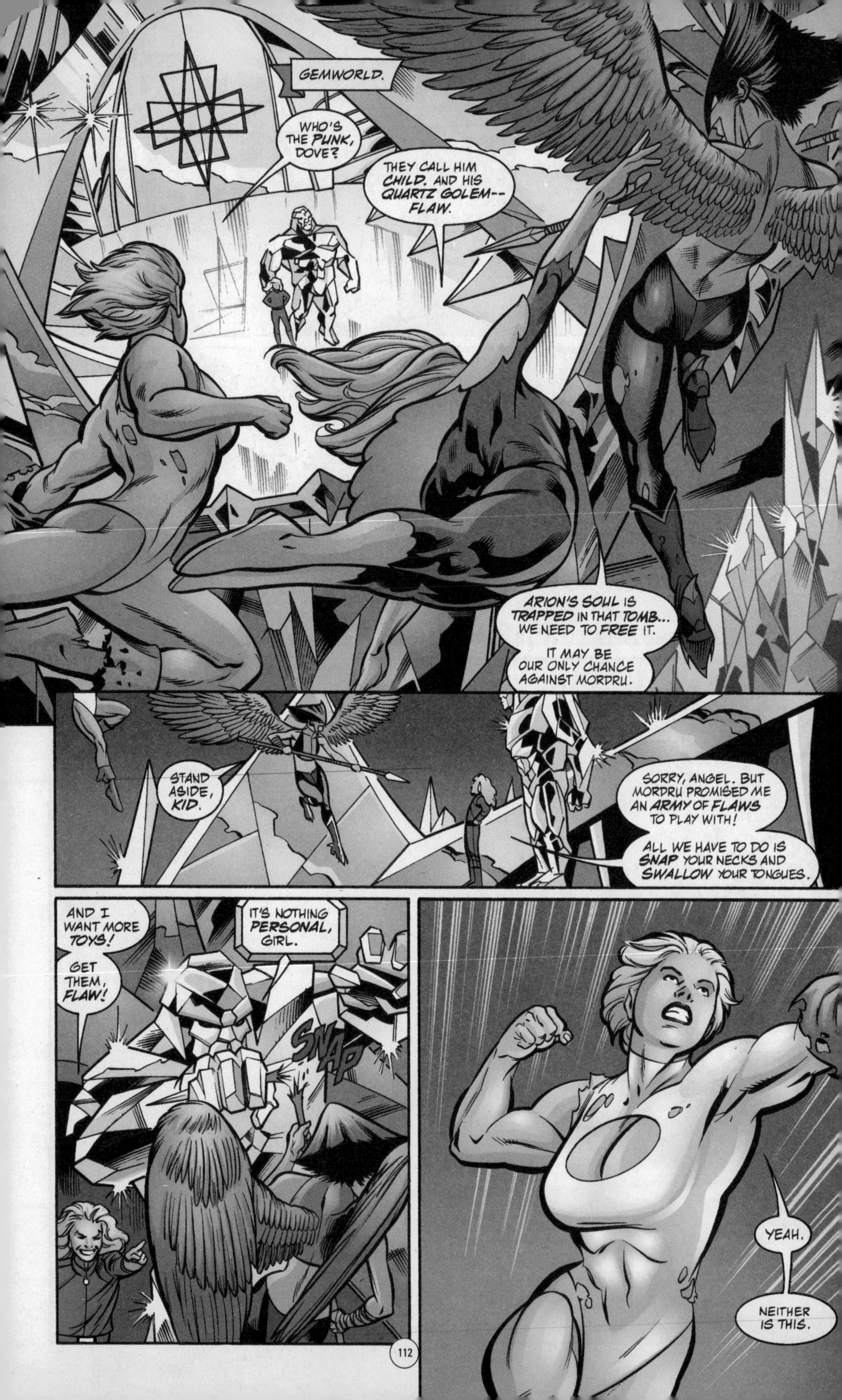
GEMWORLD.
WHO'S THE PUNK, DOVE?
THEY CALL HIM CHILD. AND HIS QUARTZ GOLEM--FLAW.
ARION'S SOUL IS TRAPPED IN THAT TOMB... WE NEED TO FREE IT.
IT MAY BE OUR ONLY CHANCE AGAINST MORDRU.
STAND ASIDE, KID.
SORRY, ANGEL. BUT MORDRU PROMISED ME AN ARMY OF FLAWS TO PLAY WITH!
ALL WE HAVE TO DO IS SNAP YOUR NECKS AND SWALLOW YOUR TONGUES.
AND I WANT MORE TOYS!
GET THEM, FLAW!
IT'S NOTHING PERSONAL, GIRL.
SNAP
YEAH.
NEITHER IS THIS.

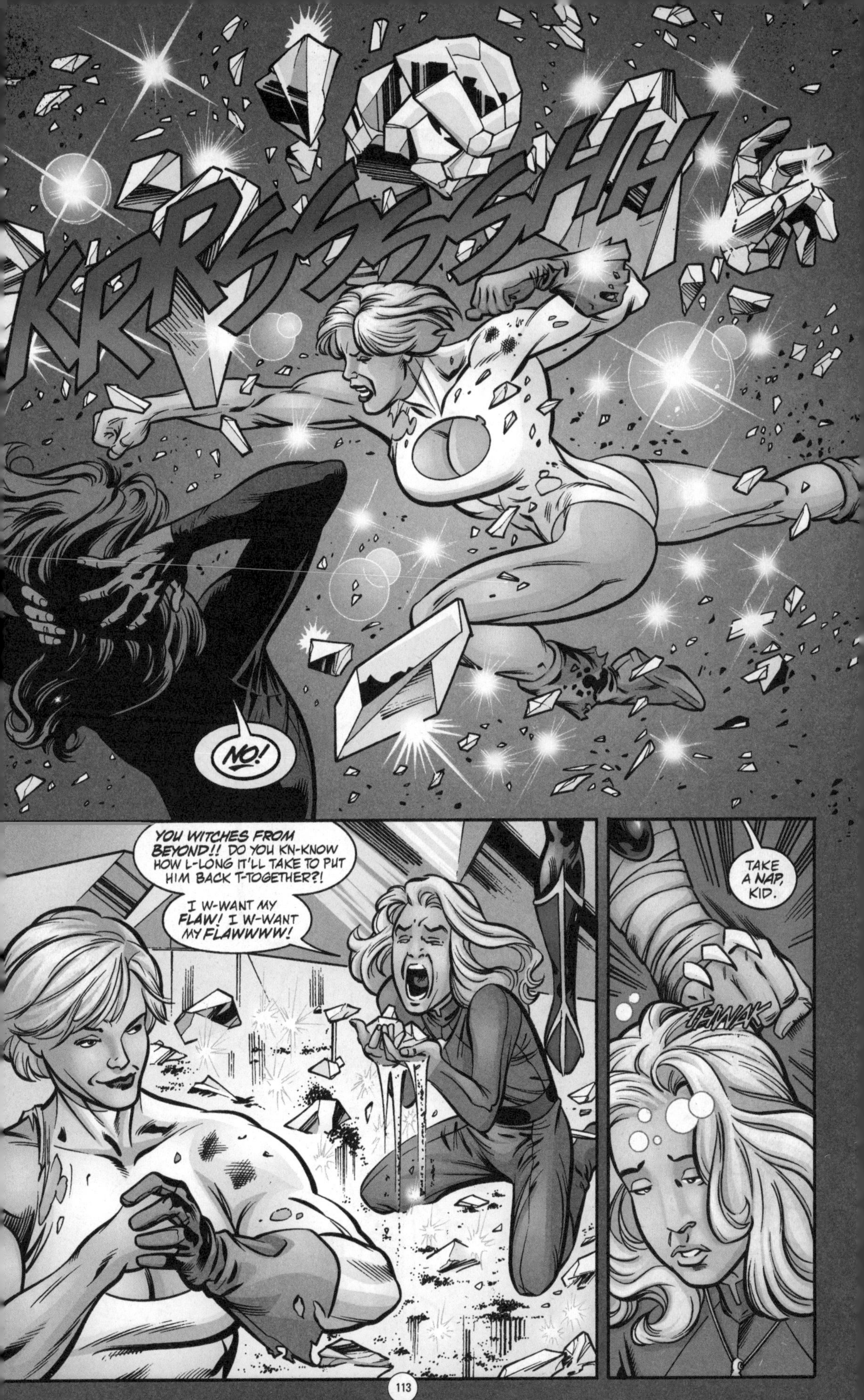
KKRSSSSHH
NO!
YOU WITCHES FROM BEYOND!! DO YOU KN-KNOW HOW L-LONG IT'LL TAKE TO PUT HIM BACK T-TOGETHER?!
I W-WANT MY FLAW! I W-WANT MY FLAWWWW!
TAKE A NAP, KID.
THWAK

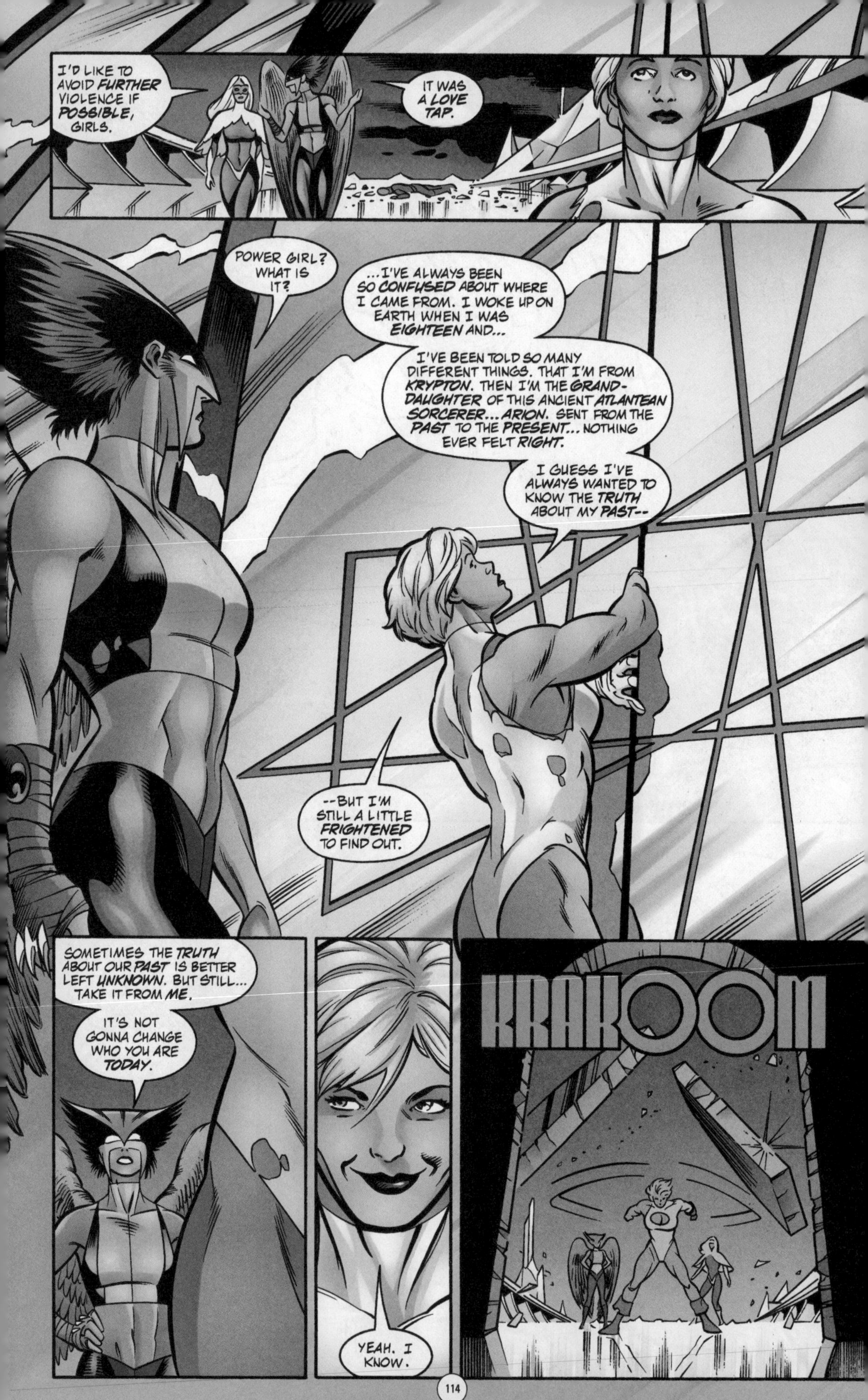
I'D LIKE TO AVOID FURTHER VIOLENCE IF POSSIBLE, GIRLS.
IT WAS A LOVE TAP.
POWER GIRL? WHAT IS IT?
...I'VE ALWAYS BEEN SO CONFUSED ABOUT WHERE I CAME FROM. I WOKE UP ON EARTH WHEN I WAS EIGHTEEN AND...
I'VE BEEN TOLD SO MANY DIFFERENT THINGS. THAT I'M FROM KRYPTON. THEN I'M THE GRAND-DAUGHTER OF THIS ANCIENT ATLANTEAN SORCERER... ARION. SENT FROM THE PAST TO THE PRESENT... NOTHING EVER FELT RIGHT.
I GUESS I'VE ALWAYS WANTED TO KNOW THE TRUTH ABOUT MY PAST--
--BUT I'M STILL A LITTLE FRIGHTENED TO FIND OUT.
SOMETIMES THE TRUTH ABOUT OUR PAST IS BETTER LEFT UNKNOWN. BUT STILL... TAKE IT FROM ME.
IT'S NOT GONNA CHANGE WHO YOU ARE TODAY.
YEAH. I KNOW.
KRAKOOM

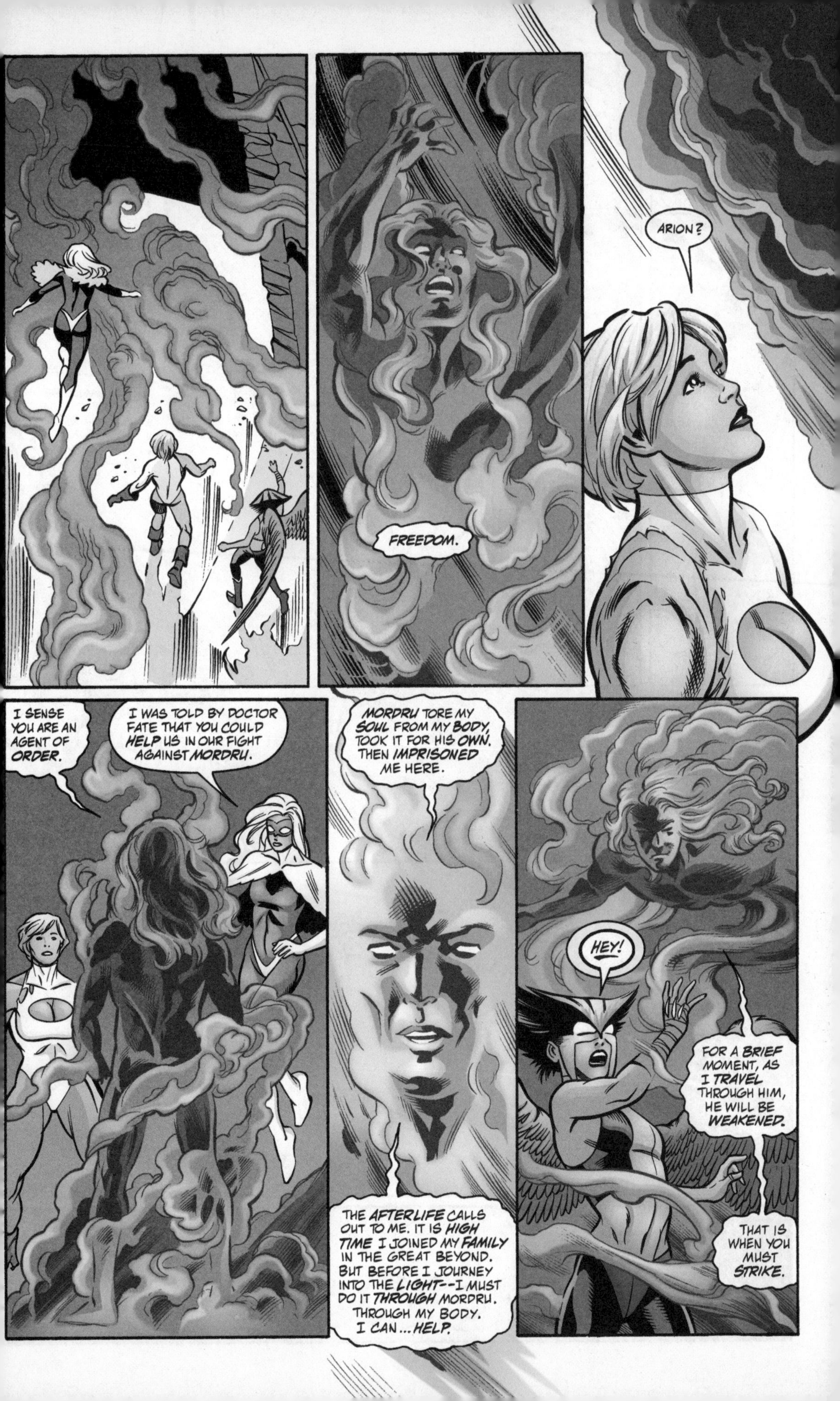
FREEDOM.
ARION?
I SENSE YOU ARE AN AGENT OF ORDER.
I WAS TOLD BY DOCTOR FATE THAT YOU COULD HELP US IN OUR FIGHT AGAINST MORDRU.
MORDRU TORE MY SOUL FROM MY BODY, TOOK IT FOR HIS OWN. THEN IMPRISONED ME HERE.
THE AFTERLIFE CALLS OUT TO ME. IT IS HIGH TIME I JOINED MY FAMILY IN THE GREAT BEYOND. BUT BEFORE I JOURNEY INTO THE LIGHT--I MUST DO IT THROUGH MORDRU. THROUGH MY BODY. I CAN... HELP.
HEY!
FOR A BRIEF MOMENT, AS I TRAVEL THROUGH HIM, HE WILL BE WEAKENED.
THAT IS WHEN YOU MUST STRIKE.

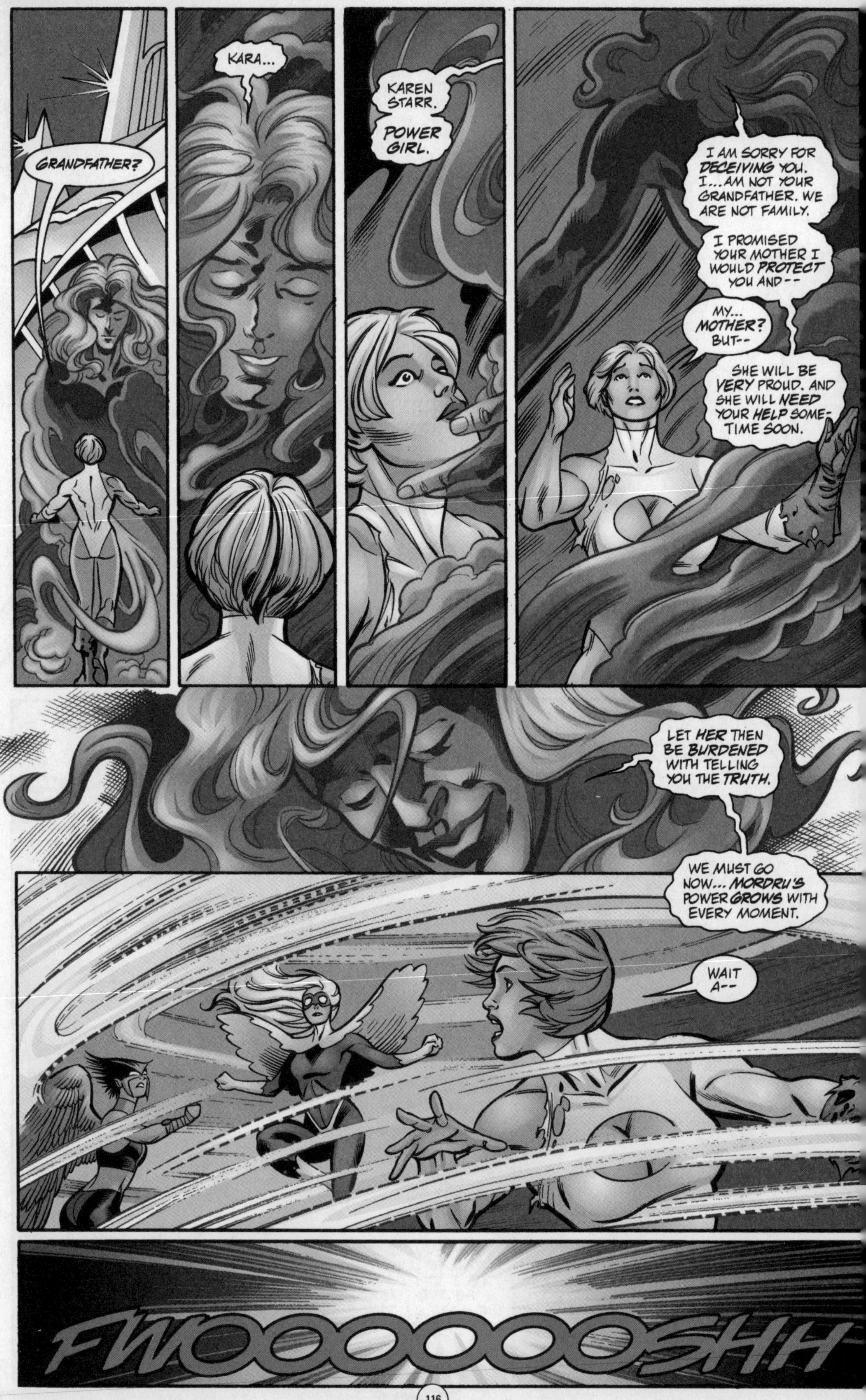

GRANDFATHER?
KARA...
KAREN STARR.
POWER GIRL.
I AM SORRY FOR DECEIVING YOU. I...AM NOT YOUR GRANDFATHER. WE ARE NOT FAMILY.
I PROMISED YOUR MOTHER I WOULD PROTECT YOU AND--
MY... MOTHER? BUT--
SHE WILL BE VERY PROUD. AND SHE WILL NEED YOUR HELP SOMETIME SOON.
LET HER THEN BE BURDENED WITH TELLING YOU THE TRUTH.
WE MUST GO NOW... MORDRU'S POWER GROWS WITH EVERY MOMENT.
WAIT A--
FWOOOOOOSHH

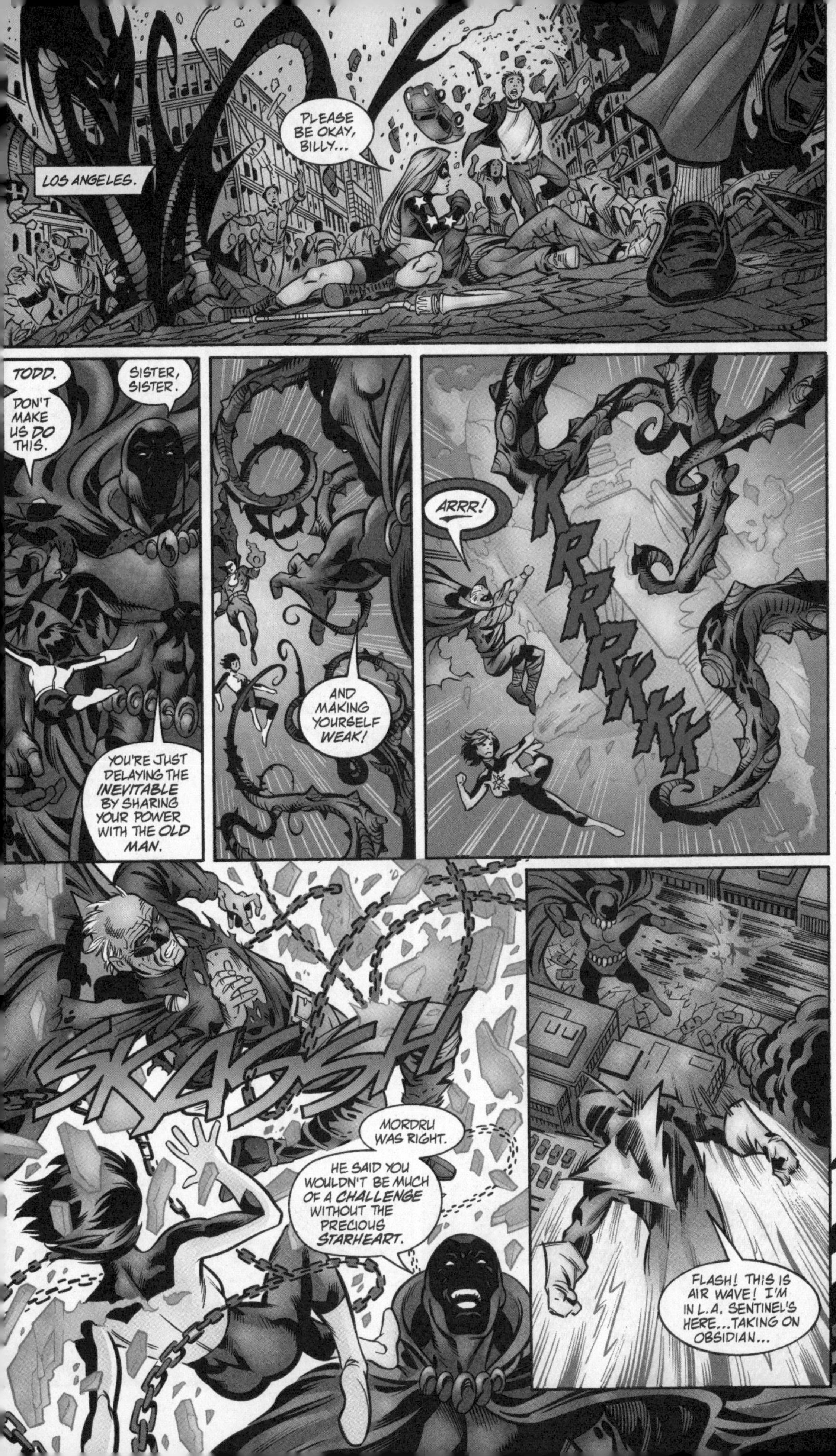

LOS ANGELES.
PLEASE BE OKAY, BILLY...
TODD.
DON'T MAKE US DO THIS.
SISTER, SISTER.
YOU'RE JUST DELAYING THE INEVITABLE BY SHARING YOUR POWER WITH THE OLD MAN.
AND MAKING YOURSELF WEAK!
ARRR!
KRRRRKKKK
SKASH
MORDRU WAS RIGHT.
HE SAID YOU WOULDN'T BE MUCH OF A CHALLENGE WITHOUT THE PRECIOUS STARHEART.
FLASH! THIS IS AIR WAVE! I'M IN L.A. SENTINEL'S HERE...TAKING ON OBSIDIAN...

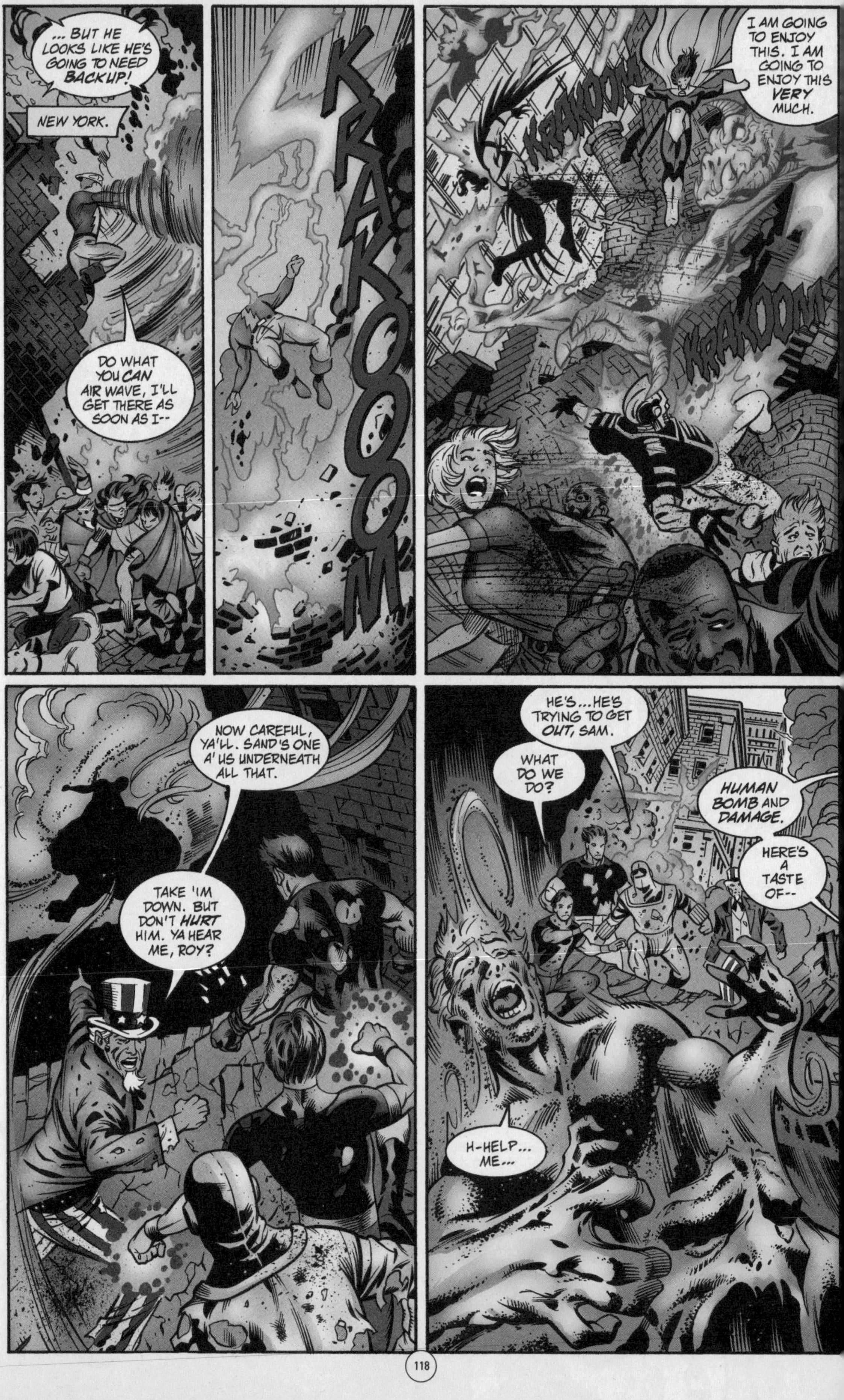
... BUT HE LOOKS LIKE HE'S GOING TO NEED BACKUP!
NEW YORK.
DO WHAT YOU CAN AIR WAVE, I'LL GET THERE AS SOON AS I--
KRAKOOOOM
KRAKOOM
I AM GOING TO ENJOY THIS. I AM GOING TO ENJOY THIS VERY MUCH.
KRAKOOM
NOW CAREFUL, YA'LL. SAND'S ONE A' US UNDERNEATH ALL THAT.
TAKE 'IM DOWN. BUT DON'T HURT HIM. YA HEAR ME, ROY?
HE'S...HE'S TRYING TO GET OUT, SAM.
WHAT DO WE DO?
HUMAN BOMB AND DAMAGE.
HERE'S A TASTE OF--
H-HELP... ME...

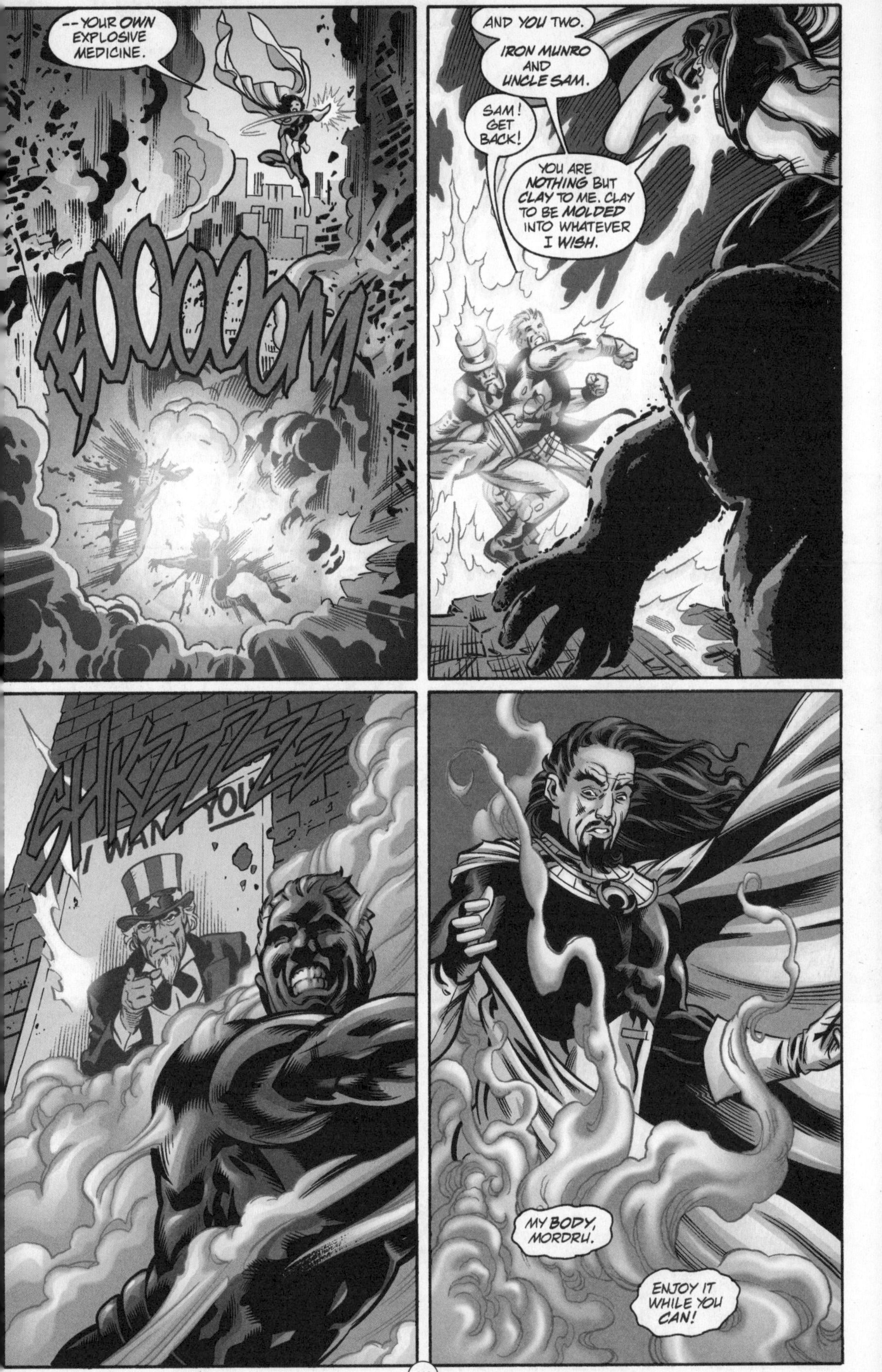

--YOUR OWN EXPLOSIVE MEDICINE.
BOOOOM
AND YOU TWO.
IRON MUNRO AND UNCLE SAM.
SAM! GET BACK!
YOU ARE NOTHING BUT CLAY TO ME. CLAY TO BE MOLDED INTO WHATEVER I WISH.
SHKZZZZZ
I WAN
YOU
MY BODY, MORDRU.
ENJOY IT WHILE YOU CAN!

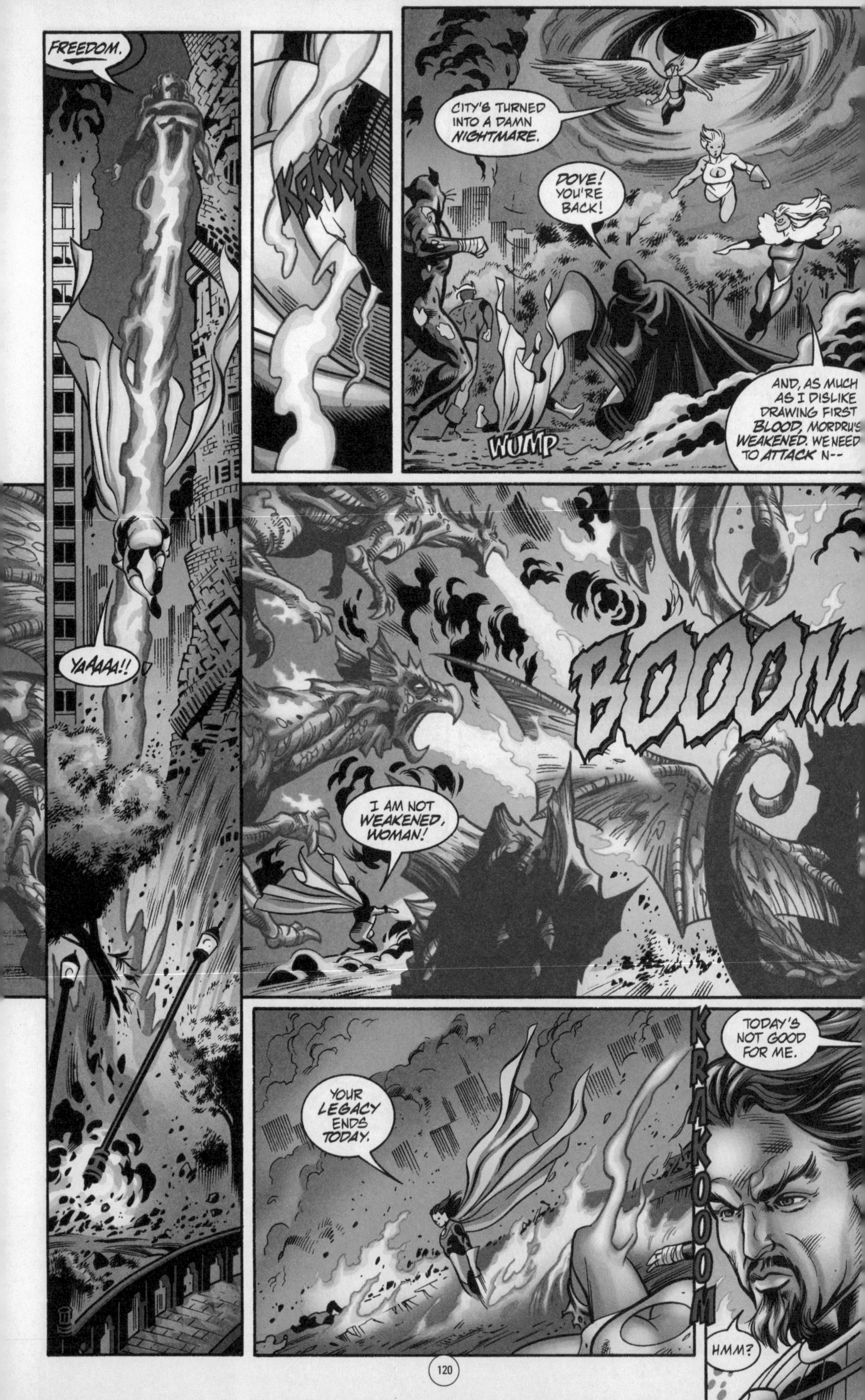
FREEDOM.
KRKKK
CITY'S TURNED INTO A DAMN NIGHTMARE.
DOVE! YOU'RE BACK!
WUMP
AND, AS MUCH AS I DISLIKE DRAWING FIRST BLOOD, MORDRU'S WEAKENED. WE NEED TO ATTACK N--
YAAAAA!!
BOOOM
I AM NOT WEAKENED, WOMAN!
YOUR LEGACY ENDS TODAY.
KRAKOOOOM
TODAY'S NOT GOOD FOR ME.
HMM?

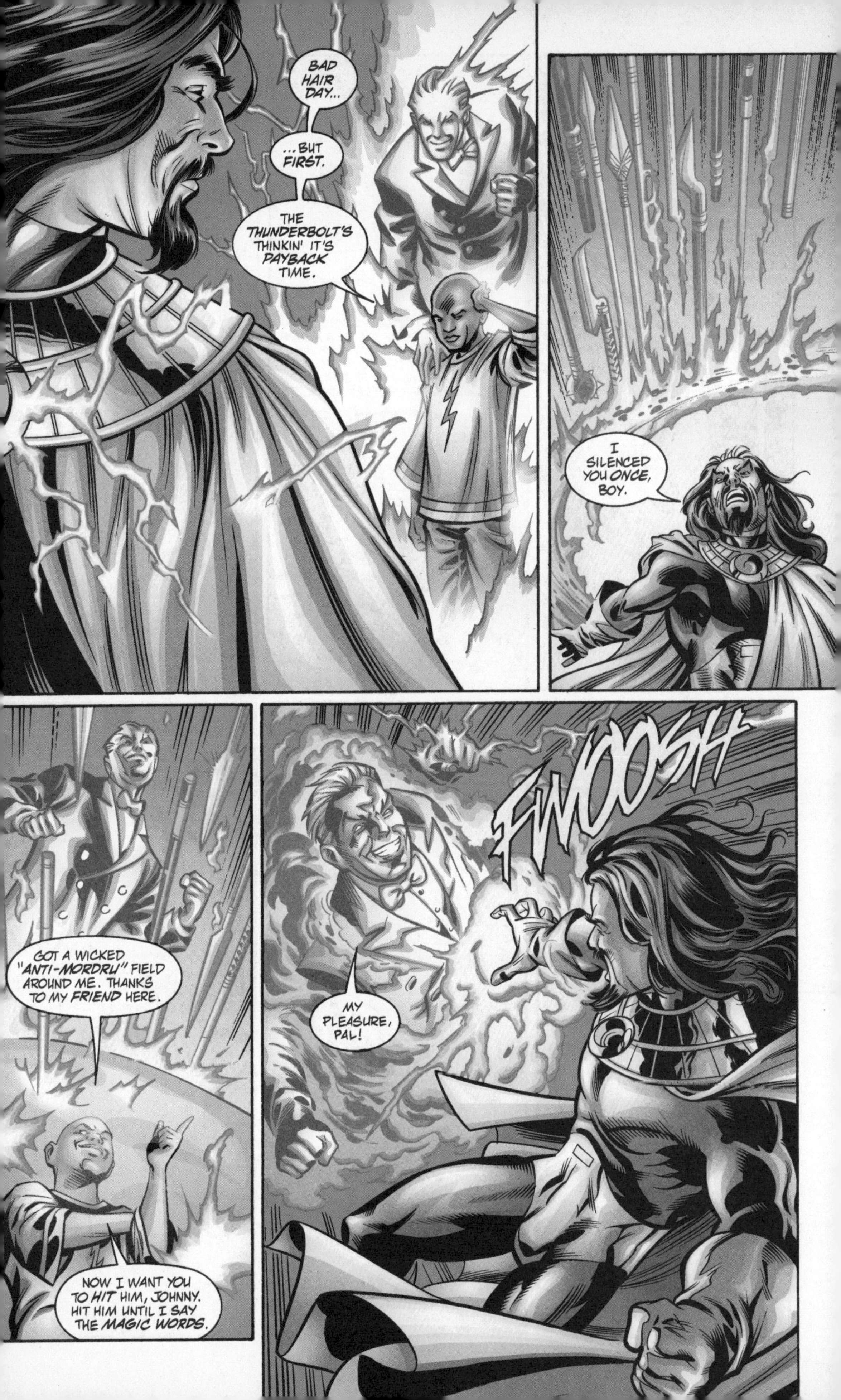
BAD HAIR DAY...
...BUT FIRST.
THE THUNDERBOLT'S THINKIN' IT'S PAYBACK TIME.
I SILENCED YOU ONCE, BOY.
GOT A WICKED "ANTI-MORDRU" FIELD AROUND ME. THANKS TO MY FRIEND HERE.
NOW I WANT YOU TO HIT HIM, JOHNNY. HIT HIM UNTIL I SAY THE MAGIC WORDS.
FWOOSH
MY PLEASURE, PAL!

YOU SHOULDN'T A' MADE JAKEEM *MAD*, DRU-MAN. KID CAN HOLD A *GRUDGE.*

BEEN TRYIN' TO *TALK* TO HIM ABOUT THAT.

YOU MAY HAVE *IMMENSE* POWER AT YOUR FINGERTIPS, BOY--

--BUT THAT POWER IS *TRAPPED* INSIDE A *FIFTH DIMENSIONAL IMP.* AN IMP WITH THE *SOUL* AND *BRAIN* OF THE JSA'S INCOMPETENT *MASCOT.*

LOOK AT *HIM.* *SMILING* LIKE AN *IDIOT.*

SMILING LIKE AN *IDIOT?*

SEE. THE THING *IS,* DRU-MAN--

--I SMILE BECAUSE I *ENJOY* LIFE.

HANGING WITH MY *FRIENDS.* MAKIN' A KID'S *WISHES* COME TRUE.

WHAM

AND PUTTIN' ARROGANT POWER-HUNGRY JERKS IN THEIR PLACE!

FZZAK

ALL RIGHT, JOHNNY. *HUG* HIM.

DID HE JUST SAY--

--*HUG* HIM?

122

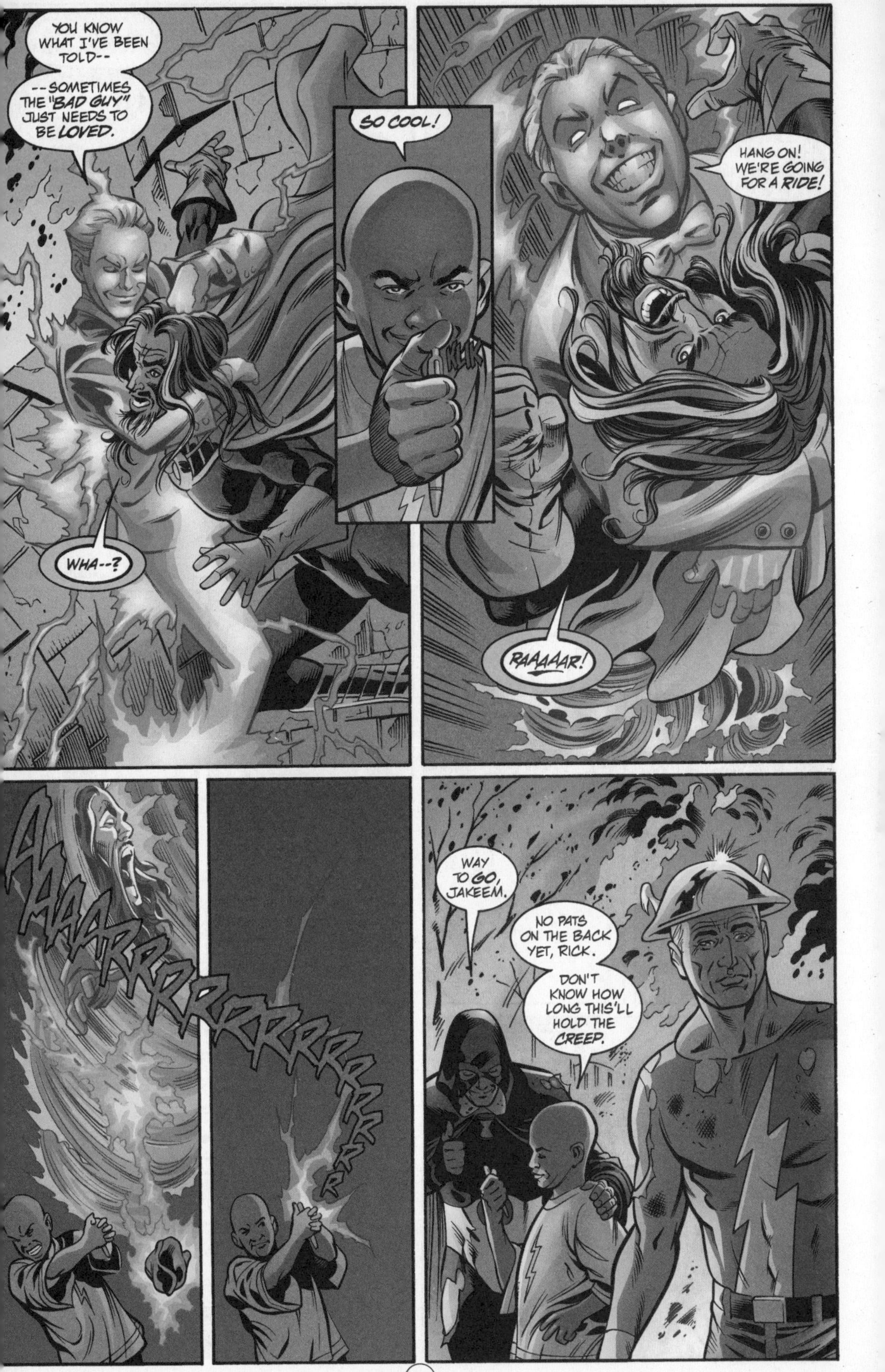
YOU KNOW WHAT I'VE BEEN TOLD--
--SOMETIMES THE "BAD GUY" JUST NEEDS TO BE LOVED.
WHA--?
SO COOL!
KLIK
HANG ON! WE'RE GOING FOR A RIDE!
RAAAAAR!
AAAARRRRRRRRRRRRRRRRR
WAY TO GO, JAKEEM.
NO PATS ON THE BACK YET, RICK.
DON'T KNOW HOW LONG THIS'LL HOLD THE CREEP.

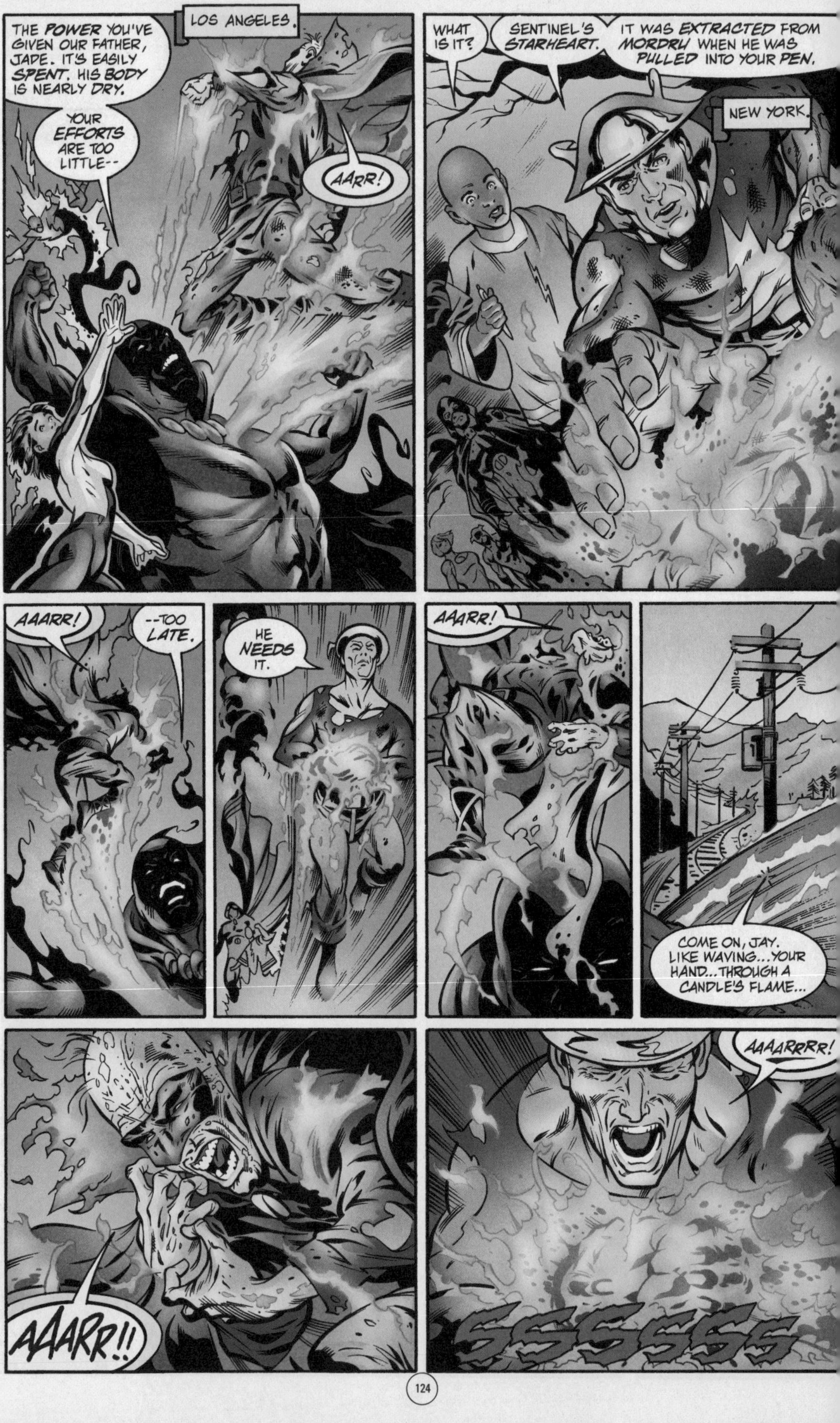
LOS ANGELES.
THE POWER YOU'VE GIVEN OUR FATHER, JADE. IT'S EASILY SPENT. HIS BODY IS NEARLY DRY.
YOUR EFFORTS ARE TOO LITTLE--
AARR!
WHAT IS IT?
SENTINEL'S STARHEART.
IT WAS EXTRACTED FROM MORDRU WHEN HE WAS PULLED INTO YOUR PEN.
NEW YORK.
AAARR!
--TOO LATE.
HE NEEDS IT.
AAARR!
COME ON, JAY. LIKE WAVING... YOUR HAND... THROUGH A CANDLE'S FLAME...
AAARR!!
AAAARRRR!
SSSSSSS

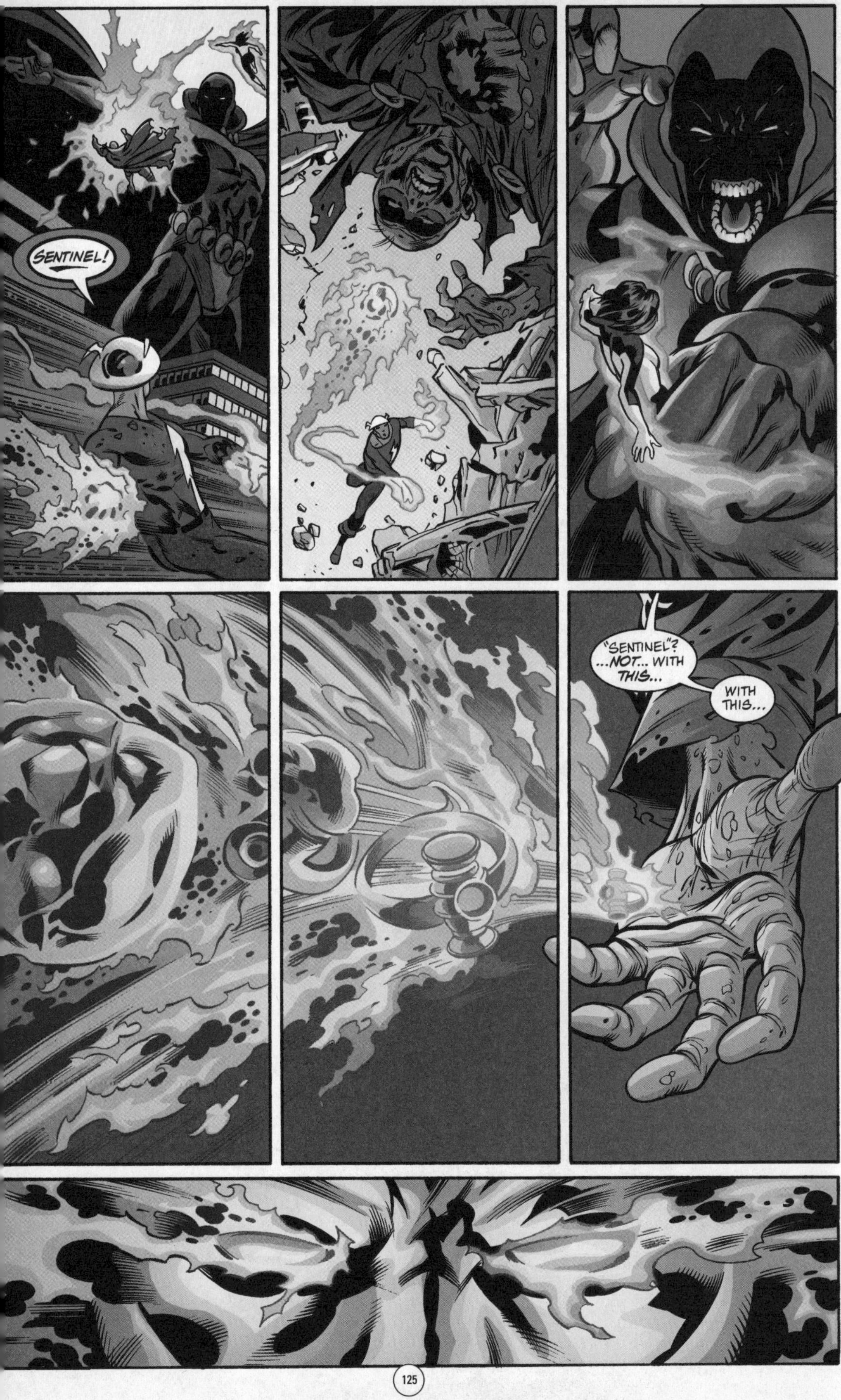
SENTINEL!
"SENTINEL"? ...NOT... WITH THIS...
WITH THIS...

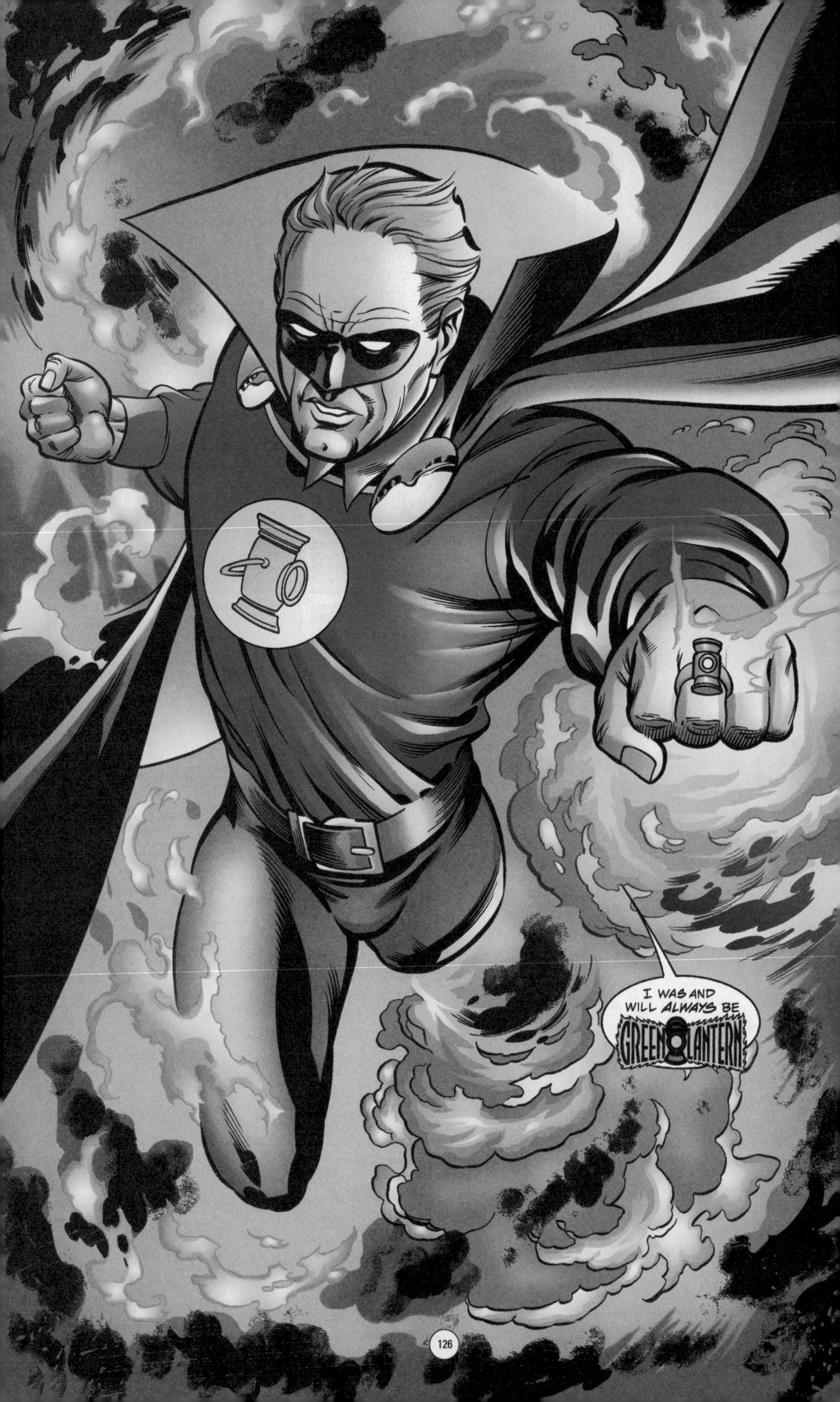
I WAS AND
WILL ALWAYS BE
GREEN LANTERN

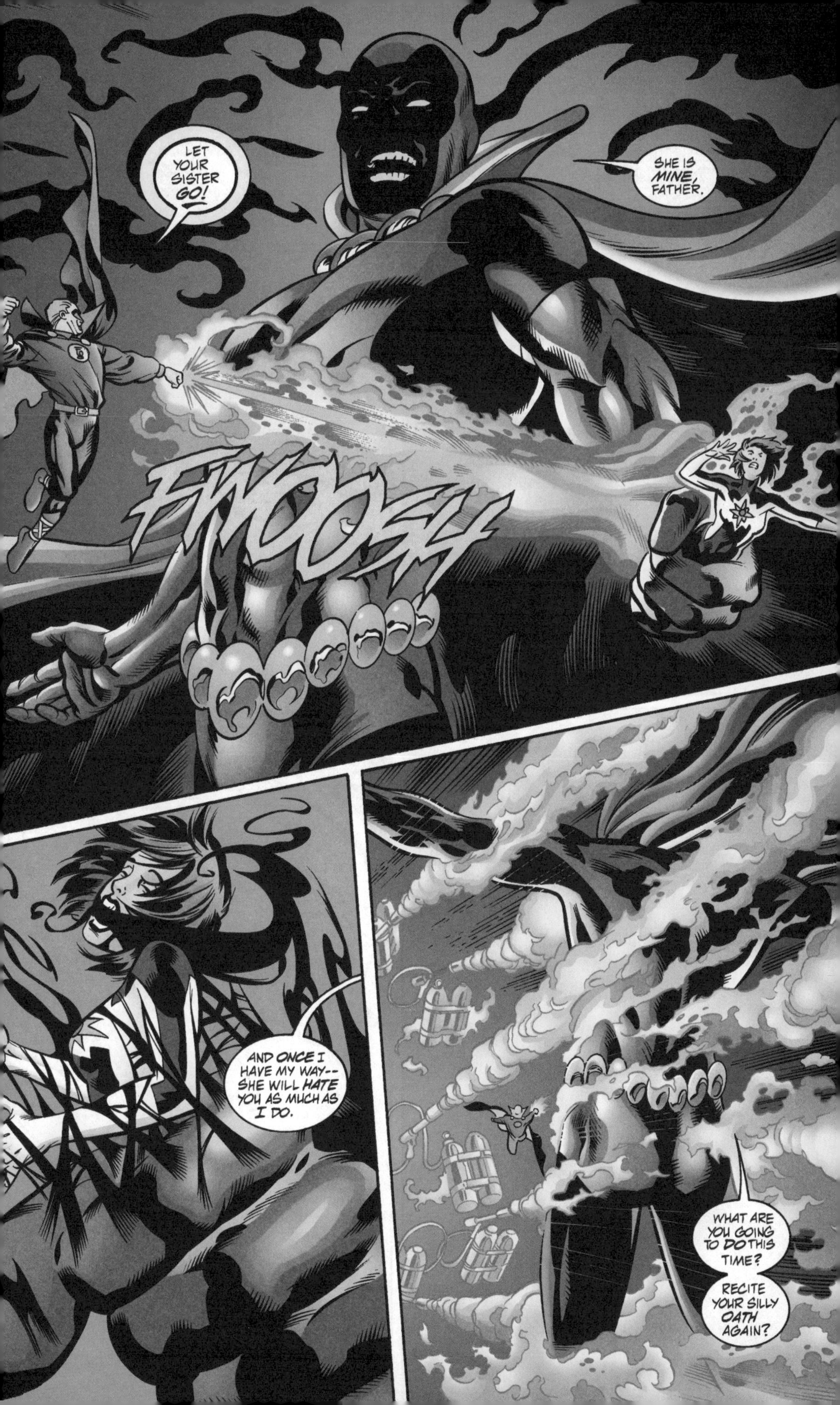
LET YOUR SISTER GO!
SHE IS MINE, FATHER.
FWOOSH
AND ONCE I HAVE MY WAY-- SHE WILL HATE YOU AS MUCH AS I DO.
WHAT ARE YOU GOING TO DO THIS TIME?
RECITE YOUR SILLY OATH AGAIN?

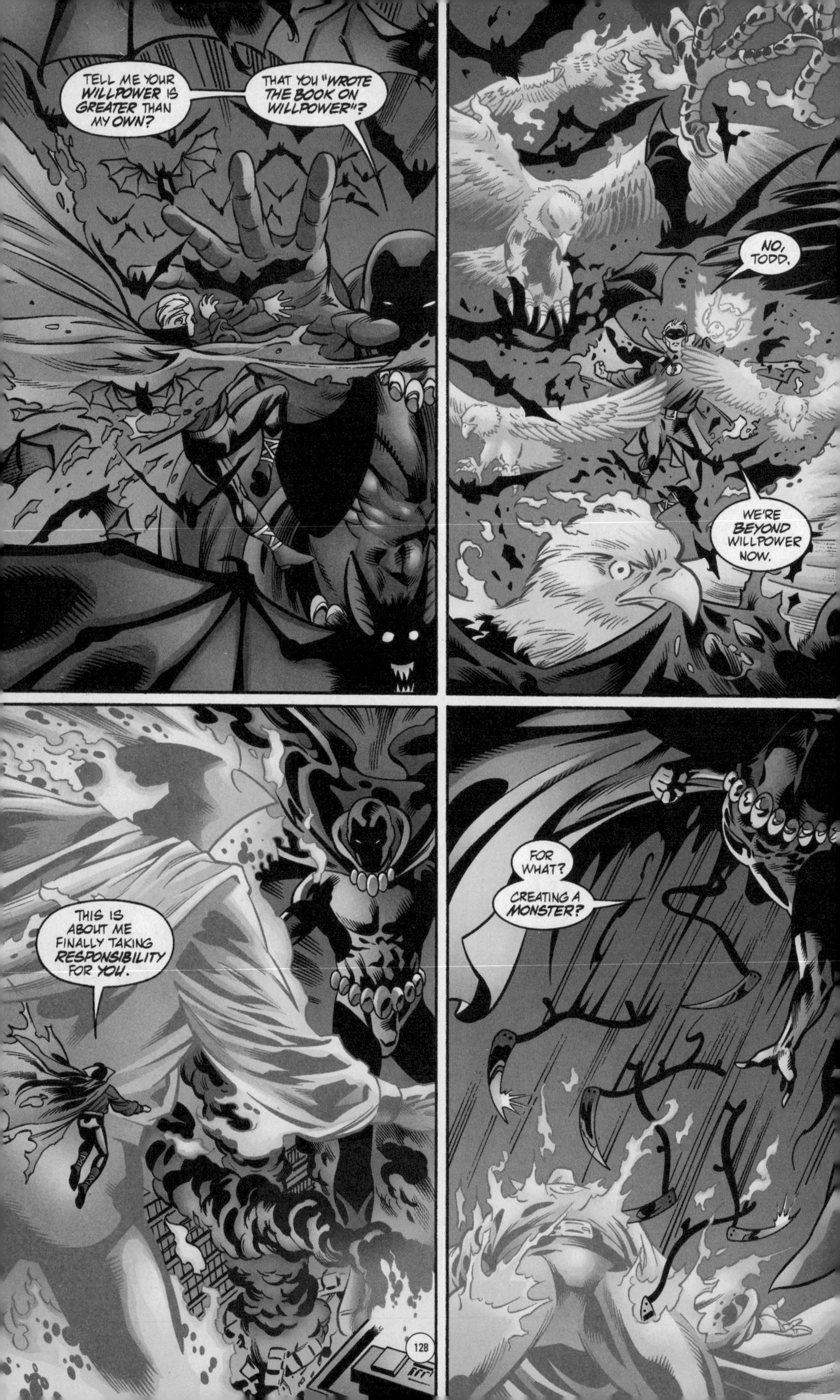
TELL ME YOUR WILLPOWER IS GREATER THAN MY OWN?
THAT YOU "WROTE THE BOOK ON WILLPOWER"?
NO, TODD.
WE'RE BEYOND WILLPOWER NOW.
THIS IS ABOUT ME FINALLY TAKING RESPONSIBILITY FOR YOU.
FOR WHAT?
CREATING A MONSTER?

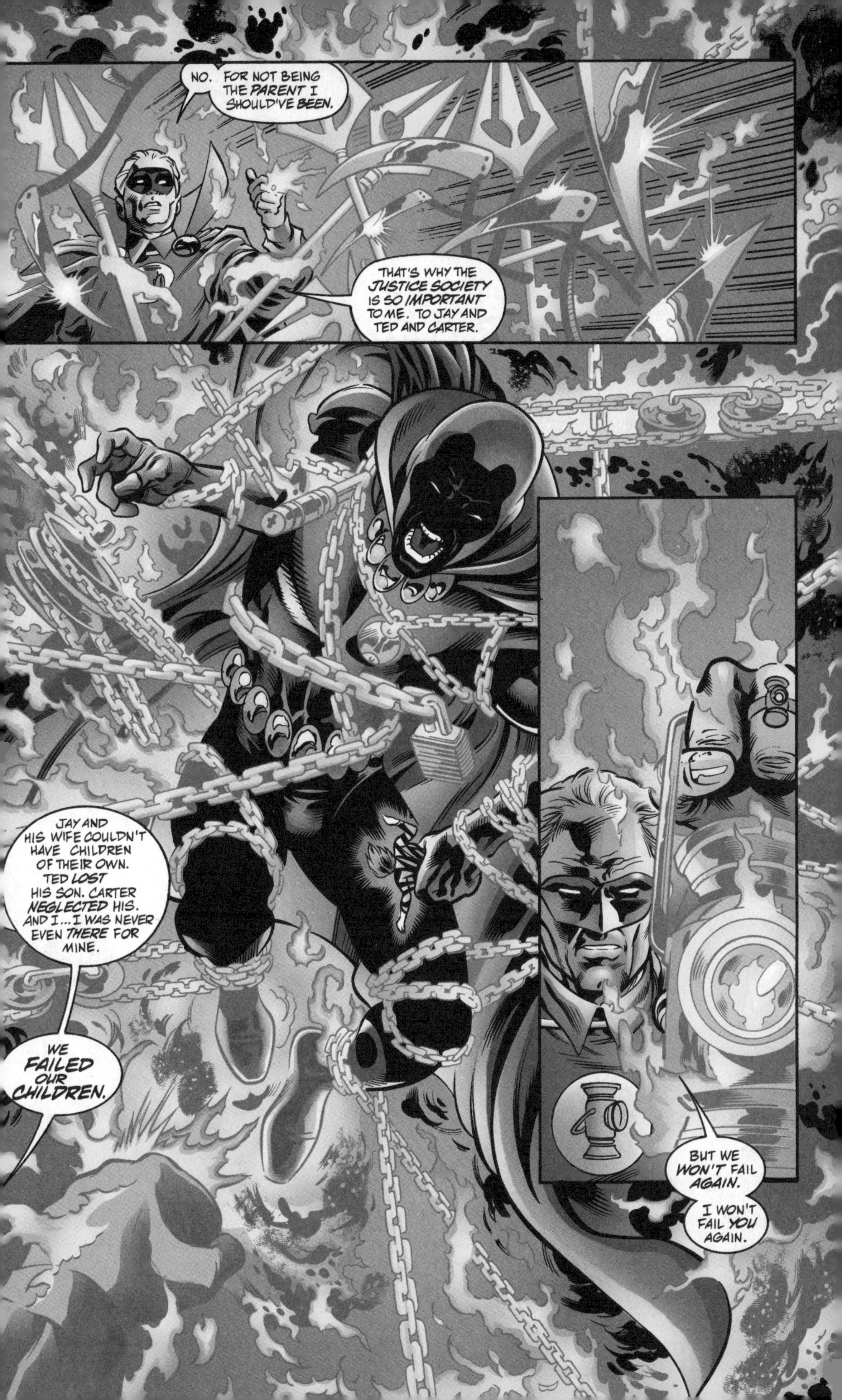

NO.
FOR NOT BEING THE PARENT I SHOULD'VE BEEN.
THAT'S WHY THE JUSTICE SOCIETY IS SO IMPORTANT TO ME. TO JAY AND TED AND CARTER.
JAY AND HIS WIFE COULDN'T HAVE CHILDREN OF THEIR OWN. TED LOST HIS SON. CARTER NEGLECTED HIS. AND I... I WAS NEVER EVEN THERE FOR MINE.
WE FAILED OUR CHILDREN.
BUT WE WON'T FAIL AGAIN.
I WON'T FAIL YOU AGAIN.

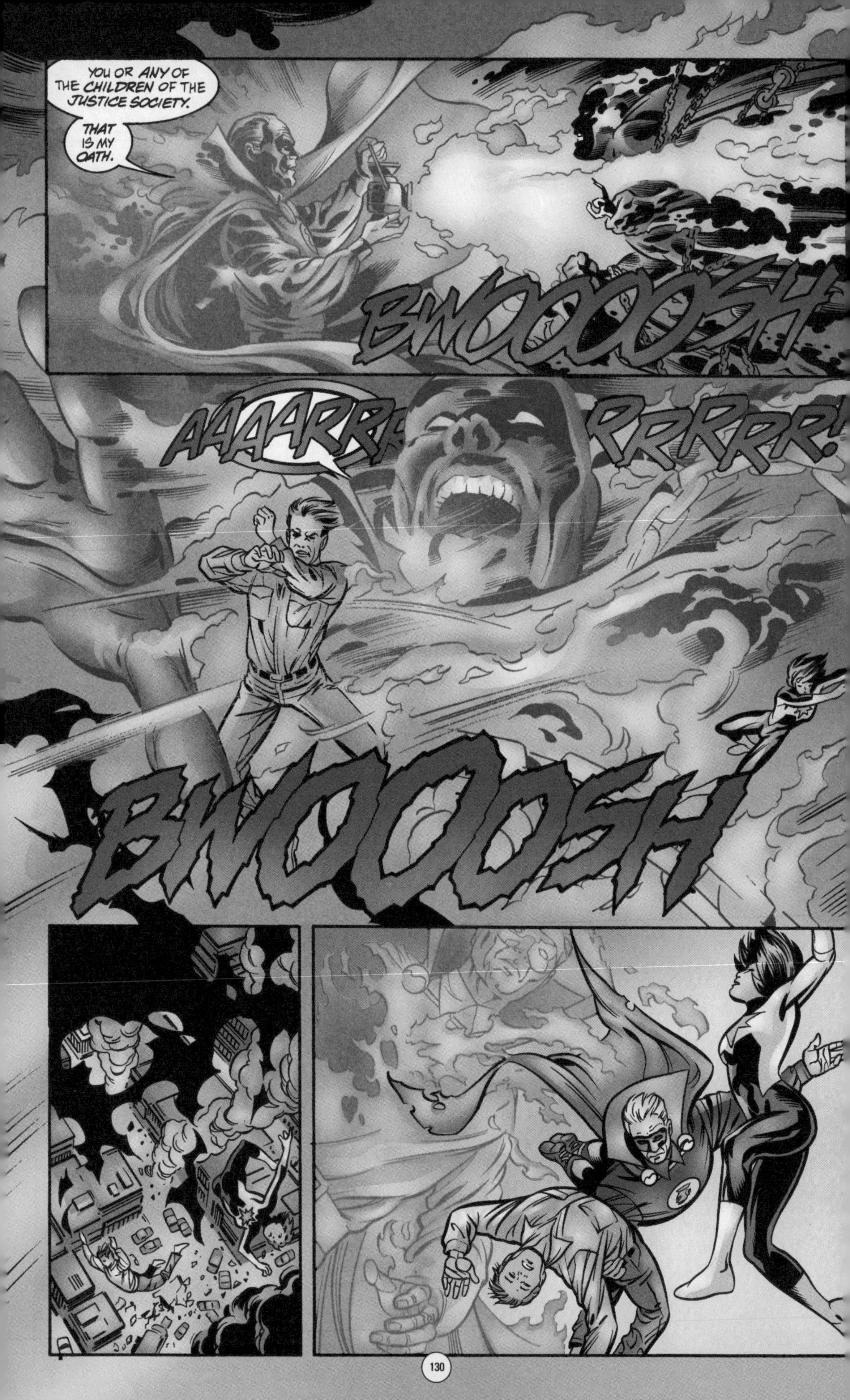
YOU OR ANY OF THE CHILDREN OF THE JUSTICE SOCIETY.
THAT IS MY OATH.
BWOOOOOSH
AAAARRRRRRRR!
BWOOOSH

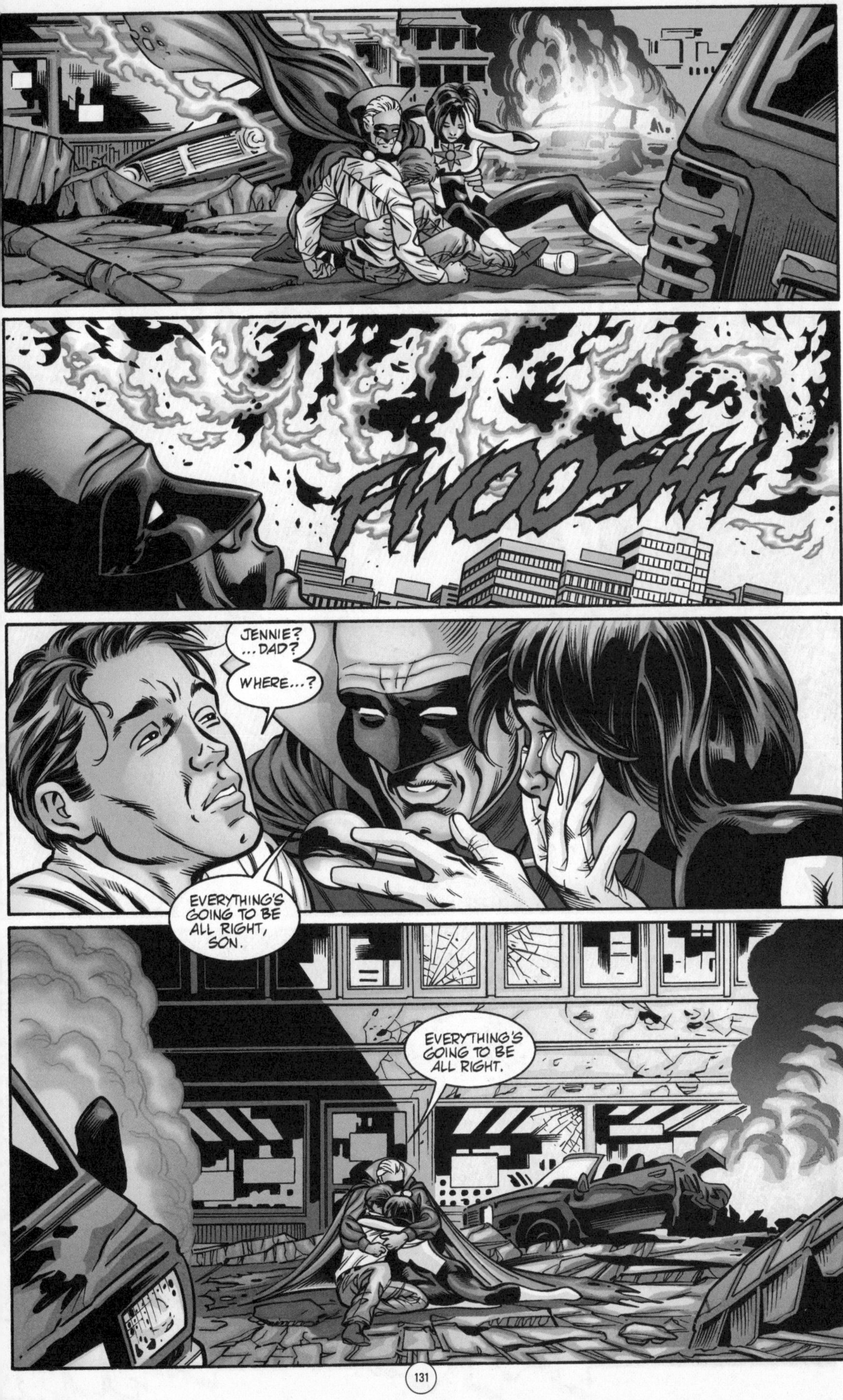
FWOOSHH
JENNIE? ...DAD?
WHERE...?
EVERYTHING'S GOING TO BE ALL RIGHT, SON.
EVERYTHING'S GOING TO BE ALL RIGHT.

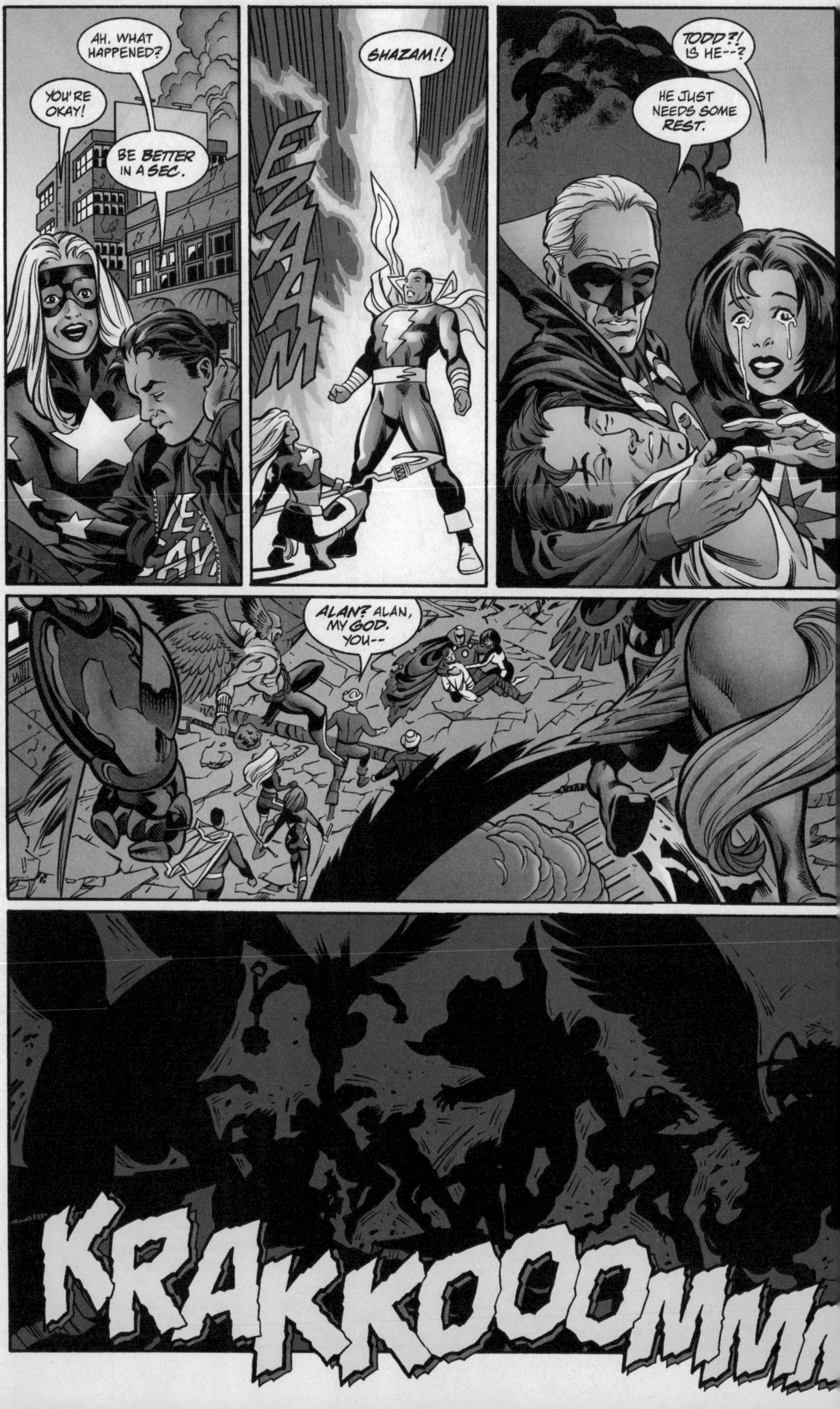

AH. WHAT HAPPENED?
YOU'RE OKAY!
BE BETTER IN A SEC.
SHAZAM!!
TODD?! IS HE--?
HE JUST NEEDS SOME REST.
ALAN? ALAN, MY GOD. YOU--
KRAKKOOOMM

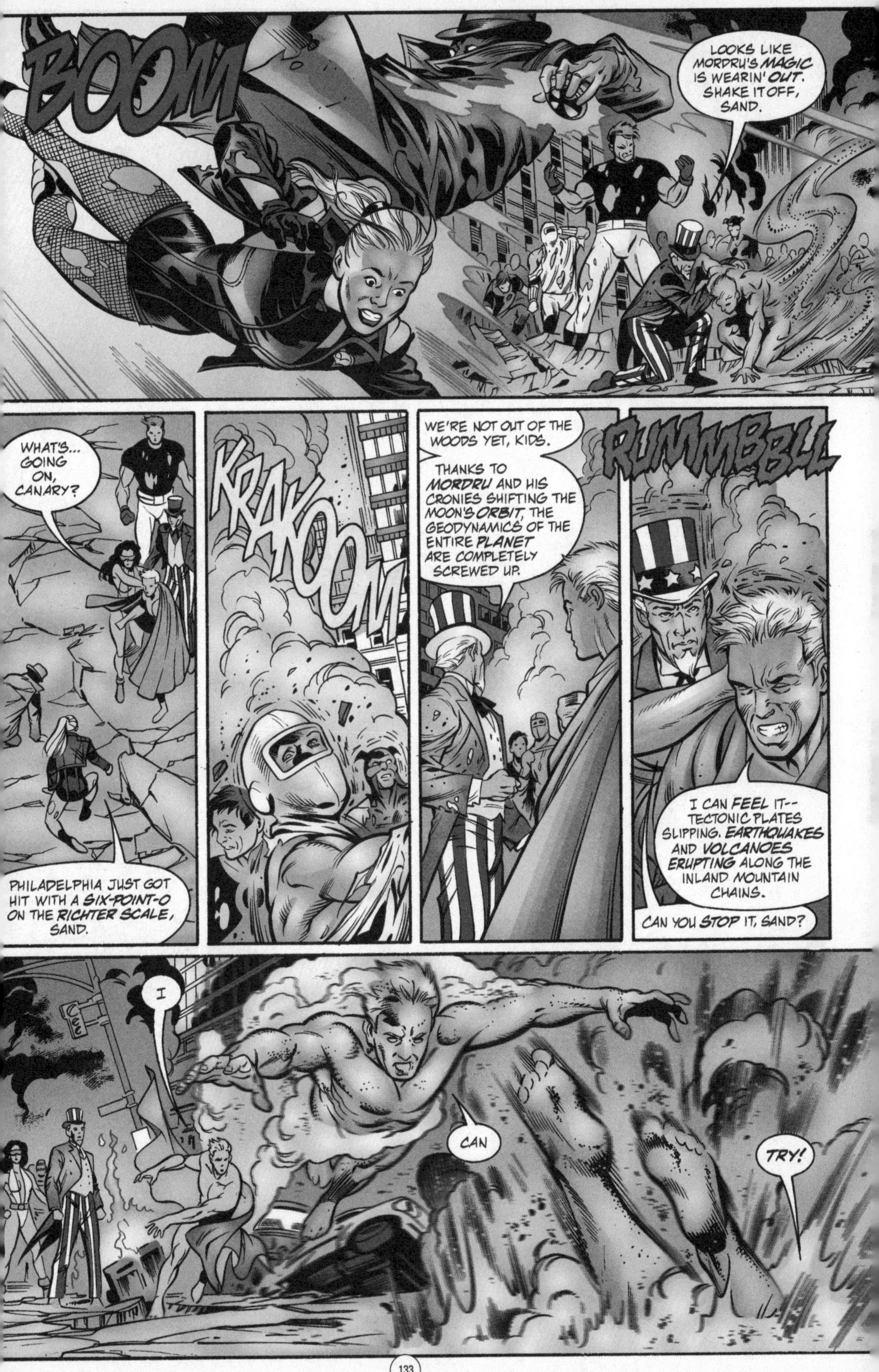
BOOM
LOOKS LIKE MORDRU'S MAGIC IS WEARIN' OUT. SHAKE IT OFF, SAND.
WHAT'S... GOING ON, CANARY?
PHILADELPHIA JUST GOT HIT WITH A SIX-POINT-O ON THE RICHTER SCALE, SAND.
KRAKOOM
WE'RE NOT OUT OF THE WOODS YET, KIDS.
THANKS TO MORDRU AND HIS CRONIES SHIFTING THE MOON'S ORBIT, THE GEODYNAMICS OF THE ENTIRE PLANET ARE COMPLETELY SCREWED UP.
RUMMBBLL
I CAN FEEL IT-- TECTONIC PLATES SLIPPING. EARTHQUAKES AND VOLCANOES ERUPTING ALONG THE INLAND MOUNTAIN CHAINS.
CAN YOU STOP IT, SAND?
I
CAN
TRY!

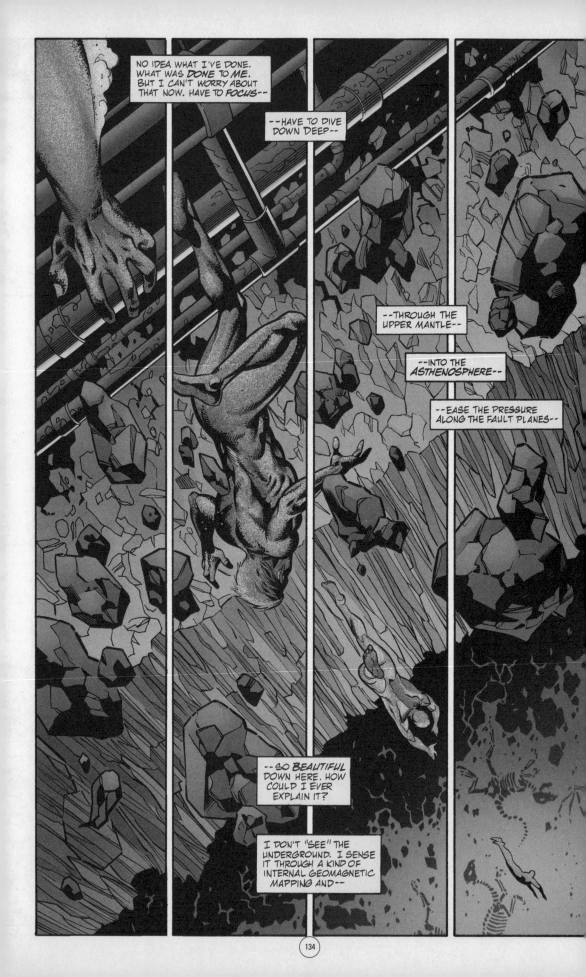

NO IDEA WHAT I'VE DONE. WHAT WAS *DONE* TO *ME*. BUT I CAN'T WORRY ABOUT THAT NOW. HAVE TO *FOCUS*--

--HAVE TO DIVE DOWN DEEP--

--THROUGH THE UPPER MANTLE--

--INTO THE *ASTHENOSPHERE*--

--EASE THE PRESSURE ALONG THE FAULT PLANES--

--SO *BEAUTIFUL* DOWN HERE. HOW COULD I EVER EXPLAIN IT?

I DON'T "SEE" THE UNDERGROUND. I SENSE IT THROUGH A KIND OF INTERNAL GEOMAGNETIC MAPPING AND--

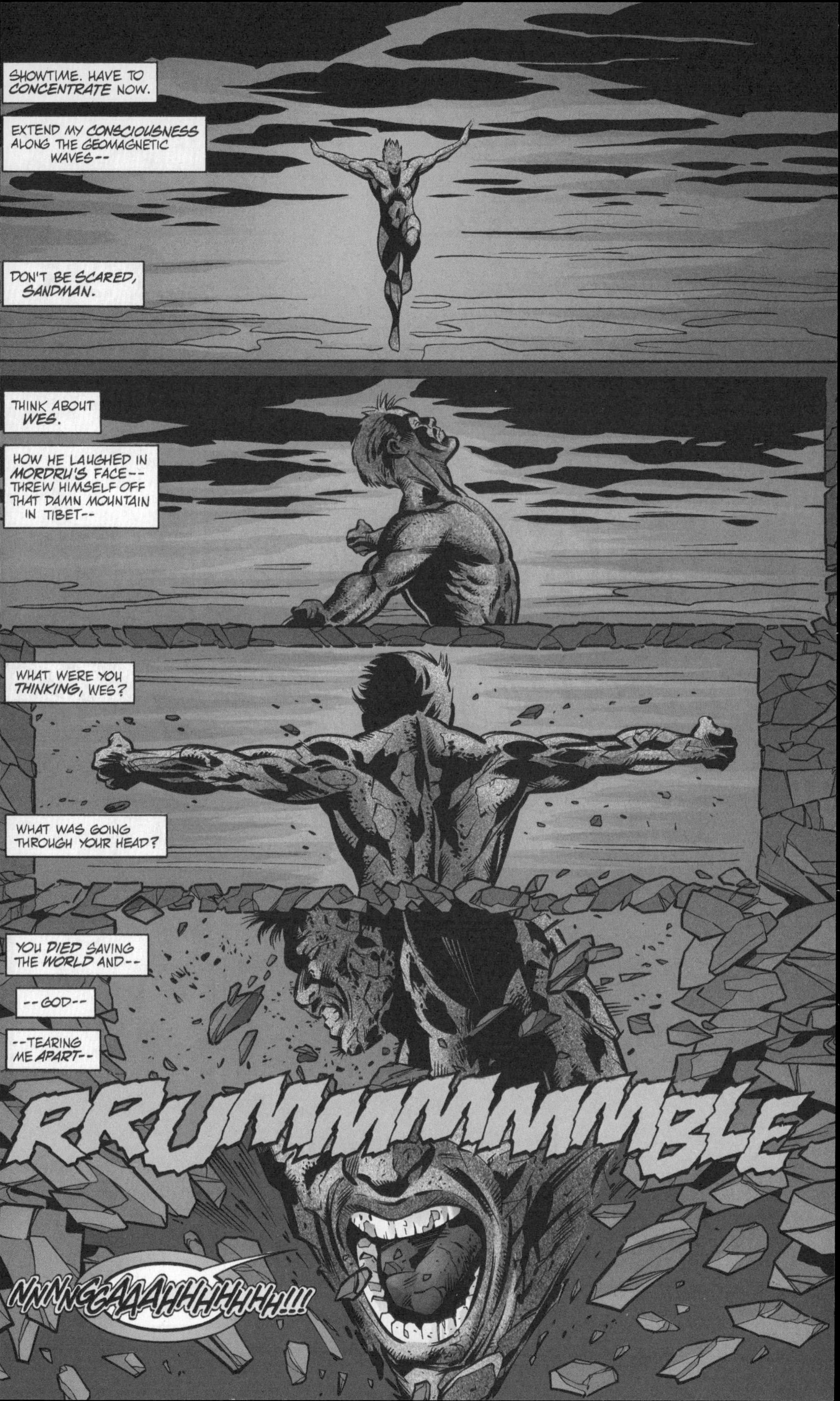
SHOWTIME. HAVE TO CONCENTRATE NOW.
EXTEND MY CONSCIOUSNESS ALONG THE GEOMAGNETIC WAVES--
DON'T BE SCARED, SANDMAN.
THINK ABOUT WES.
HOW HE LAUGHED IN MORDRU'S FACE-- THREW HIMSELF OFF THAT DAMN MOUNTAIN IN TIBET--
WHAT WERE YOU THINKING, WES?
WHAT WAS GOING THROUGH YOUR HEAD?
YOU DIED SAVING THE WORLD AND--
--GOD--
--TEARING ME APART--
RRUMMMMMMBLE
NNNNGGAAAHHHHHHH!!!

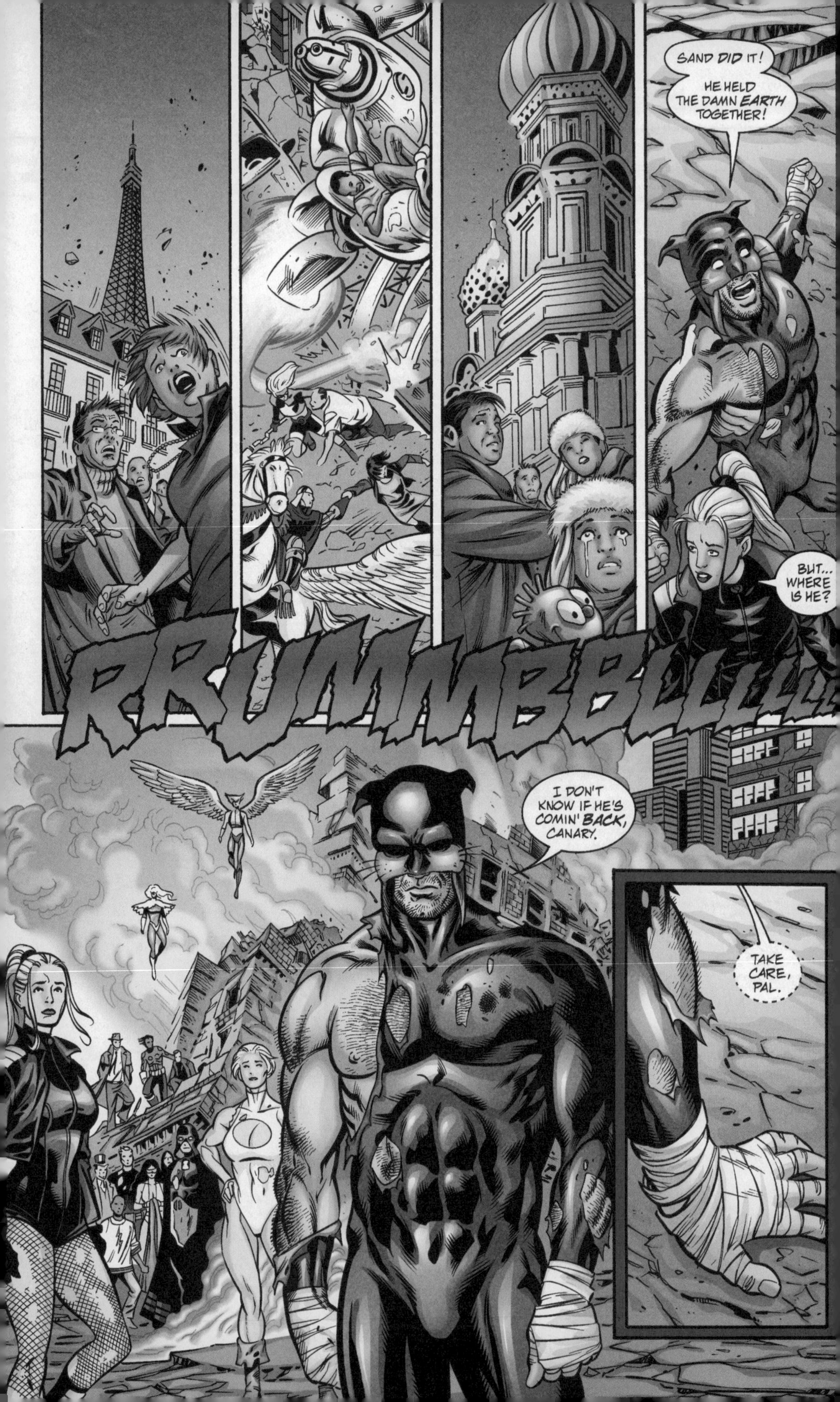
SAND DID IT!
HE HELD THE DAMN EARTH TOGETHER!
BUT... WHERE IS HE?
RRUMMBBLLLL...
I DON'T KNOW IF HE'S COMIN' BACK, CANARY.
TAKE CARE, PAL.

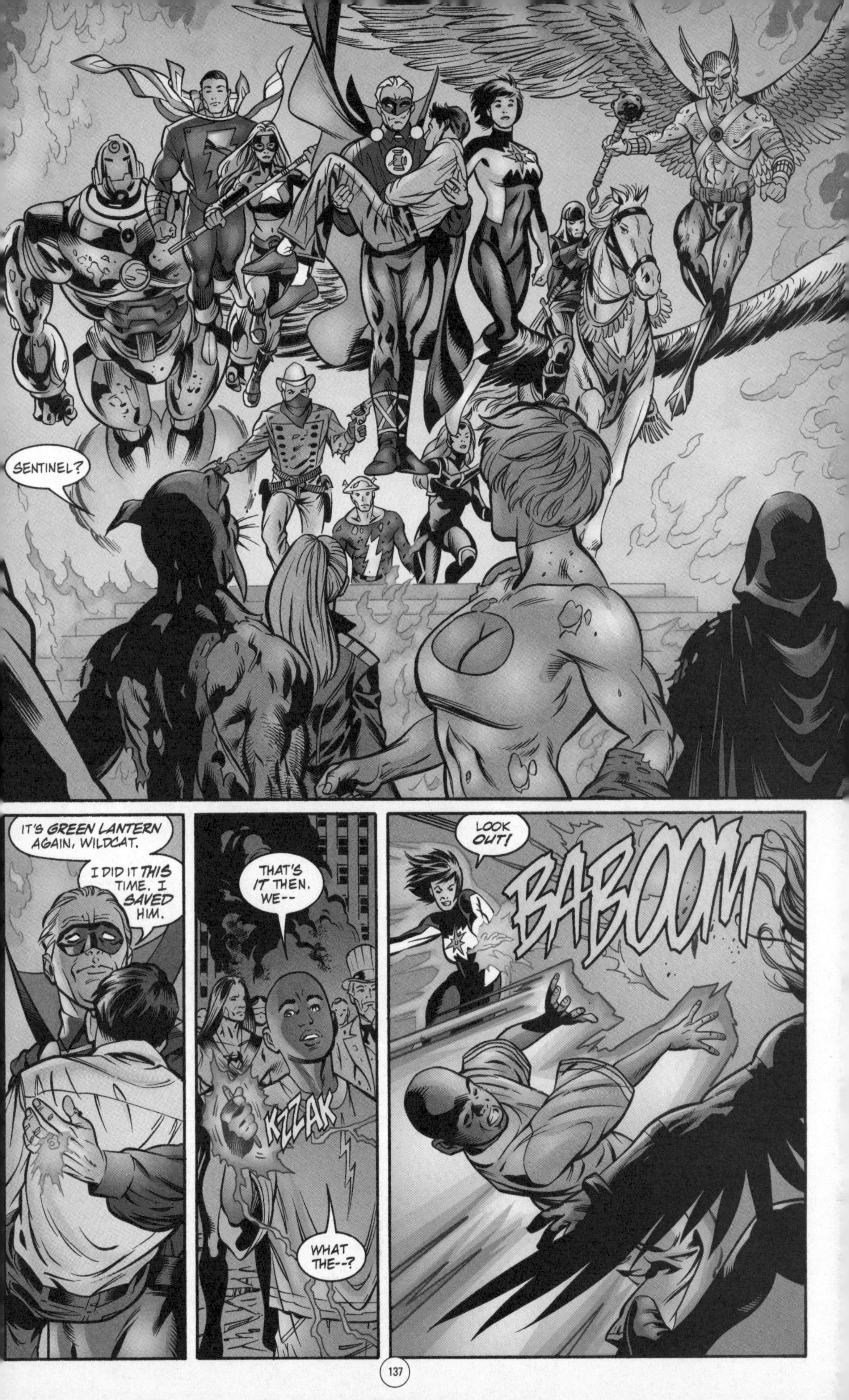
SENTINEL?
IT'S GREEN LANTERN AGAIN, WILDCAT.
I DID IT THIS TIME. I SAVED HIM.
THAT'S IT THEN. WE--
KZZAK
WHAT THE--?
LOOK OUT!
BABOOM

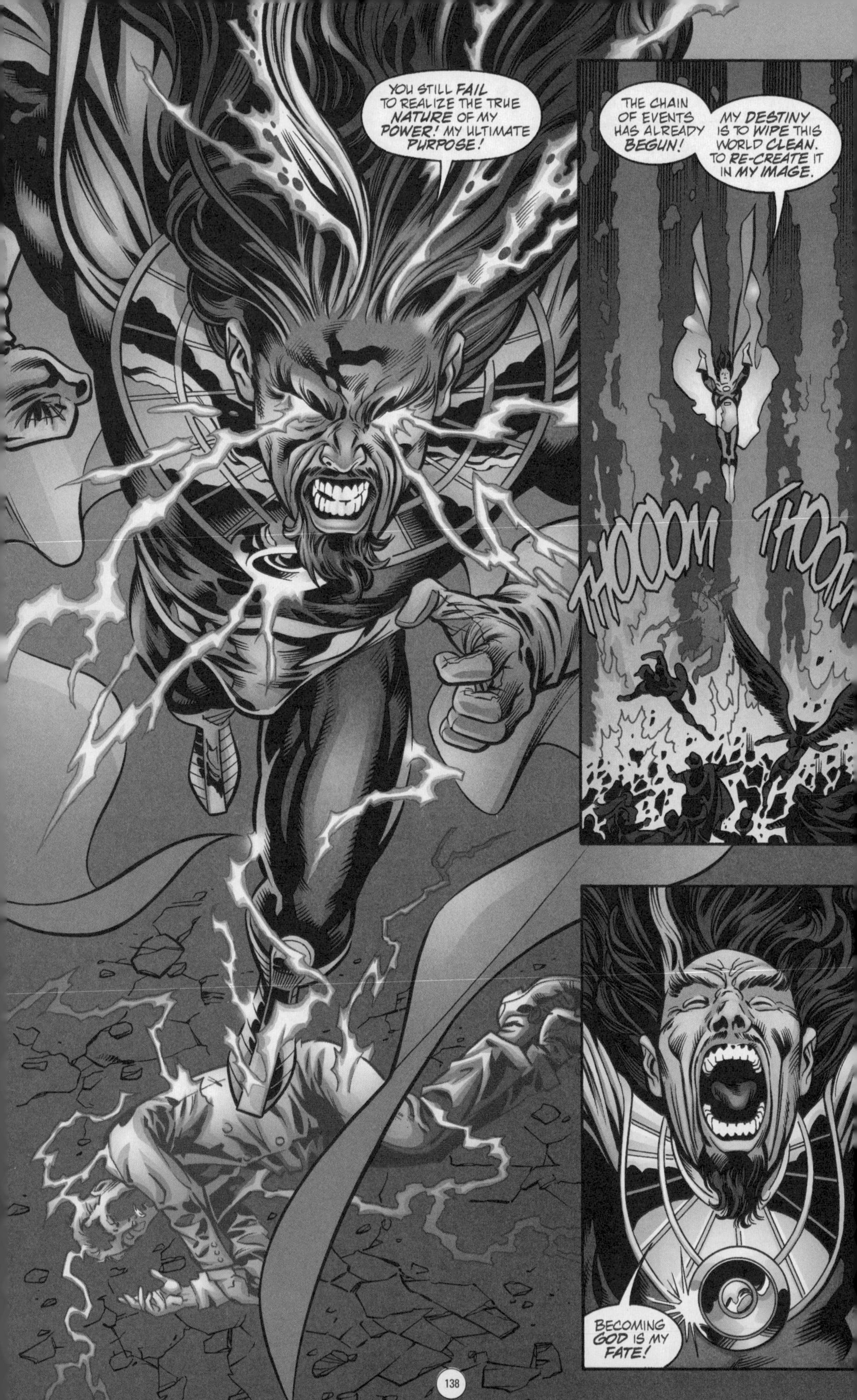
YOU STILL FAIL TO REALIZE THE TRUE NATURE OF MY POWER! MY ULTIMATE PURPOSE!
THE CHAIN OF EVENTS HAS ALREADY BEGUN!
MY DESTINY IS TO WIPE THIS WORLD CLEAN. TO RE-CREATE IT IN MY IMAGE.
THOOOM
BECOMING GOD IS MY FATE!

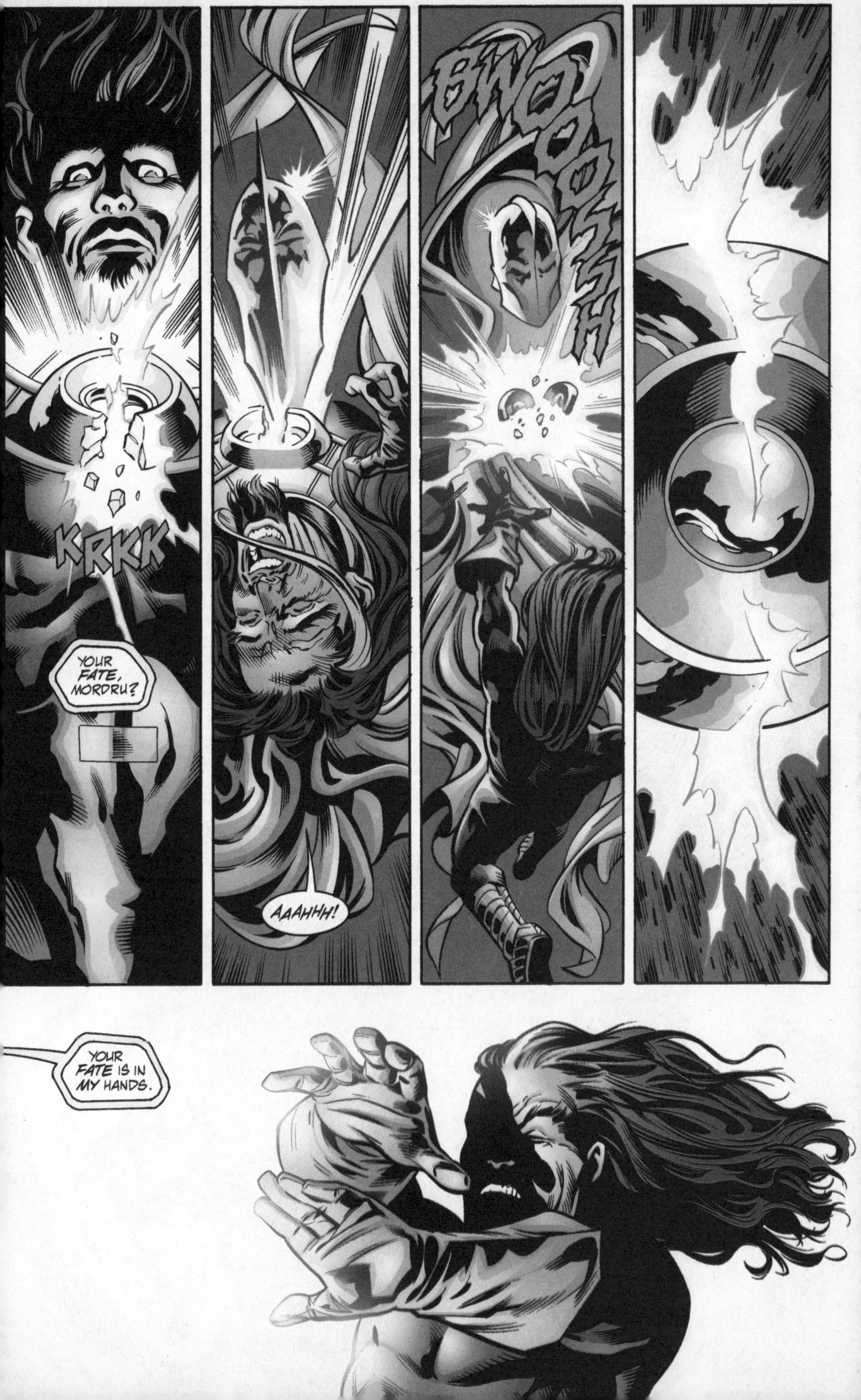

KRKK
YOUR FATE, MORDRU?
AAAHHH!
BWOOOOSH
YOUR FATE IS IN MY HANDS.

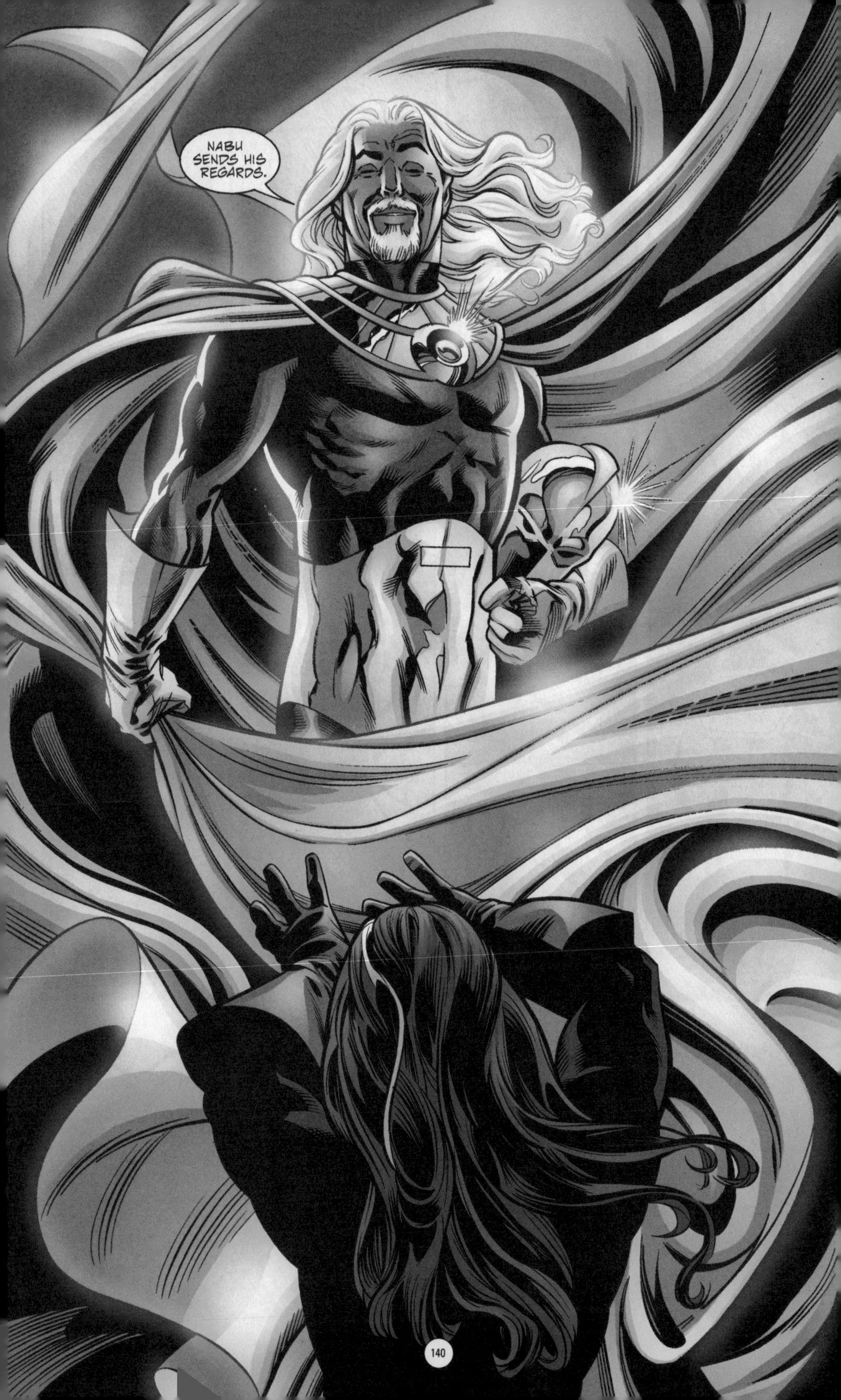
NABU SENDS HIS REGARDS.

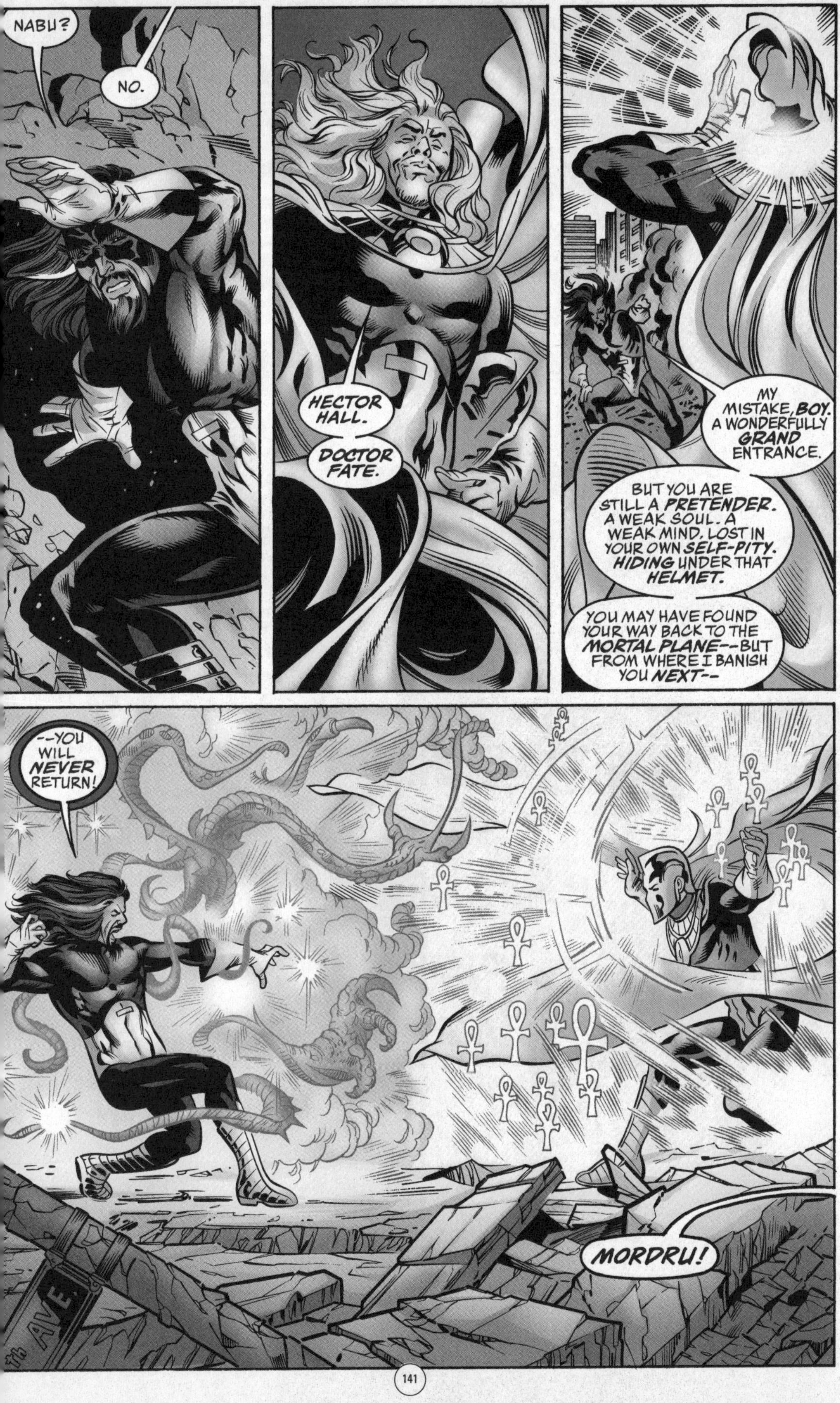
NABU?
NO.
HECTOR HALL.
DOCTOR FATE.
MY MISTAKE, BOY. A WONDERFULLY GRAND ENTRANCE.
BUT YOU ARE STILL A PRETENDER. A WEAK SOUL. A WEAK MIND. LOST IN YOUR OWN SELF-PITY. HIDING UNDER THAT HELMET.
YOU MAY HAVE FOUND YOUR WAY BACK TO THE MORTAL PLANE--BUT FROM WHERE I BANISH YOU NEXT--
--YOU WILL NEVER RETURN!
MORDRU!
AVE

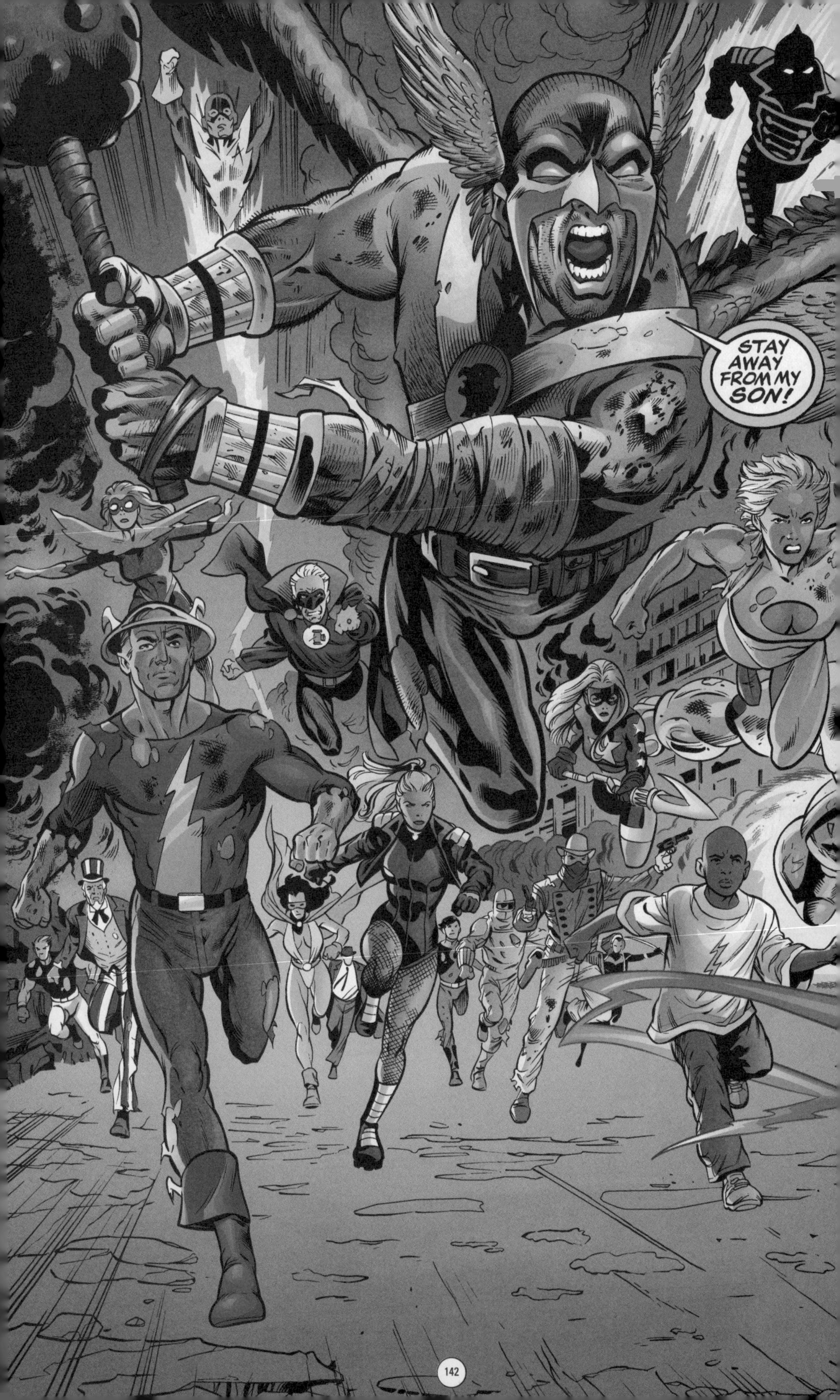
STAY AWAY FROM MY SON!

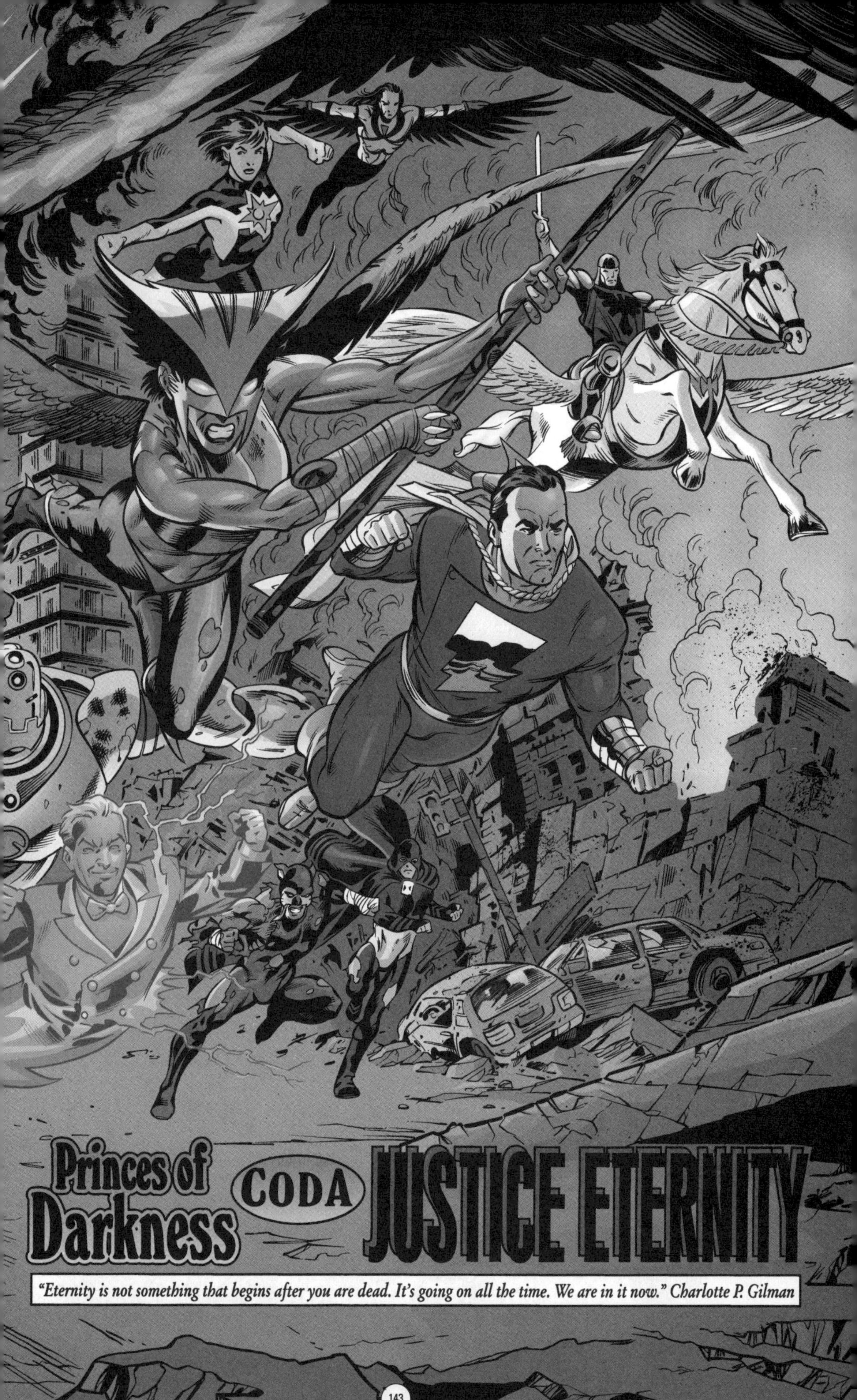

Princes of Darkness
CODA
JUSTICE ETERNITY
"Eternity is not something that begins after you are dead. It's going on all the time. We are in it now." Charlotte P. Gilman

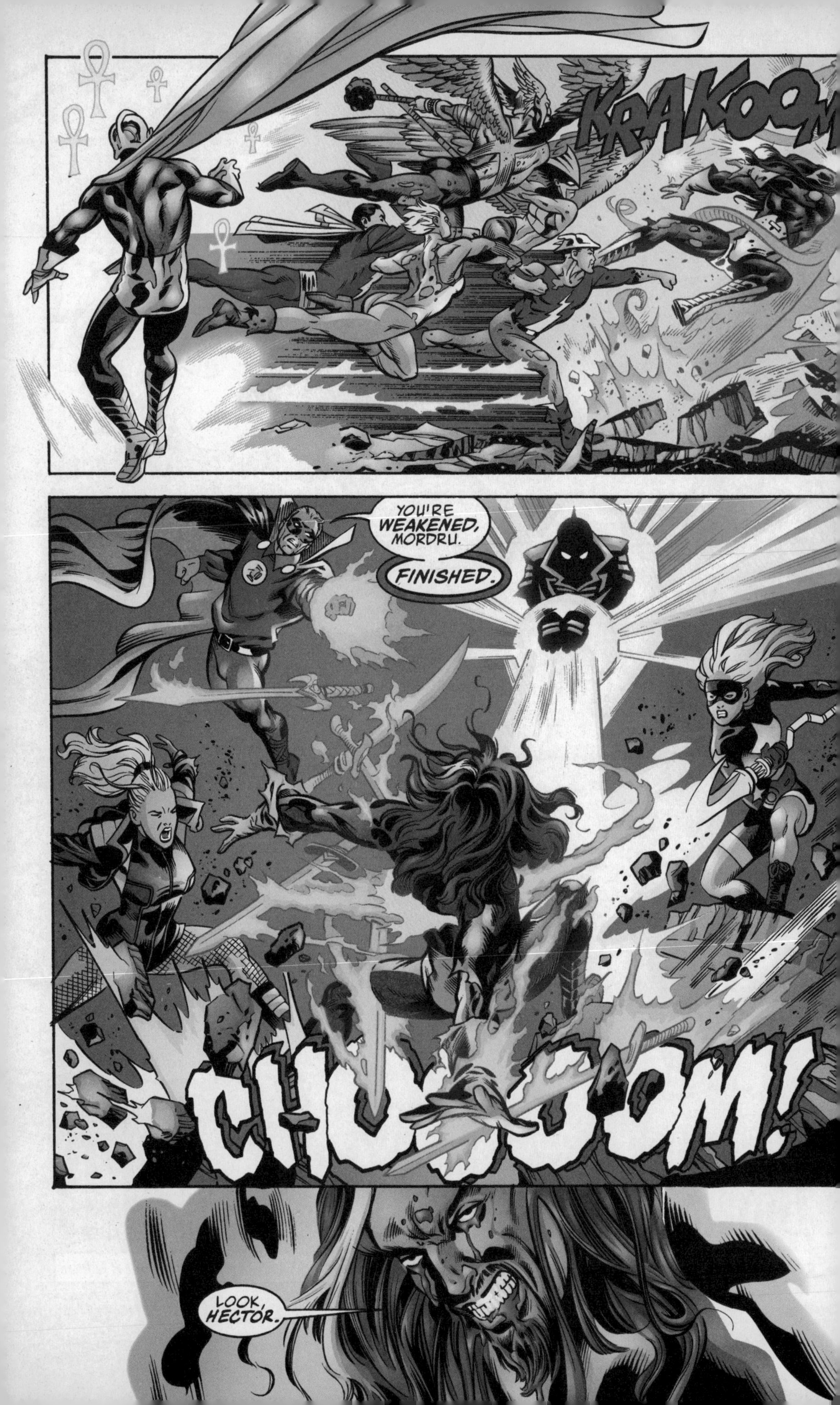
KRAKOOM
YOU'RE WEAKENED, MORDRU.
FINISHED.
LOOK, HECTOR.

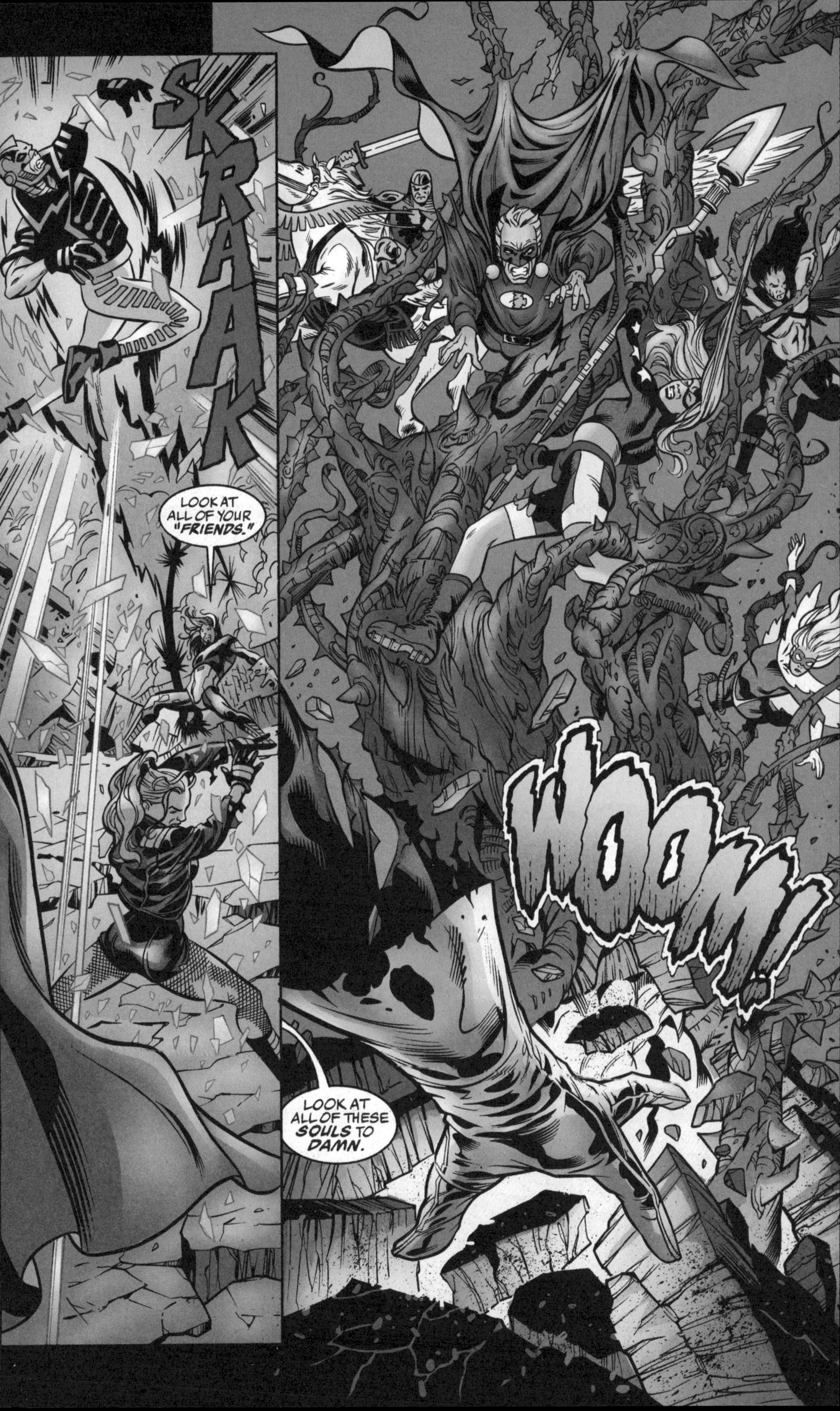
SKRAKK
LOOK AT ALL OF YOUR "FRIENDS."
WOOM!
LOOK AT ALL OF THESE SOULS TO DAMN.

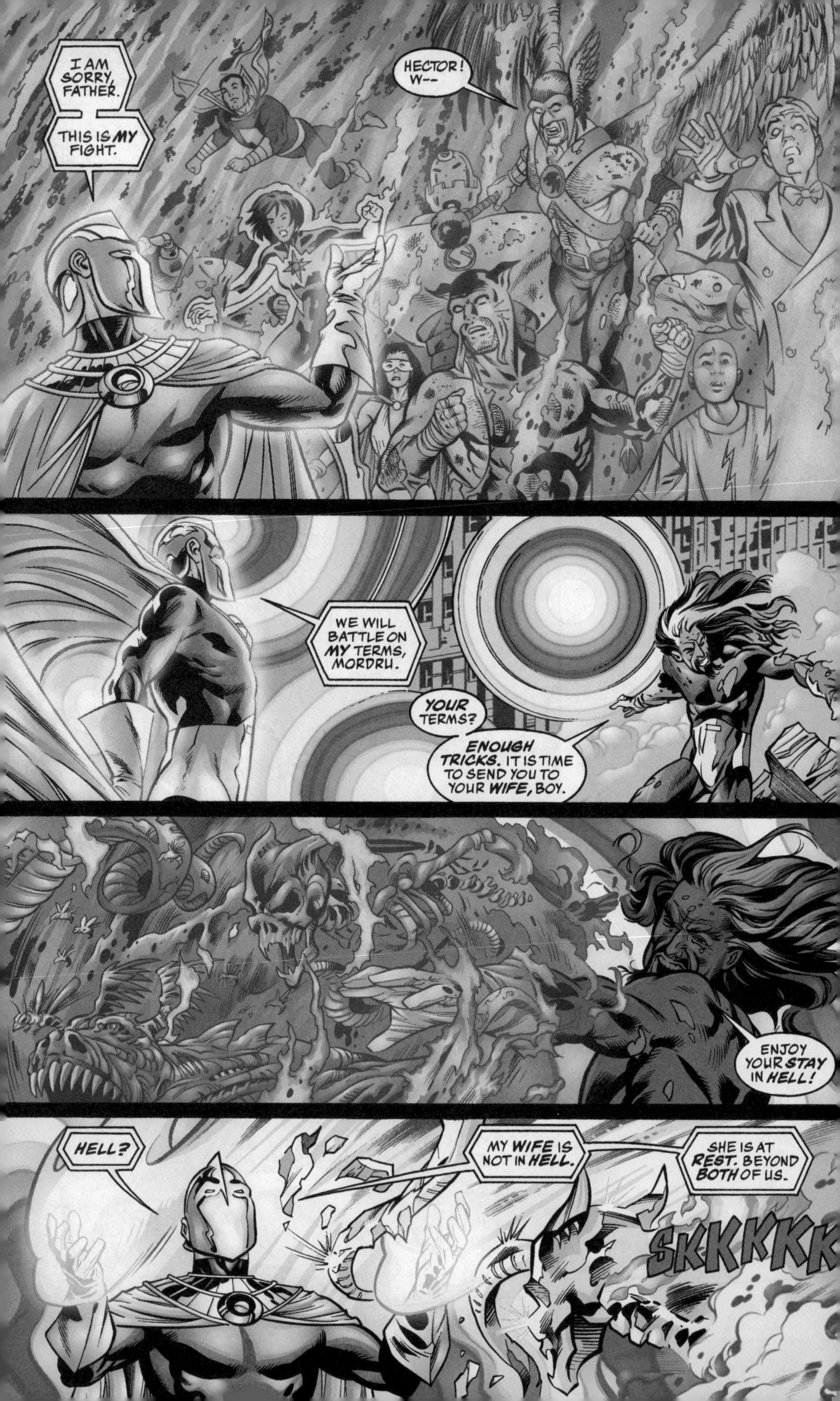

I AM SORRY, FATHER.
THIS IS MY FIGHT.
HECTOR! W--
WE WILL BATTLE ON MY TERMS, MORDRU.
YOUR TERMS?
ENOUGH TRICKS. IT IS TIME TO SEND YOU TO YOUR WIFE, BOY.
ENJOY YOUR STAY IN HELL!
HELL?
MY WIFE IS NOT IN HELL.
SHE IS AT REST. BEYOND BOTH OF US.
SKKKKK

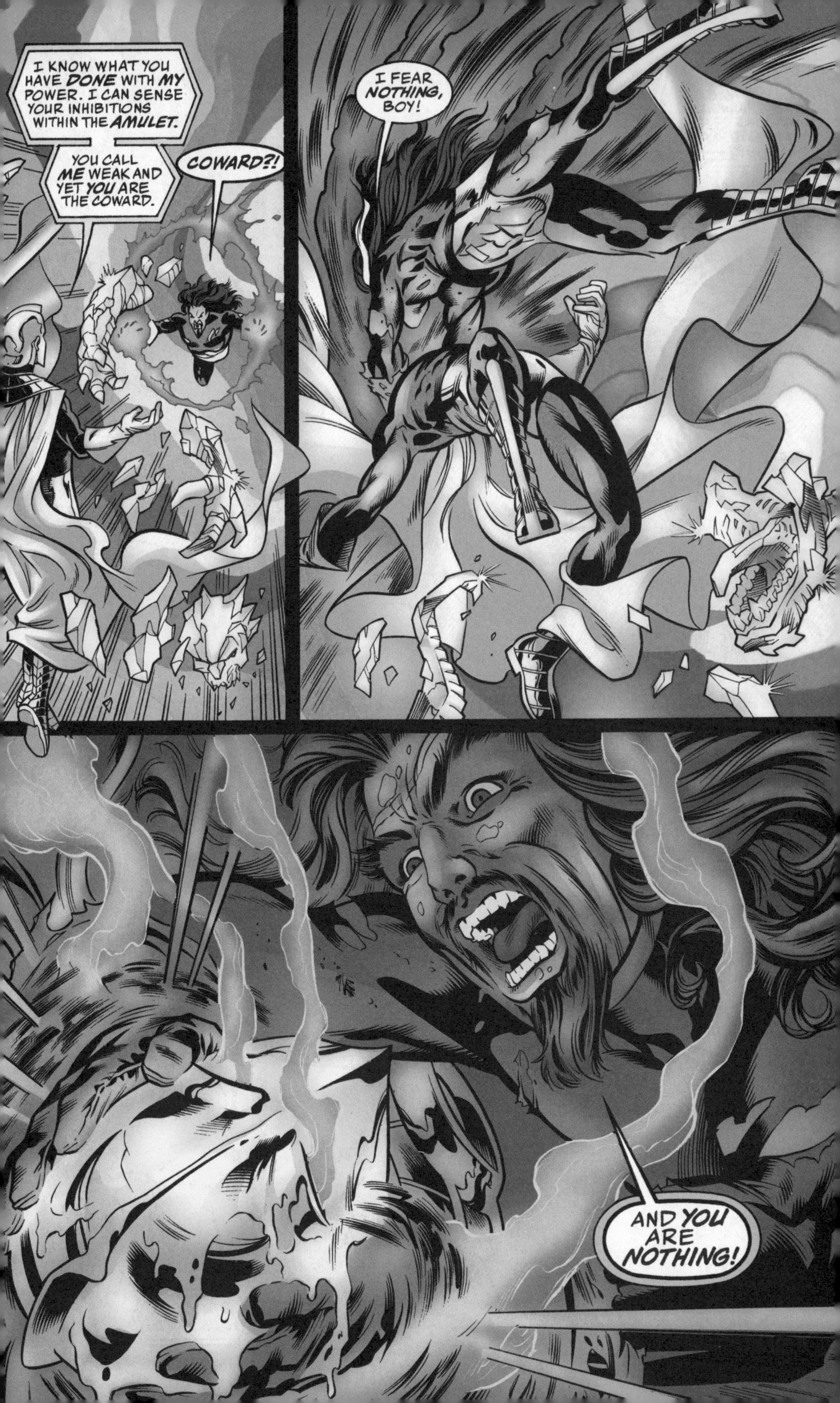
I KNOW WHAT YOU HAVE DONE WITH MY POWER. I CAN SENSE YOUR INHIBITIONS WITHIN THE AMULET.
YOU CALL ME WEAK AND YET YOU ARE THE COWARD.
COWARD?!
I FEAR NOTHING, BOY!
AND YOU ARE NOTHING!

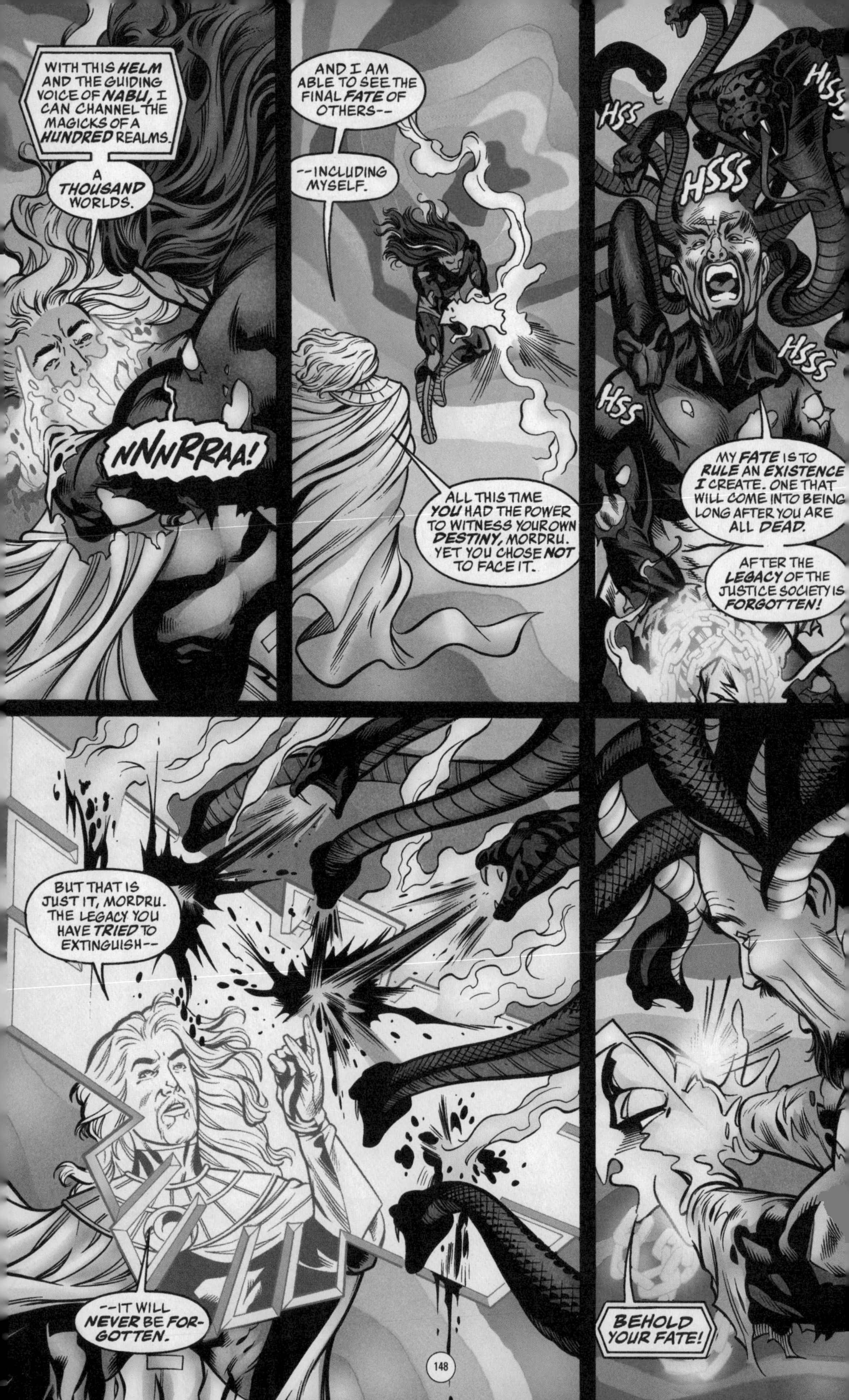
WITH THIS HELM AND THE GUIDING VOICE OF NABU, I CAN CHANNEL THE MAGICKS OF A HUNDRED REALMS.
A THOUSAND WORLDS.
NNNRRAA!
AND I AM ABLE TO SEE THE FINAL FATE OF OTHERS--
--INCLUDING MYSELF.
ALL THIS TIME YOU HAD THE POWER TO WITNESS YOUR OWN DESTINY, MORDRU. YET YOU CHOSE NOT TO FACE IT.
HSS
HISSS
HSSS
HSSS
HSS
MY FATE IS TO RULE AN EXISTENCE I CREATE. ONE THAT WILL COME INTO BEING LONG AFTER YOU ARE ALL DEAD.
AFTER THE LEGACY OF THE JUSTICE SOCIETY IS FORGOTTEN!
BUT THAT IS JUST IT, MORDRU. THE LEGACY YOU HAVE TRIED TO EXTINGUISH--
--IT WILL NEVER BE FORGOTTEN.
BEHOLD YOUR FATE!

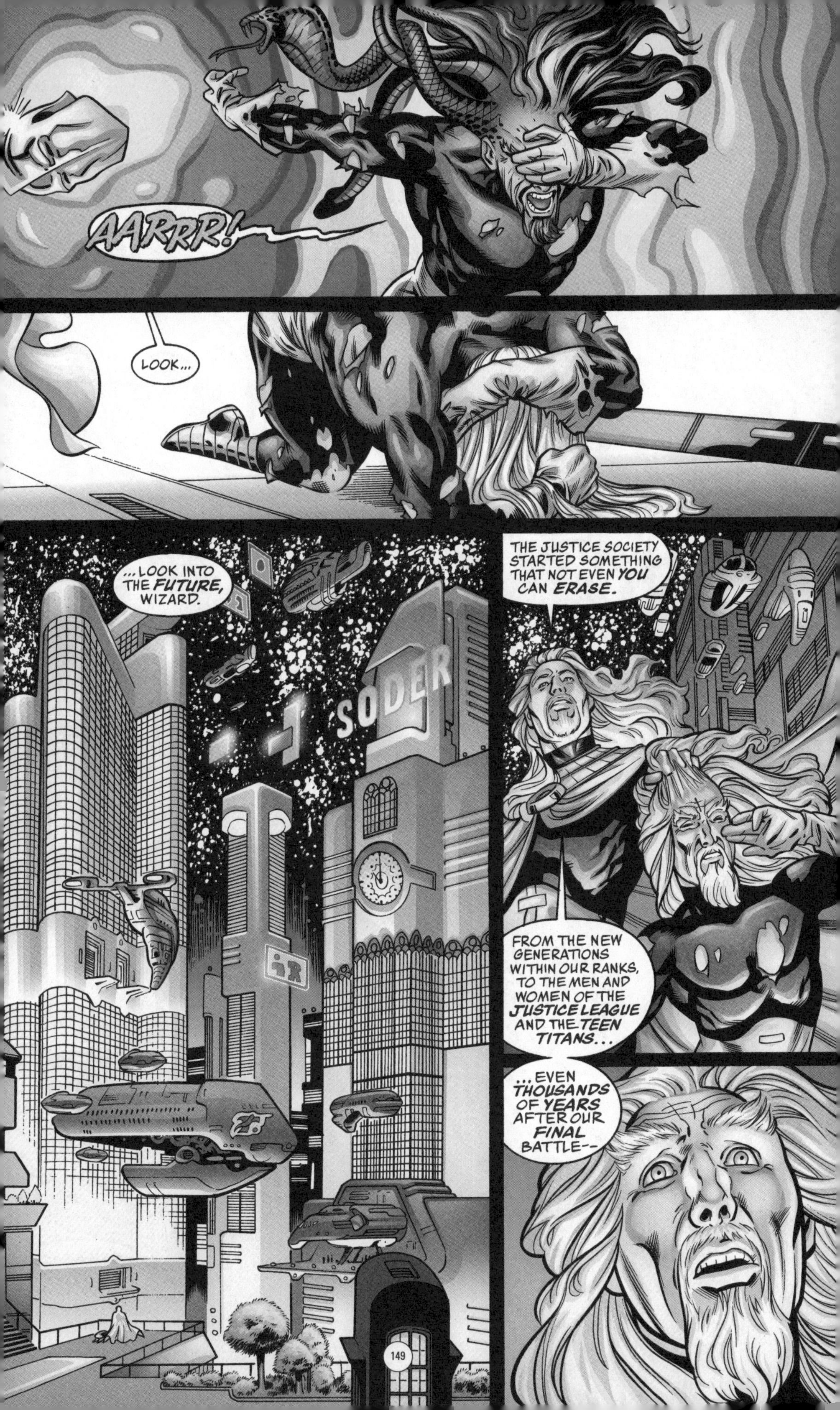

AARRR!
LOOK...
...LOOK INTO THE FUTURE, WIZARD.
SODER
THE JUSTICE SOCIETY STARTED SOMETHING THAT NOT EVEN YOU CAN ERASE.
FROM THE NEW GENERATIONS WITHIN OUR RANKS, TO THE MEN AND WOMEN OF THE JUSTICE LEAGUE AND THE TEEN TITANS...
...EVEN THOUSANDS OF YEARS AFTER OUR FINAL BATTLE--

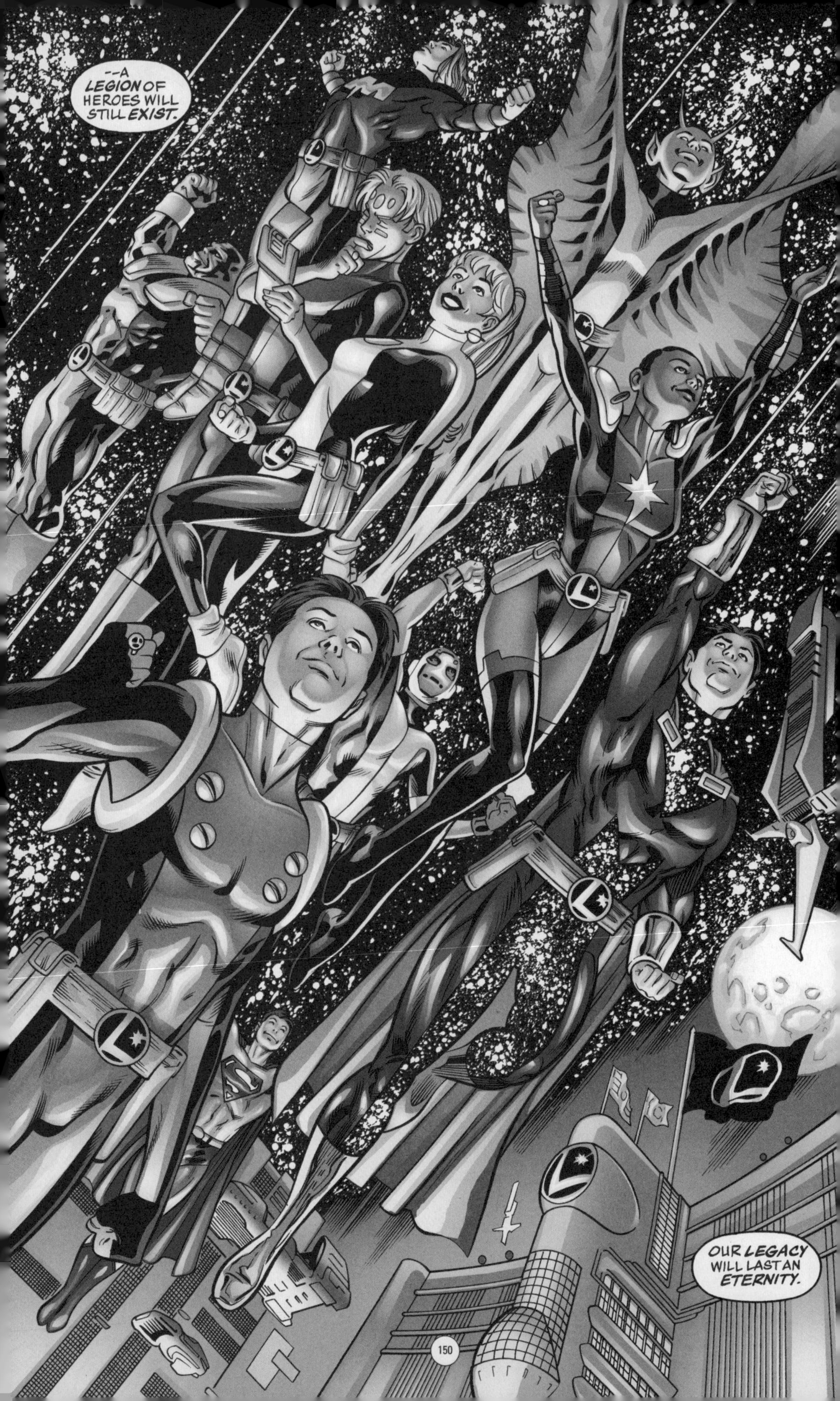
--A LEGION OF HEROES WILL STILL EXIST.
OUR LEGACY WILL LAST AN ETERNITY.

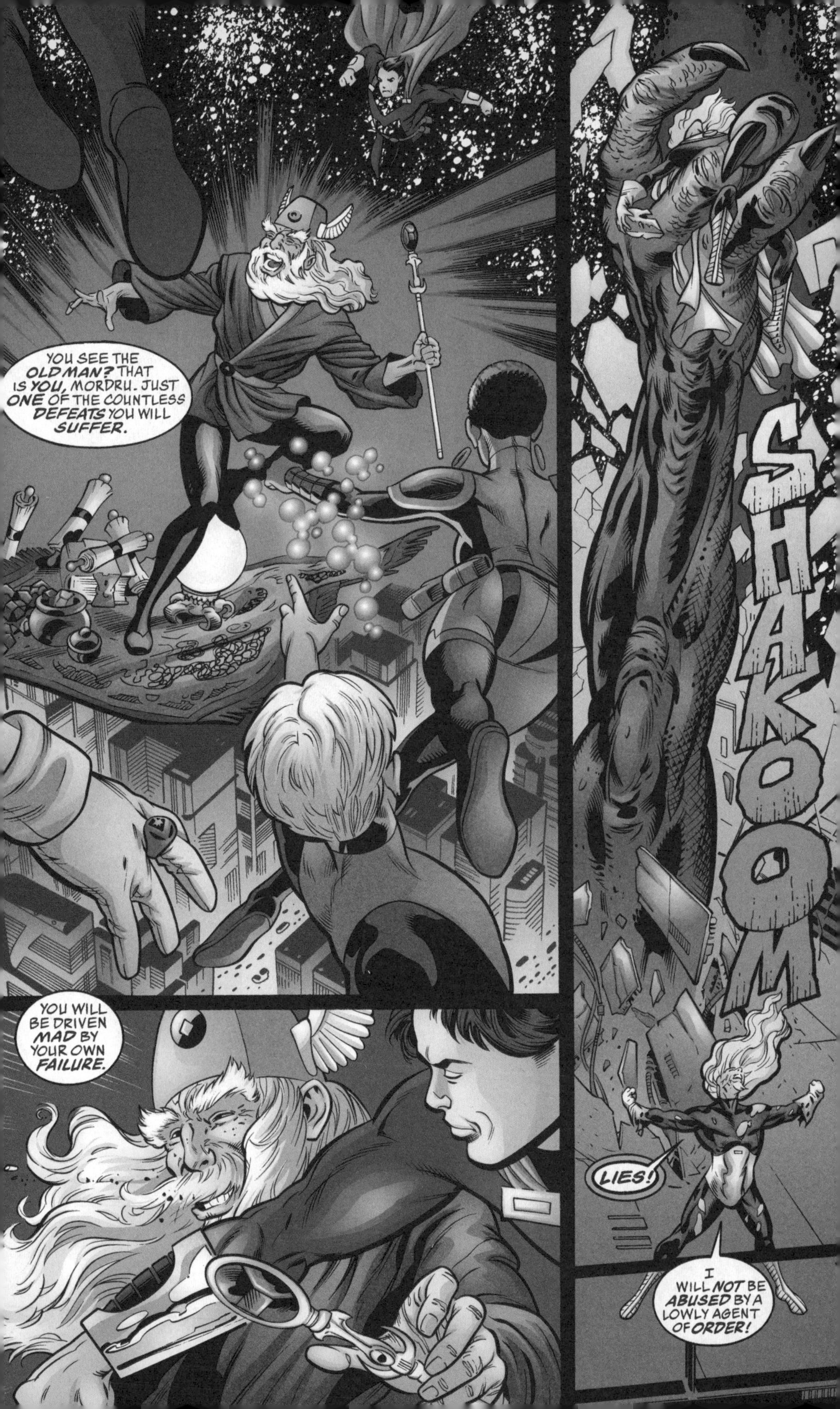
YOU SEE THE OLD MAN? THAT IS YOU, MORDRU. JUST ONE OF THE COUNTLESS DEFEATS YOU WILL SUFFER.
SHAKOOM
YOU WILL BE DRIVEN MAD BY YOUR OWN FAILURE.
LIES!
I WILL NOT BE ABUSED BY A LOWLY AGENT OF ORDER!

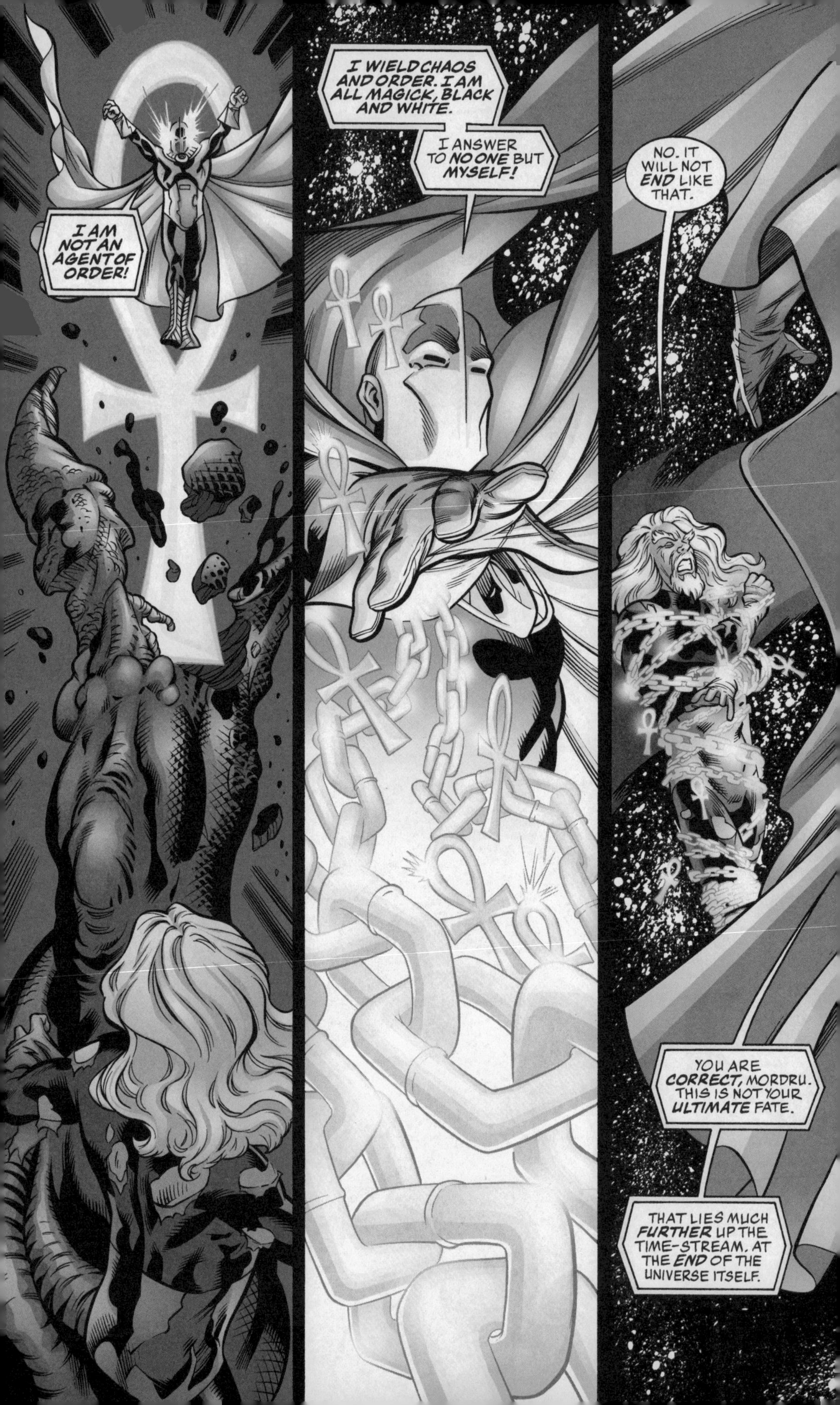
I AM NOT AN AGENT OF ORDER!
I WIELD CHAOS AND ORDER. I AM ALL MAGICK, BLACK AND WHITE.
I ANSWER TO NO ONE BUT MYSELF!
NO. IT WILL NOT END LIKE THAT.
YOU ARE CORRECT, MORDRU. THIS IS NOT YOUR ULTIMATE FATE.
THAT LIES MUCH FURTHER UP THE TIME-STREAM, AT THE END OF THE UNIVERSE ITSELF.

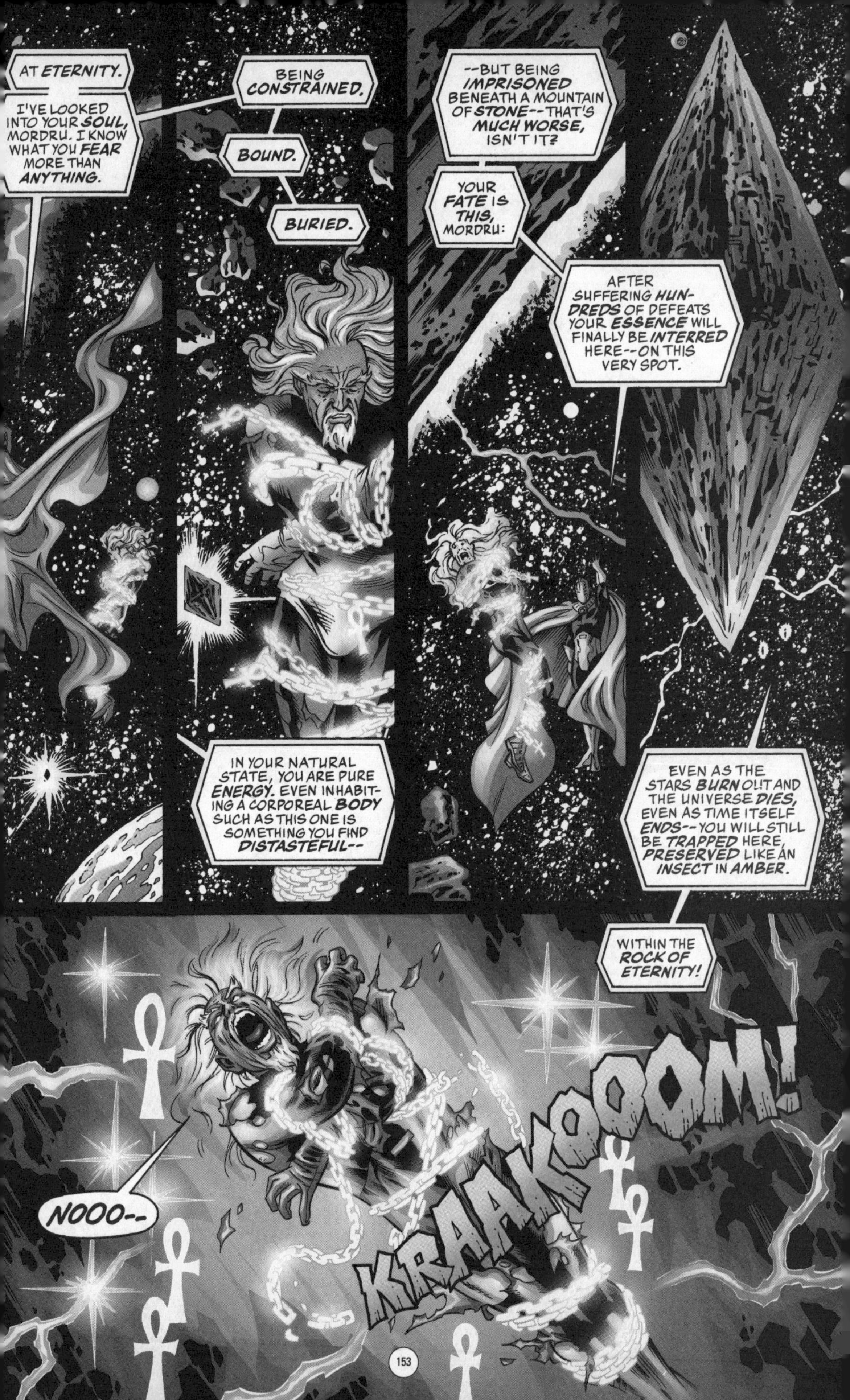

AT ETERNITY.
I'VE LOOKED INTO YOUR SOUL, MORDRU. I KNOW WHAT YOU FEAR MORE THAN ANYTHING.
BEING CONSTRAINED.
BOUND.
BURIED.
IN YOUR NATURAL STATE, YOU ARE PURE ENERGY. EVEN INHABITING A CORPOREAL BODY SUCH AS THIS ONE IS SOMETHING YOU FIND DISTASTEFUL--
--BUT BEING IMPRISONED BENEATH A MOUNTAIN OF STONE--THAT'S MUCH WORSE, ISN'T IT?
YOUR FATE IS THIS, MORDRU:
AFTER SUFFERING HUNDREDS OF DEFEATS YOUR ESSENCE WILL FINALLY BE INTERRED HERE--ON THIS VERY SPOT.
EVEN AS THE STARS BURN OUT AND THE UNIVERSE DIES, EVEN AS TIME ITSELF ENDS--YOU WILL STILL BE TRAPPED HERE, PRESERVED LIKE AN INSECT IN AMBER.
WITHIN THE ROCK OF ETERNITY!
NOOO--
KRAAKOOOM!

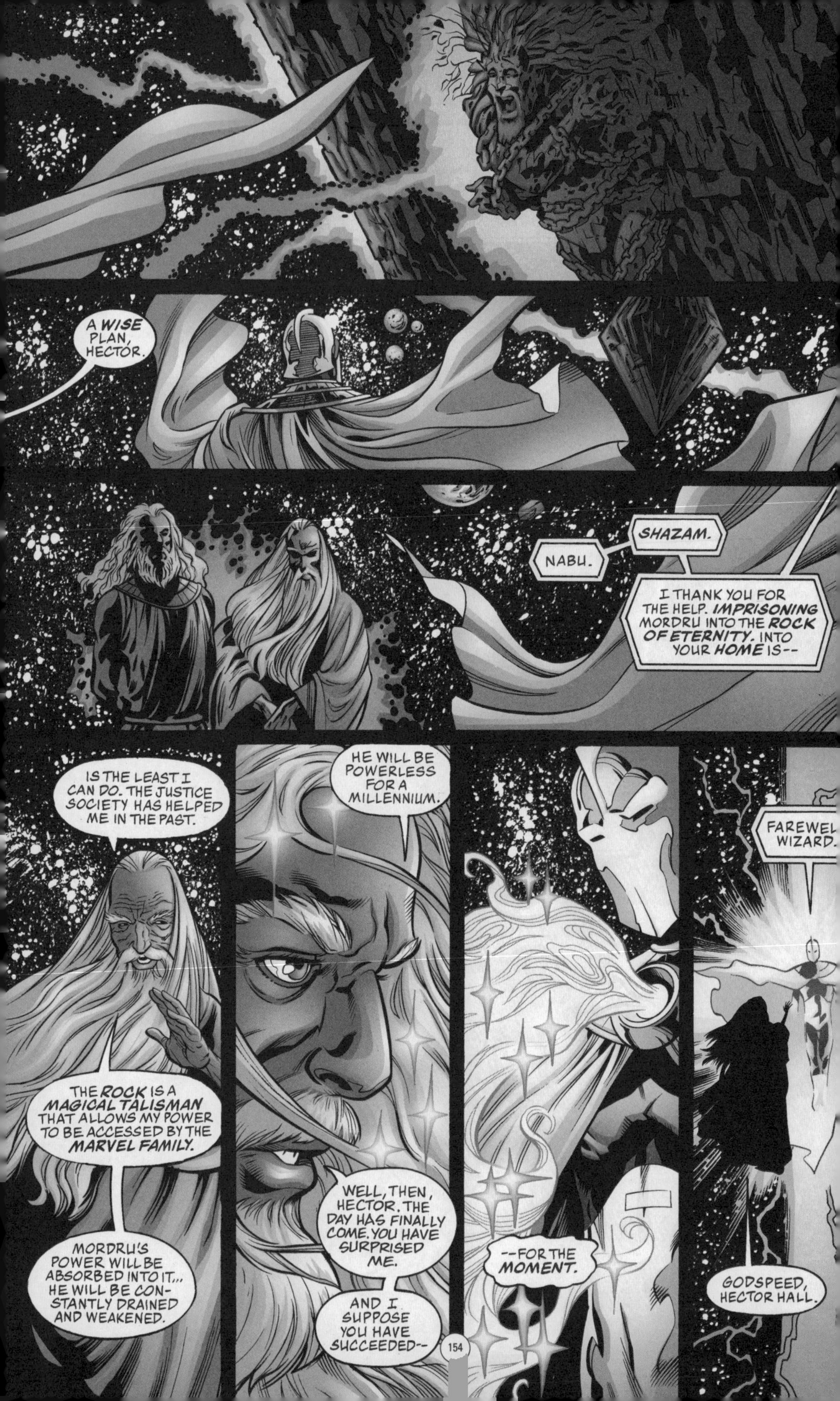

A WISE PLAN, HECTOR.
NABU.
SHAZAM.
I THANK YOU FOR THE HELP. IMPRISONING MORDRU INTO THE ROCK OF ETERNITY. INTO YOUR HOME IS--
IS THE LEAST I CAN DO. THE JUSTICE SOCIETY HAS HELPED ME IN THE PAST.
THE ROCK IS A MAGICAL TALISMAN THAT ALLOWS MY POWER TO BE ACCESSED BY THE MARVEL FAMILY.
MORDRU'S POWER WILL BE ABSORBED INTO IT... HE WILL BE CONSTANTLY DRAINED AND WEAKENED.
HE WILL BE POWERLESS FOR A MILLENNIUM.
WELL, THEN, HECTOR. THE DAY HAS FINALLY COME. YOU HAVE SURPRISED ME.
AND I SUPPOSE YOU HAVE SUCCEEDED--
--FOR THE MOMENT.
FAREWEL WIZARD.
GODSPEED, HECTOR HALL.

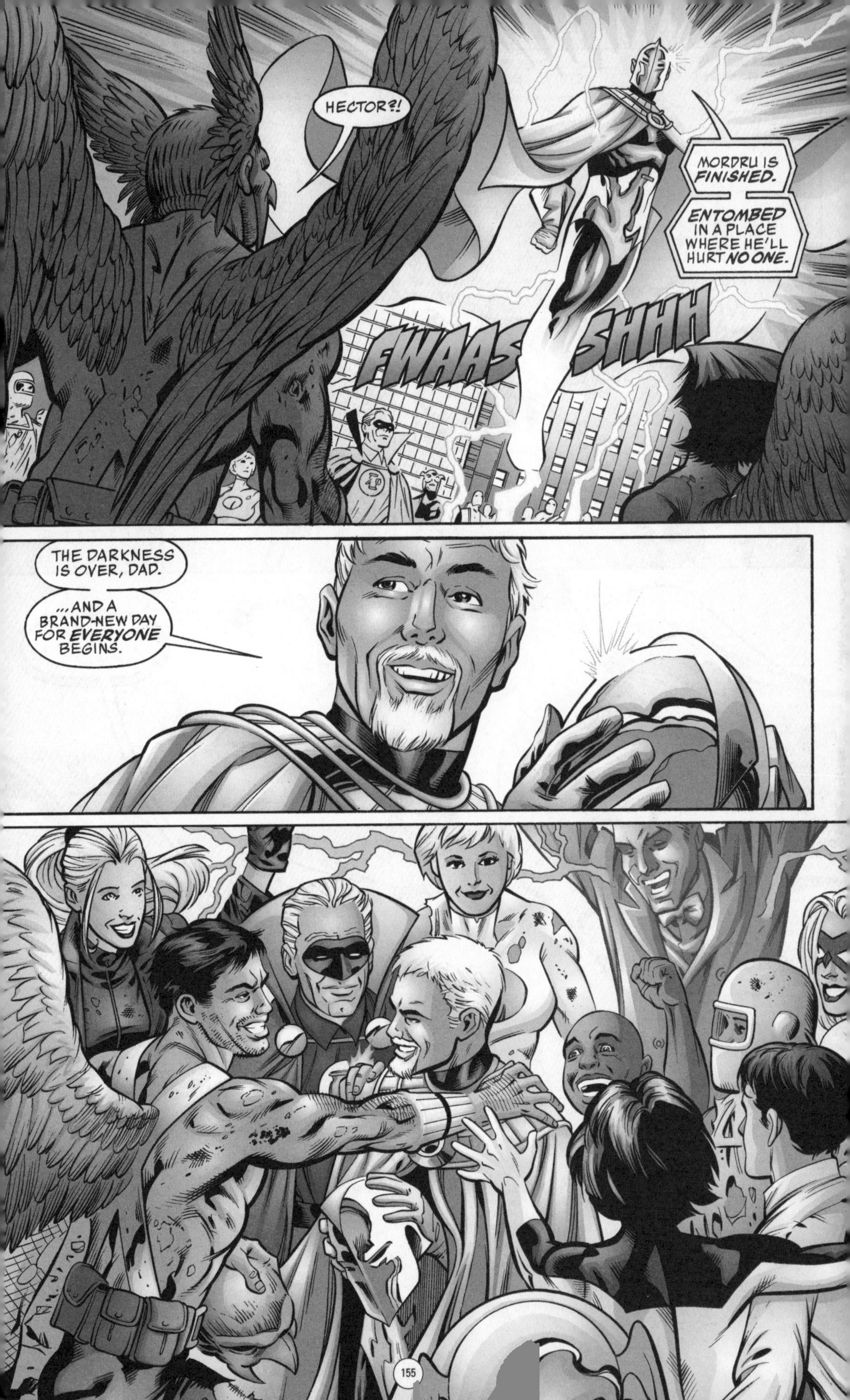
HECTOR?!
MORDRU IS FINISHED.
ENTOMBED IN A PLACE WHERE HE'LL HURT NO ONE.
FWAASSHHH
THE DARKNESS IS OVER, DAD.
...AND A BRAND-NEW DAY FOR EVERYONE BEGINS.

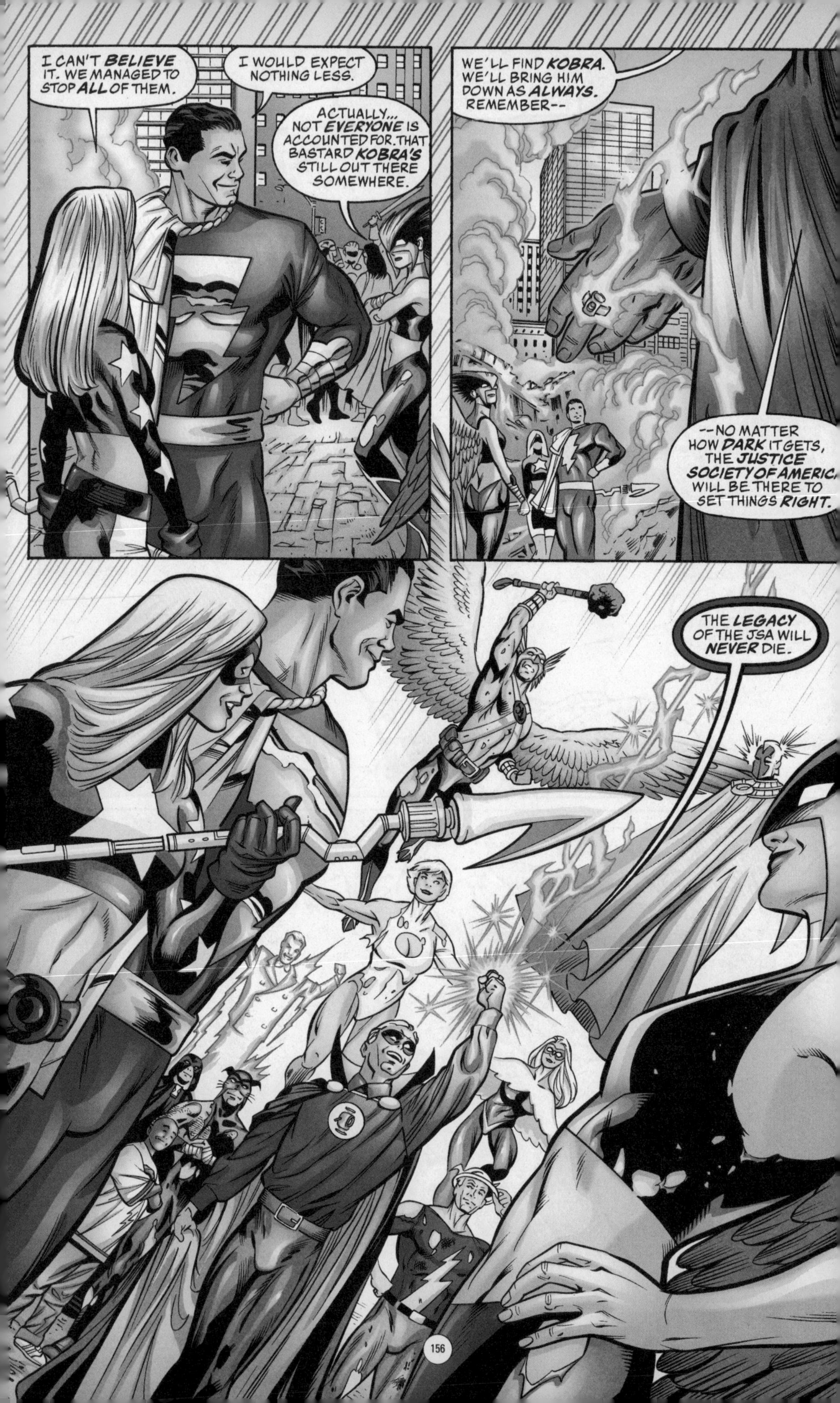

I CAN'T BELIEVE IT. WE MANAGED TO STOP ALL OF THEM.
I WOULD EXPECT NOTHING LESS.
ACTUALLY... NOT EVERYONE IS ACCOUNTED FOR. THAT BASTARD KOBRA'S STILL OUT THERE SOMEWHERE.
WE'LL FIND KOBRA. WE'LL BRING HIM DOWN AS ALWAYS. REMEMBER--
--NO MATTER HOW DARK IT GETS, THE JUSTICE SOCIETY OF AMERIC WILL BE THERE TO SET THINGS RIGHT.
THE LEGACY OF THE JSA WILL NEVER DIE.

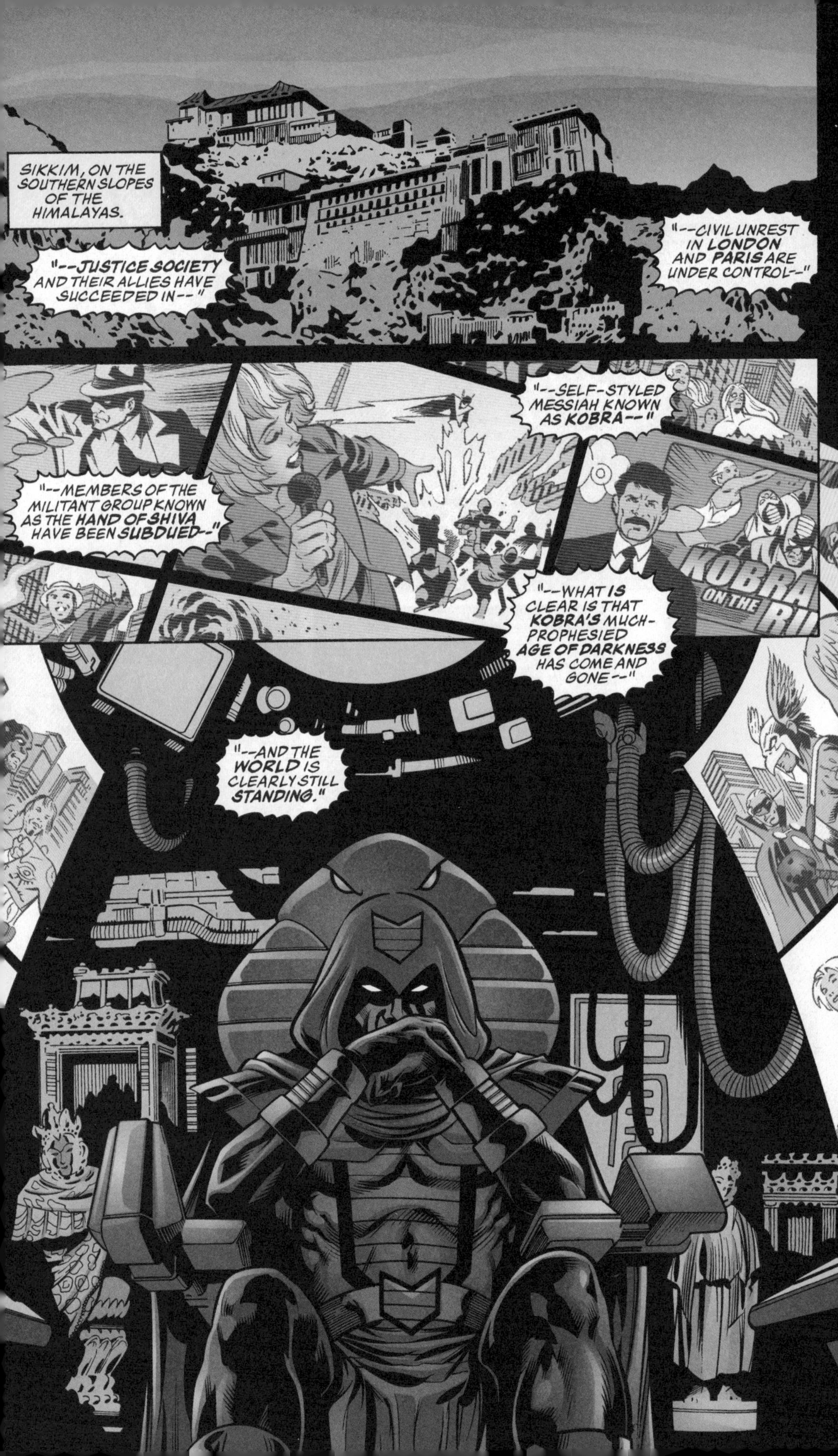

SIKKIM, ON THE SOUTHERN SLOPES OF THE HIMALAYAS.
"--JUSTICE SOCIETY AND THEIR ALLIES HAVE SUCCEEDED IN--"
"--CIVIL UNREST IN LONDON AND PARIS ARE UNDER CONTROL--"
"--SELF-STYLED MESSIAH KNOWN AS KOBRA--"
"--MEMBERS OF THE MILITANT GROUP KNOWN AS THE HAND OF SHIVA HAVE BEEN SUBDUED--"
KOBRA ON THE RU
"--WHAT IS CLEAR IS THAT KOBRA'S MUCH-PROPHESIED AGE OF DARKNESS HAS COME AND GONE--"
"--AND THE WORLD IS CLEARLY STILL STANDING."

"--A SPONTANEOUS CELEBRATION OF JOY ERUPTED--"

"--OFFICIALS HAVE YET TO RELEASE FIGURES BUT ESTIMAT-- OF THE DAMAGE MAY--"

"THIS IS JENNY FRITZ, REPORTING TO YOU LIVE FROM--"

"--UNCLEAR WHY THEY REACTED IN THIS--"

VZZZZTT

MAHADIR--?

DEVAK--?

WHY HAVE WE LOST *POWER*?

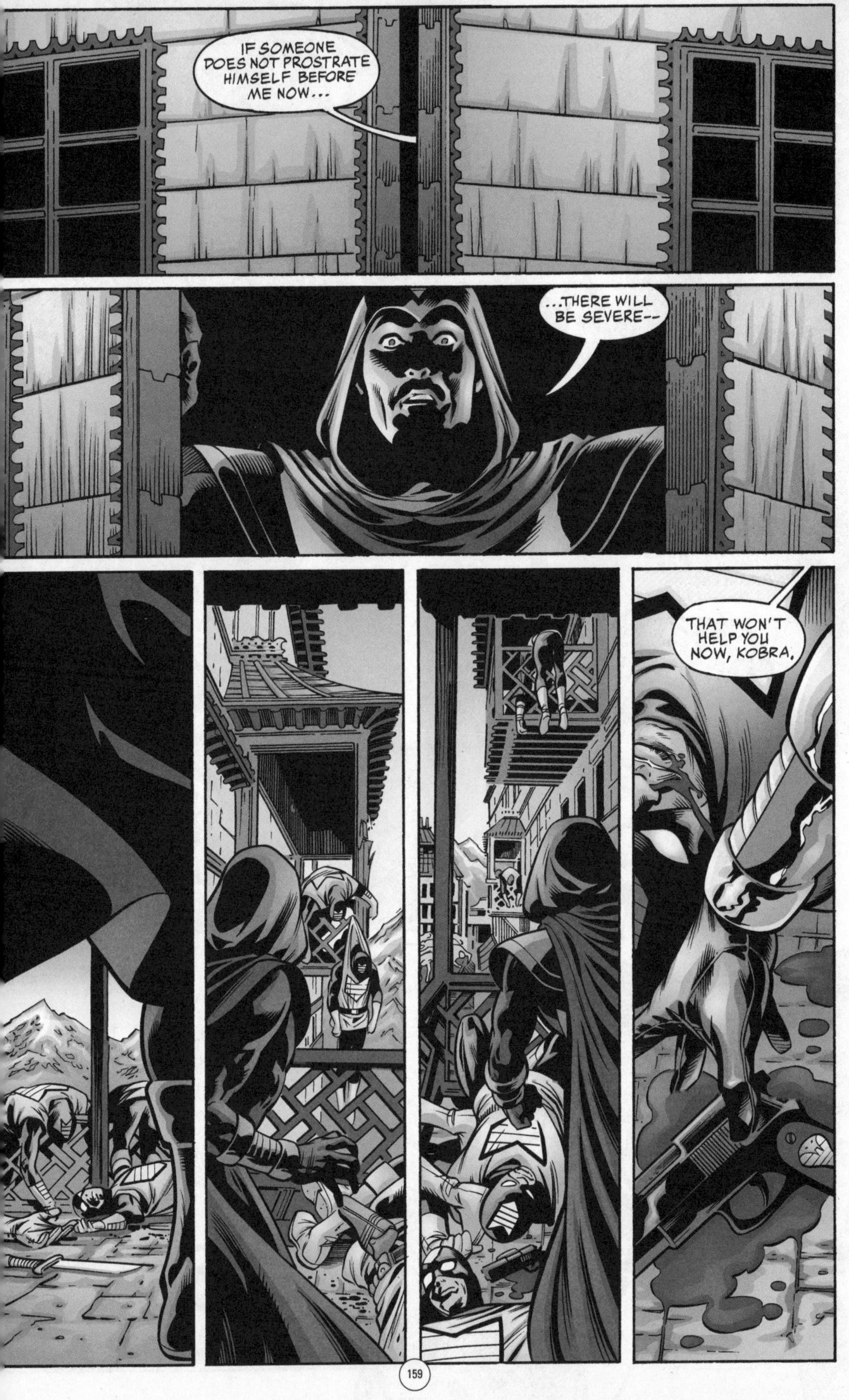
IF SOMEONE DOES NOT PROSTRATE HIMSELF BEFORE ME NOW...
...THERE WILL BE SEVERE--
THAT WON'T HELP YOU NOW, KOBRA.

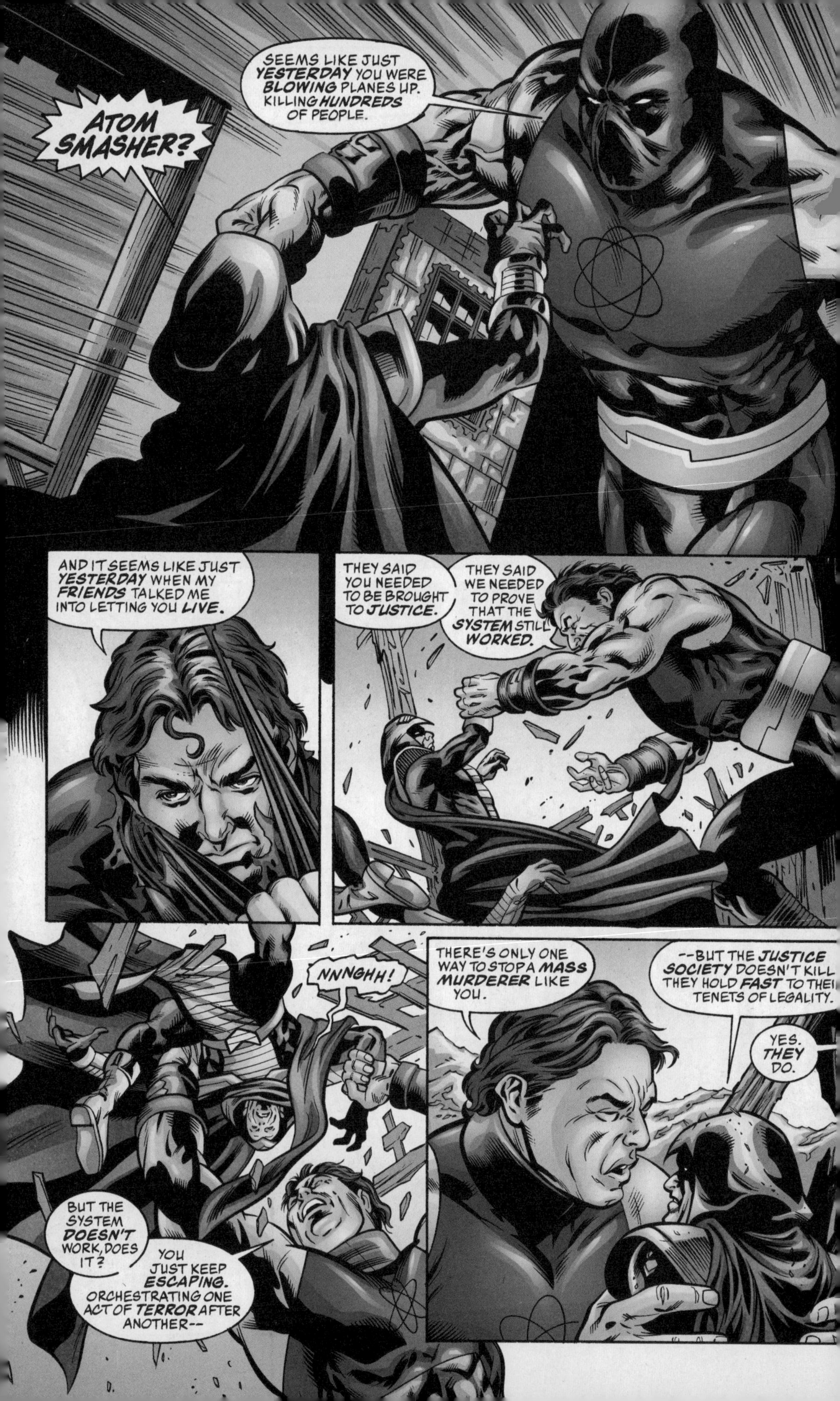
SEEMS LIKE JUST YESTERDAY YOU WERE BLOWING PLANES UP. KILLING HUNDREDS OF PEOPLE.
ATOM SMASHER?
AND IT SEEMS LIKE JUST YESTERDAY WHEN MY FRIENDS TALKED ME INTO LETTING YOU LIVE.
THEY SAID YOU NEEDED TO BE BROUGHT TO JUSTICE.
THEY SAID WE NEEDED TO PROVE THAT THE SYSTEM STILL WORKED.
NNNGHH!
BUT THE SYSTEM DOESN'T WORK, DOES IT?
YOU JUST KEEP ESCAPING. ORCHESTRATING ONE ACT OF TERROR AFTER ANOTHER--
THERE'S ONLY ONE WAY TO STOP A MASS MURDERER LIKE YOU.
--BUT THE JUSTICE SOCIETY DOESN'T KILL THEY HOLD FAST TO THEI TENETS OF LEGALITY.
YES. THEY DO.

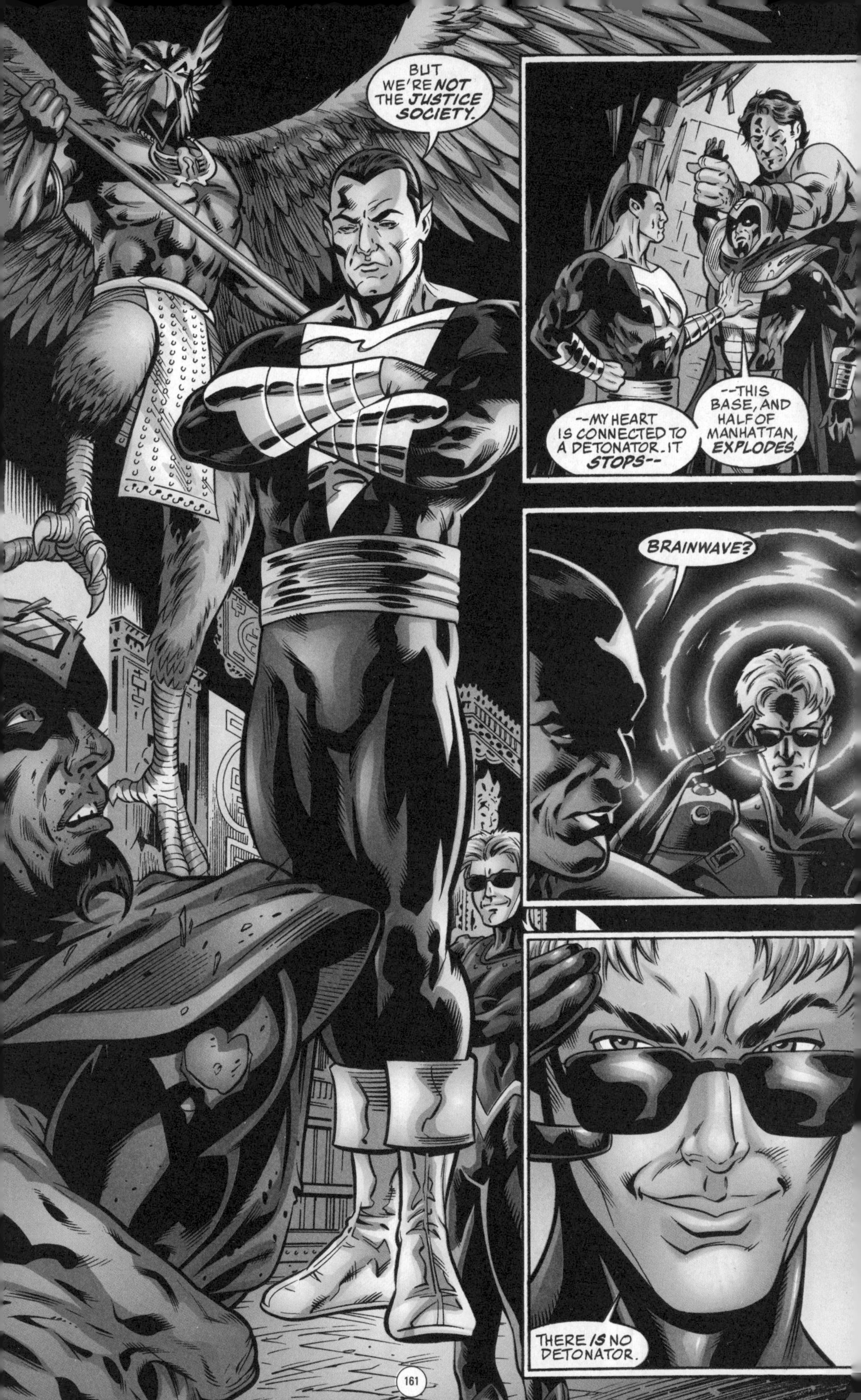
BUT WE'RE NOT THE JUSTICE SOCIETY.
--MY HEART IS CONNECTED TO A DETONATOR. IT STOPS--
--THIS BASE, AND HALF OF MANHATTAN, EXPLODES.
BRAINWAVE?
THERE IS NO DETONATOR.

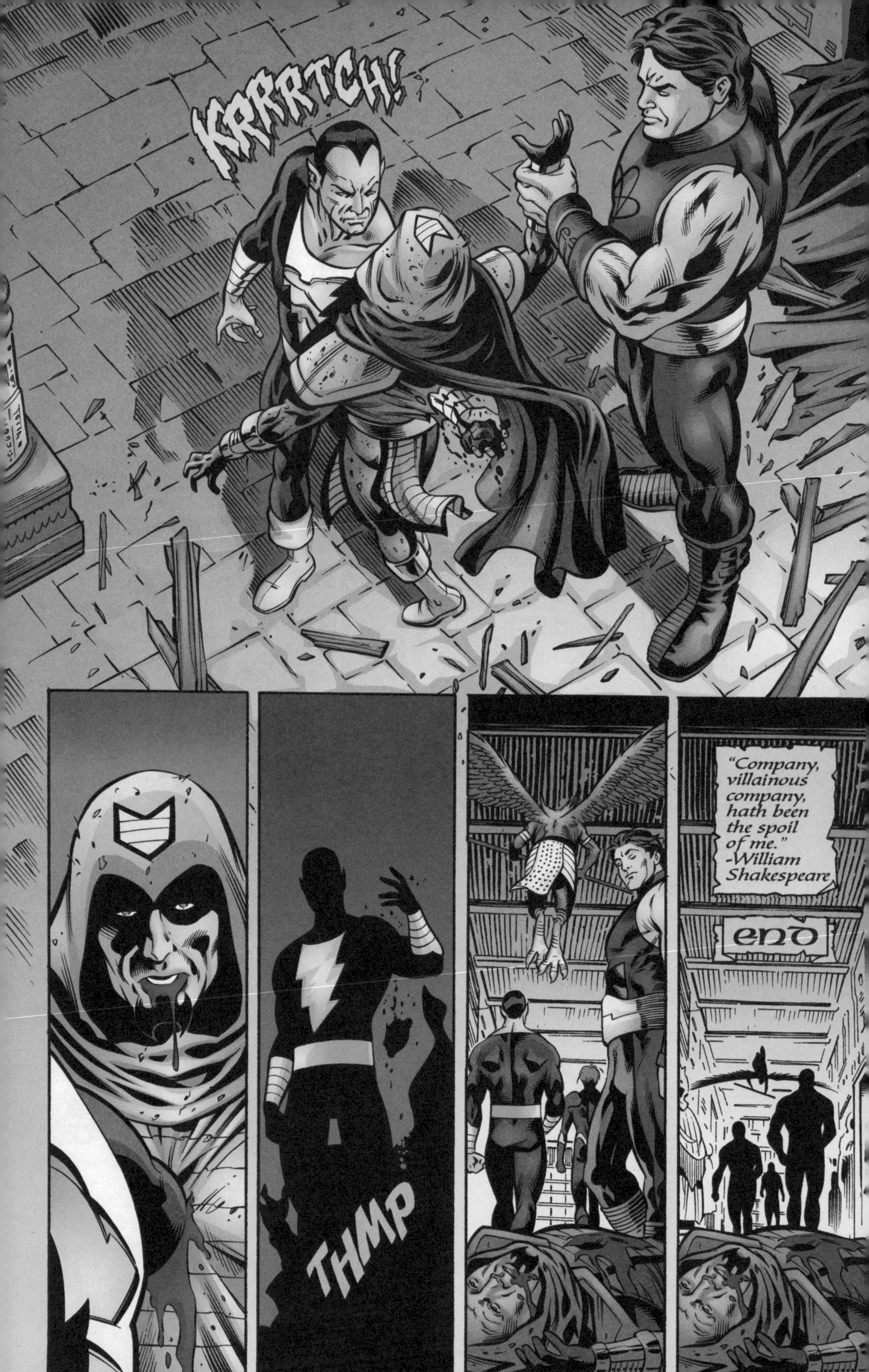
KRRRTCH!
THMP
"Company, villainous company, hath been the spoil of me."
-William Shakespeare
END

-And thanks to David Goyer for a great ride.

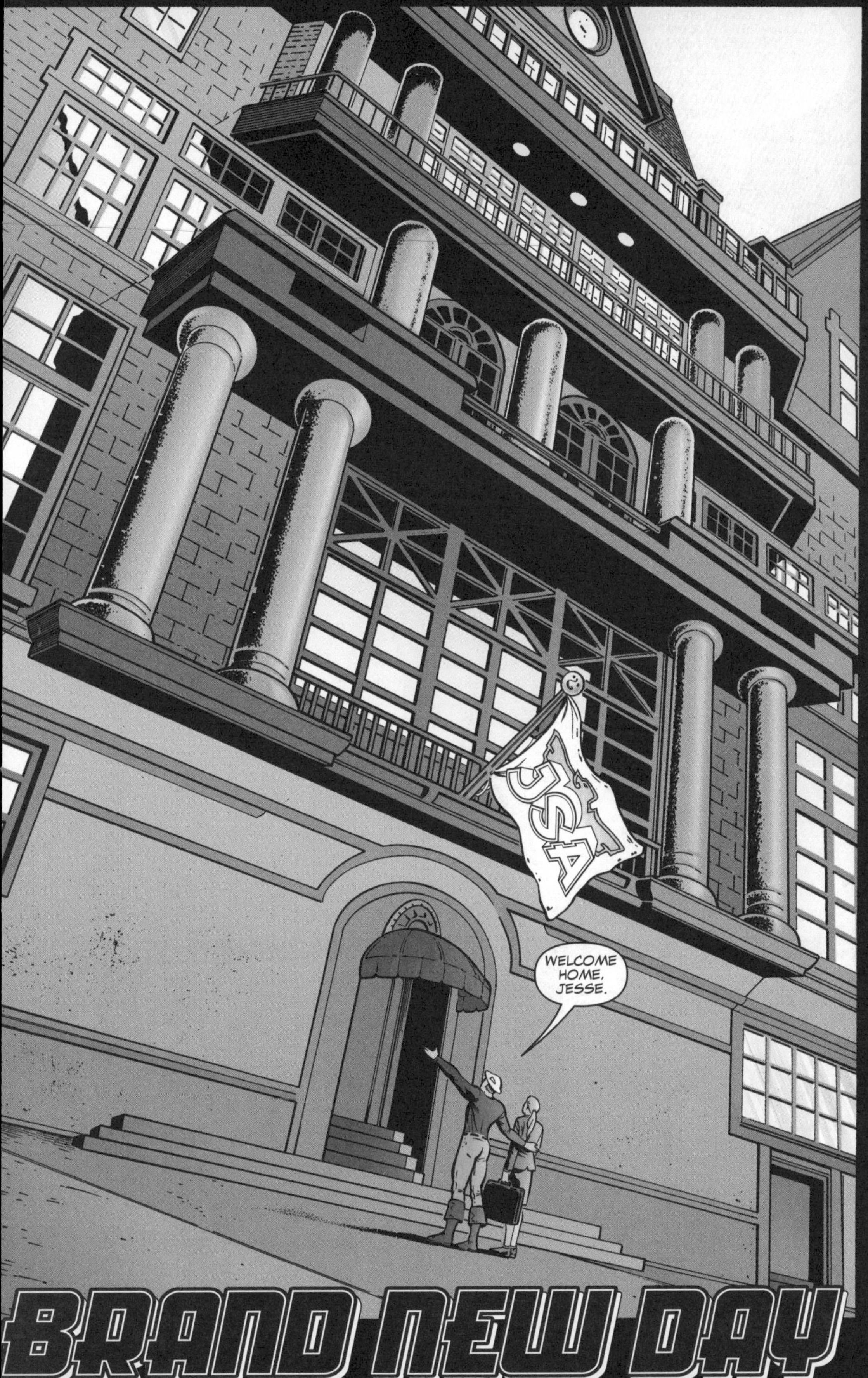
JSA
WELCOME HOME, JESSE.
BRAND NEW DAY

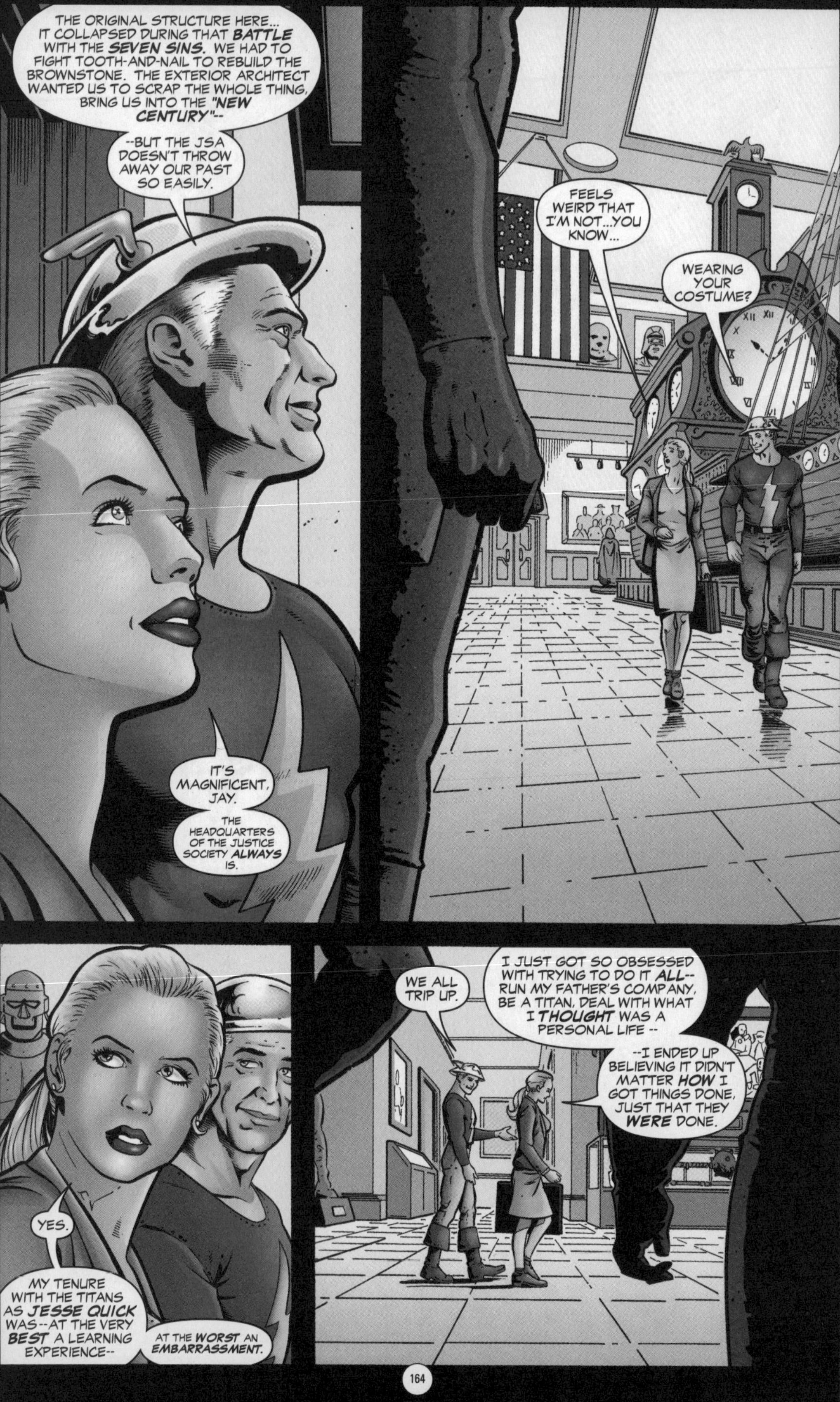
THE ORIGINAL STRUCTURE HERE... IT COLLAPSED DURING THAT BATTLE WITH THE SEVEN SINS. WE HAD TO FIGHT TOOTH-AND-NAIL TO REBUILD THE BROWNSTONE. THE EXTERIOR ARCHITECT WANTED US TO SCRAP THE WHOLE THING, BRING US INTO THE "NEW CENTURY"--
--BUT THE JSA DOESN'T THROW AWAY OUR PAST SO EASILY.
IT'S MAGNIFICENT, JAY.
THE HEADQUARTERS OF THE JUSTICE SOCIETY ALWAYS IS.
FEELS WEIRD THAT I'M NOT...YOU KNOW...
WEARING YOUR COSTUME?
YES.
MY TENURE WITH THE TITANS AS JESSE QUICK WAS--AT THE VERY BEST A LEARNING EXPERIENCE--
AT THE WORST AN EMBARRASSMENT.
WE ALL TRIP UP.
I JUST GOT SO OBSESSED WITH TRYING TO DO IT ALL-- RUN MY FATHER'S COMPANY, BE A TITAN, DEAL WITH WHAT I THOUGHT WAS A PERSONAL LIFE --
--I ENDED UP BELIEVING IT DIDN'T MATTER HOW I GOT THINGS DONE, JUST THAT THEY WERE DONE.

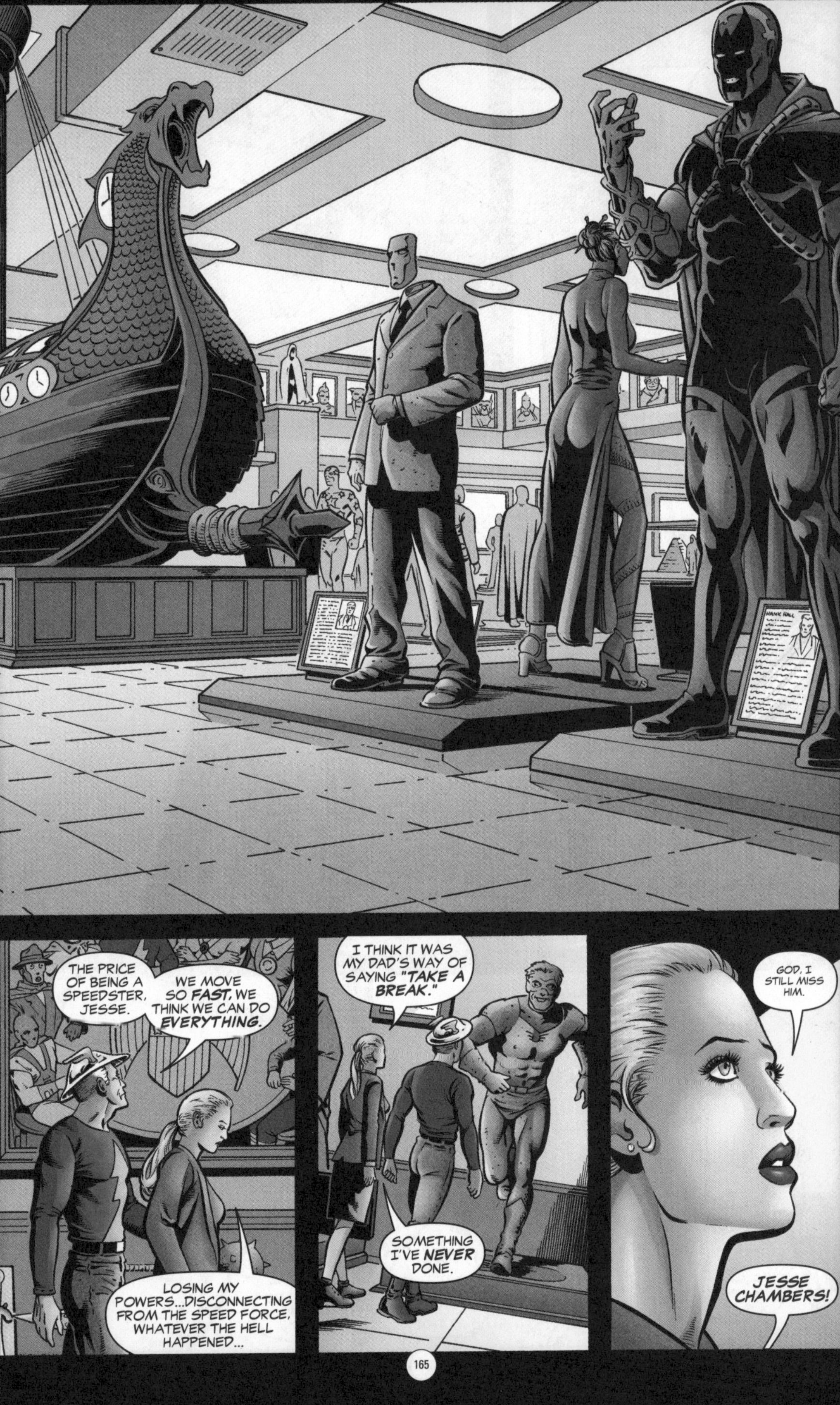
HANK HALL
THE PRICE OF BEING A SPEEDSTER, JESSE.
WE MOVE SO FAST, WE THINK WE CAN DO EVERYTHING.
LOSING MY POWERS...DISCONNECTING FROM THE SPEED FORCE, WHATEVER THE HELL HAPPENED...
I THINK IT WAS MY DAD'S WAY OF SAYING "TAKE A BREAK."
SOMETHING I'VE NEVER DONE.
GOD, I STILL MISS HIM.
JESSE CHAMBERS!

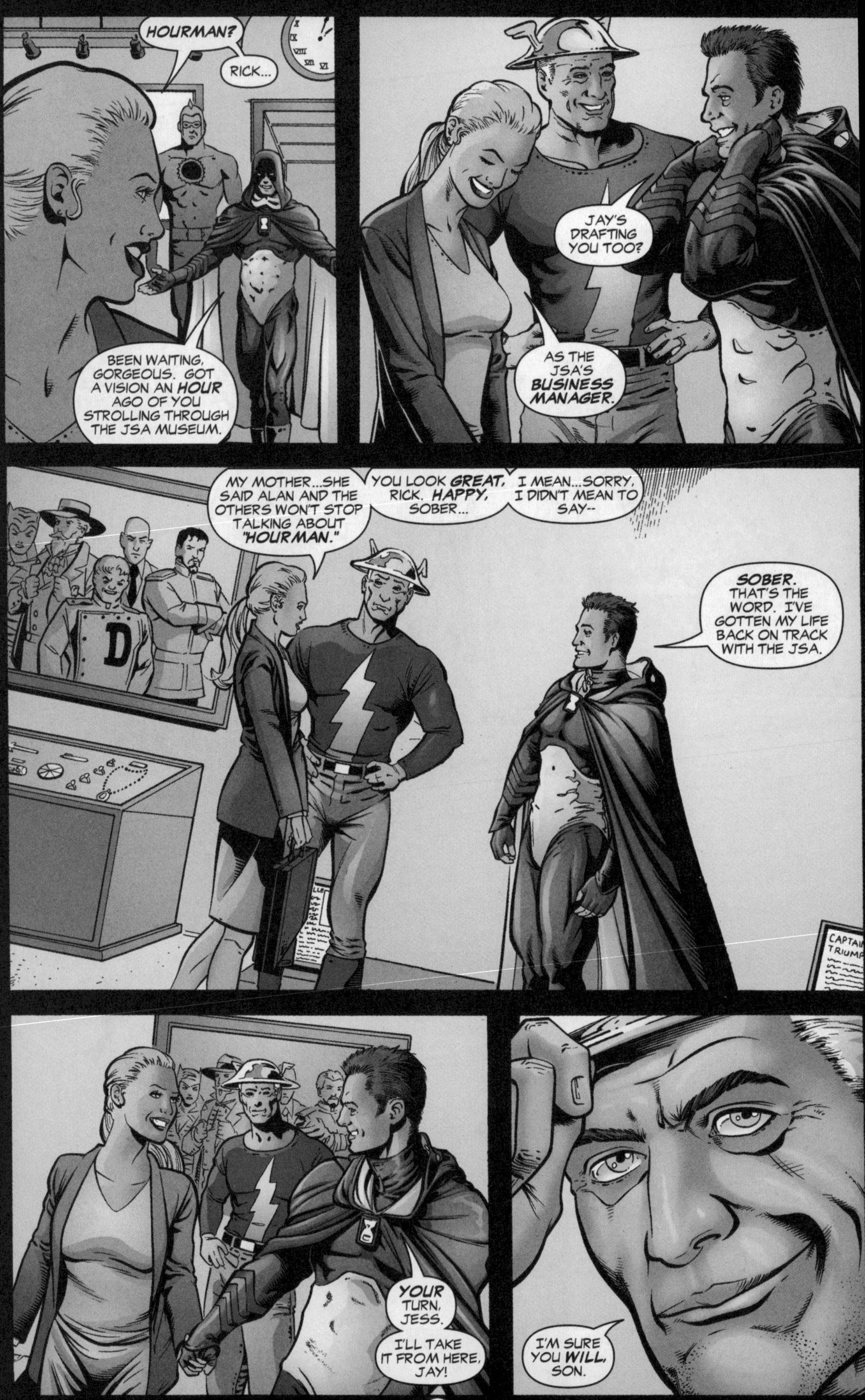

HOURMAN?
RICK...
BEEN WAITING, GORGEOUS. GOT A VISION AN HOUR AGO OF YOU STROLLING THROUGH THE JSA MUSEUM.
JAY'S DRAFTING YOU TOO?
AS THE JSA'S BUSINESS MANAGER.
MY MOTHER...SHE SAID ALAN AND THE OTHERS WON'T STOP TALKING ABOUT "HOURMAN."
YOU LOOK GREAT, RICK. HAPPY, SOBER...
I MEAN...SORRY, I DIDN'T MEAN TO SAY--
SOBER. THAT'S THE WORD. I'VE GOTTEN MY LIFE BACK ON TRACK WITH THE JSA.
D
CAPTAIN TRIUMPH
YOUR TURN, JESS.
I'LL TAKE IT FROM HERE, JAY!
I'M SURE YOU WILL, SON.

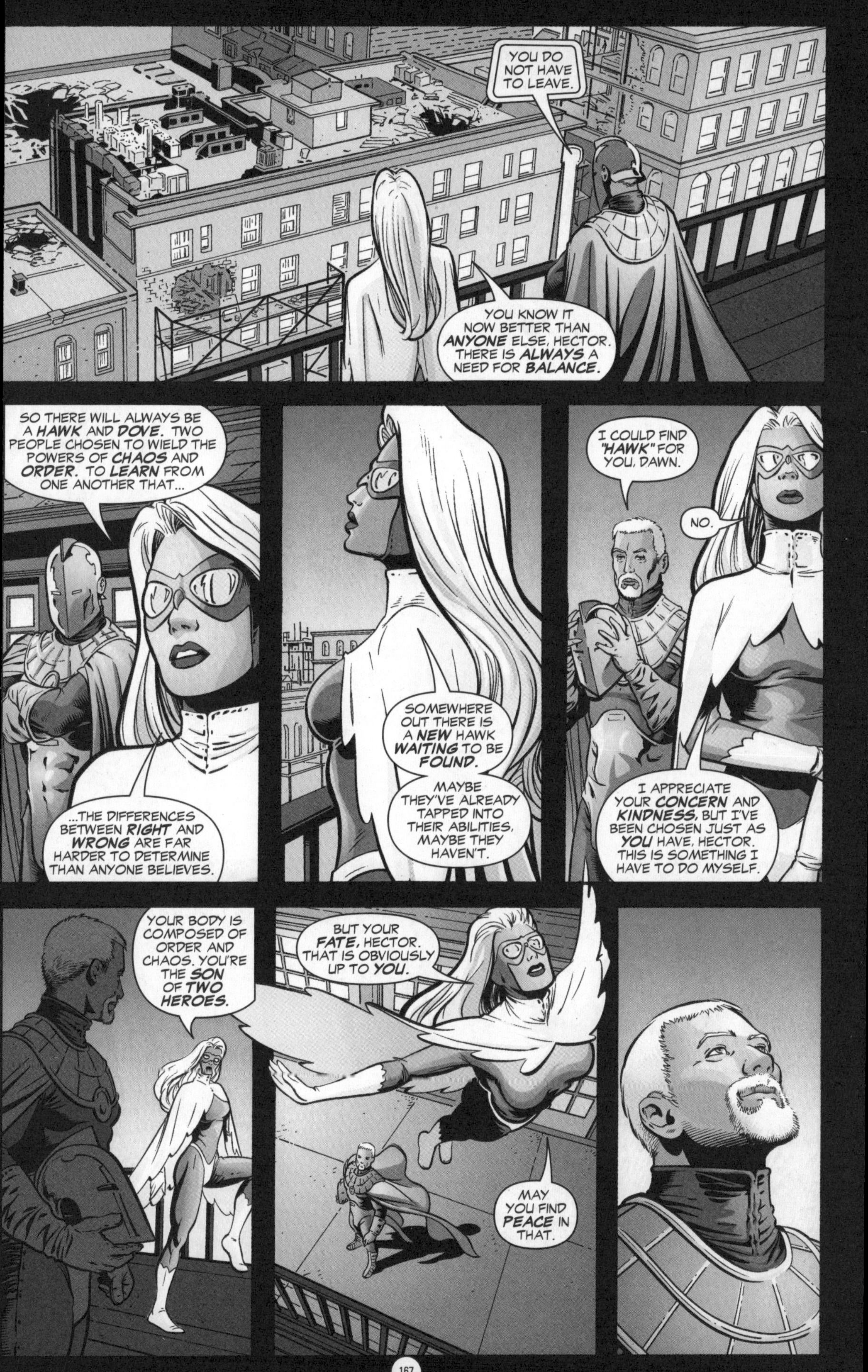

YOU DO NOT HAVE TO LEAVE.
YOU KNOW IT NOW BETTER THAN ANYONE ELSE, HECTOR. THERE IS ALWAYS A NEED FOR BALANCE.
SO THERE WILL ALWAYS BE A HAWK AND DOVE. TWO PEOPLE CHOSEN TO WIELD THE POWERS OF CHAOS AND ORDER. TO LEARN FROM ONE ANOTHER THAT...
...THE DIFFERENCES BETWEEN RIGHT AND WRONG ARE FAR HARDER TO DETERMINE THAN ANYONE BELIEVES.
SOMEWHERE OUT THERE IS A NEW HAWK WAITING TO BE FOUND.
MAYBE THEY'VE ALREADY TAPPED INTO THEIR ABILITIES, MAYBE THEY HAVEN'T.
I COULD FIND "HAWK" FOR YOU, DAWN.
NO.
I APPRECIATE YOUR CONCERN AND KINDNESS, BUT I'VE BEEN CHOSEN JUST AS YOU HAVE, HECTOR. THIS IS SOMETHING I HAVE TO DO MYSELF.
YOUR BODY IS COMPOSED OF ORDER AND CHAOS. YOU'RE THE SON OF TWO HEROES.
BUT YOUR FATE, HECTOR. THAT IS OBVIOUSLY UP TO YOU.
MAY YOU FIND PEACE IN THAT.

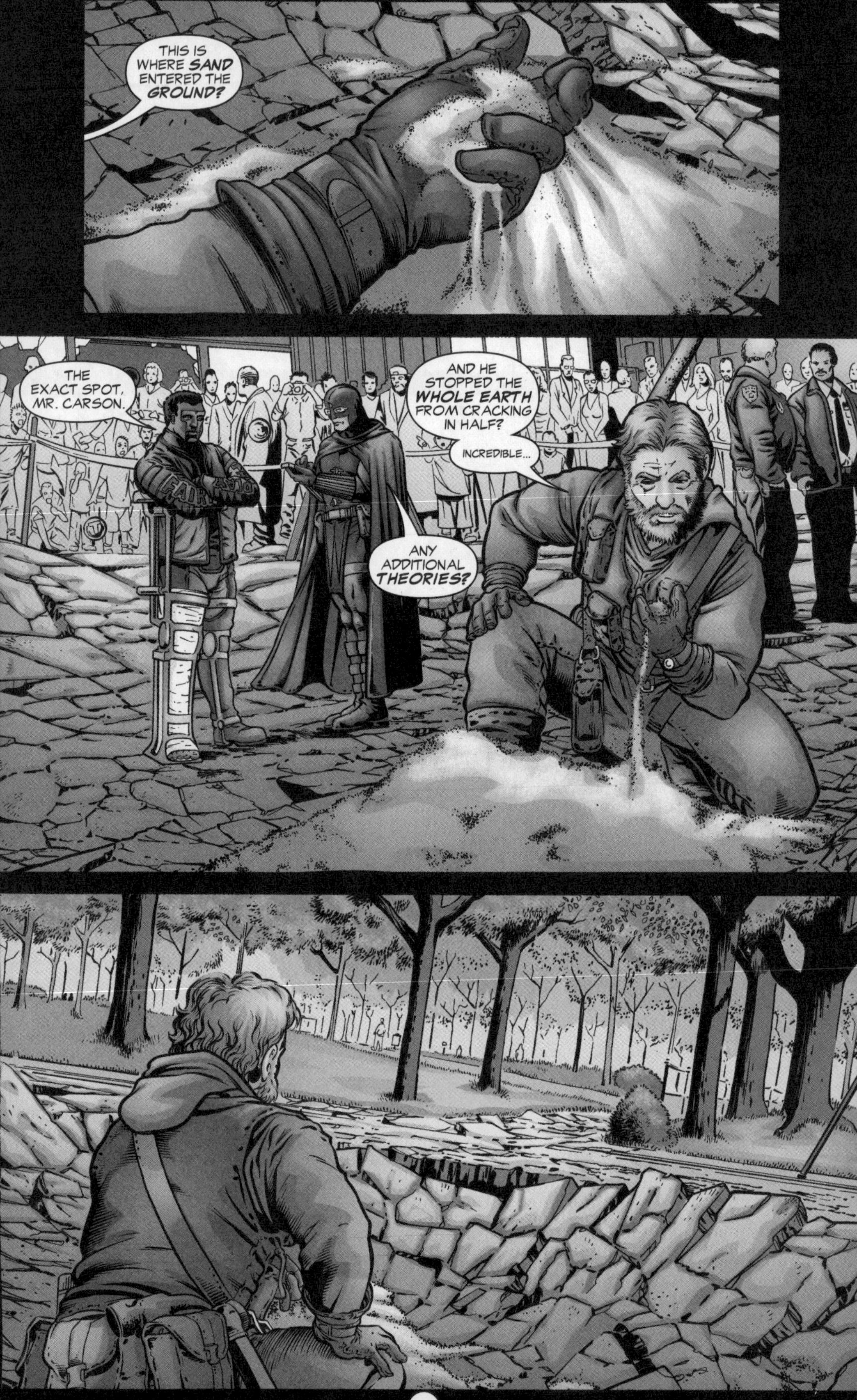
THIS IS WHERE SAND ENTERED THE GROUND?
THE EXACT SPOT, MR. CARSON.
AND HE STOPPED THE WHOLE EARTH FROM CRACKING IN HALF?
INCREDIBLE...
ANY ADDITIONAL THEORIES?

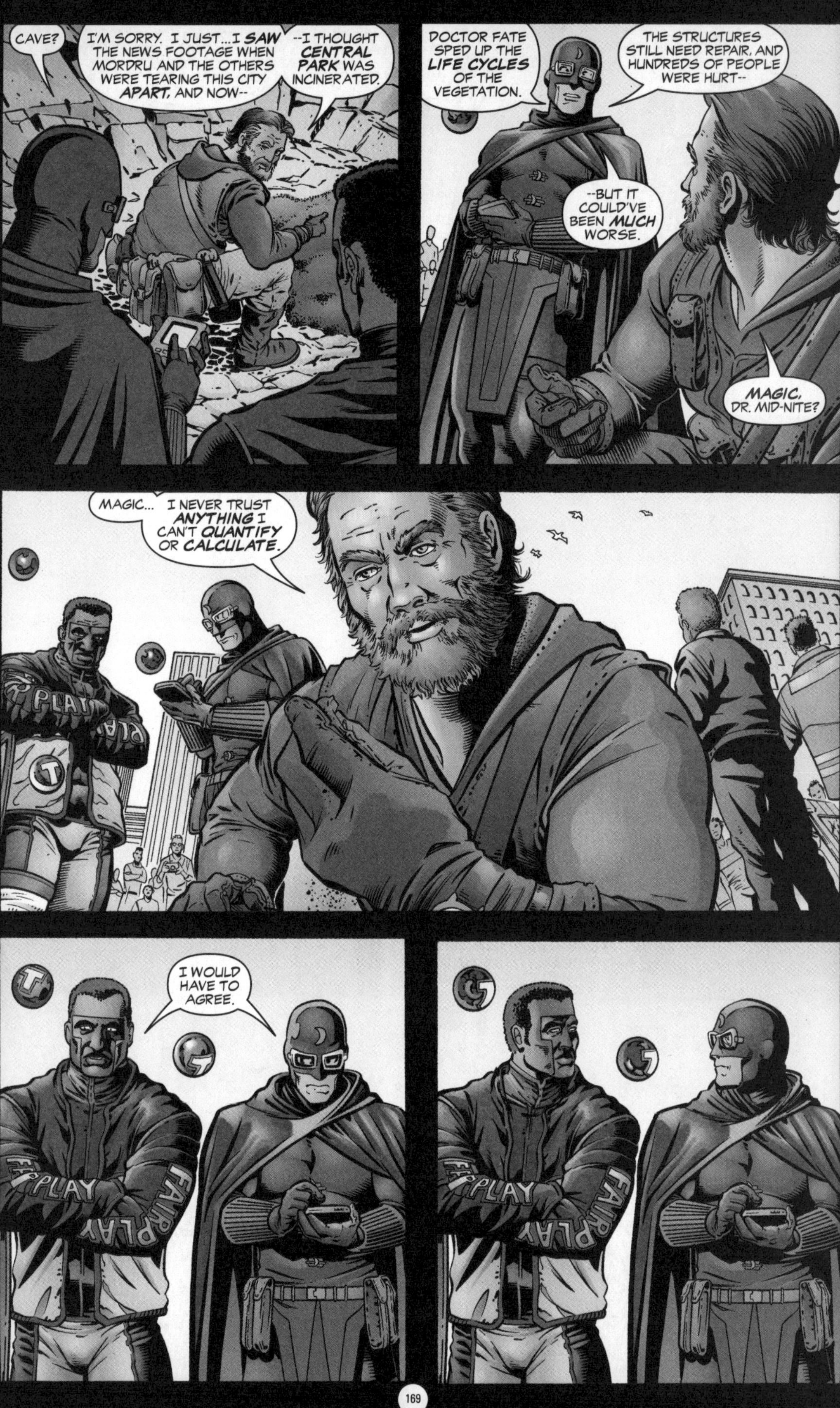
CAVE?
I'M SORRY. I JUST...I SAW THE NEWS FOOTAGE WHEN MORDRU AND THE OTHERS WERE TEARING THIS CITY APART, AND NOW--
--I THOUGHT CENTRAL PARK WAS INCINERATED.
DOCTOR FATE SPED UP THE LIFE CYCLES OF THE VEGETATION.
THE STRUCTURES STILL NEED REPAIR, AND HUNDREDS OF PEOPLE WERE HURT--
--BUT IT COULD'VE BEEN MUCH WORSE.
MAGIC, DR. MID-NITE?
MAGIC... I NEVER TRUST ANYTHING I CAN'T QUANTIFY OR CALCULATE.
I WOULD HAVE TO AGREE.

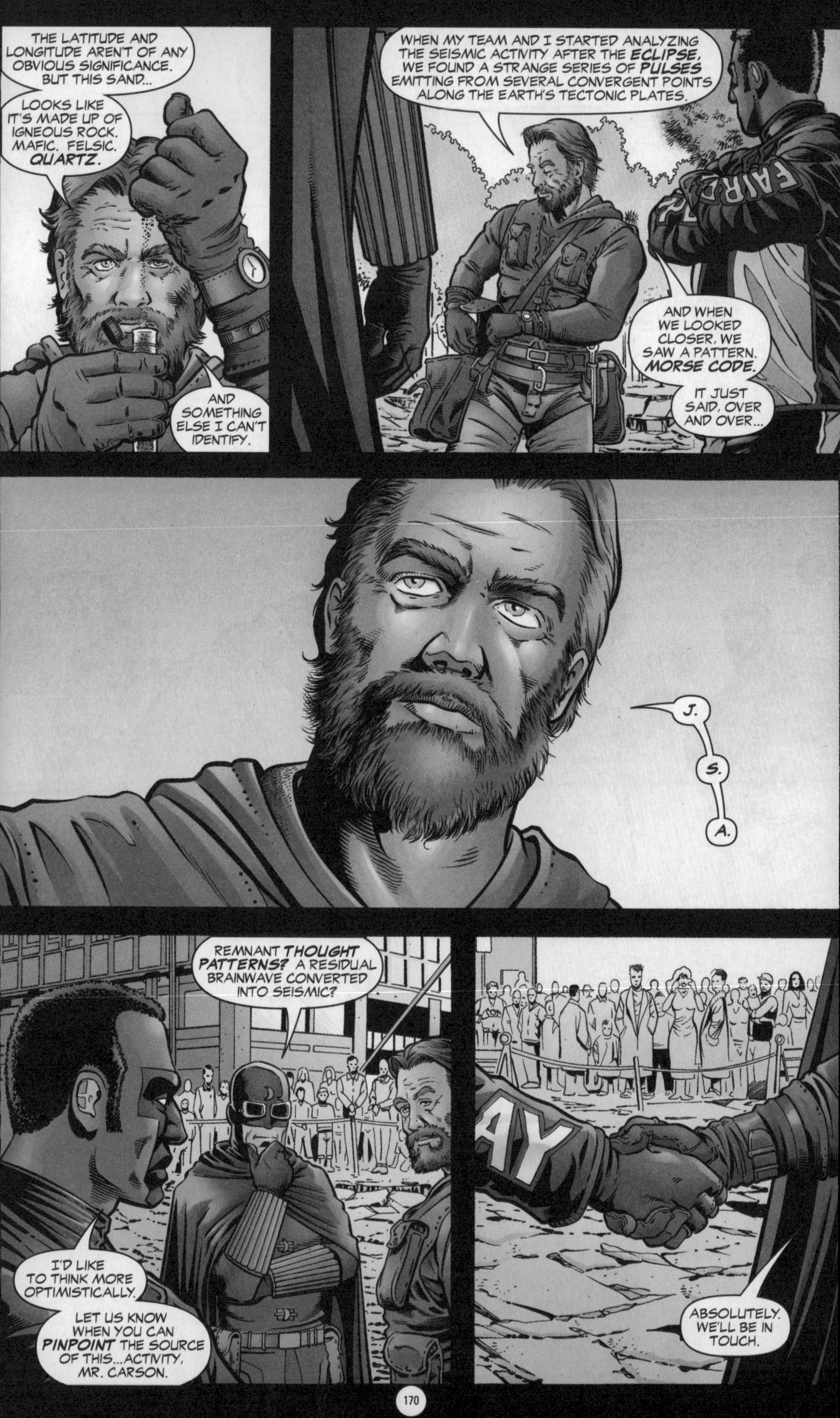
THE LATITUDE AND LONGITUDE AREN'T OF ANY OBVIOUS SIGNIFICANCE. BUT THIS SAND...
LOOKS LIKE IT'S MADE UP OF IGNEOUS ROCK. MAFIC. FELSIC. QUARTZ.
AND SOMETHING ELSE I CAN'T IDENTIFY.
WHEN MY TEAM AND I STARTED ANALYZING THE SEISMIC ACTIVITY AFTER THE ECLIPSE, WE FOUND A STRANGE SERIES OF PULSES EMITTING FROM SEVERAL CONVERGENT POINTS ALONG THE EARTH'S TECTONIC PLATES.
AND WHEN WE LOOKED CLOSER, WE SAW A PATTERN. MORSE CODE.
IT JUST SAID, OVER AND OVER...
J.
S.
A.
REMNANT THOUGHT PATTERNS? A RESIDUAL BRAINWAVE CONVERTED INTO SEISMIC?
I'D LIKE TO THINK MORE OPTIMISTICALLY.
LET US KNOW WHEN YOU CAN PINPOINT THE SOURCE OF THIS...ACTIVITY, MR. CARSON.
ABSOLUTELY. WE'LL BE IN TOUCH.

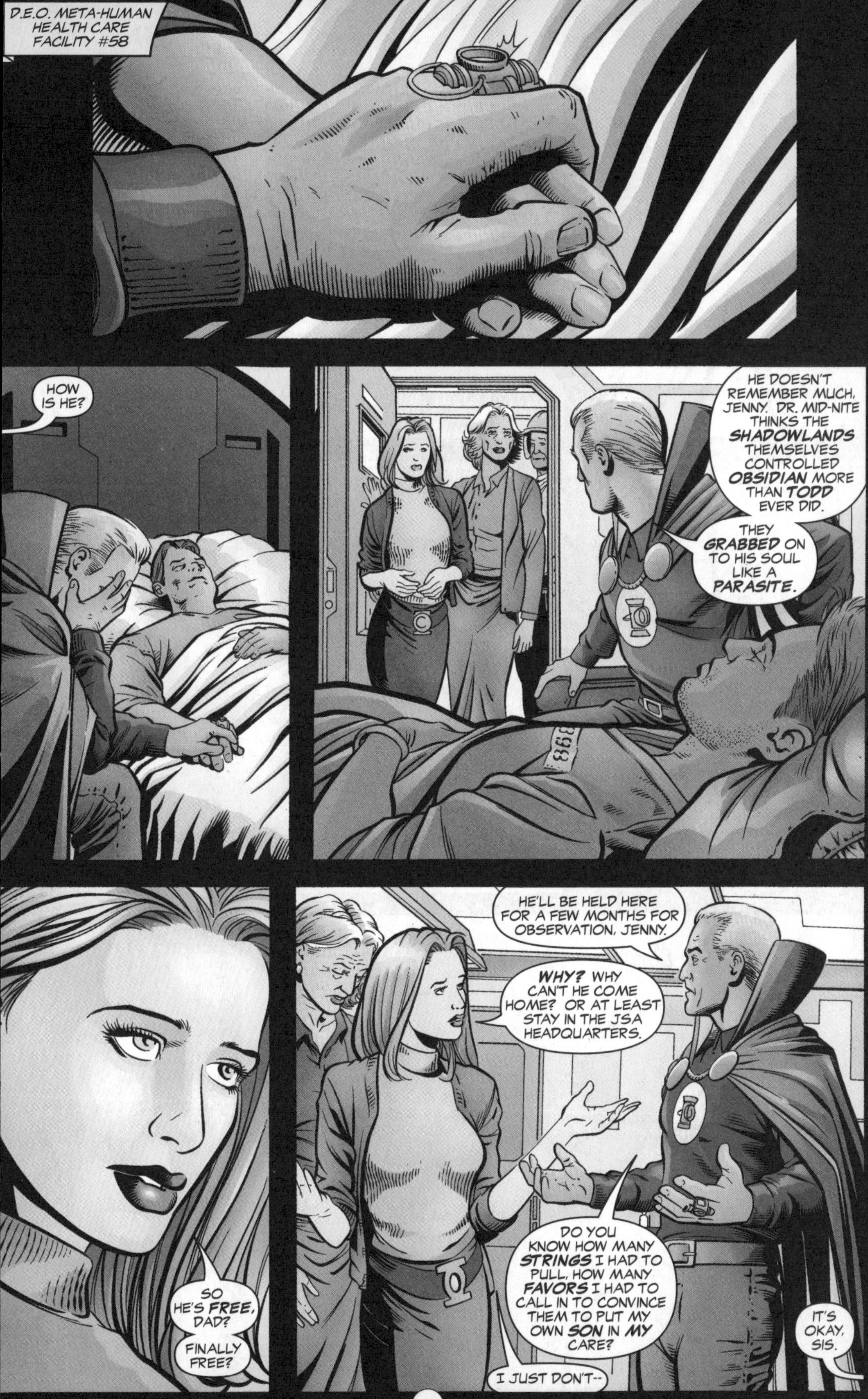
D.E.O. META-HUMAN HEALTH CARE FACILITY #58
HOW IS HE?
HE DOESN'T REMEMBER MUCH, JENNY. DR. MID-NITE THINKS THE SHADOWLANDS THEMSELVES CONTROLLED OBSIDIAN MORE THAN TODD EVER DID.
THEY GRABBED ON TO HIS SOUL LIKE A PARASITE.
SO HE'S FREE, DAD?
FINALLY FREE?
HE'LL BE HELD HERE FOR A FEW MONTHS FOR OBSERVATION, JENNY.
WHY? WHY CAN'T HE COME HOME? OR AT LEAST STAY IN THE JSA HEADQUARTERS.
DO YOU KNOW HOW MANY STRINGS I HAD TO PULL, HOW MANY FAVORS I HAD TO CALL IN TO CONVINCE THEM TO PUT MY OWN SON IN MY CARE?
I JUST DON'T--
IT'S OKAY, SIS.

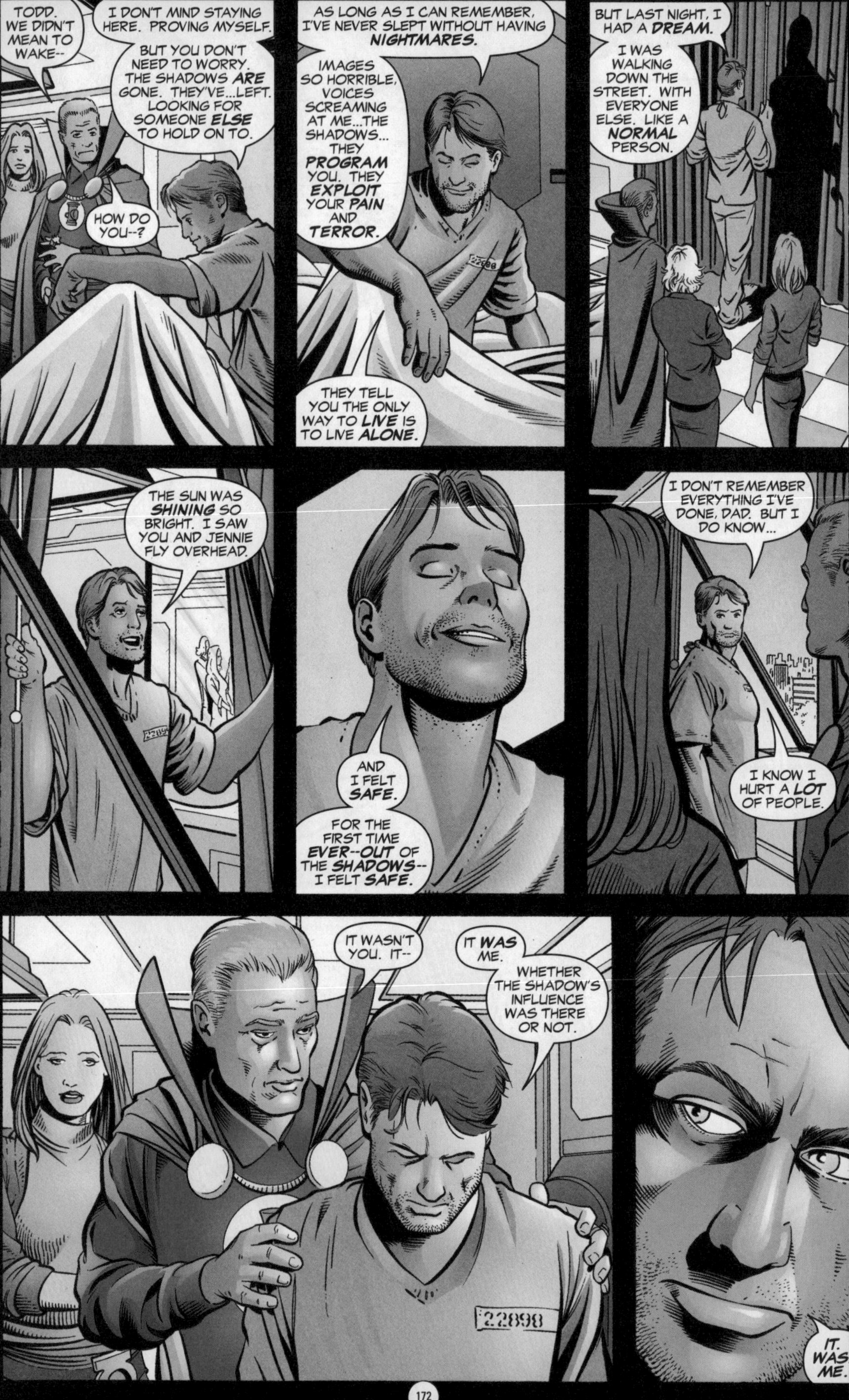
TODD. WE DIDN'T MEAN TO WAKE--
I DON'T MIND STAYING HERE. PROVING MYSELF.
BUT YOU DON'T NEED TO WORRY. THE SHADOWS ARE GONE. THEY'VE...LEFT. LOOKING FOR SOMEONE ELSE TO HOLD ON TO.
HOW DO YOU--?
AS LONG AS I CAN REMEMBER, I'VE NEVER SLEPT WITHOUT HAVING NIGHTMARES.
IMAGES SO HORRIBLE, VOICES SCREAMING AT ME...THE SHADOWS... THEY PROGRAM YOU. THEY EXPLOIT YOUR PAIN AND TERROR.
22898
THEY TELL YOU THE ONLY WAY TO LIVE IS TO LIVE ALONE.
BUT LAST NIGHT, I HAD A DREAM.
I WAS WALKING DOWN THE STREET. WITH EVERYONE ELSE. LIKE A NORMAL PERSON.
THE SUN WAS SHINING SO BRIGHT. I SAW YOU AND JENNIE FLY OVERHEAD.
AND I FELT SAFE.
FOR THE FIRST TIME EVER--OUT OF THE SHADOWS-- I FELT SAFE.
I DON'T REMEMBER EVERYTHING I'VE DONE, DAD. BUT I DO KNOW...
I KNOW I HURT A LOT OF PEOPLE.
IT WASN'T YOU. IT--
IT WAS ME.
WHETHER THE SHADOW'S INFLUENCE WAS THERE OR NOT.
22898
IT. WAS ME.

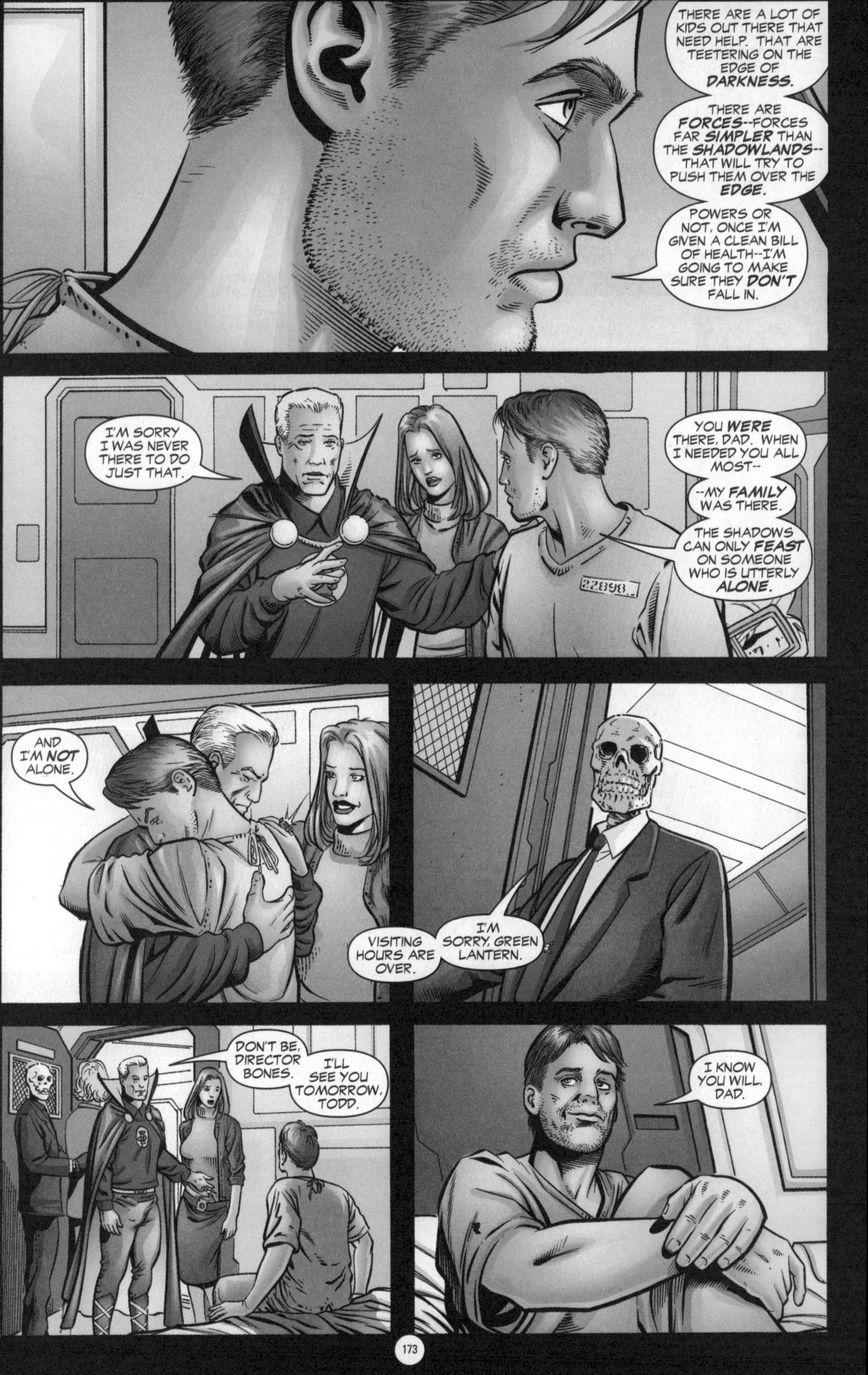
THERE ARE A LOT OF KIDS OUT THERE THAT NEED HELP. THAT ARE TEETERING ON THE EDGE OF DARKNESS.
THERE ARE FORCES--FORCES FAR SIMPLER THAN THE SHADOWLANDS--THAT WILL TRY TO PUSH THEM OVER THE EDGE.
POWERS OR NOT, ONCE I'M GIVEN A CLEAN BILL OF HEALTH--I'M GOING TO MAKE SURE THEY DON'T FALL IN.
I'M SORRY I WAS NEVER THERE TO DO JUST THAT.
YOU WERE THERE, DAD. WHEN I NEEDED YOU ALL MOST--
--MY FAMILY WAS THERE.
THE SHADOWS CAN ONLY FEAST ON SOMEONE WHO IS UTTERLY ALONE.
22898
AND I'M NOT ALONE.
I'M SORRY, GREEN LANTERN.
VISITING HOURS ARE OVER.
DON'T BE, DIRECTOR BONES.
I'LL SEE YOU TOMORROW, TODD.
I KNOW YOU WILL, DAD.

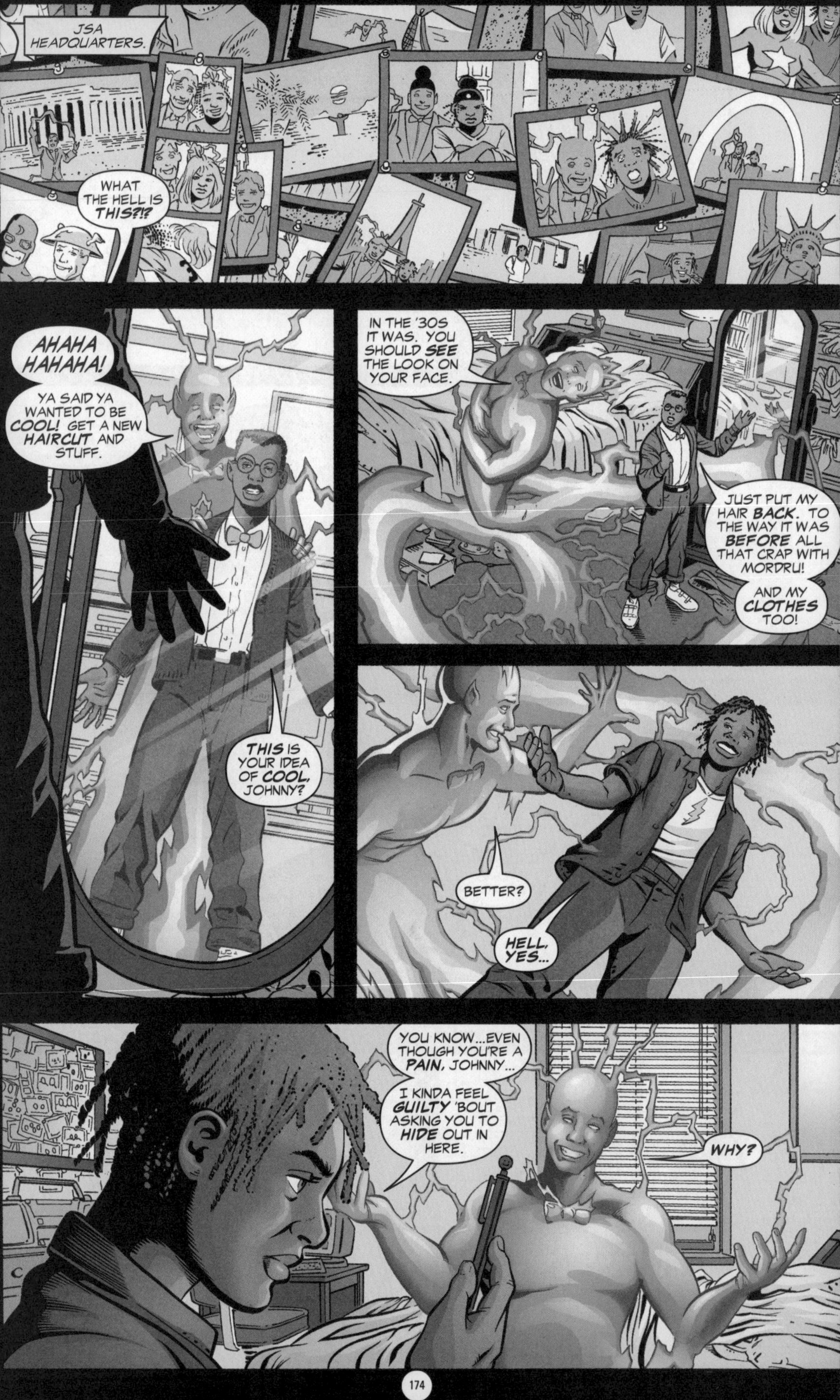
JSA HEADQUARTERS.
WHAT THE HELL IS THIS?!?
AHAHA HAHAHA!
YA SAID YA WANTED TO BE COOL! GET A NEW HAIRCUT AND STUFF.
IN THE '30S IT WAS. YOU SHOULD SEE THE LOOK ON YOUR FACE.
THIS IS YOUR IDEA OF COOL, JOHNNY?
JUST PUT MY HAIR BACK. TO THE WAY IT WAS BEFORE ALL THAT CRAP WITH MORDRU!
AND MY CLOTHES TOO!
BETTER?
HELL, YES...
YOU KNOW...EVEN THOUGH YOU'RE A PAIN, JOHNNY...
I KINDA FEEL GUILTY 'BOUT ASKING YOU TO HIDE OUT IN HERE.
WHY?

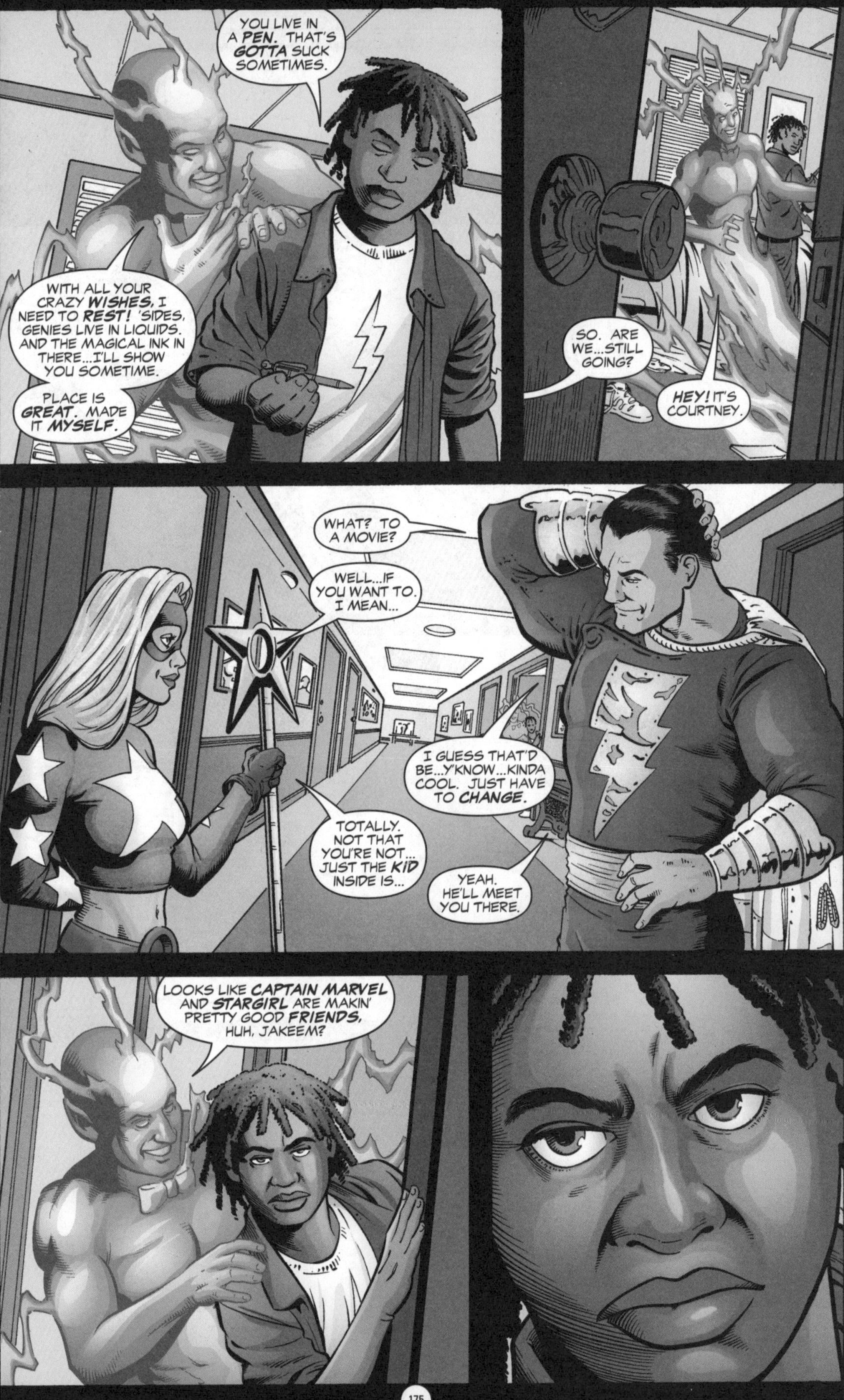
YOU LIVE IN A PEN. THAT'S GOTTA SUCK SOMETIMES.
WITH ALL YOUR CRAZY WISHES, I NEED TO REST! 'SIDES, GENIES LIVE IN LIQUIDS. AND THE MAGICAL INK IN THERE...I'LL SHOW YOU SOMETIME.
PLACE IS GREAT. MADE IT MYSELF.
SO. ARE WE...STILL GOING?
HEY! IT'S COURTNEY.
WHAT? TO A MOVIE?
WELL...IF YOU WANT TO. I MEAN...
I GUESS THAT'D BE...Y'KNOW...KINDA COOL. JUST HAVE TO CHANGE.
TOTALLY. NOT THAT YOU'RE NOT... JUST THE KID INSIDE IS...
YEAH. HE'LL MEET YOU THERE.
LOOKS LIKE CAPTAIN MARVEL AND STARGIRL ARE MAKIN' PRETTY GOOD FRIENDS, HUH, JAKEEM?

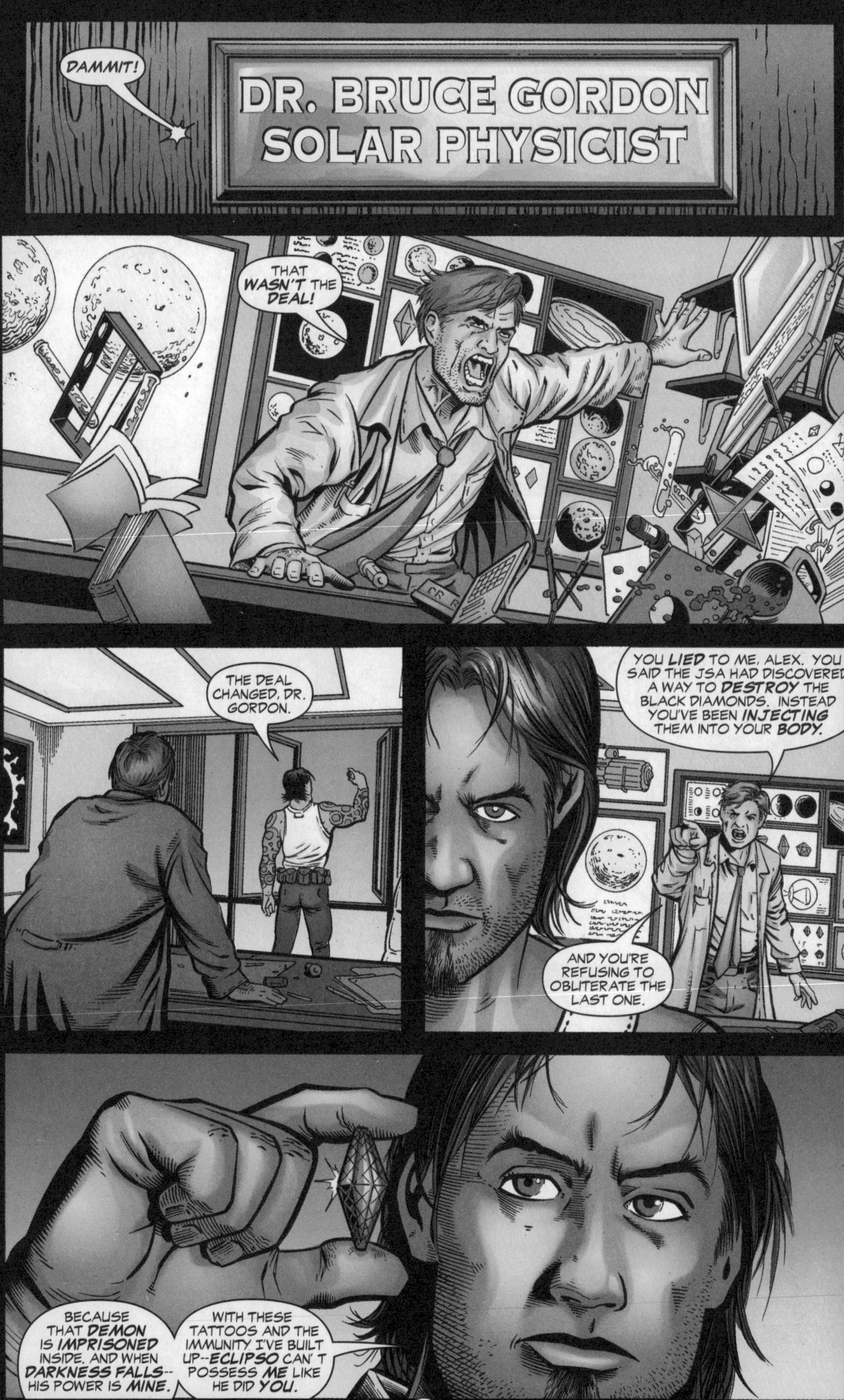
DAMMIT!
DR. BRUCE GORDON
SOLAR PHYSICIST
THAT WASN'T THE DEAL!
THE DEAL CHANGED, DR. GORDON.
YOU LIED TO ME, ALEX. YOU SAID THE JSA HAD DISCOVERED A WAY TO DESTROY THE BLACK DIAMONDS. INSTEAD YOU'VE BEEN INJECTING THEM INTO YOUR BODY.
AND YOU'RE REFUSING TO OBLITERATE THE LAST ONE.
BECAUSE THAT DEMON IS IMPRISONED INSIDE. AND WHEN DARKNESS FALLS-- HIS POWER IS MINE.
WITH THESE TATTOOS AND THE IMMUNITY I'VE BUILT UP--ECLIPSO CAN'T POSSESS ME LIKE HE DID YOU.

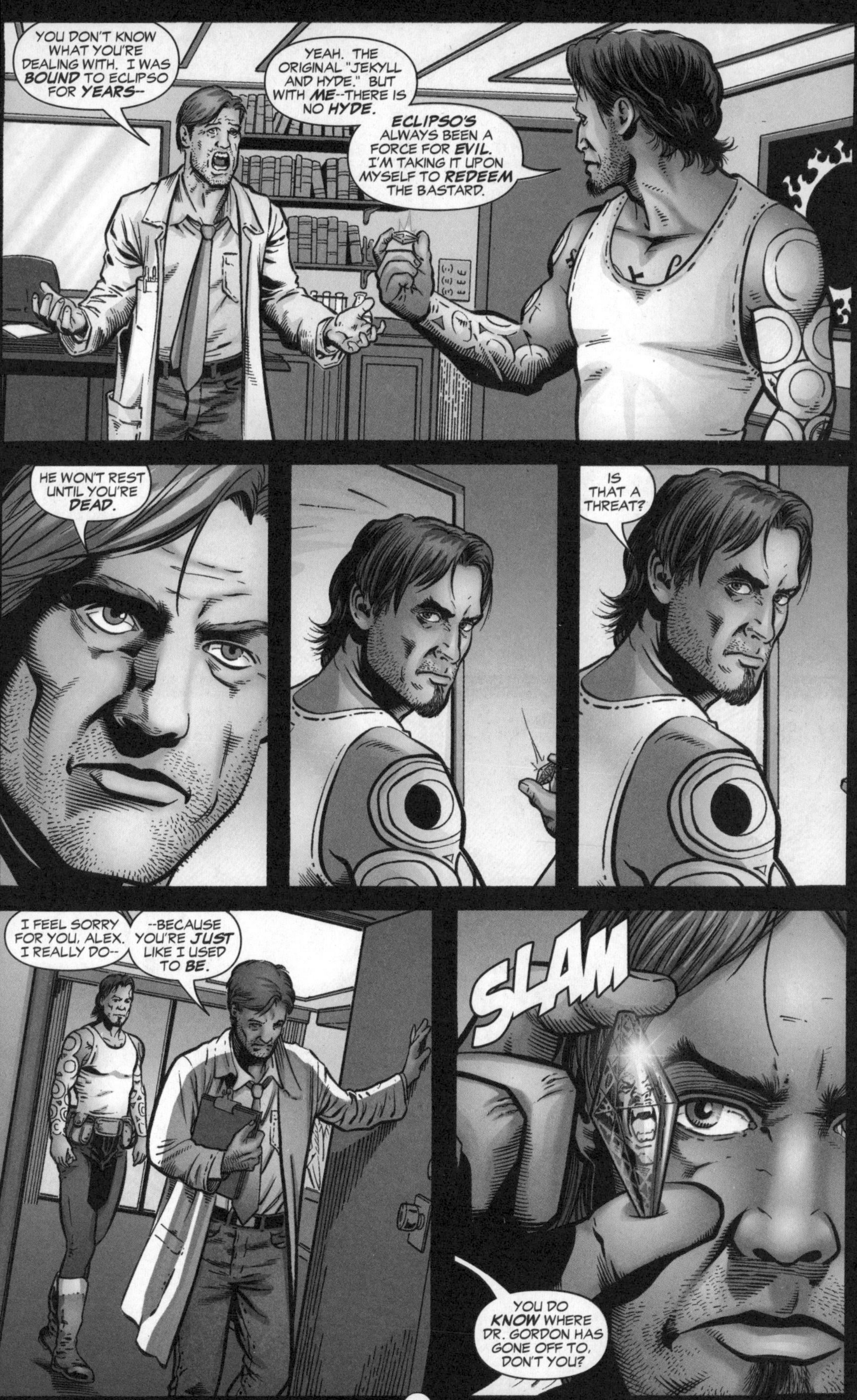
YOU DON'T KNOW WHAT YOU'RE DEALING WITH. I WAS BOUND TO ECLIPSO FOR YEARS--
YEAH. THE ORIGINAL "JEKYLL AND HYDE." BUT WITH ME--THERE IS NO HYDE.
ECLIPSO'S ALWAYS BEEN A FORCE FOR EVIL. I'M TAKING IT UPON MYSELF TO REDEEM THE BASTARD.
HE WON'T REST UNTIL YOU'RE DEAD.
IS THAT A THREAT?
I FEEL SORRY FOR YOU, ALEX. I REALLY DO--
--BECAUSE YOU'RE JUST LIKE I USED TO BE.
SLAM
YOU DO KNOW WHERE DR. GORDON HAS GONE OFF TO, DON'T YOU?

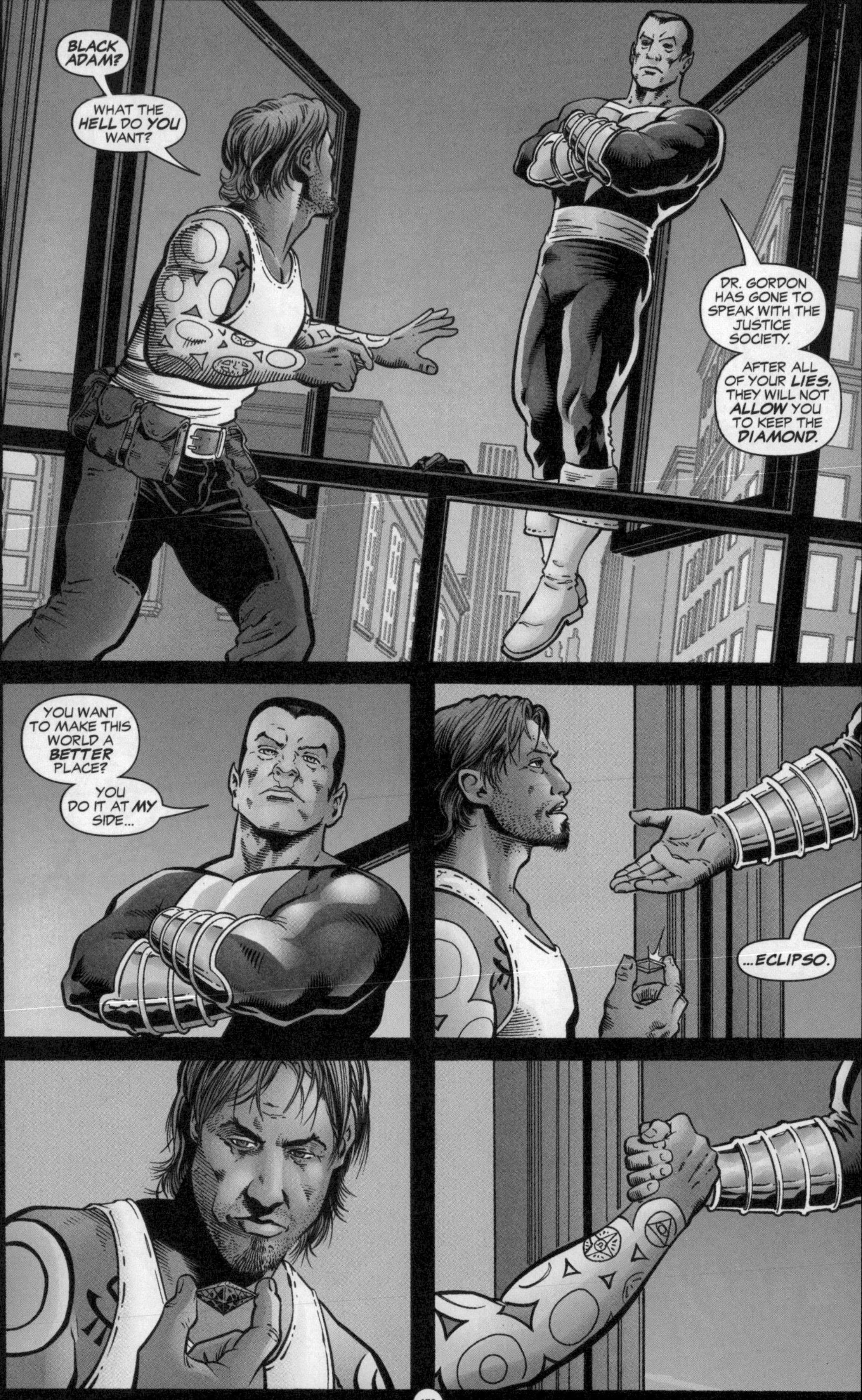
BLACK ADAM?
WHAT THE HELL DO YOU WANT?
DR. GORDON HAS GONE TO SPEAK WITH THE JUSTICE SOCIETY.
AFTER ALL OF YOUR LIES, THEY WILL NOT ALLOW YOU TO KEEP THE DIAMOND.
YOU WANT TO MAKE THIS WORLD A BETTER PLACE?
YOU DO IT AT MY SIDE...
...ECLIPSO.

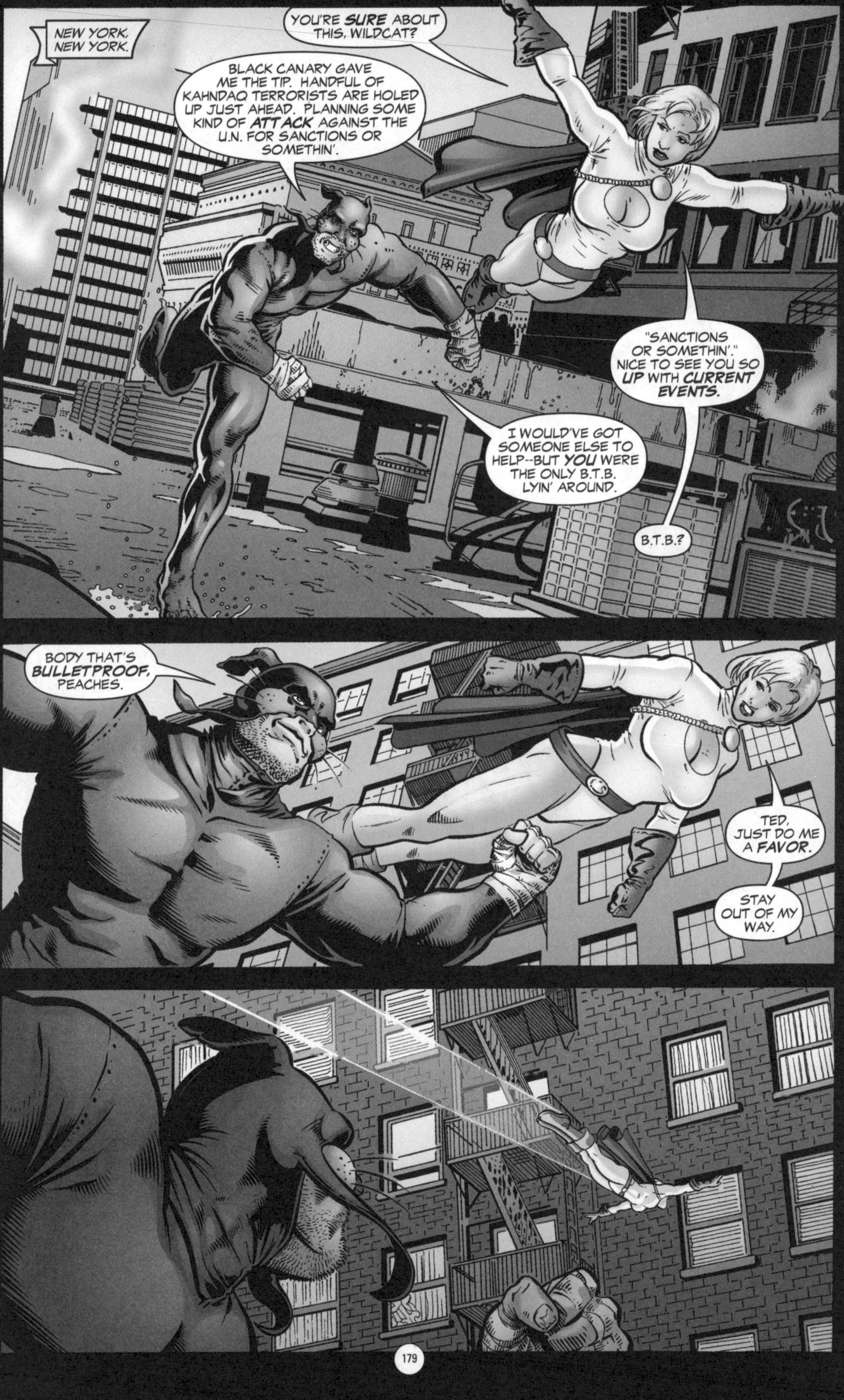

NEW YORK, NEW YORK.
YOU'RE SURE ABOUT THIS, WILDCAT?
BLACK CANARY GAVE ME THE TIP. HANDFUL OF KAHNDAQ TERRORISTS ARE HOLED UP JUST AHEAD. PLANNING SOME KIND OF ATTACK AGAINST THE U.N. FOR SANCTIONS OR SOMETHIN'.
"SANCTIONS OR SOMETHIN'." NICE TO SEE YOU SO UP WITH CURRENT EVENTS.
I WOULD'VE GOT SOMEONE ELSE TO HELP--BUT YOU WERE THE ONLY B.T.B. LYIN' AROUND.
B.T.B.?
BODY THAT'S BULLETPROOF, PEACHES.
TED, JUST DO ME A FAVOR.
STAY OUT OF MY WAY.

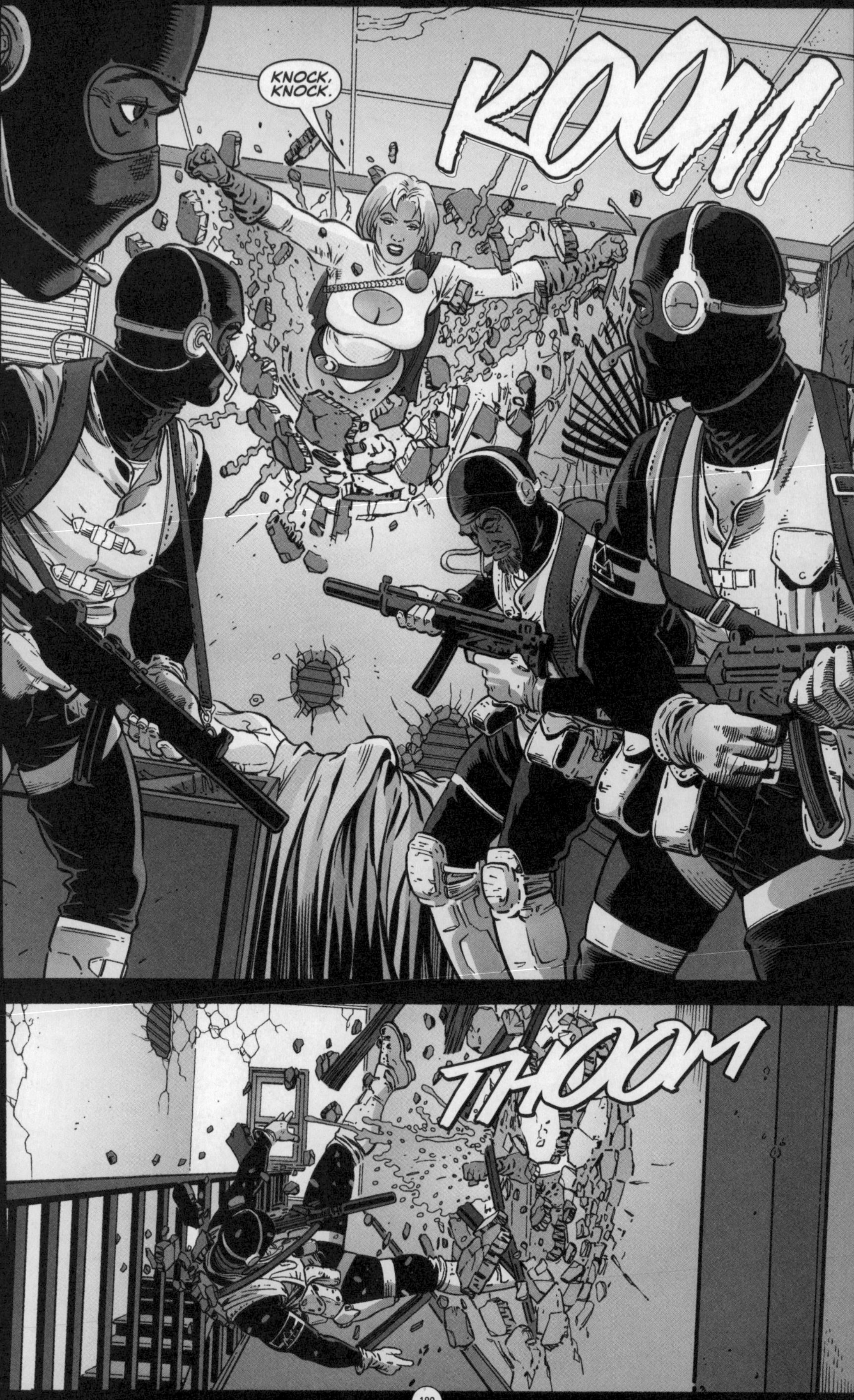
KNOCK, KNOCK.
KOOM
THOOM

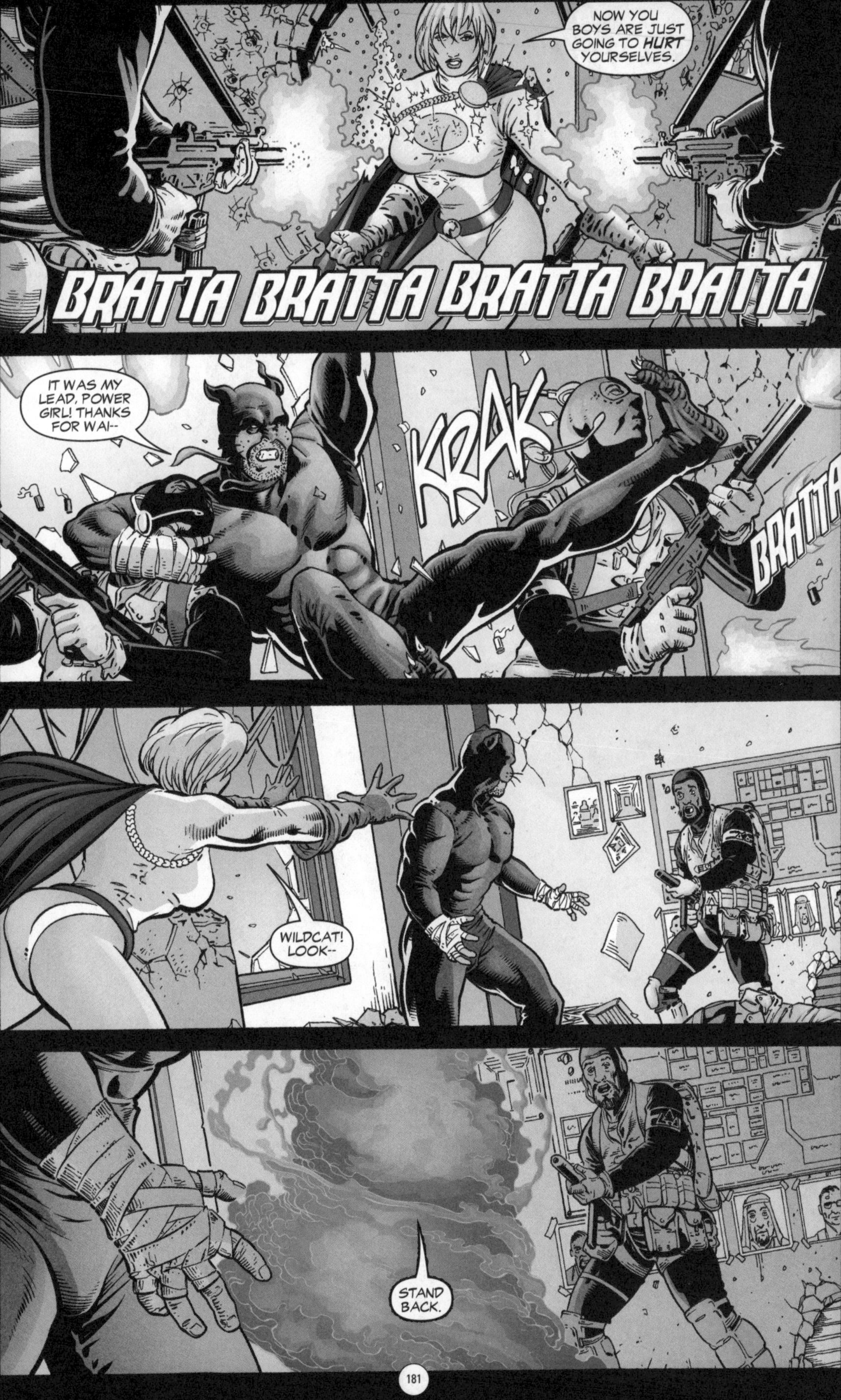
NOW YOU BOYS ARE JUST GOING TO HURT YOURSELVES.
BRATTA BRATTA BRATTA BRATTA
IT WAS MY LEAD, POWER GIRL! THANKS FOR WAI--
KRAK
BRATTA
WILDCAT! LOOK--
STAND BACK.

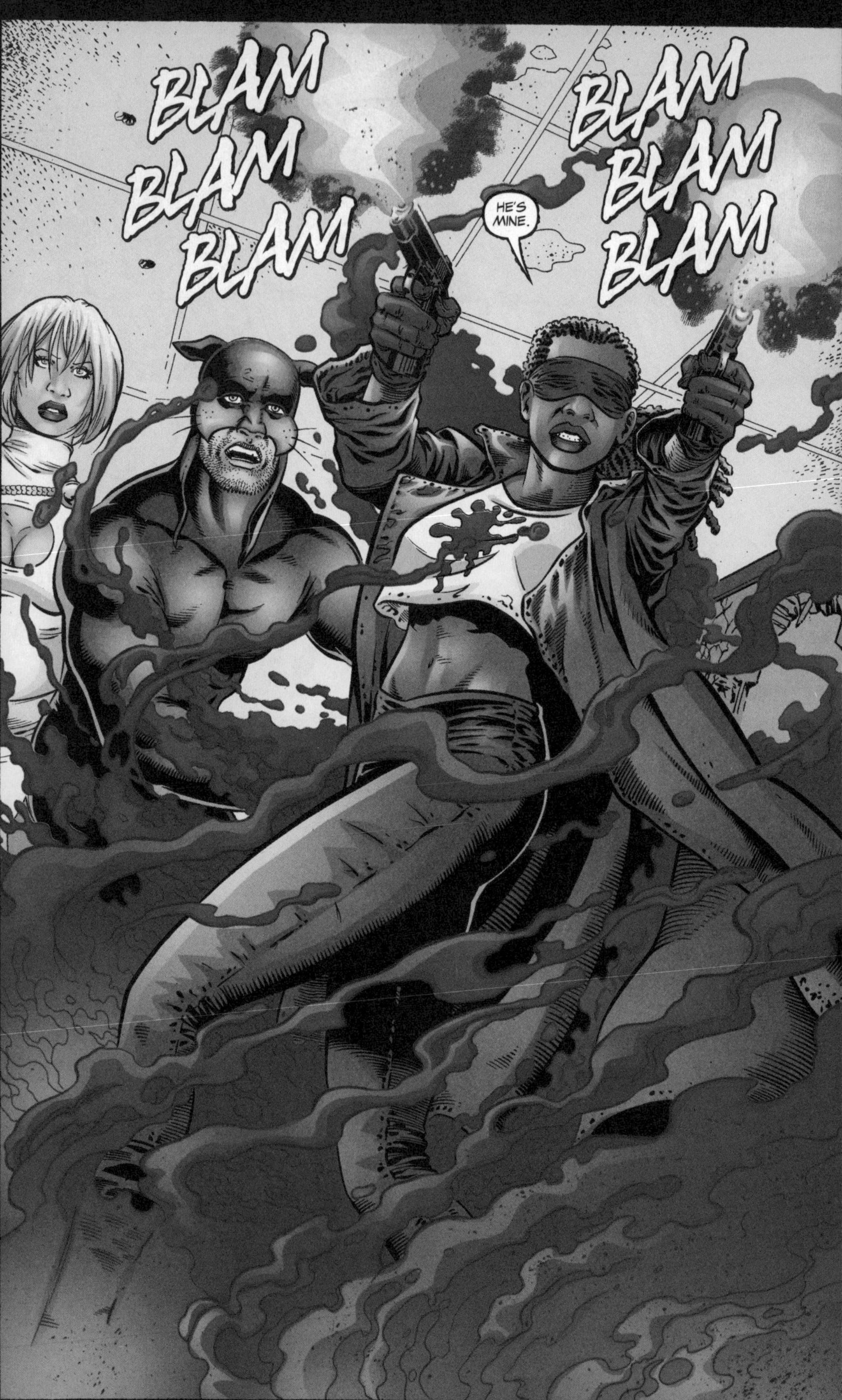
BLAM
BLAM
BLAM
HE'S MINE.
BLAM
BLAM
BLAM

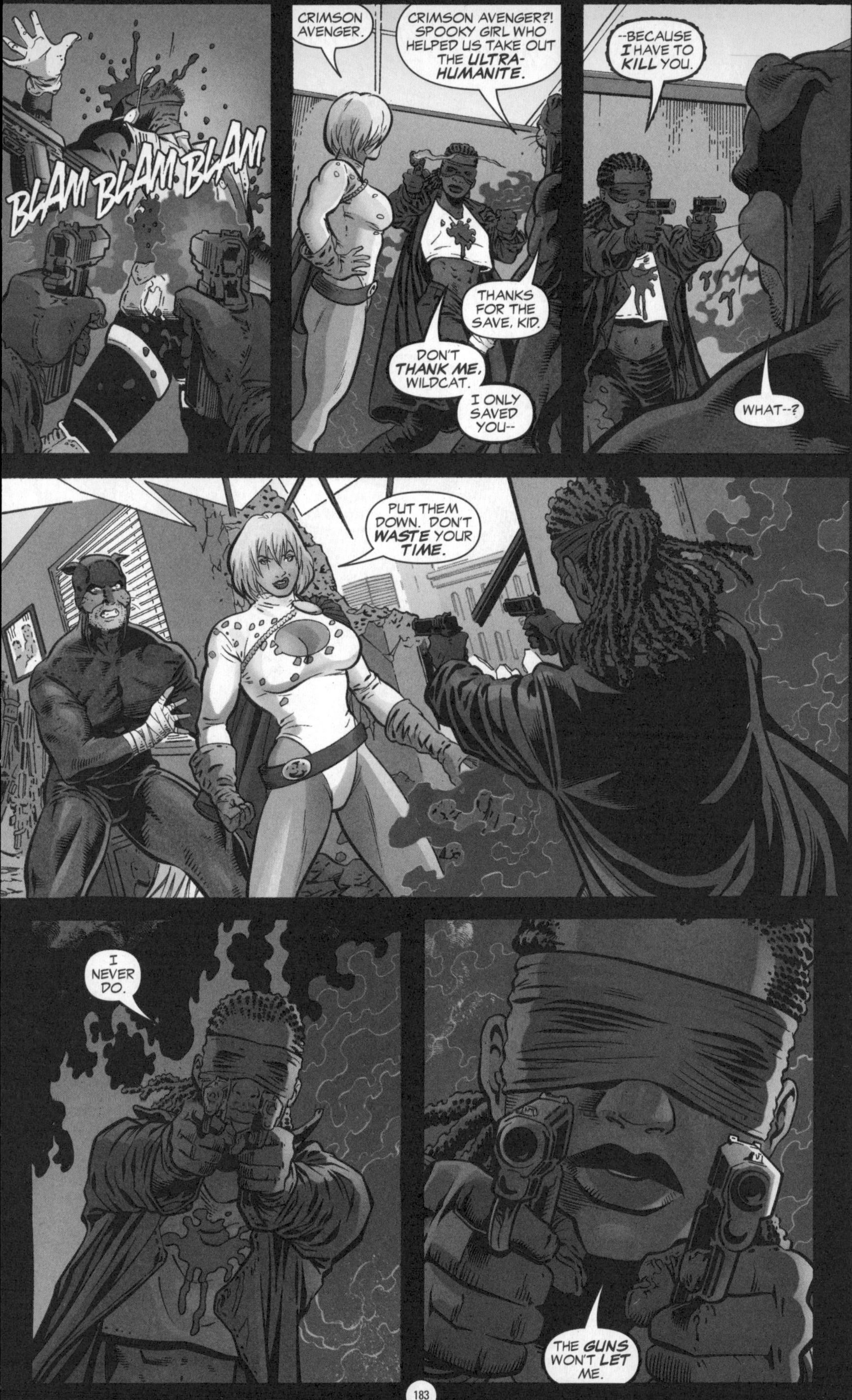
BLAM BLAM BLAM
CRIMSON AVENGER.
CRIMSON AVENGER?! SPOOKY GIRL WHO HELPED US TAKE OUT THE ULTRA-HUMANITE.
THANKS FOR THE SAVE, KID.
DON'T THANK ME, WILDCAT.
I ONLY SAVED YOU--
--BECAUSE I HAVE TO KILL YOU.
WHAT--?
PUT THEM DOWN. DON'T WASTE YOUR TIME.
I NEVER DO.
THE GUNS WON'T LET ME.

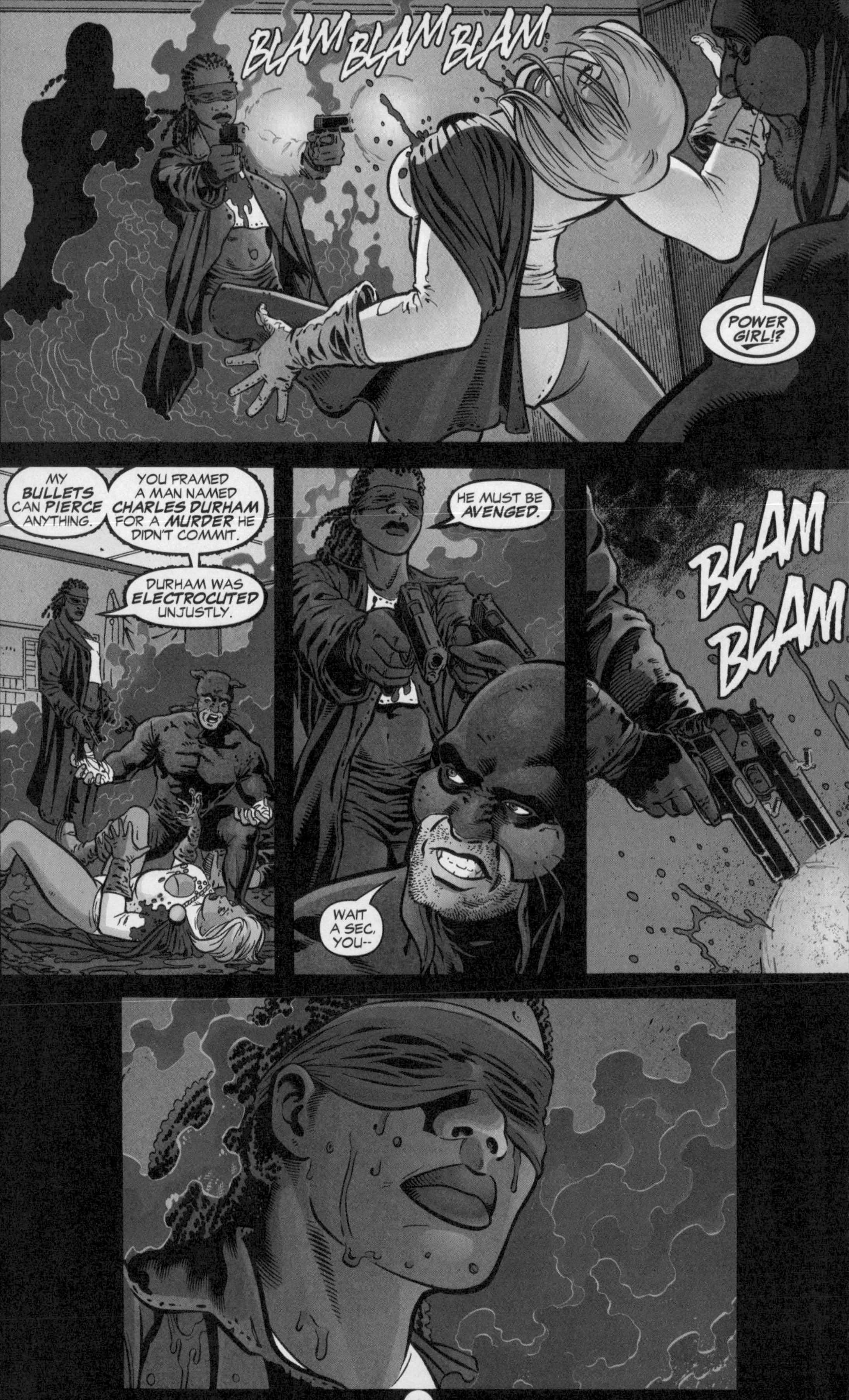
BLAM BLAM BLAM
POWER GIRL!?
MY BULLETS CAN PIERCE ANYTHING.
YOU FRAMED A MAN NAMED CHARLES DURHAM FOR A MURDER HE DIDN'T COMMIT.
DURHAM WAS ELECTROCUTED UNJUSTLY.
HE MUST BE AVENGED.
WAIT A SEC, YOU--
BLAM BLAM

DO YOU KNOW THE DIFFERENCE BETWEEN JUSTICE AND VENGEANCE?
I THOUGHT I DID. I STUDIED THE LAW. I BELIEVED IN THE LAW.
UNTIL THAT MURDERER WENT FREE. HE TOOK HIM FROM ME. HE...
I KNEW WHERE HE WAS. I KNEW WHAT HE DID.
SO I KNEW WHAT I HAD TO DO.
I REMEMBER THE KICKBACK AS I FIRED THESE GUNS. SHOT THE BULLETS INTO HIS HEART. AND THESE THINGS FOUND THEIR KILLER.
DO I REGRET IT?
I DON'T KNOW. I...I HATE THESE GUNS. THE POWER THEY HAVE OVER ME.
AND THEN THERE'S THE BLOOD. THE MEMORIES OF THE VICTIMS. THEIR SCREAMS...
THEIR PAIN... IS MY PAIN.
I AM THE CRIMSON AVENGER.
AND I HAVE LEARNED THAT JUSTICE IS VENGEANCE.
BLINDED

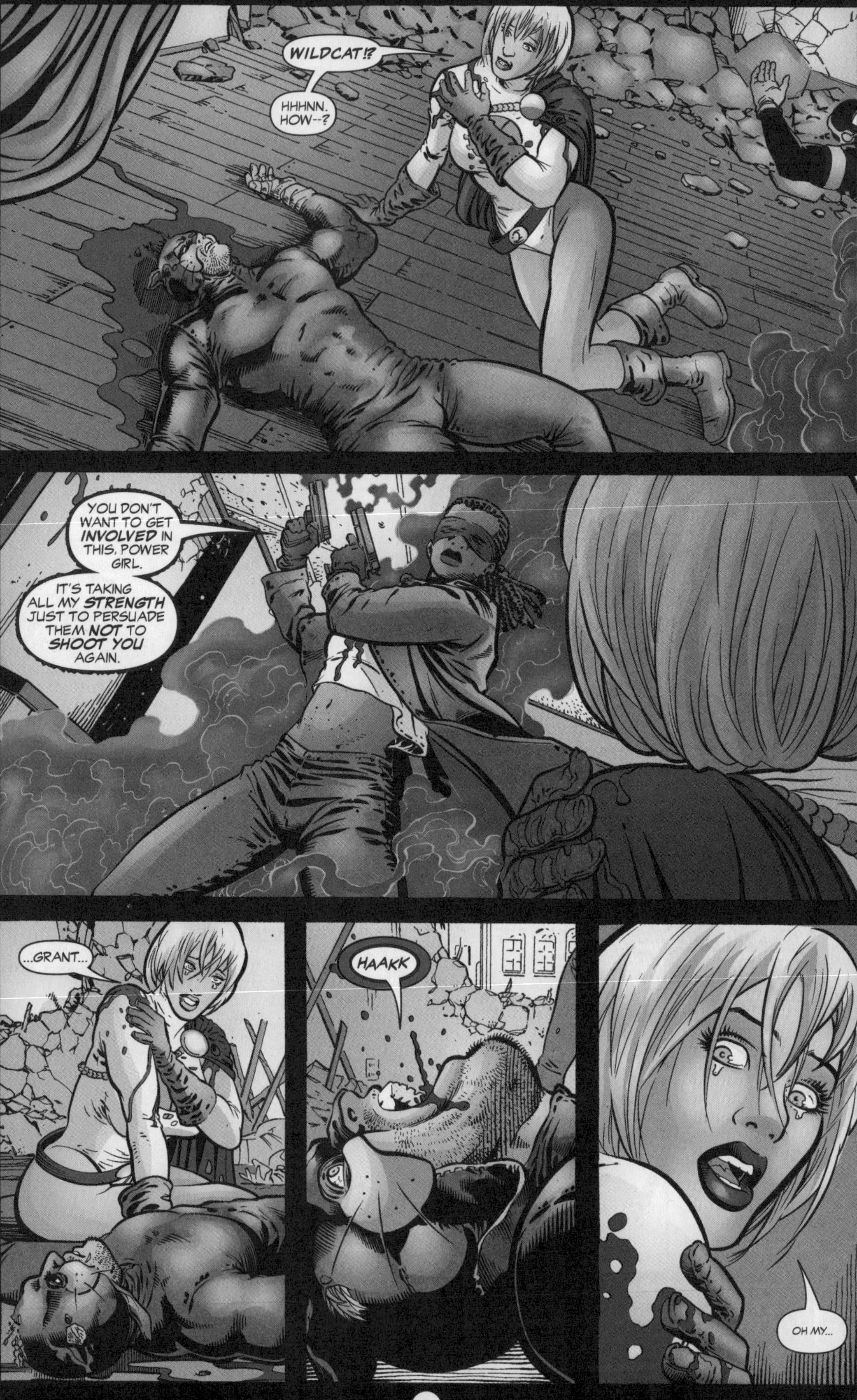
WILDCAT!?
HHHHN. HOW--?
YOU DON'T WANT TO GET INVOLVED IN THIS, POWER GIRL.
IT'S TAKING ALL MY STRENGTH JUST TO PERSUADE THEM NOT TO SHOOT YOU AGAIN.
...GRANT...
HAAKK
OH MY...

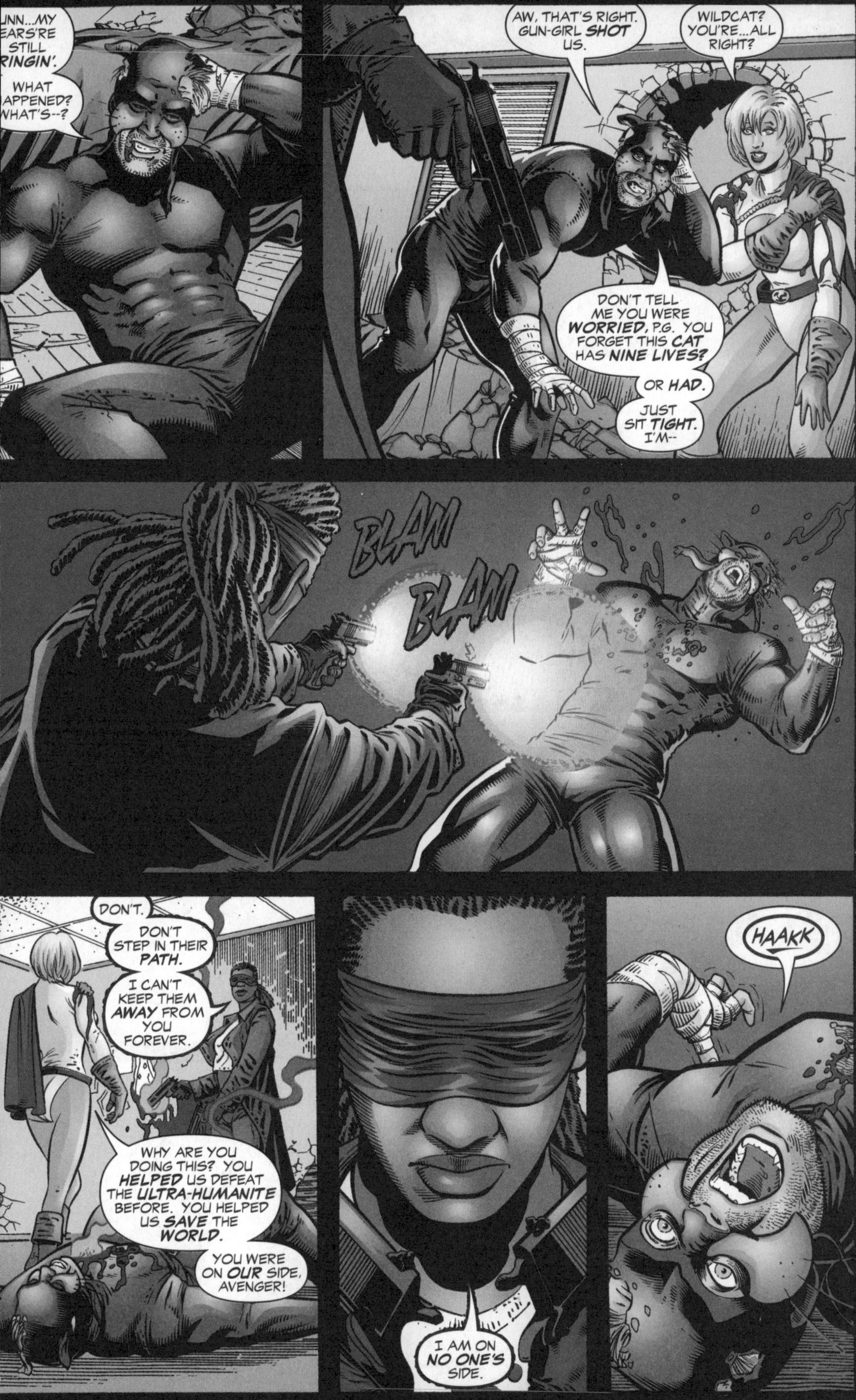
UNN...MY
EARS'RE
STILL
RINGIN'.
WHAT
APPENED?
WHAT'S--?
AW, THAT'S RIGHT. GUN-GIRL **SHOT** US.
WILDCAT? YOU'RE...ALL RIGHT?
DON'T TELL ME YOU WERE **WORRIED**, P.G. YOU FORGET THIS **CAT** HAS **NINE LIVES?**
OR **HAD**.
JUST SIT **TIGHT**. I'M--
BLAM
BLAM
DON'T.
DON'T STEP IN THEIR **PATH**.
I CAN'T KEEP THEM **AWAY** FROM YOU FOREVER.
WHY ARE YOU DOING THIS? YOU **HELPED** US DEFEAT THE **ULTRA-HUMANITE** BEFORE. YOU HELPED US **SAVE** THE **WORLD**.
YOU WERE ON **OUR** SIDE, AVENGER!
I AM ON **NO ONE'S** SIDE.
HAAKK

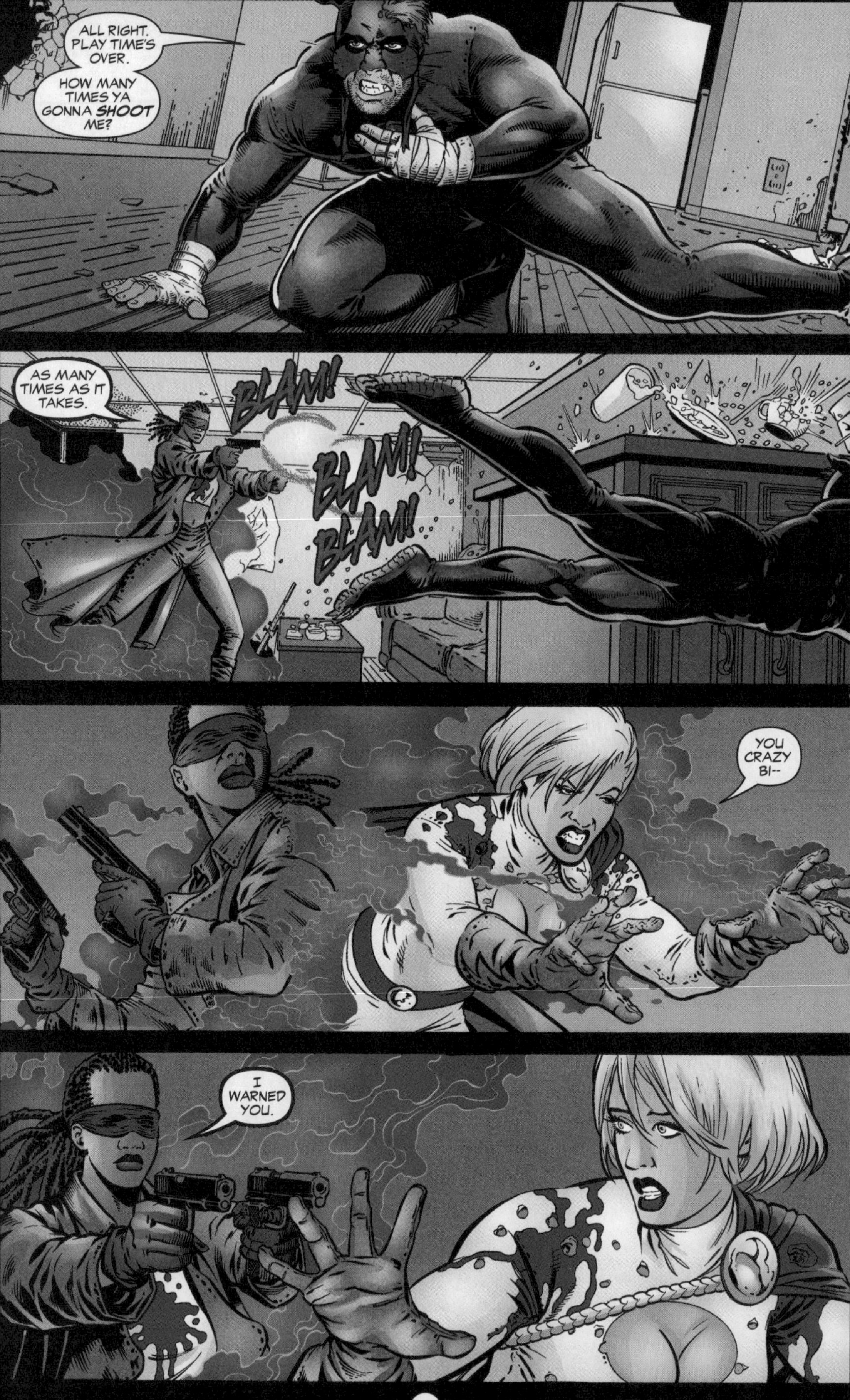
ALL RIGHT. PLAY TIME'S OVER.
HOW MANY TIMES YA GONNA **SHOOT** ME?
AS MANY TIMES AS IT TAKES.
BLAM!
BLAM!
BLAM!
YOU CRAZY BI--
I WARNED YOU.

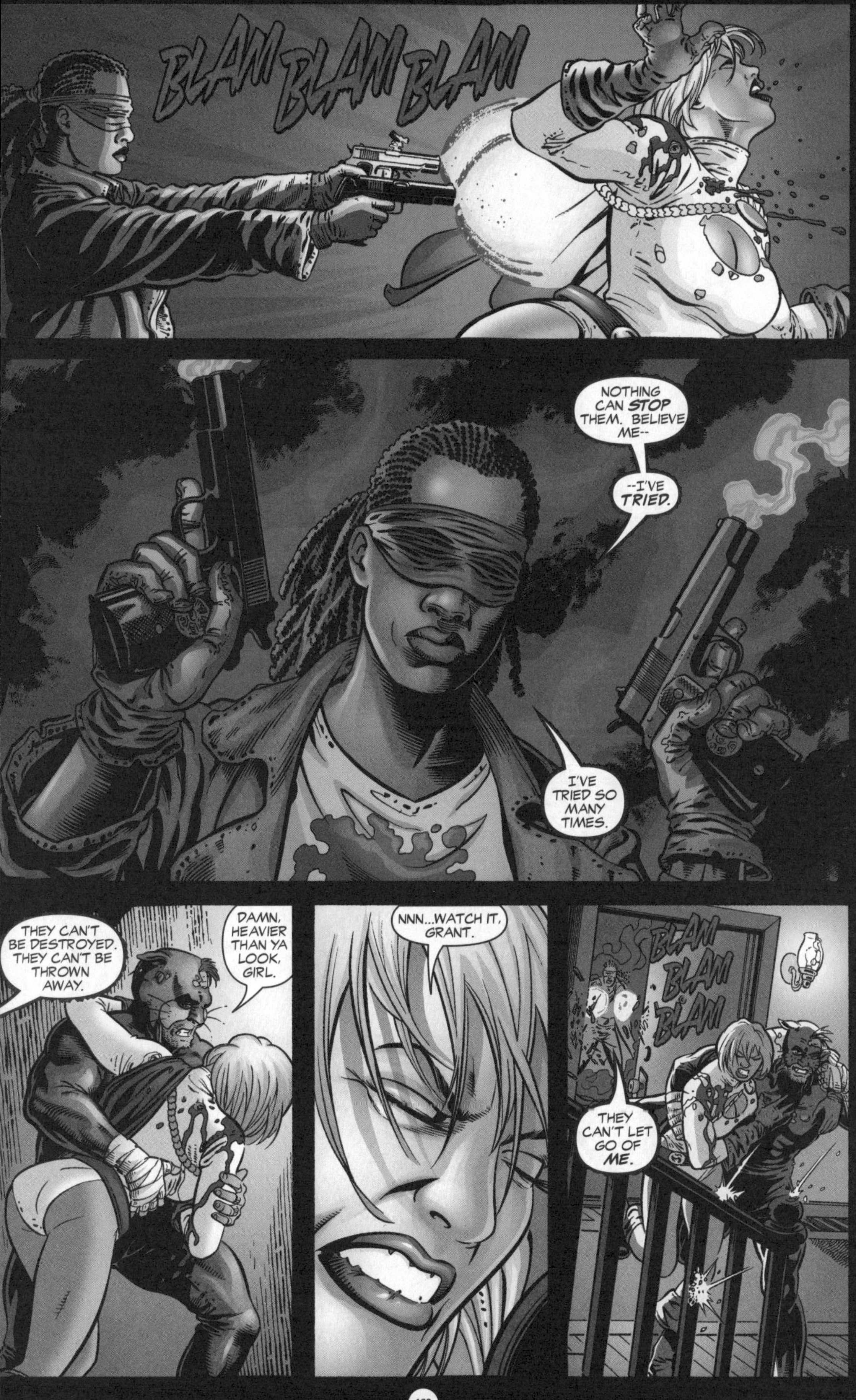
BLAM BLAM BLAM
NOTHING CAN STOP THEM. BELIEVE ME--
--I'VE TRIED.
I'VE TRIED SO MANY TIMES.
THEY CAN'T BE DESTROYED. THEY CAN'T BE THROWN AWAY.
DAMN, HEAVIER THAN YA LOOK, GIRL.
NNN...WATCH IT, GRANT.
BLAM BLAM BLAM
THEY CAN'T LET GO OF ME.

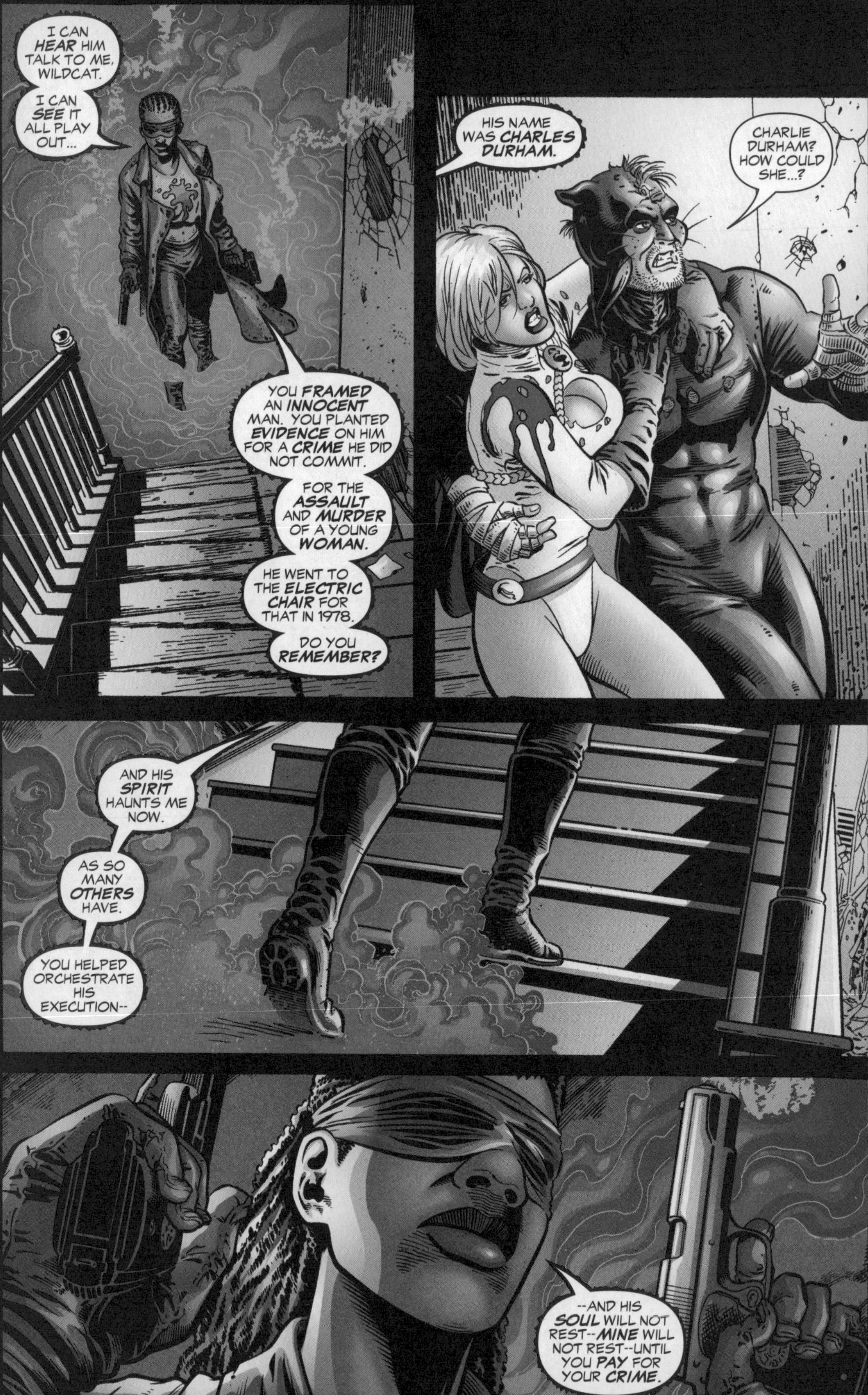

I CAN HEAR HIM TALK TO ME, WILDCAT.
I CAN SEE IT ALL PLAY OUT...
YOU FRAMED AN INNOCENT MAN. YOU PLANTED EVIDENCE ON HIM FOR A CRIME HE DID NOT COMMIT.
FOR THE ASSAULT AND MURDER OF A YOUNG WOMAN.
HE WENT TO THE ELECTRIC CHAIR FOR THAT IN 1978.
DO YOU REMEMBER?
HIS NAME WAS CHARLES DURHAM.
CHARLIE DURHAM? HOW COULD SHE...?
AND HIS SPIRIT HAUNTS ME NOW.
AS SO MANY OTHERS HAVE.
YOU HELPED ORCHESTRATE HIS EXECUTION--
--AND HIS SOUL WILL NOT REST--MINE WILL NOT REST--UNTIL YOU PAY FOR YOUR CRIME.

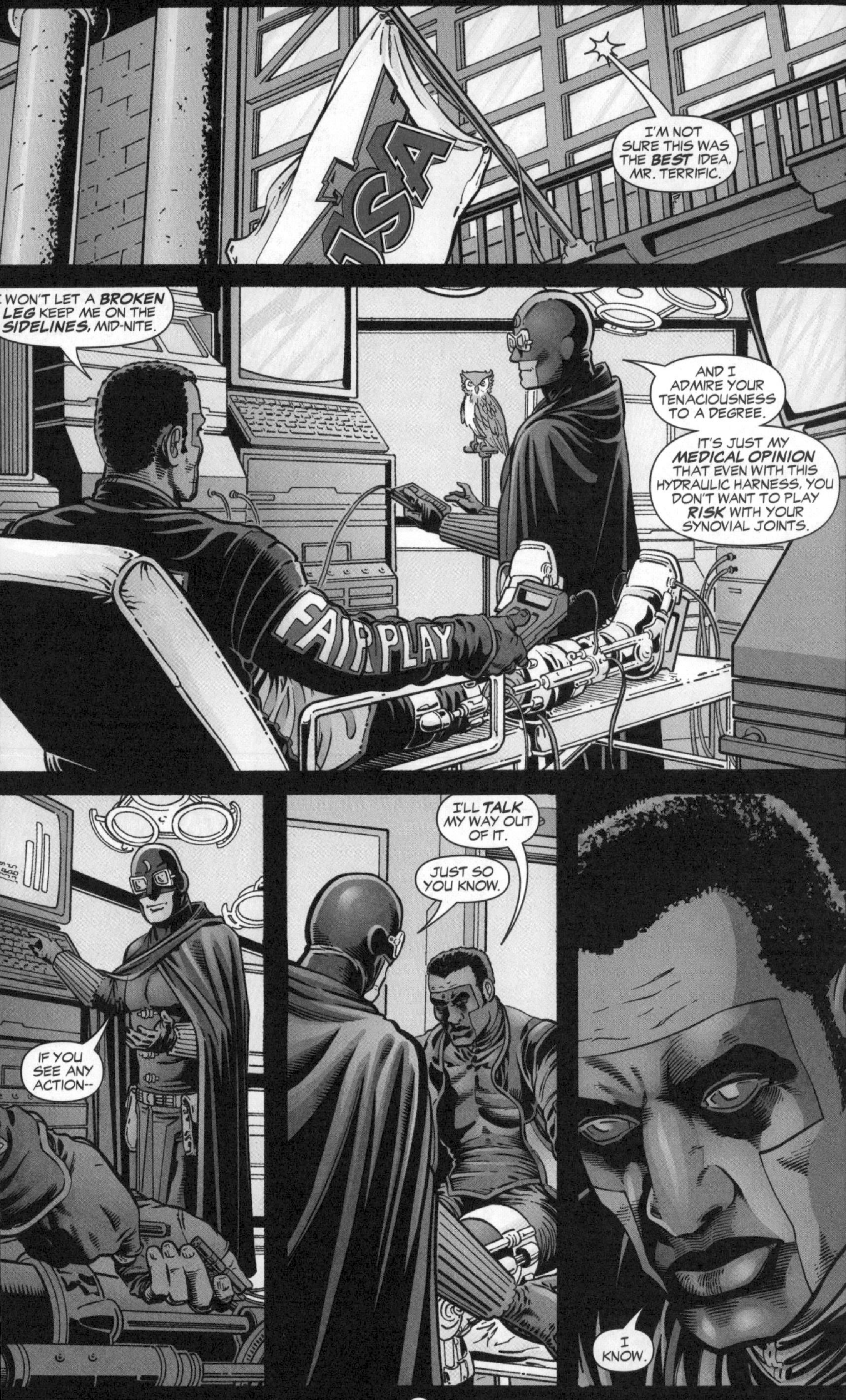
I'M NOT SURE THIS WAS THE BEST IDEA, MR. TERRIFIC.
WON'T LET A BROKEN LEG KEEP ME ON THE SIDELINES, MID-NITE.
AND I ADMIRE YOUR TENACIOUSNESS TO A DEGREE.
IT'S JUST MY MEDICAL OPINION THAT EVEN WITH THIS HYDRAULIC HARNESS, YOU DON'T WANT TO PLAY RISK WITH YOUR SYNOVIAL JOINTS.
FAIR PLAY
IF YOU SEE ANY ACTION--
I'LL TALK MY WAY OUT OF IT.
JUST SO YOU KNOW.
I KNOW.

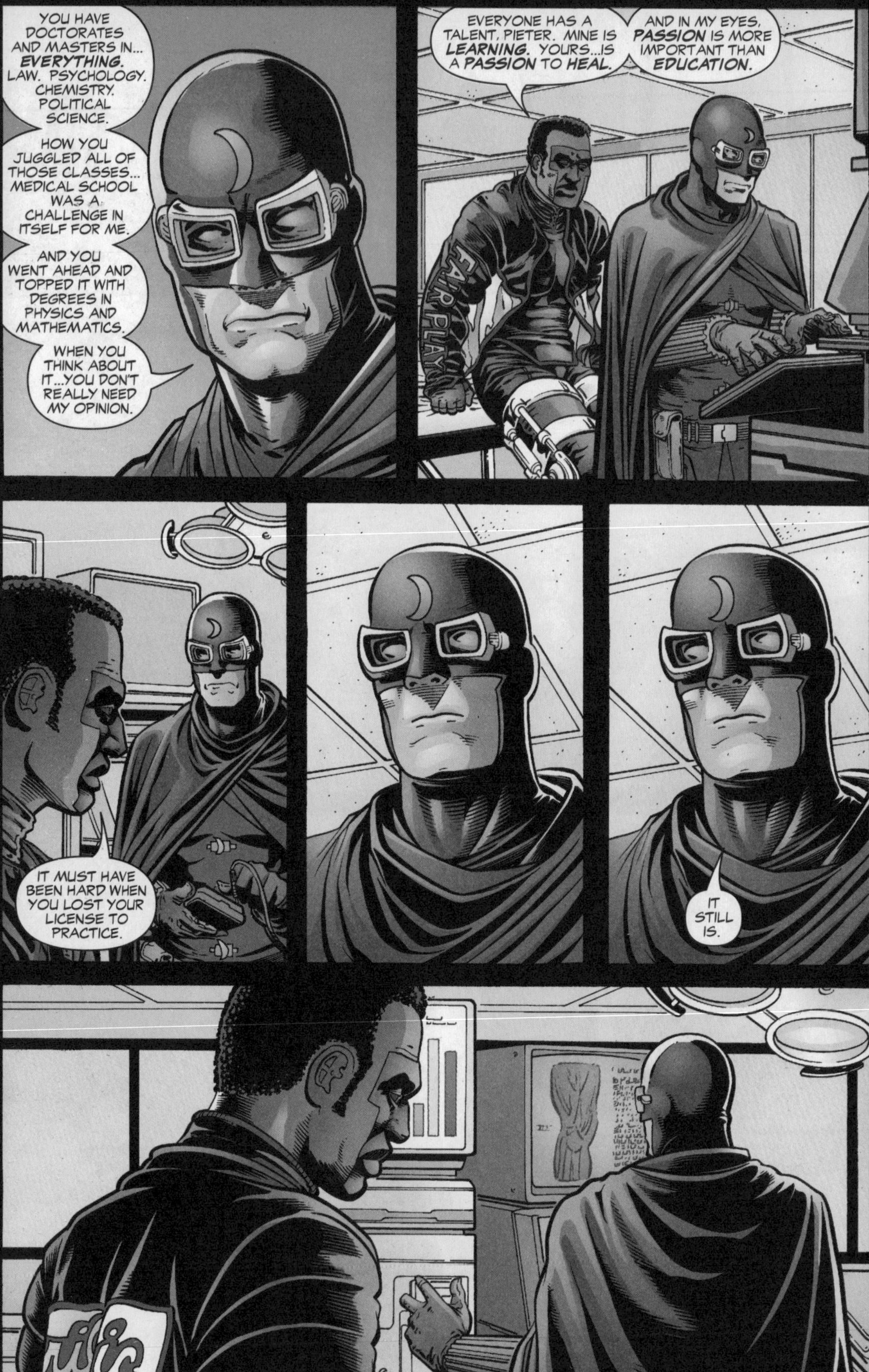
YOU HAVE DOCTORATES AND MASTERS IN... EVERYTHING. LAW. PSYCHOLOGY. CHEMISTRY. POLITICAL SCIENCE.
HOW YOU JUGGLED ALL OF THOSE CLASSES... MEDICAL SCHOOL WAS A CHALLENGE IN ITSELF FOR ME.
AND YOU WENT AHEAD AND TOPPED IT WITH DEGREES IN PHYSICS AND MATHEMATICS.
WHEN YOU THINK ABOUT IT...YOU DON'T REALLY NEED MY OPINION.
EVERYONE HAS A TALENT, PIETER. MINE IS LEARNING. YOURS...IS A PASSION TO HEAL.
AND IN MY EYES, PASSION IS MORE IMPORTANT THAN EDUCATION.
FAIR PLAY
IT MUST HAVE BEEN HARD WHEN YOU LOST YOUR LICENSE TO PRACTICE.
IT STILL IS.

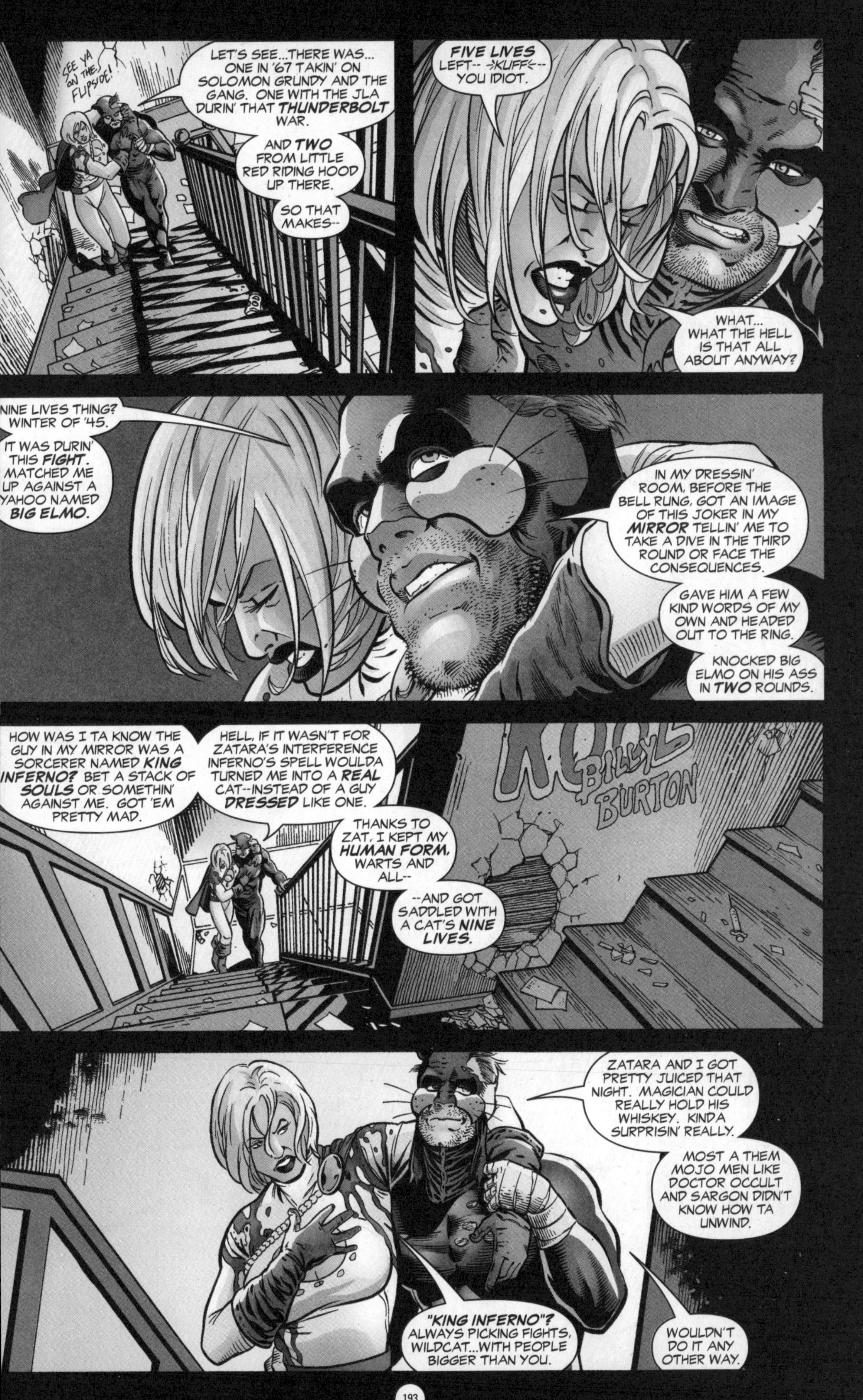
SEE YA ON THE FLIPSIDE!
LET'S SEE...THERE WAS... ONE IN '67 TAKIN' ON SOLOMON GRUNDY AND THE GANG. ONE WITH THE JLA DURIN' THAT THUNDERBOLT WAR.
AND TWO FROM LITTLE RED RIDING HOOD UP THERE.
SO THAT MAKES--
FIVE LIVES LEFT-- >KUFF< YOU IDIOT.
WHAT... WHAT THE HELL IS THAT ALL ABOUT ANYWAY?
NINE LIVES THING? WINTER OF '45.
IT WAS DURIN' THIS FIGHT. MATCHED ME UP AGAINST A YAHOO NAMED BIG ELMO.
IN MY DRESSIN' ROOM, BEFORE THE BELL RUNG, GOT AN IMAGE OF THIS JOKER IN MY MIRROR TELLIN' ME TO TAKE A DIVE IN THE THIRD ROUND OR FACE THE CONSEQUENCES.
GAVE HIM A FEW KIND WORDS OF MY OWN AND HEADED OUT TO THE RING.
KNOCKED BIG ELMO ON HIS ASS IN TWO ROUNDS.
HOW WAS I TA KNOW THE GUY IN MY MIRROR WAS A SORCERER NAMED KING INFERNO? BET A STACK OF SOULS OR SOMETHIN' AGAINST ME. GOT 'EM PRETTY MAD.
HELL, IF IT WASN'T FOR ZATARA'S INTERFERENCE INFERNO'S SPELL WOULDA TURNED ME INTO A REAL CAT--INSTEAD OF A GUY DRESSED LIKE ONE.
THANKS TO ZAT, I KEPT MY HUMAN FORM, WARTS AND ALL--
--AND GOT SADDLED WITH A CAT'S NINE LIVES.
BILLY BURTON
ZATARA AND I GOT PRETTY JUICED THAT NIGHT. MAGICIAN COULD REALLY HOLD HIS WHISKEY. KINDA SURPRISIN' REALLY.
MOST A THEM MOJO MEN LIKE DOCTOR OCCULT AND SARGON DIDN'T KNOW HOW TA UNWIND.
"KING INFERNO"? ALWAYS PICKING FIGHTS, WILDCAT...WITH PEOPLE BIGGER THAN YOU.
WOULDN'T DO IT ANY OTHER WAY.

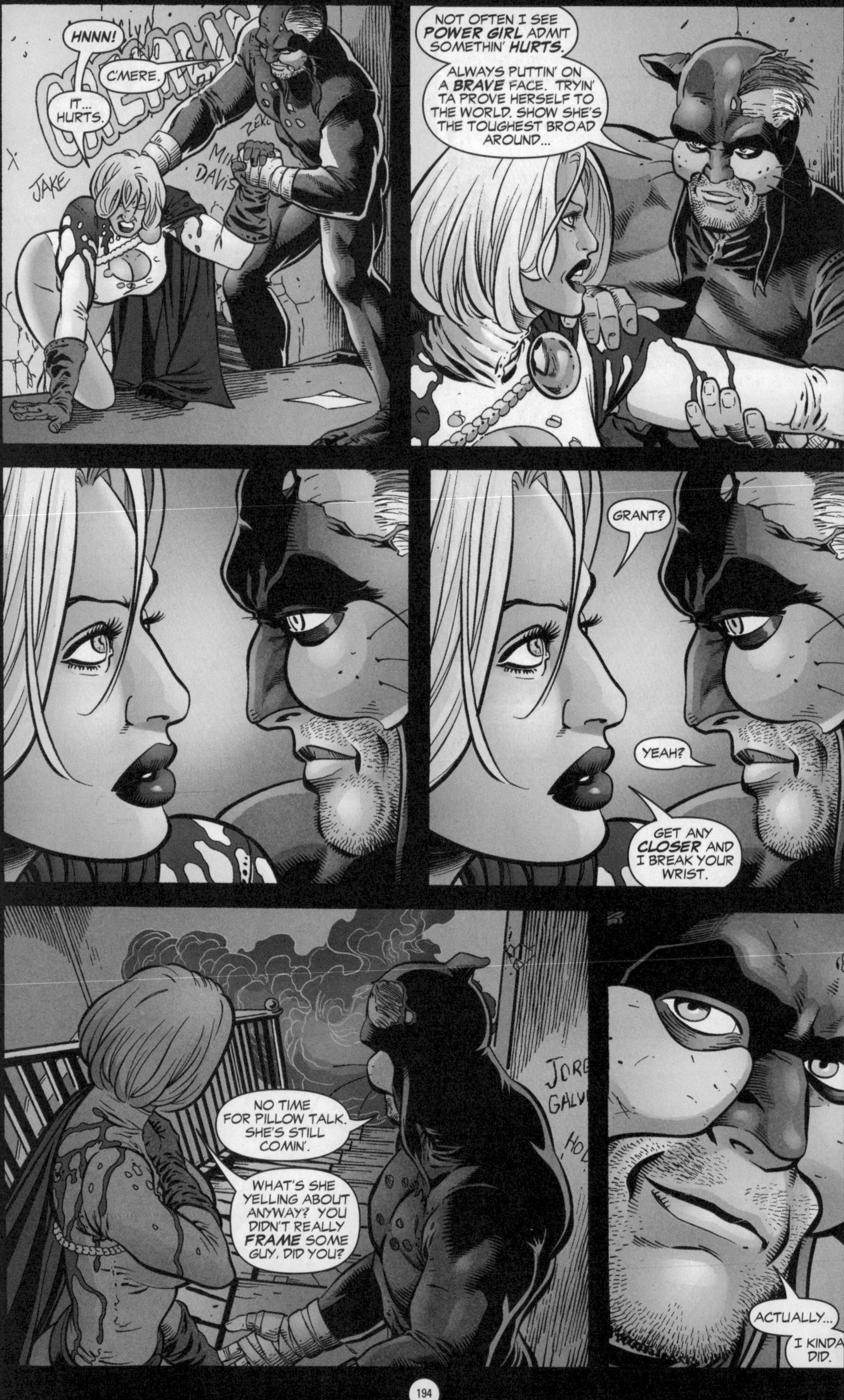
HNNN!
C'MERE.
IT... HURTS.
JAKE
DAVIS
NOT OFTEN I SEE POWER GIRL ADMIT SOMETHIN' HURTS.
ALWAYS PUTTIN' ON A BRAVE FACE. TRYIN' TA PROVE HERSELF TO THE WORLD. SHOW SHE'S THE TOUGHEST BROAD AROUND...
GRANT?
YEAH?
GET ANY CLOSER AND I BREAK YOUR WRIST.
NO TIME FOR PILLOW TALK. SHE'S STILL COMIN'.
WHAT'S SHE YELLING ABOUT ANYWAY? YOU DIDN'T REALLY FRAME SOME GUY, DID YOU?
ACTUALLY...
I KINDA DID.

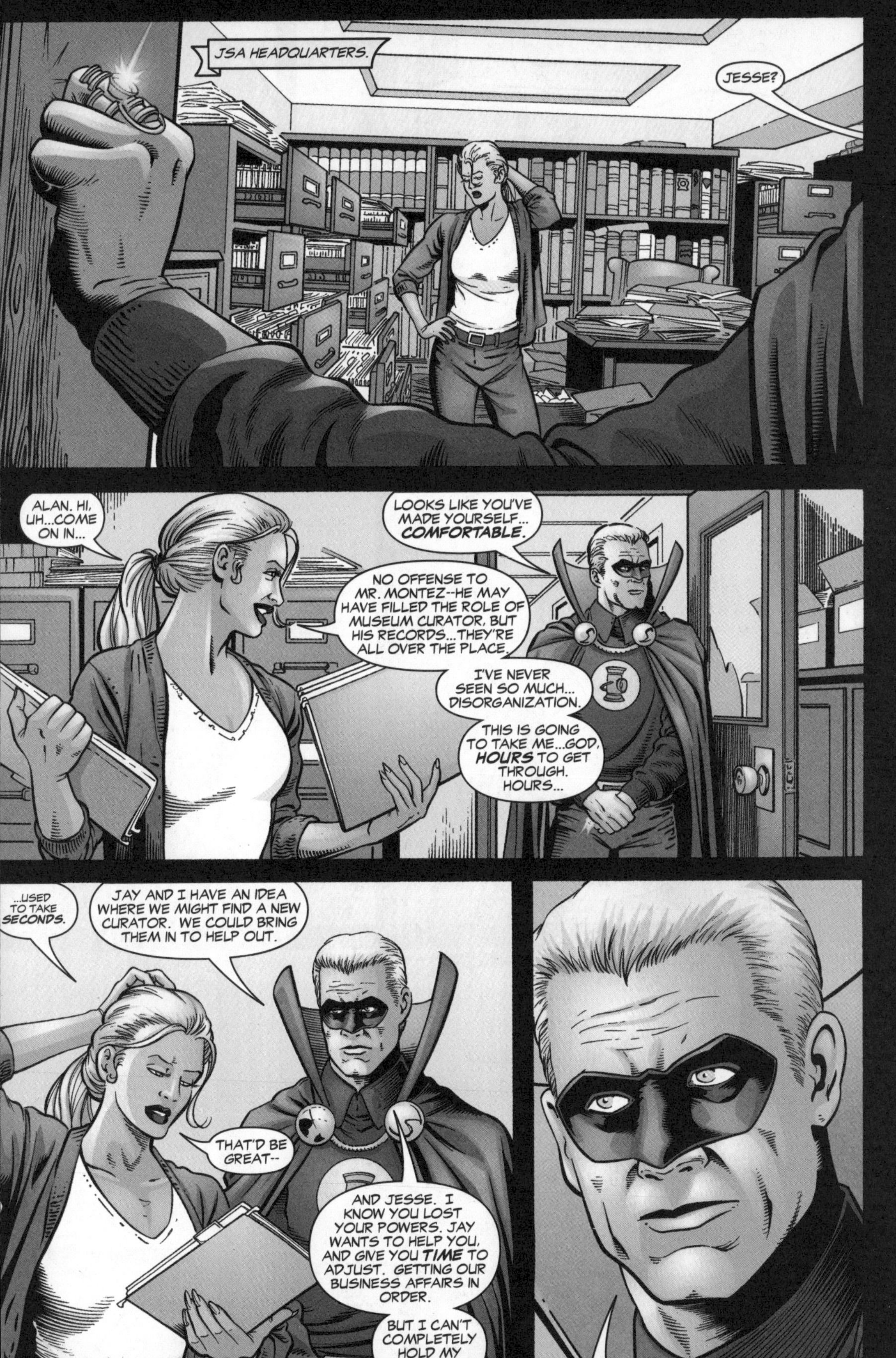
JSA HEADQUARTERS.
JESSE?
ALAN. HI, UH...COME ON IN...
LOOKS LIKE YOU'VE MADE YOURSELF... COMFORTABLE.
NO OFFENSE TO MR. MONTEZ--HE MAY HAVE FILLED THE ROLE OF MUSEUM CURATOR, BUT HIS RECORDS...THEY'RE ALL OVER THE PLACE.
I'VE NEVER SEEN SO MUCH... DISORGANIZATION.
THIS IS GOING TO TAKE ME...GOD, HOURS TO GET THROUGH. HOURS...
...USED TO TAKE SECONDS.
JAY AND I HAVE AN IDEA WHERE WE MIGHT FIND A NEW CURATOR. WE COULD BRING THEM IN TO HELP OUT.
THAT'D BE GREAT--
AND JESSE. I KNOW YOU LOST YOUR POWERS. JAY WANTS TO HELP YOU, AND GIVE YOU TIME TO ADJUST. GETTING OUR BUSINESS AFFAIRS IN ORDER.
BUT I CAN'T COMPLETELY HOLD MY TONGUE.
YOU'VE BECOME A DISAPPOINTMENT.

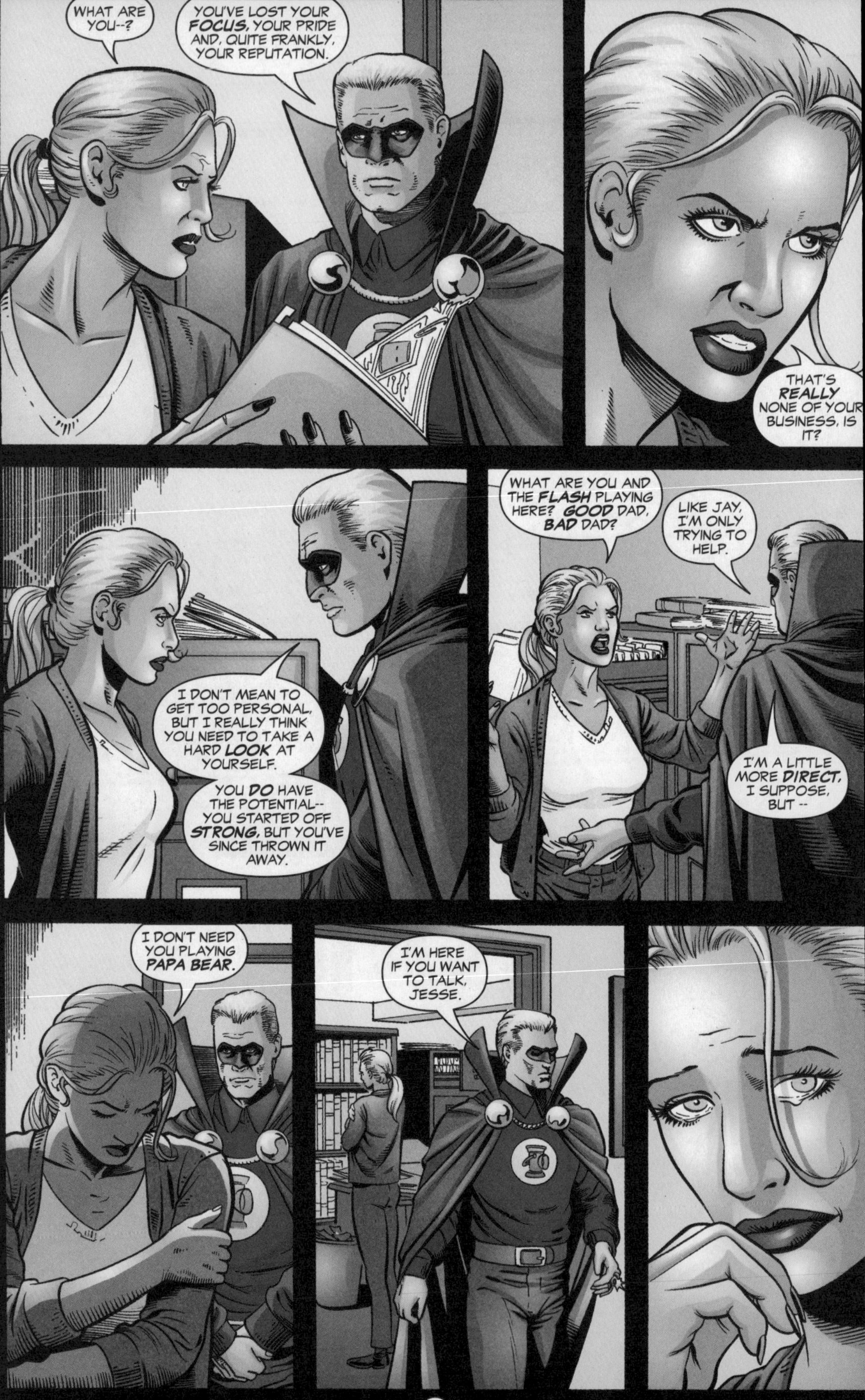
WHAT ARE YOU--?
YOU'VE LOST YOUR FOCUS, YOUR PRIDE AND, QUITE FRANKLY, YOUR REPUTATION.
THAT'S REALLY NONE OF YOUR BUSINESS, IS IT?
I DON'T MEAN TO GET TOO PERSONAL, BUT I REALLY THINK YOU NEED TO TAKE A HARD LOOK AT YOURSELF.
YOU DO HAVE THE POTENTIAL-- YOU STARTED OFF STRONG, BUT YOU'VE SINCE THROWN IT AWAY.
WHAT ARE YOU AND THE FLASH PLAYING HERE? GOOD DAD, BAD DAD?
LIKE JAY, I'M ONLY TRYING TO HELP.
I'M A LITTLE MORE DIRECT, I SUPPOSE, BUT --
I DON'T NEED YOU PLAYING PAPA BEAR.
I'M HERE IF YOU WANT TO TALK, JESSE.

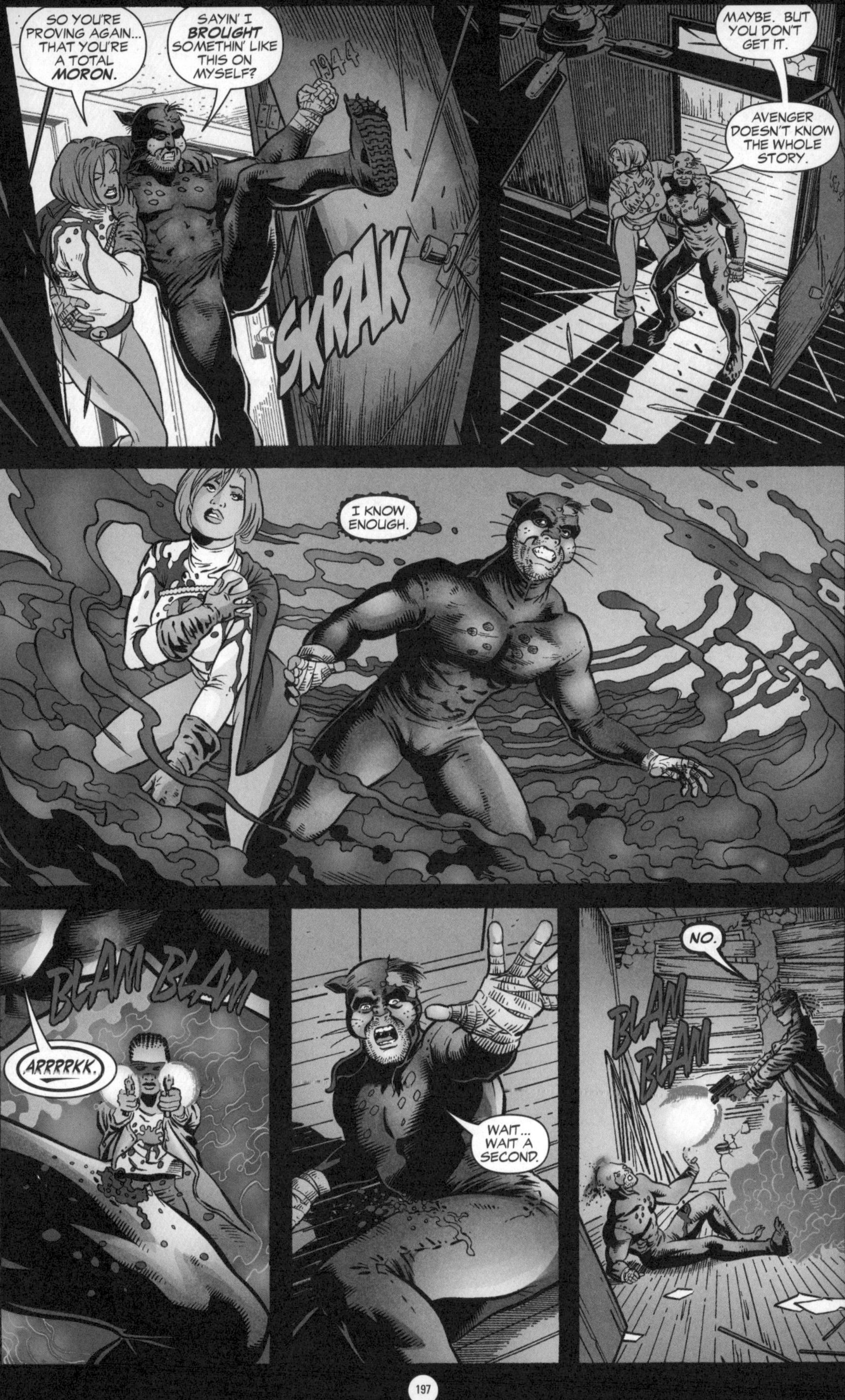
SO YOU'RE PROVING AGAIN... THAT YOU'RE A TOTAL MORON.
SAYIN' I BROUGHT SOMETHIN' LIKE THIS ON MYSELF?
1944
SKRAK
MAYBE. BUT YOU DON'T GET IT.
AVENGER DOESN'T KNOW THE WHOLE STORY.
I KNOW ENOUGH.
BLAM BLAM
ARRRRKK.
WAIT... WAIT A SECOND.
NO.
BLAM BLAM

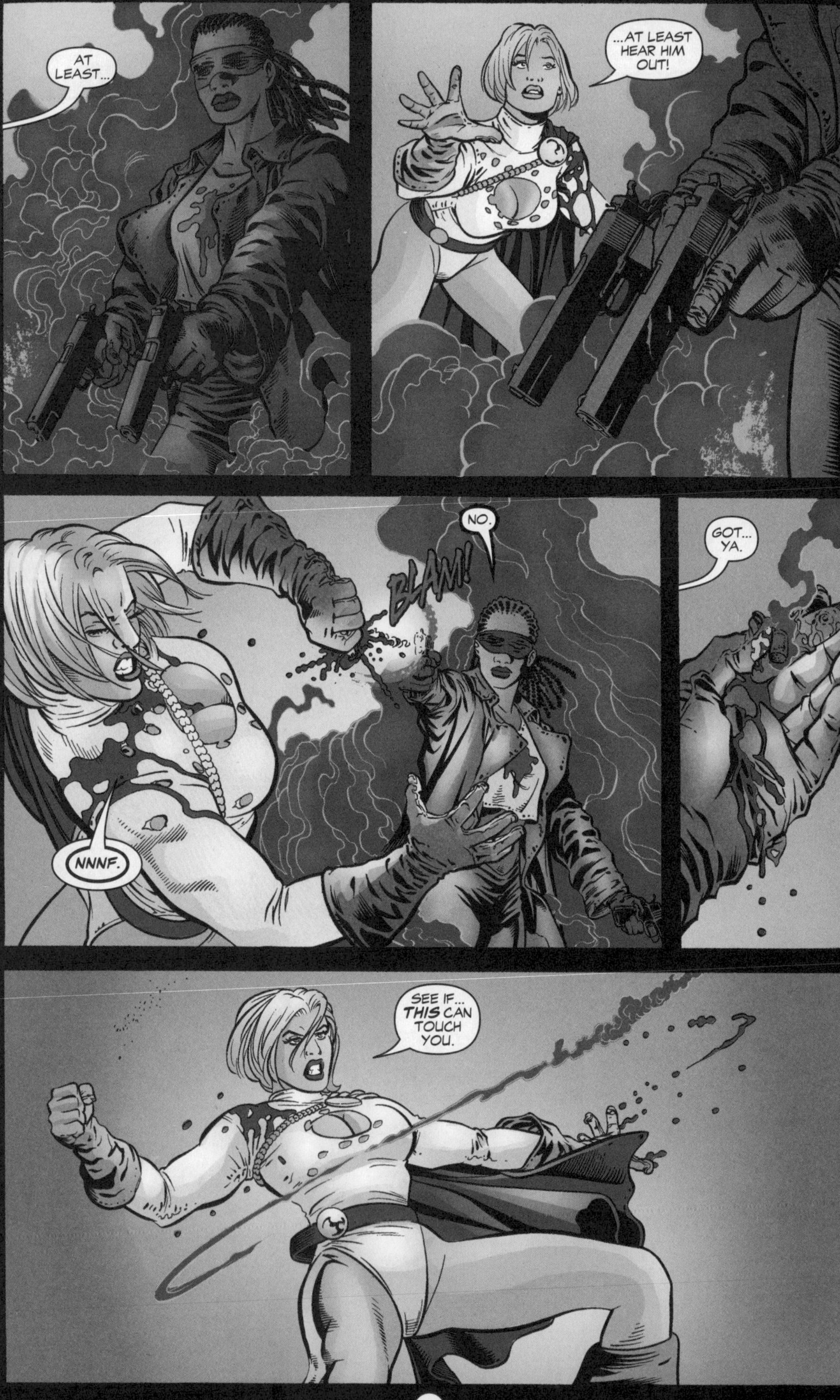
AT LEAST...
...AT LEAST HEAR HIM OUT!
NO.
BLAM!
NNNF.
GOT... YA.
SEE IF... THIS CAN TOUCH YOU.

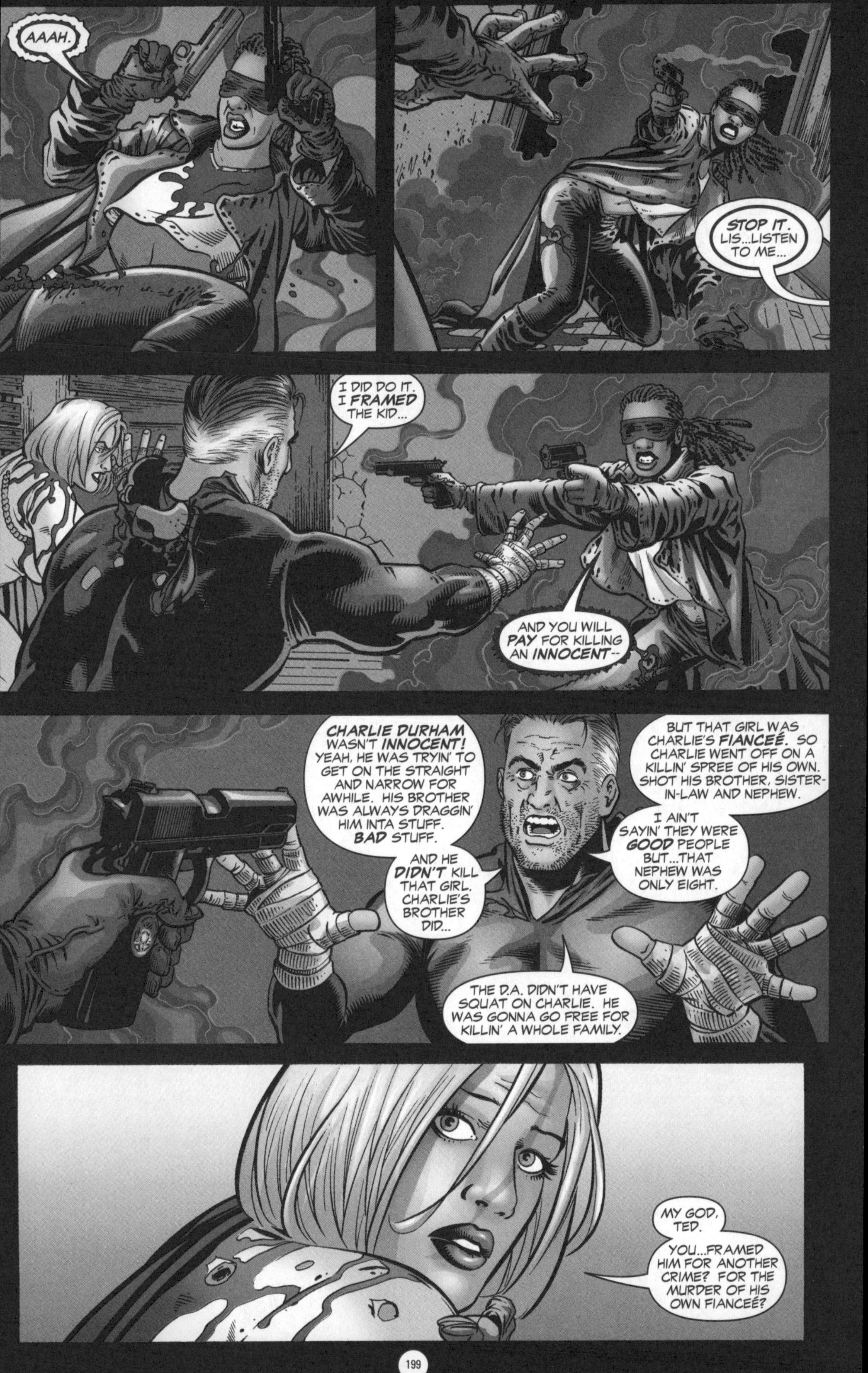
AAAH.
STOP IT. LIS...LISTEN TO ME...
I DID DO IT. I FRAMED THE KID...
AND YOU WILL PAY FOR KILLING AN INNOCENT--
CHARLIE DURHAM WASN'T INNOCENT! YEAH, HE WAS TRYIN' TO GET ON THE STRAIGHT AND NARROW FOR AWHILE. HIS BROTHER WAS ALWAYS DRAGGIN' HIM INTA STUFF. BAD STUFF.
AND HE DIDN'T KILL THAT GIRL. CHARLIE'S BROTHER DID...
BUT THAT GIRL WAS CHARLIE'S FIANCEÉ. SO CHARLIE WENT OFF ON A KILLIN' SPREE OF HIS OWN. SHOT HIS BROTHER, SISTER-IN-LAW AND NEPHEW.
I AIN'T SAYIN' THEY WERE GOOD PEOPLE BUT...THAT NEPHEW WAS ONLY EIGHT.
THE D.A. DIDN'T HAVE SQUAT ON CHARLIE. HE WAS GONNA GO FREE FOR KILLIN' A WHOLE FAMILY.
MY GOD, TED.
YOU...FRAMED HIM FOR ANOTHER CRIME? FOR THE MURDER OF HIS OWN FIANCEÉ?

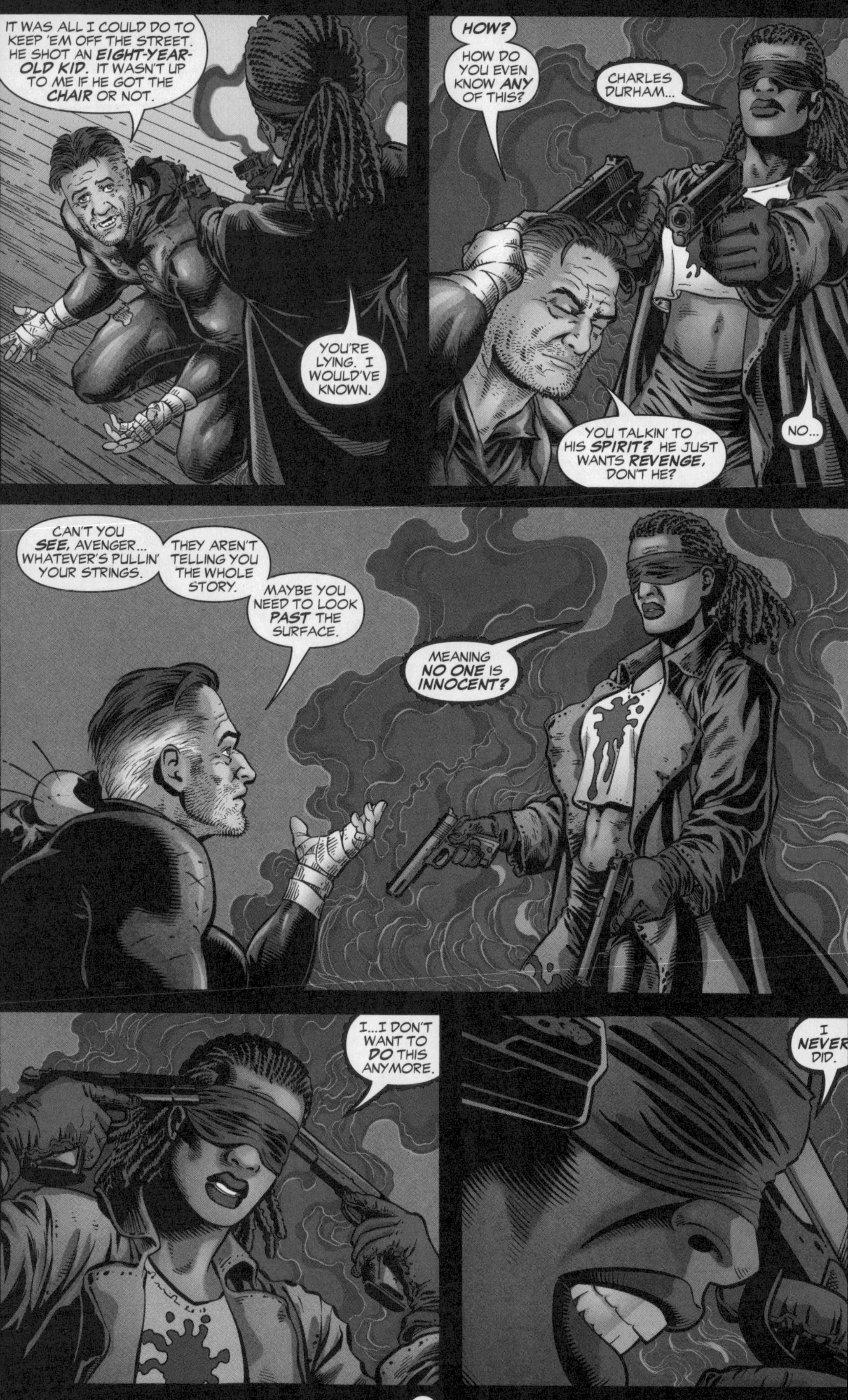
IT WAS ALL I COULD DO TO KEEP 'EM OFF THE STREET. HE SHOT AN EIGHT-YEAR-OLD KID. IT WASN'T UP TO ME IF HE GOT THE CHAIR OR NOT.
YOU'RE LYING. I WOULD'VE KNOWN.
HOW?
HOW DO YOU EVEN KNOW ANY OF THIS?
CHARLES DURHAM...
YOU TALKIN' TO HIS SPIRIT? HE JUST WANTS REVENGE, DON'T HE?
NO...
CAN'T YOU SEE, AVENGER... WHATEVER'S PULLIN' YOUR STRINGS.
THEY AREN'T TELLING YOU THE WHOLE STORY.
MAYBE YOU NEED TO LOOK PAST THE SURFACE.
MEANING NO ONE IS INNOCENT?
I...I DON'T WANT TO DO THIS ANYMORE.
I NEVER DID.

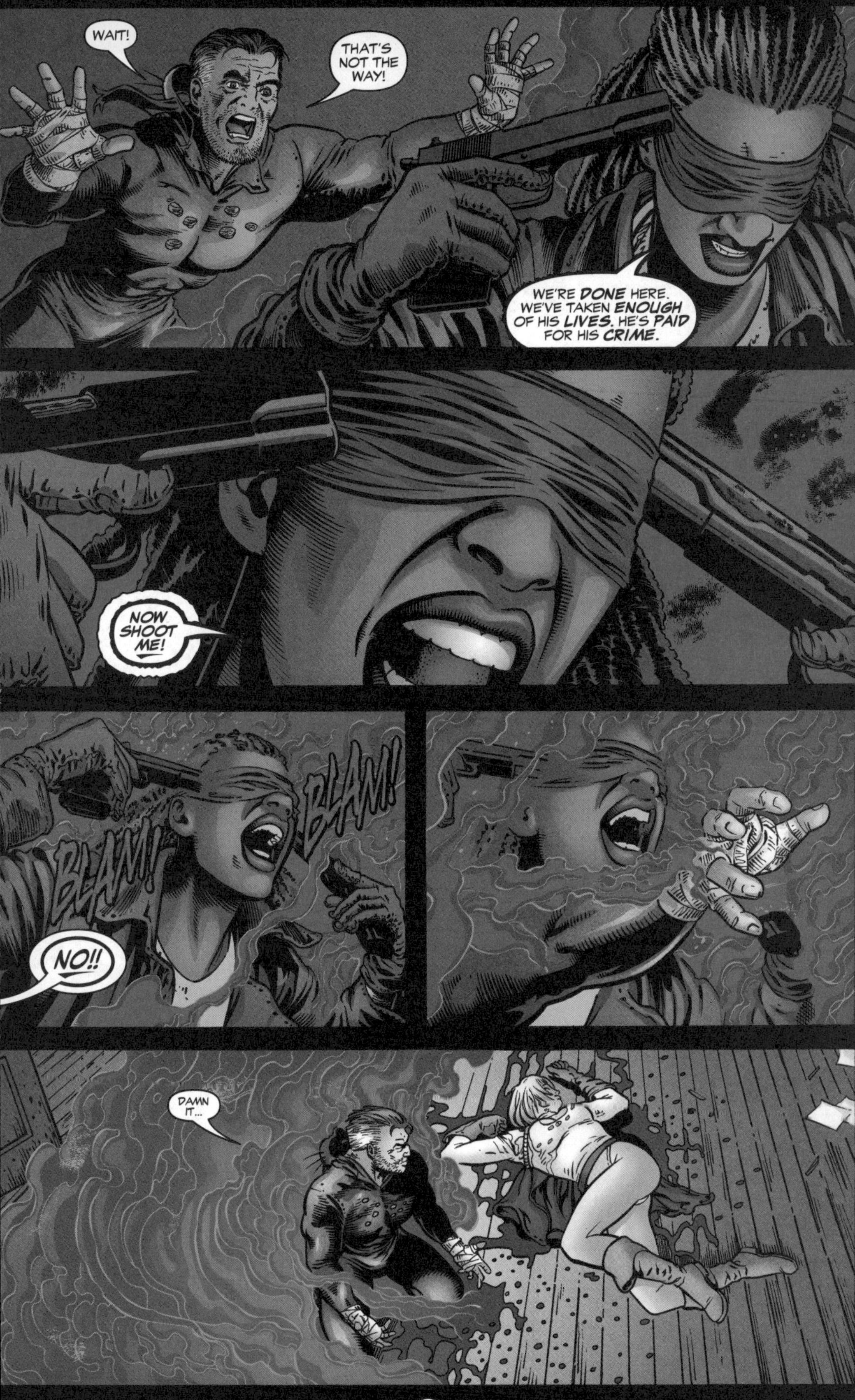
WAIT!
THAT'S NOT THE WAY!
WE'RE DONE HERE. WE'VE TAKEN ENOUGH OF HIS LIVES. HE'S PAID FOR HIS CRIME.
NOW SHOOT ME!
BLAM!
BLAM!
NO!!
DAMN IT...

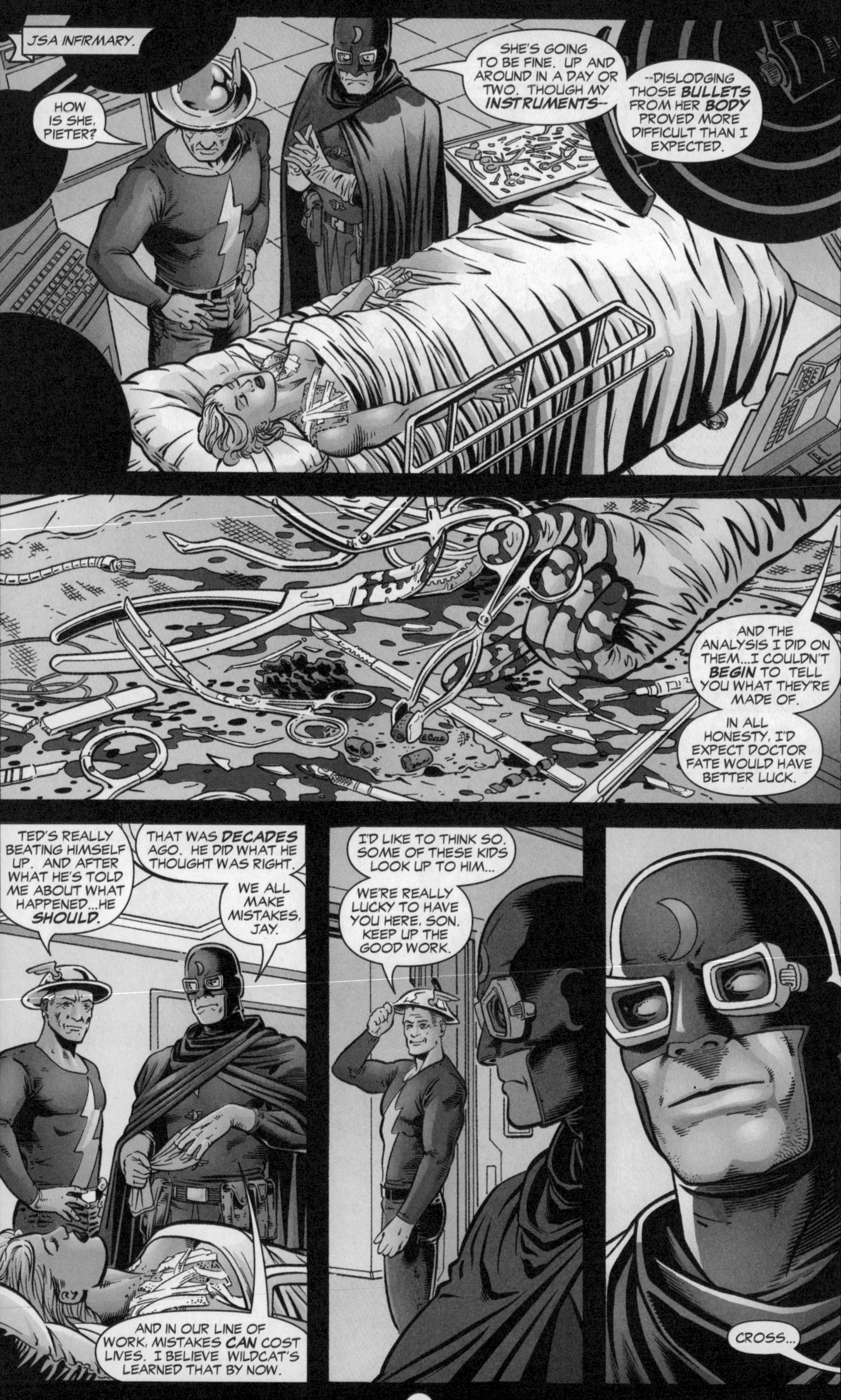
JSA INFIRMARY.
HOW IS SHE, PIETER?
SHE'S GOING TO BE FINE. UP AND AROUND IN A DAY OR TWO. THOUGH MY INSTRUMENTS--
--DISLODGING THOSE BULLETS FROM HER BODY PROVED MORE DIFFICULT THAN I EXPECTED.
AND THE ANALYSIS I DID ON THEM...I COULDN'T BEGIN TO TELL YOU WHAT THEY'RE MADE OF.
IN ALL HONESTY, I'D EXPECT DOCTOR FATE WOULD HAVE BETTER LUCK.
TED'S REALLY BEATING HIMSELF UP. AND AFTER WHAT HE'S TOLD ME ABOUT WHAT HAPPENED...HE SHOULD.
THAT WAS DECADES AGO. HE DID WHAT HE THOUGHT WAS RIGHT.
WE ALL MAKE MISTAKES, JAY.
AND IN OUR LINE OF WORK, MISTAKES CAN COST LIVES. I BELIEVE WILDCAT'S LEARNED THAT BY NOW.
I'D LIKE TO THINK SO. SOME OF THESE KIDS LOOK UP TO HIM...
WE'RE REALLY LUCKY TO HAVE YOU HERE, SON. KEEP UP THE GOOD WORK.
CROSS...

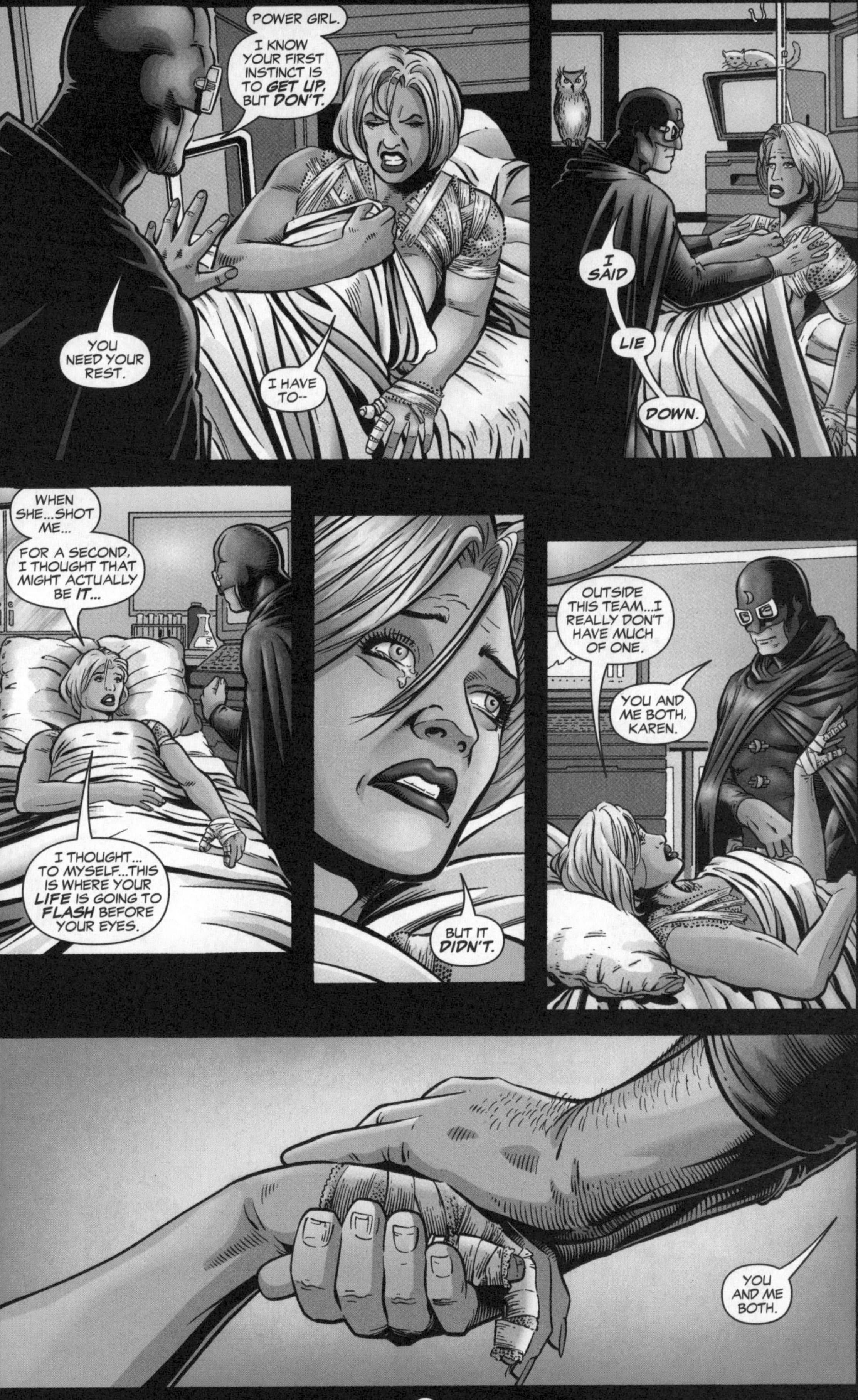

POWER GIRL.
I KNOW YOUR FIRST INSTINCT IS TO GET UP, BUT DON'T.
YOU NEED YOUR REST.
I HAVE TO--
I SAID
LIE
DOWN.
WHEN SHE...SHOT ME...
FOR A SECOND, I THOUGHT THAT MIGHT ACTUALLY BE IT...
I THOUGHT... TO MYSELF...THIS IS WHERE YOUR LIFE IS GOING TO FLASH BEFORE YOUR EYES.
BUT IT DIDN'T.
OUTSIDE THIS TEAM...I REALLY DON'T HAVE MUCH OF ONE.
YOU AND ME BOTH, KAREN.
YOU AND ME BOTH.

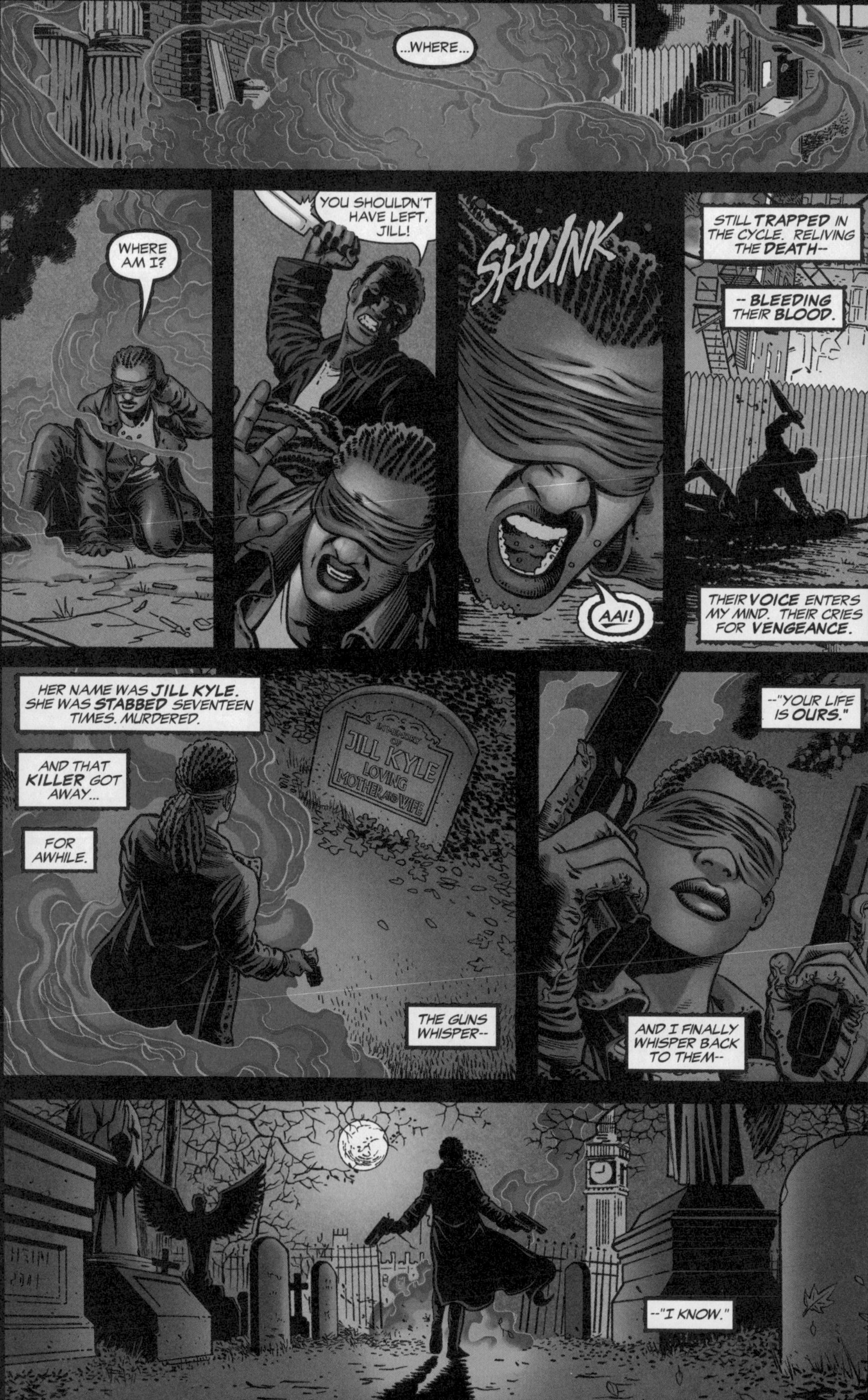

...WHERE...
WHERE AM I?
YOU SHOULDN'T HAVE LEFT, JILL!
SHUNK
AAI!
STILL TRAPPED IN THE CYCLE. RELIVING THE DEATH--
-- BLEEDING THEIR BLOOD.
THEIR VOICE ENTERS MY MIND. THEIR CRIES FOR VENGEANCE.
HER NAME WAS JILL KYLE. SHE WAS STABBED SEVENTEEN TIMES. MURDERED.
IN MEMORY OF JILL KYLE LOVING MOTHER AND WIFE
AND THAT KILLER GOT AWAY...
FOR AWHILE.
THE GUNS WHISPER--
--"YOUR LIFE IS OURS."
AND I FINALLY WHISPER BACK TO THEM--
--"I KNOW."

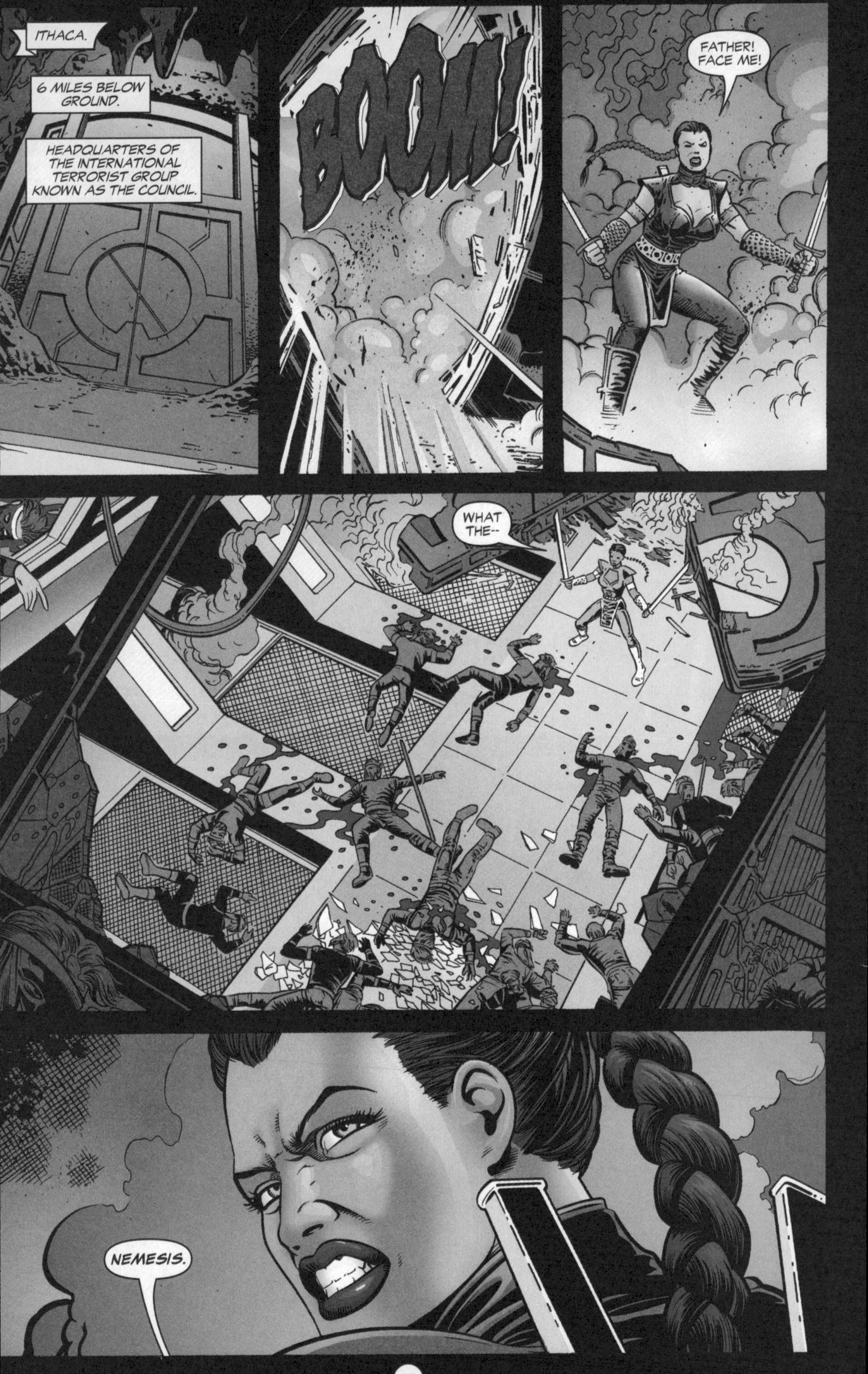
ITHACA.
6 MILES BELOW GROUND.
HEADQUARTERS OF THE INTERNATIONAL TERRORIST GROUP KNOWN AS THE COUNCIL.
BOOM!
FATHER! FACE ME!
WHAT THE--
NEMESIS.

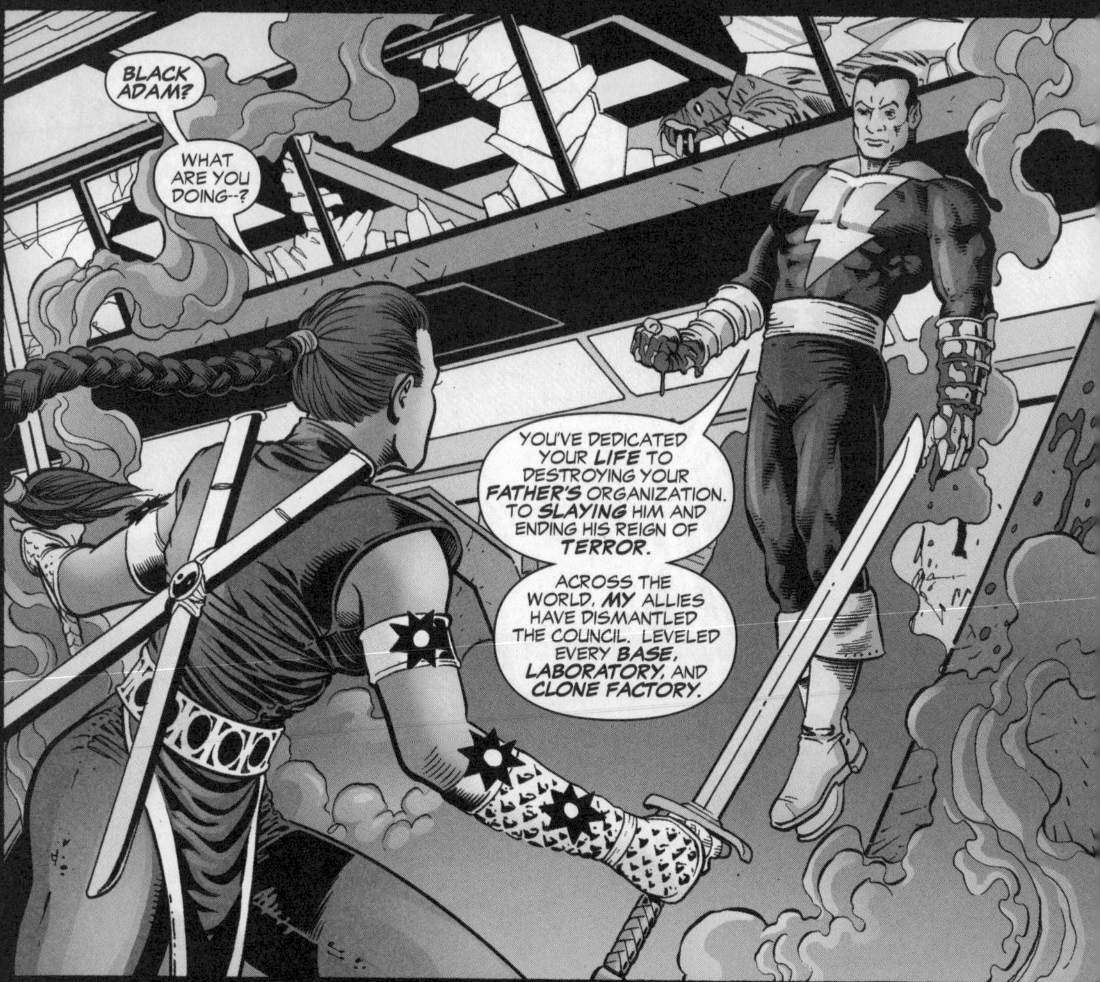
BLACK ADAM?
WHAT ARE YOU DOING--?
YOU'VE DEDICATED YOUR LIFE TO DESTROYING YOUR FATHER'S ORGANIZATION. TO SLAYING HIM AND ENDING HIS REIGN OF TERROR.
ACROSS THE WORLD, MY ALLIES HAVE DISMANTLED THE COUNCIL. LEVELED EVERY BASE, LABORATORY, AND CLONE FACTORY.

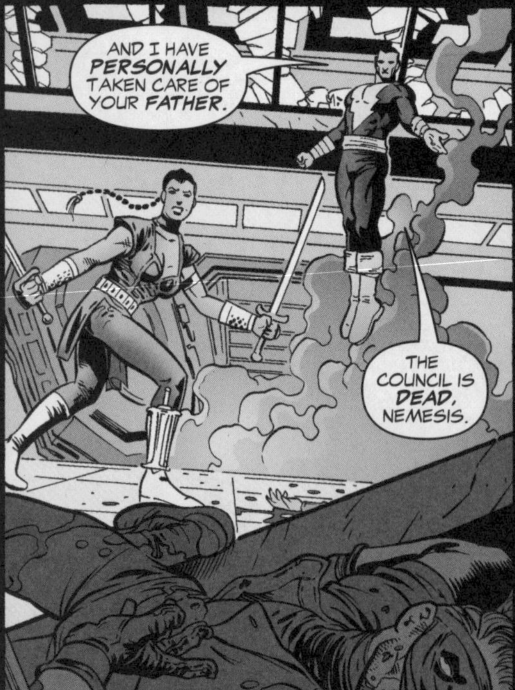
AND I HAVE PERSONALLY TAKEN CARE OF YOUR FATHER.
THE COUNCIL IS DEAD, NEMESIS.

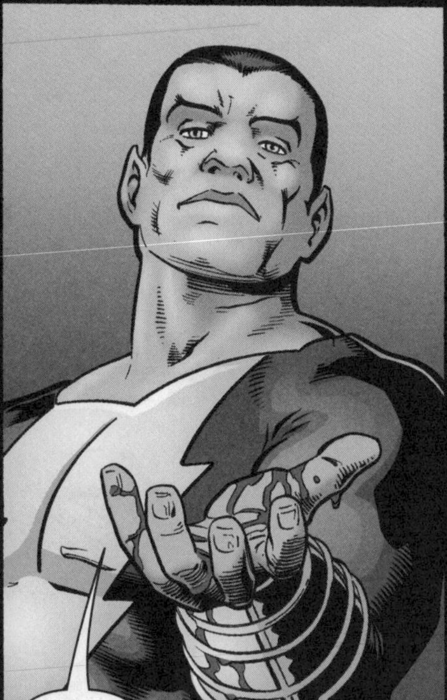
IT IS TIME TO FIND A NEW PURPOSE.

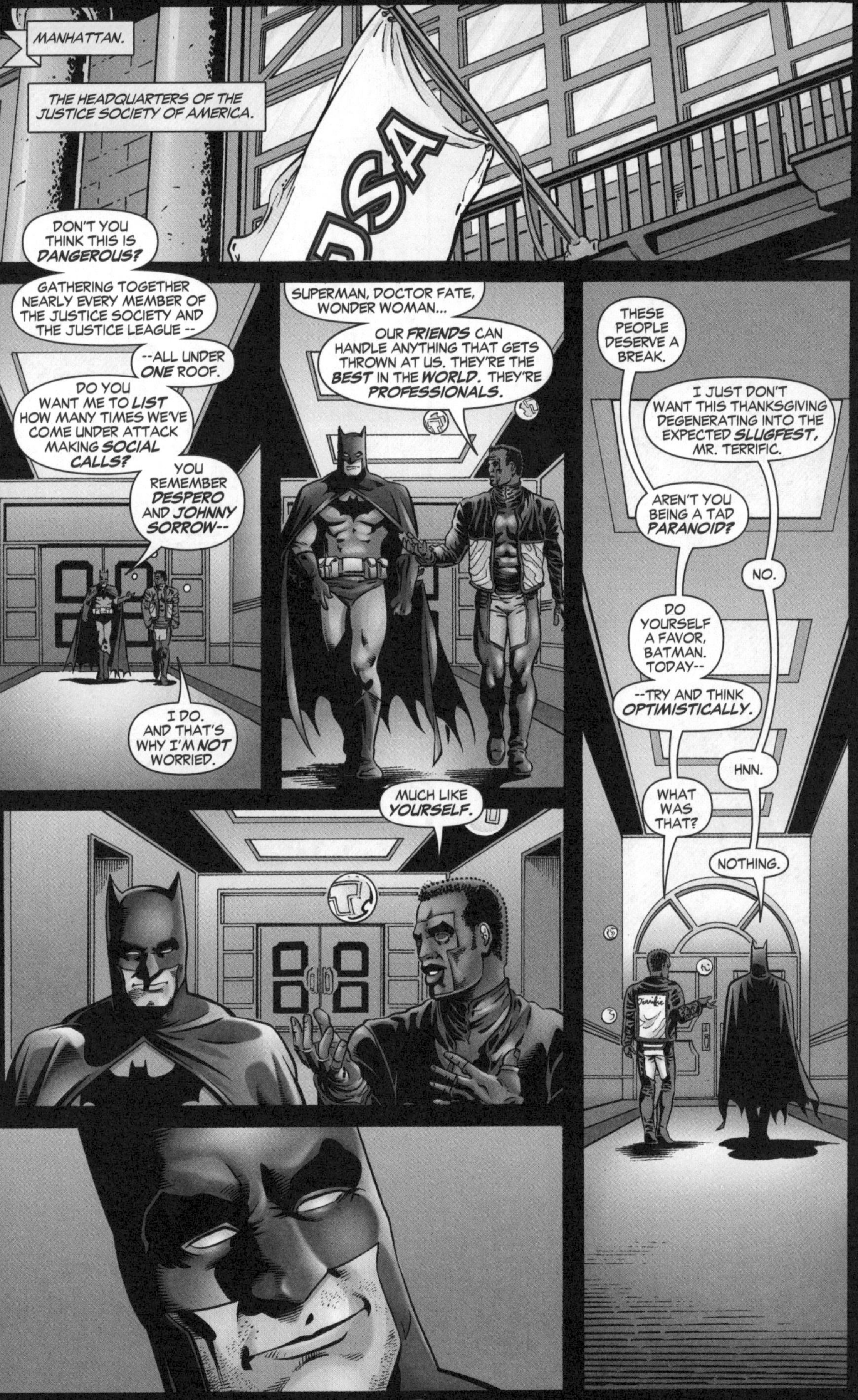
MANHATTAN.
THE HEADQUARTERS OF THE JUSTICE SOCIETY OF AMERICA.
JSA
DON'T YOU THINK THIS IS DANGEROUS?
GATHERING TOGETHER NEARLY EVERY MEMBER OF THE JUSTICE SOCIETY AND THE JUSTICE LEAGUE --
--ALL UNDER ONE ROOF.
DO YOU WANT ME TO LIST HOW MANY TIMES WE'VE COME UNDER ATTACK MAKING SOCIAL CALLS?
YOU REMEMBER DESPERO AND JOHNNY SORROW--
I DO. AND THAT'S WHY I'M NOT WORRIED.
SUPERMAN, DOCTOR FATE, WONDER WOMAN...
OUR FRIENDS CAN HANDLE ANYTHING THAT GETS THROWN AT US. THEY'RE THE BEST IN THE WORLD. THEY'RE PROFESSIONALS.
MUCH LIKE YOURSELF.
THESE PEOPLE DESERVE A BREAK.
I JUST DON'T WANT THIS THANKSGIVING DEGENERATING INTO THE EXPECTED SLUGFEST, MR. TERRIFIC.
AREN'T YOU BEING A TAD PARANOID?
NO.
DO YOURSELF A FAVOR, BATMAN. TODAY--
--TRY AND THINK OPTIMISTICALLY.
HNN.
WHAT WAS THAT?
NOTHING.
Terrific

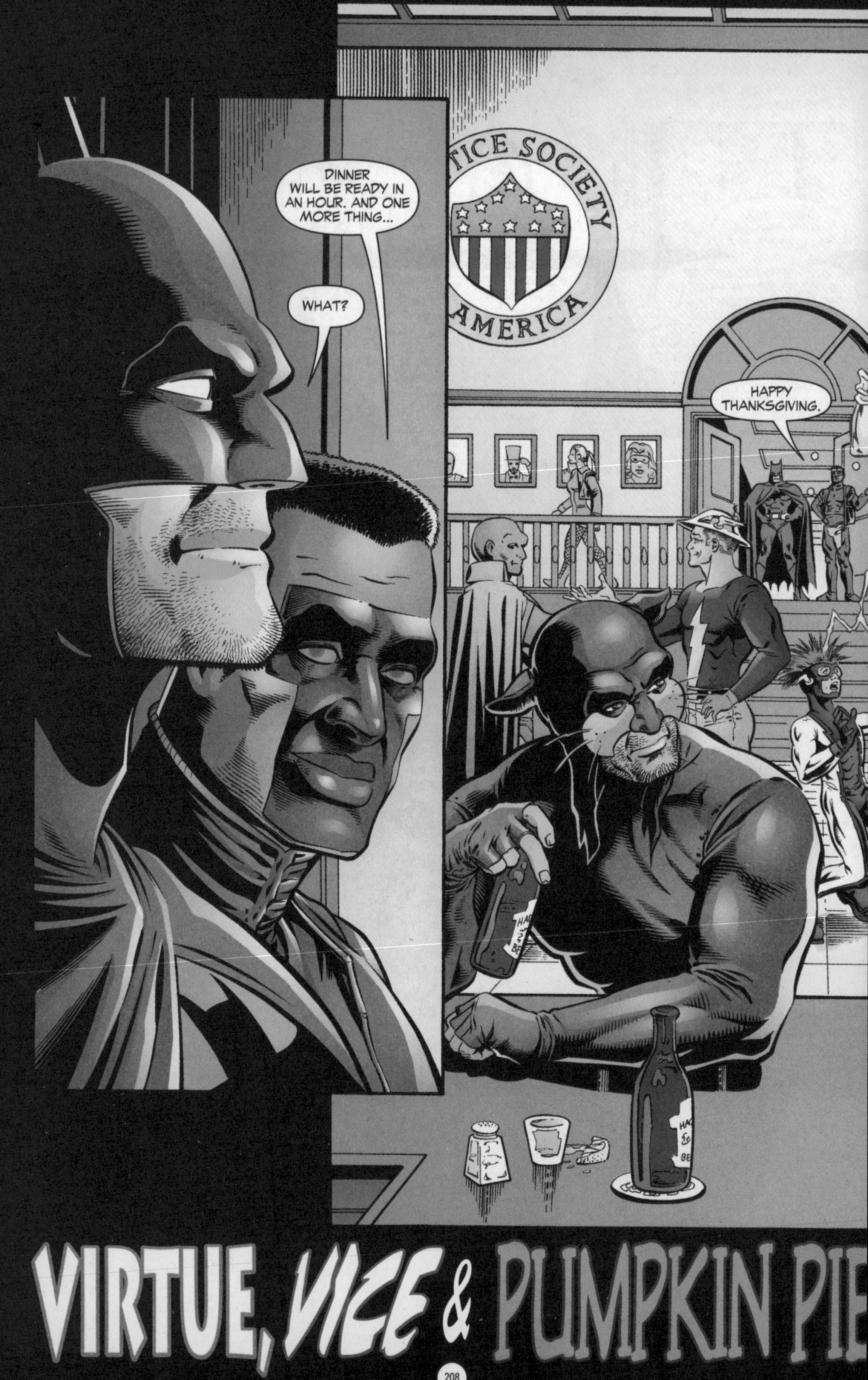
DINNER WILL BE READY IN AN HOUR. AND ONE MORE THING...
WHAT?
HAPPY THANKSGIVING.
VIRTUE, VICE & PUMPKIN PIE

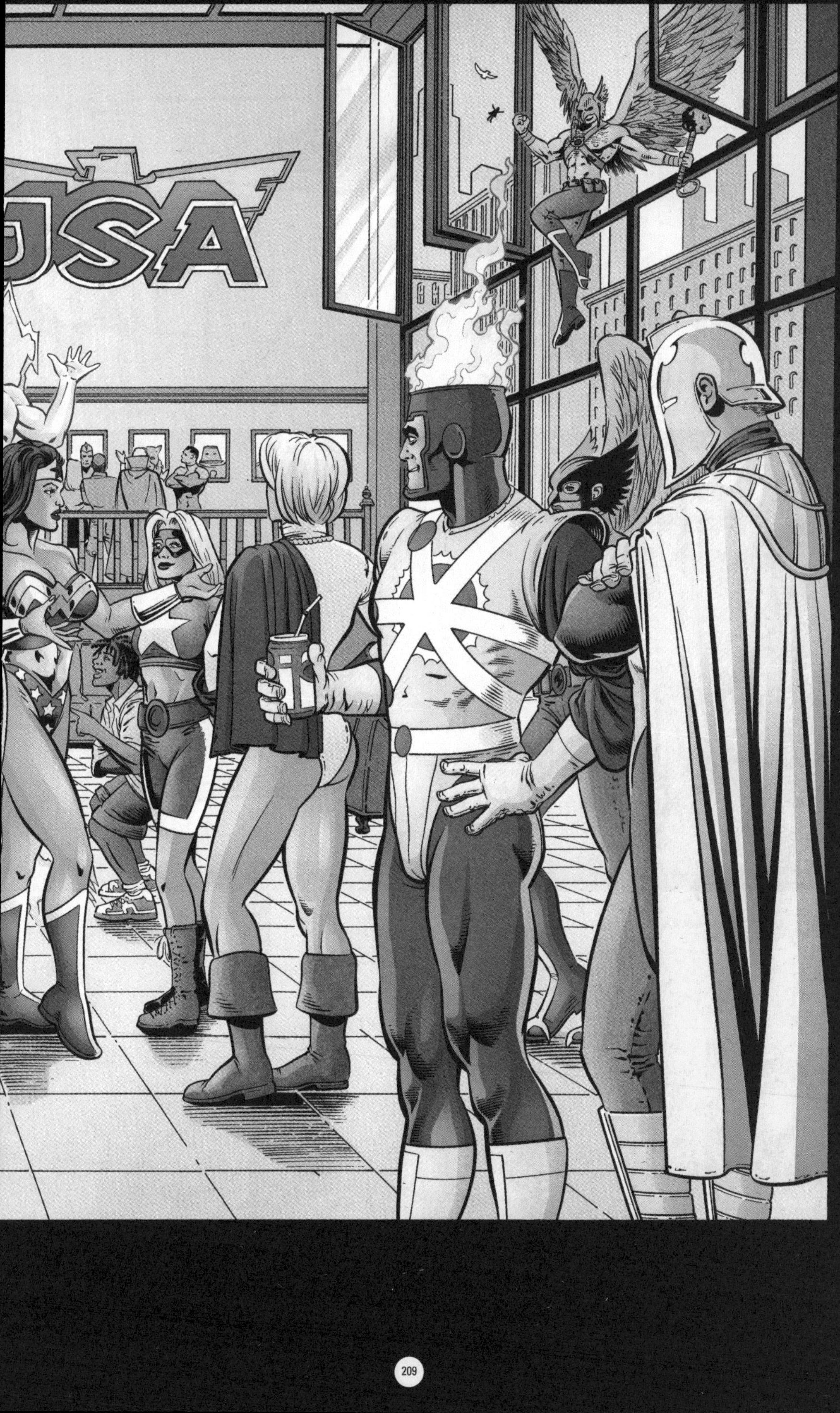

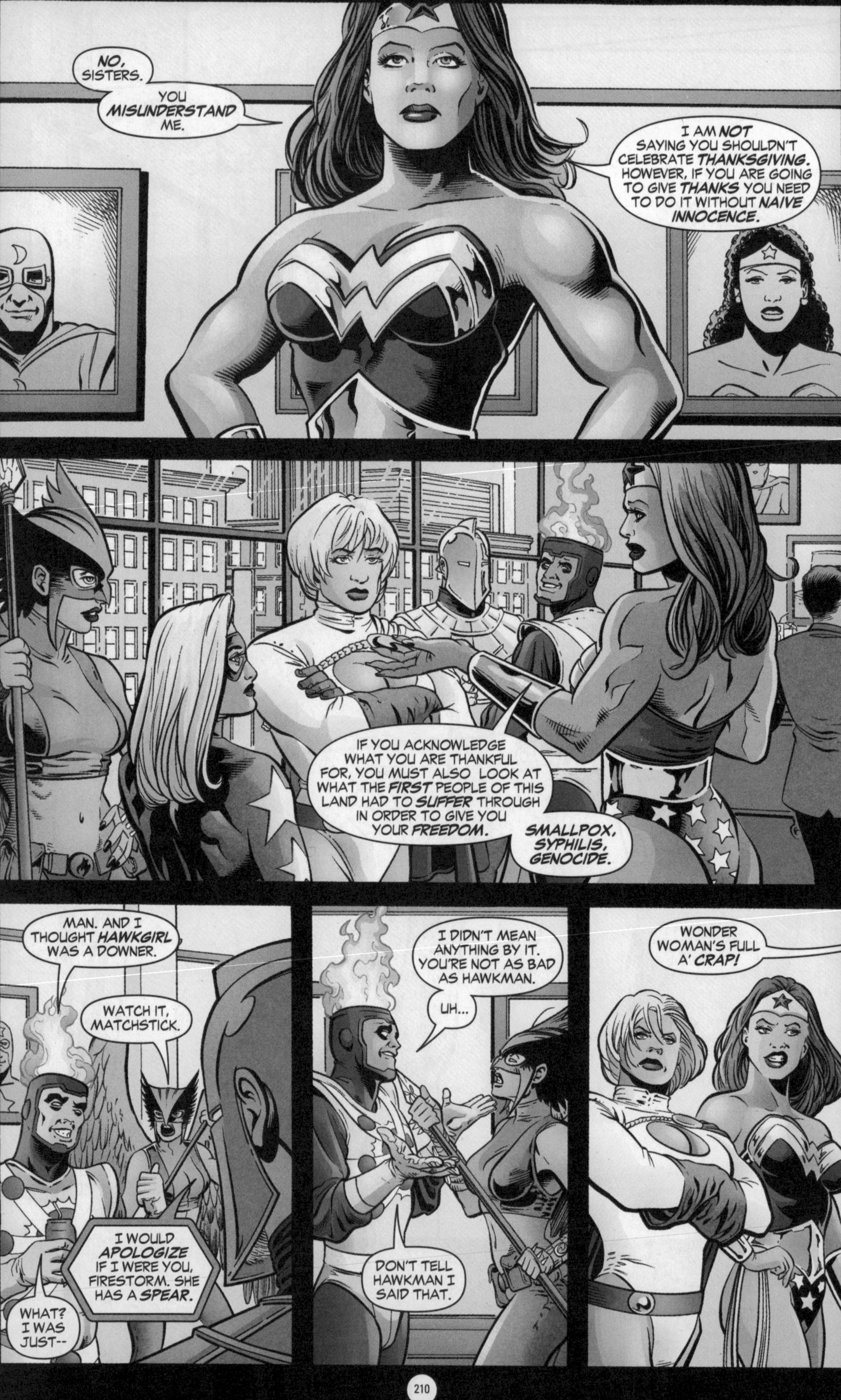

NO, SISTERS.
YOU MISUNDERSTAND ME.
I AM NOT SAYING YOU SHOULDN'T CELEBRATE THANKSGIVING. HOWEVER, IF YOU ARE GOING TO GIVE THANKS YOU NEED TO DO IT WITHOUT NAIVE INNOCENCE.
IF YOU ACKNOWLEDGE WHAT YOU ARE THANKFUL FOR, YOU MUST ALSO LOOK AT WHAT THE FIRST PEOPLE OF THIS LAND HAD TO SUFFER THROUGH IN ORDER TO GIVE YOU YOUR FREEDOM.
SMALLPOX, SYPHILIS, GENOCIDE.
MAN. AND I THOUGHT HAWKGIRL WAS A DOWNER.
WATCH IT, MATCHSTICK.
I WOULD APOLOGIZE IF I WERE YOU, FIRESTORM. SHE HAS A SPEAR.
WHAT? I WAS JUST--
I DIDN'T MEAN ANYTHING BY IT. YOU'RE NOT AS BAD AS HAWKMAN.
UH...
DON'T TELL HAWKMAN I SAID THAT.
WONDER WOMAN'S FULL A' CRAP!

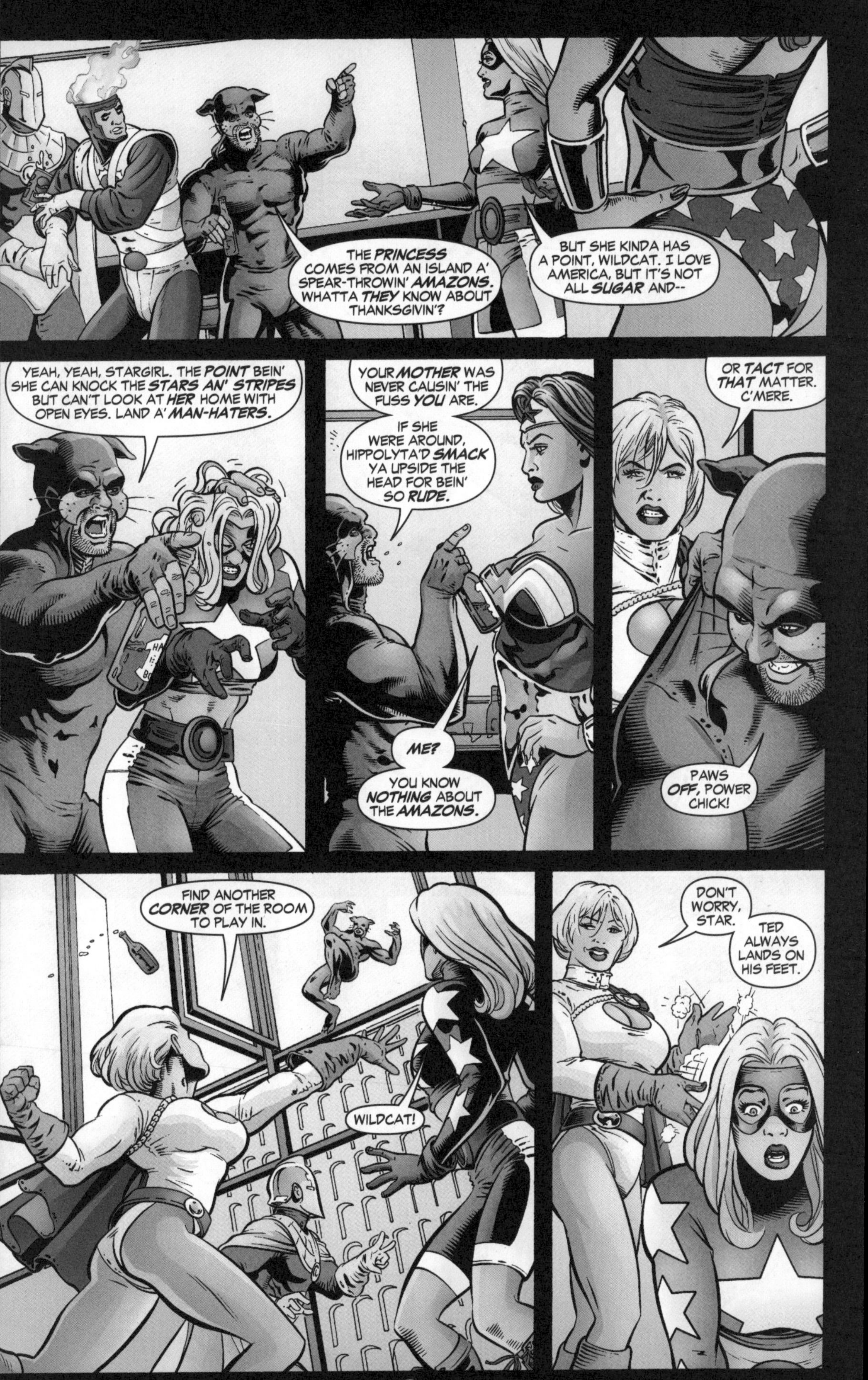
THE PRINCESS COMES FROM AN ISLAND A' SPEAR-THROWIN' AMAZONS. WHATTA THEY KNOW ABOUT THANKSGIVIN'?
BUT SHE KINDA HAS A POINT, WILDCAT. I LOVE AMERICA, BUT IT'S NOT ALL SUGAR AND--
YEAH, YEAH, STARGIRL. THE POINT BEIN' SHE CAN KNOCK THE STARS AN' STRIPES BUT CAN'T LOOK AT HER HOME WITH OPEN EYES. LAND A' MAN-HATERS.
YOUR MOTHER WAS NEVER CAUSIN' THE FUSS YOU ARE.
IF SHE WERE AROUND, HIPPOLYTA'D SMACK YA UPSIDE THE HEAD FOR BEIN' SO RUDE.
ME?
YOU KNOW NOTHING ABOUT THE AMAZONS.
OR TACT FOR THAT MATTER. C'MERE.
PAWS OFF, POWER CHICK!
FIND ANOTHER CORNER OF THE ROOM TO PLAY IN.
WILDCAT!
DON'T WORRY, STAR.
TED ALWAYS LANDS ON HIS FEET.

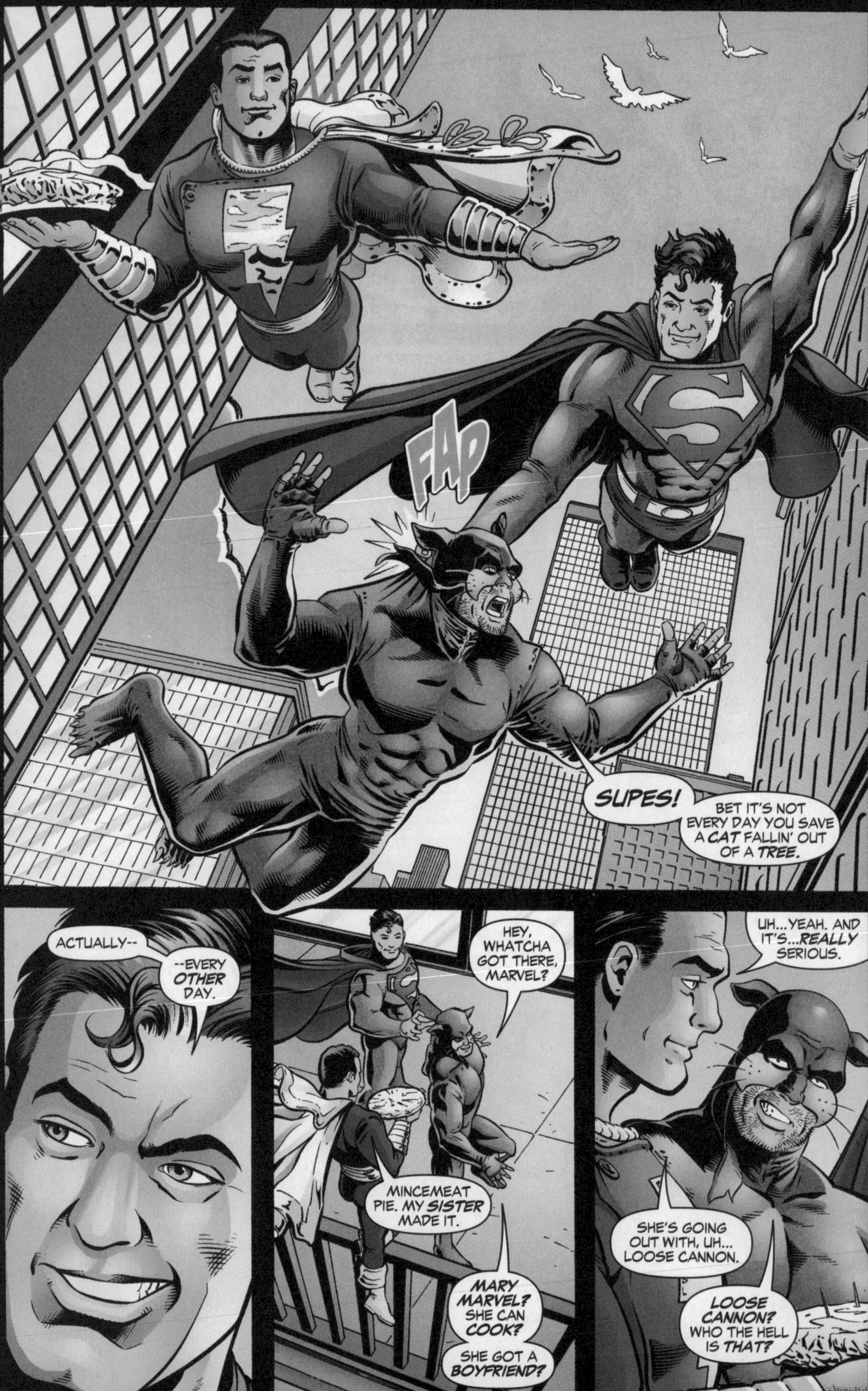
FAP
SUPES!
BET IT'S NOT EVERY DAY YOU SAVE A CAT FALLIN' OUT OF A TREE.
ACTUALLY--
--EVERY OTHER DAY.
HEY, WHATCHA GOT THERE, MARVEL?
MINCEMEAT PIE. MY SISTER MADE IT.
MARY MARVEL? SHE CAN COOK?
SHE GOT A BOYFRIEND?
UH...YEAH. AND IT'S...REALLY SERIOUS.
SHE'S GOING OUT WITH, UH... LOOSE CANNON.
LOOSE CANNON? WHO THE HELL IS THAT?

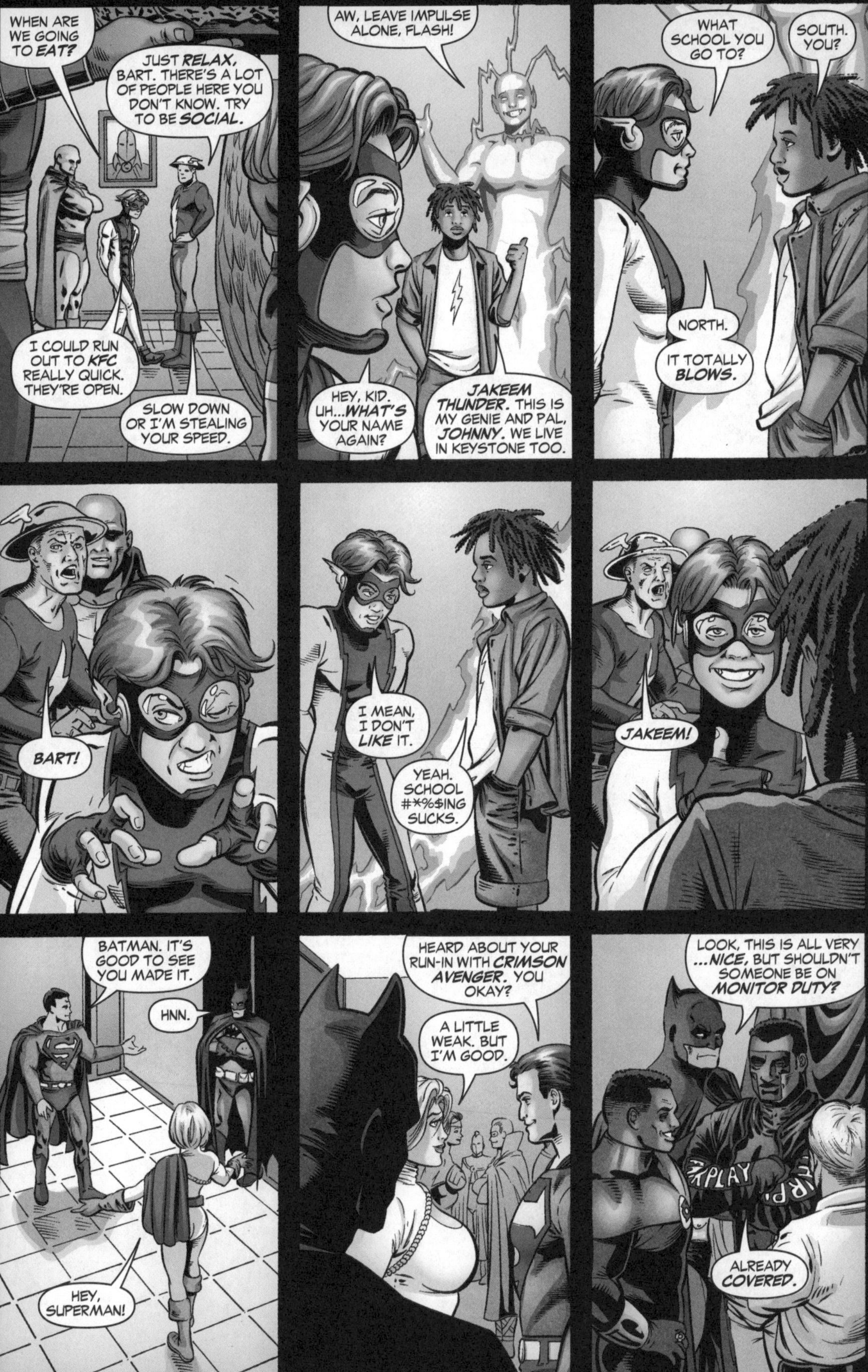
WHEN ARE WE GOING TO EAT?
JUST RELAX, BART. THERE'S A LOT OF PEOPLE HERE YOU DON'T KNOW. TRY TO BE SOCIAL.
I COULD RUN OUT TO KFC REALLY QUICK. THEY'RE OPEN.
SLOW DOWN OR I'M STEALING YOUR SPEED.
AW, LEAVE IMPULSE ALONE, FLASH!
HEY, KID. UH...WHAT'S YOUR NAME AGAIN?
JAKEEM THUNDER. THIS IS MY GENIE AND PAL, JOHNNY. WE LIVE IN KEYSTONE TOO.
WHAT SCHOOL YOU GO TO?
SOUTH. YOU?
NORTH.
IT TOTALLY BLOWS.
BART!
I MEAN, I DON'T LIKE IT.
YEAH. SCHOOL #*%$ING SUCKS.
JAKEEM!
BATMAN. IT'S GOOD TO SEE YOU MADE IT.
HNN.
HEY, SUPERMAN!
HEARD ABOUT YOUR RUN-IN WITH CRIMSON AVENGER. YOU OKAY?
A LITTLE WEAK. BUT I'M GOOD.
LOOK, THIS IS ALL VERY ...NICE, BUT SHOULDN'T SOMEONE BE ON MONITOR DUTY?
ALREADY COVERED.

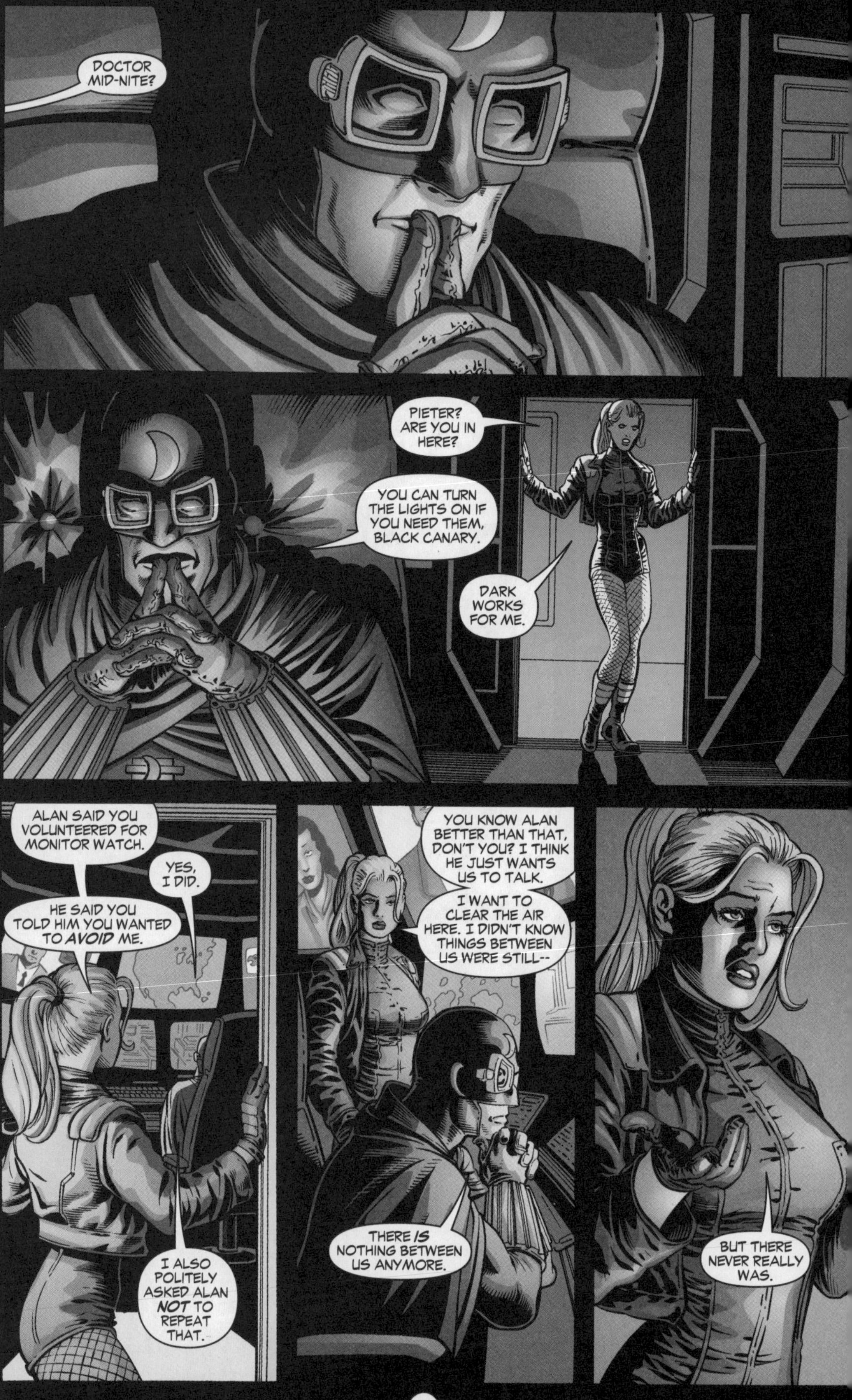
DOCTOR MID-NITE?
PIETER? ARE YOU IN HERE?
YOU CAN TURN THE LIGHTS ON IF YOU NEED THEM, BLACK CANARY.
DARK WORKS FOR ME.
ALAN SAID YOU VOLUNTEERED FOR MONITOR WATCH.
YES, I DID.
HE SAID YOU TOLD HIM YOU WANTED TO AVOID ME.
I ALSO POLITELY ASKED ALAN NOT TO REPEAT THAT.
YOU KNOW ALAN BETTER THAN THAT, DON'T YOU? I THINK HE JUST WANTS US TO TALK.
I WANT TO CLEAR THE AIR HERE. I DIDN'T KNOW THINGS BETWEEN US WERE STILL--
THERE IS NOTHING BETWEEN US ANYMORE.
BUT THERE NEVER REALLY WAS.

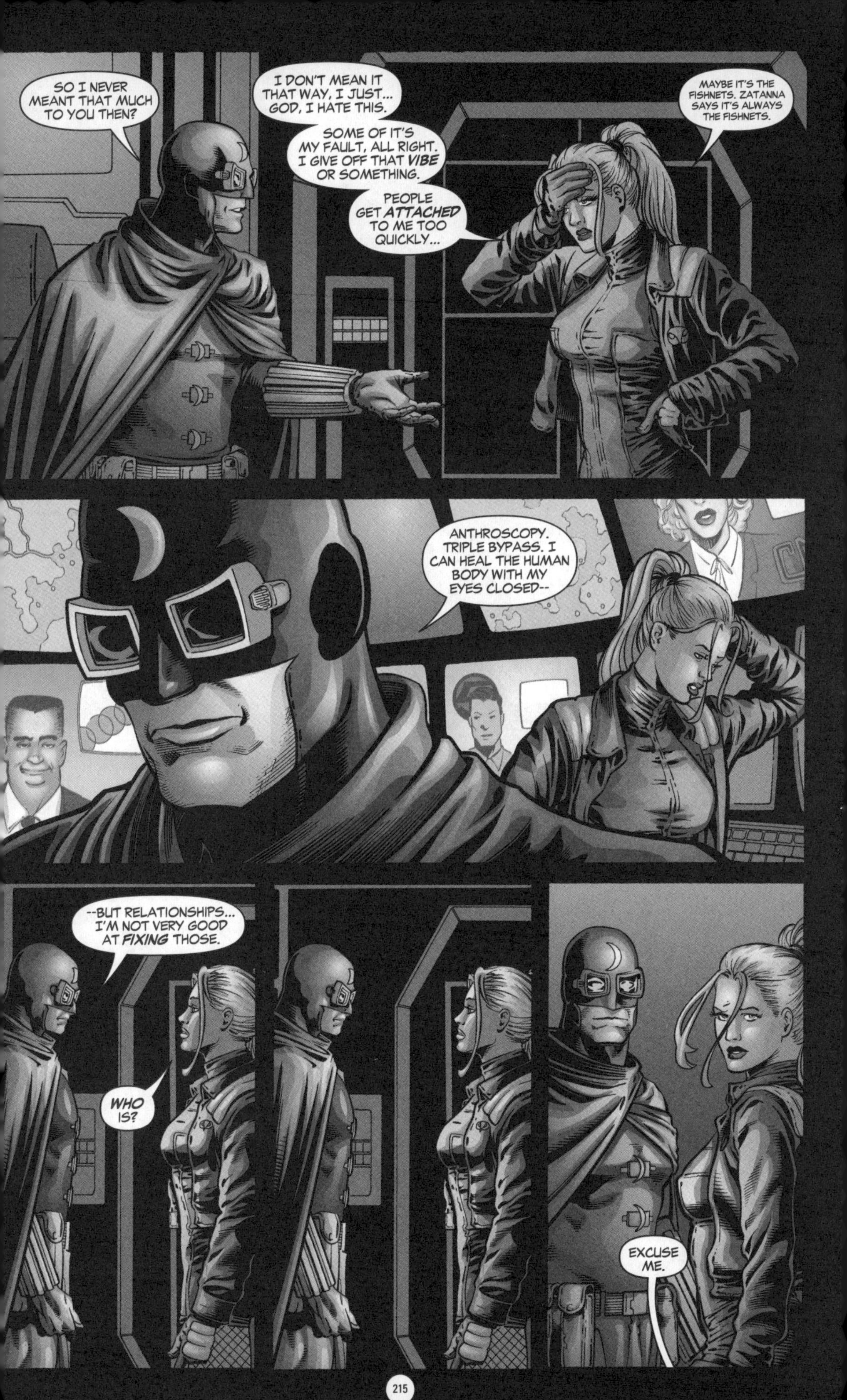
SO I NEVER MEANT THAT MUCH TO YOU THEN?
I DON'T MEAN IT THAT WAY, I JUST... GOD, I HATE THIS.
SOME OF IT'S MY FAULT, ALL RIGHT. I GIVE OFF THAT VIBE OR SOMETHING.
PEOPLE GET ATTACHED TO ME TOO QUICKLY...
MAYBE IT'S THE FISHNETS. ZATANNA SAYS IT'S ALWAYS THE FISHNETS.
ANTHROSCOPY. TRIPLE BYPASS. I CAN HEAL THE HUMAN BODY WITH MY EYES CLOSED--
--BUT RELATIONSHIPS... I'M NOT VERY GOOD AT FIXING THOSE.
WHO IS?
EXCUSE ME.

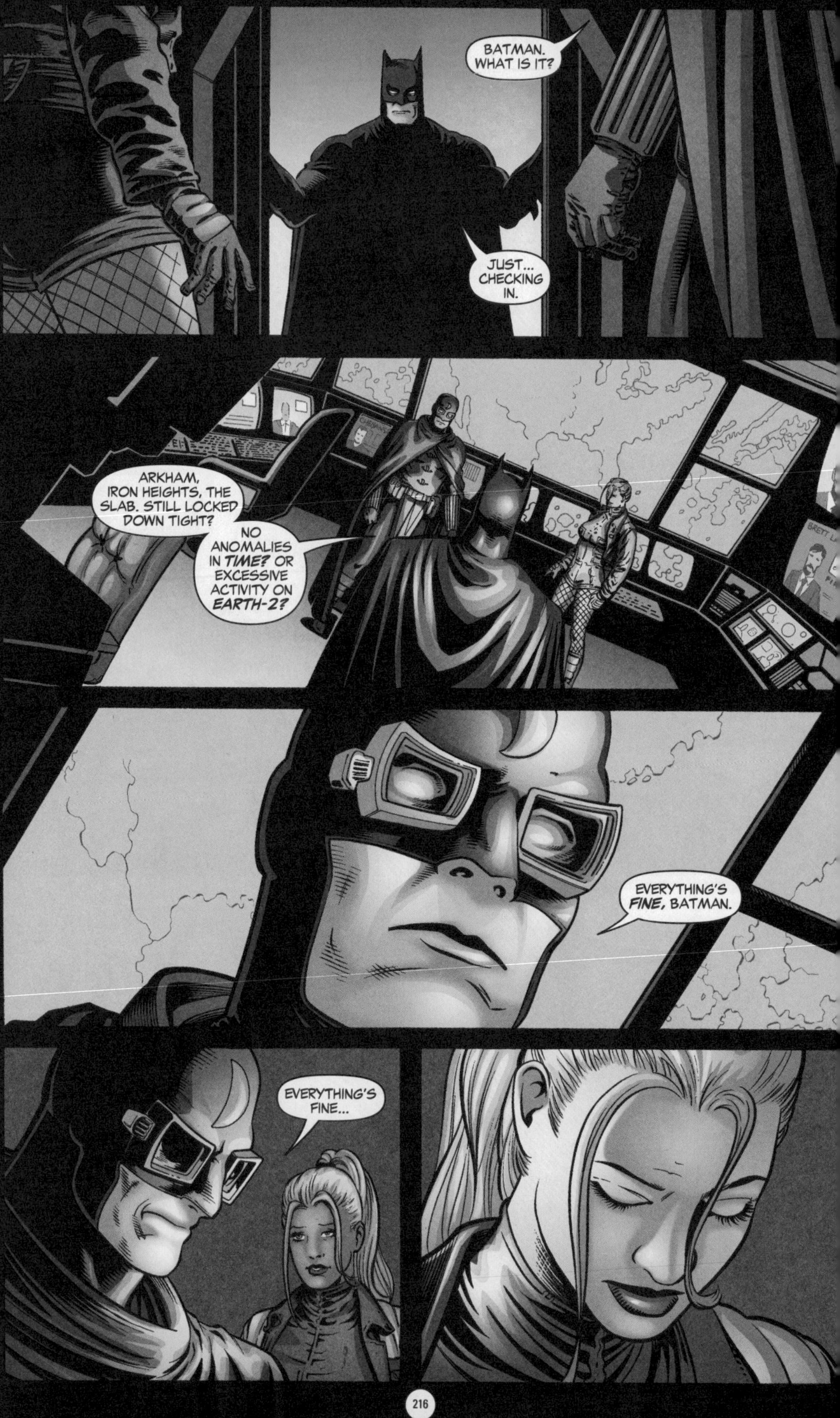
BATMAN. WHAT IS IT?
JUST... CHECKING IN.
ARKHAM, IRON HEIGHTS, THE SLAB. STILL LOCKED DOWN TIGHT?
NO ANOMALIES IN TIME? OR EXCESSIVE ACTIVITY ON EARTH-2?
EVERYTHING'S FINE, BATMAN.
EVERYTHING'S FINE...

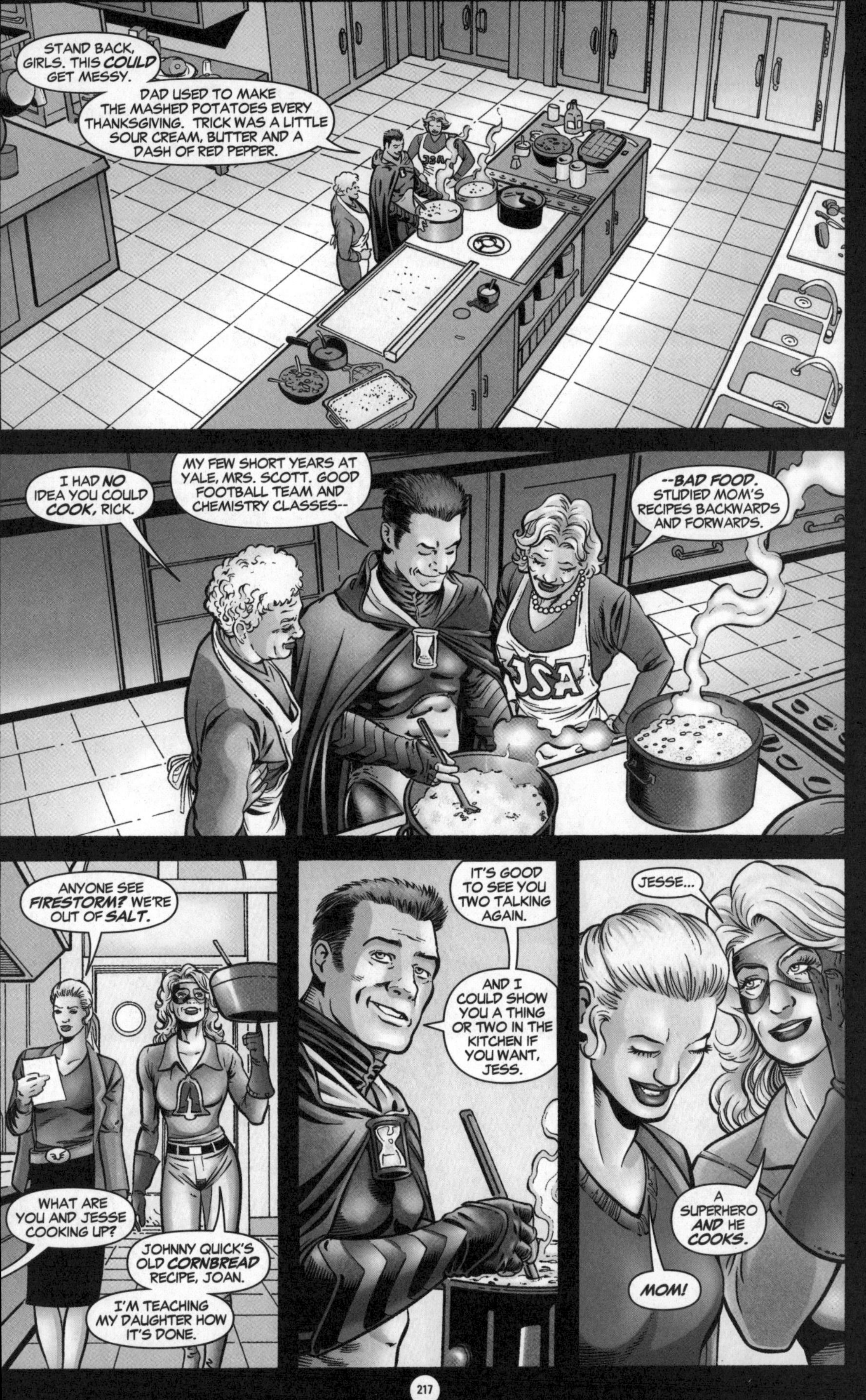

STAND BACK, GIRLS. THIS COULD GET MESSY.
DAD USED TO MAKE THE MASHED POTATOES EVERY THANKSGIVING. TRICK WAS A LITTLE SOUR CREAM, BUTTER AND A DASH OF RED PEPPER.
I HAD NO IDEA YOU COULD COOK, RICK.
MY FEW SHORT YEARS AT YALE, MRS. SCOTT. GOOD FOOTBALL TEAM AND CHEMISTRY CLASSES--
--BAD FOOD. STUDIED MOM'S RECIPES BACKWARDS AND FORWARDS.
ANYONE SEE FIRESTORM? WE'RE OUT OF SALT.
WHAT ARE YOU AND JESSE COOKING UP?
JOHNNY QUICK'S OLD CORNBREAD RECIPE, JOAN.
I'M TEACHING MY DAUGHTER HOW IT'S DONE.
IT'S GOOD TO SEE YOU TWO TALKING AGAIN.
AND I COULD SHOW YOU A THING OR TWO IN THE KITCHEN IF YOU WANT, JESS.
JESSE...
A SUPERHERO AND HE COOKS.
MOM!

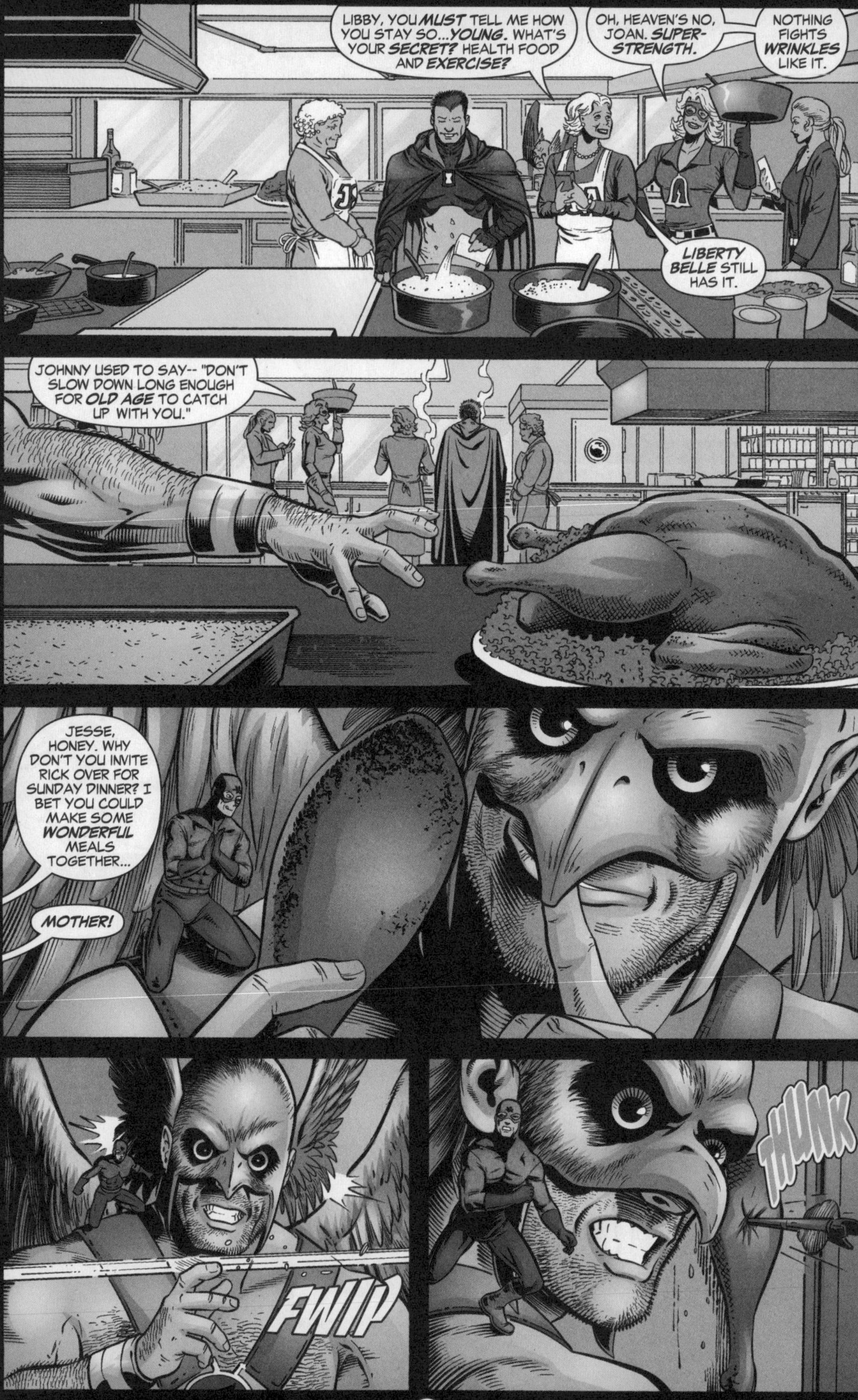
LIBBY, YOU MUST TELL ME HOW YOU STAY SO...YOUNG. WHAT'S YOUR SECRET? HEALTH FOOD AND EXERCISE?
OH, HEAVEN'S NO, JOAN. SUPER-STRENGTH.
NOTHING FIGHTS WRINKLES LIKE IT.
LIBERTY BELLE STILL HAS IT.
JOHNNY USED TO SAY-- "DON'T SLOW DOWN LONG ENOUGH FOR OLD AGE TO CATCH UP WITH YOU."
JESSE, HONEY. WHY DON'T YOU INVITE RICK OVER FOR SUNDAY DINNER? I BET YOU COULD MAKE SOME WONDERFUL MEALS TOGETHER...
MOTHER!
FWIP
THUNK

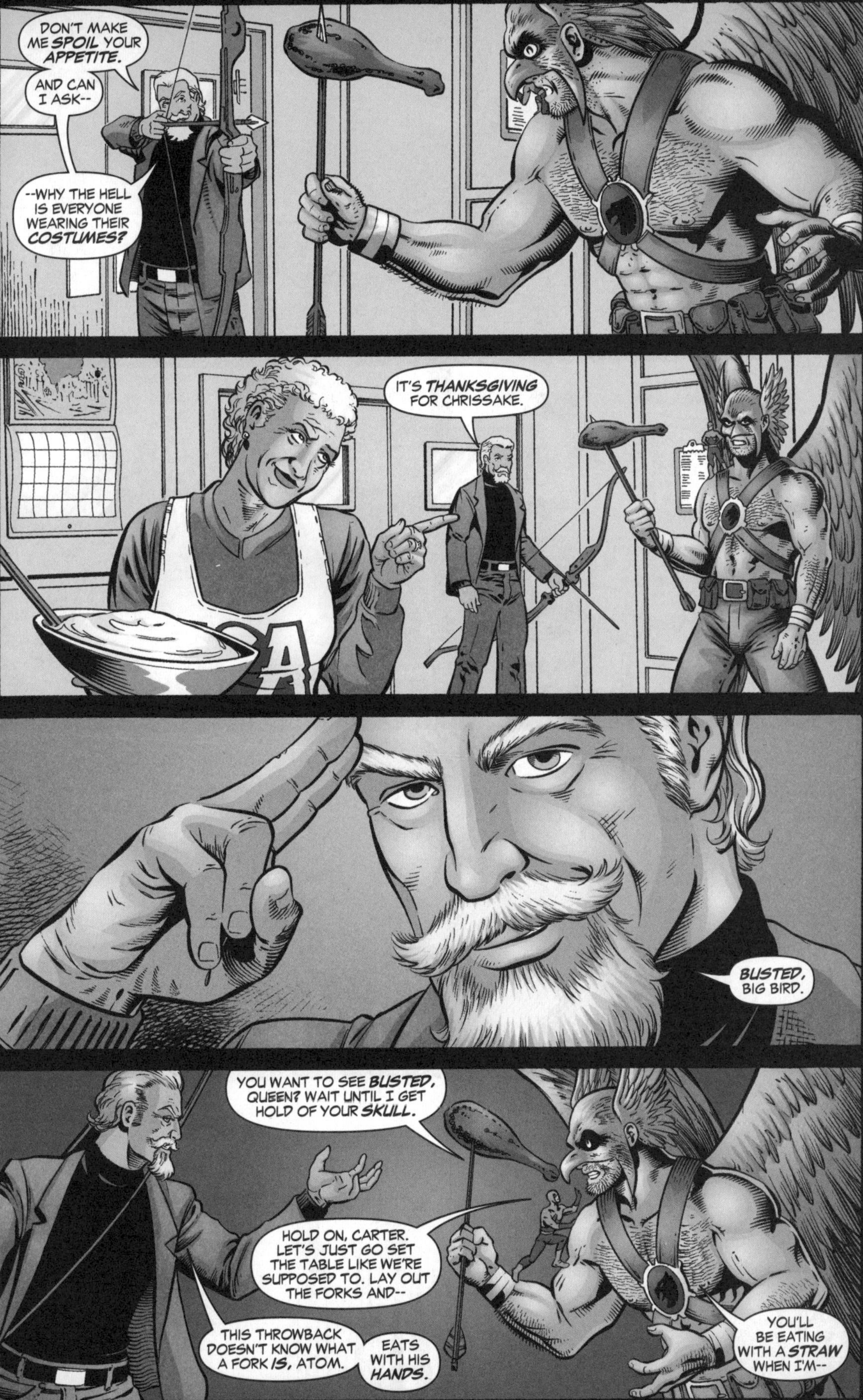
DON'T MAKE ME SPOIL YOUR APPETITE.
AND CAN I ASK--
--WHY THE HELL IS EVERYONE WEARING THEIR COSTUMES?
IT'S THANKSGIVING FOR CHRISSAKE.
BUSTED, BIG BIRD.
YOU WANT TO SEE BUSTED, QUEEN? WAIT UNTIL I GET HOLD OF YOUR SKULL.
HOLD ON, CARTER. LET'S JUST GO SET THE TABLE LIKE WE'RE SUPPOSED TO. LAY OUT THE FORKS AND--
THIS THROWBACK DOESN'T KNOW WHAT A FORK IS, ATOM.
EATS WITH HIS HANDS.
YOU'LL BE EATING WITH A STRAW WHEN I'M--

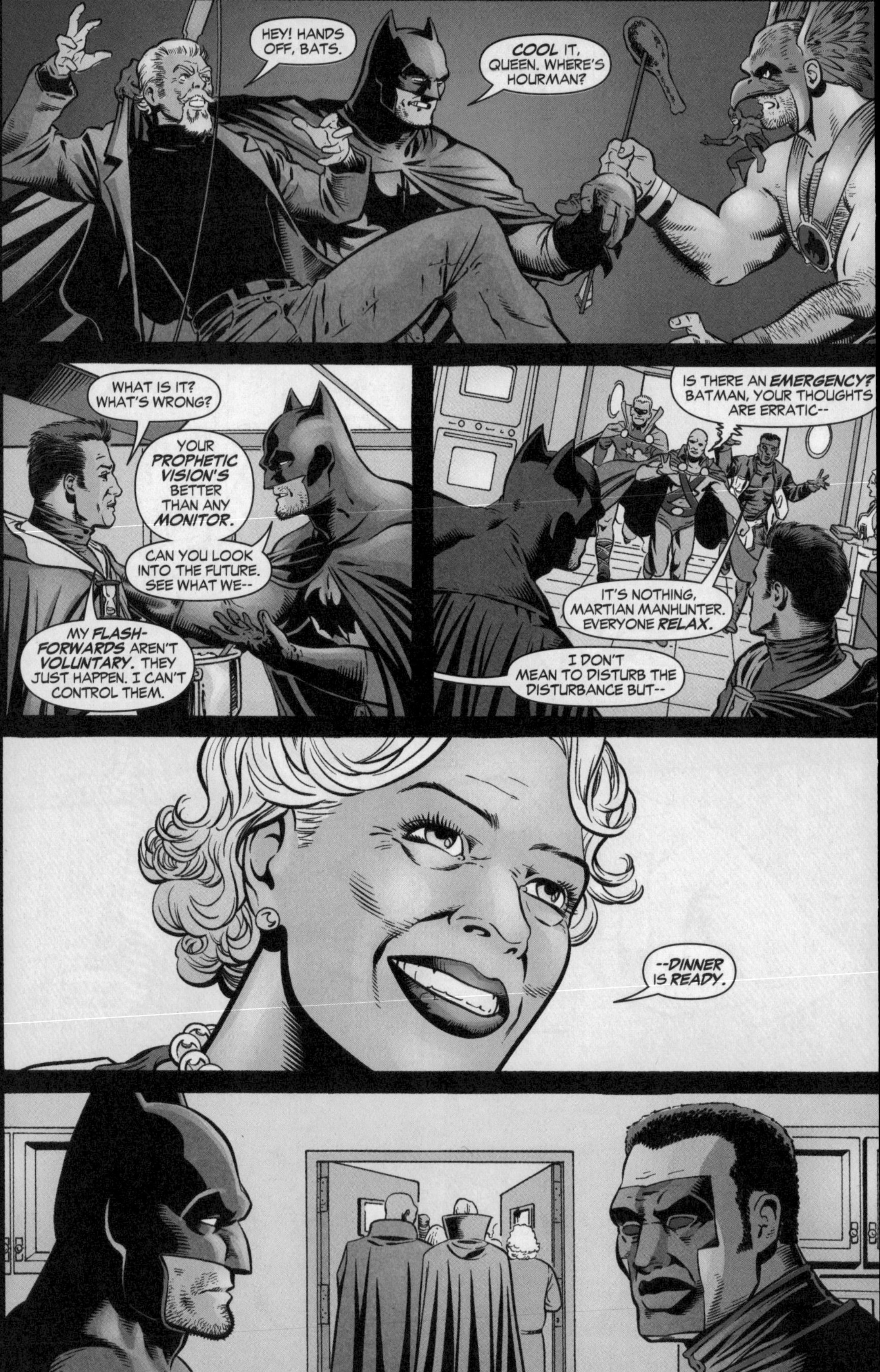
HEY! HANDS OFF, BATS.
COOL IT, QUEEN. WHERE'S HOURMAN?
WHAT IS IT? WHAT'S WRONG?
YOUR PROPHETIC VISION'S BETTER THAN ANY MONITOR.
CAN YOU LOOK INTO THE FUTURE. SEE WHAT WE--
MY FLASH-FORWARDS AREN'T VOLUNTARY. THEY JUST HAPPEN. I CAN'T CONTROL THEM.
IS THERE AN EMERGENCY? BATMAN, YOUR THOUGHTS ARE ERRATIC--
IT'S NOTHING, MARTIAN MANHUNTER. EVERYONE RELAX.
I DON'T MEAN TO DISTURB THE DISTURBANCE BUT--
--DINNER IS READY.

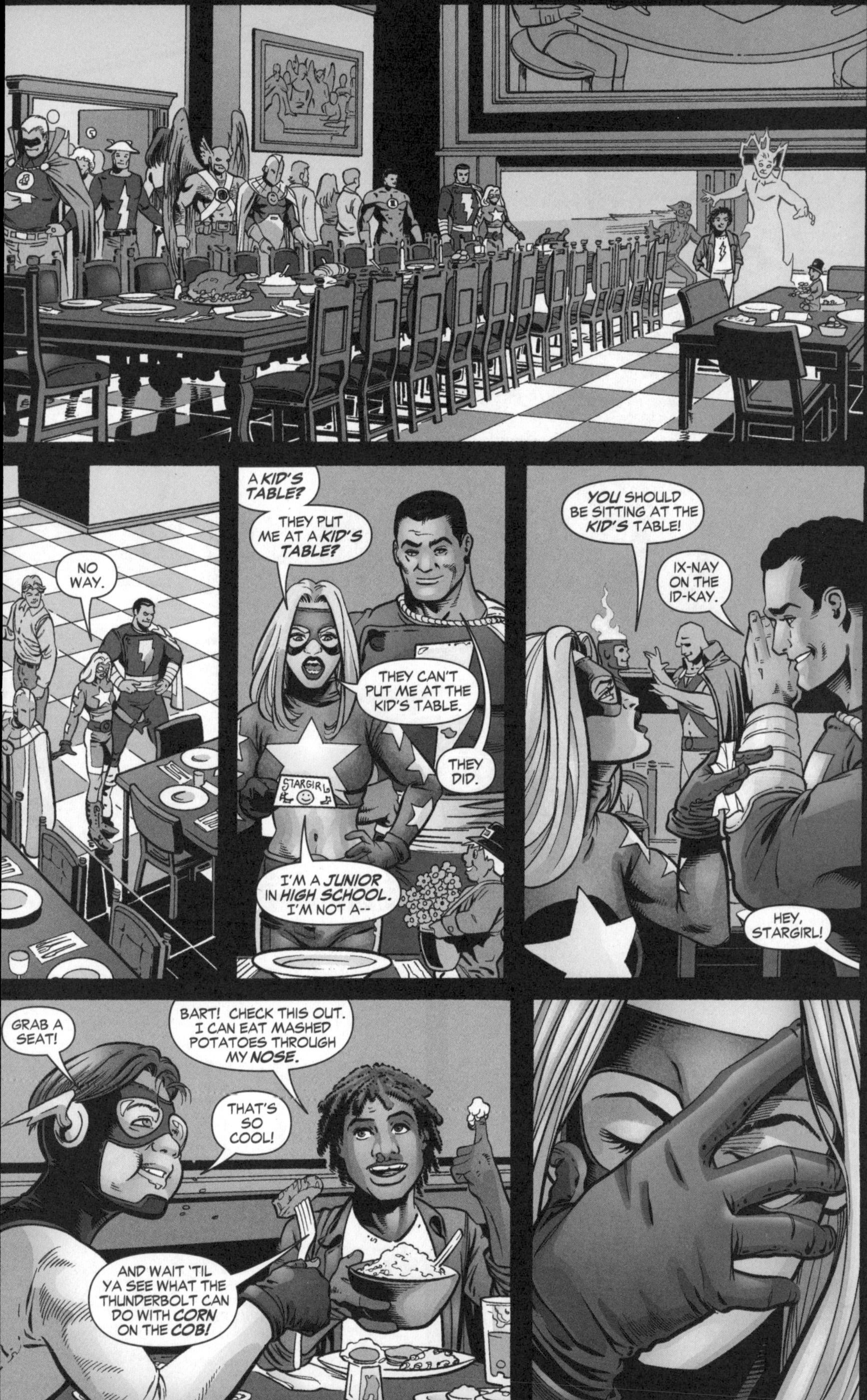

NO WAY.
A KID'S TABLE?
THEY PUT ME AT A KID'S TABLE?
THEY CAN'T PUT ME AT THE KID'S TABLE.
THEY DID.
I'M A JUNIOR IN HIGH SCHOOL. I'M NOT A--
YOU SHOULD BE SITTING AT THE KID'S TABLE!
IX-NAY ON THE ID-KAY.
HEY, STARGIRL!
GRAB A SEAT!
BART! CHECK THIS OUT. I CAN EAT MASHED POTATOES THROUGH MY NOSE.
THAT'S SO COOL!
AND WAIT 'TIL YA SEE WHAT THE THUNDERBOLT CAN DO WITH CORN ON THE COB!

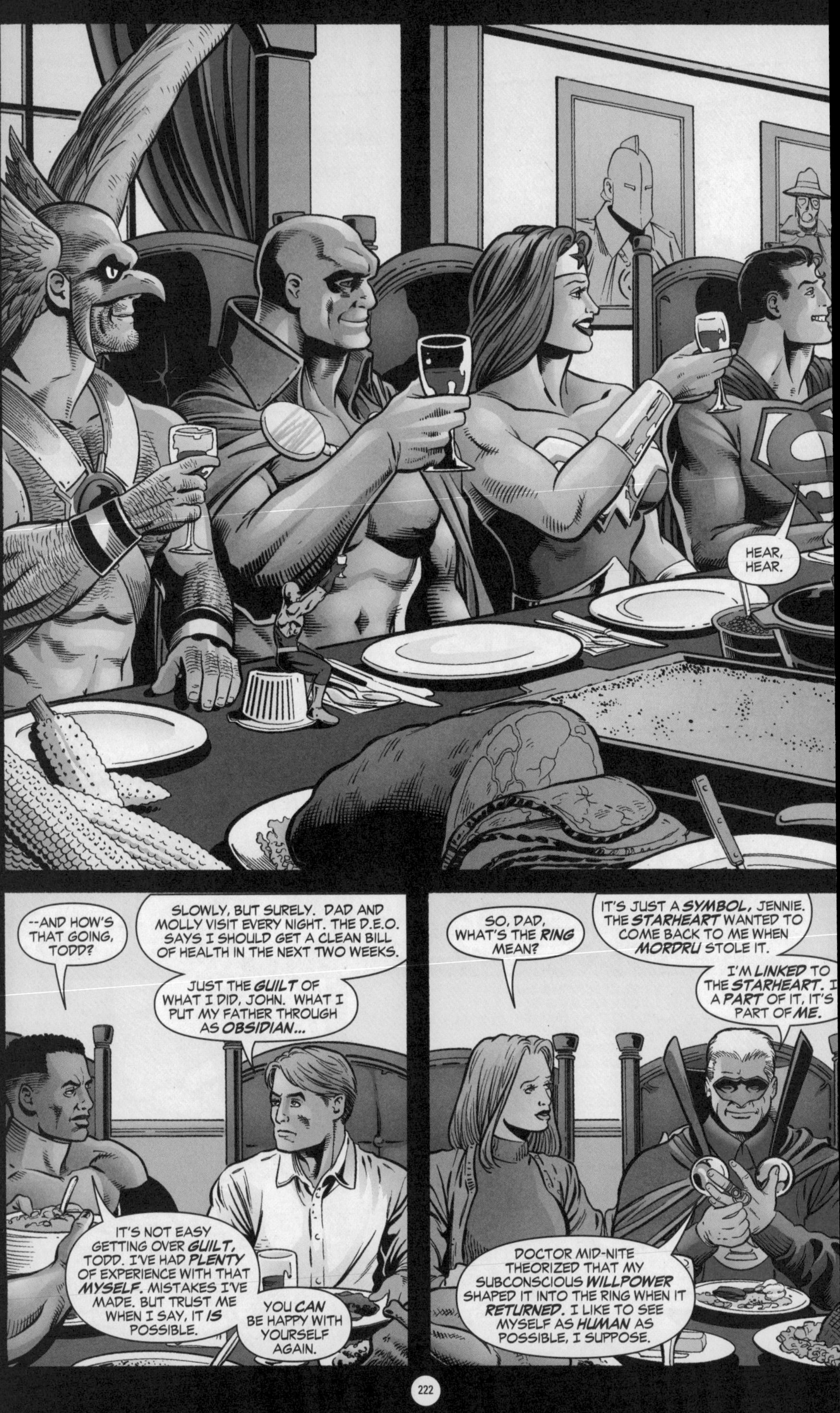
HEAR, HEAR.
--AND HOW'S THAT GOING, TODD?
SLOWLY, BUT SURELY. DAD AND MOLLY VISIT EVERY NIGHT. THE D.E.O. SAYS I SHOULD GET A CLEAN BILL OF HEALTH IN THE NEXT TWO WEEKS.
JUST THE GUILT OF WHAT I DID, JOHN. WHAT I PUT MY FATHER THROUGH AS OBSIDIAN...
IT'S NOT EASY GETTING OVER GUILT, TODD. I'VE HAD PLENTY OF EXPERIENCE WITH THAT MYSELF. MISTAKES I'VE MADE. BUT TRUST ME WHEN I SAY, IT IS POSSIBLE.
YOU CAN BE HAPPY WITH YOURSELF AGAIN.
SO, DAD, WHAT'S THE RING MEAN?
IT'S JUST A SYMBOL, JENNIE. THE STARHEART WANTED TO COME BACK TO ME WHEN MORDRU STOLE IT.
I'M LINKED TO THE STARHEART. I A PART OF IT, IT'S PART OF ME.
DOCTOR MID-NITE THEORIZED THAT MY SUBCONSCIOUS WILLPOWER SHAPED IT INTO THE RING WHEN IT RETURNED. I LIKE TO SEE MYSELF AS HUMAN AS POSSIBLE, I SUPPOSE.

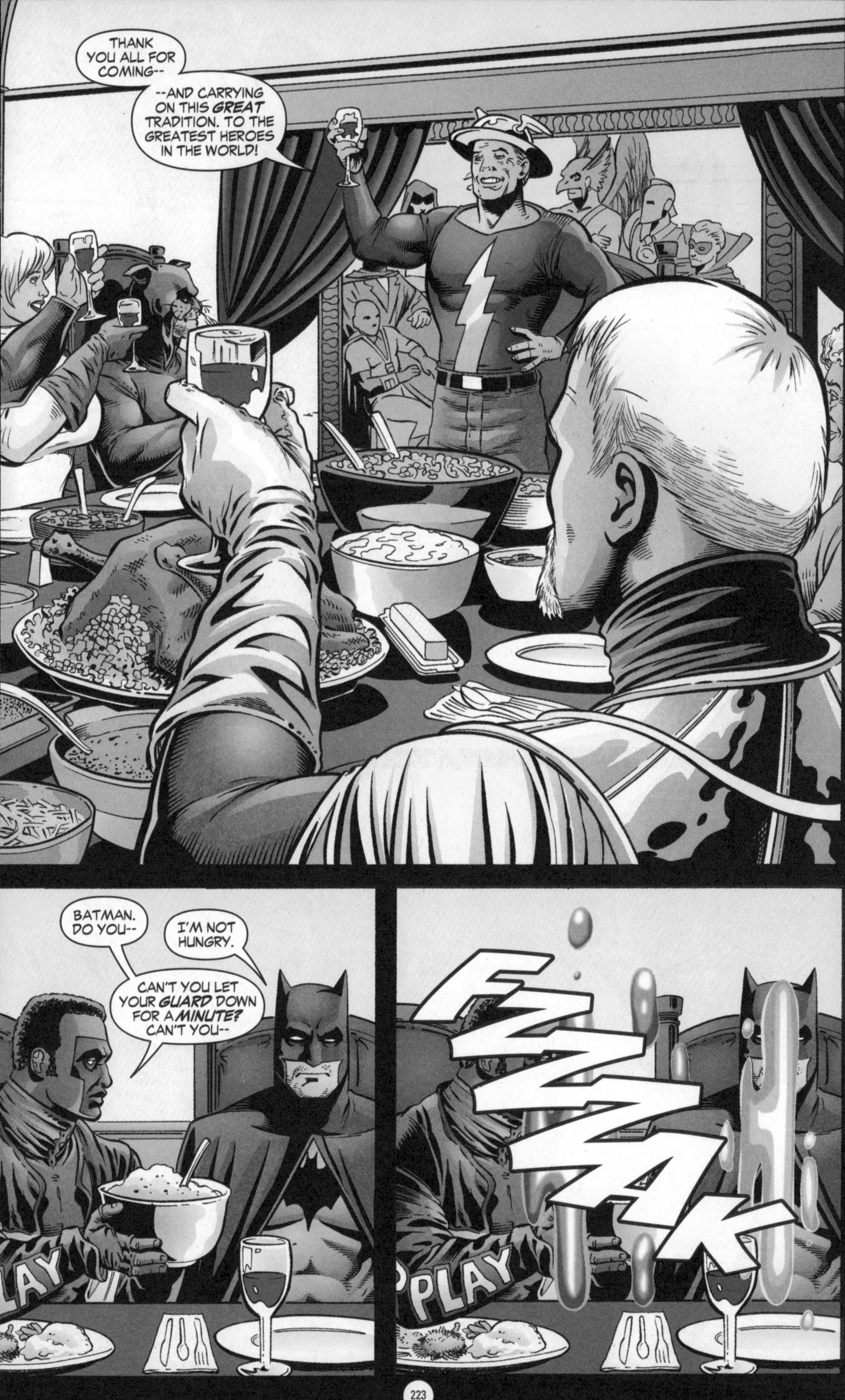
THANK YOU ALL FOR COMING--
--AND CARRYING ON THIS GREAT TRADITION. TO THE GREATEST HEROES IN THE WORLD!
BATMAN. DO YOU--
I'M NOT HUNGRY.
CAN'T YOU LET YOUR GUARD DOWN FOR A MINUTE? CAN'T YOU--
PLAY
FZZZAK
PPLAY

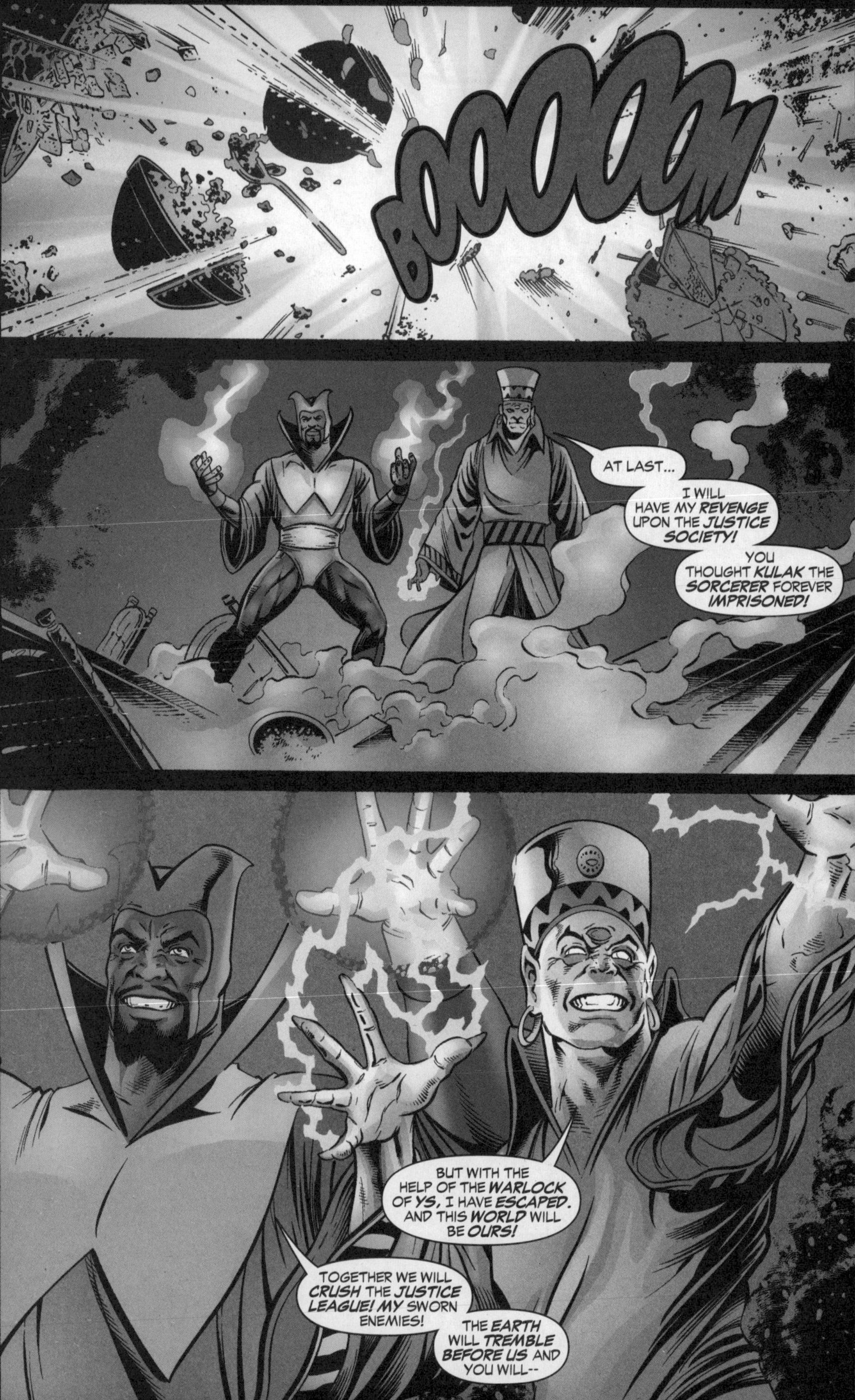
BOOOOOM
AT LAST...
I WILL HAVE MY REVENGE UPON THE JUSTICE SOCIETY!
YOU THOUGHT KULAK THE SORCERER FOREVER IMPRISONED!
BUT WITH THE HELP OF THE WARLOCK OF YS, I HAVE ESCAPED. AND THIS WORLD WILL BE OURS!
TOGETHER WE WILL CRUSH THE JUSTICE LEAGUE! MY SWORN ENEMIES!
THE EARTH WILL TREMBLE BEFORE US AND YOU WILL--

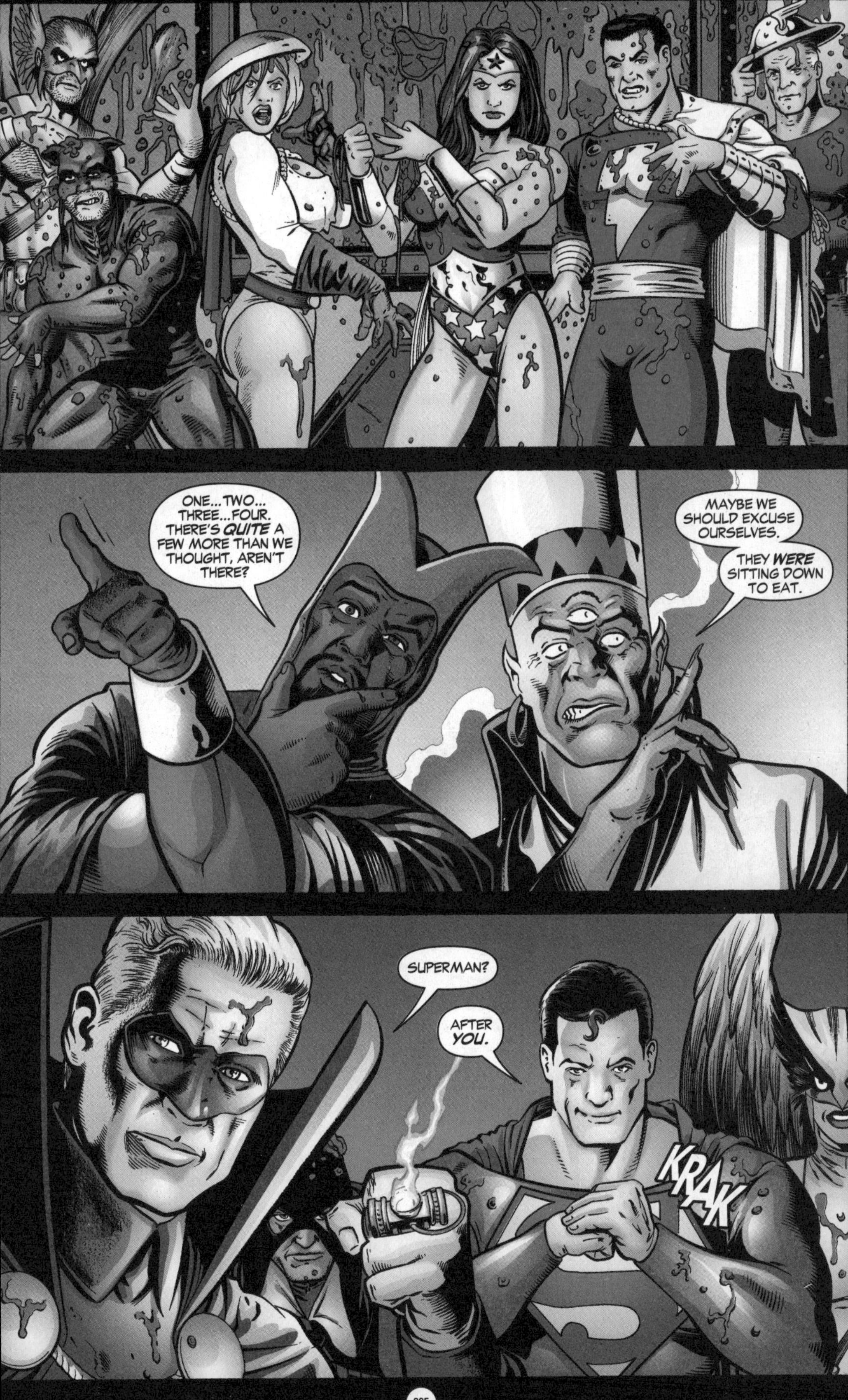

ONE...TWO... THREE...FOUR. THERE'S *QUITE* A FEW MORE THAN WE THOUGHT, AREN'T THERE?
MAYBE WE SHOULD EXCUSE OURSELVES.
THEY *WERE* SITTING DOWN TO EAT.
SUPERMAN?
AFTER *YOU*.
KRAK

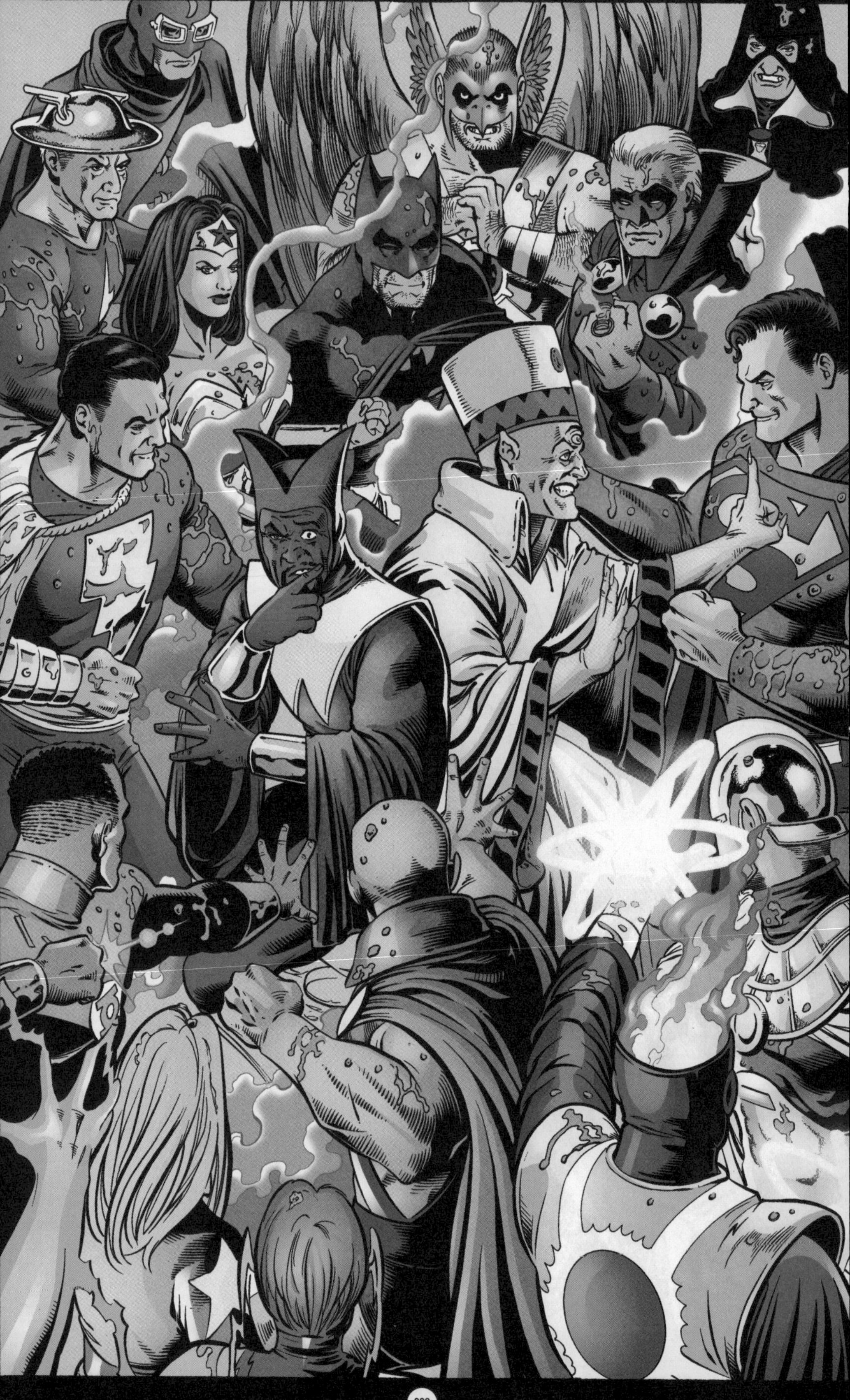

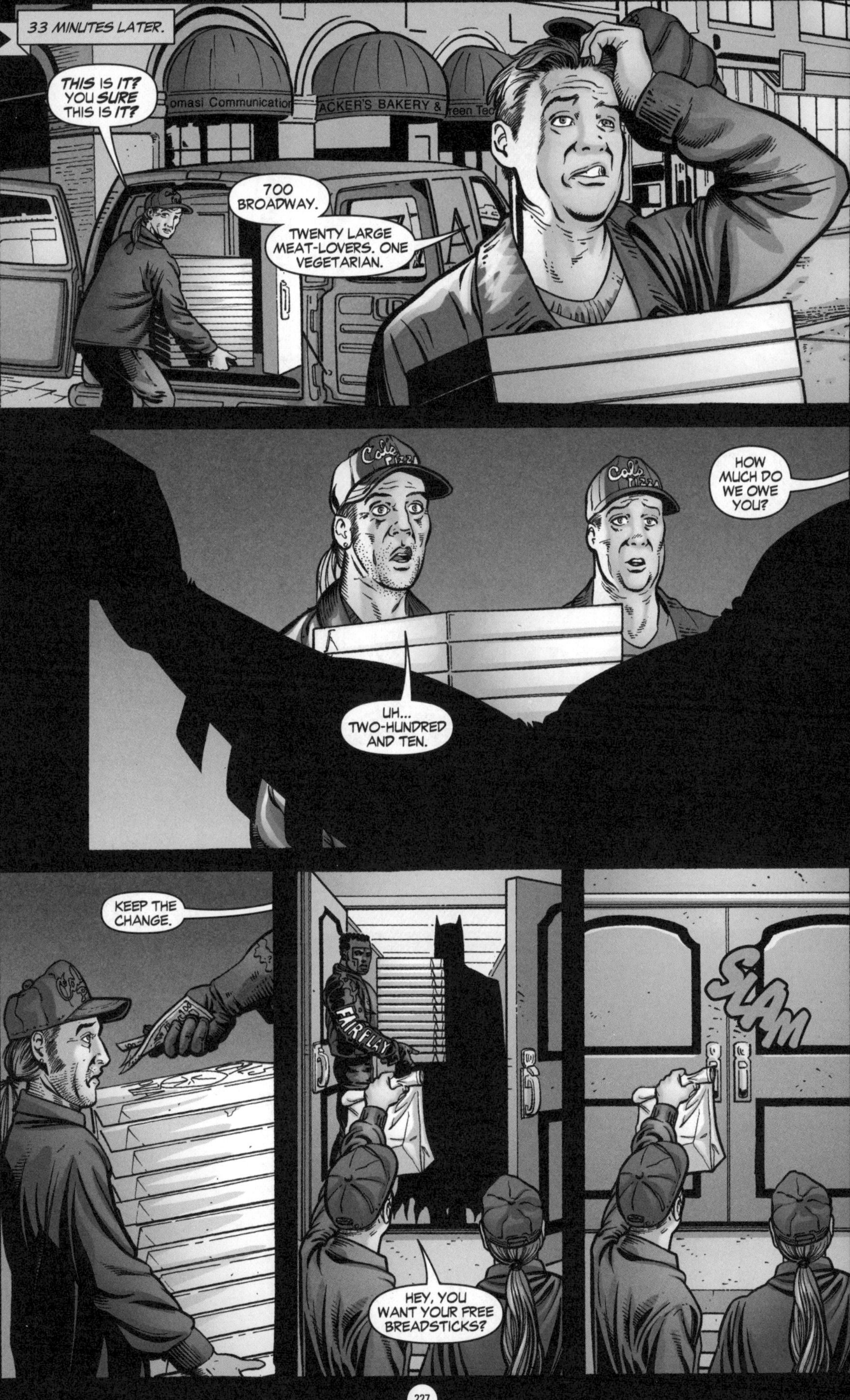

33 MINUTES LATER.
THIS IS IT? YOU SURE THIS IS IT?
omasi Communicatio
ACKER'S BAKERY &
reen Tec
700 BROADWAY.
TWENTY LARGE MEAT-LOVERS. ONE VEGETARIAN.
HOW MUCH DO WE OWE YOU?
UH... TWO-HUNDRED AND TEN.
KEEP THE CHANGE.
FAIRPLAY
SLAM
HEY, YOU WANT YOUR FREE BREADSTICKS?

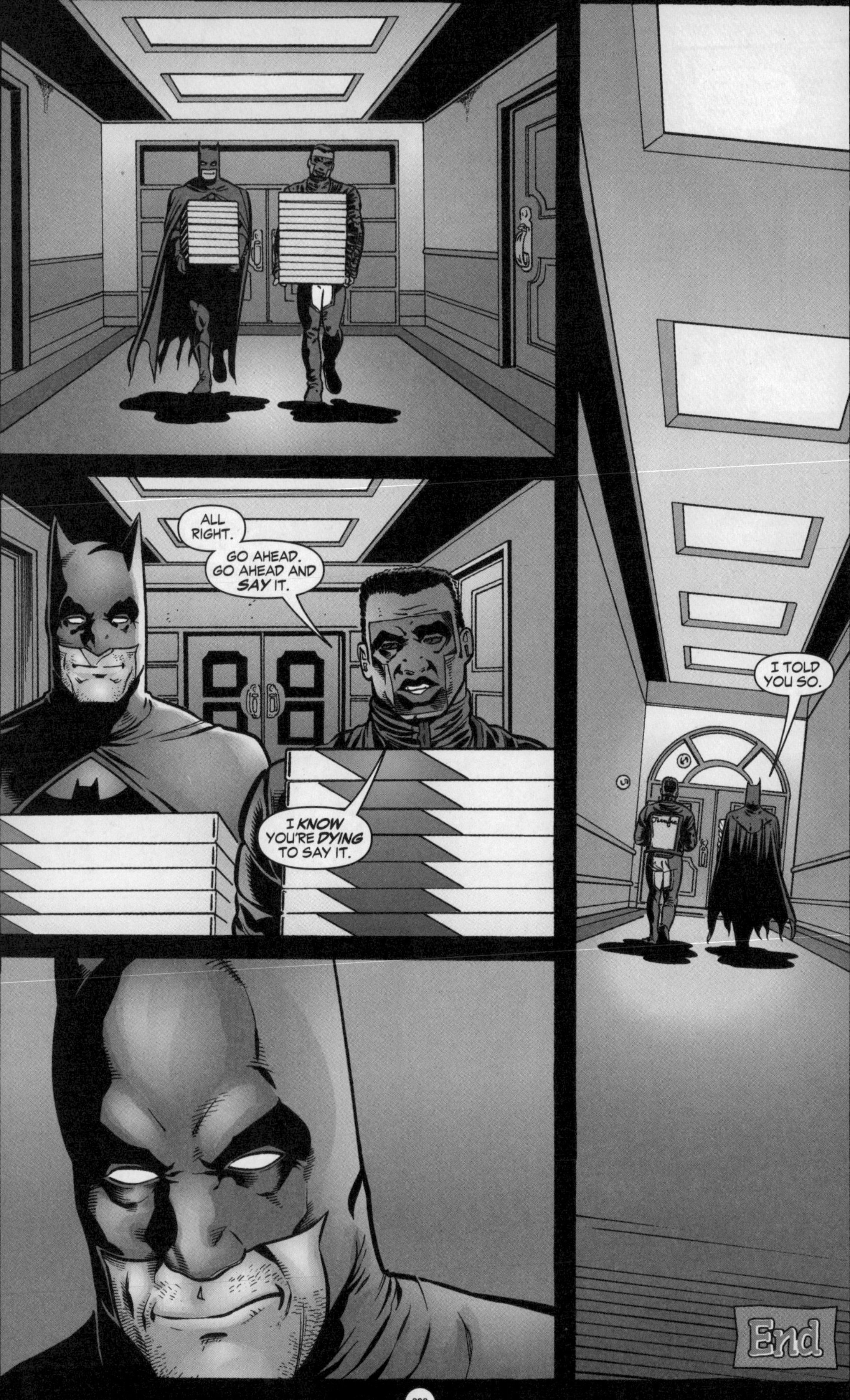
ALL RIGHT.
GO AHEAD. GO AHEAD AND SAY IT.
I KNOW YOU'RE DYING TO SAY IT.
I TOLD YOU SO.
End

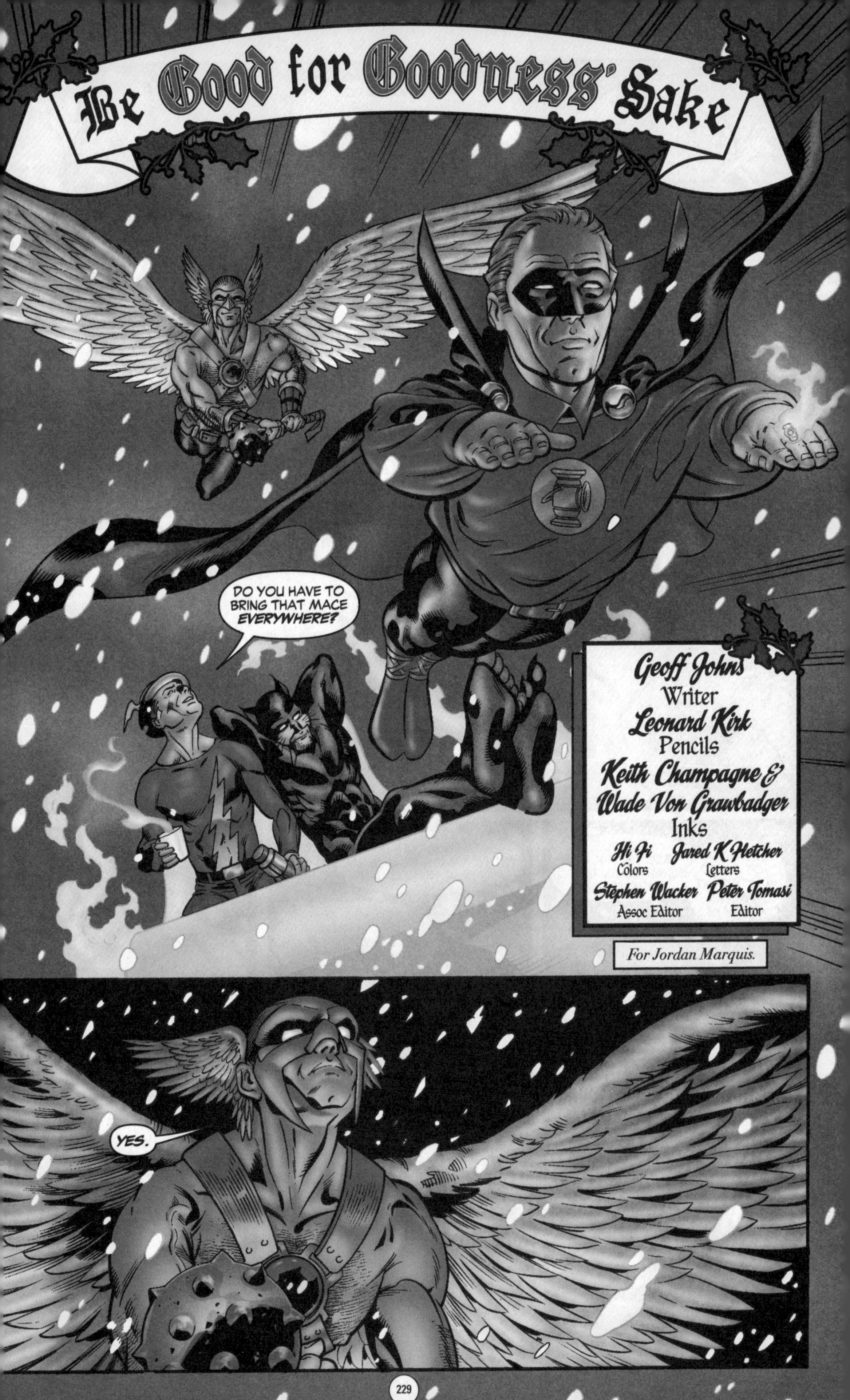
Be Good for Goodness' Sake
DO YOU HAVE TO BRING THAT MACE EVERYWHERE?
Geoff Johns Writer
Leonard Kirk Pencils
Keith Champagne & Wade Von Grawbadger Inks
Hi Fi Colors
Jared K Fletcher Letters
Stephen Wacker Assoc Editor
Peter Tomasi Editor
For Jordan Marquis.
YES.

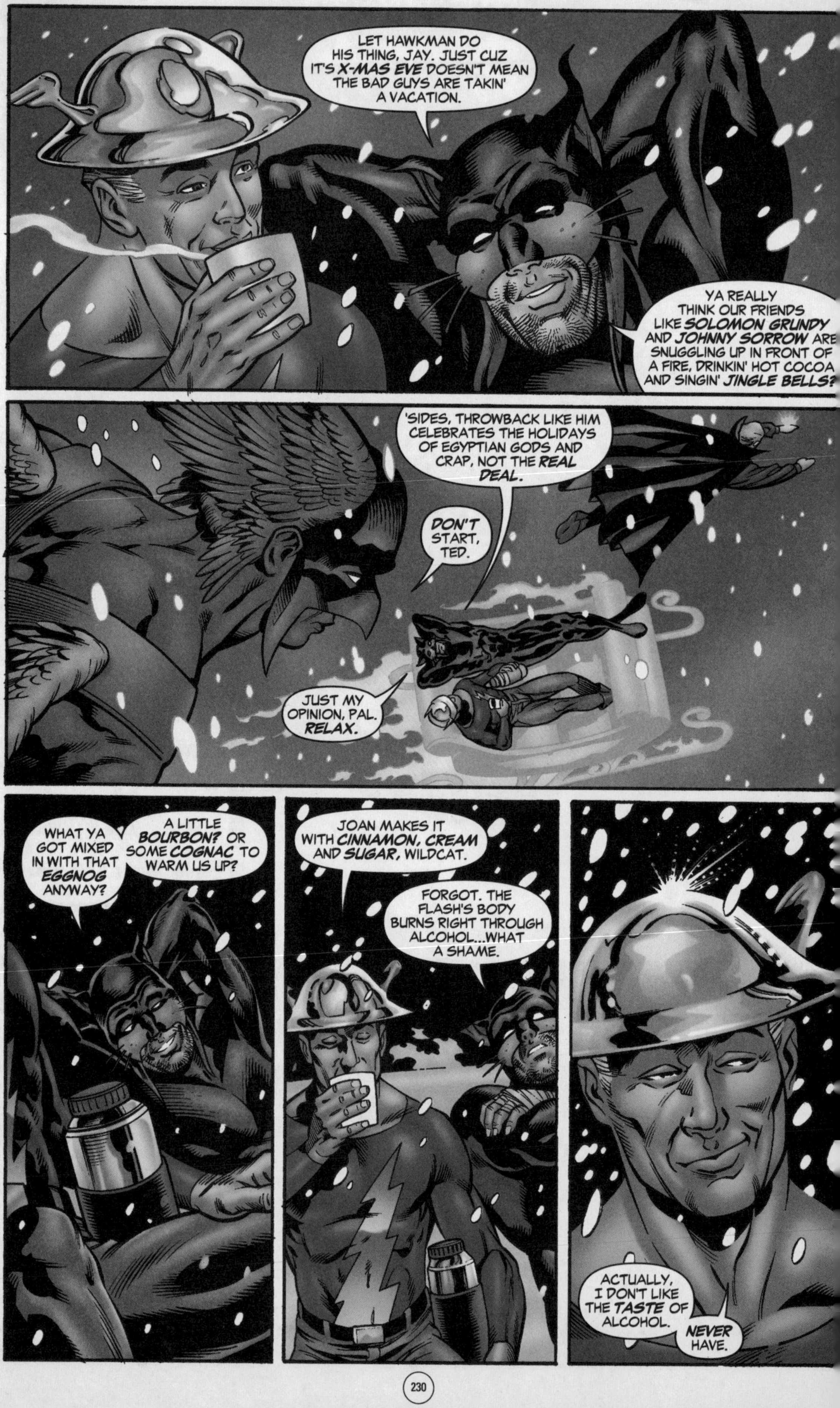

LET HAWKMAN DO HIS THING, JAY. JUST CUZ IT'S X-MAS EVE DOESN'T MEAN THE BAD GUYS ARE TAKIN' A VACATION.
YA REALLY THINK OUR FRIENDS LIKE SOLOMON GRUNDY AND JOHNNY SORROW ARE SNUGGLING UP IN FRONT OF A FIRE, DRINKIN' HOT COCOA AND SINGIN' JINGLE BELLS?
'SIDES, THROWBACK LIKE HIM CELEBRATES THE HOLIDAYS OF EGYPTIAN GODS AND CRAP, NOT THE REAL DEAL.
DON'T START, TED.
JUST MY OPINION, PAL. RELAX.
WHAT YA GOT MIXED IN WITH THAT EGGNOG ANYWAY?
A LITTLE BOURBON? OR SOME COGNAC TO WARM US UP?
JOAN MAKES IT WITH CINNAMON, CREAM AND SUGAR, WILDCAT.
FORGOT. THE FLASH'S BODY BURNS RIGHT THROUGH ALCOHOL...WHAT A SHAME.
ACTUALLY, I DON'T LIKE THE TASTE OF ALCOHOL. NEVER HAVE.

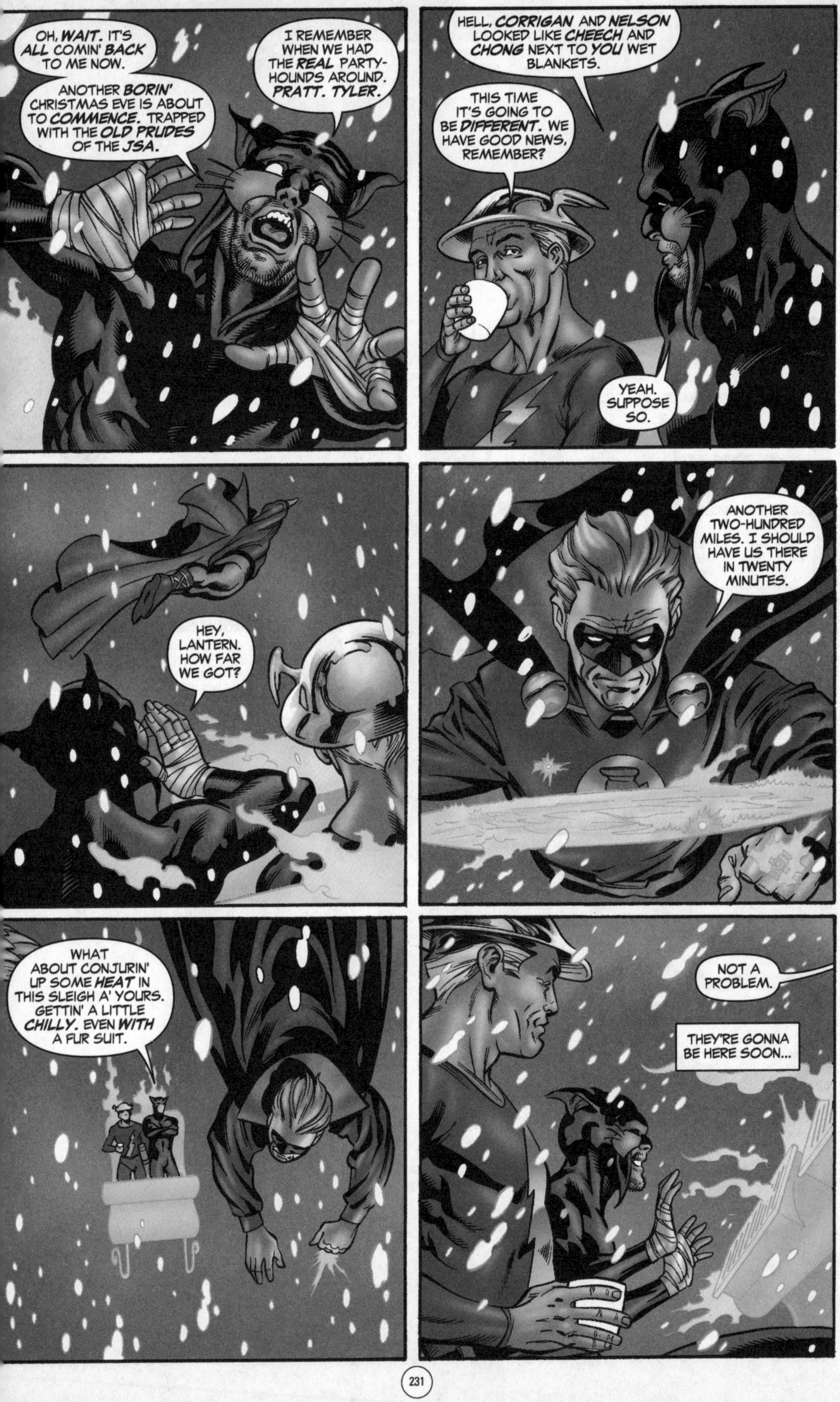
OH, WAIT. IT'S ALL COMIN' BACK TO ME NOW.
ANOTHER BORIN' CHRISTMAS EVE IS ABOUT TO COMMENCE. TRAPPED WITH THE OLD PRUDES OF THE JSA.
I REMEMBER WHEN WE HAD THE REAL PARTY-HOUNDS AROUND. PRATT. TYLER.
HELL, CORRIGAN AND NELSON LOOKED LIKE CHEECH AND CHONG NEXT TO YOU WET BLANKETS.
THIS TIME IT'S GOING TO BE DIFFERENT. WE HAVE GOOD NEWS, REMEMBER?
YEAH. SUPPOSE SO.
HEY, LANTERN. HOW FAR WE GOT?
ANOTHER TWO-HUNDRED MILES. I SHOULD HAVE US THERE IN TWENTY MINUTES.
WHAT ABOUT CONJURIN' UP SOME HEAT IN THIS SLEIGH A' YOURS. GETTIN' A LITTLE CHILLY. EVEN WITH A FUR SUIT.
NOT A PROBLEM.
THEY'RE GONNA BE HERE SOON...

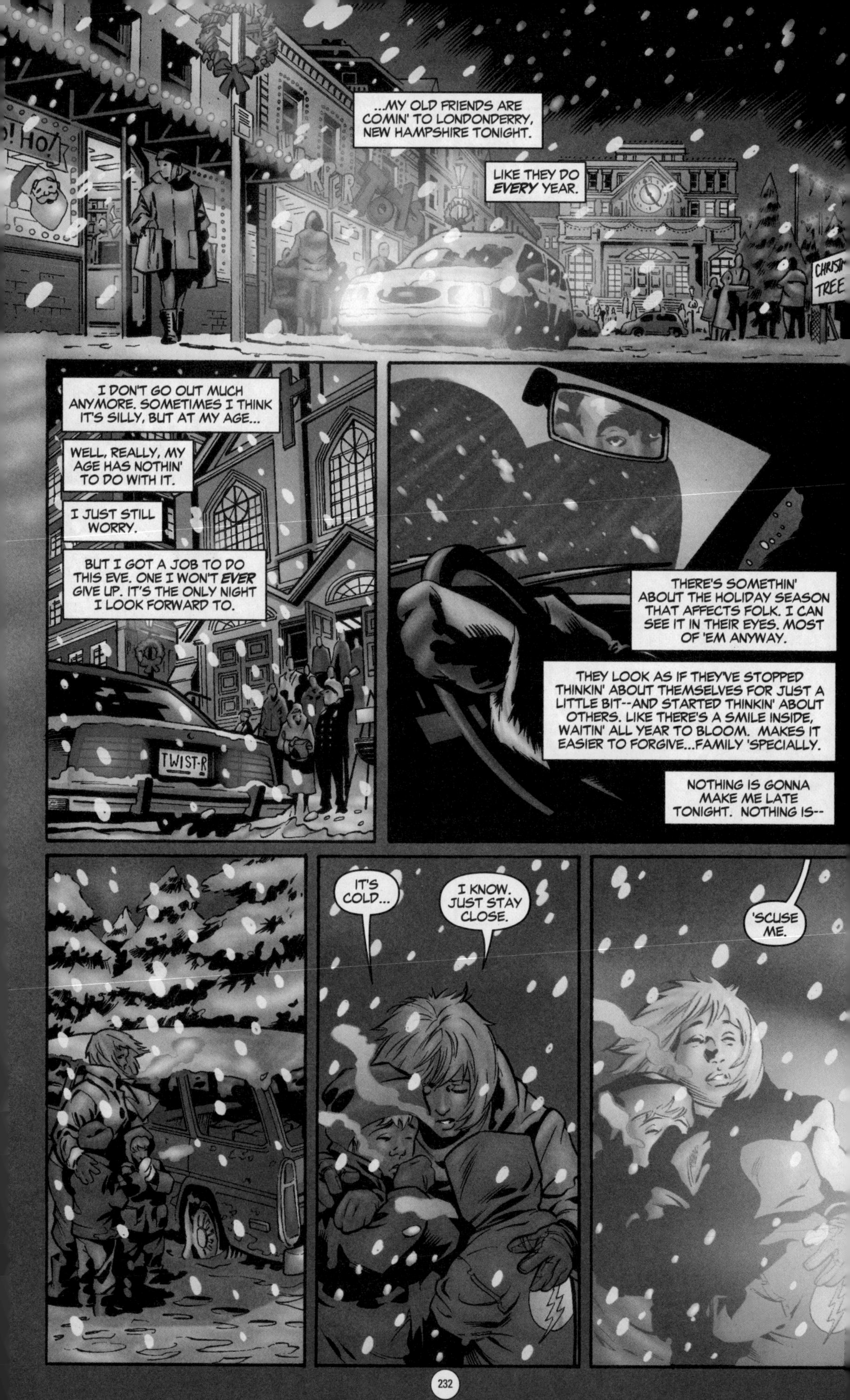

...MY OLD FRIENDS ARE COMIN' TO LONDONDERRY, NEW HAMPSHIRE TONIGHT.
LIKE THEY DO *EVERY* YEAR.
CHRISTM TREE
I DON'T GO OUT MUCH ANYMORE. SOMETIMES I THINK IT'S SILLY, BUT AT MY AGE...
WELL, REALLY, MY AGE HAS NOTHIN' TO DO WITH IT.
I JUST STILL WORRY.
BUT I GOT A JOB TO DO THIS EVE. ONE I WON'T *EVER* GIVE UP. IT'S THE ONLY NIGHT I LOOK FORWARD TO.
TWIST-R
THERE'S SOMETHIN' ABOUT THE HOLIDAY SEASON THAT AFFECTS FOLK. I CAN SEE IT IN THEIR EYES. MOST OF 'EM ANYWAY.
THEY LOOK AS IF THEY'VE STOPPED THINKIN' ABOUT THEMSELVES FOR JUST A LITTLE BIT--AND STARTED THINKIN' ABOUT OTHERS. LIKE THERE'S A SMILE INSIDE, WAITIN' ALL YEAR TO BLOOM. MAKES IT EASIER TO FORGIVE...FAMILY 'SPECIALLY.
NOTHING IS GONNA MAKE ME LATE TONIGHT. NOTHING IS--
IT'S COLD...
I KNOW. JUST STAY CLOSE.
'SCUSE ME.

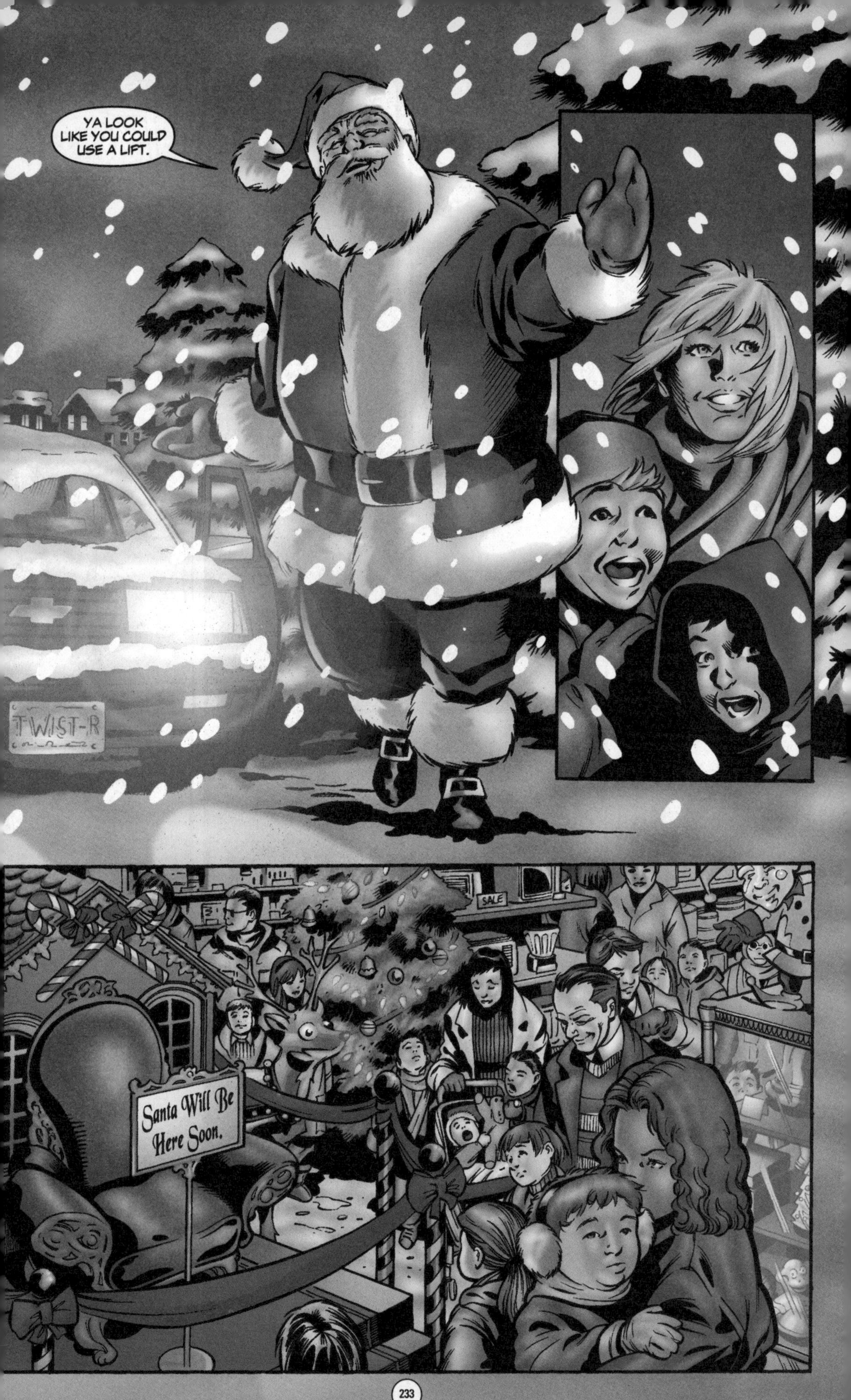

YA LOOK LIKE YOU COULD USE A LIFT.
TWIST-R
Santa Will Be Here Soon.
SALE

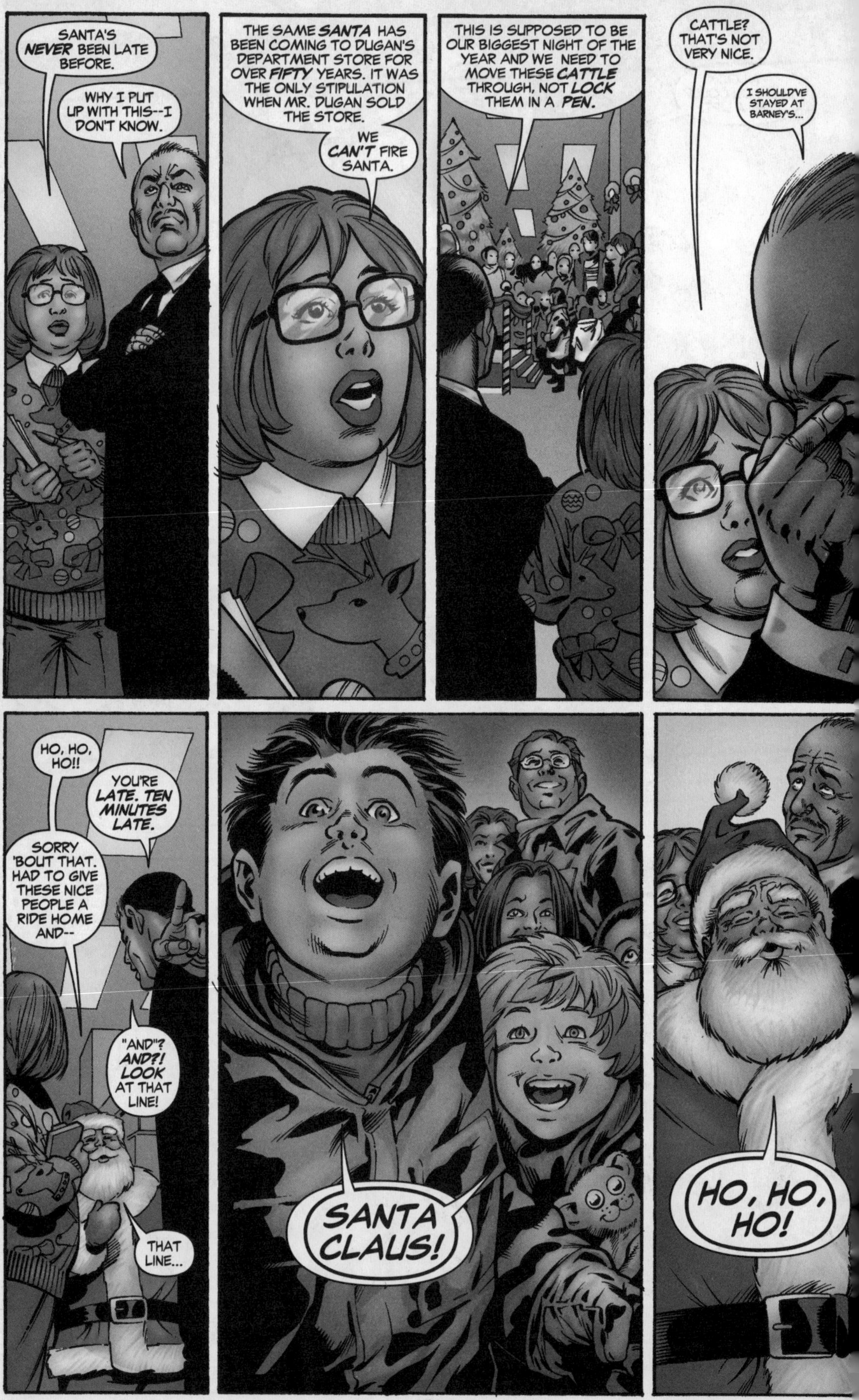
SANTA'S NEVER BEEN LATE BEFORE.
WHY I PUT UP WITH THIS--I DON'T KNOW.
THE SAME SANTA HAS BEEN COMING TO DUGAN'S DEPARTMENT STORE FOR OVER FIFTY YEARS. IT WAS THE ONLY STIPULATION WHEN MR. DUGAN SOLD THE STORE.
WE CAN'T FIRE SANTA.
THIS IS SUPPOSED TO BE OUR BIGGEST NIGHT OF THE YEAR AND WE NEED TO MOVE THESE CATTLE THROUGH, NOT LOCK THEM IN A PEN.
CATTLE? THAT'S NOT VERY NICE.
I SHOULD'VE STAYED AT BARNEY'S...
HO, HO, HO!!
YOU'RE LATE. TEN MINUTES LATE.
SORRY 'BOUT THAT. HAD TO GIVE THESE NICE PEOPLE A RIDE HOME AND--
"AND"? AND?! LOOK AT THAT LINE!
THAT LINE...
SANTA CLAUS!
HO, HO, HO!

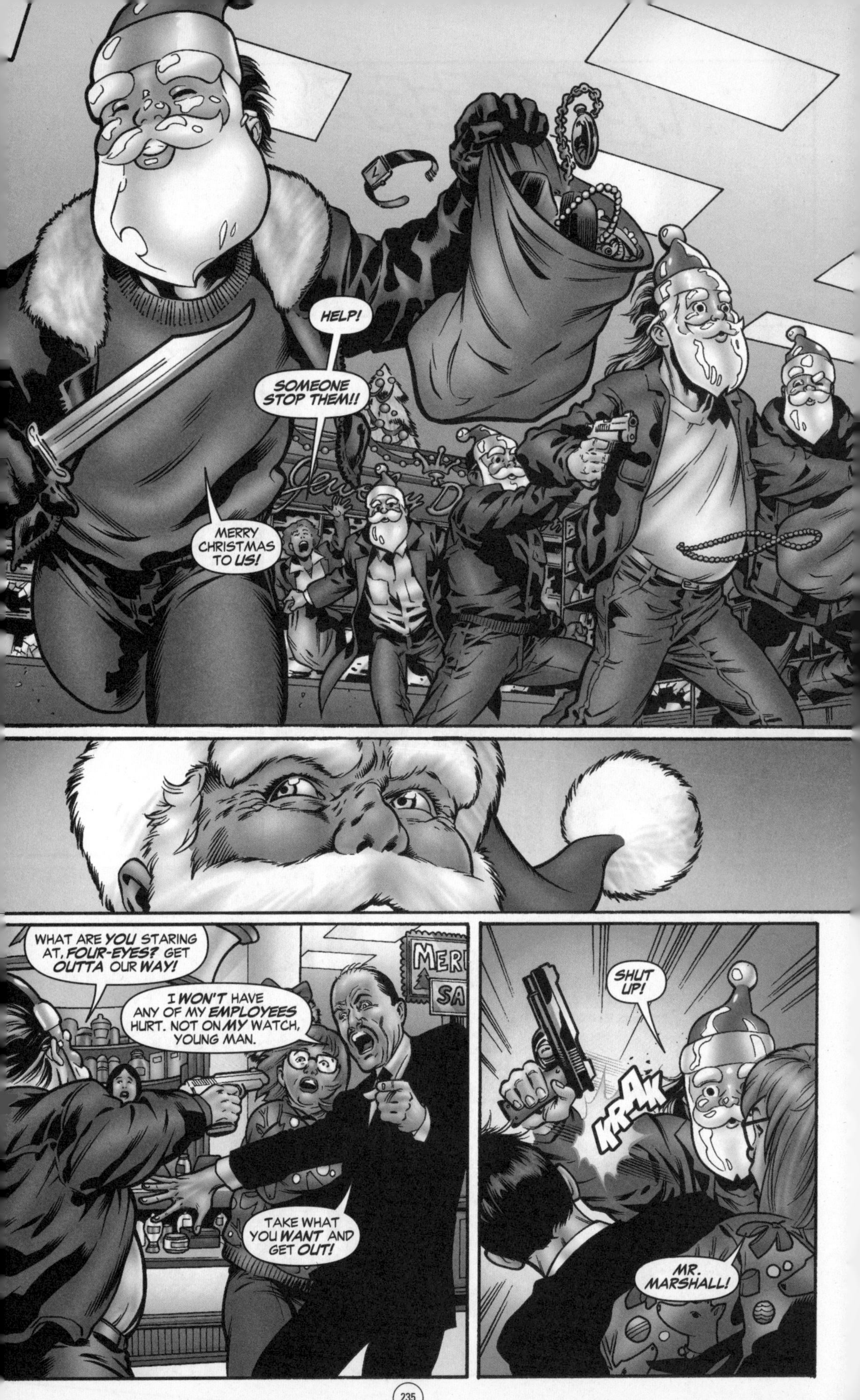
HELP!
SOMEONE STOP THEM!!
MERRY CHRISTMAS TO US!
WHAT ARE YOU STARING AT, FOUR-EYES? GET OUTTA OUR WAY!
I WON'T HAVE ANY OF MY EMPLOYEES HURT. NOT ON MY WATCH, YOUNG MAN.
TAKE WHAT YOU WANT AND GET OUT!
SHUT UP!
KRAK
MR. MARSHALL!

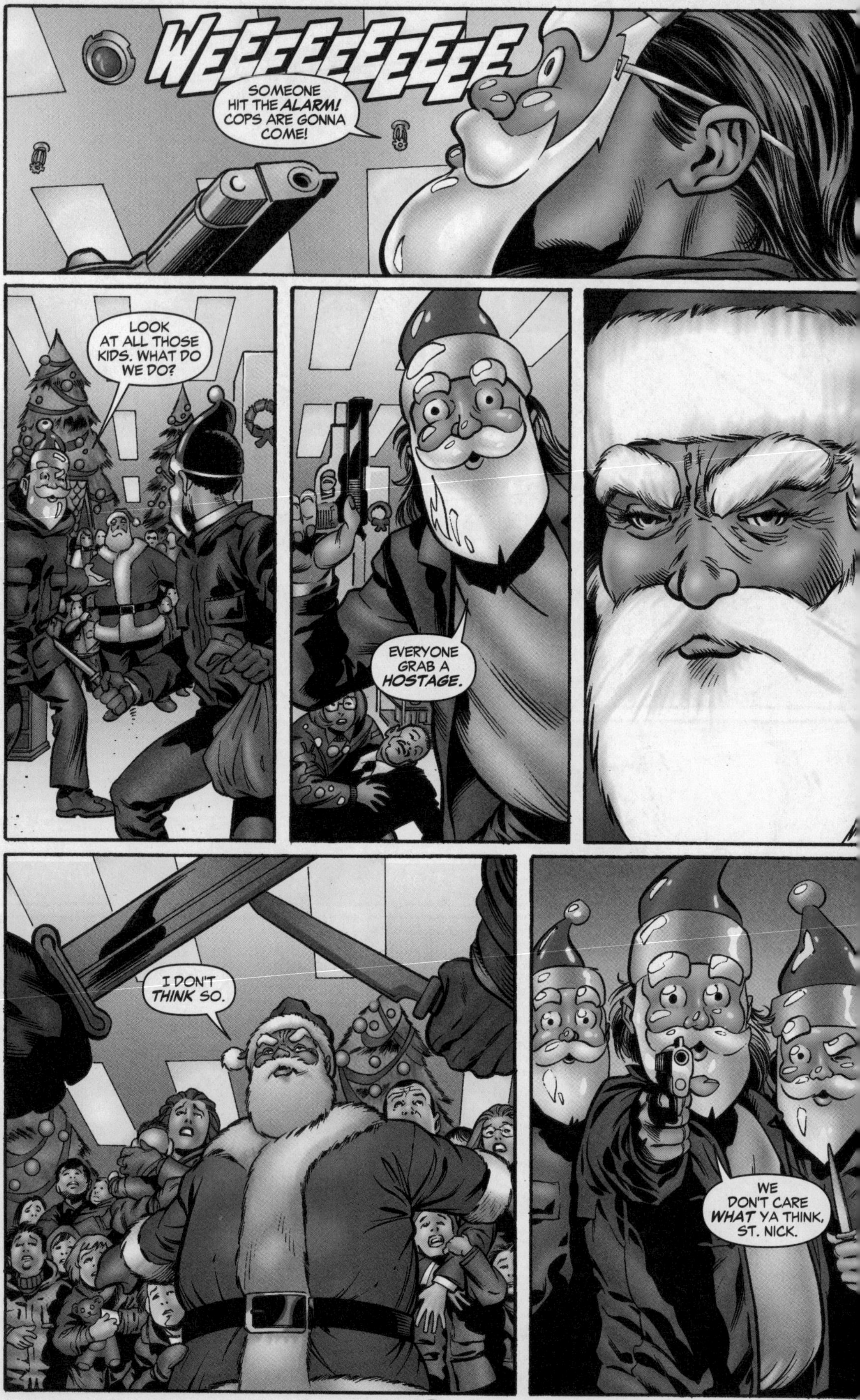
WEEEEEEEEEEE
SOMEONE HIT THE *ALARM!* COPS ARE GONNA COME!
LOOK AT ALL THOSE KIDS. WHAT DO WE DO?
EVERYONE GRAB A *HOSTAGE.*
I DON'T *THINK* SO.
WE DON'T CARE *WHAT* YA THINK, ST. NICK.

THEY GOT HERE EARLY THIS YEAR.

WHAT A NICE SURPRISE.

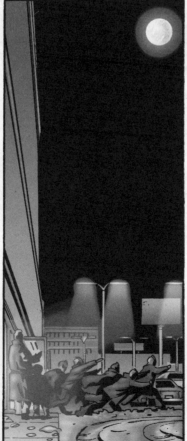

LOOK AT *THIS...*

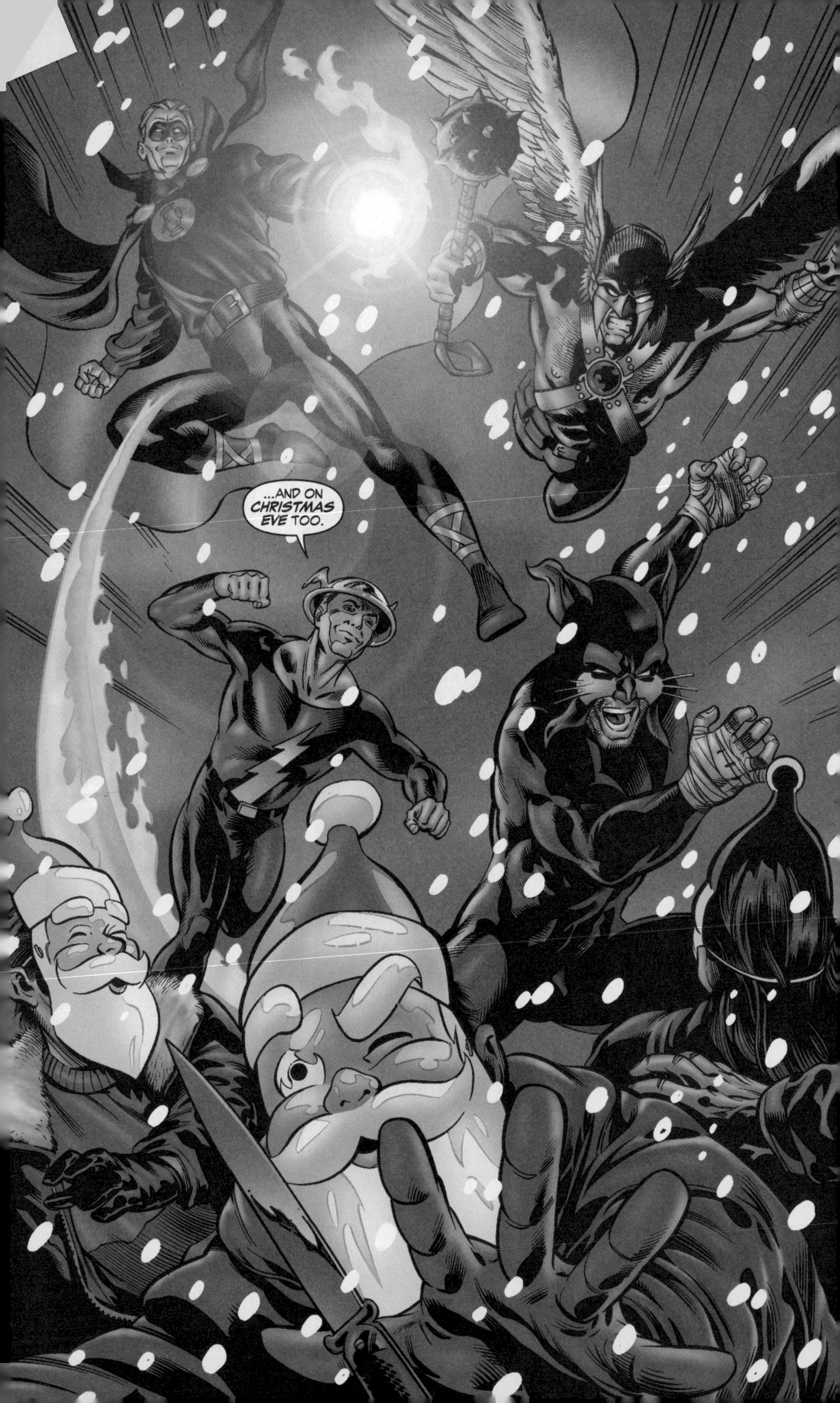
...AND ON CHRISTMAS EVE TOO.

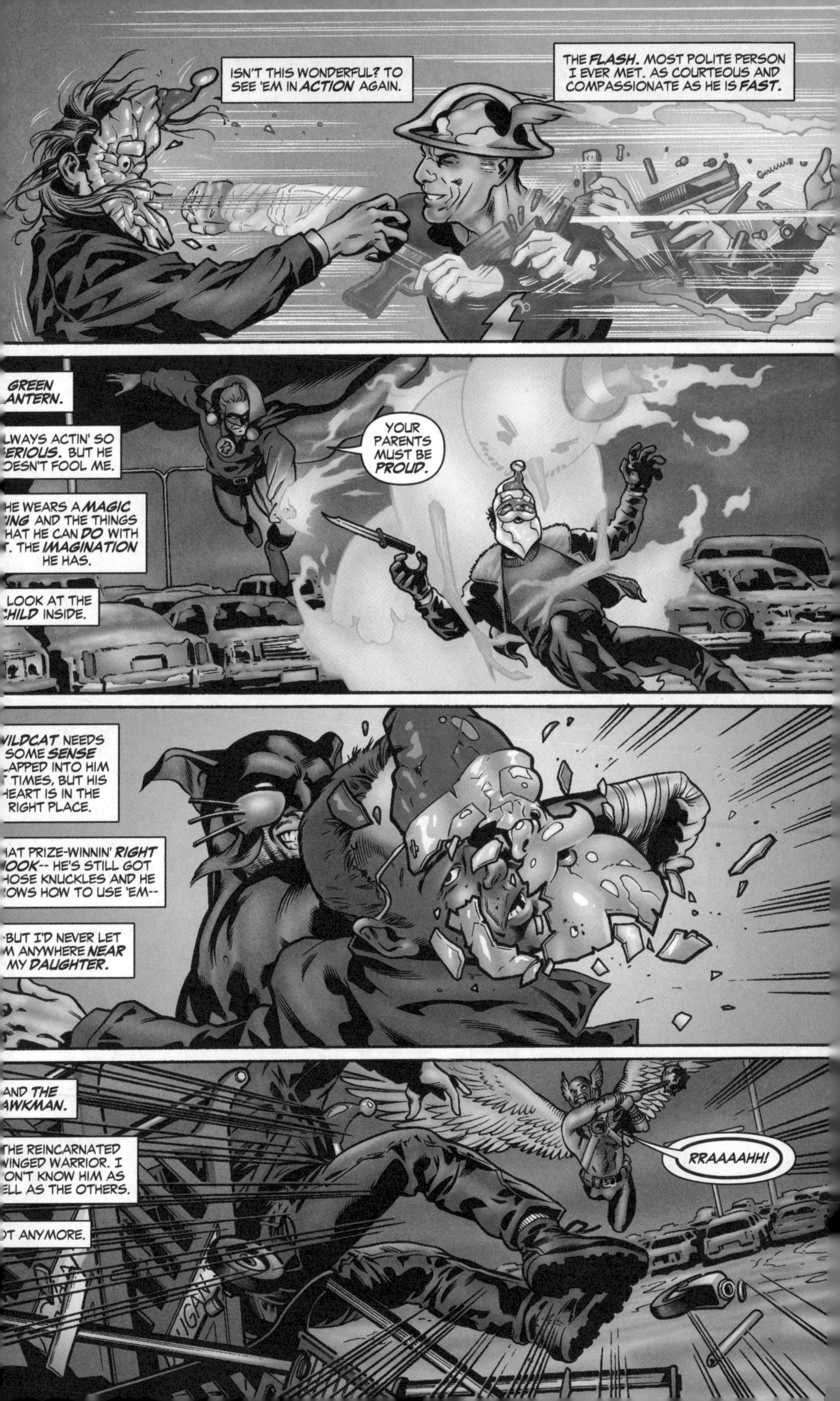

ISN'T THIS WONDERFUL? TO SEE 'EM IN *ACTION* AGAIN.
THE *FLASH*. MOST POLITE PERSON I EVER MET. AS COURTEOUS AND COMPASSIONATE AS HE IS *FAST*.
GREEN ANTERN.
LWAYS ACTIN' SO *ERIOUS*. BUT HE OESN'T FOOL ME.
YOUR PARENTS MUST BE *PROUD*.
HE WEARS A *MAGIC ING* AND THE THINGS HAT HE CAN *DO* WITH T. THE *IMAGINATION* HE HAS.
LOOK AT THE *HILD* INSIDE.
VILDCAT NEEDS SOME *SENSE* LAPPED INTO HIM T TIMES, BUT HIS HEART IS IN THE RIGHT PLACE.
HAT PRIZE-WINNIN' *RIGHT OOK*-- HE'S STILL GOT HOSE KNUCKLES AND HE OWS HOW TO USE 'EM--
-BUT I'D NEVER LET M ANYWHERE *NEAR* MY *DAUGHTER*.
AND *THE AWKMAN.*
THE REINCARNATED VINGED WARRIOR. I ON'T KNOW HIM AS ELL AS THE OTHERS.
RRAAAAHH!
OT ANYMORE.

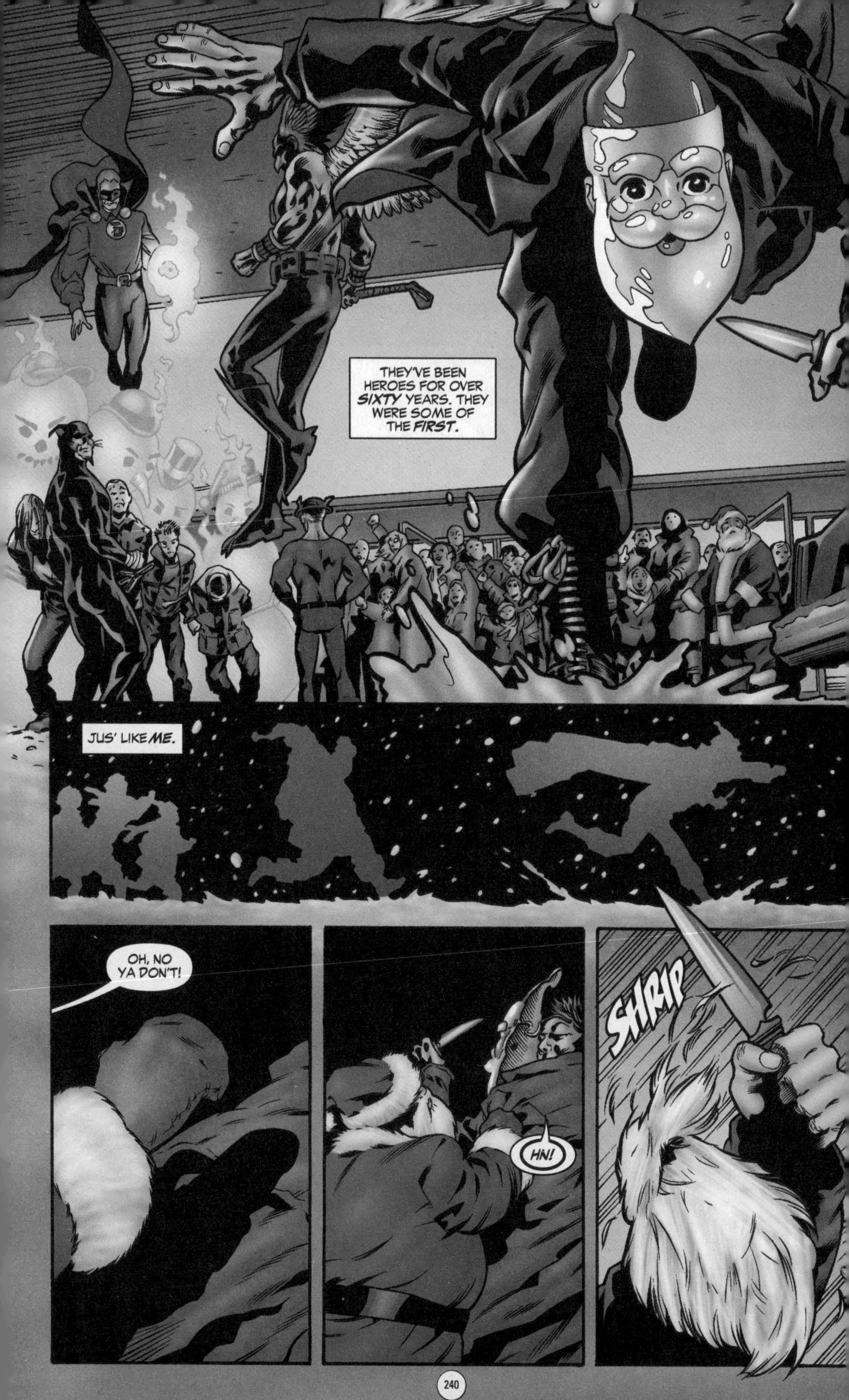

THEY'VE BEEN HEROES FOR OVER SIXTY YEARS. THEY WERE SOME OF THE FIRST.
JUS' LIKE ME.
OH, NO YA DON'T!
HN!
SHRIP

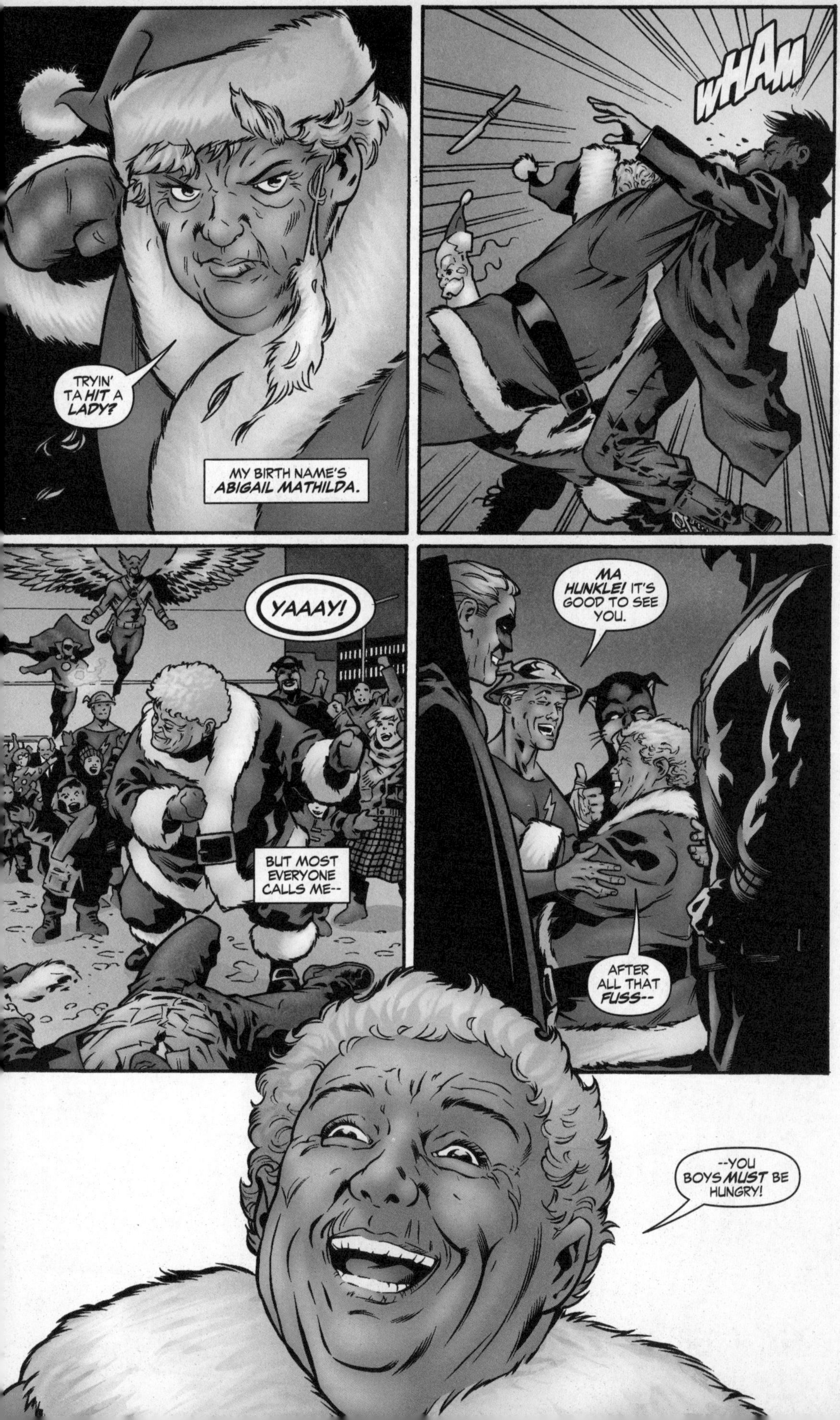
TRYIN' TA HIT A LADY?
MY BIRTH NAME'S ABIGAIL MATHILDA.
WHAM
YAAAY!
BUT MOST EVERYONE CALLS ME--
MA HUNKLE! IT'S GOOD TO SEE YOU.
AFTER ALL THAT FUSS--
--YOU BOYS MUST BE HUNGRY!

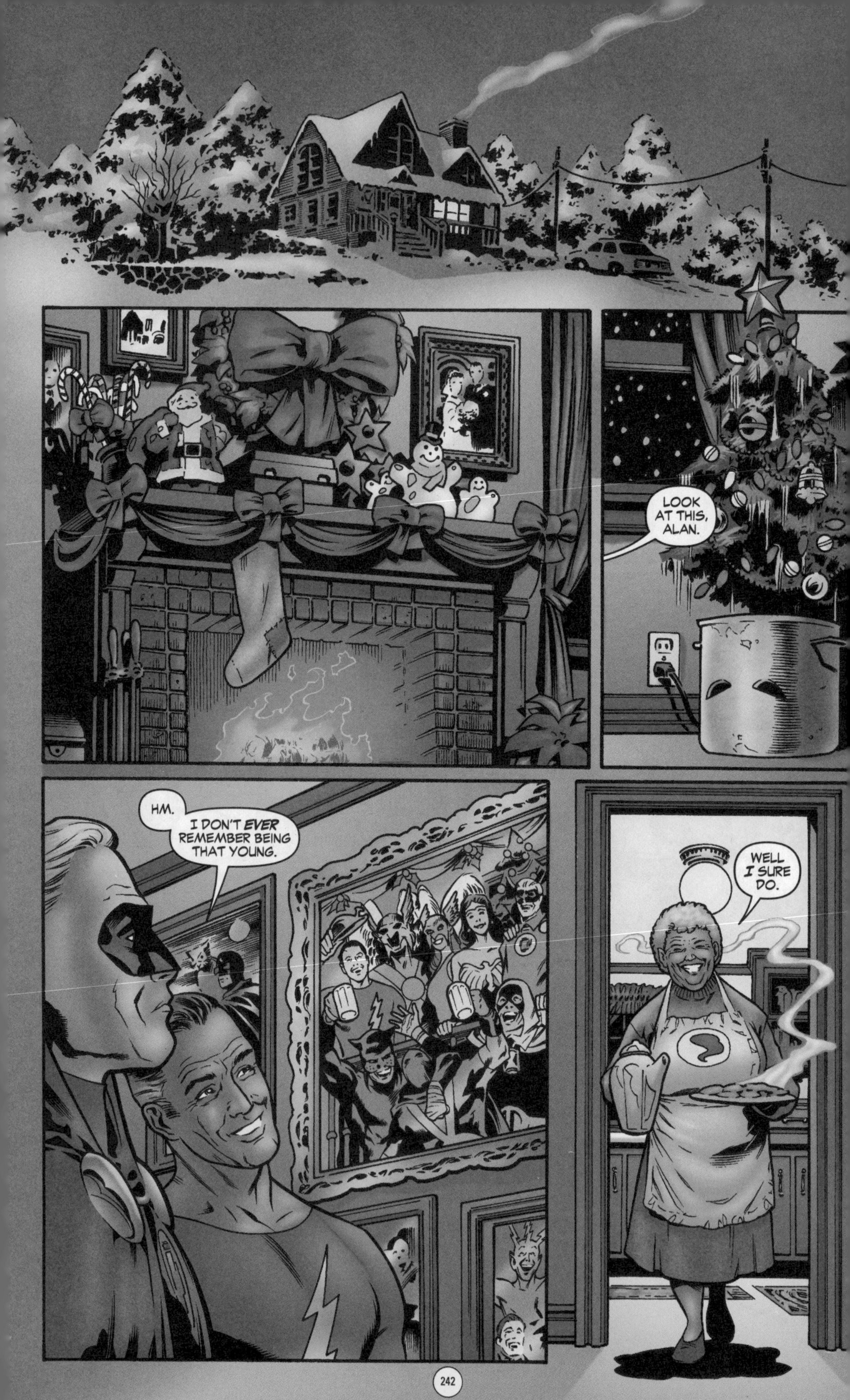
LOOK AT THIS, ALAN.
HM.
I DON'T EVER REMEMBER BEING THAT YOUNG.
WELL I SURE DO.

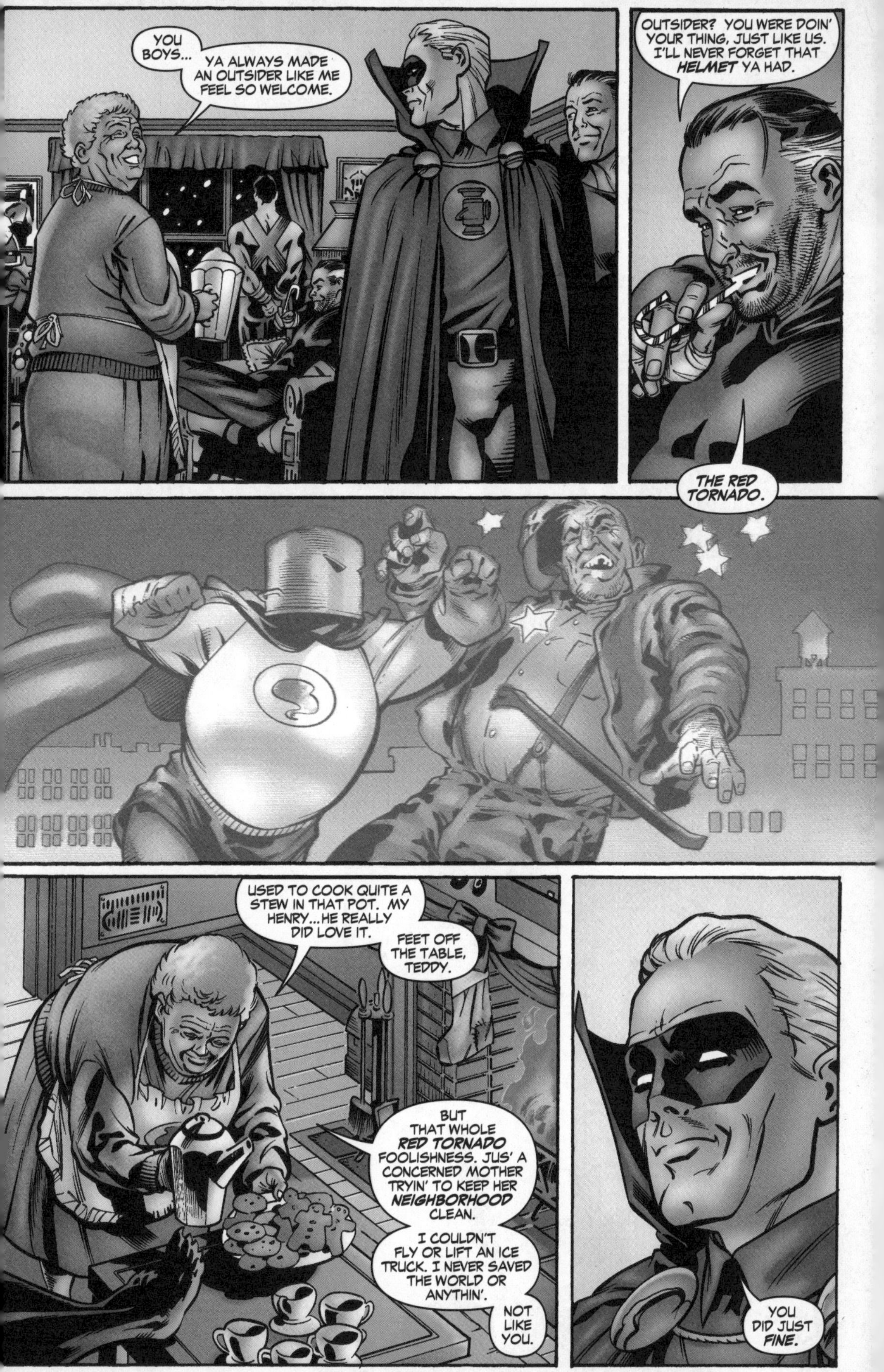
YOU BOYS...
YA ALWAYS MADE AN OUTSIDER LIKE ME FEEL SO WELCOME.
OUTSIDER? YOU WERE DOIN' YOUR THING, JUST LIKE US. I'LL NEVER FORGET THAT HELMET YA HAD.
THE RED TORNADO.
USED TO COOK QUITE A STEW IN THAT POT. MY HENRY...HE REALLY DID LOVE IT.
FEET OFF THE TABLE, TEDDY.
BUT THAT WHOLE RED TORNADO FOOLISHNESS. JUS' A CONCERNED MOTHER TRYIN' TO KEEP HER NEIGHBORHOOD CLEAN.
I COULDN'T FLY OR LIFT AN ICE TRUCK. I NEVER SAVED THE WORLD OR ANYTHIN'.
NOT LIKE YOU.
YOU DID JUST FINE.

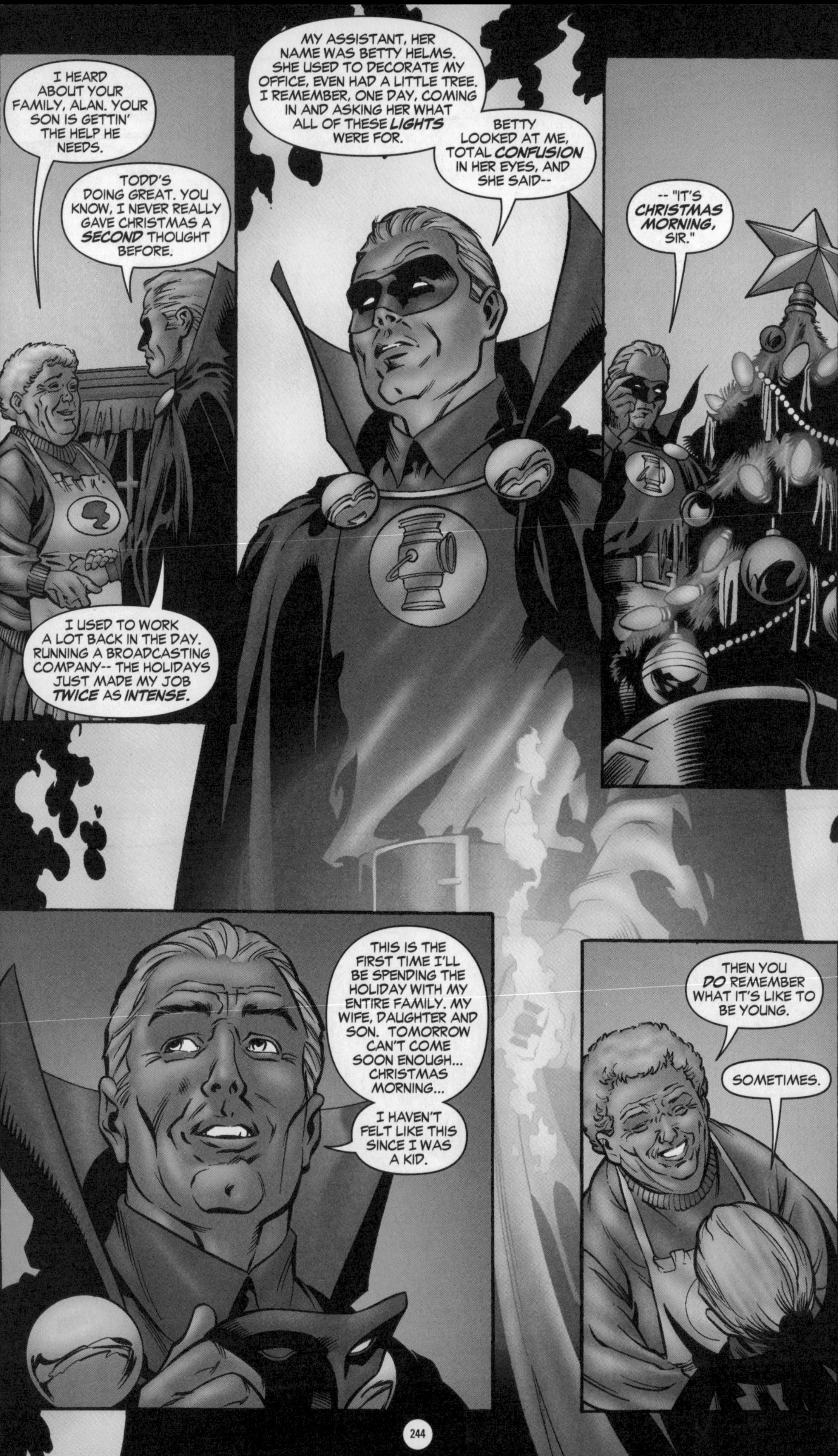
I HEARD ABOUT YOUR FAMILY, ALAN. YOUR SON IS GETTIN' THE HELP HE NEEDS.
TODD'S DOING GREAT. YOU KNOW, I NEVER REALLY GAVE CHRISTMAS A SECOND THOUGHT BEFORE.
I USED TO WORK A LOT BACK IN THE DAY. RUNNING A BROADCASTING COMPANY-- THE HOLIDAYS JUST MADE MY JOB TWICE AS INTENSE.
MY ASSISTANT, HER NAME WAS BETTY HELMS. SHE USED TO DECORATE MY OFFICE, EVEN HAD A LITTLE TREE. I REMEMBER, ONE DAY, COMING IN AND ASKING HER WHAT ALL OF THESE LIGHTS WERE FOR.
BETTY LOOKED AT ME, TOTAL CONFUSION IN HER EYES, AND SHE SAID--
-- "IT'S CHRISTMAS MORNING, SIR."
THIS IS THE FIRST TIME I'LL BE SPENDING THE HOLIDAY WITH MY ENTIRE FAMILY. MY WIFE, DAUGHTER AND SON. TOMORROW CAN'T COME SOON ENOUGH... CHRISTMAS MORNING...
I HAVEN'T FELT LIKE THIS SINCE I WAS A KID.
THEN YOU DO REMEMBER WHAT IT'S LIKE TO BE YOUNG.
SOMETIMES.

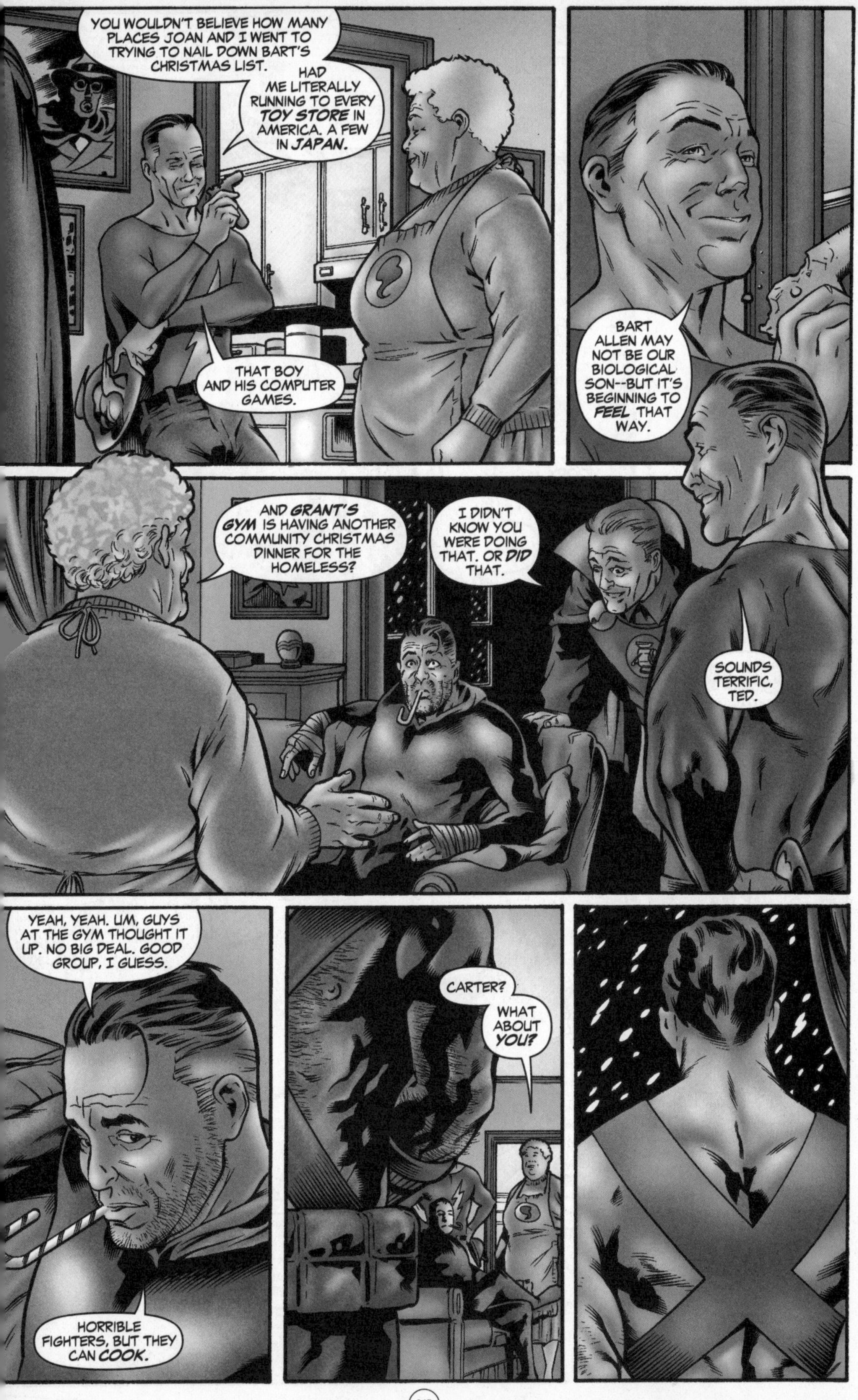
YOU WOULDN'T BELIEVE HOW MANY PLACES JOAN AND I WENT TO TRYING TO NAIL DOWN BART'S CHRISTMAS LIST.
HAD ME LITERALLY RUNNING TO EVERY TOY STORE IN AMERICA. A FEW IN JAPAN.
THAT BOY AND HIS COMPUTER GAMES.
BART ALLEN MAY NOT BE OUR BIOLOGICAL SON--BUT IT'S BEGINNING TO FEEL THAT WAY.
AND GRANT'S GYM IS HAVING ANOTHER COMMUNITY CHRISTMAS DINNER FOR THE HOMELESS?
I DIDN'T KNOW YOU WERE DOING THAT. OR DID THAT.
SOUNDS TERRIFIC, TED.
YEAH, YEAH. UM, GUYS AT THE GYM THOUGHT IT UP. NO BIG DEAL. GOOD GROUP, I GUESS.
HORRIBLE FIGHTERS, BUT THEY CAN COOK.
CARTER?
WHAT ABOUT YOU?

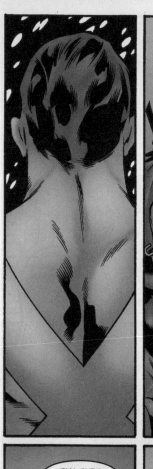

CARTER...

HE'S MOODY TODAY.

HUSH, TEDDY.

I USED TO SPEND CHRISTMAS WITH HAWKGIRL. DESPITE OUR RELIGIOUS BELIEFS, IT WAS A DAY WE CHERISHED TOGETHER.

TOMORROW, KENDRA IS GOING TO HER GRANDFATHER'S. TO VISIT HER COUSIN. MIA... OR SOMETHING.

WHY DON'T YOU--

INVITE MYSELF? THAT WOULD BE SELFISH. SHE DESERVES TIME ALONE WITH HER FAMILY.

I'M SURE WILDCAT COULD USE HELP AT THE GYM.

KRAK

WHA'?

WELL...

GUESS WE COULD USE AN EXTRA HAND. HELP PASS EVERYTHING OUT. THAT IS--

--IF YOU'RE INTERESTED, CARTER.

MAYBE. ...THANKS, TED.

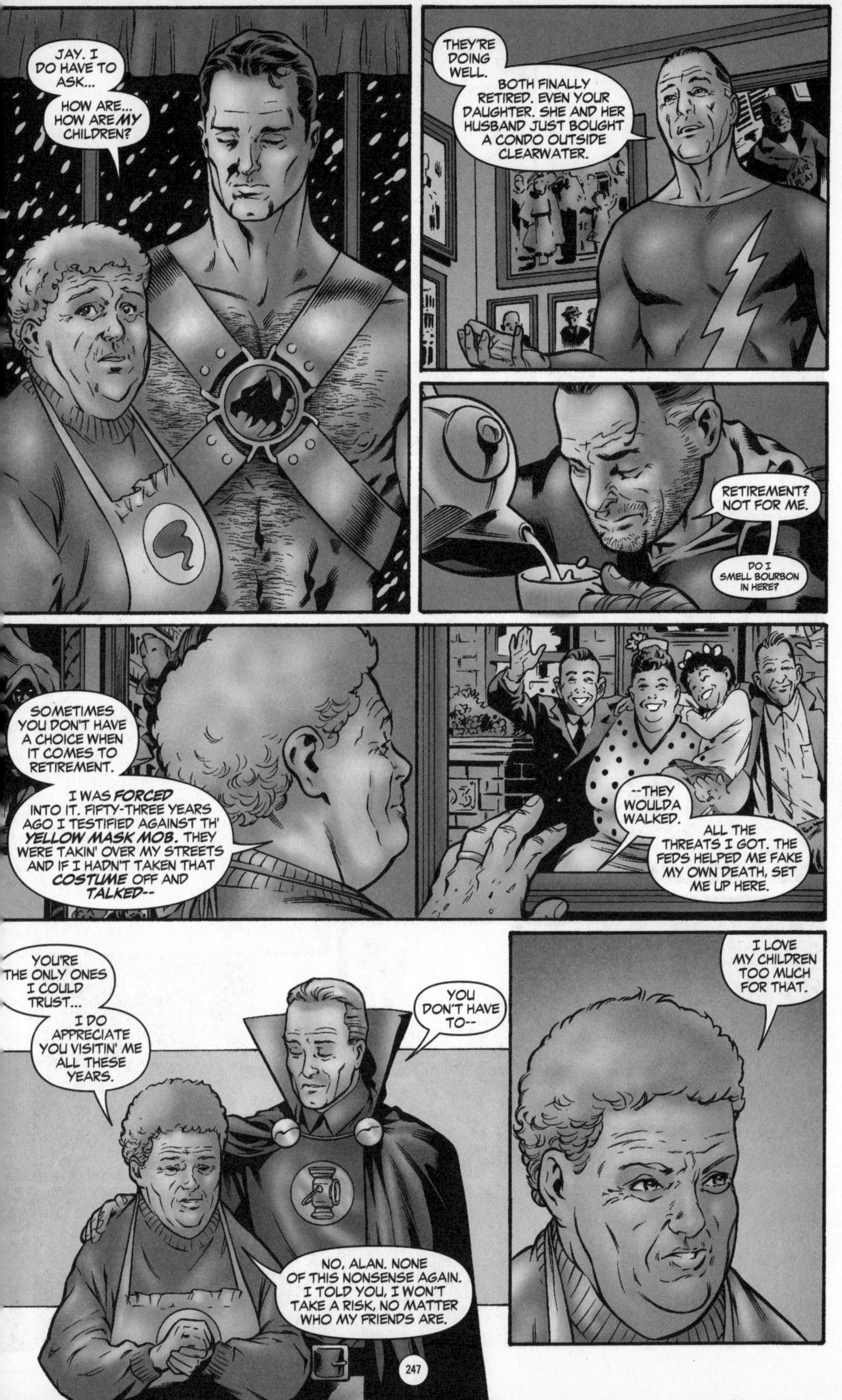

JAY. I DO HAVE TO ASK...
HOW ARE... HOW ARE MY CHILDREN?
THEY'RE DOING WELL.
BOTH FINALLY RETIRED. EVEN YOUR DAUGHTER. SHE AND HER HUSBAND JUST BOUGHT A CONDO OUTSIDE CLEARWATER.
FAIR PLAY
RETIREMENT? NOT FOR ME.
DO I SMELL BOURBON IN HERE?
SOMETIMES YOU DON'T HAVE A CHOICE WHEN IT COMES TO RETIREMENT.
I WAS FORCED INTO IT. FIFTY-THREE YEARS AGO I TESTIFIED AGAINST TH' YELLOW MASK MOB. THEY WERE TAKIN' OVER MY STREETS AND IF I HADN'T TAKEN THAT COSTUME OFF AND TALKED--
--THEY WOULDA WALKED.
ALL THE THREATS I GOT. THE FEDS HELPED ME FAKE MY OWN DEATH, SET ME UP HERE.
YOU'RE THE ONLY ONES I COULD TRUST...
I DO APPRECIATE YOU VISITIN' ME ALL THESE YEARS.
YOU DON'T HAVE TO--
NO, ALAN. NONE OF THIS NONSENSE AGAIN. I TOLD YOU, I WON'T TAKE A RISK, NO MATTER WHO MY FRIENDS ARE.
I LOVE MY CHILDREN TOO MUCH FOR THAT.

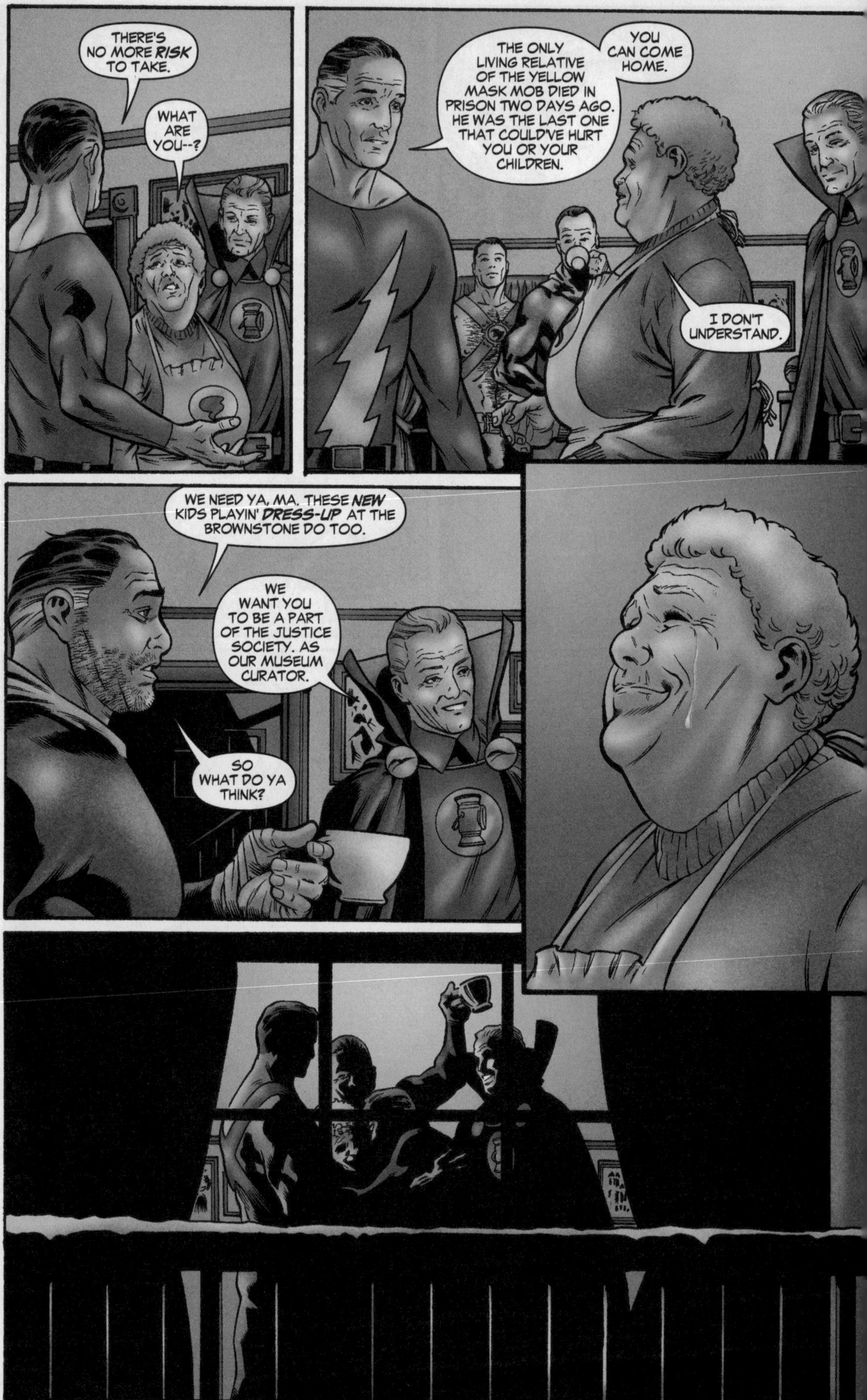
THERE'S NO MORE RISK TO TAKE.
WHAT ARE YOU--?
THE ONLY LIVING RELATIVE OF THE YELLOW MASK MOB DIED IN PRISON TWO DAYS AGO. HE WAS THE LAST ONE THAT COULD'VE HURT YOU OR YOUR CHILDREN.
YOU CAN COME HOME.
I DON'T UNDERSTAND.
WE NEED YA, MA. THESE NEW KIDS PLAYIN' DRESS-UP AT THE BROWNSTONE DO TOO.
WE WANT YOU TO BE A PART OF THE JUSTICE SOCIETY. AS OUR MUSEUM CURATOR.
SO WHAT DO YA THINK?

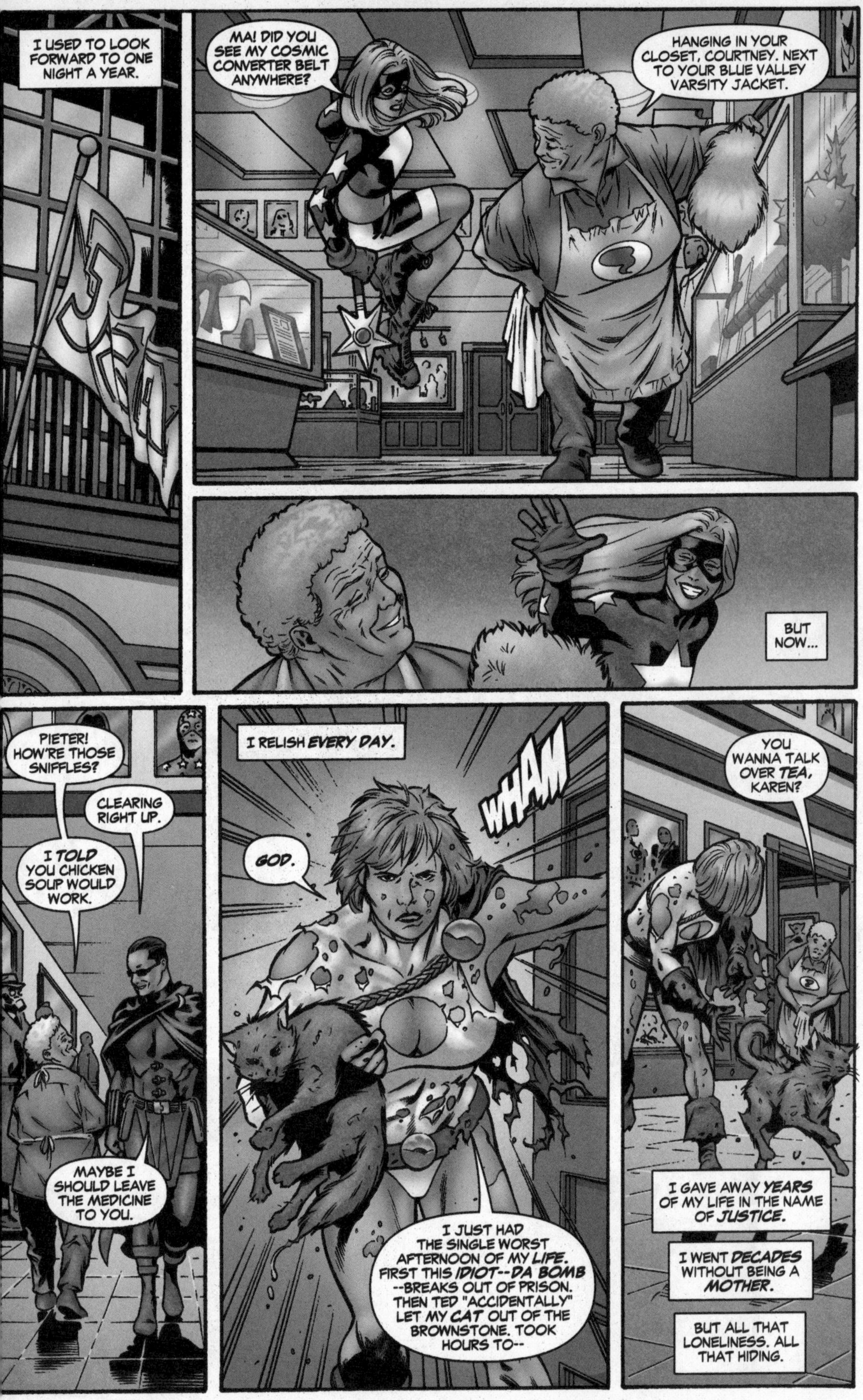

I USED TO LOOK FORWARD TO ONE NIGHT A YEAR.
MA! DID YOU SEE MY COSMIC CONVERTER BELT ANYWHERE?
HANGING IN YOUR CLOSET, COURTNEY. NEXT TO YOUR BLUE VALLEY VARSITY JACKET.
BUT NOW...
PIETER! HOW'RE THOSE SNIFFLES?
CLEARING RIGHT UP.
I TOLD YOU CHICKEN SOUP WOULD WORK.
MAYBE I SHOULD LEAVE THE MEDICINE TO YOU.
I RELISH EVERY DAY.
WHAM
GOD.
I JUST HAD THE SINGLE WORST AFTERNOON OF MY LIFE. FIRST THIS IDIOT--DA BOMB --BREAKS OUT OF PRISON. THEN TED "ACCIDENTALLY" LET MY CAT OUT OF THE BROWNSTONE. TOOK HOURS TO--
YOU WANNA TALK OVER TEA, KAREN?
I GAVE AWAY YEARS OF MY LIFE IN THE NAME OF JUSTICE.
I WENT DECADES WITHOUT BEING A MOTHER.
BUT ALL THAT LONELINESS. ALL THAT HIDING.

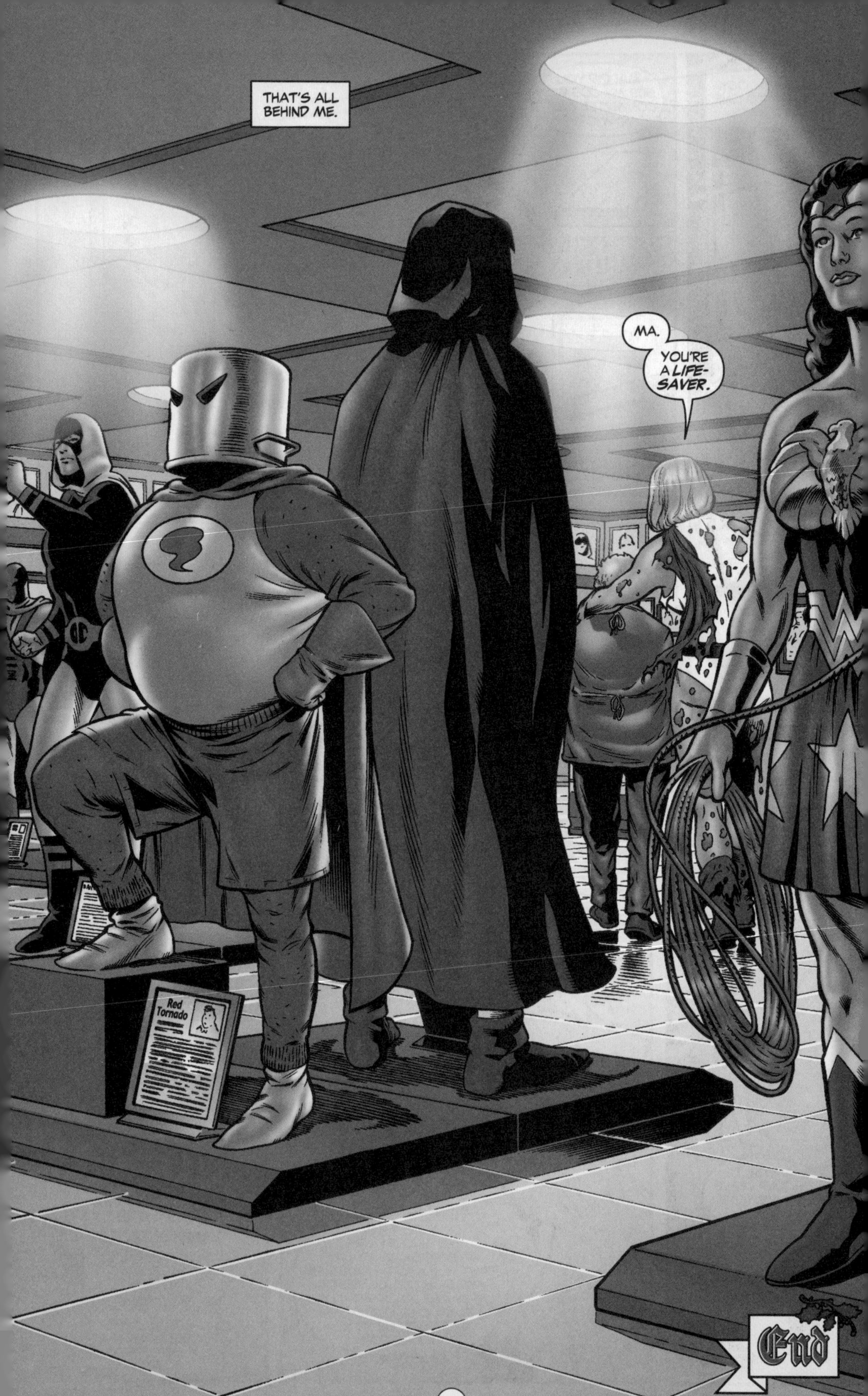
THAT'S ALL BEHIND ME.
MA.
YOU'RE A LIFE-SAVER.
Red Tornado
End

COVER GALLERY

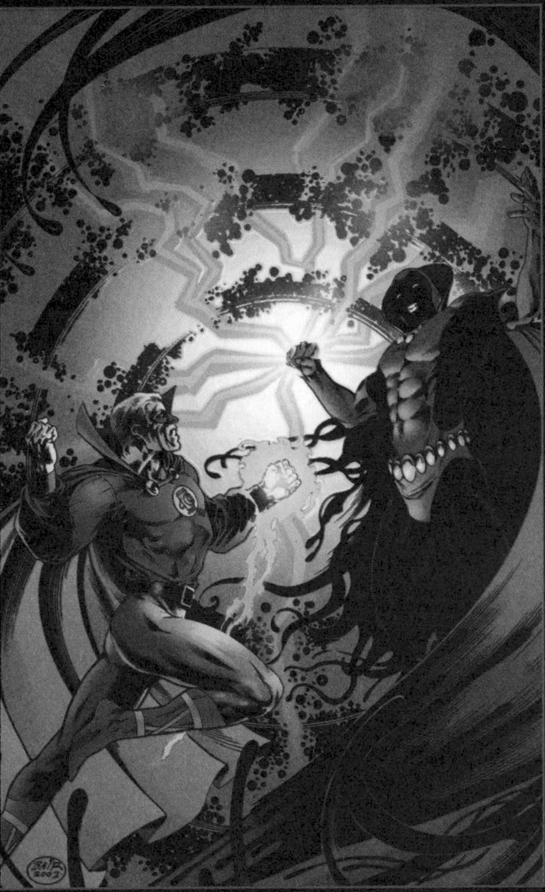

JSA #46

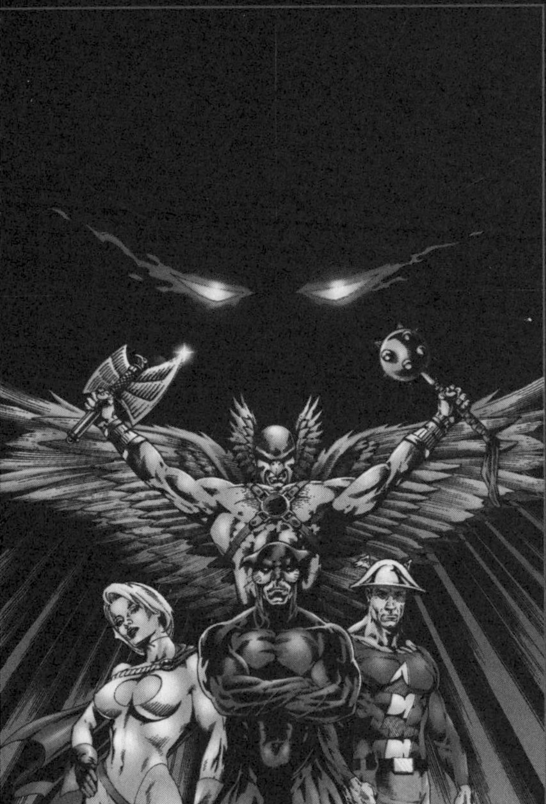

JSA #47

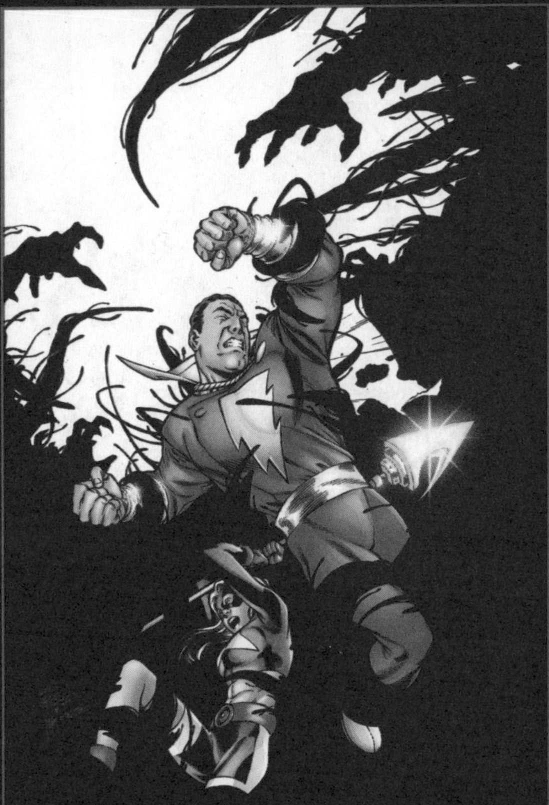

JSA #48

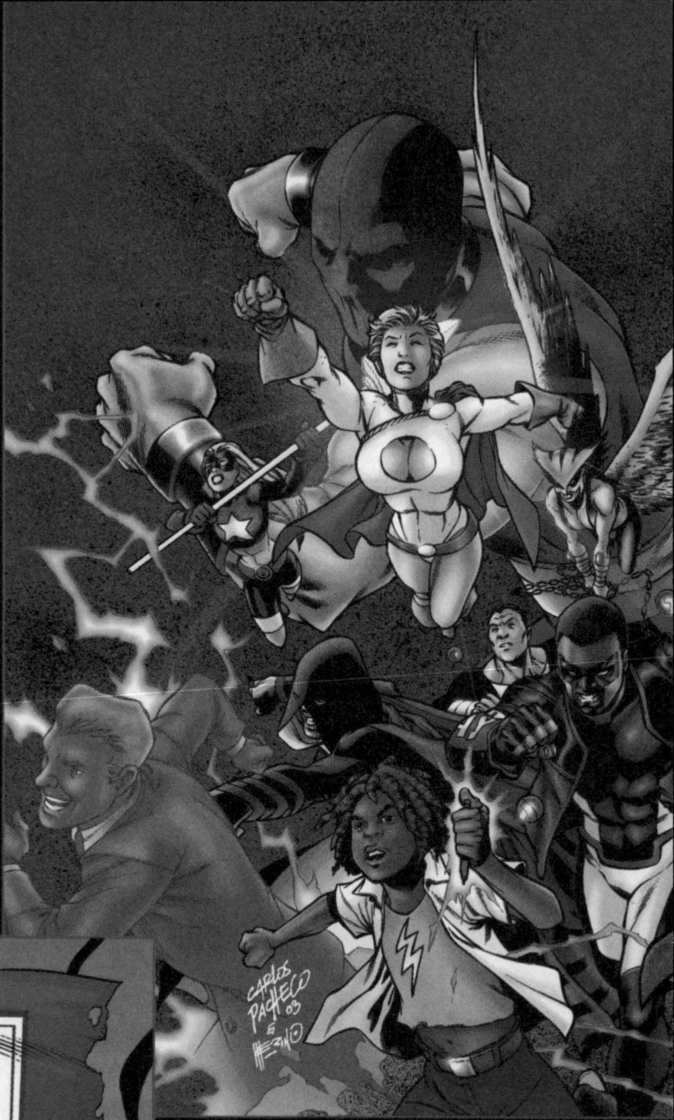

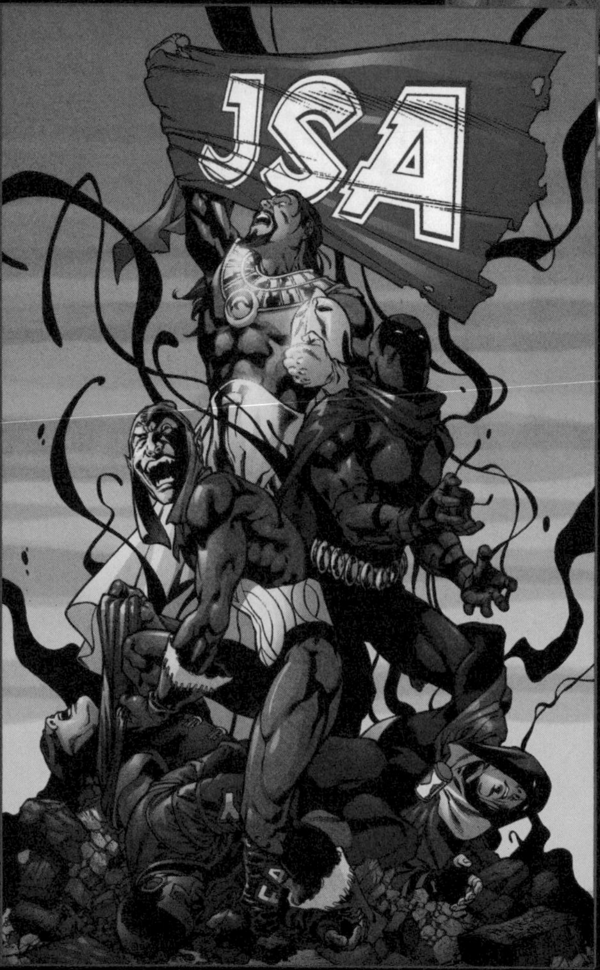
JSA

JSA #49

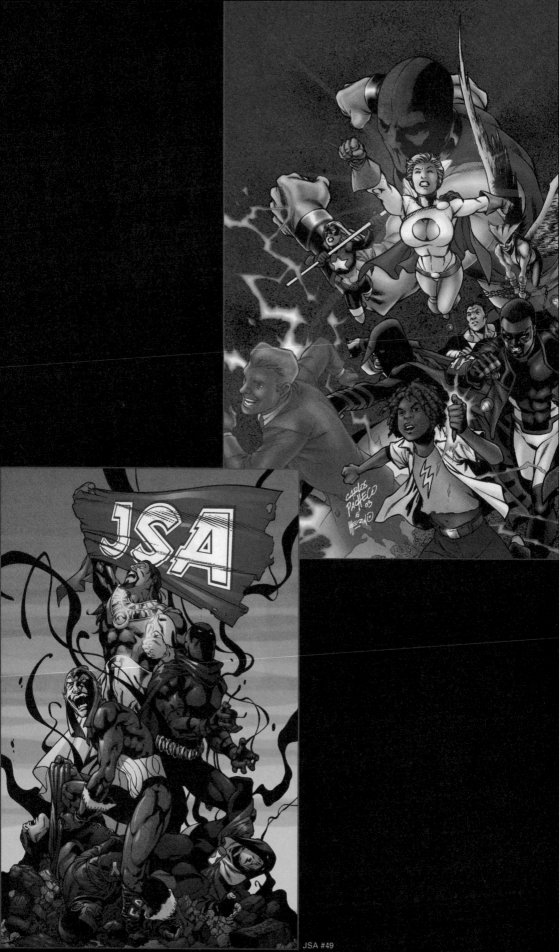

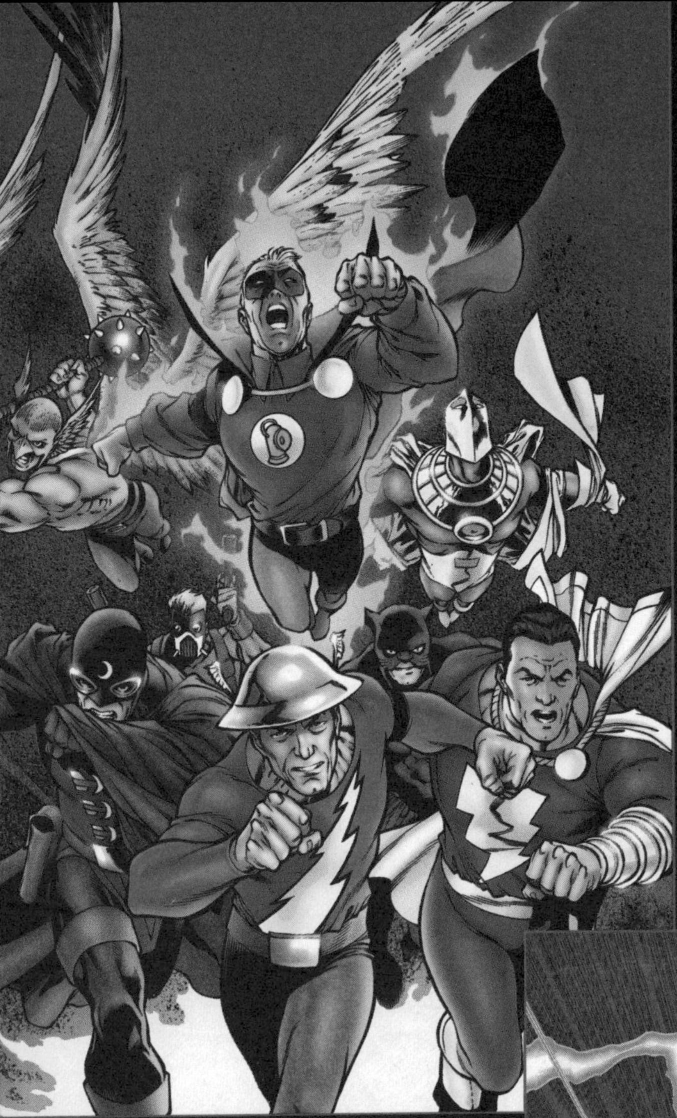

JSA #50

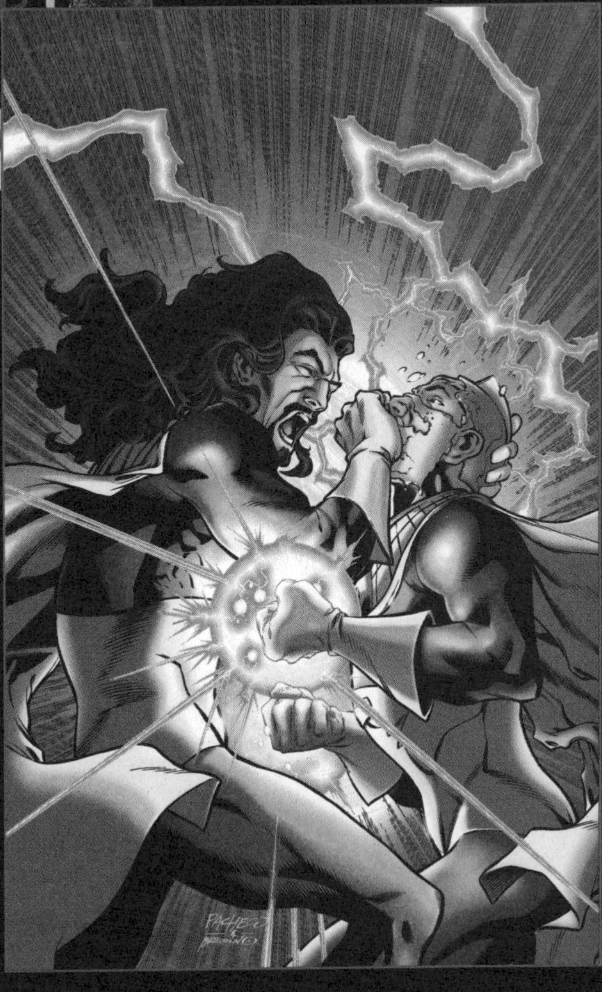

JSA #51

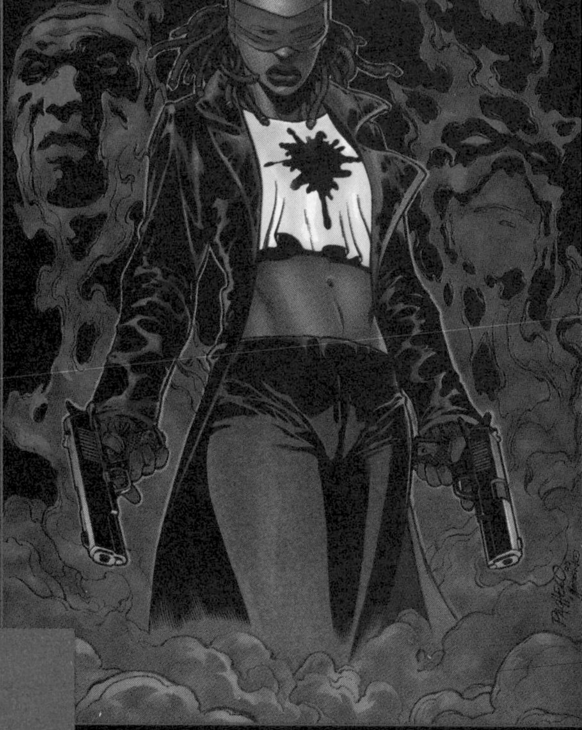

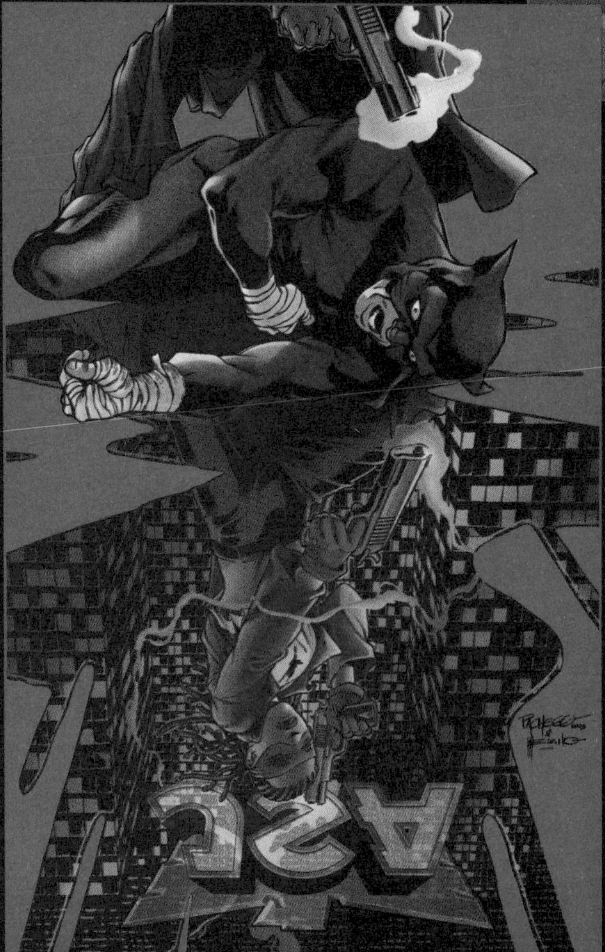

JSA #53

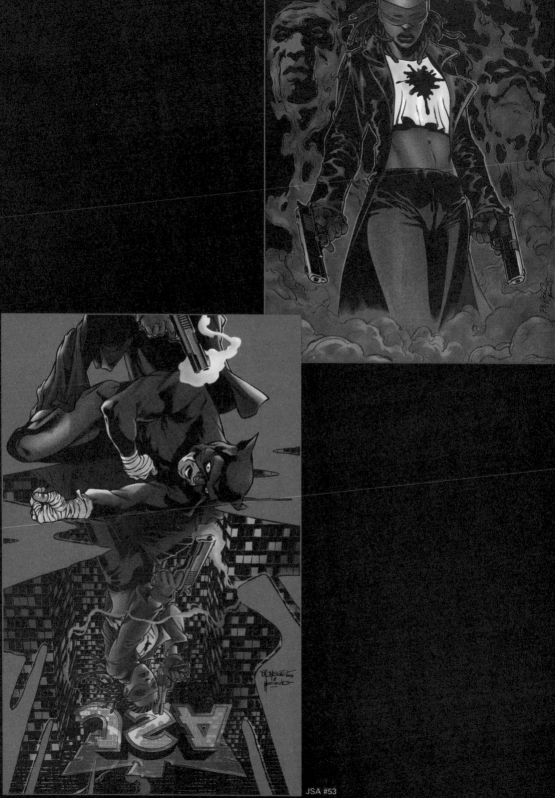

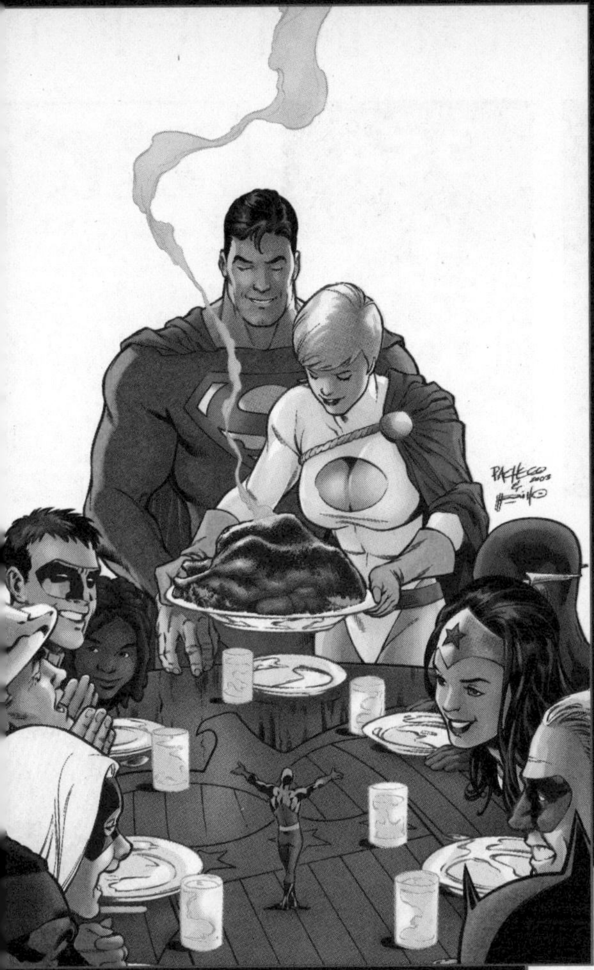

JSA #54

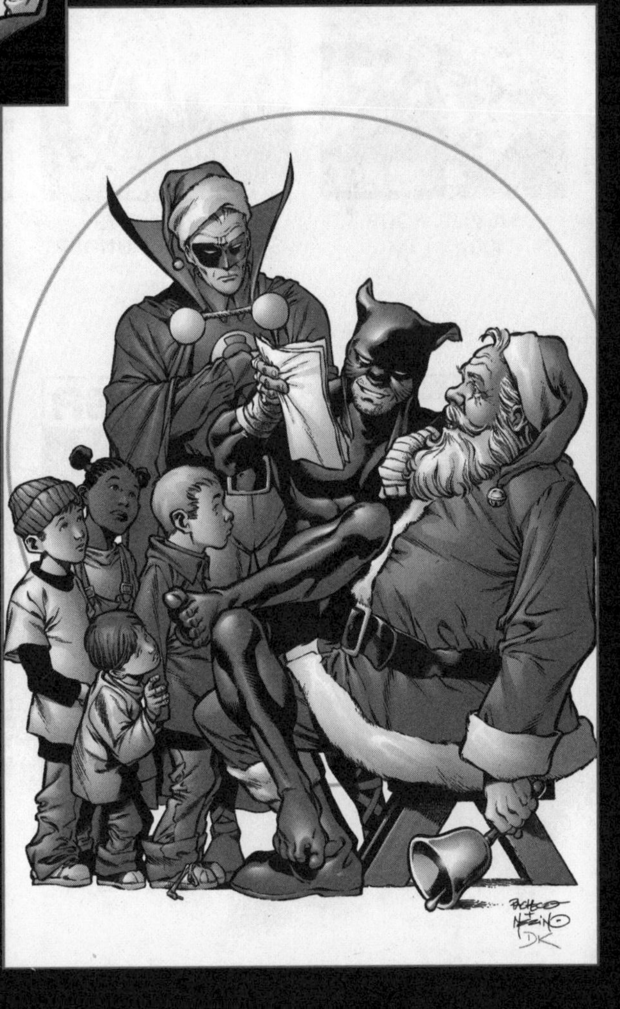

JSA #55

THE JSA LIBRARY

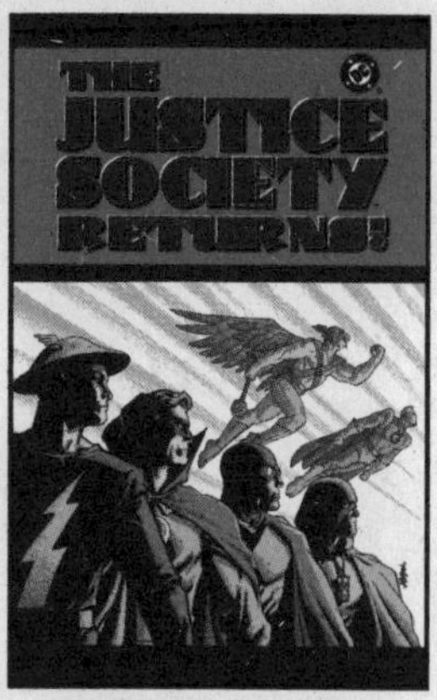
THE JUSTICE SOCIETY RETURNS!

JUSTICE SOCIETY RETURNS

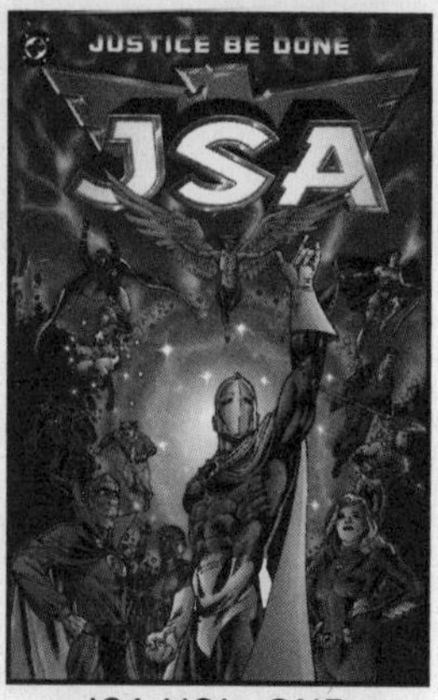
JUSTICE BE DONE
JSA

JSA VOL. ONE: JUSTICE BE DONE

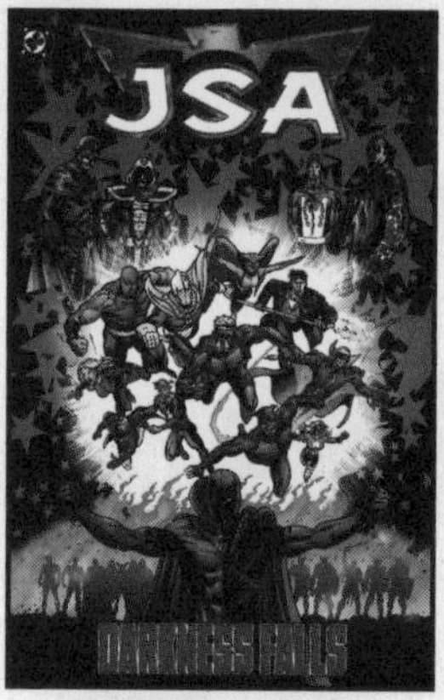
JSA
DARKNESS FALLS

JSA VOL. TWO: DARKNESS FALLS

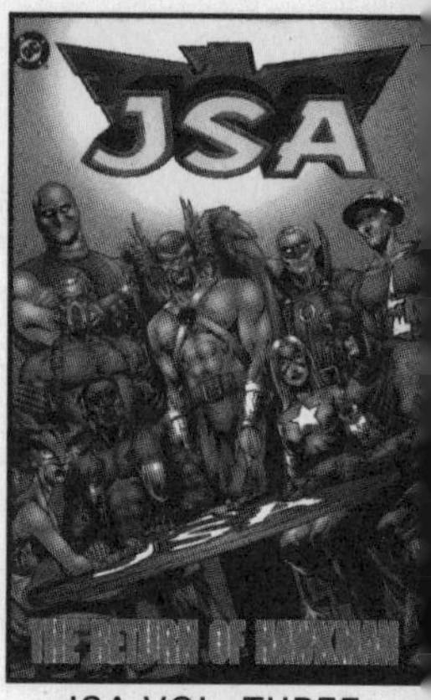
JSA
THE RETURN OF HAWKMAN

JSA VOL. THREE: THE RETURN OF HAWKMAN

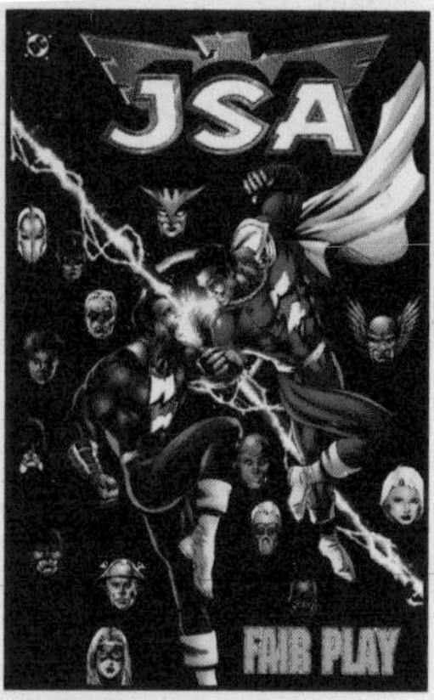
JSA
FAIR PLAY

JSA VOL. FOUR: FAIR PLAY

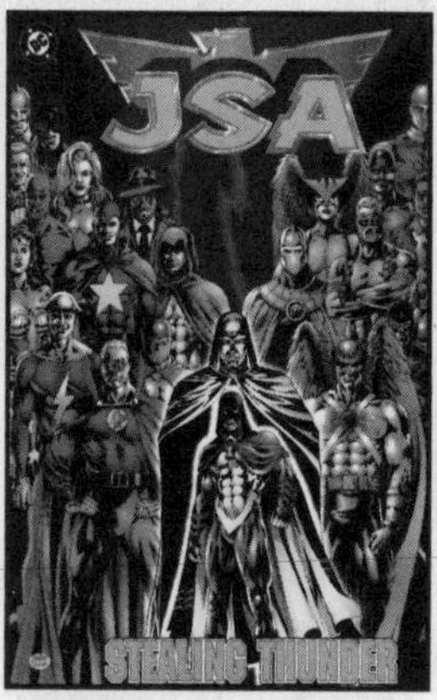
JSA
STEALING THUNDER

JSA VOL. FIVE: STEALING THUNDER

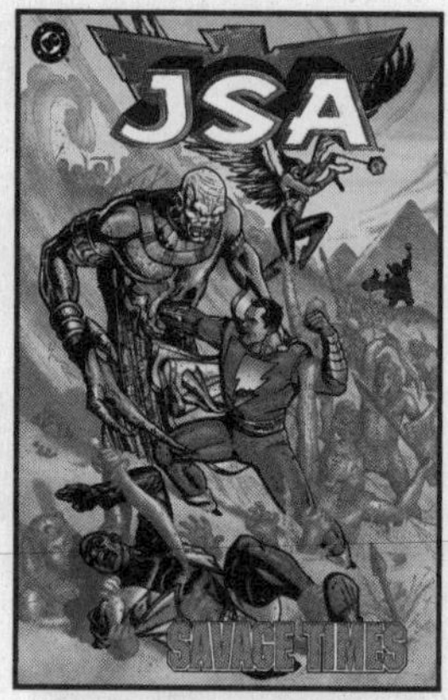
JSA
SAVAGE TIMES

JSA VOL. SIX: SAVAGE TIMES

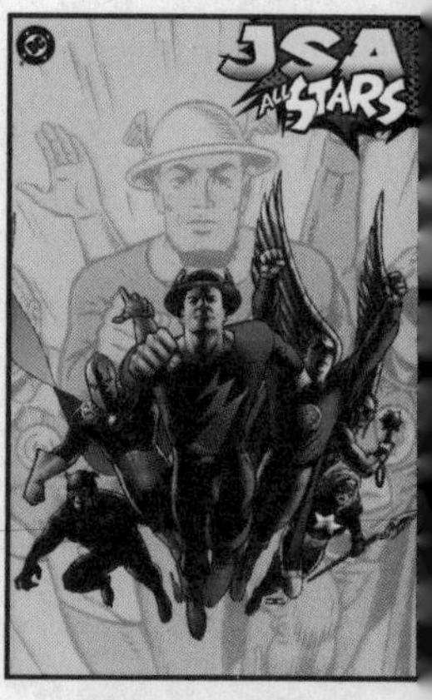
JSA
ALL STARS

JSA ALL STARS

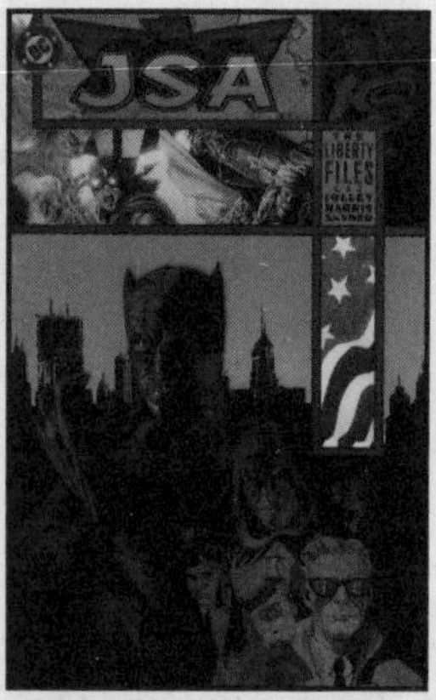
JSA
LIBERTY FILES

JSA: LIBERTY FILES

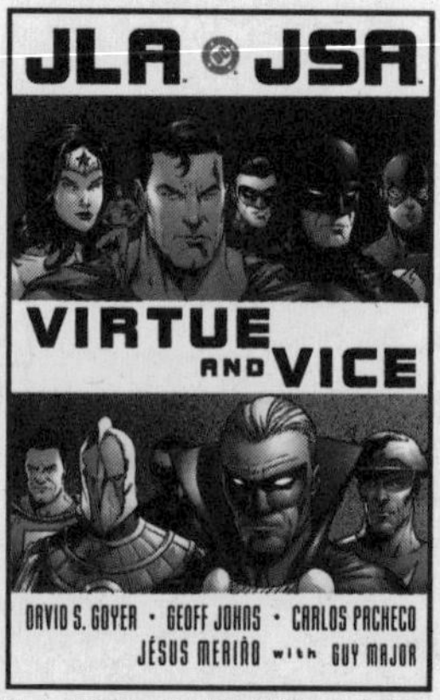
JLA JSA
VIRTUE AND VICE
DAVID S. GOYER · GEOFF JOHNS · CARLOS PACHECO
JÉSUS MERIÑO with GUY MAJOR

JLA/JSA: VIRTUE & VICE

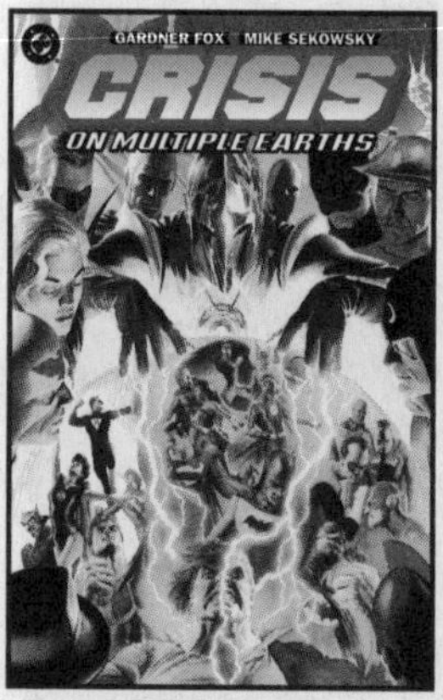
GARDNER FOX | MIKE SEKOWSKY
CRISIS
ON MULTIPLE EARTHS

CRISIS ON MULTIPLE EARTHS VOLS. ONE - THREE

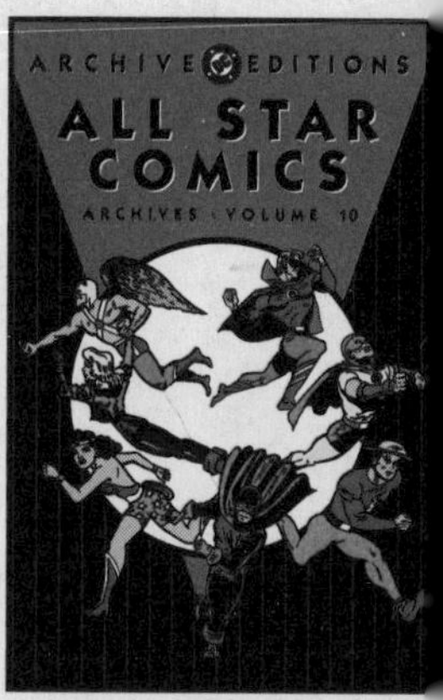
ARCHIVE EDITIONS
ALL STAR COMICS
ARCHIVES VOLUME 10

ALL STAR ARCHIVES VOLS. ONE - ELEVEN

collecting all 55 issues of the Golden Age JSA!